Gross Private Investment				Exports			Imports				
Machinery and equipment	Total Inventory Investment	Investment in non-farm inventories	Investment in farm inventories	Total Exports of goods and services	Exports of goods	Exports of services	Total Imports of goods and services	Imports of goods	Imports of services	Statistical discrepancy	Final domestic demand
2144	104	501	-397	7310	6274	1036	7517	5982	1535	-90	41438
2368	674	436	238	7951	6798	1153	8048	6491	1557	48	44133
2642	735	457	278	8730	7473	1257	8389	6806	1583	-46	47041
3234	647	743	-96	10137	8752	1385	9522	7745	1777	-98	51544
3947	1303	1244	59	10772	9247	1525	10840	8917	1923	-124	56949
4854	1277	1066	211	12574	10808	1766	12554	10389	2165	-253	63898
4926	177	184	-7	14161	11797	2364	13451	11079	2372	-130	69049
4581	708	473	235	16161	14144	2017	15235	12642	2593	-93	74714
5149	1473	994	479	17818	15476	2342	17732	14533	3199	208	82233
5497	253	377	-124	20124	17471	2653	17831	14299	3532	-481	88315
5814	410	388	22	21110	18351	2759	19490	15778	3712	-626	97266
6538	765	1049	-284	23820	20955	2865	22824	18843	3981	-2	108349
8220	1881	1703	178	29892	26503	3389	28075	23359	4716	305	125208
10246	3566	3808	-242	37760	33522	4238	37544	31805	5739	1032	149450
12130	1337	1057	280	38950	34365	4585	41994	34960	7034	649	174920
13413	2290	1918	372	44293	39133	5160	45723	37607	8116	941	198454
14188	1821	1760	61	51229	45629	5600	51613	42522	9091	-435	220313
15978	894	498	396	61336	54739	6597	60424	50105	10319	177	243485
19738	4734	4570	164	75153	67111	8042	73585	62520	11065	250	273697
22612	-748	-274	-474	88288	78993	9295	82462	69703	12759	743	309355
28370	1178	668	510	97027	86219	10808	94413	79683	14730	1540	356228
25912	-10016	-9907	-109	97586	86698	10888	82791	68041	14750	723	375222
25338	-2567	-2019	-548	104735	92914	11821	91339	75443	15896	-869	402471
26875	3950	5281	-1331	128759	115674	13085	112913	95405	17508	-772	431687
30196	3544	3190	354	137379	122804	14575	126077	106597	19480	95	471970
33547	2690	1950	740	142758	125173	17585	137782	115194	22588	-572	506746
37854	2689	3087	-398	149913	131484	18429	143316	119325	23991	-1304	552446
44158	3403	3998	-595	163842	143533	20309	159117	132714	26403	1795	604543
47472	4066	3533	533	168936	146962	21974	168723	139216	29507	387	654607
45478	-2727	-3352	625	175513	152056	23457	174624	141000	33624	20	683408
41932	-5845	-5898	53	172161	147670	24491	176093	140658	35435	13	696772
41715	-6522	-5810	-712	189784	163464	26320	192393	154428	37965	-1532	713096
41411	-947	-2153	1206	219664	190213	29451	219673	177121	42552	-1967	732507
46897	450	775	-325	262127	228168	33959	253014	207875	45139	-1167	764432
50787	8883	8705	178	302480	265334	37146	276618	229938	46680	-826	778511
53453	2341	1577	764	321248	280079	41169	287553	237689	49864	-626	803656
67346	8175	9174	-999	348604	303379	45225	331271	277727	53544	-71	859580
73881	5813	6284	-471	377349	326180	51169	360261	303377	56884	142	892849
78685	3909	3853	56	418542	365234	53308	386025	326845	59180	156	938684
85555	7144	7407	-263	479450	422562	56888	426223	363278	62945	535	995080
84728	-6022	-4794	-1228	469355	412510	56845	413812	351004	62808	289	1.03E+06

· MACROECONOMICS ·

SECOND CANADIAN EDITION

David C. Colander
Middlebury College

Peter S. Sephton
Queen's University

Charlene Richter
British Columbia Institute of Technology

McGraw-Hill Ryerson

Toronto   Montréal   Burr Ridge, IL   Dubuque, IA   Madison, WI   New York
San Francisco   St. Louis   Bangkok   Bogotá   Caracas   Kuala Lumpur   Lisbon
London   Madrid   Mexico City   Milan   New Delhi   Santiago   Seoul   Singapore
Sydney   Taipei

McGraw-Hill
Ryerson Limited

A Subsidiary of The **McGraw·Hill** *Companies*

Dedicated to the memory of Frank Knight and Thorstein Veblen, both of whose economics have significantly influenced the contents of this book.

Macroeconomics, Second Canadian Edition

Copyright © 2003, 1997 by McGraw-Hill Ryerson Limited, a Subsidiary of The McGraw-Hill Companies, Inc. All rights reserved. Copyright © 2001, 1998, 1995, 1993 by The McGraw-Hill Companies, Inc. All rights reserved. No part of this publication may be reproduced or transmitted in any form or by any means, or stored in a data base or retrieval system, without the prior written permission of McGraw-Hill Ryerson Limited, or in the case of photocopying or other reprographic copying, a licence from CANCOPY (the Canadian Copyright Licensing Agency), 6 Adelaide Street East, Suite 900, Toronto, Ontario, M5C 1H6.

Statistics Canada information is used with the permission of the Minister of Industry, as Minister responsible for Statistics Canada. Information on the availability of the wide range of data from Statistics Canada can be obtained from Statistics Canada's Regional Offices, its World Wide Web site at http://www.statcan.ca, and its toll-free access number 1-800-263-1136.

ISBN: 0-07-090110-4

1 2 3 4 5 6 7 8 9 10 TCP 0 9 8 7 6 5 4 3

Printed and bound in Canada

Care has been taken to trace ownership of copyright material contained in this text; however, the publisher will welcome any information that enables them to rectify any reference or credit for subsequent editions.

Cover Art:
• Alexander Calder (1898–1976)
• *Little Ball with Counterweight* ca. 1931
• Painted sheet metal, wire and wood
• 63¾ x 12½ x 12½ in. (161.9 x 31.8 x 31.8 cm)
• Collection of Whitney Museum of American Art, New York
• Promised 50th Anniversary Gift of Mr. and Mrs. Leonard J. Howich
• © 1999 Estate of Alexander Calder/Artists Rights Society (ARS), New York
• Photography by: Jerry L. Thompson

Interior Artist: Alexander Calder (1898–1976)
• *Yellow Whale*, 1958
• Painted sheet metal, wire and paint, 26 x 25 inches (66 cm x 114.3 cm)
• Collection of Peter and Beverly Lipman
• © 1999 Estate of Alexander Calder/Artists Rights Society (ARS), New York
• Photography by: Jerry L. Thompson

Vice President and Editorial Director: Pat Ferrier
Senior Sponsoring Editor: Lynn Fisher
Developmental Editor: Maria Chu
Economics Editor: Ron Doleman
Marketing Manager: Kelly Smyth
Supervising Editor: Anne Macdonald
Copy Editor: Susan Broadhurst
Production Coordinator: Jennifer Wilkie
Composition: First Folio Resource Group, Inc.
Cover Design: Greg Devitt
Printer: Transcontinental Printing Group

National Library of Canada Cataloguing in Publication Data

Colander, David C.
    Macroeconomics/David C. Colander, Peter Sephton, Charlene Richter.—2nd Canadian ed.

Includes index.
ISBN 0-07-090110-4

Macroeconomics. I. Sephton, Peter S. II. Richter, Charlene, 1956- III. Title.

HB172.5.C64 2002   339   C2002-902248-7

ABOUT THE
AUTHORS

David Colander is the Christian A. Johnson Distinguished Professor of Economics at Middlebury College. He has authored, co-authored, or edited 35 books and over 100 articles on a wide range of economic topics.

He earned his B.A. at Columbia College and his M.Phil and Ph.D. at Columbia University. He also studied at the University of Birmingham in England and at Wilhelmsburg Gymnasium in Germany. Professor Colander has taught at Columbia College, Vassar College, and the University of Miami, as well as having been a consultant to Time-Life Films, a consultant to Congress, a Brookings Policy Fellow, and Visiting Scholar at Nuffield College, Oxford.

He belongs to a variety of professional associations and has served on the board of directors and as vice president and president of both the History of Economic Thought Society and the Eastern Economics Association. He has also served on the editorial boards of the *Journal of Economic Perspectives, The Journal of Economic Education, The Journal of Economic Methodology, The Journal of the History of Economic Thought,* and *The Eastern Economics Journal.*

He is married to a pediatrician, Patrice, who has a private practice in Middlebury, Vermont. In their spare time, the Colanders designed and built their oak post-and-beam house on a ridge overlooking the Green Mountains to the east and the Adirondacks to the west. The house is located on the site of a former drive-in movie theatre. (They replaced the speaker poles with fruit trees and used the I-beams from the screen as support for the second story of the carriage house and the garage. Dave's office and library are in the former projection room.)

Peter Sephton is a Professor in the School of Business at Queen's University and the Director of the Queen's National Executive MBA program. He has authored or co-authored several books as well as over three dozen articles on a wide range of topics.

He earned his B.A. at McMaster University and his M.A. and Ph.D. from Queen's University. Professor Sephton has taught at the University of Regina, the University of New Brunswick, and St. Thomas University. He has also been a visiting scholar at the International Monetary Fund as well as the Federal Reserve Bank of St. Louis. He has acted as a consultant to provincial governments and environmental engineering firms. In addition, he has provided advice in legal cases that involved estimating damages for personal injury and fatal accident claims. He has also held positions at the Bank of Canada, the Ontario Ministry of Treasury and Economics, and the Federal Business Development Bank.

Charlene Richter currently teaches in the School of Business at the British Columbia Institute of Technology in Burnaby; teaching various introductory and advanced economics courses to (very bright) students in the Financial Management and Advanced Studies in Business programs. Previously, Charlene worked as an economist with Bell Canada where she analyzed industrial strategy and competition policy. She was also a member of a collaborative research team at the Centre for Trade Policy and Law in Ottawa that quantified the effects of North American free trade on Canadian manufacturing industries, and assessed the significance of international technology transfers between Canadian and U.S. high tech firms. She received B.A. and M.A. degrees from Simon Fraser University, and is a provincially certified teacher holding a British Columbia Professional Teaching Certificate. She has written several economics course manuals and designed and delivered distance education courses. Charlene is the co-author of several academic papers, and a recipient of an award for excellence in teaching. Besides her interest in Canadian industrial policy and international trade, Charlene has many other fascinations: photography, art, architecture, wine, fitness and the stock market. However, Charlene has discovered that her recreational activities are—most unfortunately—subject to irascible and unsympathetic budget constraints.

BRIEF CONTENTS

Preface xiv

I

INTRODUCTION: THINKING LIKE AN ECONOMIST

1 Economics and Economic Reasoning 4
Appendix A: The Language of Graphs 20

2 The Economic Organization of Society 27
Appendix A: The History of Economic Systems 47

3 The Canadian Economy in a Global Setting 55
Appendix A: Valuing Stocks and Bonds 78

4 Supply and Demand 82

5 Using Supply and Demand 104
Appendix A: Algebraic Representation of Supply, Demand, and Equilibrium 127

II

MACROECONOMICS

I MACROECONOMIC ISSUES

6 Economic Growth, Business Cycles, Unemployment, and Inflation 134
Appendix A: Nonmainstream Approaches to Macro 159

7 National Income Accounting 162
Appendix A: Calculating Real GDP 185

II THE MACROECONOMIC FRAMEWORK

8 Growth, Productivity, and the Wealth of Nations 187

9 Aggregate Demand, Aggregate Supply, and Modern Macroeconomics 210

10 The Multiplier Model 234
Appendix A: An Algebraic Presentation of the Expanded Multiplier Model 256
Appendix B: The Multiplier Model and the AS/AD Model 257

III POLICY ISSUES

11 Demand Management Policy: The Fiscal Approach 260

12 Politics, Surpluses, Deficits, and Debt 284
Appendix A: Changes in the Debt-to-GDP Ratio 303

13 Money, Banking, and the Financial Sector 305
Appendix A: A Closer Look at Financial Institutions and Financial Markets 326
Appendix B: Creation of Money Using T-Accounts 335

14 Monetary Policy and the Debate about Macro Policy 338
Appendix A: The Effect of Monetary Policy Using T-Accounts 358

15 Inflation and Its Relationship to Unemployment and Growth 360

IV INTERNATIONAL POLICY ISSUES

16 Open Economy Macro: Exchange Rate and Trade Policy 382
Appendix A: History of Exchange Rate Systems 413

17 International Dimensions of Monetary and Fiscal Policies 416

V COMBINING THE FRAMEWORK WITH POLICY

18 Tools, Rules, and Policy 432

CONTENTS

Preface xiv

INTRODUCTION: THINKING LIKE AN ECONOMIST

1 ECONOMICS AND ECONOMIC REASONING 4

What Economics Is 5

A Guide to Economic Reasoning 6
   Marginal Costs and Marginal Benefits 6

KNOWING THE TOOLS: Economic Knowledge in
   One Sentence: TANSTAAFL 7
   Economics and Passion 7
   Opportunity Cost 8
   Economic and Market Forces 9

BEYOND THE TOOLS: Economics in Perspective 10

Economic Terminology 11

Economic Insights 11
   The Invisible Hand Theory 12

APPLYING THE TOOLS: Winston Churchill and
   Lady Astor 13
   Economic Theory and Stories 13
   Microeconomics and Macroeconomics 13

KNOWING THE TOOLS: Dealing with
   Math Anxiety 14

Economic Institutions 14

Economic Policy Options 15
   Objective Policy Analysis 16
   Policy and Social and Political Forces 17

Conclusion 17

Chapter Summary 17
   Key Terms 18
   Questions for Thought and Review 18
   Problems and Exercises 18
   Web Questions 19
   Answers to Margin Questions 19

Appendix A: The Language of Graphs 20

2 THE ECONOMIC ORGANIZATION OF SOCIETY 27

Capitalism 28
   Reliance on the Market 28
   What's Good about the Market? 29

Socialism 29
   Socialism in Theory 29
   Socialism in Practice 30

The Production Possibility Curve and Economic
Reasoning 30

APPLYING THE TOOLS: Tradition and Today's
   Economy 31
   The Production Possibility Table 31

BEYOND THE TOOLS: The Rise of Markets in
   Perspective 32
   The Production Possibility Curve 32

KNOWING THE TOOLS: Production Possibility
   Curves 35

Some Examples of Shifts in the Production Possibility
Curve 37
The Production Possibility Curve and Economic
Systems 38
The Production Possibility Curve and
Tough Choices 39
Comparative Advantage, Specialization, and Trade 39
The Division of Labour 41
Markets, Specialization, and Growth 42
Conclusion 42
Chapter Summary 43
Key Terms 43
Questions for Thought and Review 43
Problems and Exercises 44
Web Questions 46
Answers to Margin Questions 46
Appendix A: The History of Economic Systems 47

3 THE CANADIAN ECONOMY IN A
GLOBAL SETTING 55

The Canadian Economy 56
Business 57
Consumer Sovereignty and Business 57
Forms of Business 58
BEYOND THE TOOLS: Is Canada a Postindustrial
Society? 58
Finance and Business 59
KNOWING THE TOOLS: The Stock Market 60
E-Commerce and the Digital Economy 60
Households 61
The Power of Households 61
Suppliers of Labour 62
Government 62
Government as an Actor 63
Government as a Referee 64
The Global Setting 65
Global Corporations 66
International Trade 66
APPLYING THE TOOLS: A World Economic
Geography Quiz 67
BEYOND THE TOOLS: International Issues in
Perspective 70
KNOWING THE TOOLS: Our International
Competitors 71
How International Trade Differs from Domestic Trade 71
Institutions Supporting Free Trade 73

Free Trade Organizations 73
International Economic Policy Organizations 74
Conclusion 74
Chapter Summary 75
Key Terms 75
Questions for Thought and Review 75
Problems and Exercises 76
Web Questions 77
Answers to Margin Questions 77
Appendix A: Valuing Stocks and Bonds 78

4 SUPPLY AND DEMAND 82

Demand 83
The Law of Demand 83
The Demand Curve 84
Shifts in Demand versus Movements along a Demand
Curve 84
Shift Factors of Demand 85
A Review 86
The Demand Table 87
From a Demand Table to a Demand Curve 87
Individual and Market Demand Curves 88
KNOWING THE TOOLS: Six Things to Remember
When Considering a Demand Curve 89
Supply 89
The Law of Supply 90
The Supply Curve 90
Shifts in Supply versus Movements along a Supply
Curve 91
Shift Factors of Supply 91
Shift in Supply versus a Movement along a Supply
Curve 92
A Review 93
The Supply Table 93
KNOWING THE TOOLS: Six Things to Remember
When Considering a Supply Curve 94
From a Supply Table to a Supply Curve 94
Individual and Market Supply Curves 94
The Marriage of Supply and Demand 95
Excess Supply 95
Excess Demand 95
Price Adjusts 95
The Graphical Marriage of Supply and Demand 96
Equilibrium 97
What Equilibrium Is 97
What Equilibrium Isn't 97
Desirable Characteristics of Supply/Demand
Equilibrium 97

APPLYING THE TOOLS: The Supply and Demand for
    Children 99

Conclusion 99

Chapter Summary 99
    Key Terms 100
    Questions for Thought and Review 100
    Problems and Exercises 101
    Web Questions 102
    Answers to Margin Questions 102

5 USING SUPPLY AND DEMAND 104

The Power of Supply and Demand 104
    Six Real-World Examples 106
KNOWING THE TOOLS: Supply and
    Demand in Action 109
    A Review 109
Government Interventions: Price Ceilings and Floors 111
    Price Ceilings 111
    Price Floors 114
Government Interventions: Taxes, Tariffs, and
Quotas 116
    Excise Taxes and Tariffs 116
    Quotas 117
    The Relationship between a Quota and a Tariff 117
The Limitations of Supply and Demand Analysis 118
    Other Things Don't Remain Constant 118
    The Fallacy of Composition 119
The Roles of Government 119
BEYOND THE TOOLS: Laissez-Faire Is Not
    Anarchy 120
    Provide a Stable Set of Institutions and Rules 120
    Promote Effective and Workable Competition 120
    Correct for Externalities 121
    Ensure Economic Stability and Growth 122
    Provide for Public Goods 122
    Adjust for Undesired Market Results 122
    Market Failures and Government Failures 123
Conclusion 123

Chapter Summary 124
    Key Terms 124
    Questions for Thought and Review 124
    Problems and Exercises 125
    Web Questions 126
    Answers to Margin Questions 126
Appendix A: Algebraic Representation of Supply, Demand,
    and Equilibrium 127

MACROECONOMICS

I MACROECONOMIC ISSUES

**6 ECONOMIC GROWTH, BUSINESS
CYCLES, UNEMPLOYMENT, AND
INFLATION 134**

Two Frameworks: The Long Run and the Short Run 135
Growth 135
KNOWING THE TOOLS: Your Consumption and
    Average Consumption 136
    Global Experiences with Growth 136
    The Benefits and Costs of Growth 137
Business Cycles 138
    The Phases of the Business Cycle 138
    Why Do Business Cycles Occur? 140
    Leading Indicators 141
Unemployment 141
    Unemployment as a Social Problem 142
    Unemployment as Government's Problem 143
    Why the Target Rate of Unemployment Changed 143
BEYOND THE TOOLS: From Full Employment to the
    Target Rate of Unemployment 144
    Whose Responsibility Is Unemployment? 144
APPLYING THE TOOLS: Categories of
    Unemployment 145
    How Is Unemployment Measured? 146
    Unemployment and Potential Output 148
    Microeconomic Categories of Unemployment 149
Inflation 149
    Measurement of Inflation 150
KNOWING THE TOOLS: Measurement Problems with
    the Consumer Price Index 152
    Real and Nominal Concepts 154
    Expected and Unexpected Inflation 154
    Costs of Inflation 155
Conclusion 156

Chapter Summary 156
    Key Terms 157
    Questions for Thought and Review 157
    Problems and Exercises 157
    Web Questions 158

Answers to Margin Questions 159

Appendix A: Nonmainstream Approaches to Macro 159

7 NATIONAL INCOME ACCOUNTING 162

National Income Accounting 163
  Measuring Total Economic Output of Goods and
    Services 163
  Calculating GDP 164
BEYOND THE TOOLS: Is GDP Biased Against
  Women? 168
Two Methods of Calculating GDP 168
  The National Income Accounting Identity 168
  The Expenditures Approach 168
  The Factor Incomes Approach 171
  Equality of Income and Expenditure 173
  Other Income Terms 173
APPLYING THE TOOLS: National Income
  Accounting 175
Using GDP Figures 175
  Comparing GDP among Countries 175
  Economic Welfare over Time 176
  Real and Nominal GDP 176
Some Limitations of National Income Accounting 177
  GDP Measures Market Activity, Not Welfare 178
APPLYING THE TOOLS: The Happiness Index 178
  Measurement Errors 179
  Misinterpretation of Subcategories 179
  Genuine Progress Indicators 180
APPLYING THE TOOLS: The Underground
  Economy 180
Conclusion 181
Chapter Summary 181
  Key Terms 182
  Questions for Thought and Review 182
  Problems and Exercises 182
  Web Questions 184
  Answers to Margin Questions 184
Appendix A: Calculating Real GDP 185

II THE MACROECONOMIC FRAMEWORK

8 GROWTH, PRODUCTIVITY, AND THE WEALTH OF NATIONS 187

General Observations about Growth 188
  Growth and the Economy's Potential Output 188

The Importance of Growth for Living Standards 188
BEYOND THE TOOLS: Is Growth Good? 189
  Markets, Specialization, and Growth 190
  Economic Growth, Distribution, and Markets 190
  Per Capita Growth 191
The Sources of Growth 192
  Investment and Accumulated Capital 192
  Available Resources 193
  Growth-Compatible Institutions 194
  Technological Development 194
  Entrepreneurship 195
  Turning the Sources of Growth into Growth 195
The Production Function and Theories of Growth 195
  The Standard Theory of Growth—the Classical
    Growth Model 196
APPLYING THE TOOLS: Is the 21st Century the Age of
  Technology or One of Many Ages of Technology? 198
  New Growth Theory 199
Economic Policies to Encourage Per Capita Growth 202
  Policies to Encourage Saving and Investment 202
  Policies to Control Population Growth 203
  Policies to Increase the Level of Education 204
  Policies to Create Institutions That Encourage
    Technological Innovation 204
  Policies to Provide Funding for Basic Research 206
  Policies to Increase the Economy's Openness to
    Trade 206
Conclusion 206
Chapter Summary 207
  Key Terms 207
  Questions for Thought and Review 207
  Problems and Exercises 208
  Web Questions 209
  Answers to Margin Questions 209

9 AGGREGATE DEMAND, AGGREGATE SUPPLY, AND MODERN MACROECONOMICS 210

The Historical Development of Modern Macro 211
  From Classical to Keynesian Economics 212
  Classical Economists 212
  The Layperson's Explanation for Unemployment 212
  The Essence of Keynesian Economics 213
KNOWING THE TOOLS: In the Long Run, We're All
  Dead 213
The *AS/AD* Model 214
The Aggregate Demand Curve 215

The Slope of the *AD* Curve 215
Shifts in the *AD* Curve 217

The Aggregate Supply Curve 219
The Slope of the *SAS* Curve 220
Shifts in the *SAS* Curve 221

The Long-Run Aggregate Supply Curve 221

Equilibrium in the Aggregate Economy 222
Short-Run Equilibrium 222
Long-Run Equilibrium 223
Integrating the Short-Run and Long-Run
Frameworks 223

KNOWING THE TOOLS: Why Are Prices
Inflexible? 224

KNOWING THE TOOLS: A Review of the *AS/AD*
Model 226
Some Additional Policy Examples 227

Why Macro Policy Is More Complicated Than the
AS/AD Model Makes It Look 227
Three Policy Ranges 228
The Problem of Estimating Potential Output 229
Some Real-World Examples 229
Debates about Potential Output 230

Conclusion 231

Chapter Summary 231
Key Terms 232
Questions for Thought and Review 232
Problems and Exercises 232
Web Questions 233
Answers to Margin Questions 233

10 THE MULTIPLIER MODEL 234

BEYOND THE TOOLS: Econometric Models 235

The Multiplier Model 235

BEYOND THE TOOLS: History of the Multiplier
Model 236
Aggregate Production 236
Aggregate Expenditures 237

Determining the Equilibrium Level of Aggregate
Income 241

KNOWING THE TOOLS: Solving for Equilibrium
Income Algebraically 242
The Multiplier Equation 242
The Multiplier Process 243
The Circular Flow Model and the Intuition behind the
Multiplier Process 245

The Multiplier Model in Action 246

The Steps of the Multiplier Process 247
Examples of the Effects of Shifts in Aggregate
Expenditures 247

KNOWING THE TOOLS: Determinants of the AE
Curve 249

Limitations of the Multiplier Model 249
The Multiplier Model Is Not a Complete Model of the
Economy 250
Shifts Are Not as Great as Intuition Suggests 250
The Price Level Will Often Change in Response to
Shifts in Demand 250
People's Forward-Looking Expectations Make
the Adjustment Process Much More
Complicated 252
Shifts in Expenditures Might Reflect Desired Shifts in
Supply and Demand 252
Expenditures Depend on Much More Than Current
Income 252

Conclusion 253

Chapter Summary 253
Key Terms 254
Questions for Thought and Review 254
Problems and Exercises 254
Web Questions 255
Answers to Margin Questions 255

*Appendix A: An Algebraic Presentation of the Expanded
Multiplier Model 256*

*Appendix B: The Multiplier Model and the AS/AD
Model 257*

III POLICY ISSUES

**11 DEMAND MANAGEMENT POLICY: THE
FISCAL APPROACH 260**

The Story of Fiscal Policy 261
Aggregate Demand Management 261

BEYOND THE TOOLS: Keynes and Fiscal Policy 262
Fighting Recession: Expansionary Fiscal Policy 262
Fighting Inflation: Contractionary Fiscal Policy 264
The Questionable Effectiveness of Fiscal Policy 264

APPLYING THE TOOLS: Using Taxes Rather Than
Expenditures as the Tool of Fiscal Policy 266

Alternatives to Fiscal Policy 266
Directed Investment Policies: Policy Affecting
Expectations 267

KNOWING THE TOOLS: Government Demand
   Management Policies 268
   Trade Policy and Export-Led Growth 268
   Autonomous Consumption Policy 270

Real-World Examples 270
   Fiscal Policy in the Second World War 270
   Recent Fiscal Policy 271

Problems with Fiscal and Other Activist Policies 272
   1. Financing the Deficit Doesn't Have Offsetting
     Effects 272
   2. Knowing What the Situation Is 274
   3. Knowing the Level of Potential Income 274
   4. The Government's Flexibility in Changing Taxes
     and Spending 275

APPLYING THE TOOLS: Tax Breaks for the Middle
   Class 276
   5. Size of the Government Debt Doesn't Matter 276
   6. Fiscal Policy Doesn't Negatively Affect Other
     Government Goals 276
   Summary of the Problems 277

Fiscal Policy When the Price Level Is Flexible 277

Building Fiscal Policies into Institutions 279

Conclusion 279

Chapter Summary 280
   Key Terms 281
   Questions for Thought and Review 281
   Problems and Exercises 281
   Web Questions 282
   Answers to Margin Questions 283

**12 POLITICS, SURPLUSES, DEFICITS, AND
   DEBT 284**

Defining Surpluses and Deficits 286
   Financing the Deficit 286
   Arbitrariness of Defining Surpluses and Deficits 286
   Surpluses and Deficits as Summary Measures 287

Nominal and Real Surpluses and Deficits 287

Structural and Passive Surpluses and Deficits 289

The Definition of Debt and Assets 289
   Debt Management 290
   Difference between Individual and Government
     Debt 291

Canadian Government Deficits and Debt: The Historical
Record 292
   The Debt Burden 292
   Canadian Debt Relative to Other Countries 293

Interest Rates and Debt Burden 294

The Modern Debate about the Surplus 296
   Why Did the Surplus Come About? 296

KNOWING THE TOOLS: Four Important Points about
   Deficits and Debt 296
   The Federal Deficit and Debt Are Only Part of the
     Picture 297
   A Different Type of Crowding Out 297
   Is The Deficit a Good Measure of the Stance of Fiscal
     Policy? 299

BEYOND THE TOOLS: Inflation and Indexed Bonds
299

BEYOND THE TOOLS: The Stock Market Crash of
2014? 301

Conclusion 301

Chapter Summary 301
   Key Terms 302
   Questions for Thought and Review 302
   Problems and Exercises 302
   Web Questions 303
   Answers to Margin Questions 303

Appendix A: Changes in the Debt-to-GDP Ratio 303

**13 MONEY, BANKING, AND THE
   FINANCIAL SECTOR 305**

Why Is the Financial Sector Important to Macro? 306
   The Role of Interest Rates in the Financial Sector 307
   Saving That Escapes the Circular Flow 308

The Definition and Functions of Money 308
   The Canadian Central Bank: The Bank of Canada 308
   Functions of Money 309

Alternative Measures of Money 311
   M_1 311

KNOWING THE TOOLS: Characteristics of a Good
   Money 312
   M_2 312
   Beyond M_2: "The Pluses" 312
   Distinguishing between Money and Credit 313

Banks and the Creation of Money 314
   How Banks Create Money 315

APPLYING THE TOOLS: Financial Innovation 315
   The Money Multiplier 317
   Faith as the Backing of Our Money Supply 320

APPLYING THE TOOLS: The Real-World Money
   Multiplier and Recent Reforms in Banking 321

Regulation of Banks and the Financial Sector 321
    Financial Panics 321
    Anatomy of a Financial Panic 322
    Government Policy to Prevent Panic 322
    The Benefits and Problems of Guarantees 323

Conclusion 324

Chapter Summary 324
    Key Terms 324
    Questions for Thought and Review 324
    Problems and Exercises 325
    Web Questions 325
    Answers to Margin Questions 326

Appendix A: A Closer Look at Financial Institutions and Financial Markets 326

KNOWING THE TOOLS: Do Financial Assets Make Society Richer 329

Appendix B: Creation of Money Using T-Accounts 335

14 MONETARY POLICY AND THE DEBATE ABOUT MACRO POLICY 338

Duties and Structure of the Bank of Canada 340
    Structure of the Bank 340

APPLYING THE TOOLS: Central Banks in Other Countries 342

BEYOND THE TOOLS: History of the Canadian Banking System 344
    Duties of the Bank 345
    The Importance of Monetary Policy 345

APPLYING THE TOOLS: Three Letters 345
    The Conduct of Monetary Policy 346

Tools of Monetary Policy 346
    The Overnight Financing Rate 346
    Cash Management Operations 348

KNOWING THE TOOLS: Fancy Lingo 349

Monetary Policy in the *AS/AD* Model 350
    Monetary Policy in the Circular Flow 351
    The Emphasis on the Interest Rate 352
    Real and Nominal Interest Rates 352
    Real and Nominal Interest Rates and Monetary Policy 353

Problems in the Conduct of Monetary Policy 353
    Knowing What Policy to Use 353
    Understanding the Policy You're Using 354
    Lags in Monetary Policy 354
    Political Pressure 355

Conflicting International Goals 355

Conclusion 355

Chapter Summary 355
    Key Terms 356
    Questions for Thought and Review 356
    Problems and Exercises 356
    Web Questions 357
    Answers to Margin Questions 357

Appendix A: The Effect of Monetary Policy Using T-Accounts 358

15 INFLATION AND ITS RELATIONSHIP TO UNEMPLOYMENT AND GROWTH 360

Some Basics about Inflation 361
    The Distributional Effects of Inflation 361
    Expectations of Inflation 361
    Productivity, Inflation, and Wages 362

Theories of Inflation 362
    The Quantity Theory of Money and Inflation 362

KNOWING THE TOOLS: Demand-Pull and Cost-Push Inflation 363

BEYOND THE TOOLS: The Keeper of the Classical Faith: Milton Friedman 367
    The Institutional Theory of Inflation 368

KNOWING THE TOOLS: Dieting and Fighting Inflation 371

Inflation and Unemployment: The Phillips Curve 371
    History of the Phillips Curve 372
    The Breakdown of the Short-Run Phillips Curve 372
    The Long-Run and Short-Run Phillips Curves 372
    Stagflation and the Phillips Curve 375
    The New Economy: The Late 1990s and Early 2000s 376

The Relationship between Inflation and Growth 376
    Quantity Theory and the Inflation/Growth Trade-Off 376
    Institutional Theory and the Inflation/Growth Trade-Off 377

Conclusion 378

Chapter Summary 378
    Key Terms 379
    Questions for Thought and Review 379
    Problems and Exercises 379
    Web Questions 380
    Answers to Margin Questions 381

IV INTERNATIONAL POLICY ISSUES

16 OPEN ECONOMY MACRO: EXCHANGE RATE AND TRADE POLICY 382

The Balance of Payments 383
    The Current Account 384
    The Capital and Financial Account 385
    Balance of Payments Equilibrium 386

Exchange Rates 387
    Exchange Rates and the Balance of
        Payments 388
    Fundamental Forces Determining Exchange
        Rates 388
    Why Exchange Rate Determination Is More
        Complicated Than Supply/Demand Analysis
        Makes It Seem 390
    International Trade Problems from Shifting Values of
        Currencies 391
    KNOWING THE TOOLS: Exchange Rates Set by
        Law: Nonconvertible Currencies and Capital
        Controls 391
    How a Fixed Exchange Rate System Works 392

APPLYING THE TOOLS: The Value of the Canadian
    Dollar 394

Advantages and Disadvantages of Alternative Exchange
Rate Systems 395
    Fixed Exchange Rates 396
    Flexible Exchange Rates 397
    Partially Flexible Exchange Rates 398
    Which View Is Right? 398

Monetary Union in North America 398

APPLYING THE TOOLS: The Euro 399
    Possible Options 399

Adjusting the Economy to the Exchange Rate via Trade
Policy 402
    Varieties of Trade Restrictions 402
    Economists' Dislike of Trade Restriction
        Policies 405
    Strategic Trade Policies 405

International Trade Ageements Affecting Canada 406
    The Canada–U.S. Free Trade Agreement 406
    The North American Free Trade Agreement 408
    Free Trade Areas of the Americas 408

Conclusion 409
Chapter Summary 409
    Key Terms 410
    Questions for Thought and Review 410
    Problems and Exercises 411
    Web Questions 411
    Answers to Margin Questions 412
Appendix A: History of Exchange Rate Systems 413

17 INTERNATIONAL DIMENSIONS OF MONETARY AND FISCAL POLICIES 416

The Ambiguous International Goals of Macroeconomic
Policy 417
    The Exchange Rate Goal 417
    The Trade Balance Goal 417

APPLYING THE TOOLS: Canadian Trade: Dominated
by the United States 418
    International versus Domestic Goals 418

Monetary and Fiscal Policy with Fixed Exchange
Rates 419
    Increase the Private Demand for Euros via
        Contractionary Monetary Policy 419
    Decrease the Private Supply of Euros via
        Contractionary Monetary and Fiscal Policy 420

Monetary and Fiscal Policy with Flexible or Partially
Flexible Exchange Rate Regimes 420
    Monetary Policy's Effect on Exchange Rates 420
    Monetary Policy's Effect on the Trade Balance 422
    Fiscal Policy's Effect on Exchange Rates 424
    Fiscal Policy's Effect on the Trade Deficit 425

International Phenomena and Domestic Goals 426
    International Monetary and Fiscal Coordination 426

KNOWING THE TOOLS: Monetary and Fiscal Policy's
    Effect on International Goals 427
    Coordination Is a Two-Way Street 427
    Crowding Out and International Considerations 427

Conclusion 428
Chapter Summary 429
    Questions for Thought and Review 429
    Problems and Exercises 430
    Web Questions 430
    Answers to Margin Questions 431

V COMBINING THE FRAMEWORK WITH POLICY

18 TOOLS, RULES, AND POLICY 432

Models 433
    Micro Models 433
    Macro Models 435
KNOWING THE TOOLS: Key Models in Introductory Macroeconomics 439
Using Models to Understand and Discuss Policy 439
    Policies and Institutions 439
    Worldviews and Policy 441
    Keynesian and Classical Policy Views 442
    Monetary and Fiscal Policy 444
    Policy Process and Credibility 445
    Has the Economy Entered a New Era? 447
BEYOND THE TOOLS: The Stock Market Boom and the Economy 449

Conclusion 450
Chapter Summary 450
    Key Terms 451
    Questions for Thought and Review 451
    Problems and Exercises 451
    Web Questions 452
    Answers to Margin Questions 452

GLOSSARY G-1

COLLOQUIAL GLOSSARY CG-2

PHOTO CREDITS PC-1

INDEX I-1

PREFACE

"I actually enjoyed reading this book. As I read the chapter I felt like the professor was in the room." We received e-mails like these as we began work on this edition. They capture what we believe to be the most distinctive feature of our book—students enjoy reading it.

Our first edition was well received; it was, in large part, a standard book in both tone and structure. Students liked it, but it was seen by some as a bit idiosyncratic; it had its own presentation of AS/AD, some novel metaphors, significantly more history and information about institutions than most books had, and unfortunately, some problems during the production stage that allowed a number of pesky errors to make their way into the finished product.

NEW TO THE SECOND EDITION

We've introduced a number of changes in this edition. One that we're really excited about is the addition of a new co-author, Charlene Richter. Charlene has over 20 years of experience in the classroom and is one of the best teachers of economics around. We're excited she's joined us and we know that many of the improvements over the first edition are directly due to Charlene.

The second Canadian edition is the most teachable yet. It is shorter; it reflects many recent changes in the economy and the profession; many of its more challenging presentations have been simplified; and the production team has done a fantastic job of coordinating a geographically disperse author team. The following sections review the major changes.

● Shorter

When developing this edition we asked instructors which chapters they assign. The instructors told us that they liked many of the chapters but didn't have time to teach everything, so we cut out tangents from chapters so students could focus on the core content. This left a cleaner, shorter, more straightforward presentation of the central ideas of economics. For example, Chapter 3, The Canadian Economy in a Global Setting, combines first-edition Chapters 4 and 5. The combined chapter is much shorter and surveys the issues while saving the analysis for the macro core chapters.

● Innovation and Globalization

The economy has changed significantly in the last few years and this edition reflects that change. The revisions emphasize the digital revolution, which affects both technology and innovation, and globalization and its affect on growth. Nearly every chapter includes some discussion of one or the other or both. An entire chapter, Chapter 8, Growth, Productivity, and the Wealth of Nations, focusses on technology and growth.

● Changes in Style and Pedagogy

In response to reviewer feedback, the second edition contains fewer nonstandard terms and presentations. For example, the first edition used metaphors—the invisible handshake and the invisible foot—to describe the social and political forces that influence the economy. Instructors thought they were distracting, so we eliminated them. We still discuss social and political factors—we just don't use the metaphors.

We've also added World Wide Web icons to the margins, which direct students to questions at the end of each chapter that require some on-line research and investigation.

What's Good about the Market?

Is the market a good way to coordinate individuals' activities? Much of this book will be devoted to answering that question. The answer that we, and most Canadian economists, come to is: Yes, it is a reasonable way. True, it has problems; the market can be unfair, mean, and arbitrary, and sometimes it is downright awful. Why then do economists support it? For the same reason that Oliver Wendell Holmes supported democracy—it is a lousy system, but, based on experience with alternatives, it is better than all the others we've thought of. 2.1

see page 46

We've also reduced the number of terms defined in the margin so that students can focus on the core material, and we've made sure that these terms are clearly and consistently defined from chapter to chapter.

This edition also presents a learning structure that is clean and logical from the ground up. Here are some examples of the changes: Chapter 4, Supply and Demand, now discusses shift factors of demand and supply individually, and Chapter 5 immediately gives students the opportunity to apply those shift factors to the real world where multiple shift factors may move simultaneously. Chapter 9, Aggregate Demand, Aggregate Supply, and Modern Macroeconomics, offers a careful, uncomplicated, and standard explanation of the shift factors of aggregate demand, and then shows students how to apply the models to the real world. Here we've departed from the model used in the American edition of the text to include an upward-sloping short-run aggregate supply curve as well as a traditional aggregate demand curve. Why? Because the Canadian economy isn't a mirror image of the U.S. economy. Our models must be relevant to our environment so we can better understand the how and why of macroeconomics and macroeconomic policy.

Learning depends on organization, so we've worked hard to make elements dovetail within chapters. **Learning Objectives**, which match the structure of each chapter, serve as a quick chapter introduction and can be used by students as self-quizzes. Judiciously chosen key terms are carefully defined in context, and **Chapter Summaries** consolidate main points within the Learning Objectives framework. **Questions for Thought and Review** reinforce the Learning Objectives as they test student comprehension.

2

After reading this chapter, you should be able to:

- Define capitalism and explain how it relies on markets to coordinate economic activities.
- Define socialism and explain how in practice it solves the three coordination problems.
- Describe how economic systems have evolved from the eighth century to today.
- Demonstrate opportunity cost with a production possibility curve.
- State the principle of increasing marginal opportunity cost.

Chapter Summary

- Any economic system must solve three central problems:
  What, and how much, to produce.
  How to produce it.
  For whom to produce it.
- Capitalism is based on private property and the market; socialism is based on individuals' goodwill toward others.

- In welfare capitalism, the market, the government, and tradition each rule components of the economy.
- The production possibility curve measures the maximum combination of outputs that can be obtained from a given number of inputs. It embodies the opportunity cost concept.
- In general, in order to get more and more of something,

Pedagogy should reinforce content and help students do well on exams. This requires not only a clearly written book, but also a book that gives students an opportunity to try out their new knowledge. In addition to the critical thinking questions that were a hallmark of the previous edition, this edition includes more fundamental questions so that students can be sure they understand the basics.

Portable tutor: A pedagogical aid that uses the text margins to highlight important concepts and to ask questions that reinforce the Learning Objectives. These margin questions are answered at the end of each chapter.

CAPITALISM

Capitalism is an economic system based on private property and the market in which, in principle, individuals decide how, what, and for whom to produce. Under capitalism, individuals are encouraged to follow their own self-interest, while market forces of supply and demand are relied on to coordinate those individual pursuits. Distribution of goods is to each individual according to his or her ability, effort, and inherited property.

Reliance on market forces doesn't mean that political, social, and historical forces play no role in coordinating economic decisions. These other forces do influence how the market works. For example, for a market to exist, government must allocate and defend **private property rights**—*the control a private individual or firm has over an asset or a right.* The concept of private ownership must exist and must be accepted by individuals in society. When you say, "This car is mine," it means that it is unlawful for someone else to take it without your permission. If someone takes it without your permission, he or she is subject to punishment through the legal system.

> Capitalism is an economic system based on private property and the market. It gives private property rights to individuals, and relies on market forces to coordinate economic activity.

Reliance on the Market

Markets work through a system of rewards and payments. If you do something, you get paid for doing that something; if you take something, you pay for that something. How much you get is determined by how much you give. This relationship seems fair to most people. But there are instances when it doesn't seem fair. Say someone is unable to work. Should that person get nothing? How about Joe down the street, who was given $10 million by his parents? Is it fair that he gets lots of toys, like Corvettes and skiing

> **Q.₁** John, your study partner, is telling you that the best way to allocate property rights is through the market. How do you respond?

Each chapter ends with a set of **Web questions** that directs students to a variety of Web sites from think tanks to government data sites to business-related sites. These new questions fill many roles: They help students see how the concepts in the chapter really do relate to real-world issues; they familiarize students with the mass of information on the Internet; and they give students a chance to apply the concepts they're learning.

Web Questions

1. The Canada Pension Plan is significant to the evolution of capitalism in Canada. Go to the Human Resources Development Canada home page (www.hrdc-drhc.gc.ca/ips/common/home.shtml) and describe how changes in the plan have moved the Canadian economy toward welfare capitalism. What changes have been made that will alter the nature of CPP? What does this say about the evolution of capitalism today?

a. With how many countries does Canada trade?
b. What are its three largest trading partners?
c. How does this trade affect the world production possibility curve?

3. Visit the Adam Smith Institute's Web site (www.adam-smith.org/uk) and skim through Book One of *The Wealth of Nations*.
a. In which chapter does the quotation in the text

In another pedagogical change, we've reorganized the boxed material to fit the theme of "tools, not rules." The boxes in this edition are of three types—Knowing the Tools, Applying the Tools, and Beyond the Tools. Each of the core theory chapters contains a Knowing the Tools box that reviews the chapter's most important concepts, models, and definitions.

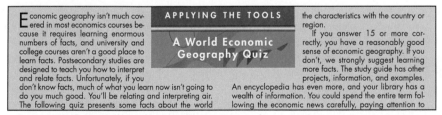

KNOWING THE TOOLS

Six Things to Remember When Considering a Demand Curve

- A demand curve had better follow the law of demand: When price rises, quantity demanded falls; and vice versa.
- The horizontal axis—quantity—has a time dimension.
- The quantities are of the same quality.
- The vertical axis—price—assumes all other prices remain the same.
- The curve assumes everything else is held constant.
- Effects of price changes are shown by movements along the demand curve. Effects of anything else on demand (shift factors) are shown by shifts of the entire demand curve.

Applying the Tools boxes provide real-world applications or information related to the chapter.

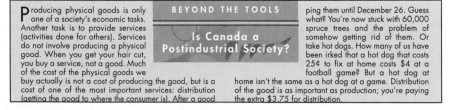

APPLYING THE TOOLS

A World Economic Geography Quiz

Economic geography isn't much covered in most economics courses because it requires learning enormous numbers of facts, and university and college courses aren't a good place to learn facts. Postsecondary studies are designed to teach you how to interpret and relate facts. Unfortunately, if you don't know facts, much of what you learn now isn't going to do you much good. You'll be relating and interpreting air. The following quiz presents some facts about the world the characteristics with the country or region.

If you answer 15 or more correctly, you have a reasonably good sense of economic geography. If you don't, we strongly suggest learning more facts. The study guide has other projects, information, and examples. An encyclopedia has even more, and your library has a wealth of information. You could spend the entire term following the economic news carefully, paying attention to

Material that places a concept in a broader or more institutional context appears in Beyond the Tools boxes.

BEYOND THE TOOLS

Is Canada a Postindustrial Society?

Producing physical goods is only one of a society's economic tasks. Another task is to provide services (activities done for others). Services do not involve producing a physical good. When you get your hair cut, you buy a service, not a good. Much of the cost of the physical goods we buy actually is not a cost of producing the good, but is a cost of one of the most important services: distribution (getting the good to where the consumer is). After a good ping them until December 26. Guess what? You're now stuck with 60,000 spruce trees and the problem of somehow getting rid of them. Or take hot dogs. How many of us have been irked that a hot dog that costs 25¢ to fix at home costs $4 at a football game? But a hot dog at home isn't the same as a hot dog at a game. Distribution of the good is as important as production; you're paying the extra $3.75 for distribution.

These carefully defined boxes help students organize complementary material as they read through the chapters.

We've also added a glossary of colloquial terms so that students whose first language isn't English will broaden and strengthen their understanding of the common usage of English.

● Major Changes

The three biggest changes in this text are (1) a restructuring of the macro presentation to a long-run first presentation, (2) the change to a more traditional treatment of the *AS/AD* model, and (3) the focus on a single model with fewer Keynesian/Classical distinctions.

- *Expanded and earlier coverage of growth.*   New Chapter 8, Growth, Productivity, and the Wealth of Nations, presents the long-run framework that determines potential income and growth before presenting the short-run framework relevant for fluctuations. This change reflects the growing interest in the long run and sets the stage for an integrated discussion of macro policy. The growth presentation is an intuitive one, emphasizing gains from trade, specialization, and division of labour, not an analytic one based on the Solow growth model. The chapter presents the empirical evidence showing a correlation between markets and growth, and discusses why markets lead to growth. It concludes with a discussion of government policies that promote growth.

- *Surrender to AS/AD terminology.*   Those of you familiar with our book and with us know that we have battled against the way *AS/AD* is presented in the text. In this edition we surrender. Our alternative terminology did not catch on at the principles level; it involved simply too much analytics for students to learn, and so in this edition we use standard *AS/AD* terminology. We don't regard the fight as a total loss. In some ways we, together with a large number of other economists who wrote technical articles, won the battle; all principles books now do a much better job of presenting the *AS/AD* model and distinguishing it from a micro supply/demand model, so using it is not so objectionable.

- *The AS/AD modification required major changes.*   In Chapter 9, Aggregate Demand, Aggregate Supply, and Modern Macroeconomics, we first simplified the presentation of both the *AS* and *AD* curves. The *AD* curve is presented clearly with a minimum of technical additions. Similarly, to keep the presentation as simple as possible, at first, the short-run *AS* curve is presented as perfectly elastic, with changes in price levels coming from changes in factor prices in excess of rising productivity. Combined, these two curves create a simple model that can be easily applied to discuss policy issues and extended to the case of an upward-sloping short-run *AS* curve. Moreover, because we developed potential income in the previous chapter we now use the *AS/AD* model to bring together the short-run and long-run frameworks.

- *Fewer Keynesian/Classical distinctions.*   Modern economics has arrived at a combined macro model that most economists support; this edition focuses on that model and downplays the Keynesian/ Classical policy debates that were central in the first edition. There are still differences of opinion, but they are differences of interpretations within a model, not differences of models.

- *Repositioned money and banking chapter.*   Chapter 13, Money, Banking, and the Financial Sector, now forms part of a more standard sequence. It comes after the discussion of theory and immediately before the monetary policy chapter.

- *A change in focus from deficits to surpluses.*   The revised, briefer Chapter 12, Politics, Surpluses, Deficits, and Debt, reflects current reality by shifting emphasis from deficits to surpluses. In order to facilitate an early discussion of the integration of long-run and short-run budgetary issues, it comes just after the fiscal policy chapter.

- *A simplified presentation of inflation.*   Chapter 15, Inflation and Its Relationship to Unemployment and Growth, has been simplified considerably. The first half of the chapter replaces the previous Keynesian/Classical inflation arguments with a simpler presentation of the basics of inflation. The chapter is given a contemporary policy focus with examples from Chile, Finland, Brazil, and New Zealand. The connection between the short-run and long-run Phillips curve has also been simplified.

- *A new summary chapter.* New Chapter 18, Tools, Rules, and Policy, capitalizes on the second edition's thoroughly integrated theory and policy discussions and helps students prepare for the final exam by tying together tools, institutions, and policy discussions. It first reviews the models and then uses them to explain and discuss policy. It emphasizes policy regimes and contemporary policy expectations, including the need for credibility. The chapter ends by addressing the question "Has the economy entered a new era?"

Every chapter has been updated with the latest possible statistics and the most up-to-date policy discussions.

● Design

Besides being different, the second Canadian edition also *looks* different. The design is more open and the typeface more reader-friendly. A lighter colour palette makes the graphs and charts easier to read. The Tools boxes are more integrated so students are less likely to skip over them.

WHAT WE'VE KEPT

The above discussion may make this seem like a whole new book; it isn't. *Macroeconomics* is still written by us with the same essential elements that differentiate it from other books. This includes the focus on teaching economic sensibility and the maintenance of our collective voice, both in the examples and in the passionate writing style.

Finally, while institutions and history receive less coverage, they are still important to us, so you will still find more historical and institutional issues in this book than in almost any other principles book.

ANCILLARIES

All reviewers agreed that the first edition ancillaries could be improved, so that's what we did. Thus, in this edition we have consolidated and significantly expanded and improved the previous edition's supplements into an accessible, convenient package.

For The Instructor

● The Instructor's Online Learning Centre

The OLC at www.mcgrawhill.ca/college/colander includes a password-protected Web site for Instructors. The site offers downloadable supplements and PageOut, the McGraw-Hill Ryerson course Web site development centre.

● Instructor's CD-ROM

This CD-ROM contains all of the necessary Instructor Supplements, including:

Instructor's Manual

The Instructor's Manual offers eight new features that make class preparation easier than ever. "Chapter Overview" and "What's New" provide a quick review of each chapter. "What's New" will be invaluable when modifying lecture notes to fit the new edition. "Discussion Starters" will help engage students and keep them thinking. "Tips for Teaching Large Sections" offers innovative ideas for teaching very large classes. "Student Stumbling Blocks" provides additional explanations or examples that help clarify difficult concepts. "Ties to the Tools" helps bring those text boxes into the classroom. "Pop Quiz" will help students prepare for exams. The "Case Studies" provide contemporary, real-world economic examples.

Computerized Test Bank

The test banks (micro and macro) have been adapted by Andrew Secord of St. Thomas University. The Test Bank contains over 5,000 questions and each question is categorized by chapter learning objective; level of difficulty (easy, medium, hard); skill being tested (recall, comprehension, application); and type of question (word problem, calculation, graph). They are available in the Diploma electronic test generating system.

PowerPoint Presentations

Adapted by Sonja Novkovic of St. Mary's University, this package includes all text exhibits and key concepts.

● CBC Video Cases

Prepared by Kevin Richter of Douglas College is a series of video segments drawn from CBC broadcasts. These videos have been chosen to assist students in applying economic concepts to real-world events. A set of instructor notes accompanies each video segment and is available at the Instructor's Online Learning Centre. The video segments will be available in VHS format and through video-streaming from the Online Learning Centre which is accessible to both instructors and students.

● PageOut

Visit www.mhhe.com/pageout to create a Web page for your course using our resources. PageOut is the McGraw-Hill Ryerson Web site development centre. This Web-page-generation software is free to adopters and is designed to help faculty create an online course complete with assignments, quizzes, links to relevant Web sites, lecture notes, and more, in a matter of minutes.

In addition, content cartridges are also available for course management systems, such as *WebCT* and *Blackboard*.

For The Student

● Study Guide [ISBN 007-090109-0]

Adapted by Oliver Franke of Athabasca University, the Study Guide reviews the main concepts from each chapter and applies those concepts in a variety of ways: short-answer questions; matching terms with definitions; problems and applications; a brain-teaser; multiple-choice questions; and potential essay questions. Since students learn best not by just knowing the right answer but by understanding how to get there, each answer comes with an explanation. Timed cumulative pretests help students prepare for exams. Ask for it at your bookstore!

● Student Online Learning Centre

Prepared by Oliver Franke of Athabasca University, this electronic learning aid located at www.mcgrawhill.ca/college/colander offers a wealth of materials including: CBC Video Cases; Learning Objectives; Online Quizzing (Pre-test and Post-test); Tutorial; Practice Exercises; Web Notes; Sample Exam Questions with answers; Key Terms and Searchable Glossary; PowerPoint slides; and a link to CANSIM II database.

● **GradeSummit** [www.gradesummit.com]

GradeSummit is an Internet-based self-assessment service that offers a variety of ways for students to analyze what they know and don't know. By revealing subject strengths and weaknesses and by providing detailed feedback and direction, GradeSummit enables students to focus their study time on those areas where they are most in need of improvement. GradeSummit provides data about how much students know while they study for an exam—not after they take it. It helps the professor measure an individual student's progress and assess that progress relative to others in their class.

ACKNOWLEDGEMENTS

The entire team at McGraw-Hill Ryerson deserves credit for embracing the idea of this revision and for keeping the project moving in a timely fashion. But Maria Chu, our Developmental Editor, deserves special mention for guiding the manuscript through two revisions with patience and tact. We thank Pat Ferrier, Editorial Director, Lynn Fisher, Senior Sponsoring Editor, and Ron Doleman, Economics Editor, for making this textbook a priority project and for supporting our suggestions for improvement. We would also like to thank Susan James and Susan Broadhurst, Copy Editors, for their attention to detail and accurate copy editing on *Microeconomics* and *Macroeconomics* respectively. We are grateful to Anne Macdonald, Supervising Editor, for transforming the final manuscript into a handsome book and to Kelly Smyth, Marketing Manager, for promoting it with such enthusiasm. And we appreciate the outstanding work of the McGraw-Hill Ryerson production team: Jennifer Wilkie, Production Coordinator, Dianna Little, Art Director, and Greg Devitt, Designer.

This textbook makes use of a wide range of macroeconomic data, mostly from Statistics Canada's CANSIM II database. Statistics Canada information is used with the kind permission of Statistics Canada.

Our sincere thanks go to Study Guide author Oliver Franke of Athabasca University. And to Maurice Tugwell of Acadia University and Audrey Laporte of the University of Toronto, who provided technical reviews of the manuscript.

Last, but not least, we thank the following teachers and colleagues, whose thorough reviews and thoughtful suggestions led to innumerable substantive improvements:

Keir Armstrong
Carleton University

Jeff Davidson
University of Lethbridge

Brian Ferguson
University of Guelph

Oliver Franke
Athabasca University

Raimo Marttala
Malaspina College

Kevin Richter
Douglas College

Gary Riser
Memorial University

Harvey Schwartz
York University

Andrew Secord
St. Thomas University

James Sentance
University of Prince Edward Island

Annie Spears
University of Prince Edward Island

Maurice Tugwell
Acadia University

We would also like to thank our families and friends for allowing us to indulge in long absences while working on the book. Their contributions cannot be quantified, nor can we thank them adequately for their sacrifices. They helped us keep our work in perspective and provided a loving environment in which to work.

In addition, we'd like to thank generations of students for asking good questions. We'd particularly like to thank those students who developed a passionate interest in the economic world around them, and in economics itself.

McGraw-Hill Ryerson
Online Learning Centre

McGraw-Hill Ryerson offers you an online resource that combines the best content with the flexibility and power of the Internet. Organized by chapter, the COLANDER Online Learning Centre (OLC) offers the following features to enhance your learning and understanding of economics:

- Pre-test and Post-test Quizzes
- Web Links
- Student Tutorials
- Practice Exercises
- Sample Exam Questions with Answers
- Interactive Graphing Exercises
- Microsoft® PowerPoint® Powernotes

- CBC Video Cases **CBC**
- Learning Objectives
- Chapter Summary
- Searchable Key Terms and Glossary
- Links to CANSIM II Database
- EconGraphKit

By connecting to the "real world" through the OLC, you will enjoy a dynamic and rich source of current information that will help you get more from your course and improve your chances for success, both in economics and in the future.

For the Instructor

Downloadable Supplements

All key supplements, including Instructor's Manual and Microsoft® PowerPoint® Presentations, are available, password-protected for instant access!

PageOut

Create your own course Web page for free, quickly and easily. Your professionally designed Web site links directly to OLC material, allows you to post a class syllabus, offers an online gradebook, and much more! Visit www.pageout.net

Online Resources

Primis Online gives you access to our resources in the best medium for your students: printed textbooks or electronic ebooks. There are over 350,000 pages of content available from which you can create customized learning tools from our online database at www.mhhe.com/primis

eServices

McGraw-Hill Ryerson offers a unique services package designed for Canadian faculty. Our mission is to equip providers of higher education with superior tools and resources required for excellence in teaching. For additional information visit
http://www.mcgrawhill.ca/highereducation/eservices/

ning Centre

For the Student

Interactive Graphing Exercises

Selected chapters include graphs that can be manipulated to solve exercises like those in the textbook. Students can actually see curves shift based on changes to the data.

Online Quizzes

Do you understand the material? You'll know after taking an Online Quiz! Try the Multiple Choice and True/False questions for each chapter. They're auto-graded with feedback and the option to send results directly to faculty. A pre-test and post-test is provided for each chapter.

Microsoft® PowerPoint® Powernotes

View and download presentations created for each text. Great for pre-class preparation and post-class review.

Link to CANSIM II Database Σ-STAT

Provides free-of-charge access to Statistics Canada's Computerized database and information retrieval service through ΣSTAT, Statistics Canada's educational resource that allows you to review socio-economic and demographic data in charts, graphs, and maps.

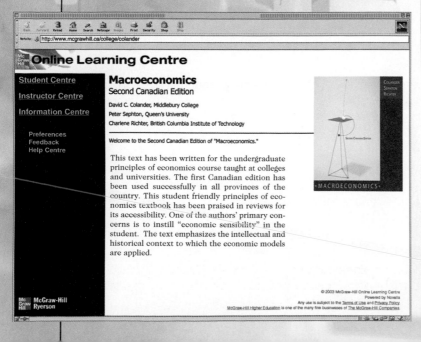

Your Internet companion to the most exciting educational tools on the Web!

The Online Learning Centre can be found at:

www.mcgrawhill.ca/college/colander

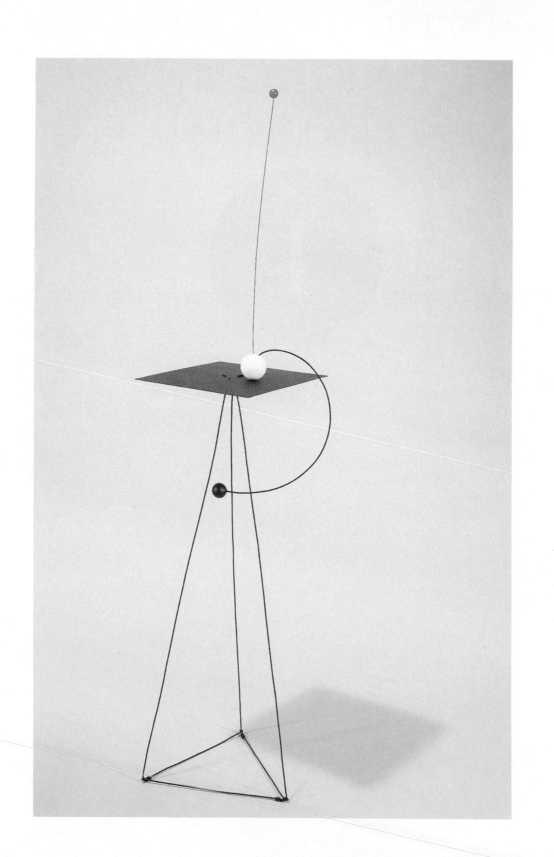

INTRODUCTION: THINKING LIKE AN ECONOMIST

I

Chapter 1   Economics and Economic Reasoning

Chapter 2   The Economic Organization of Society

Chapter 3   The Canadian Economy in a Global Setting

Chapter 4   Supply and Demand

Chapter 5   Using Supply and Demand

Part I is an introduction, and an introduction to an introduction seems a little funny. Other sections have introductions, so it seemed a little funny not to have an introduction to Part I, and besides, as you will see, we're a little funny ourselves (which, in turn, has two interpretations; we're sure you'll decide which of the two is appropriate). It will, however, be a very brief introduction, consisting of questions you probably have and some answers to those questions.

SOME QUESTIONS AND ANSWERS

Why study economics?
Because it's neat and interesting and helps provide insight into events that are constantly going on around you.

Why is this book so big?
Because there's a lot of important information in it and because the book is designed so your instructor can pick and choose. You'll likely not be required to read all of it – but once you start it, you'll probably read it all anyhow. (Would you believe?)

Why does this book cost so much?
To answer this question you'll have to read the book.

Will this book make me rich?
No.

Will this book make me happy?
It depends.

This book doesn't seem to be written in a normal textbook style. What gives?
Learning economics is fun, so why write a book that's hard to read? We're passionate when it comes to conveying our love for economics. (OK, we need to get out more). We'll try hard to keep your interest and convince you that thinking like an economist is pretty easy once you get the hang of it.

Will the entire book be like this?
No, the introduction is just trying to rope you in! Much of this book will be hard going. Learning happens to be a difficult task – no pain, no gain. But the authors aren't sadists – we try to make learning as pleasantly painful as possible.

What do the authors' students think of them?
Fair, interesting, and sincerely interested in getting students to learn. (Answer written by some of our students).

So, there you have it. Answers to the questions that you might never have thought of if they hadn't been put in front of you. We hope they give you a sense of the approach we'll use in this book. There are some neat ideas in it. Let's now briefly consider what's in the first five chapters.

A SURVEY OF THE FIRST FIVE CHAPTERS

This first section is really an introduction to the rest of the book. It gives you the background necessary so that the later chapters will make sense. Chapter 1 gives you an overview of the entire field of economics as well as an introduction to our style. Chapter 2 gives you some history of economic systems and shows you how important institutions are. It gives you a sense of how economic forces interact with political and social forces. Chapter 3 introduces you to the institutions of the Canadian economy and discusses how our economy must be viewed in a global setting. Chapters 4 and 5 introduce you to supply and demand, and show you not only the power of those two concepts, but also their limitations.

Now let's get on with the show.

Economics and Economic Reasoning

1

After reading this chapter, you should be able to:

- Define economics and list three coordination problems that an economy must solve.

- Explain how to make decisions by comparing marginal costs and marginal benefits.

- Define opportunity cost and explain its relationship to economic reasoning.

- Explain real-world events in terms of economic forces, social forces, and political forces.

- Differentiate between microeconomics and macroeconomics.

- Distinguish among positive economics, normative economics, and the art of economics.

*In my vacations, I visited the poorest quarters
of several cities and walked through one street after
another, looking at the faces of the poorest people.
Next I resolved to make as thorough a study
as I could of Political Economy.*

Alfred Marshall

When an artist looks at the world, he sees colour. When a musician looks at the world, she hears music. An economist looks at the world and sees a symphony of costs and benefits. The economist's world might not be as colourful or as melodic as the artist's or musician's worlds, but it's more practical. If you want to understand what's going on in the world that's really out there, you need to know economics.

WHAT ECONOMICS IS

Economics is *the study of how human beings coordinate their wants and desires, given the decision-making mechanisms, social customs, and political realities of their society.* One of the key words in the definition of the term "economics" is *coordination.* Coordination can mean many things. In the study of economics, coordination refers to how the three central problems facing any economy are solved. These central problems are:

1. What, and how much, to produce.

2. How to produce it.

3. For whom to produce it.

In answering these questions, economists generally find that individuals want more than is available, given how much they're willing to work. That means that in our economy there is a problem of **scarcity**—*the goods available are too few to satisfy individuals' desires.* Wants are unlimited but resources are limited.

Scarcity has two elements—our wants and our means of fulfilling those wants. These can be interrelated since wants are changeable and partially determined by society. The way we fulfill wants can affect those wants. For example, if you work on Bay Street you will probably want upscale and trendy clothes. If you work in Calgary, you may be quite happy wearing Levi's and cowboy boots.

The degree of scarcity is constantly changing. The quantity of goods, services, and usable resources depends on technology and human action, which underlie production. Individuals' imagination, innovativeness, and willingness to do what needs to be done can greatly increase available goods and resources. Who knows what technologies lie in our future—nanites or micromachines that change atoms into whatever we want could conceivably eliminate scarcity of goods we currently consume. But they would not eliminate scarcity entirely since new wants are constantly developing.

In all known economies, coordination has involved coercion—limiting people's wants and increasing the amount of work individuals are willing to do to fulfill those wants. The reality is that many people would rather play than help solve society's problems. So the basic economic problem involves inspiring people to do things that other people want them to do, and not to do things that other people don't want them to do. Thus, an alternative definition of economics is that it is the study of how to get people to do things they're not wild about doing (such as studying) and not to do things they are wild about doing (such as eating all the lobster they like), so that the things some people want to do are consistent with the things other people want to do.

To understand an economy you need to learn:

1. *Economic reasoning.*

2. *Economic terminology.*

3. *Economic insights* that economists have about issues, and theories that lead to those insights.

4. Information about *economic institutions*.

5. Information about the *economic policy options* facing society today.

Let's consider each in turn.

Three central coordination problems any economy must solve are what to produce, how to produce it, and for whom to produce it.

The quantity of goods, services, and usable resources depends on technology and human action.

To understand an economy you need to learn:

1. Economic reasoning.
2. Economic terminology.
3. Economic insights.
4. Economic institutions.
5. Economic policy options.

A GUIDE TO ECONOMIC REASONING

People trained in economics think in a certain way. They analyze everything critically; they compare the costs and the benefits of every issue and make decisions based on those costs and benefits. For example, say you're trying to decide whether protecting baby seals is a good policy or not. Economists are trained to set their emotions aside and ask: What are the costs of protecting baby seals, and what are the benefits? Thus, they are open to the argument that the benefits of allowing baby seals to be killed might exceed the costs. To think like an economist is to address almost all issues using a cost/benefit approach. Economic reasoning—how to think like an economist, making decisions on the basis of costs and benefits—is the most important lesson you'll learn from this book.

Economic reasoning, once learned, is infectious. If you're susceptible, being exposed to it will change your life. It will influence your analysis of everything, including issues normally considered outside the scope of economics. For example, you will likely use economic reasoning to decide the possibility of getting a date for Saturday night, and who will pay for dinner. You will likely use it to decide whether to read this book, whether to attend class, whom to marry, and what kind of work to go into after you graduate. This is not to say that economic reasoning will provide all the answers. As you will see throughout this book, real-world questions are inevitably complicated, and economic reasoning simply provides a framework within which to approach a question. In the economic way of thinking, every choice has costs and benefits, and decisions are made by comparing them.

Marginal Costs and Marginal Benefits

The relevant costs and relevant benefits to economic reasoning are the expected *incremental* or additional costs incurred and the expected *incremental* benefits that result from a decision. Economists use the term *marginal* when referring to additional or incremental. Marginal costs and marginal benefits are key concepts.

A **marginal cost** is *the additional cost to you over and above the costs you have already incurred.* That means eliminating **sunk costs**—*costs that have already been incurred and cannot be recovered*—from the relevant costs when making a decision. Consider, for example, attending class. You've already paid your tuition; it is a sunk cost. So the marginal (or additional) cost of going to class does not include tuition.

Similarly with marginal benefit. A **marginal benefit** is *the additional benefit above what you've already derived.* The marginal benefit of reading this chapter is the *additional* knowledge you get from reading it. If you already knew everything in this chapter before you picked up the book, the marginal benefit of reading it now is zero. The marginal benefit is not zero if by reading the chapter you learn that you are prepared for class; before, you might only have suspected you were prepared.

Comparing marginal (additional) costs with marginal (additional) benefits will often tell you how you should adjust your activities to be as well off as possible. Just follow the **economic decision rule:**

If the marginal benefits of doing something exceed the marginal costs, do it.

If the marginal costs of doing something exceed the marginal benefits, don't do it.

As an example, let's consider a discussion we might have with a student who tells us that she is too busy to attend our classes. We respond, "Think about the tuition you've spent for this class—it works out to about $30 a lecture." The student answers that the

---

Economic reasoning is making decisions on the basis of costs and benefits.

1.1

see page 19

If the relevant benefits of doing something exceed the relevant costs, do it. If the relevant costs of doing something exceed the relevant benefits, don't do it.

Q.1 Say you bought stock A for $10 and stock B for $20. The price of each is currently $15. Assuming taxes are not an issue, which would you sell if you need $15?

Once upon a time, Tanstaafl was made king of all the lands. His first act was to call his economic advisers and tell them to write up all the economic knowledge the society possessed. After years of work, they presented their monumental effort: 25 volumes, each about 400 pages long. But in the interim, King Tanstaafl had become a very busy man, what with running a kingdom of all the lands and everything. Looking at the lengthy volumes, he told his advisers to summarize their findings in one volume.

Despondently, the economists returned to their desks, wondering how they could summarize what they'd been so careful to spell out. After many more years of rewriting, they were finally satisfied with their one-volume effort, and tried to make an appointment to see the king. Unfortunately, affairs of state had become even more pressing than before, and the king couldn't take the time to see them. Instead he sent word to them that he couldn't be bothered with a whole volume, and ordered them, under threat of death (for he had become a tyrant), to reduce the work to one sentence.

The economists returned to their desks, shivering in their sandals and pondering their impossible task. Thinking about their fate if they were not successful, they decided to send out for one last meal. Unfortunately, when they were collecting money to pay for the meal, they discovered they were broke. The disgusted delivery man took the last meal back to the cook, and the economists started down the path to the beheading station. On the way, the delivery man's parting words echoed in their ears. They looked at each other and suddenly they realized the truth. "We're saved!" they screamed. "That's it! That's economic knowledge in one sentence!" They wrote the sentence down and presented it to the king, who thereafter fully understood all economic problems. (He also gave them a good meal.) The sentence?

There **A**in't **N**o **S**uch **T**hing **A**s **A** **F**ree **L**unch— **TANSTAAFL**

book she reads for class is a book that we wrote, and that we wrote it so clearly she fully understands everything. She goes on:

> I've already paid the tuition and whether I go to class or not, I can't get any of the tuition back, so the tuition is a sunk cost and doesn't enter into my decision. The marginal cost to me is what I could be doing with the hour instead of spending it in class. I value my time at $75 an hour [people who understand everything value their time highly], and even though I've heard that your lectures are super, I estimate that the marginal benefit of your class is only $50. The marginal cost, $75, exceeds the marginal benefit, $50, so I don't attend class.

We would congratulate her on her diplomacy and her economic reasoning, but tell her that we give a quiz every week, that students who miss a quiz fail the quiz, that those who fail all the quizzes fail the course, and that those who fail the course do not graduate. In short, she is underestimating the marginal benefits of attending our classes. Correctly estimated, the marginal benefits of attending class exceed the marginal costs. So she should attend classes.

Economics and Passion

Recognizing that everything has a cost is reasonable, but it's a reasonableness that many people don't like. It takes some of the passion out of life. It leads you to consider possibilities like these:

- Saving some people's lives with liver transplants might not be worth the additional cost. The money might be better spent on nutritional programs that would save 20 lives for every 2 lives you might save with transplants.

- Maybe we shouldn't try to eliminate all pollution, because the additional cost of doing so may be too high. To eliminate all pollution might be to forgo too much of some other worthwhile activity.

- Buying a stock that went up 20 percent wasn't necessarily the greatest investment if in doing so you had to forgo some other investment that would have paid you a 30 percent return.

- It might make sense for the automobile industry to save $12 per car by not installing a safety device, even though without the safety device some people will be killed.

You get the idea. This kind of reasonableness is often criticized for being cold-hearted. But, not surprisingly, economists disagree; they argue that their reasoning leads to a better society for the majority of people.

Opportunity Cost

Putting economists' cost/benefit rules into practice isn't easy. To do so, you have to be able to choose and measure the costs and benefits correctly. Economists have devised the concept of **opportunity cost** to help you do that. The opportunity cost of undertaking an activity is *the benefit forgone by undertaking that activity.* The benefit forgone is the benefit that you might have gained from choosing the next-best alternative. To obtain the benefit of something, you must give up (forgo) something else—namely, the next-best alternative. All activities that have a next-best alternative have an opportunity cost.

Let's consider some examples. The opportunity cost of going out once with Natalia (or Nathaniel), the most beautiful woman (attractive man) in the world, might well be losing your solid steady, Margo (Mike). The opportunity cost of cleaning up the environment might be a reduction in the money available to assist low-income individuals. The opportunity cost of having a child might be two boats, three cars, and a two-week vacation each year for five years.

Examples are endless, but let's consider two that are particularly relevant to you: your choice of courses and your decision about how much to study. Let's say you're a full-time student and at the beginning of the term you had to choose four or five courses to take. Taking one precluded taking some other, and the opportunity cost of taking an economics course may well have been not taking a course on theatre. Similarly with studying: you have a limited amount of time to spend studying economics, studying some other subject, sleeping, or partying. The more time you spend on one activity, the less time you have for another. That's opportunity cost.

Notice how neatly the opportunity cost concept takes into account costs and benefits of all other options, and converts these alternative benefits into costs of the decision you're now making.

The relevance of opportunity cost isn't limited to your individual decisions. Opportunity costs are also relevant to government's decisions, which affect everyone in society. A common example is the guns-versus-butter debate. The resources that a society has are limited; therefore, its decision to use those resources to have more guns (more weapons) means that it must have less butter (fewer consumer goods). Thus, when society decides to spent $5 billion more on an improved health care system, the opportunity cost of that decision is $5 billion not spent on helping the homeless, paying off some of the national debt, or providing for national defense.

The opportunity cost concept has endless implications. It can even be turned upon itself. For instance, it takes time to think about alternatives; that means that there's a cost to being reasonable, so it's only reasonable to be somewhat unreasonable. If you fol-

---

Economic reasoning is based on the premise that everything has a cost.

Q-2 Can you think of a reason why a cost/benefit approach to a problem might be inappropriate? Can you give an example?

Opportunity cost is the basis of cost/benefit economic reasoning; it is the benefit forgone, or the cost, of the next-best alternative to the activity you've chosen. In economic reasoning, that cost is less than the benefit of what you've chosen.

Opportunity costs have always made choice difficult, as we see in the early-19th-century engraving, "One or the Other."

Q-3 John, your math study partner, has just said that the opportunity cost of studying one math chapter is about 1/40 the price you paid for your math book, since the chapter is about 1/40 of the book. Is he right? Why or why not?

lowed that argument, you've caught the economic bug. If you didn't, don't worry. Just remember the opportunity cost concept for now; we'll infect you with economic thinking in the rest of the book.

Economic and Market Forces

The opportunity cost concept applies to all aspects of life and is fundamental to understanding how society reacts to scarcity. When goods are scarce, those goods must be rationed. That is, a mechanism must be chosen to determine who gets what. Society must deal with the scarcity, thinking about and deciding how to allocate the scarce good.

Let's consider some specific real-world rationing mechanisms. Dormitory rooms are often rationed by lottery, and permission to register in popular classes is often rationed by a first-come, first-registered rule. Food in Canada, however, is generally rationed by price. If price did not ration food, there wouldn't be enough food to go around. All scarce goods or rights must be rationed in some fashion. These rationing mechanisms are examples of **economic forces,** *the necessary reactions to scarcity.*

One of the important choices that a society must make is whether to allow these economic forces to operate freely and openly or to try to rein them in. A **market force** is *an economic force that is given relatively free rein by society to work through the market.* Market forces ration by changing prices. When there's a shortage, the price goes up. When there's a surplus, the price goes down. Much of this book will be devoted to analyzing how the market works like an invisible hand, guiding economic forces to coordinate individual actions and allocate scarce resources. The **invisible hand** is *the price mechanism, the rise and fall of prices that guides our actions in a market.*

Societies can't choose whether or not to allow economic forces to operate—economic forces are always operating. However, societies may choose whether to allow market forces to predominate. Other forces play a major role in deciding whether to let market forces operate. Economic reality is determined by a contest among these forces.

Let's consider an example in which social forces prevent an economic force from becoming a market force: the problem of getting a date for Saturday night. If a school (or a society) has significantly more people of one sex than the other (let's say more men than women), some men may well find themselves without a date—that is, men will be in excess supply—and will have to find something else to do, say study or go to a movie by themselves. An "excess supply" person could solve the problem by paying someone to go out with him or her, but that would probably change the nature of the date in unacceptable ways. It would be revolting to the person who offered payment and to the person who was offered payment. That unacceptability is an example of the complex social and cultural norms that guide and limit our activities. People don't try to buy dates because social forces prevent them from doing so.

Now let's consider another example in which political and legal influences stop economic forces from becoming market forces. Say you decide that you can make some money delivering mail in your neighborhood. You try to establish a small business, but suddenly you are confronted with the law. Canada Post has a legal exclusive right to deliver regular mail, so you'll be prohibited from delivering regular mail in competition with the post office. Economic forces—the desire to make money—led you to want to enter the business, but in this case political forces quash the invisible hand.

Often political and social forces work together against the invisible hand. For example, in Canada there aren't enough babies to satisfy all the couples who desire them. Babies born to particular sets of parents are rationed—by luck. Consider a group of parents, all of whom want babies. Those who can, have a baby; those who can't have one, but want one, try to adopt. Adoption agencies ration the available babies. Who gets a

Q.4 Ali, your study partner, states that charging a user fee for health care is immoral—that health care should be freely available to all individuals in society. How would you respond?

When an economic force operates through the market, it becomes a market force.

Economic reality is controlled by three forces:
1. Economic forces (the invisible hand);
2. Social and cultural forces; and
3. Political and legal forces.

Social and cultural forces can play a significant role in the economy.

Q.5 Your study partner, Joan, states that market forces are always operative. Is she right? Why or why not?

Economic forces are always operative; society may allow market forces to operate.

BEYOND THE TOOLS

Economics in Perspective

All too often, students study economics out of context. They're presented with sterile analysis and boring facts to memorize, and are never shown how economics fits into the larger scheme of things. That's bad: it makes economics seem boring—but economics is not boring. Every so often throughout this book, sometimes in the appendixes and sometimes in boxes, we'll step back and put the analysis in perspective, giving you an idea of where the analysis sprang from and its historical context. In educational jargon, this is called *enrichment*.

We begin here with economics itself.

First, its history: In the 1500s there were few universities. Those that existed taught theology, Latin, Greek, philosophy, history, and mathematics. No economics. Then came the *Enlightenment* (about 1700), in which reasoning replaced God as the explanation of why things were the way they were. Pre-Enlightenment thinkers would answer the question, "Why am I poor?" with "Because God wills it." Enlightenment scholars looked for a different explanation. "Because of the nature of land ownership" is one answer they found.

Such reasoned explanations required more knowledge of the way things were, and the amount of information expanded so rapidly that it had to be divided or categorized for an individual to have any hope of knowing a subject. Soon philosophy was subdivided into science and philosophy. In the 1700s, the sciences were split into natural sciences and social sciences. The amount of knowledge kept increasing, and in the late 1800s and early 1900s social science itself split into subdivisions: economics, political science, history, geography, sociology, anthropology, and psychology. Many of the insights about how the economic system worked were codified in Adam Smith's *The Wealth of Nations,* written in 1776. Notice that this was written before economics as a subdiscipline developed, and Adam Smith could also be classified as an anthropologist, a sociologist, a political scientist, and a social philosopher.

Throughout the 18th and 19th centuries, economists such as Adam Smith, Thomas Malthus, John Stuart Mill, David Ricardo, and Karl Marx were more than economists; they were social philosophers who covered all aspects of social science. These writers were subsequently called *classical economists*. Alfred Marshall continued in that classical tradition and his book, *Principles of Economics,* published in the late 1800s, was written with the other social sciences much in evidence. But Marshall also changed the questions economists ask; he focussed on those questions that could be asked in a graphical supply/demand framework.

This book falls solidly in the Marshallian tradition. It sees economics as a way of thinking—as an engine of analysis used to understand real-world phenomena.

Marshallian economics is an art, not a science. It is primarily about policy, not theory. It sees institutions as well as political and social dimensions of reality as important, and it shows you how economics ties in to those dimensions.

baby depends on criteria set by the adoption agency and on the desires of the birth mother, who can often specify the socioeconomic background (and many other characteristics) of the family in which she wants her baby to grow up. That's the economic force in action; it gives more power to the supplier of something that's in short supply.

1.2

see page 19

If our society allowed individuals to buy and sell babies, that economic force would be translated into a market force. The invisible hand would see to it that the quantity of babies supplied would equal the quantity of babies demanded at some price. The market, not the adoption agencies, would do the rationing.[1]

---

[1]Even though it's against the law, some babies are nonetheless "sold" on a semilegal market, also called a grey market. In the United States, at the turn of the century, the "market price" for a healthy baby was about U.S. $30,000. If it were legal to sell babies (and if people didn't find it morally repugnant to have babies in order to sell them), the price would be much lower, because there would be a larger supply of babies. (It was not against the law in the U.S. to sell human eggs in the late 1990s, and one human egg was sold for U.S. $50,000. The average price was much lower; it varied with donor characteristics such as academic performance and athletic accomplishments.)

Most people, including us, find the idea of selling babies repugnant. But why? It's the strength of social forces backed up and strengthened by political forces.

What is and isn't allowable differs from one society to another. For example, in Russia, until recently, private businesses were against the law, so not many people started their own businesses. In the United States, until the 1970s, it was against the law to hold gold except in jewelry and for certain limited uses such as dental supplies, so most people refrained from holding gold. Ultimately a country's laws and social norms determine whether the invisible hand will be allowed to work.

Social and political forces are active in all parts of your life. Political forces influence many of your everyday actions. You don't practice medicine without a license; you don't sell body parts or certain addictive drugs. These actions are against the law. But many people do sell alcohol; that's not against the law if you have a permit. Social forces also influence us. You don't make profitable loans to your friends (you don't charge your friends interest); you don't charge your children for their food (parents are supposed to feed their children); many sports and media stars don't sell their autographs (some do, but many consider the practice tacky); you don't lower the wage you'll accept in order to take a job away from someone else. The list is long. You cannot understand economics without understanding the limitations that political and social forces place on economic actions.

In summary, what happens in a society can be seen as the reaction to, and interaction of, these three forces: economic forces, political and legal forces, and social and historical forces. Economics has a role to play in sociology, history, and politics, just as sociology, history, and politics have roles to play in economics.

Economics is about the real world. Throughout this book we'll use the forces just described to talk about real-world events and the interrelationships of economics, history, sociology, and politics.

> What happens in society can be seen as a reaction to, and interaction of, economic forces, political forces, social forces, and historical forces.

ECONOMIC TERMINOLOGY

Economic terminology needs little discussion. It simply needs learning. As terms come up, you'll begin to recognize them. Soon you'll begin to understand them, and finally you'll begin to feel comfortable using them. In this book we're trying to describe how economics works in the real world, so we introduce you to many of the terms that occur in business and in discussions of the economy. Whenever possible we'll integrate the introduction of new terms into the discussion so that learning them will seem painless. In fact, we've already introduced you to a number of economic terms: *opportunity cost, the invisible hand, market forces, economic forces,* to name just a few. By the end of the book we'll have introduced you to many more.

ECONOMIC INSIGHTS

Economists have thought about the economy for a long time, so it's not surprising that they've developed some insights into the way it works.

These insights are often based on generalizations, called theories, about the workings of an abstract economy. Theories tie together economists' terminology and knowledge about how an economy operates. Theories are inevitably too abstract to apply in specific cases, and thus a theory is often embodied in an **economic model**—*a framework that places the generalized insights of the theory in a more specific contextual setting*—or in an **economic principle**—*a commonly held economic insight stated as a law or general assump-*

> Theories, models, and principles must be combined with a knowledge of real-world economic institutions to arrive at specific policy recommendations.

tion. Then these theories, models, and principles are empirically tested (as best one can) to ensure that they correspond to reality. While these models and principles are less general than theories, they are still usually too general to apply in specific cases. Theories, models, and principles must be combined with a knowledge of real-world economic institutions to arrive at specific policy recommendations. An example? Early in 2002, many stores in Moncton, N.B. were open on Sundays, yet shops in Amherst, N.S., a short drive away, were not allowed to open on Sundays. Our theories and models need to take these institutional features into account if they are going to be of use in answering economic questions.

To see the importance of principles, think back to when you learned to add. You didn't memorize the sum of 147 and 138; instead you learned a principle of addition. The principle says that when adding 147 and 138, you first add 7 + 8, which you memorized was 15. You write down the 5 and carry the 1, which you add to 4 + 3 to get 8. Then add 1 + 1 = 2. So the answer is 285. When you know just one principle, you know how to add millions of combinations of numbers.

The Invisible Hand Theory

In the same way, knowing a theory gives you insight into a wide variety of economic phenomena, even though you don't know the particulars of each phenomenon. For example, much of economic theory deals with the *pricing mechanism* and how the market operates to coordinate *individuals' decisions.* Economists have come to the following insights:

When the quantity supplied is greater than the quantity demanded, price has a tendency to fall.

When the quantity demanded is greater than the quantity supplied, price has a tendency to rise.

Using these generalized insights, economists have developed a theory of markets that leads to the further insight that, under certain conditions, markets are efficient. That is, the market will coordinate individuals' decisions, allocating scarce resources to their best possible use. **Efficiency** means *achieving a goal as cheaply as possible.* Economists call this insight the **invisible hand theory**—*a market economy, through the price mechanism, will allocate resources efficiently.*

Theories, and the models used to represent them, are enormously efficient methods of conveying information, but they're also necessarily abstract. They rely on simplifying assumptions, and *if you don't know the assumptions, you don't know the theory.* The result of forgetting assumptions could be similar to what happens if you forget that you're supposed to add numbers in columns. Forgetting that, yet remembering all the steps, can lead to a wildly incorrect answer. For example,

$$147$$
$$+ \ \ 138$$
$$\overline{}$$
1,608 is wrong.

Knowing the assumptions of theories and models allows you to progress beyond gut reaction and better understand the strengths and weaknesses of various economic systems. Let's consider a central economic assumption: the assumption that individuals behave rationally—that what they choose reflects what makes them happiest, given the constraints they face, such as level of income. If that assumption doesn't hold, the invisible hand theory doesn't hold.

Q-6 There has been a superb growing season and the quantity of tomatoes supplied exceeds the quantity demanded. What is likely to happen to the price of tomatoes?

There are many stories about Nancy Astor, the first woman elected to Britain's Parliament. A vivacious, fearless American woman, she married into the English aristocracy and, during the 1930s and 1940s, became a bright light on the English social and political scenes, which were already quite bright.

One story told about Lady Astor is that she and Winston Churchill, the unorthodox genius who had a long and distinguished political career and who was Britain's prime minister during World War II, were sitting in a pub having a theoretical discussion about morality. Churchill suggested that as a thought experiment Lady Astor ponder the question: If a man were to promise her a huge amount of money—say a million pounds—for the privilege, would she sleep with him? Lady Astor did ponder the question for a while and finally answered, yes, she would, if the money were guaranteed. Churchill then asked her if she would sleep with him for five pounds. Her response was sharp: "Of course not. What do you think I am—a prostitute?" This time Churchill won the battle of wits by answering, "We have already established that fact; we are now simply negotiating about price."

One moral that economists might draw from this story is that economic incentives, if high enough, can have a powerful influence on behaviour. An equally important moral of the story is that noneconomic incentives can also be very strong. Why do most people feel it's wrong to sell sex for money, even if they would be willing to do so if the price were high enough? Keeping this second moral in mind will significantly increase your economic understanding of real-world events.

Economic Theory and Stories

Economic theory, and the models in which that theory is presented, often developed as a shorthand way of telling a story. These stories are important; they make the theory come alive and convey the insights that give economic theory its power. In this book we present plenty of theories and models, but they're accompanied by stories that provide the context that makes them relevant.

Theory is a shorthand way of telling a story.

At times, because there are many new terms, discussing models and theories takes up much of the presentation time and becomes a bit oppressive. That's the nature of the beast. As Albert Einstein said, "Theories should be as simple as possible, but not more so." When a theory or a model becomes oppressive, pause and think about the underlying story that the theory is meant to convey. That story should make sense and be concrete. If you can't translate the theory into a story, you don't understand the theory.

Often economic theories are presented in mathematical—graphical or algebraic—models. In this book we keep models to a minimum, but we cannot avoid them completely. Graphical models are used so much by economists that they must be included. So part of the course will consist of translating the verbal discussions of the economy into graphical models. To prepare you for these graphical models we have written a brief introduction to the basics of graphical presentation in Appendix A of this chapter.

Microeconomics and Macroeconomics

Economic theory is divided into two parts: microeconomic theory and macroeconomic theory. Microeconomic theory considers economic reasoning from the viewpoint of individuals and firms and builds up from there to an analysis of the whole economy. We define **microeconomics** as *the study of individual choice, and how that choice is influenced by economic forces.* Microeconomics studies such things as the pricing policies of firms, households' decisions of what to buy, and how markets allocate resources among alternative ends. Our discussion of opportunity cost was based on microeconomic theory. The invisible hand theory comes from microeconomics.

Microeconomics is the study of how individual choice is influenced by economic forces.

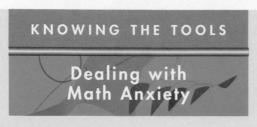

Knowing our own students, we can see the red flags rising, the legs tensing up, the fear flooding over many of you. Here it comes—the math and the graphs.

We wish we could change things by saying to you, "Don't worry— mathematics and graphical analysis are easy." But we can't. That doesn't mean math and graphical analysis aren't wonderful tools that convey ideas neatly and efficiently. They are. But we've had enough teaching experience to know that somewhere back in elementary school some teacher blew it and put about 40 percent of you off mathematics for life. A tool that scares you to death is not useful; it can be a hindrance, not a help, to learning. Nothing your current teacher or we now can say, write, or do is going to com-

pletely reassure you, but we'll do our best to relieve your anxiety.

Try to follow the numerical and graphical examples carefully, because they not only cement the knowledge into your minds, they also present in a rigorous manner the ideas we're discussing. The ideas conveyed in the numerical and graphical examples will be explained in words—and the graphical analysis (the type of mathematical explanation most used in introductory economics) generally will simply be a more precise presentation of the accompanying discussion in words. In most economics courses the exams pose the questions in graphical terms, so there's no getting around the need to understand the ideas graphically. And it is easier than you think. (Appendix A at the end of this chapter discusses the basics of graphical analysis.)

As one builds up from microeconomic analysis to an analysis of the entire economy, everything gets rather complicated. Many economists try to uncomplicate matters by taking a different approach—a macroeconomic approach—first looking at the aggregate, or whole, and then breaking it down into components. We define **macroeconomics** as *the study of the economy as a whole, which includes inflation, unemployment, business cycles, and growth*. Macroeconomics focusses on aggregate relationships, such as how household consumption is related to income and how government policies can affect growth. A micro approach would analyze a person by looking first at each individual cell and then building up. A macro approach would start with the person and then go on to his or her components—arms, legs, fingernails, feelings, and so on. Put simply, microeconomics analyzes from the parts to the whole; macroeconomics analyzes from the whole to the parts.

> Macroeconomics is the study of inflation, unemployment, business cycles, and growth; it focusses on aggregate relationships.

Microeconomics and macroeconomics are very much interrelated. Clearly, what happens in the economy as a whole is based on individual decisions, but individual decisions are made within an economy and can be understood only within that context. For example, whether a firm decides to expand production capacity will depend on what the owners expect will happen to the demand for their products. Those expectations are determined by macroeconomic conditions. Likewise, decisions by the federal government to change social assistance programs in the mid-1990s had to be made based on how those changes would affect the decisions of millions of individuals. Because microeconomics focusses on the individual and macroeconomics focusses on the whole economy, traditionally microeconomics and macroeconomics are taught separately, even though they are interrelated.

Q-7 Classify the following topics as macroeconomic or microeconomic:

1. The impact of a tax increase on aggregate output.
2. The relationship between two competing firms' pricing behaviour.
3. A farmer's decision to plant soy beans or wheat.
4. The effect of trade on economic growth.

ECONOMIC INSTITUTIONS

To know whether you can apply economic theory to reality, you must know about economic institutions. Corporations, governments, and cultural norms are all economic institutions. Many economic institutions have social, political, and religious dimensions. For example, your job often influences your social standing. In addition, many social institutions, such as the family, have economic functions. If any institution significantly affects economic decisions, we include it as an economic institution because you must understand that institution if you are to understand how the economy functions.

Economic institutions differ significantly among countries. For example, in Germany banks are allowed to own companies; in the United States they cannot. This contributes to a difference in the flow of resources into investment in Germany as compared to the flow in the United States. Or alternatively, in Japan, competition laws (laws under which companies can combine or coordinate their activities) are loose; in Canada they are more restrictive. This causes differences in the nature of competition in the two countries.

Economic institutions sometimes seem to operate in ways quite different than economic theory predicts. For example, economic theory says that prices are determined by supply and demand. However, businesses say that prices are set by rules of thumb—often by what are called cost-plus-markup rules. That is, you determine what your costs are, multiply by 1.4 or 1.5, and the result is the price you set. Economic theory says that supply and demand determine who's hired; experience suggests that hiring is often done on the basis of who you know, not by economic forces.

These apparent contradictions have two complementary explanations. First, economic theory abstracts from many issues. These issues may account for the differences. Second, there's no contradiction; economic principles often affect decisions from behind the scenes. For instance, supply and demand pressures determine what the price markup over cost will be. In all cases, however, to apply economic theory to reality—to gain the full value of economic insights—you've got to have a sense of economic institutions.

To apply economic theory to reality, you've got to have a sense of economic institutions.

ECONOMIC POLICY OPTIONS

Economic policies are *actions (or inaction) taken by government to influence economic actions.* The final goal of the course is to present the economic policy options facing our society today. For example, should the government restrict mergers between firms? Should it run a budget deficit? Should it do something about the international trade surplus? Should it decrease taxes?

We saved this discussion for last because there's no sense talking about policy options unless you know some economic terminology, some economic theory, and something about economic institutions. Once you know something about them, you're in a position to consider the policy options available for dealing with the economic problems our society faces.

To carry out economic policy effectively one must understand how institutions might change as a result of the economic policy.

Policies operate within institutions, but policies can also influence the institutions within which they operate. Let's consider an example: employment insurance and seasonal workers. In 1956 Canada introduced legislation to protect workers from short periods of unemployment (The Canadian Unemployment Assistance Act). That program evolved to the point where nearly 80 percent of the claimants were people who had previously received benefits. The initial aim of the program was to provide *temporary assistance* to the unemployed, but it had become a means of stabilizing incomes for those working in seasonal industries (fishing, lumber, etc). In the 1990s the federal government changed the program (now called employment insurance) and it tightened up the conditions under which repeat use was allowed. This is not to say that we shouldn't have programs to protect seasonal workers against unemployment; it is only to say that we must build into our policies their effect on institutions. When employment and unemployment insurance programs motivate people towards repeat use, the government might want to consider whether separate programs and premiums should apply to industries dominated by repeat users. Policies affect institutions; with a potential for feedback from institutions to policies.

Q.8 True or false? Economists should focus their policy analysis on institutional changes because such policies offer the largest gains.

Q.9 John, your study partner, is a free market advocate. He argues that the invisible hand theory tells us that the government should not interfere with the economy. Do you agree? Why or why not?

1.3

see page 19

Positive economics is the study of what is, and how the economy works.

Normative economics is the study of what the goals of the economy should be.

The *art of economics* is the application of the knowledge learned in positive economics to the achievement of the goals determined in normative economics.

Q.10 State whether the following five statements belong in positive economics, normative economics, or the art of economics.

1. We should support the market because it is efficient.
2. Given certain conditions, the market achieves efficient results.
3. Based on past experience and our understanding of markets, if one wants a reasonably efficient result, markets should probably be relied on.
4. The distribution of income should be left to markets.
5. Markets allocate income according to contributions of factors of production.

Some policies are designed to change institutions directly. While these policies are much more difficult to implement than policies that don't, they also offer the largest potential for gain. Let's consider an example. In the 1990s, a number of countries decided to replace socialist institutions with market economies. The result: output in those countries fell enormously as the old institutions fell apart. Eventually, these countries hope, once the new market institutions are predominant, output will bounce back and further gains will be made. The temporary hardship these countries are experiencing shows the enormous difficulty of implementing policies involving major institutional changes.

Objective Policy Analysis

Good economic policy analysis is objective; that is, it keeps the analyst's value judgments separate from the analysis. Objective analysis does not say, "This is the way things should be," reflecting a goal established by the analyst. That would be subjective analysis because it would reflect the analyst's view of how things should be. Instead, objective analysis says, "This is the way the economy works, and if society (or the individual or firm for whom you're doing the analysis) wants to achieve a particular goal, this is how it might go about doing so." Objective analysis keeps, or at least tries to keep, subjective views—value judgments—separate.

To make clear the distinction between objective and subjective analysis, economists have divided economics into three categories: *positive economics, normative economics,* and the *art of economics.* **Positive economics** is *the study of what is, and how the economy works.* It asks such questions as: How does the market for pork bellies work? How do price restrictions affect market forces? These questions fall under the heading of economic theory. **Normative economics** is *the study of what the goals of the economy should be.* Normative economics asks such questions as: What should the distribution of income be? What should tax policy be designed to achieve? In discussing such questions, economists must carefully delineate whose goals they are discussing. One cannot simply assume that one's own goals for society are society's goals.

The **art of economics** is *the application of the knowledge learned in positive economics to the achievement of the goals one has determined in normative economics.* It looks at such questions as: To achieve a certain distribution of income, how would you go about it, given the way the economy works?[2] Most policy discussions fall under the art of economics.

In each of these three branches of economics, economists separate their own value judgments from their objective analysis as much as possible. The qualifier "as much as possible" is important, since some value judgments inevitably sneak in. We are products of our environment, and the questions we ask, the framework we use, and the way we interpret empirical evidence all embody value judgments and reflect our backgrounds.

Maintaining objectivity is easiest in positive economics, where one is working with abstract models to understand how the economy works. Maintaining objectivity is harder in normative economics. You must always be objective about whose normative values you are using. It's easy to assume that all of society shares your values, but that assumption is often wrong.

It's hardest to maintain objectivity in the art of economics because it embodies the problems of both positive and normative economics. Because noneconomic forces affect policy, to practice the art of economics we must make judgments about how these

---

[2] This three-part distinction was made back in 1896 by a famous economist, John Neville Keynes, father of John Maynard Keynes, the economist who developed macroeconomics. This distinction was instilled into modern economics by Milton Friedman and Richard Lipsey in the 1950s. They, however, downplayed the art of economics, which J. N. Keynes had seen as central to understanding the economist's role in policy making.

noneconomic forces work. These judgments are likely to embody our own value judgments. So we must be exceedingly careful to be as objective as possible in practicing the art of economics.

Policy and Social and Political Forces

When you think about the policy options facing society, you'll quickly discover that the choice of policy options depends on much more than economic theory. You must take into account historical precedent plus social, cultural, and political forces. In an economics course, we don't have time to analyze these forces in as much depth as we'd like. That's one reason there are separate history, political science, sociology, and anthropology courses.

We don't pretend that these forces play an insignificant role in policy decisions, but specialization is necessary. In economics, we focus the analysis on the invisible hand, and much of economic theory is devoted to how the economy would operate if the invisible hand were the only force operating. But as soon as we apply theory to reality and policy, we must take into account political and social forces as well.

An example will make our point more concrete. Most economists agree that holding down or eliminating tariffs (taxes on imports) and quotas (numerical limitations on imports) makes good economic sense. They strongly advise governments to follow a policy of free trade. Do governments follow free trade policies? Almost invariably they do not. Politics leads society in a different direction. If you're advising a policy maker, you need to point out that these other forces must be taken into account, and how other forces should (if they should) and can (if they can) be integrated with your recommendations.

CONCLUSION

There's tons more that could be said by way of introducing you to economics, but an introduction must remain an introduction. As it is, this chapter should have:

1. Introduced you to economic reasoning.

2. Surveyed what we're going to cover in this book.

This introduction was our opening line. We hope it also conveyed the importance and relevance that belong to economics. If it did, it has served its intended purpose. Economics is tough, but tough can be fun.

Chapter Summary

- The three coordination problems any economy must solve are what to produce, how to produce it, and for whom to produce it. In solving these problems economies have found that there is a problem of scarcity.

- Economic reasoning structures all questions in a cost/benefit frame: If the marginal benefits of doing something exceed the marginal costs, do it. If the marginal costs exceed the marginal benefits, don't do it.

- Sunk costs are not relevant to the economic decision rule.

- The opportunity cost of undertaking an activity is the benefit you might have gained from choosing the next-best alternative.

- "There ain't no such thing as a free lunch" (TANSTAAFL) embodies the opportunity cost concept.

- Economic forces, the forces of scarcity, are always working. Market forces, which ration by changing prices, are not always allowed to work.

- Economic reality is controlled and directed by three types of forces: economic forces, political forces, and social forces.

- Under certain conditions the market, through its price mechanism, will allocate scarce resources efficiently.

- Economics can be divided into microeconomics and macroeconomics. Microeconomics is the study of individual choice and how that choice is influenced by eco-nomic forces. Macroeconomics is the study of the economy as a whole, which includes inflation, unemployment, business cycles, and growth.

- Economics can be subdivided into positive economics, normative economics, and the art of economics. Positive economics is the study of what is, normative economics is the study of what should be, and the art of economics relates positive to normative economics.

Key Terms

art of economics *(16)*

economic decision rule *(6)*

economic forces *(9)*

economic model *(11)*

economic policies *(15)*

economic principle *(11)*

economics *(5)*

efficiency *(12)*

invisible hand *(9)*

invisible hand theory *(12)*

macroeconomics *(14)*

marginal benefit *(6)*

marginal cost *(6)*

market force *(9)*

microeconomics *(13)*

normative economics *(16)*

opportunity cost *(8)*

positive economics *(16)*

scarcity *(5)*

sunk costs *(6)*

Questions for Thought and Review

1. Why did we focus the definition of economics on co-ordination rather than on scarcity?

2. List two recent choices you made and explain why you made those choices in terms of marginal benefits and marginal costs.

3. At times we all regret decisions. Does this necessarily mean we did not use the economic decision rule when making the decision?

4. What is the opportunity cost of buying a $20,000 car?

5. Name three ways a limited number of dormitory rooms could be rationed. How would economic forces determine individual behaviour in each? How would social or legal forces determine whether those economic forces become market forces?

6. Give two examples of social forces and explain how they keep economic forces from becoming market forces.

7. Give two examples of political or legal forces and explain how they might interact with the invisible hand.

8. What is an economic model? What besides a model do economists need to make policy recommendations?

9. Does economic theory prove that the free market system is best? Why?

10. List two microeconomic and two macroeconomic problems.

11. Name an economic institution and explain how it either embodies economic principles or affects economic decision making.

12. Is a good economist always objective? Why?

Problems and Exercises

1. You rent a car for $29.95. The first 150 km are free, but each km thereafter costs 15 cents. You drive it 200 km. What is the marginal cost of driving the car?

2. Calculate, using the best estimates you can:
   a. Your opportunity cost of attending school.
   b. Your opportunity cost of taking this course.
   c. Your opportunity cost of attending yesterday's lecture in this course.

3. Individuals have two kidneys but most of us need only one. People who have lost both kidneys through accident or disease must be hooked up to a dialysis machine, which cleanses waste from their bodies. Say a person who has two good kidneys offers to sell one of them to someone whose kidney function has been totally destroyed. The seller asks $30,000 for the kidney, and the person who has lost both kidneys accepts the offer. Who benefits from the deal? Who is hurt? Should a society allow such market transactions? Why?

4. For some years, China has had a one-child-per-family policy. For cultural reasons, there are now many more male than female children born in China. How is this likely to affect who pays the cost of dates in China in 15 or 20 years? Explain your response.

5. In some provinces shopping on Sundays is legal while in others it is not. Can economics be used to explain this fact? Why?

6. Go to two stores: a supermarket and a convenience store.
   a. Write down the cost of a litre of milk in each.
   b. The prices are most likely different. Using the terminology used in this chapter, explain why that is the case and why anyone would buy milk in the store with the higher price.
   c. Do the same exercise with shirts or dresses in Wal-Mart (or its equivalent) and The Bay (or its equivalent).

7. In the mid-1990s, the German comedian Harald Schmidt attempted to mimic the successful David Letterman show in Germany. The format didn't entertain its German audience. What economic policy lesson can be learned from Harald Schmidt's failure?

8. State whether the following statements belong in positive economics, normative economics, or the art of economics.

   a. In a market, when quantity supplied exceeds quantity demanded, price tends to fall.
   b. When determining tax rates, the government should take into account the income needs of individuals.
   c. What society feels is fair is determined largely by cultural norms.
   d. When deciding which rationing mechanism is best (lottery, price, first-come/first-served), one must take into account the goals of society.
   e. Suppose Ontario rations water to farmers at subsidized prices. If Ontario allows the trading of water rights, it will allow economic forces to be a market force.

9. Adam Smith, who wrote *The Wealth of Nations* and is seen as the father of modern economics, also wrote *The Theory of Moral Sentiments*, in which he argued that society would be better off if people weren't so selfish and were more considerate of others. How does this view fit with the discussion of economic reasoning presented in the chapter?

Web Questions

1. Find an employment Web page (an example is www.monster.ca) and search for available jobs using "economist" as a keyword. List five jobs that economists have and write a one-sentence description of each.

2. Use an online periodical (an example is www.canadianbusiness.com) to find two examples of political or legal forces at work. Do those forces keep economic forces from becoming market forces?

3. Using an Internet mapping page (an example is ca.maps.yahoo.com), create a map of your neighborhood and answer the following questions:
   a. How is the map like a model?
   b. What are the limitations of the map?
   c. Could you use this map to determine change in elevation in your neighbourhood? Distance from one place to another? Traffic speed? What do your answers suggest about what to consider when using a map or a model?

Answers to Margin Questions

The numbers in parentheses refer to the page number of each margin question.

1. Since the price of both stocks is now $15, it doesn't matter which one you sell (assuming no differential capital gains taxation). The price you bought them for doesn't matter; it's a sunk cost. Marginal analysis refers to the future gain, so what you expect to happen to future prices of the stocks—not past prices—should determine which stock you decide to sell.   (6)

2. A cost/benefit analysis requires that you put a value on a good, and placing a value on a good can be seen as demeaning it. Consider love. Try telling an acquaintance that you'd like to buy his or her spiritual love, and see what response you get.   (8)

3. John is wrong. The opportunity cost of reading the chapter is primarily the time you spend reading it. Reading the book prevents you from doing other things. Assuming that you already paid for the book, the original price is no longer part of the opportunity cost; it is a sunk cost. Bygones are bygones.   (8)

4. Whenever there is scarcity, the scarce good must be rationed by some means. Free health care has an opportunity cost in other resources. So if health care is not rationed, to get the resources to supply that care, other goods would have to be more tightly rationed than they currently are. It is likely that the opportunity cost of supplying free health care would be larger than most societies would be willing to pay. Hence, some procedures deemed "non-essential" involve a fee not covered by Canada's medicare system.   (9)

5. Joan is wrong. Economic forces are always operative; market forces are not. *(9)*

6. According to the invisible hand theory, the price of tomatoes will likely fall. *(12)*

7. (1) Macroeconomics; (2) Microeconomics; (3) Microeconomics; (4) Macroeconomics. *(14)*

8. False. While such changes have the largest gain, they may also have the largest cost. The policies economists should focus on are those that offer the largest net gain—benefits minus costs—to society. *(16)*

9. He is wrong. The invisible hand theory is a positive theory and does not tell us anything about policy. To do so would be to violate Hume's dictum that a "should" cannot be derived from an "is." This is not to say that government should or should not interfere; whether government should interfere is a very difficult question. *(16)*

10. (1) Normative; (2) Positive; (3) Art; (4) Normative; (5) Positive. *(16)*

APPENDIX A

The Language of Graphs

A picture is worth 1,000 words. Economists, being efficient, like to present ideas in **graphs,** *pictures of points in a coordinate system in which points denote relationships between two or more variables.* But a graph is worth 1,000 words only if the person looking at the graph knows the graphical language. Graphs are usually written on graph paper.

We have enormous sympathy for students who don't understand graphs. A number of our students get thrown for a loop by graphs. They understand the idea, but graphs confuse them. This appendix is for them, and for those of you like them. It's a primer on graphs.

TWO WAYS TO USE GRAPHS

In this book we use graphs in two ways:

1. To present an economic model or theory visually; to show how two variables interrelate.

2. To present real-world data visually. To do this, we use primarily bar charts, line charts, and pie charts.

Actually, these two ways of using graphs are related. They are both ways of presenting visually the *relationship* between two things.

Graphs are built around a number line, or axis, like the one in Figure A1-1(a). The numbers are generally placed in order, equal distances from one another. That number line allows us to represent a number at an appropriate point on the line. For example, point A represents the number 4.

The number line in Figure A1-1(a) is drawn horizontally, but it doesn't have to be; it can also be drawn vertically, as in Figure A1-1(b).

Figure A1-1 (a, b, and c)   **HORIZONTAL AND VERTICAL NUMBER LINES AND A COORDINATE SYSTEM**

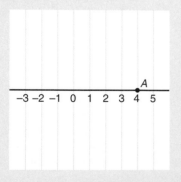

(a) Horizontal number line

(b) Vertical number line

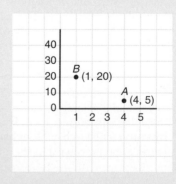

(c) Coordinate system

How we divide our axes, or number lines, into intervals, is up to us. In Figure A1-1(a), we called each interval 1; in Figure A1-1(b), we called each interval 10. Point A appears after 4 intervals of 1 (starting at 0 and reading from left to right), so it represents 4. In Figure A1-1(b), where each interval represents 10, to represent 5, we place point B halfway in the interval between 0 and 10.

So far, so good. Graphs combine a vertical and a horizontal number line, as in Figure A1-1(c). When the horizontal and vertical number lines are put together, they're called *axes*. (Each line is an axis. *Axes* is the plural of *axis*.) We now have a **coordinate system**—*a two-dimensional space in which one point represents two numbers*. For example, point A in Figure A1-1(c) represents the numbers (4, 5): 4 on the horizontal number line and 5 on the vertical number line. Point B represents the numbers (1, 20). (By convention, the horizontal numbers are always written first.)

Being able to represent two numbers with one point is useful because it allows the relationships between two numbers to be presented visually instead of having to be expressed verbally, which is often cumbersome. For example, say the cost of producing 6 units of something is $4 per unit and the cost of producing 10 units is $3 per unit. By putting both these points on a graph, we can visually see that producing 10 units costs less per unit than producing 6 units.

Another way to use graphs to present real-world data visually is to use the horizontal line to represent time. Say that we let each horizontal interval equal a year. and each vertical interval equal $100 in income. By graphing your income each year, you can obtain a visual representation of how your income has changed over time.

Using Graphs in Economic Modelling

We use graphs throughout the book as we present economic models, or simplifications of reality. A few terms are often used in describing these graphs, and we'll now go over them. Consider Figure A1-2(a), on the next page, which lists the number of pens bought per day (column 2) at various prices (column 1).

We can present the table's information in a graph by combining the pairs of numbers in the two columns of the table and representing, or plotting, them on two axes. We do that in Figure A1-2(b).

By convention, when graphing a relationship between price and quantity, economists place price on the vertical axis and quantity on the horizontal axis.

We can now connect the points, producing a line like the one in Figure A1-2(c). With this line, we interpolate the numbers between the points (which makes for a nice visual presentation). That is, we make the **interpolation assumption**—*the assumption that the relationship between variables is the same between points as it is at the points*. The interpolation assumption allows us to think of a line as a collection of points and therefore to connect the points into a line.

Even though the line in Figure A1-2(c) is straight, economists call any such line drawn on a graph a *curve*. Because it's straight, the curve in A1-2(c) is called a **linear curve**—*a curve that is drawn as a straight line*. Notice that this curve starts high on the left-hand side and goes down to the right. Economists say that any curve that looks like that is *downward-sloping*. They also say that a downward-sloping curve represents an **inverse relationship**—*a relationship between two variables in which whenever one goes up, the other goes down*. In this example, the line demonstrates an inverse relationship between price and quantity—that is, when the price of pens goes up, the quantity bought goes down.

Figure A1-2(d) presents a **nonlinear curve**—*a curve that is drawn as a curved line*. This curve, which really is curved, starts low on the left-hand side and goes up to the right. Economists say any curve that goes up to the right is *upward-sloping*. An upward-sloping curve represents a **direct relationship**—*a relationship in which when one variable goes up, the other goes up too*. The direct relationship we're talking about here is the one between the two variables (what's measured on the horizontal and vertical lines). *Downward-sloping* and *upward-sloping* are terms you need to memorize if you want to keep graphically in your mind the image of the relationships they represent.

Slope

One can, of course, be far more explicit about how much the curve is sloping upward or downward by defining it in terms of **slope**—*the change in the value on the vertical axis divided by the change in the value on the horizontal axis*. Sometimes the slope is presented as "rise over run":

$$\text{Slope} = \frac{\text{Rise}}{\text{Run}} = \frac{\text{Change in value on vertical axis}}{\text{Change in value on horizontal axis}}$$

Slopes of Linear Curves

In Figure A1-3 (on page 23), we present five linear curves and measure their slope. Let's go through an example to show how we can measure slope. To do so, we must pick two points. Let's use points A (6, 8) and B (7, 4) on curve *a*. Looking at these points, we see that as we move from 6 to 7 on the horizontal axis, we move from 8 to 4 on the

Figure A1-2 (a, b, c, and d)   **A TABLE AND GRAPHS SHOWING THE RELATIONSHIPS BETWEEN PRICE AND QUANTITY**

	Price per pen	Quantity of pens bought per day
A	$3.00	4
B	2.50	5
C	2.00	6
D	1.50	7
E	1.00	8

(a) Price quantity table

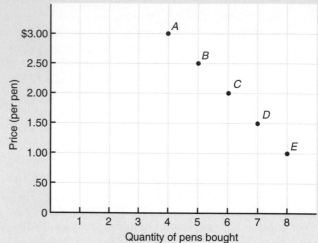

(b) From a table to a graph (1)

(c) From a table to a graph (2)

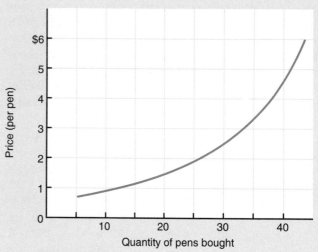

(d) Nonlinear curve

vertical axis. So when the number on the vertical axis falls by 4, the number on the horizontal axis increases by 1. That means the slope is −4 divided by 1, or −4.

Notice that the inverse relationships represented by the two downward-sloping curves, *a* and *b*, have negative slopes, and that the direct relationships represented by the two upward-sloping curves, *c* and *d*, have positive slopes. Notice also that the flatter the curve, the smaller the numerical value of the slope; and the more vertical, or steeper, the curve, the larger the numerical value of the slope. There are two extreme cases:

1. When the curve is horizontal (flat), the slope is zero.

2. When the curve is vertical (straight up and down), the slope is infinite (larger than large).

Knowing the term *slope* and how it's measured lets us describe verbally the pictures we see visually. For example, if we say a curve has a slope of zero, you should picture in your mind a flat line; if we say "a curve with a slope of minus one," you should picture a falling line that makes a 45° angle with the horizontal and vertical axes. (It's the hypotenuse of an isosceles right triangle with the axes as the other two sides.)

Figure A1-3　SLOPES OF CURVES

The slope of a curve is determined by rise over run. The slope of curve *a* is shown in the graph. The rest are shown below:

	Rise	÷	Run	=	Slope
b	−1		+2		−.5
c	1		1		1
d	4		1		4
e	1		1		1

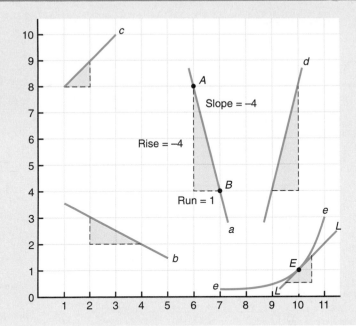

Slopes of Nonlinear Curves

The preceding examples were of *linear (straight) curves*. With *nonlinear curves*—the ones that really do curve—the slope of the curve is constantly changing. As a result, we must talk about the slope of the curve at a particular point, rather than the slope of the whole curve. How can a point have a slope? Well, it can't really, but it can almost, and if that's good enough for mathematicians, it's good enough for us.

Defining the slope of a nonlinear curve is a bit more difficult. The slope at a given point on a nonlinear curve is determined by the slope of a linear (or straight) line that's tangent to that curve. (A line that's tangent to a curve is a line that just touches the curve, and touches it only at one point in the immediate vicinity of the given point.) In Figure A1-3, the line *LL* is tangent to the curve *ee* at point *E*. The slope of that line, and hence the slope of the curve at the one point where the line touches the curve, is +1.

Maximum and Minimum Points

Two points on a nonlinear curve deserve special mention. These points are the ones for which the slope of the curve is zero. We demonstrate those in Figure A1-4(a) and (b). At point A, we're at the top of the curve so it's at a maximum point; at point B, we're at the bottom of the curve so it's at a minimum point. These maximum and minimum points are referred to often by economists, and it's important to realize that the value of the slope of the curve at each of these points is zero.

There are, of course, many other types of curves, and much more can be said about the curves we've talked about. We won't do so because, for purposes of this course, we won't need to get into those refinements. We've presented as much on graphing as you need to know for this book.

KNOWING THE TOOLS

Inverse and Direct Relationships

Inverse relationship:
When X goes up, Y goes down.
When X goes down, Y goes up.

Direct relationship:
When X goes up, Y goes up.
When X goes down, Y goes down.

Figure A1-4 (a and b) **A MAXIMUM AND A MINIMUM POINT**

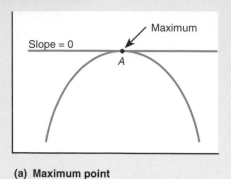

(a) Maximum point

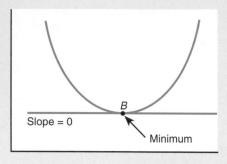

(b) Minimum point

PRESENTING REAL-WORLD DATA IN GRAPHS

The previous discussion covered terms that economists use in presenting models that focus on hypothetical relationships. Economists also use graphs in presenting actual economic data. Say, for example, that you want to show how exports have changed over time. Then you would place years on the horizontal axis (by convention) and exports on the vertical axis, as in Figure A1-5(a) and (b). Having done so, you have a couple of choices: you can draw a **line graph**—*a graph where the data are connected by a continuous line*; or you can make a **bar graph**—*a graph where the area*

under each point is filled in to look like a bar. Figure A1-5(a) shows a line graph and Figure A1-5(b) shows a bar graph.

Another type of graph is a **pie chart**—*a circle divided into "pie pieces," where the undivided pie represents the total amount and the pie pieces reflect the percentage of the whole pie that the various components make up.* This type of graph is useful in visually presenting how a total amount is divided. Figure A1-5(c) shows a pie chart, which happens to represent the division of grades on a test we gave. Notice that 5 percent of the students got As.

There are other types of graphs, but they're all variations on line and bar graphs and pie charts. Once you understand these three basic types of graphs, you shouldn't have any trouble understanding the other types.

Figure A1-5 (a, b, and c) **PRESENTING INFORMATION VISUALLY**

(a) Line graph

(b) Bar graph

(c) Pie chart

Figure A1-6 (a and b)　THE IMPORTANCE OF SCALES

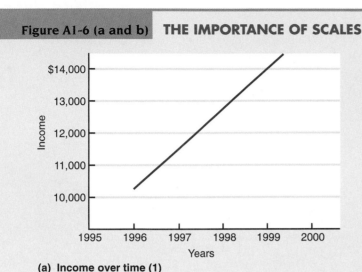

(a) Income over time (1)

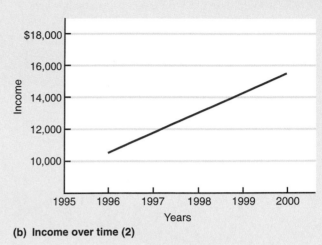

(b) Income over time (2)

INTERPRETING GRAPHS ABOUT THE REAL WORLD

Understanding graphs is important because, if you don't, you can easily misinterpret the meaning of graphs. For example, consider the two graphs in Figure A1-6 (a) and (b). Which graph demonstrates the larger rise in income? If you said (a), you're wrong. The intervals in the vertical axes differ, and if you look carefully you'll see that the curves in both graphs represent the same combination of points. So when considering graphs, always make sure you understand the markings on the axes. Only then can you interpret the graph.

Let's now review what we've covered.

- A graph is a picture of points on a coordinate system in which the points denote relationships between numbers.

- A downward-sloping line represents an inverse relationship or a negative slope.

- An upward-sloping line represents a direct relationship or a positive slope.

- Slope is measured by rise over run, or a change of y (the number measured on the vertical axis) over a change in x (the number measured on the horizontal axis).

- The slope of a point on a nonlinear curve is measured by the rise over run of a line tangent to that point.

- At the maximum and minimum points of a nonlinear curve, the value of the slope is zero.

- In reading graphs, one must be careful to understand what's being measured on the vertical and horizontal axes.

Key Terms

bar graph *(24)*	graph *(20)*	inverse relationship *(21)*	nonlinear curve *(21)*
coordinate system *(21)*	interpolation assumption *(21)*	line graph *(24)*	pie chart *(24)*
direct relationship *(21)*		linear curve *(21)*	slope *(21)*

Questions for Thought and Review

1. Create a coordinate space on graph paper and label the following points:
   a. $(0, 5)$
   b. $(-5, -5)$
   c. $(2, -3)$
   d. $(-1, 1)$

2. Graph the following costs per unit, and answer the questions that follow.

Horizontal Axis: Output	Vertical Axis: Cost per Unit
1	$30
2	20
3	12
4	6
5	2
6	6
7	12
8	20
9	30

   a. Is the relationship between cost per unit and output linear or nonlinear? Why?
   b. In what range in output is the relationship inverse? In what range in output is the relationship direct?
   c. In what range in output is the slope negative? In what range in output is the slope positive?
   d. What is the slope between 1 and 2 units?

3. Within a coordinate space, draw a line with:
   a. Zero slope.
   b. Infinite slope.
   c. Positive slope.
   d. Negative slope.

4. Calculate the slope of lines *a* to *e* in the following co-ordinate system.

   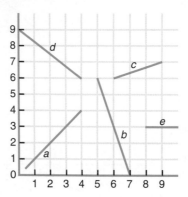

5. Given the following nonlinear curve, answer the following questions:

   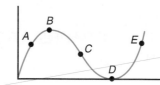

   a. At what point(s) is the slope negative?
   b. At what point(s) is the slope positive?
   c. At what point(s) is the slope zero?
   d. What point is the maximum? What point is the minimum?

6. State what type of graph or chart you would use to show the following real-world data:
   a. Interest rates from 1929 to 2000.
   b. Median income levels of various ethnic groups in Canada.
   c. Total federal expenditures by selected categories.
   d. Total costs of producing 100–800 shoes.

The Economic Organization of Society

2

After reading this chapter, you should be able to:

- Define capitalism and explain how it relies on markets to coordinate economic activities.

- Define socialism and explain how in practice it solves the three coordination problems.

- Describe how economic systems have evolved from the eighth century to today.

- Demonstrate opportunity cost with a production possibility curve.

- State the principle of increasing marginal opportunity cost.

- Explain why economic reasoning must be considered in context that requires a knowledge of history and institutions.

- Relate the concept of comparative advantage to the production possibility curve.

In capitalism man exploits man;
in socialism it's the other way round.

Abba Lerner

Every economy must solve three main coordination problems:

1. What, and how much, to produce.
2. How to produce it.
3. For whom to produce it.

Societies face a universal problem when trying to solve the three problems: Usually what individuals want to do isn't consistent with what "society" wants them to do. Society would often like people to consider what's good for society when making their individual decisions, and to agree that what society wants for them is what they want, too. For example, say society has garbage, and society determines that your neighbourhood is the best place to set up a garbage dump. Even if you agree a garbage dump is needed, you probably won't want it in your neighbourhood. This attitude of **NIMBY** (*Not In My Back Yard*)—*a mindset of approving a project but not wanting it to be nearby*—is found throughout our society.

Individual goals and social goals also conflict when decisions are being made about how much to produce and consume. Individuals generally like to consume much more than they like to produce. So a society must provide incentives for its members to produce more and consume less to alleviate that scarcity. A sure sign that an economic system isn't working is when people perceive that there are important things that need to be done, but are sitting around doing nothing because the system doesn't provide them with the incentive to do them.

How hard is it to make the three decisions we've listed? Imagine for a moment the problem of living in a family: the fights, arguments, and questions that come up. "Do I have to do the dishes?" "Why can't I have piano lessons?" "Bobby got a new sweater. How come I didn't?" "Mom likes you best." Now multiply the size of the family by millions. The same fights, the same arguments, the same questions—only for society the problems are millions of times more complicated than for one family.

How are these complicated coordination problems solved? The two main economic systems the world has used in the past 50 years—capitalism and socialism—answer this question differently.

The coordination problems faced by society are immense.

CAPITALISM

Capitalism is *an economic system based on private property and the market in which, in principle, individuals decide how, what, and for whom to produce.* Under capitalism, individuals are encouraged to follow their own self-interest, while market forces of supply and demand are relied on to coordinate those individual pursuits. Distribution of goods is to each individual according to his or her ability, effort, and inherited property.

Reliance on market forces doesn't mean that political, social, and historical forces play no role in coordinating economic decisions. These other forces do influence how the market works. For example, for a market to exist, government must allocate and defend **private property rights**—*the control a private individual or firm has over an asset or a right*. The concept of private ownership must exist and must be accepted by individuals in society. When you say, "This car is mine," it means that it is unlawful for someone else to take it without your permission. If someone takes it without your permission, he or she is subject to punishment through the legal system.

Capitalism is an economic system based on private property and the market. It gives private property rights to individuals, and relies on market forces to coordinate economic activity.

Reliance on the Market

Markets work through a system of rewards and payments. If you do something, you get paid for doing that something; if you take something, you pay for that something. How much you get is determined by how much you give. This relationship seems fair to most people. But there are instances when it doesn't seem fair. Say someone is unable to work. Should that person get nothing? How about Joe down the street, who was given $10 million by his parents? Is it fair that he gets lots of toys, like Corvettes and skiing

Q.1 John, your study partner, is telling you that the best way to allocate property rights is through the market. How do you respond?

trips to Whistler, and doesn't have to work, while the rest of us have to work 40 hours a week and maybe go to school at night?

We'll put those questions about fairness off at this point—they are very difficult questions. For now, all we want to present is the underlying concept of fairness that capitalism embodies: "Them that works, gets; them that don't, starves."[1] In capitalism, individuals are encouraged to follow their own self-interest.

In capitalist economies, individuals are free to do whatever they want as long as it's legal. The market is relied on to see that what people want to get, and want to do, is consistent with what's available. Price is the mechanism through which people's desires are coordinated and goods are rationed. If there's not enough of something to go around, its price goes up; if more of something needs to get done, the price given to individuals willing to do it goes up. If something isn't wanted or doesn't need to be done, its price goes down. Under capitalism, fluctuations in prices play a central role in coordinating individuals' wants.

Under capitalism, fluctuations in prices play a central role in coordinating individuals' wants.

What's Good about the Market?

Is the market a good way to coordinate individuals' activities? Much of this book will be devoted to answering that question. The answer that we, and most Canadian economists, come to is: Yes, it is a reasonable way. True, it has problems; the market can be unfair, mean, and arbitrary, and sometimes it is downright awful. Why then do economists support it? For the same reason that Oliver Wendell Holmes supported democracy—it is a lousy system, but, based on experience with alternatives, it is better than all the others we've thought of.

2.1

see page 46

The primary debate among economists is not about using markets; it is about how markets should be structured, and whether they should be modified and adjusted by government regulation. Those are much harder questions, and on these questions, opinions differ enormously.

The primary debate among economists is not about using markets but about how markets are structured.

SOCIALISM

The view that markets are a reasonable way to organize society has not always been shared by all economists. Throughout history strong arguments have been made against markets. These arguments are both philosophical and practical. The philosophical argument against the market is that it brings out the worst in people—it glorifies greed. It encourages people to beat out others rather than to be cooperative. As an alternative some economists have supported **socialism**—which is, in theory, *an economic system based on individuals' goodwill toward others, not on their own self-interest, and in which, in principle, society decides what, how, and for whom to produce.*

Socialism in Theory

You can best understand the idea behind theoretical socialism by thinking about how decisions are made in a family. In most families, benevolent parents decide who gets

---

[1]How come the authors get to use rotten grammar but scream when they see rotten grammar in your papers? Well, that's fairness for you. Actually, we should say a bit more about writing style. All writers are expected to know correct grammar; if they don't, they don't deserve to be called writers. Once you know grammar, you can individualize your writing style, breaking the rules of grammar where the meter and flow of the writing require it. Right now, you're still proving that you know grammar, so in papers handed in to your instructor, you shouldn't break the rules of grammar until you've proved to the instructor that you know them. We've done lots of books, so our editors give us a bit more leeway than your instructors will give you.

Q.2   Are there any activities in a family that you believe should be allocated by a market? What characteristics do those activities have?

what, based on the needs of each member of the family. When Sabin gets a new coat and his sister Sally doesn't, it's because Sabin needs a coat while Sally already has two coats that fit her and are in good condition. Victor may be slow as molasses, but from his family he still gets as much as his superefficient brother Jerry gets. In fact, Victor may get more than Jerry because he needs extra help.

Markets have little role in most families. In our families, when food is placed on the table we don't bid on what we want, with the highest bidder getting the food. In our families, every person can eat all he or she wants, although if one child eats more than a fair share, that child gets a lecture from us on the importance of sharing. "Be thoughtful; be considerate. Think of others first," are lessons that many families try to teach.

Socialism is, in theory, an economic system that tries to organize society in the same way as most families are organized—all people contribute what they can, and all get what they need.

In theory, socialism is an economic system that tries to organize society in the same way as these families are organized, trying to see that individuals get what they need. Socialism tries to take other people's needs into account and adjust people's own wants in accordance with what's available. In socialist economies, individuals are urged to look out for the other person; if individuals' inherent goodness won't make them consider the general good, government will make them. In contrast, a capitalist economy expects people to be selfish; it relies on markets and competition to direct that selfishness to the general good.[2]

Socialism in Practice

Q.3   Which would be more likely to attempt to foster individualism: socialism or capitalism?

Soviet-style socialism is an economic system that uses administrative control or central planning to solve the coordination problems: what, how, and for whom.

Q.4   What is the difference between socialism in theory and socialism in practice?

Few economists argue directly in favour of greed. Most accept that it would be great if everyone wanted to be good to others. However, they point out that in practice, economic systems based upon people's goodwill have tended to break down. This is certainly true of the major countries that tried socialism starting in the 1900s. In practice, socialist governments had to take a strong role in guiding the economy. Socialism became an economic system based on government ownership of the means of production, with economic activity governed by central planning. What we are describing as "socialism in practice" is often called **Soviet-style socialism**—*an economic system that uses administrative control or central planning to solve the coordination problems: what, how, and for whom*—because it was the system used by the Soviet Union. Under that Soviet-style socialist economic system, government planning boards set society's goals and then directed individuals and firms as to how to achieve those goals.

THE PRODUCTION POSSIBILITY CURVE AND ECONOMIC REASONING

The choices that a society must make are often presented in terms of a production possibility curve. The production possibility curve is related to the concept of opportunity cost that you were introduced to in Chapter 1. It is a tool that shows the trade-offs among choices we make. It can be used nicely to discuss choices societies must make about economic systems. Applying economic reasoning outside of any historical and institutional context, however, has difficulties and we'll discuss these difficulties too.

[2]As you probably surmised, the above distinction is too sharp. Even capitalist societies want people to be selfless, but not too selfless. Children in capitalist societies are generally taught to be selfless at least in dealing with friends and family. The difficulties parents and societies face is finding a midpoint between the two positions: selfless but not too selfless; selfish but not too selfish.

In a tradition-based society, the social and cultural forces give a society inertia (a tendency to resist change) that predominates over economic and political forces.

"Why did you do it that way?"

"Because that's the way we've always done it."

Tradition-based societies had markets, but they were peripheral, not central, to economic life. In feudal times what was produced, how it was produced, and for whom it was produced were primarily decided by tradition.

In today's Canadian economy, the market plays the central role in economic decisions. But that doesn't mean that tradition is dead. As we said in Chapter 1, tradition still plays a significant role in today's society, and, in many aspects of society, tradition still overwhelms the invisible hand. Consider the following:

1. The persistent view that women should be home-makers rather than factory workers, consumers rather than producers.

2. The raised eyebrows when a man is introduced as a nurse, secretary, homemaker, or member of any other profession conventionally identified as women's work.

3. Society's unwillingness to permit the sale of individuals or body organs.

4. Parents' willingness to care for their children without financial compensation.

Each of these tendencies reflects tradition's influence in Western society. Some are so deep-rooted that we see them as self-evident. Some of tradition's effects we like; others we don't—but we often take them for granted. Economic forces may work against these traditions, but the fact that they're still around indicates the continued strength of tradition in our market economy.

The Production Possibility Table

As we discussed in Chapter 1, the concept of opportunity cost—every decision has a cost in forgone opportunities—lies at the centre of economic reasoning. Opportunity cost can be seen numerically with a **production possibility table**—*a table that lists the maximum combination of outputs that can be obtained from a given number of inputs.* An **output** is simply *a result of an activity,* and an **input** is *what you put into a production process to achieve an output.* For example, your grade in a course is an output and your study time is an input.

Let's present the study-time/grades example numerically. Say you have exactly 20 hours a week to devote to two courses: economics and history. (So, maybe we're a bit optimistic.) Grades are given numerically and you know that the following relationships exist: if you study 20 hours in economics, you'll get a grade of 100; 18 hours, 94; and so forth.[3]

Let's say that the best you can do in history is a 98 with 20 hours of study a week; 19 hours of study guarantees a 96, and so on. The production possibility table in Figure 2-1(a) shows the highest combination of grades you can get with various allocations of the 20 hours available for studying the two subjects. One possibility is getting 100 in economics and 58 in history. Another is getting 70 in economics and 78 in history.

Notice that the opportunity cost of studying one subject rather than the other is embodied in the production possibility table. The information in the table comes from experience: we are assuming that you've discovered that if you transfer an hour of study

A production possibility table lists the maximum combination of outputs that can be obtained from a given number of inputs.

Markets can be as sophisticated as the Toronto Stock Exchange or as informal as a yard sale.

---

[3]Throughout the book we'll be presenting numerical examples to help you understand the concepts. The numbers we choose are often arbitrary. After all, you have to choose something. As an exercise, you might choose different numbers than we did, numbers that apply to your own life, and work out the argument using those numbers.

The Rise of Markets in Perspective

Back in the Middle Ages, markets developed spontaneously. "You have something I want; I have something you want. Let's trade" is a basic human attitude we see in all aspects of life. Even children quickly get into trading: chocolate ice cream for vanilla, two Pokémon cards for a ride on a motor scooter. Markets institutionalize such trading by providing a place where people know they can go to trade. New markets are continually being formed. Today there are markets for hockey cards, pork bellies (which become bacon and pork chops), rare coins, and so on. The Internet, with sites like eBay, is expanding markets enormously, allowing ordinary people to trade with people thousands of miles away.

Throughout history, societies have tried to prevent some markets from operating because they feel those markets are ethically wrong or have undesirable side effects. Societies have the power to prevent markets, to make some kinds of markets illegal. In Canada, the addictive drug market, the baby market, and the sex market, to name a few, are illegal. In socialist countries, markets in a much wider range of goods (such as clothes, cars, and soft drinks) and activities (such as private business for individual profit) have been illegal.

But, even if a society prevents the market from operating, society cannot escape the invisible hand. If there's excess supply, there will be downward pressure on prices; if there's excess demand, there will be upward pressure on prices. To maintain an equilibrium in which the quantity supplied does not equal the quantity demanded, a society needs a strong force to prevent the invisible hand from working. In the Middle Ages, that strong force was religion. The Church told people that if they got too far into the market mentality—if they followed their self-interest—they'd go to Hell.

Until recently, in socialist society the state provided the preventive force. The educational system in socialist countries emphasized a communal set of values. They taught students that a member of socialist society does not try to take advantage of other human beings but, rather, lives by the philosophy "From each according to his ability; to each according to his need."

For whatever reason—whether it be that true socialism wasn't really tried, or that people's self-interest is too strong—the "from each according to his ability; to each according to his need" approach didn't work in socialist countries. They have switched (some say succumbed) to greater reliance on the market.

from economics to history, you'll lose 3 points on your grade in economics and gain 2 points in history. Thus, the opportunity cost of a 2-point rise in your history grade is a 3-point decrease in your economics grade.

The Production Possibility Curve

The production possibility curve is a curve measuring the maximum combination of outputs that can be obtained from a given number of inputs.

The information in the production possibility table can also be presented graphically in a diagram called a production possibility curve. A **production possibility curve** is *a curve measuring the maximum combination of outputs that can be obtained from a given number of inputs*. It is a graphical presentation of the opportunity cost concept.

A production possibility curve is created from a production possibility table by mapping the table in a two-dimensional graph. We've taken the information from the table in Figure 2-1(a) and mapped it into Figure 2-1(b). The history grade is mapped, or plotted, on the horizontal axis; the economics grade is on the vertical axis.

As you can see from the bottom row of Figure 2-1(a), if you study economics for all 20 hours and study history for 0 hours, you'll get grades of 100 in economics and 58 in history. Point A in Figure 2-1(b) represents that choice. If you study history for all 20 hours and study economics for 0 hours, you'll get a 98 in history and a 40 in economics. Point E represents that choice. Points B, C, and D represent three possible choices between these two extremes.

Notice that the production possibility curve slopes downward from left to right. That means that there is an inverse relationship (a trade-off) between grades in

Figure 2-1 (a and b) A PRODUCTION POSSIBILITY TABLE AND CURVE FOR GRADES IN ECONOMICS AND HISTORY

The production possibility table (a) shows the highest combination of grades you can get with only 20 hours available for studying economics and history.

The information in the production possibility table in (a) can be plotted on a graph, as is done in (b). The grade received in economics is on the vertical axis, and the grade received in history is on the horizontal axis.

Hours of study in history	Grade in history	Hours of study in economics	Grade in economics
20	98	0	40
19	96	1	43
18	94	2	46
17	92	3	49
16	90	4	52
15	88	5	55
14	86	6	58
13	84	7	61
12	82	8	64
11	80	9	67
10	78	10	70
9	76	11	73
8	74	12	76
7	72	13	79
6	70	14	82
5	68	15	85
4	66	16	88
3	64	17	91
2	62	18	94
1	60	19	97
0	58	20	100

(a) Production possibility table

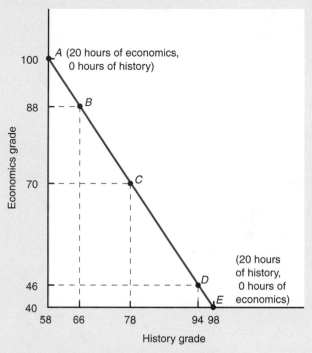

(b) Production possibility curve

economics and grades in history. The better the grade in economics, the worse the grade in history, and vice versa. That downward slope represents the opportunity cost concept—you get more of one benefit only if you get less of another benefit.

The production possibility curve not only demonstrates the opportunity cost concept, it also measures the opportunity cost. For example, in Figure 2-1(b), say you want to raise your grade in history from a 94 to a 98 (move from point *D* to point *E*). The opportunity cost of that 4-point increase would be a 6-point decrease in your economics grade, from 46 to 40.

To summarize, the production possibility curve demonstrates that:

1. There is a limit to what you can achieve, given the existing institutions, resources, and technology.

2. Every choice you make has an opportunity cost. You can get more of something only by giving up something else.

Increasing Marginal Opportunity Cost We chose an unchanging trade-off in the study-time/grade example because it made the initial presentation of the production possibility curve easier. Since, by assumption, you could always trade two points on your history grade for three points on your economics grade, the production possibility curve was a straight line and opportunity cost was constant. But is that the way we'd expect

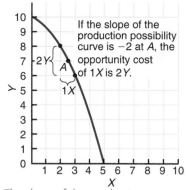

If the slope of the production possibility curve is −2 at *A*, the opportunity cost of 1*X* is 2*Y*.

The slope of the production possibility curve tells you the opportunity cost of good *X* in terms of good *Y*. You have to give up 2*Y* to get 1*X* when you're around point *A*.

Q.5 If a production possibility curve is a straight line, is opportunity cost constant?

Figure 2-2 (a and b) A PRODUCTION POSSIBILITY TABLE AND CURVE

The table in (**a**) contains information on the trade-off between the production of burgers and DVDs. This information has been plotted on the graph in (**b**). Notice in (**b**) that as we move along the production possibility curve from *A* to *F*, trading DVDs for burgers, we get fewer and fewer burgers for each pound of DVDs given up. That is, the opportunity cost of choosing burgers over DVDs increases as we increase the production of burgers. This concept is called the principle of increasing marginal opportunity cost. The phenomenon occurs because some resources are better suited for the production of DVDs than for the production of burgers, and we use the better ones first.

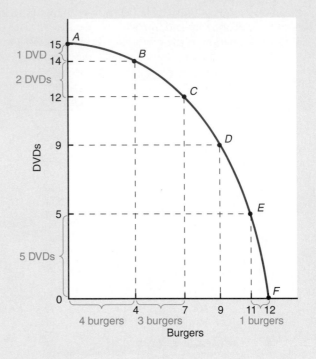

% of resources devoted to production of burgers	Number of burgers	% of resources devoted to production of DVDs	DVDs	Row
0	0	100	15	A
20	4	80	14	B
40	7	60	12	C
60	9	40	9	D
80	11	20	5	E
100	12	0	0	F

(a) Production possibility table

(b) Production possibility curve

Q-6 If no resource had a comparative advantage in the production of any good, what would the shape of the production possibility curve be? Why?

reality to be? Probably not. The production possibility curve is generally bowed outward, as in Figure 2-2(b).

Why? Because some resources are better suited for the production of certain kinds of goods than they are for the production of other kinds of goods. To make the answer more concrete, let's talk specifically about society's choice between burgers and DVDs. The graph in Figure 2-2(b) is derived from the table in Figure 2-2(a).

Let's see what the shape of the curve means in terms of numbers. Let's start with society producing only DVDs (point A). Giving up a DVD initially gains us a lot of burgers (4), moving us to point B. The next 2 DVDs we give up gains us slightly fewer burgers (point C). If we continue to trade DVDs for burgers, we find that at point D we gain very few burgers from giving up a DVD. The opportunity cost of choosing burgers over DVDs increases as we increase the production of burgers.

The reason the opportunity cost of burgers increases as we consume more burgers is that some resources are relatively better suited to producing burgers, while others are relatively better suited to producing DVDs. Put in economists' terminology, some resources have a **comparative advantage** over other resources—*the ability to be better suited to the production of one good than to the production of another good.* In this example, some resources have a comparative advantage over other resources in the production of DVDs, while other resources have a comparative advantage in the production of burgers.

When making small amounts of burgers and large amounts of DVDs, in the production of those burgers we use the resources whose comparative advantage is in the

KNOWING THE TOOLS

Production Possibility Curves

Definition	Shape	Shifts	Points In, Out, and On
The production possibility curve is a curve that measures the maximum combination of outputs that can be obtained with a given number of inputs	Most are outward bowed because of increasing marginal opportunity cost; if opportunity cost doesn't change, the production possibility curve is a straight line	Increases in inputs or increases in the productivity of inputs shift the production possibility curve out; decreases have the opposite effect; the production possibility curve shifts along the axis whose input is changing	Points inside the production possibility curve are points of inefficiency; points on the production possibility curve are points of efficiency; points outside the production possibility curve are not obtainable

production of burgers. All other resources are devoted to producing DVDs. Because the resources used in producing burgers aren't good at producing DVDs, we're not giving up many DVDs to get those burgers. As we produce more and more of a good, we must use resources whose comparative advantage is in the production of the other good—in this case, more suitable for producing DVDs than for producing burgers. As we remove resources from the production of DVDs to get the same additional amount of burgers, we must give up increasing numbers of DVDs. An alternative way of saying this is that the opportunity cost of producing burgers becomes greater as the production of burgers increases. As we continue to increase the production of burgers, the opportunity cost of more burgers becomes very high because we're using resources to produce burgers that have a strong comparative advantage for producing DVDs.

For many of the choices society must make, opportunity costs tend to increase as we choose more and more of an item. The reason is that resources are not easily adaptable from the production of one good to the production of another. Such a phenomenon about choice is so common, in fact, that it has acquired a name: the **principle of increasing marginal opportunity cost.** That principle states:

> *In order to get more of something, one must give up ever-increasing quantities of something else.*

In other words, initially the opportunity costs of an activity are low, but they increase the more we concentrate on that activity. Sometimes this law is called the flowerpot law because, if it didn't hold, all the world's food could be grown in a flowerpot. But it can't be. As we add more seeds to a fixed amount of soil, there won't be enough nutrients or room for the roots, so output per seed decreases.

Efficiency We would like, if possible, to get as much output as possible from a given amount of inputs or resources. That's **productive efficiency**—*achieving as much output as possible from a given amount of inputs or resources.* We would like to be efficient. The production possibility curve helps us see what is meant by productive efficiency. Consider point A in Figure 2-3(a), which is inside the production possibility curve. If we are producing at point A, we are using all our resources to produce 6 burgers and 4 DVDs,

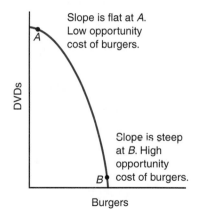

Remember: when the slope is flat, there's a low opportunity cost of burgers (a high opportunity cost of DVDs). When the slope is steep, there's a high opportunity cost of burgers (a low opportunity cost of DVDs).

The principle of increasing marginal opportunity cost states that opportunity costs increase the more you concentrate on the activity. In order to get more of something, one must give up ever-increasing quantities of something else.

Figure 2-3 (a, b, and c) EFFICIENCY, INEFFICIENCY, AND TECHNOLOGICAL CHANGE

The production possibility curve helps us see what is meant by efficiency. At point A, in (a), all inputs are used to make 4 DVDs and 6 burgers. This is inefficient since there is a way to obtain more of one without giving up any of the other, that is, to obtain 6 DVDs and 6 burgers (point C) or 8 burgers and 4 DVDs (point B). All points inside the production possibility curve are inefficient. With fixed inputs and given technology, we cannot go beyond the production possibility curve. For example, point D is unattainable.

A technological change that improves production techniques will shift the production possibility curve outward, as shown in both (b) and (c). How the curve shifts outward depends on how technology improves. For example, if we become more efficient in the production of both burgers and DVDs, the curve will shift out as in (b). If we become more efficient in producing DVDs, but not in producing burgers, then the curve will shift as in (c).

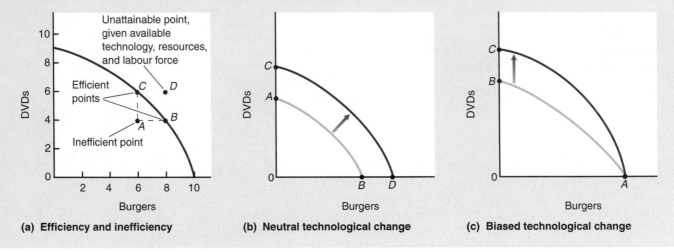

(a) **Efficiency and inefficiency**   (b) **Neutral technological change**   (c) **Biased technological change**

Point A represents **inefficiency**—*getting less output from inputs which, if devoted to some other activity, would produce more output.* That's because with the same inputs we could be getting either 8 burgers and 4 DVDs (point B) or 6 DVDs and 6 burgers (point C). As long as we prefer more to less, both points B and C represent **efficiency**—*achieving a goal using as few inputs as possible.* We always want to move our production out to a point on the production possibility curve.

Why not move out farther, to point D? If we could, we would, but by definition the production possibility curve represents the most output we can get from a certain combination of inputs. So point D is unattainable, given our resources and technology.

When technology improves, when more resources are discovered, or when the economic institutions get better at fulfilling our wants, we can get more output with the same inputs. What this means is that when technology or an economic institution improves, the entire production possibility curve shifts outward from AB to CD in Figure 2-3(b). How the production possibility curve shifts outward depends on how the technology improves. For example, say we become more efficient in producing DVDs, but not more efficient in producing burgers. Then the production possibility curve shifts outward to AC in Figure 2-3(c).

Policies that costlessly shift the production possibility curve outward are the most desirable policies because they don't require us to decrease our consumption of one good to get more of another. Alas, such policies are the most infrequent. Improving technology and institutions and discovering more resources are not costless; generally there's an opportunity cost of doing so that must be taken into account.

Efficiency involves achieving a goal as cheaply as possible. Efficiency has meaning only in relation to a specified goal.

Figure 2-4   EXAMPLES OF SHIFTS IN PRODUCTION POSSIBILITY CURVES

Each of these curves reflects a different type of shift. Your assignment is to match these shifts with the situations given in the text on pages 37 and 38.

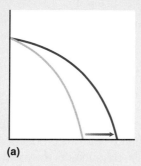
(a)

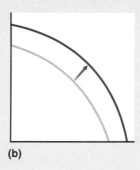
(b)

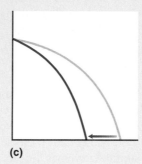
(c)

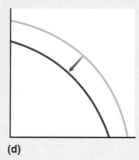
(d)

Distribution and Productive Efficiency In discussing the production possibility curve, we avoided questions of distribution: Who gets what? But such questions cannot be ignored in real-world situations. Specifically, if the method of production is tied to a particular income distribution and choosing one method will help some people but hurt others, we can't say that one method of production is efficient and the other inefficient, even if one method produces more total output than the other. As we stated above, the term *efficiency* involves achieving a goal as cheaply as possible. The term has meaning only in regard to a specified goal. Say, for example, that we have a society of ascetics who believe that consumption above some minimum is immoral. For such a society, producing more for less (productive efficiency) would not be efficient since consumption is not its goal. Or say that we have a society that cares that what is produced is fairly distributed. An increase in output that goes to only one person and not to anyone else would not necessarily be efficient.

In our society, however, most people prefer more to less, and many policies have relatively small distributional consequences. On the basis of the assumption that more is better than less, economists use their own kind of shorthand for such policies and talk about efficiency as identical to productive efficiency—increasing total output. But it's important to remember the assumption under which that shorthand is used: that the distributional effects that accompany the policy aren't undesirable and that we, as a society, prefer more output.

Some Examples of Shifts in the Production Possibility Curve

To see whether you understand the production possibility curve, let us now consider some situations that can be shown with the production possibility curve. In Figure 2-4 we demonstrate four situations with production possibility curves. Below, we list five situations. To test your understanding of the curve, match each situation to one of the curves in Figure 2-4 (a graph can match more than one situation).

1. A new genetic material is found that doubles the speed at which agricultural goods grow.

2. Nanites (micromachines) are perfected that lower the cost of manufactured goods.

3. A meteor hits the earth and destroys half the world's natural resources.

Q-7 Your firm is establishing a trucking business in Saudi Arabia. The firm has noticed that women are generally paid much less than men in Saudi Arabia, and the firm suggests that hiring women would be more efficient than hiring men. What should you respond?

Expanding technology and capacities to produce shifts out the production possibilities curve.

Q.8 When a natural disaster hits the prairies, where most of Canada's wheat is produced, what happens to the Canadian production possibility curve for wheat and butter?

4. A world trade war erupts and trade restrictions increase enormously.

5. Soviet-style socialist countries give up on the socialist system and switch to a market system.

The correct answers are: 1–a; 2–a; 3–d; 4–d; 5–d.

If you got them all right, you are well on your way to understanding the production possibility curve.

The Production Possibility Curve and Economic Systems

Some of you may have rightly wondered about one of the answers in the above examples, specifically, the last one. (If you wondered about the others, a review is in order for you.) The appropriate wondering is the following: According to what we have said previously, the shift by socialist countries toward markets should shift the production possibility curve out, not in; so wouldn't the correct answer be that it shifts the production possibility curve out because it introduces markets that allow trade?

The answer to that question is: Yes, it should *eventually* shift the production possibility curve out. But in the short and medium run (i.e., within 5 to 10 years) the change will shift it in. The explanation of why this is so brings us back to our discussion of economic systems and allows us to tie together that discussion with the discussion of opportunity costs as represented by the production possibility curve.

The production possibility curve presents choices in a timeless fashion, but most choices are dependent upon previous choices.

The production possibility curve presents choices in a timeless fashion and therefore makes opportunity costs clear-cut; there are two choices, one with a higher cost and one with a lower cost. The reality is that most choices are dependent on other choices; they are made sequentially with a time dimension. With sequential choices you cannot simply reverse your decision. Once you have started on a path, to take another path you have to return to the beginning. Thus, following one path often lowers the costs of options along that path, but it raises the costs of options along another path.

Such sequential decisions can best be seen within the framework of a **decision tree**—*a visual description of sequential choices.* A decision tree is shown in Figure 2-5.

Q.9 Draw a decision tree that shows the choices you have faced when pursuing your undergraduate studies. Which choices were most costly?

Once you make the initial decision to go on path A, the costs of path B options become higher; they include the costs of reversing your path and starting over. The decision trees of life have thousands of branches; each decision you make rules out other paths, or at least increases your costs highly. (Remember that day you decided to blow off your homework? That decision may have changed your future life.)

Another way of putting this same point is that all *decisions are made in context:* What makes sense in one context may not make sense in another. For example, say you're answering the question "Would society be better off if students were taught literature or if

---

Figure 2-5   A DECISION TREE

Decisions are often made sequentially. Decisions made at low levels of the decision tree preclude, or at least significantly increase the costs of, other decisions.

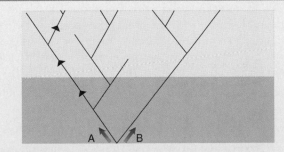

they were taught agriculture?" The answer depends on the institutional context. In a developing country whose goal is large increases in material output, teaching agriculture may make sense. In a developed country, where growth in material output is less important, teaching literature may make sense.

Recognizing the contextual nature of decisions is important when interpreting the production possibility curve. Because decisions are contextual, what the production possibility curve for a particular decision looks like depends on the existing institutions, and the analysis can be applied only in institutional and historical context. The production possibility curve is not a purely technical phenomenon. The curve is an engine of analysis to make contextual choices, not a definitive tool to decide what one should do in all cases.

> Because decisions are contextual, what the production possibility curve for a particular decision looks like depends on the existing institutions, and the analysis can be applied only in an institutional and historical context.

From the above discussion, it should be clear where economic systems fit into this discussion. The choice of economic systems is not the type of decision that the production possibility curve is designed to address. Usually, the curve takes the system as given. The production possibility curve is most useful when analyzing questions that involve policy decisions given existing systems and institutions—slight movements in the production of one good or another.

The Production Possibility Curve and Tough Choices

The production possibility curve represents the tough choices society must make. Look at questions such as: Should we save the spotted owl or should we allow logging in the Western forests? Should we expand the government health care system or should we strengthen our national defense system? Should we emphasize policies that allow more consumption now or should we emphasize policies that allow more consumption in the future? Such choices involve difficult trade-offs that can be pictured by the production possibility curve.

> The production possibility curve represents the tough choices society must make.

Not everyone recognizes these choices. For example, politicians often talk as if the production possibility curve were nonexistent. They promise voters the world, telling them, "If you elect me, you can have more of everything." When they say that, they obscure the hard choices and increase their probability of getting elected.

Economists do the opposite. They promise little except that life is tough, and they continually point out that seemingly free lunches often involve significant hidden costs. Alas, political candidates who exhibit such reasonableness seldom get elected. Economists' reasonableness has earned economics the nickname *the dismal science*.

> Economists continually point out that seemingly free lunches often involve significant hidden costs.

COMPARATIVE ADVANTAGE, SPECIALIZATION, AND TRADE

The same comparative advantage argument we used to explain the shape of the production possibility curve can be used to show how trade (and hence how the markets that facilitate trade) make society better off. Let's start with an international example. Say Canada can produce widgets at a cost of $4 apiece and wadgets at $4 apiece, while Korea can produce widgets at a cost of 300 won (won is the Korean currency) apiece and wadgets at a cost of 100 won apiece. In Canada, the opportunity cost of one widget is one wadget. (Since each costs $4, Canada must reduce its production of wadgets by one to produce another widget.) In Korea, the opportunity cost of a widget is three wadgets, since it costs three times as much to produce a widget as it does to produce a wadget. Because Canada's opportunity cost of producing widgets is lower than Korea's, Canada is said to have a comparative advantage in producing widgets. Similarly, Korea

> A country has a comparative advantage in a good if it can produce that good at a lower *opportunity* cost than another country can. (Remember, it is a lower opportunity cost, not necessarily a lower absolute cost.)

is said to have comparative advantage in producing wadgets because its opportunity cost of wadgets is one-third of a widget, while Canada's opportunity cost of wadgets is one widget.

If one country has a comparative advantage in one good, the other country must necessarily have a comparative advantage in the other good. Notice how comparative advantage hinges on opportunity cost, not total cost. Even if one country can produce all goods cheaper than another country, trade between them is still possible since the opportunity costs of various goods differ.

The same reasoning can be applied to trade among individuals. To keep the analysis simple, let's consider two individuals. Sunder is a whiz at creative writing; he can turn out four creative writing papers a day or one economics paper a day, or any proportional combination thereof. Ti is an economics whiz; she can turn out four economics papers a day or one creative writing paper a day, or any proportional combination thereof. Figure 2-6(a) shows how many papers each can write in a day.

Sunder and Ti's teacher has given each of them a weekly assignment to do four economics and four creative writing papers. Ti spends four days writing four creative writing papers and one day writing four economics papers. Sunder does the reverse. This will leave no time for partying.

The following week their teacher allows Ti and Sunder to collaborate on their assignment. The team must turn in eight creative writing papers and eight economics papers. Ti and Sunder will receive a collective grade. The question facing Ti and Sunder is how to divide up the work. If they work as they did the week before, it will take each of them all week.

Fortunately Ti is taking an economics course and has just learned about comparative advantage. She points out to Sunder that they can do much better if they avail themselves of their comparative advantages. Since Ti has a comparative advantage in economics and Sunder has a comparative advantage in creative writing, it pays for them to specialize in their respective strengths. Let's say they do that. Their new production possibility table per day is shown in Figure 2-6(b). They both specialize, and in one day the team can turn out four economics papers and four creative writing papers. Now it takes them only two days to do their assignment, leaving them three days to party (or to study for other courses, or to work at a part-time job to pay for their education).

The benefits of collaboration and specialization can also be shown with production possibility curves. Production possibility curves show all the possible combinations of dividing up each student's time and possible combinations when dividing up the work.

Sunder and Ti's respective paper-writing production possibility curves per day are shown in Figure 2-6(c). The blue line represents Sunder's production possibility curve; the red line represents Ti's production possibility curve. The curve connecting points A, B, and C shows the production possibilities if Ti and Sunder collaborate. You should be able to explain the individual production possibility curves. The combined curve is a little more complicated. This curve tells you what they can write when working together. If they both spent the day writing economics papers, they would end up with 5 economics papers and no creative writing papers—point A. If instead, they both wrote creative writing papers, they would have 5 creative writing papers and no economics papers—point C. At these endpoints one person is not taking advantage of his or her comparative advantage. If, instead, they take advantage of their own special skills, Sunder would write 4 creative writing papers and Ti would write 4 economics papers in one day—point B. Connecting points A, B, and C shows all combinations of papers both can write together in one day.

Notice that the combined production possibility curve is shifted out significantly. When individuals collaborate, using their comparative advantages, their production

Q-10 Show, using production possibility curves, that Steve and Sarah would be better off specializing in their baking activities, and then trading, rather than baking only for themselves, given the following production possibility tables.

(a) Steve's Production per Day		(b) Sarah's Production per Day	
Loaves of Bread	Dozens of Cookies	Loaves of Bread	Dozens of Cookies
4	0	4	0
3	2	3	1
2	4	2	2
1	6	1	3
0	8	0	4

2.2 see page 46

Figure 2-6 (a, b, and c)   **THE GAINS FROM TRADE**

Trade makes people better off. In this figure we compare individuals' combined production possibilities under two alternative assumptions. The table in (**a**) shows the number of economics and creative writing papers each student can produce in a day. The table in (**b**) shows their maximum possibilities when the students collaborate. The graph in (**c**) plots the production possibility curves associated with the tables in (**a**) and (**b**). Notice what trade does to the production possibility frontier. The combined curve is bowed out, reflecting the principle of increasing marginal opportunity costs.

(a) Sunder and Ti's individual possibilities

	Economics papers per day	Creative writing papers per day
Sunder	1	4
Ti	4	1

(b) Sunder and Ti's joint possibilities

	Economics papers per day	Creative writing papers per day
A	5	0
B	4	4
C	0	5

(c) Production possibility curves (numbers of papers per day)

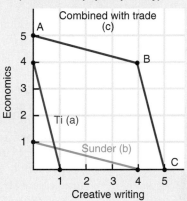

possibilities expand. By collaborating and specializing, each can reach beyond his or her individual production possibility curve. This shifting out of the production possibility curve comes from using comparative advantage and is a geometric representation of the gains to trade.

> When individuals trade using their comparative advantages, their combined production possibility curve shifts outward.

2.3

see page 46

The Division of Labour

The above examples give a visual sense of the power of markets to make people better off. Markets allow people to trade—to utilize their comparative advantages and specialize in what they do best—and thereby to improve society's combined production possibility curve. Adam Smith, the founder of modern economics, saw this aspect of markets and trade as what differentiated human beings from animals. He wrote:

> This division of labour, from which so many advantages are derived, is not originally the effect of any human wisdom, which foresees and intends that general opulence to which it gives occasion. It is the necessary, though very slow and gradual consequence, of a certain propensity in human nature which has in view no such extensive utility; the propensity to truck, barter, and exchange one thing for another. . . . [This propensity] is common to all men, and to be found in no other race of animals, which seem to know neither this nor any other species of contracts. . . . Nobody ever saw a dog make a fair and deliberate exchange of one bone for another with another dog. Nobody ever saw one animal by its gestures and natural cries signify to another, this is mine, that yours; I am willing to give this for that.

The argument that the division of labour and trade makes individuals better off also holds for countries. Trade shifts out countries' production possibility curves, making them better off. There are, of course, exceptions to this proposition. (Remember all models are dependent on the assumptions of the model.) These exceptions are consid-

Markets allow specialization and the division of labour. They allow individuals to develop their comparative advantages, thereby increasing the production possibilities of society.

ered later in microeconomics courses when trade is looked at in more depth. But the general argument that trade and markets make people better off because they allow individuals and economies to assert their comparative advantages carries through and is a primary reason why economists generally support markets.

Markets, Specialization, and Growth

We can see the effect of markets on our well-being empirically by considering the growth of economies. As you can see from Figure 2-7, for 1700 years the world economy grew very slowly. Then, at the end of the 18th century, the world economy started to grow, and it has grown at an increasing rate since then.

What changed? The introduction of markets and democracy. There's something about markets that leads to economic growth. Markets allow specialization and encourage trade. The bowing out of the production possibilities from trade is part of the story, but a minor part. As individuals compete and specialize they learn by doing, becoming even better at what they do. Markets also foster competition, which pushes individuals to find better ways of doing things. They devise new technologies that further the growth process.

The new millennium is offering new ways for individuals to specialize and compete. More and more businesses are trading on the Internet. For example, schools, such as the University of Phoenix and Athabasca University are providing online competition for traditional schools. Similarly, online bookstores and drugstores are proliferating. As Internet technology becomes built into our economy, we can expect more specialization, more division of labour, and the economic growth that follows.

CONCLUSION

As we will emphasize throughout this book, the tools you will be learning here are powerful but simple, and that simplicity means that much care must be used in their application—to see that the tools fit the situation for which they are used. Businesses tell us that they have much more of a problem with new employees who think they understand things, but actually don't, than they do with new employees who recognize how little they know—who are willing to learn the institutional ropes—and recognize that the time for changing institutions is only when they understand the structural role that the institutions play.

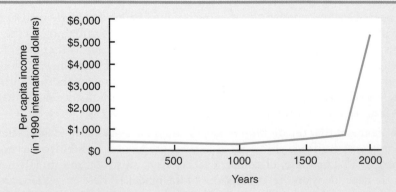

Figure 2-7   GROWTH IN THE PAST TWO MILLENNIA

Source: Angus Maddison, *Monitoring the World Economy*, OECD, 1995; Angus Maddison, "Poor Until 1820," *The Wall Street Journal*, January 11, 1999.

What this means is that economic reasoning is extraordinarily strong, and it really helps you if you apply it in the appropriate time and context. It remains strong when inappropriately applied; but it leads you to the wrong conclusion. The reality is that history and institutions are fundamentally important for making good economic decisions. Economic reasoning alone does not tell anyone, "This is right and this is wrong policy." What economic reasoning does is to provide a framework of analysis that focusses the decision on precisely what are the opportunity costs, and what are the alternative ways of measuring those costs. Fitting that reasoning together with your gut intuitive sense of what is right and wrong is what makes a good economist.

Chapter Summary

- Any economic system must solve three central problems:
  - What, and how much, to produce.
  - How to produce it.
  - For whom to produce it.
- Capitalism is based on private property and the market; socialism is based on individuals' goodwill toward others.
- In capitalism, the what, how, and for whom problems are solved by the market.
- In Soviet-style socialism, the what, how, and for whom problems were solved by government planning boards.
- Political, social, and economic forces are active in both capitalism and socialism.
- Economic systems are in a constant state of evolution.
- Markets use the price mechanism to coordinate economic activity.
- In feudalism, tradition rules; in mercantilism, the government rules; in capitalism, the market rules.

- In welfare capitalism, the market, the government, and tradition each rule components of the economy.
- The production possibility curve measures the maximum combination of outputs that can be obtained from a given number of inputs. It embodies the opportunity cost concept.
- In general, in order to get more and more of something, we must give up ever-increasing quantities of something else. This is the principle of increasing marginal opportunity cost.
- Production possibility curves must be interpreted within the contextual nature of decisions.
- Trade allows people to use their comparative advantage and shift out society's production possibility curve.
- The rise of markets has coincided with significant increases in output. Specialization, trade, and competition have all contributed to the increase.

Key Terms

capitalism   (28)

comparative
 advantage   (34)

decision tree   (38)

efficiency   (36)

inefficiency   (36)

input   (31)

NIMBY   (28)

output   (31)

principle of increasing
 marginal opportunity
 cost (35)

private property rights   (28)

production possibility
 curve   (32)

production possibility
 table   (31)

productive efficiency   (35)

socialism   (29)

Soviet-style socialism   (30)

Questions for Thought and Review

1. What three problems must any economic system solve?

2. How does capitalism solve these three problems?

3. How does Soviet-style socialism solve these three problems?

4. Is capitalism or socialism the better economic system? Why?

5. What arguments can you give for supporting a socialist organization of a family and a capitalist organization of the economy?

6. Design a grade production possibility table and curve that embody the principle of increasing marginal opportunity cost.

7. What would the production possibility curve look like if there were decreasing marginal opportunity costs? Explain. What is an example of decreasing marginal opportunity costs?

8. Show how a production possibility curve would shift if a society became more productive in its output of widgets but less productive in its output of wadgets.

9. How does the theory of comparative advantage relate to production possibility curves?

10. When all people use economic reasoning, inefficiency is impossible, because if the benefit of reducing that inefficiency were greater than the cost, the efficiency would be eliminated. Thus, if people use economic reasoning, it's impossible to be on the interior of a production possibility curve. Is this statement true or false? Why?

11. Why, in the near term, would a switch of socialist countries to a market system cause their production possibility curves to shift in? What institutional and societal characteristics are necessary to carry through that switch successfully?

12. If trade shifts the production possibility curve out, why do some politicians oppose actions to promote trade?

Problems and Exercises

1. Poland, Bulgaria, and Hungary (all former socialist countries) were in the process of changing to a market economy in the 1990s.
   a. Go to the library and find the latest information about their transitions.
   b. Explain what has happened in the markets, political structures, and social customs of those countries.

2. Economists Edward Lazear and Robert Michael have calculated that the average family spends two and a half times as much on each adult as they do on each child.
   a. Does this mean that children are deprived and that the distribution is unfair?
   b. Do you think these percentages change with family income? If so, how?
   c. Do you think that the allocation would be different in a family in a Soviet-style socialist country than in a capitalist country? Why?

3. One of the specific problems Soviet-style socialist economies had was keeping up with capitalist countries technologically.
   a. Can you think of any reason inherent in a centrally planned economy that would make innovation difficult?
   b. Can you think of any reason inherent in a capitalist country that would foster innovation?
   c. Joseph Schumpeter, a famous Harvard economist of the 1930s, predicted that as firms in capitalist societies grew in size they would innovate less. Can you suggest what his argument might have been?
   d. Schumpeter's prediction did not come true. Modern capitalist economies have had enormous innovations. Can you provide explanations as to why?

4. A country has the following production possibility table:

Resources Devoted to Clothing	Output of Clothing	Resources Devoted to Food	Output of Food
100%	20	0%	0
80	16	20	5
60	12	40	9
40	8	60	12
20	4	80	14
0	0	100	15

   a. Draw the country's production possibility curve.
   b. What's happening to marginal opportunity costs as output of food increases?
   c. Say the country gets better at the production of food. What will happen to the production possibility curve?
   d. Say the country gets equally better at producing both food and clothing. What will happen to the production possibility curve?

5. Suppose a country has the following production possibility table:

Resources Devoted to Clothing	Output of Clothing	Resources Devoted to Food	Output of Food
100%	15	0%	0
80	14	20	4
60	12	40	8
40	9	60	12
20	5	80	16
0	0	100	20

   a. Draw the country's production possibility curve.
   b. What is the combined production possibility curve for this country and the country in question 4 if the

countries do not trade and they devote equal proportionate resources to produce each good?

c. What would be the combined production possibility
curve of the two countries if they took advantage of
their comparative advantages?

6. Assume Canada can produce Toyotas at the cost of
$8,000 per car and Chevrolets at $6,000 per car. In
Japan, Toyotas can be produced at 1,000,000 yen and
Chevrolets at 500,000 yen.

a. In terms of Chevrolets, what is the opportunity cost of
producing Toyotas in each country?

b. Who has the comparative advantage in producing
Chevrolets?

c. Assume Canadians purchase 50,000 Chevrolets and
30,000 Toyotas each year. The Japanese purchase far
fewer of each. Using productive efficiency as the
guide, who should most likely produce Chevrolets and
who should produce Toyotas, assuming Chevrolets are
going to be produced in one country and Toyotas in
the other?

7. Lawns produce no crops but occupy more land in Canada
than any single crop, such as corn. This means that
Canada is operating inefficiently and hence is at a point
inside the production possibility curve. Right? If not,
what does it mean?

8. Groucho Marx is reported to have said, "The secret of
success is honest and fair dealing. If you can fake those,
you've got it made." What would likely happen to society's production possibility curve if everyone could fake
honesty? Why? (Hint: Remember that society's production possibility curve reflects more than just technical
relationships.)

9. Suppose Wombatland has the following production possibilities table:

Label	Resources Devoted to Thingamabobs	Output of Thingamabobs	Resources Devoted to Whatsits	Output of Whatsits
A	0%	0	100	10
B	20	6	80	8
C	40	11	60	6
D	60	15	40	4
E	80	18	20	2
F	100	20	0	0

a. Draw the production possibilities curve with the quantity of Whatsits on the vertical axis, and mark the
points A through F using the labels in the table.

b. Is the opportunity cost of a Thingamabob constant?
How can you tell without making any calculations?

c. Calculate the opportunity cost of a Thingamabob
between points A and B, B and C, C and D, D and
E, and E and F.

10. Refer to the data in the table in Problem 9 above. Suppose there is a technological innovation that increases
the production of both Thingamabobs and Whatsits by
100 percent.

a. Draw the new production possibilities curve.

b. Has technological change affected the opportunity
cost of Thingamabobs?

c. Explain why. Use calculations between points A and
B, B and C, and so on to support your answer.

11. The Kingdom of Kent has the following production possibilities table:

Label	Resources Devoted to Dohickies	Output of Dohickies	Resources Devoted to Thingies	Output of Thingies
A	0%	0	100%	980
B	25	70	75	840
C	50	140	50	630
D	75	210	25	350
E	100	280	0	0

a. Draw the production possibilities curve with the quantity of Dohickies on the horizontal axis and label the
points A through E.

b. Does the opportunity cost of a Dohickie change as more
and more Dohickies are produced? If so, how, and why?

c. Calculate the opportunity cost of a Dohickie between
points A and B; B and C; C and D; and D and E. Are
you finding what you expected given your answer to
part b?

d. Without performing the calculations, how can you determine the opportunity cost of a Thingie between
points E and D; D and C; C and B; and B and A?
Should opportunity costs be rising between points E
and A? Why?

e. Now calculate the opportunity cost of a Thingie between the points considered in part d. Is your answer
what you expected? Explain.

Web Questions

1. The Canada Pension Plan is significant to the evolution of capitalism in Canada. Go to the Human Resources Development Canada home page (www.hrdc-drhc.gc.ca/ips/common/home.shtml) and describe how changes in the plan have moved the Canadian economy toward welfare capitalism. What changes have been made that will alter the nature of CPP? What does this say about the evolution of capitalism today?

2. Starting from the Department of Foreign Affairs and International Trade Web site (www.dfait-maeci.gc.ca/trade/menu-e.asp),

a. With how many countries does Canada trade?
b. What are its three largest trading partners?
c. How does this trade affect the world production possibility curve?

3. Visit the Adam Smith Institute's Web site (www.adam-smith.org/uk) and skim through Book One of *The Wealth of Nations*.
a. In which chapter does the quotation in the text appear?
b. What did Smith say limited the division of labour? Why?

Answers to Margin Questions

1. He is wrong. Property rights are required for a market to operate. Once property rights are allocated, the market will allocate goods, but the market cannot distribute the property rights that are required for the market to operate. *(28)*

2. Most families allocate basic needs through control and command. The parents do (or try to do) the controlling and commanding. Generally they are well-intentioned, trying to meet their perception of their children's needs. However, some family activities that are not basic needs might be allocated through the market. For example, if one child wants a go-cart and is willing to do extra work at home in order to get it, go-carts might be allocated through the market, with the child earning chits that can be used for such nonessentials. *(30)*

3. Capitalism places much more emphasis on fostering individualism. Socialism tries to develop a system in which the individual's needs are placed second to society's needs. *(30)*

4. In theory, socialism is an economic system based upon individuals' goodwill. In practice, socialism follows the Soviet model and involves central planning and government ownership of the primary means of production. *(30)*

5. The slope of the production possibilities curve tells us the opportunity cost of one good in terms of another. A straight line has a constant slope, so opportunity costs would be fixed (constant). *(33)*

6. If no resource had a comparative advantage, the production possibility curve would be a straight line connecting the points of maximum production of each product, as in the graph below.

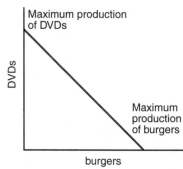

At all points along this curve, the opportunity cost of producing burgers and DVDs is equal. *(34)*

7. We remind them of the importance of cultural forces. In Saudi Arabia women are not allowed to drive. *(37)*

8. The production possibility curve shifts along the wheat axis as in the graph below. *(38)*

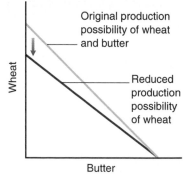

9. A decision tree showing your choices as an undergraduate might look like this: *(38)*

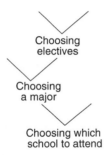

(a) Combined, No Trade		(b) Combined, Trade	
Loaves of Bread	Dozens of Cookies	Loaves of Bread	Dozens of Cookies
8	0	8	0
6	3	6	4
4	6	4	8
2	9	2	10
0	12	0	12

10. If Steve and Sarah do not trade, and divide their time identically, their combined production possibility table is shown in (**a**). If they do collaborate, their production possibility table is shown in (**b**). The corresponding production possibility curves are drawn beneath the tables. The production possibility curve with trade is further to the right than the one without trade. Steve and Sarah can each end up with more bread and cookies if they trade than if they work on their own.   *(40)*

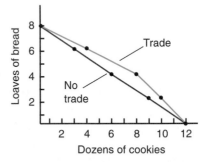

APPENDIX A

The History of Economic Systems

Remember the distinction between market and economic forces: Economic forces have always existed—they operate in all aspects of our lives; but market forces have not always existed. Markets are social creations societies use to coordinate individuals' actions. Markets developed, sometimes spontaneously, sometimes by design, because they offered a better life for at least some—and usually a large majority of—individuals in a society.

To understand why markets developed, it is helpful to look briefly at the history of the economic systems from which our own system descended.

EVOLVING ECONOMIC SYSTEMS

Capitalism and socialism have not existed forever. Capitalism came into widespread existence in the mid-1700s; socialism came into existence in the early 1900s. Before capitalism and socialism, other forms of economic systems existed, including **feudalism**—*an economic system in which traditions rule*. In feudalism if your parents were serfs (small farmers who lived on a manor), you would be a serf. Feudalism dominated the Western world from about the 8th century to the 15th century.

Throughout the feudalistic period merchants and artisans (small manufacturers who produced goods by hand) grew in importance and wealth and, eventually, their increased importance led to a change in the economic system from feudalism to **mercantilism**—*an economic system in which government determines the what, how, and for whom decisions by doling out the rights to undertake certain economic activities*. Mercantilism remained the dominant economic system until the 1700s, when the **Industrial Revolution**—*a time when technology and machines rapidly modernized industrial production and mass-produced goods replaced handmade goods*—led to a decrease in the power of small producers, an increase in the power of capitalists, and eventually to a revolution instituting capitalism as the dominant economic system.

Some economists prefer to call the system that evolved from mercantilism a *market economic system* rather than capitalism. Their justification for doing so is that the key element of the new system is not the power of the capitalists but the central reliance on markets to coordinate economic activities. They argue that the market system is not fundamentally changed if the power shifts from a small group of capitalists to corporations, or even to nonprofit organizations, as long as the market remains central. We agree with their argument, but we prefer the term *capitalism* because of its widespread usage, not because we believe that capitalist control is the central element of our modern market economy.

We mention feudalism and mercantilism because aspects of both continue in economies today. For example, governments in Japan and Germany play significant roles in directing their economies. Their economic systems are sometimes referred to as *neomercantilist economies*.

The Need for Coordination in an Economic System

As economic systems evolved from mercantilism to a market economy, many people asked: Who will coordinate economic activities if the government does not? It was in answering this question that modern economics developed. To answer that question, a British moral philosopher named Adam Smith developed, in his famous book *The Wealth of Nations* (1776), the concept of the invisible hand, and used it to explain how markets could coordinate the economy without the active involvement of government. Smith wrote:

> Man has almost constant occasion for the help of his brethren, and it is in vain for him to expect it from their benevolence only. He will be more likely to prevail, if he can interest their self-love in his favour, and show them that it is for their own advantage to do for him what he requires of them. Whoever offers to another a bargain of any kind proposes to do this. Give me that which I want, and you shall have that which you want, is the meaning of every such offer; and it is in this manner that we obtain from one another the far greater part of those good offices which we stand in need of. It is not from the benevolence of the butcher, the brewer, or the baker, that we expect our dinner, but from their regard to their own interest. We address ourselves, not to their humanity but to their self-love, and never talk to them of our own necessities but of their advantages.

Smith argued that the market's invisible hand would guide suppliers' actions toward the general good. No government coordination was necessary.

Evolutionary Changes within Systems

Revolutionary shifts that give rise to new economic systems are not the only way economic systems change. Systems also evolve. For example, both capitalism and socialism have changed over the years, evolving with changes in social customs, political forces, and the strength of markets. A brief look at their evolution will give us a good sense of the struggles between them that dominate our lives. In the 1930s, during the Great Depression, capitalist countries integrated a number of what might be called socialist institutions into their existing institutions. Distribution of goods was no longer, even in theory, only according to ability; need also played a role. Governments began to play a larger role in the economy, taking control over some of the *how, what,* and *for whom* decisions. For example, most capitalist nations established welfare and social security systems, providing an economic safety net for people whose incomes could not fill their needs. Capitalism became what is sometimes called **welfare capitalism**—*an economic system in which the market is allowed to operate but in which government plays dual roles in determining distribution and making the what, how, and for whom decisions*. In some countries the governments played such an important role that they could reasonably be called market-modified socialist economies. Some countries that allow markets today, such as Sweden, call their economic system a socialist, rather than a capitalist, system.

In the 1980s, in socialist countries the reverse process took place: socialism integrated capitalist institutions into its existing institutions. By the 1990s, most of the former socialist countries had given up Soviet-style socialism and had begun to let the market determine the what, how, and for whom decisions. Some government activities in former socialist economies were privatized—sold to the private sector. Similarly in the 1990s, in capitalist countries governments became even more market-oriented and tried to pull back their involvement in the market in favour of private enterprise. For example, governments in Western Europe and the United States tried to eliminate some aspects of their welfare systems. In the 1980s and 1990s economic systems moved more toward the capitalist end of the spectrum.

A Blurring of the Distinction between Capitalism and Socialism

The result of these recent changes has been a blending of economic systems and a blurring of the distinctions between capitalism and socialism. China still ostensibly has a socialist system, but a recent trip to China convinced one of us that it is a very capitalist type of socialism. If the trend toward use of market mechanisms in socialist countries continues, in the 21st century only one general type of economic structure may exist. It won't be pure socialism and it won't be pure capitalism. It will be a blend of the two.

FEUDAL SOCIETY: RULE OF TRADITION

Let's go back in time to the year 1000 when Europe had no nation-states as we now know them. (Ideally, we would have gone back farther and explained other economic systems, but, given the limited space, we had to draw the line somewhere—an example of trade-off.) The predominant economic system at that time was feudalism. There was no coordinated central government, no unified system of law, no national patriotism, no national defense, although a strong religious institution simply called the Church fulfilled some of these roles. There were few towns; most individuals lived in walled manors or "estates." These manors "belonged to" the "lord of the manor." (Occasionally the "lord" was a lady, but not often.) We say "belonged to" rather than "were owned by" because most of the empires or federations at that time were not formal nation-states that could organize, administer, and regulate ownership. No documents or deeds gave ownership of the land to an individual. Instead, tradition ruled, and in normal times nobody questioned the lord's right to the land. The land "belonged to" the lord because the land "belonged to" him—that's the way it was.

Without a central nation-state, the manor served many functions a nation-state would have served had it existed. The lord provided protection, often within a walled area surrounding the manor house or, if the manor was large enough, a castle. He provided administration and decided disputes. He also decided *what* would be done, *how* it would be done, and *who* would get what, but these decisions were limited. In the same way that the land belonged to the lord because that's the way it always had been, what people did and how they did it were determined by what they always had done. Tradition ruled the manor more than the lord did

Problems of a Tradition-Based Society

Feudalism developed about the 8th and 9th centuries and lasted until about the 15th century, though in isolated countries such as Russia it continued well into the 19th century, and in all European countries its influence lingered for hundreds of years (as late as about 140 years ago in some parts of Germany). Such a long-lived system must have done some things right, and feudalism did: it solved the what, how, and for whom problems in an acceptable way.

But a tradition-based society has problems. In a traditional society, because someone's father was a baker, the son must also be a baker, and because a woman was a homemaker, she wouldn't be allowed to be anything but a homemaker. But what if Joe Blacksmith, Jr., the son of Joe Blacksmith, Sr., is a lousy blacksmith and longs to knead dough, while Joe Baker, Jr., would make a superb blacksmith but hates kneading pastry? Tough. Tradition dictated who did what. In fact, tradition probably arranged things so that we will never know whether Joe Blacksmith, Jr., would have made a superb baker.

As long as a society doesn't change too much, tradition operates reasonably well, although not especially efficiently, in holding the society together. However, when a society must undergo change, tradition does not work. Change means that the things that were done before no longer need to be done, while new things do need to get done. But if no one has traditionally done these new things, then they don't get done. If the change is important but a society can't figure out some way for the new things to get done, the society falls apart. That's what happened to feudal society. It didn't change when change was required.

The life of individuals living on the land, called *serfs*, was difficult, and feudalism was designed to benefit the lord. Some individuals in feudal society just couldn't take life on the manor, and they set off on their own. Because there was no organized police force, they were unlikely to be caught and forced to return to the manor. Going hungry, being killed, or both, however, were frequent fates of an escaped serf. One place to which serfs could safely escape, though, was a town or city—the remains of what in Roman times had been thriving and active cities. These cities, which had been decimated by plagues, plundering bands, and starvation in the preceding centuries, nevertheless remained an escape hatch for runaway serfs because they relied far less on tradition than did manors. City dwellers had to live by their wits; many became merchants who lived predominantly by trading. They were middlemen; they would buy from one group and sell to another.

Trading in towns was an alternative to the traditional feudal order because trading allowed people to have an income independent of the traditional social structure. Markets broke down tradition. Initially merchants traded using barter (exchange of one kind of good for another): silk and spices from the Orient for wheat, flour, and artisan products in Europe. But soon a generalized purchasing power (money) developed as a medium of exchange. Money greatly expanded the possibilities of trading because its use meant that goods no longer needed to be bartered. They could be sold for money, which could then be spent to buy other goods.

In the beginning, land was not traded, but soon the feudal lord who just had to have a silk robe but had no money was saying, "Why not? I'll sell you a small piece of land so I can buy a shipment of silk." Once land became tradable, the traditional base of the feudal society was undermined. Tradition that can be bought and sold is no longer tradition—it's just another commodity.

FROM FEUDALISM TO MERCANTILISM

Toward the end of the Middle Ages (mid-15th century), markets went from being a sideshow, a fair that spiced up people's lives, to being the main event. Over time, some traders and merchants started to amass fortunes that dwarfed those of the feudal lords. Rich traders settled down; existing towns and cities expanded and new towns were formed. As towns grew and as fortunes shifted from feudal lords to merchants, power in society shifted to the towns. And with that shift came a change in society's political and economic structure.

As these traders became stronger politically and economically, they threw their support behind a king (the strongest lord) in the hope that the king would expand their ability to trade. In doing so, they made the king even stronger. Eventually, the king became so powerful that his will prevailed over the will of the other lords and even over the will of the Church. As the king consolidated his power, nation-states as we know them today evolved. *The government became an active influence on economic decision making*.

As markets grew, feudalism evolved into mercantilism. The evolution of feudal systems into mercantilism occurred in somewhat this way: As cities and their markets grew in size and power relative to the feudal manors and the traditional economy, a whole new variety of possible economic activities developed. It was only natural that individuals began to look to a king to establish a new tra-

dition that would determine who would do what. Individuals in particular occupations organized into groups called *guilds*, which were similar to strong labour unions today. These guilds, many of which had financed and supported the king, now expected the king and his government to protect their interests.

As new economic activities, such as trading companies, developed, individuals involved in these activities similarly depended on the king for the right to trade and for help in financing and organizing their activities. For example, in 1492, when Christopher Columbus had the wild idea that by sailing west he could get to the East Indies and trade for their riches, he went to Spain's Queen Isabella and King Ferdinand for financial support.

Since many traders had played and continued to play important roles in financing, establishing, and supporting the king, the king was usually happy to protect their interests. The government doled out the rights to undertake a variety of economic activities. This was the era in which the Hudson's Bay Company received its charter. By the late 1400s, Western Europe had evolved from a feudal to a mercantilist economy.

The mercantilist period was marked by the increased role of government, which could be classified in two ways: by the way it encouraged growth, and by the way it limited growth. Government legitimized and financed a variety of activities, thus encouraging growth. But government also limited economic activity in order to protect the monopolies of those it favoured, thus limiting growth. So mercantilism allowed the market to operate, but it kept the market under its control. The market was not allowed to respond freely to the laws of supply and demand.

FROM MERCANTILISM TO CAPITALISM

Mercantilism provided the source for major growth in Western Europe, but mercantilism also unleashed new tensions within society. Like feudalism, mercantilism limited entry into economic activities. It used a different form of limitation—politics rather than social and cultural tradition—but individuals who were excluded still felt unfairly treated.

The most significant source of tension was the different roles played by craft guilds and owners of new businesses, who were called industrialists or **capitalists**—*businesspeople who have acquired large amounts of money and use it to invest in businesses*. Craft guild members were artists in their own crafts: pottery, shoemaking, and the like. New business owners destroyed the art of production by devising machines to replace hand production. Machines produced goods cheaper and faster than craftsmen.[1] The result was an increase in supply and a downward pressure on the price, which was set by the government. Craftsmen didn't want to be replaced by machines. They argued that machine-manufactured goods didn't have the same quality as hand-crafted goods, and that the new machines would disrupt the economic and social life of the community.

Industrialists were the outsiders with a vested interest in changing the existing system. They wanted the freedom to conduct business as they saw fit. Because of the enormous cost advantage of manufactured goods over hand-crafted goods, a few industrialists overcame government opposition and succeeded within the mercantilist system. They earned their fortunes and became an independent political power.

Once again the economic power base shifted, and two groups competed with each other for power—this time, the guilds and the industrialists. The government had to decide whether the support the industrialists (who wanted government to loosen its power over the country's economic affairs) or the craftsmen and guilds (who argued for strong government limitations and for maintaining traditional values of workmanship). This struggle raged in the 1700s and 1800s. But during this time, governments themselves were changing. This was the Age of Revolutions, and the kings' powers were being limited by democratic reform movements—revolutions supported and financed in large part by the industrialists.

The Need for Coordination in an Economy

Craftsmen argued that coordination of the economy was necessary, and the government had to be involved. If government wasn't going to coordinate economic activity, who would? To answer that question, a British moral philosopher named Adam Smith developed the concept of the invisible hand, in his famous book *The Wealth of Nations* (1776), and used it to explain how markets could coordinate the economy without the active involvement of government.

As stated earlier in the chapter, Smith argued that the market's invisible hand would guide suppliers' actions toward the general good. No government coordination was necessary.

With the help of economists such as Adam Smith, the industrialists' view won out. Government pulled back from its role in guiding the economy and adopted a **laissez-faire** policy—*the economic policy of leaving coordination of individuals' wants to be controlled by the market.* (*Laissez-faire*, a French term, means "Let events take their course; leave things alone.")

The Industrial Revolution

The invisible hand worked; capitalism thrived. Beginning about 1750 and continuing through the late 1800s, machine production increased enormously, almost totally replacing hand production. This phenomenon has been given a name: the Industrial Revolution. The economy grew faster than ever before. Society was forever transformed. New inventions changed all aspects of life. James Watt's steam engine (1769) made manufacturing and travel easier. Eli Whitney's cotton gin (1793) changed the way cotton was processed. James Kay's flying shuttle (1733),[2] James Hargreaves' spinning jenny (1765), and Richard Arkwright's power loom (1769), combined with the steam engine, changed the way cloth was processed and the clothes people wore.

The need to mine vast amounts of coal to provide power to run the machines changed the economic and physical landscapes. The repeating rifle changed the nature of warfare. Modern economic institutions replaced guilds. Stock markets, insurance companies, and corporations all became important. Trading was no longer financed by government; it was privately financed—although government policies, such as colonial policies giving certain companies (such as the famous East India Company) monopoly trading rights with a country's colonies, helped in that trading. The Industrial Revolution, democracy, and capitalism all arose in the middle and late 1700s. By the 1800s, they were part of the institutional landscape of Western society. Capitalism had arrived.

---

[1]Throughout this section we use *men* to emphasize that these societies were strongly male-dominated. There were almost no business-women. In fact, a woman had to turn over her property to a man upon her marriage, and the marriage contract was written as if she were owned by her husband!

[2]The invention of the flying shuttle frustrated the textile industry because it enabled workers to weave so much cloth that the spinners of thread from which the cloth was woven couldn't keep up. This challenge to the textile industry was met by offering a prize to anyone who could invent something to increase the thread spinners' productivity. The prize was won when the spinning jenny was invented.

Welfare Capitalism
FROM CAPITALISM TO ~~SOCIALISM~~

Capitalism was marked by significant economic growth in the Western world. But it was also marked by human abuses—18-hour workdays, low wages, children as young as five years old slaving long hours in dirty, dangerous factories and mines—to produce enormous wealth for an elite few. Such conditions and inequalities led to criticism of the capitalist or market economic system.

Marx's Analysis

The best-known critic of this system was Karl Marx, a German philosopher, economist, and sociologist who wrote in the 1800s and who developed an analysis of the dynamics of change in economic systems. Marx argued that economic systems are in a constant state of change, and that capitalism would not last. Workers would revolt, and capitalism would be replaced by a socialist economic system.

Marx saw an economy marked by tensions between economic classes. He saw capitalism as an economic system controlled by the capitalist class (businessmen). His class analysis was that capitalist society is divided into capitalist and worker classes. He said constant tension between these economic classes causes changes in the system. The capitalist class made large profits by exploiting the **proletariat** class—*the working class*—and extracting what he called *surplus value* from workers who, according to Marx's labour theory of value, produced all the value inherent in goods. Surplus value was the additional profit, rent, or interest that, according to Marx's normative views, capitalists added to the price of goods. What economic analysis sees as recognizing a need that society has and fulfilling it, Marx saw as exploitation.

Marx argued that this exploitation would increase as production facilities became larger and larger and as competition among capitalists decreased. At some point, he believed, exploitation would lead to a revolt by the proletariat, who would overthrow their capitalist exploiters.

By the late 1800s, some of what Marx predicted had occurred, although not in the way that he thought it would. Production moved from small to large factories. Corporations developed, and classes became more distinct from one another. Workers were significantly differentiated from owners. Small firms merged and were organized into monopolies and trusts (large combinations of firms). The trusts developed ways to prevent competition among themselves and ways to limit entry of new competitors into the market. Marx was right in his predictions about these developments, but he was wrong in his prediction about society's response to them.

The Revolution that Did Not Occur

Western society's response to the problems of capitalism was not a revolt by the workers. Instead, governments stepped in to stop the worst abuses of capitalism. The hard edges of capitalism were softened.

Evolution, not revolution, was capitalism's destiny. The democratic state did not act, as Marx argued it would, as a mere representative of the capitalist class. Competing pressure groups developed; workers gained political power that offset the economic power of businesses.

In the late 1930s and the 1940s, workers dominated the political agenda. During this time, capitalist economies developed an economic safety net that included government-funded programs, such as public welfare and unemployment insurance, and established an extensive set of regulations affecting all aspects of the economy. Today, depressions are met with direct government policy. Competition laws, regulatory agencies, and social programs of government softened the hard edges of capitalism. Laws were passed prohibiting child labour, mandating a certain minimum wage, and limiting the hours of work. Capitalism became what is sometimes called welfare capitalism.

Due to these developments, federal government spending now accounts for about a fifth of all spending in Canada, and for more than half in some European countries. Were an economist from the late 1800s to return from the grave, he'd probably say socialism, not capitalism, exists in Western societies. Most modern-day economists wouldn't go that far, but they would agree that our economy today is better described as a welfare capitalist economy than as a capitalist, or even a market, economy. Because of these changes, the North American and Western European economies are a far cry from the competitive "capitalist" economy that Karl Marx criticized. Markets operate, but they are constrained by the government: they are regulated.

The concept of *capitalism* was developed to denote a market system controlled by one group in society, the capitalists. Looking at Western societies today, we see that domination by one group no longer characterizes Western economies. Although in theory capitalists control corporations through their ownership of shares of stock, in practice corporations are controlled in large part by managers.

There remains an elite group who control business, but *capitalist* is not a good term to describe them. Managers, not capitalists, exercise primary control over business, and even their control is limited by laws or the fear of laws being passed by governments.

Governments in turn are influenced by a variety of pressure groups. Sometimes one group has more influence; at other times, another. Government policies similarly fluctuate. Sometimes they are pro-worker, sometimes pro-industrialist, sometimes pro-government, and sometimes pro-society.

FROM FEUDALISM TO SOCIALISM

You probably noticed that we crossed out *Socialism* in the previous section's heading and replaced it with *Welfare Capitalism*. That's because capitalism did not evolve to socialism as Karl Marx predicted it would. Instead, Marx's socialist ideas took root in feudalist Russia, a society that the Industrial Revolution had in large part bypassed. Arriving at a different place and a different time than Marx predicted it would, you shouldn't be surprised to read that socialism arrived in a different way than Marx predicted. The proletariat did not revolt to establish socialism. Instead, the First World War, which the Russians were losing, crippled Russia's feudal economy and government. A small group of socialists overthrew the czar (Russia's king) and took over the government in 1917. They quickly pulled Russia out of the war, and then set out to organize a socialist society and economy.

Russian socialists tried to adhere to Marx's ideas, but they found that Marx had concentrated on how capitalist economies operate, not on how a socialist economy should be run. Thus, Russian socialists faced a huge task with little guidance. Their most immediate problem was how to increase production so that the economy could emerge from feudalism into the modern industrial world. In Marx's analysis, capitalism was a necessary stage in the evolution toward the ideal state for a very practical reason. The capitalists exploit the workers, but in doing so capitalists extract the necessary surplus—an amount of production in excess of what is consumed. That surplus had to be extracted in order to provide the factories and machinery upon which a socialist economic system would be built. But since capitalism did not exist in Russia, a true socialist state could not be established immediately. Instead, the socialists created **state socialism**—*an economic system in which government sees to it that people work for the common good until they can be relied upon to do that on their own.*

Socialists saw state socialism as a transition stage to pure socialism. This transition stage still exploited the workers; when Joseph Stalin took power in Russia in the late 1920s, he took the peasants' and small farmers' land and turned it into collective farms. The government then paid farmers low prices for their produce. When farmers balked at the low prices, millions of them were killed.

Simultaneously, Stalin created central planning agencies that told individuals what to produce and how to produce it, and decided for whom things would be produced. During this period, *socialism* became synonymous with *central economic planning,* and Soviet-style socialism became the model of socialism in practice.

Also during this time, Russia took control of a number of neighbouring states and established the Union of Soviet Socialist Republics (USSR), the formal name of the Soviet Union. The Soviet Union also installed Soviet-dominated governments in a number of Eastern European countries. In 1949 most of China, under the rule of Mao Zedong, adopted Soviet-style socialist principles.

Since the late 1980s, the Soviet socialist economic and political structure has fallen apart. The Soviet Union as a political state broke up, and its former republics became autonomous. Eastern European countries were released from Soviet control. Now they faced a new problem: transition from socialism to a market economy. Why did the Soviet socialist economy fall apart? Because workers lacked incentives to work; production was inefficient; consumer goods were either unavailable or of poor quality; and high Soviet officials were exploiting their positions, keeping the best jobs for themselves and moving themselves up in the waiting lists for consumer goods. In short, the parents of the socialist family (the Communist party) were not acting benevolently; they were taking many of the benefits for themselves.

Recent political and economic upheavals in Eastern Europe and the former Soviet Union suggest that the kind of socialism these societies tried did not work. However, that failure does not mean that socialist goals are bad; nor does it mean that no type of socialism can ever work. To overthrow socialist-dominated governments it is not necessary to accept capitalism, and many citizens of these countries are looking for an alternative to both systems. Most, however, want to establish market economies.

FROM SOCIALISM TO . . . ?

The upheavals in the former Soviet Union and Eastern Europe have left China as the only major power using a socialist economic system. But even in China there have been changes, and the Chinese economy is socialist in name only. Almost uncontrolled markets exist in numerous sectors of the economy. These changes have led some socialists to modify their view that state socialism is the path from capitalism to true socialism, and instead to joke: "Socialism is the longest path from capitalism to capitalism."

Key Terms

capitalists *(50)*

laissez-faire *(51)*

proletariat *(52)*

state socialism *(53)*

feudalism *(47)*

Industrial Revolution *(47)*

mercantilism *(47)*

welfare capitalism *(48)*

The Canadian Economy in a Global Setting

3

After reading this chapter, you should be able to:

- Describe how businesses, households, and government interact in a market economy.

- Summarize briefly the advantages and disadvantages of various types of businesses.

- Explain why, even though households have the ultimate power, much of the economic decision making is done by business and government.

- List two general roles of government.

- List the primary areas with which Canada trades.

- State two ways international trade differs from intranational trade.

- List three important global trade organizations.

- List four important international policy organizations.

Letting a hundred flowers blossom and a hundred schools of thought contend is the policy for promoting progress in the arts and sciences and a flourishing socialist culture in our land.

Mao Zedong

The Canadian economic machine generates enormous economic activity and provides a high standard of living (compared to most other countries) for almost all its inhabitants. It also provides economic security for its citizens. Starvation is far from most

Ultimately the Canadian economy's strength is its people and
its other resources.

people's minds. Ultimately, what underlies the Canadian economy's strength is its people and its other resources. Canada has vast central plains that are extraordinarily fer-
tile, as are areas in its East and West. It is the world's largest producer, and largest
exporter, of zinc. It has excellent ports and almost a million kilometres of highways.

The positive attributes of the Canadian economy don't mean that Canada has no
problems. Critics point out that crime and drugs are omnipresent, economic resources
such as oil and minerals are declining, the environment is deteriorating, the distribution
of income is skewed toward the rich, regional disparities persist even though governments have spent billions to fight them, and enormous economic effort goes into economic gamesmanship (real estate deals, stock market deals, deals about deals) that
seems simply to reshuffle existing wealth, not create new wealth.

THE CANADIAN ECONOMY

Figure 3-1 diagrams a market economy such as that of Canada. Notice that it's divided
up into three groups: businesses, households, and government. Households supply
labour and other factors of production to businesses and are paid by businesses for doing
so. The market where this interaction takes place is called a *factor market*. Businesses
produce goods and services and sell them to households and government. The market
where this interaction takes place is called the *goods market*.

Notice also the arrows going out to and coming in from both business and households. Those arrows represent the connection of an economy to the world economy. It
consists of interrelated flows of goods (exports and imports) and money (capital flows).
Finally, consider the arrows connecting government with households and business.

Q-1 Into what three groups are
market economies generally broken up?

*Income earned by households goes to
purchasing goods and services
produced by business.*

Figure 3-1   DIAGRAMMATIC REPRESENTATION OF A MARKET ECONOMY

This circular flow diagram of the economy is a good way to organize your thinking about the aggregate economy.
As you can see, the three sectors—households, government, and business—interact in a variety of ways.

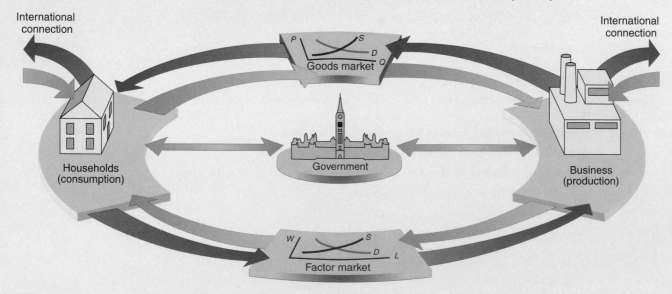

Government taxes business and households. It buys goods and services from business and buys labour services from households. Then, with some of its tax revenue, it provides services (e.g., roads, education) to both business and households and gives some of its tax revenue directly back to individuals. In doing so, it redistributes income. But government also serves a second function. It oversees the interaction of business and households in the goods and factor markets. Government, of course, is not independent. Canada is a democracy, so households vote to determine who will govern.

Now let's look briefly at the individual components.

BUSINESS

Business is responsible for about 80 percent of Canadian production. (Government is responsible for the other 20 percent.) In fact, any time a household decides to produce something, it becomes a business. **Business** is simply the name given to *private producing units in our society.*

3.1
see page 77

Businesses in Canada decide *what* to produce, *how* much to produce, and *for whom* to produce it. They make these central economic decisions on the basis of their own feelings, which are influenced by market incentives. Anyone who wants to can start a business, provided he or she can come up with the required cash and meet the necessary regulatory requirements. Each year thousands of businesses are started.

Businesses in Canada decide *what* to produce, *how much* to produce, and *for whom* to produce it.

Don't think of business as something other than people. Businesses are ultimately made up of a group of people organized together to accomplish some end. Although corporations account for a large part of all sales, in terms of numbers of businesses, most are one- or two-person operations. Home-based businesses are easy to start. All you have to do is say you're in business, and you are. However, some businesses require licenses, permits, and approvals from various government agencies. That's one reason why **entrepreneurship** (*the ability to organize and get something done*) is an important part of business.

Consumer Sovereignty and Business

To say that businesses decide what to produce isn't to say that **consumer sovereignty** (*the consumer's wishes rule what's produced*) doesn't reign in Canada. Businesses decide what to produce based on what they believe will sell. A key question a person in Canada should ask about starting a business is: Can I make a profit from it? **Profit** is *what's left over from total revenues after all the appropriate costs have been subtracted.* Businesses that guess correctly what the consumer wants generally make a profit. Businesses that guess wrong generally operate at a loss.

Although businesses decide what to produce, they are guided by consumer sovereignty.

People are free to start businesses for whatever purposes they want. No one asks them: "What's the social value of your term paper assistance business, your Twinkies business, your pornography business, or your textbook publishing business?" Yet the Canadian economic system is designed to channel individuals' desire to make a profit into the general good of society. That's the invisible hand at work. As long as the business doesn't violate a law and does conform to regulations, people in Canada are free to start whatever business they want, if they can get the money to finance it.

Q-2 In Canada the invisible hand ensures that only socially valuable businesses are started. True or false? Why?

Research at Statistics Canada indicates that from 1984 to 1994, at least half of new businesses in Canada went out of business after less than one year, and only one-fifth of them survived a decade. The average business life during this period was about six years. That's the invisible hand — it may be brutal, but it works.[1]

---

[1]http://www.statcan.ca/english/IPS/Data/61-526-XIE.htm

Producing physical goods is only one of a society's economic tasks. Another task is to provide services (activities done for others). Services do not involve producing a physical good. When you get your hair cut, you buy a service, not a good. Much of the cost of the physical goods we buy actually is not a cost of producing the good, but is a cost of one of the most important services: distribution (getting the good to where the consumer is). After a good is produced, it has to get to the individuals who are going to consume it at the time they need it. If the distribution system gets botched up, it's as if the good had never been produced.

Let's consider a couple of examples. Take Christmas trees. Say you're sitting on 60,000 cut spruce trees in New Brunswick, but an ice storm prevents you from shipping them until December 26. Guess what? You're now stuck with 60,000 spruce trees and the problem of somehow getting rid of them. Or take hot dogs. How many of us have been irked that a hot dog that costs 25¢ to fix at home costs $4 at a football game? But a hot dog at home isn't the same as a hot dog at a game. Distribution of the good is as important as production; you're paying the extra $3.75 for distribution.

The importance of the service economy can be seen in modern technology companies. They provide information and methods of handling information, not physical goods. Operating systems, such as Linux and Windows, can be supplied over the Internet; no physical production is necessary. So, yes, it is fair to say that our economy is a postindustrial economy.

Forms of Business

The three primary forms of business are sole proprietorships, partnerships, and corporations. **Sole proprietorships**—*businesses that have only one owner*—are the easiest to start and have the fewest bureaucratic hassles. **Partnerships**—*businesses with two or more owners*—create possibilities for sharing the burden, but they also create unlimited liability for each of the partners. **Corporations**—*businesses that are treated as a person and are legally owned by their stockholders, who are not liable for the actions of the corporate "person"*—are the largest form of business when measured in terms of receipts.

The advantages and disadvantages of each are summarized in the following table:

Advantages and Disadvantages of Various Forms of For-Profit Businesses

	Sole Proprietor	Partnership	Corporation
Advantages	1. Minimum bureaucratic hassle 2. Direct control by owner	1. Ability to share work and risks 2. Relatively easy to form	1. No personal liability 2. Increasing ability to get funds 3. Ability to shed personal income and gain added expenses
Disadvantages	1. Limited ability to get funds 2. Unlimited personal liability	1. Unlimited personal liability (even for partner's blunder) 2. Limited ability to get funds	1. Legal hassle to organize 2. Possible double taxation of income 3. Monitoring problems

Since corporations are the most complex, let's consider them more carefully. When a corporation is formed, it issues **stock** (*certificates of ownership in a company*), which is sold or given to individuals. Proceeds of the sale of that stock make up what is called the *equity capital* of a company. Ownership of stock entitles you to vote in the election of a corporation's directors.

Corporations were developed as institutions to make it easier for company owners to be separated from company management. A corporation provides the owners with **limited liability**—*the stockholder's liability is limited to the amount that stockholder has invested in the company*. With the other two forms of business, owners can lose everything they possess, even if they have only a small amount invested in the company, but in a corporation the owners can lose only what they have invested in that corporation. If you've invested $100, you can lose only $100. In the other kinds of business, even if you've invested only $100, you could lose everything; the business's losses must be covered by the individual owners. Corporations' limited liability makes it easier for them to attract investment capital. Corporations pay taxes, but they also offer their individual owners ways of legally avoiding taxes.

A corporation's stock can be distributed among a few people or among millions of stockholders. Stocks can be bought and sold either in an independent transaction between two people (an *over-the-counter* trade) or through a broker and a *stock exchange*.

In corporations, ownership is separated from control of the firm. Most stockholders have little input into the decisions a corporation makes. Instead, corporations are often controlled by their managers, who often run them for their own benefit as well as for the owners'. The reason is that owners' control of management is limited.

A large percentage of most corporations' stock is not even controlled by the owners; instead, it is controlled by financial institutions such as mutual funds (financial institutions that invest individuals' money for them) and by pension funds (financial institutions that hold people's money for them until it is to be paid out to them upon their retirement). Thus, ownership of corporations is another step removed from individuals.

Why is the question of who controls a firm important? Because economic theory assumes the goal of business owners is to maximize profits, which would be true of corporations if stockholders made the decisions. Managers don't have the same incentives to maximize profits that owners do. There's pressure on managers to maximize profits, but that pressure can often be weak or ineffective. An example of how firms deal with this problem involves stock options. Many companies give their managers stock options—rights to buy stock at a low price—to encourage them to worry about the price of their company's stock. But these stock options dilute the value of company ownership and decrease profits per share.

Finance and Business

Much of what you hear in the news about business concerns financial assets—assets that acquire value from an obligation of someone else to pay. Stocks are one example of a financial asset; bonds are another. Financial assets are traded in markets such as the Toronto Stock Exchange. Trading in financial markets can make people rich (or poor) quickly. Stocks and bonds can also provide a means through which corporations can finance expansions and new investments.

Recently there has been much in the news about one part of these financial markets—initial public offerings (IPOs), in which a company first offers some of its stock to the general public, with the owners keeping a large portion for themselves. This is an example of how financial markets work to fund companies, allowing the economy to grow.

Q.3 Many businesses in Canada end with "Ltd.," while in the United States many end in "Inc." Why?

Most corporations are controlled by managers, with little effective stockholder control.

Q.4 It is obvious that all for-profit businesses in Canada will maximize profit. True or false? Why?

 3.2

see page 77

Stocks are usually traded on a *stock exchange*—a formal market in which stocks are bought and sold.

In order to buy or sell a stock, you contact a stockbroker (or simply contact the company through the Web—it's cheaper that way) and say you want to buy or sell whatever stock you've decided on—say Ford Motor Company. The commission you're charged for having the broker sell you the stock (or sell it for you) varies. It usually starts at some minimum between $10 and $30, and then is so much per share.

There are a number of stock exchanges. The largest and most familiar one in Canada is the Toronto Stock Exchange.

To judge how stocks as a whole are doing, a number of indexes have been developed. These include the TSX, and in the U.S., Standard and Poor's (S&P 500), the Wilshire Index, the Russell 2000, and the Dow Jones Industrial Average. The TSX replaced the TSE300 index in May 2002. It's the one you are most likely to hear about in the news.

KNOWING THE TOOLS

The Stock Market

When a share of a corporation's existing stock is sold on the stock exchange, corporations get no money from that sale. The sale is simply a transfer of ownership from one individual (or organization) to another. The only time a corporation gets money from the sale of stock is when it first issues the shares.

HOW TO READ THE STOCK TABLES

Get all your quotes throughout the day at www.nationalpost.com

Lines in boldface indicate that the stock closed at least 5% higher or lower than the previous board lot closing price. Stocks must close at a minimum $1 and trade at least 500 shares to qualify.

Underlined stocks have traded 500% or more above their 60-day average daily volume.
1. **Up/down arrows** indicate a new 52-week high or low in the day's trading
2. **52-week high/low:** Highest and lowest inter-day price reached in the previous 52 weeks
3. **Stock names** have been abbreviated
4. **Ticker:** Basic trading symbol for primary issues (usually common)
5. **Dividend:** Indicated annual rate. See footnotes
6. **Yield %:** Annual dividend rate or amount paid in past 12 months as a percentage of closing price in past 12 months
7. **P/E:** Price earnings ratio, closing price divided by earnings per share in past 12 months. Figures reported in US$ converted to C$
8. **Volume:** Number of shares traded in 00s; z – odd lot; e – exact no. of shares
9. **High:** Highest inter-day trading price
10. **Low:** Lowest inter-day trading price

		3	4		6	7	8	9	10	11	12
52W high	**52W low**	**Stock**	**Ticker**	**Div**	**Yield %**	**P/E**	**Vol 00s**	**High**	**Low**	**Close**	**Net chg**
↑x29.25	21.15	MaxStockna	MAX	f0.50	1.96	7.4	210501	27.25	27.05	27.20	+0.10
n 39.25	31.15	MaxStockna	...MAX	f1.00	2.83	10.3	210501	37.25	37.05	37.20	+0.10
↓s49.25	41.15	MaxStockna	MAX	f1.50	3.30	13.2	210501	47.25	47.05	47.20	+0.10

11. **Close:** Closing price
12. **Net change:** Change between board lot closing price and previous board lot closing price

If a Canadian listed stock doesn't trade, its last bid and ask price can be found in the bid/ask table

Footnotes
* – traded in $US x – stock is trading ex-dividend n – stock is newly listed on exchange in past year s – stock has split in past year c – stock has consolidated in past year – spinoff company distributed as shares ÷ – shares carry unusual voting rights † – denotes tier I

stocks on CDNX (tier III stocks on CDNX have a **Y** as first letter of ticker)

Dividend footnotes
r – dividend in arrears u – US$ p – paid in the past 12 months including extras y – dividend paid in stock, cash equivalent f – floating rate, annualized v – variable rate, annualized based on last payment

Data supplied by CGI
905-479-STAR and FP DataGroup
416-350-6500
Historical Nasdaq supplied by DataStream

———— **How to read the options, index options, futures prices and futures options tables** ————

P/C – Option put or call. Futures prices open interest reflects previous trading day. **CBOT** – Chicago Board of Trade, **CDNX** – Canadian Venture Exchange, **CME** – Chicago Mercantile Exchange, **COMEX** – New York Commodity Exchange, **FINEX** – Financial Instruments Exchange, **IMM** – International Money Market, **CSCE** – Coffee, Sugar, Cocoa Exchange, **KBOT** – Kansas City Board of Trade, **MPLS** – Minneapolis Grain Exchange, **NYCE** – New York Cotton Exchange, **NYME** – New York Mercantile Exchange, **NYFE** – New York Futures Exchange, **r** – option not traded, **s** – no option offered, **TSE** – Toronto Stock Exchange, **TFE** – Toronto Futures Exchange, **WPG** – Winnipeg Commodity Exchange.

Source: *The National Post*, used with permission.

In the late 1990s, the stock prices of many of the ".com" (read: dot com) companies, which are firms in some way related to the Internet, exploded. The stocks sold for enormous values—values that many economists felt could not last. (See Appendix A at the end of this chapter for a discussion of how economists value financial assets.) They saw what is called a financial bubble—a situation in which financial assets' valuations are based on what almost everyone believes are insupportable expectations—and were expecting the bubble to burst, or at least to shrink down to a supportable size. That, in fact, is what happened late in 2000 and during 2001. Some firms that had been trading for $150 a share fell to $7. Most market-watchers think the bubble has burst, although late in 2001 some investment gurus predicted stock prices would continue to fall well into 2002.

E-Commerce and the Digital Economy

To say that many of the Internet companies were overvalued is not to say that e-commerce—buying and selling over the Internet—will not make an enormous difference to the economy, and to the nature of business. Almost all economists believe it will. E-commerce adds heavy competition to the economy, and will place pressure on existing firms to compete with low prices. If they don't, they will lose their customers. More and more individuals are buying cars, books, prescription drugs, and even groceries on the Web, and the range of what is bought will expand. One reason is that the Internet removes the importance of geography and location for firms. In doing so it reduces the value of firms whose comparative advantage depends on geography, while increasing the value of firms whose comparative advantage does not depend on geography.

Some goods are more conducive to being sold on the Internet than others. For example, there are certain goods customers want to see before they buy them. Until virtual reality is perfected, that is impossible with the Internet. The practice of going to see goods at local stores but then buying them on the Internet will likely lead to some changes in the nature of businesses. Consider cars; because the Internet allows car buyers to compare prices and get a better deal than the local dealer generally gives, more and more people are buying cars over the Internet. Before they do so, however, they generally visit the local car dealership to see and test-drive the car. As Internet car buying expands, such practices are unlikely to continue. The future may well include car showrooms that charge you to test-drive, or even look at, a car (with the charge being rebated by the selling company if you actually buy the car).

E-commerce has grown enormously in the early 2000s, and a terminology developed that is captured in the table below. Initially, B2B (business selling to business) activity grew, but B2C (business selling to consumers) was also growing. Auction sites C2C (consumers selling to consumers) and bidding sites for consumers (C2B) were also beginning to grow.

B2B	B2C
C2B	C2C

HOUSEHOLDS

The second classification we'll consider in this overview of Canadian economic institutions is households. **Households** (*groups of individuals living together and making joint decisions*) are the most powerful economic institution. They ultimately influence government and business, the other two economic institutions. Households' votes in the political arena determine government policy; their decisions about supplying labour and capital determine what businesses will have available to work with; and their spending decisions or expenditures (the "votes" they cast with their dollars) determine what business will be able to sell.

In the economy, households vote with their dollars.

The Power of Households

While the ultimate power does in principle lie with the people and households, much of that power has been assigned to representatives. As we discussed above, corporations are only partially responsive to owners of their stocks, and much of that ownership is once-removed from individuals. Ownership of 1,000 shares in a company with a total of 2 million shares isn't going to get you any influence over the corporation's activities. As a stockholder, you simply accept what the corporation does.

A major decision that corporations make independently of their stockholders concerns what to produce. Ultimately households decide whether to buy what business produces, but business spends a lot of money telling us what services we want, what products make us "with it," what books we want to read, and the like. Most economists believe that consumer sovereignty reigns—that we are not fooled or controlled by advertising. Still, it is an open question in some economists' minds whether we, the people, control business or the business representatives control people.

Consumer sovereignty reigns, but it works indirectly by influencing businesses.

Because of this assignment of power to other institutions, in many spheres of the economy households are not active producers of output but merely passive recipients of income, primarily in their role as suppliers of labour.

Suppliers of Labour

The largest source of household income is wages and salaries (the income households get from labour). Households supply the labour with which businesses produce and government governs. The total Canadian labour force is about 16 million people, about 7 percent (1.1 million) of whom were unemployed in 2001. The average Canadian work week is about 39 hours. The average pay in Canada was nearly $700 per week, which translates to about $18.00 per hour. Of course, that average has enormous variability and depends on the occupation and region of the country where one is employed. For example, lawyers often earn $100,000 per year; physicians earn about $150,000 per year; and CEOs of large corporations may make $2 million per year or more. A beginning McDonald's employee generally makes about $12,000 per year.

The table below shows current and predicted labour market conditions (in 2004) by skill level and skill type. The skill level refers to the minimum level of education and training required to work in those occupations, while the skill type refers to a broad industry category. Primary industry and sales and services are both expected to decline, whereas labour market conditions in almost every other market are expected to remain at their current levels or improve.

Skill Types	Skill Levels										
	Managerial		Professional		Technical, paraprofessional & skilled		Intermediate		Labouring & elemental		All
	Current	2004	Current	2004	Current	2004	Current	2004	Current	2004	Current	2004
Business, Finance & Administration	Good	Good	Good	Good	Good	Good	Fair	Fair	--	--	Good	Good
Natural & Applied Sciences	Good	Good	Good	Good	Good	Good	--	--	--	--	Good	Good
Health	Good	Good	Good	Good	Fair	Fair	Fair	Fair	--	--	Good	Good
Social Science, Education, Government Service & Religion	Good	Good	Fair	Fair	Fair	Fair	--	--	--	--	Fair	Fair
Art, Culture, Recreation & Sport	Good	Good	Fair	Fair	Fair	Fair	--	--	--	--	Fair	Fair
Sales & Services	Good	Good	--	--	Fair	Good	Fair	Limited	Limited	Limited	Fair	Limited
Trades, Transport & Equipment Operators	Fair	Good	--	--	Fair	Fair	Fair	Fair	Limited	Limited	Fair	Fair
Primary Industry	Good	Fair	--	--	Fair	Fair	Limited	Limited	Limited	Limited	Fair	Fair
Processing, Manufacturing & Utilities	Good	Good	--	--	Good	Good	Fair	Fair	Limited	Limited	Fair	Fair
All	Good	Good	Good	Good	Fair	Fair	Fair	Fair	Limited	Limited	Fair	Fair

Source: Human Resources Development Canada, Job Futures 2000 World of Work, http://jobfutures.ca/doc/jf/lmo/part1/en/table1.shtml

GOVERNMENT

The third major Canadian economic institution we'll consider is government. Government plays two general roles in the economy. It's both a referee (setting the rules that determine relations between business and households) and an actor (collecting money in taxes and spending that money on its own projects, such as health care and education). Let's first consider government's role as an actor.

Government as an Actor

Canada has a federal government system, which means we have various levels of government (federal, provincial, and local), each with its own powers. Together they consume about 20 percent of the country's total output and employ about 800,000 individuals. The various levels of government also have a number of programs that redistribute income through taxation or through an array of social welfare and assistance programs designed to help specific groups.

Provincial and Local Government Provincial and local governments employ over 450,000 people and spend over $250 billion a year. As you can see in Figure 3-2(a), provincial and local governments get much of their income from taxes: property taxes, sales taxes, and provincial income taxes. They spend their tax revenues on social services, health care, and education (education through high school is available free in public schools), and roads, as Figure 3-2(b) shows.

Federal Government Probably the best way to get an initial feel for the federal government and its size is to look at the various categories of its tax revenues and expenditures in Figure 3-3(a). Notice income taxes make up about 63 percent of the federal government's revenue, while sales taxes make up about 20 percent. That's more than 80 percent of the federal government's revenues, most of which shows up as a deduction from your paycheque. In Figure 3-3(b), notice that the federal government's two largest categories of spending are social services and debt charges, with transfer payments well behind.

What are transfer payments? You'll notice there are two categories of revenues in Figure 3-2(a) listed as general purpose transfers and special purpose transfers. **Transfer payments** are payments by governments to individuals that are not in return for goods and services, with the federal government making transfers to the provinces, and the provinces making transfers to the municipalities.

3.3

see page 77

Q.5 The largest percentage of federal expenditure is in what general category?

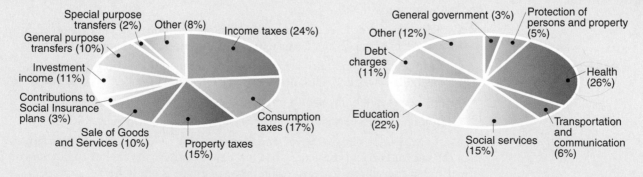

Figure 3-2 (a and b) INCOME AND EXPENDITURES OF PROVINCIAL AND LOCAL GOVERNMENTS, 2001

The charts give you a sense of the importance of provincial and local governments—where they get (a), and where they spend (b), their revenues.

(a) Income

Special purpose transfers (2%) Other (8%) Income taxes (24%)
General purpose transfers (10%)
Investment income (11%)
Contributions to Social Insurance plans (3%)
Sale of Goods and Services (10%)
Property taxes (15%)
Consumption taxes (17%)

(b) Expenditures

General government (3%) Protection of persons and property (5%)
Other (12%)
Debt charges (11%)
Education (22%)
Social services (15%)
Health (26%)
Transportation and communication (6%)

Source: Statistics Canada, Cansim II, Table 385-001

Figure 3-3 (a and b) INCOME AND EXPENDITURES OF THE FEDERAL GOVERNMENT, 2001

The pie charts show the sources and uses of federal government revenue. It is important to note that, when the government runs a deficit, expenditures exceed income and the difference is made up by borrowing, so the size of the income and expenditure pies may not be equal.

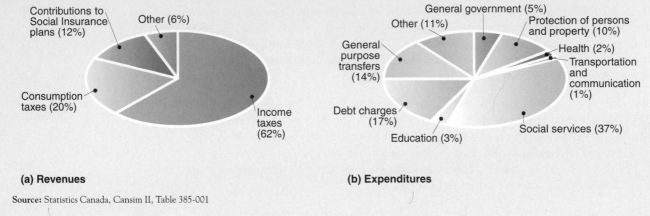

(a) Revenues

(b) Expenditures

Source: Statistics Canada, Cansim II, Table 385-001

General purpose transfers are equalization payments that are meant to reduce disparities between the "have" and the "have not" provinces. They are supposed to allow all provinces to provide similar services at comparable levels of taxation. Special purpose transfers are primarily aimed at funding social spending on health care, welfare, and post-secondary education. The special purpose transfers are known as the Canada Health and Social Transfer.

Government as a Referee

Even if government spending made up only a small proportion of total expenditures, government would still be central to the study of economics. The reason is that, in a market economy, government sets the rules of interaction between households and businesses, and acts as a referee, changing the rules when it sees fit. Government decides whether economic forces will be allowed to operate freely.

Some examples of Canadian laws regulating the interaction between households and businesses today are:

1. Businesses are not free to hire and fire whomever they want. They must comply with labour laws. Even closing a plant requires notice for many kinds of firms.

2. Many working conditions are subject to government regulation: safety rules, wage rules, overtime rules, hours-of-work rules, and the like.

3. Businesses cannot meet with other businesses to agree on prices they will charge.

4. In some businesses workers must join a union to work at certain jobs.

Most of these laws evolved over time. Up until the 1930s, household members, in their roles as workers and consumers, had few rights. Businesses were free to hire and fire at will and, if they chose, to deceive and take advantage of consumers.

Over time, new laws to curb business abuses have been passed, and government agencies have been formed to enforce these laws. Many people think the pendulum has swung too far the other way. They believe businesses are saddled with too many regulatory burdens.

Figure 3-4   THE CANADIAN ECONOMY IN A GLOBAL SETTING

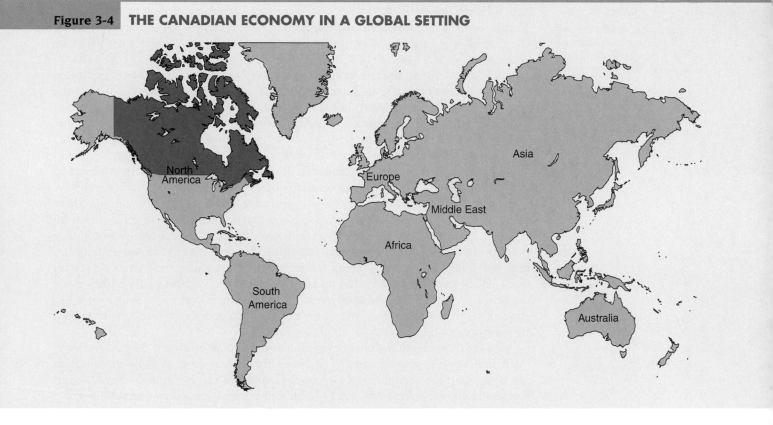

One big question that we'll address throughout this book is: What referee role should the government play in an economy? For example, should government use its taxing powers to redistribute income from the rich to the poor? Should it allow mergers between companies? Should it regulate air traffic? Should it regulate prices? Should it attempt to stabilize fluctuations of aggregate income?

THE GLOBAL SETTING

We now turn to a discussion of how international issues affect the Canadian economy. Nearly every decision facing Canada or a firm operating in Canada involves international issues. The Canadian economy is integrated with the world economy, and we cannot reasonably discuss Canadian economic issues without discussing the role that international considerations play in these issues.

International issues must be taken into account in just about any economic decision a country or a firm faces.

Probably the best way to put the Canadian economy into perspective is to look at a map of the world, such as the one in Figure 3-4. Notice the physical size of Canada. Compared to the world, it's relatively small. Alternatively, consider population; the Canadian population is about 31 million; the world population is 6 billion, so the Canadian population is about 0.5 percent of the world population. The importance of Canada increases somewhat when we consider that Canadian production accounts for nearly 2 percent of world output, but it is important for Canadians to remember that there is a whole world out there, and Canada is simply a part of that world.

Global Corporations

Global corporations are corporations with substantial operations on both the production and sales sides in more than one country.

The importance of the world to the Canadian economy can also be seen by considering the clothes on your back. Most likely they were made abroad. Similarly with the cars you drive. It's likely that half of you drive a car that was made abroad. Of course, it's often difficult to tell. Just because a car has a Japanese or German name doesn't mean that it was produced abroad. Some Japanese and German companies have manufacturing plants in Canada. Others, such as Chrysler and Daimler Benz (they make Mercedes) have merged. When goods are produced by **global corporations** (*corporations with substantial operations in both production and sales in more than one country*), corporate names don't always tell much about where a good is produced. As global corporations' importance has grown, most manufacturing decisions have come to be made in reference to the international market, not the Canadian domestic market.

Global corporations offer enormous benefits for countries. They create jobs; they bring new ideas and new technologies to a country, and they provide competition for domestic companies, keeping them on their toes. But global corporations also pose a number of problems for governments. One is their implication for domestic and international policy. A domestic corporation exists within a country and can be dealt with using policy measures within that country. A global corporation exists within many countries and there is no global government to regulate or control it. If it doesn't like the policies in one country—say taxes are too high or regulations too tight—it can shift its operations to other countries.

At times it seems that global corporations are governments unto themselves, especially in relation to poorer countries. In terms of sales, a number of global corporations are larger than the economies of middle-size countries. For example, General Motors has a total annual revenue of U.S. $177 billion; Ecuador has a total annual income of U.S. $60 billion. This comparison is not quite accurate, since sales do not necessarily reflect power; but when a company's decisions can significantly affect what happens in a country's economy, that company has significant economic power.

When global corporations have such power, it is not surprising that they can sometimes dominate a country. The corporation can use its expertise and experience to direct a small country to do its bidding rather than the other way around.

Before you condemn globals, remember: Globals don't have it so easy either. Customs and laws differ among countries. Trying to meet the differing laws and ambiguous limits of acceptable action in various countries is often impossible. For example, in many countries bribery is an acceptable part of doing business. If you want to get permission to sell a good, you must pay the appropriate officials *baksheesh* (as it's called in Egypt) or *la mordita* (as it's called in Mexico). In Canada, such payments are called bribes and are illegal. Given these differing laws, the only way a Canadian company can do business in some foreign countries is to break Canadian laws.

Moreover, global corporations often work to maintain close ties among countries and to reduce international tension. If part of your company is in an Eastern European country and part is in Canada, you want the two countries to be friends. So beware of making judgments about whether global corporations are good or bad. They're both simultaneously.

International Trade

The volume and value of world trade have grown substantially over the last century but there have been significant fluctuations around this trend. Sometimes trade has grown rapidly; at other times it has grown slowly or has even fallen off.

In part, fluctuations in world trade result from fluctuations in world output. When output rises, international trade rises; when output falls, international trade falls.

Economic geography isn't much covered in most economics courses because it requires learning enormous numbers of facts, and university and college courses aren't a good place to learn facts. Postsecondary studies are designed to teach you how to interpret and relate facts. Unfortunately, if you don't know facts, much of what you learn now isn't going to do you much good. You'll be relating and interpreting air. The following quiz presents some facts about the world economy. Below we list characteristics of 20 countries or regions in random order. Beneath the characteristics, in alphabetical order, we list 20 countries or regions. Associate the characteristics with the country or region.

If you answer 15 or more correctly, you have a reasonably good sense of economic geography. If you don't, we strongly suggest learning more facts. The study guide has other projects, information, and examples. An encyclopedia has even more, and your library has a wealth of information. You could spend the entire term following the economic news carefully, paying attention to where various commodities are produced, and picturing in your mind a map whenever you hear about an economic event.

1. Former British colony, now small independent island country famous for producing rum.

2. Large sandy country contains world's largest known oil reserves.

3. Very large country with few people; produces 25 percent of the world's wool.

4. Temperate country ideal for producing wheat, soybeans, fruits, vegetables, wine, and meat.

5. Small tropical country produces abundant coffee and bananas.

6. Has world's largest population and world's largest hydropower potential.

7. Second-largest country in Europe; famous for wine and romance.

8. Former Belgian colony with vast copper mines.

9. European country; exports luxury clothing, footwear, and automobiles.

10. Country that has depleted many of its natural resources but that has the highest level of GDP of any country in the world.

11. Long, narrow country of four main islands; most thickly populated country in the world; exports majority of the world's electronics products.

12. Recently politically reunified country; one important product is steel.

13. Second-largest country in the world; leading zinc exporter.

14. European country for centuries politically repressed; now becoming industrialized; chemicals are one of its leading exports.

15. 96 percent of its people live on 4 percent of the land; much of the world's finest cotton comes from here.

16. Politically and radically troubled African nation has world's largest concentration of gold.

17. Huge, heavily populated country eats most of what it raises but is a major tea exporter.

18. Country that is a top producer of oil and gold; has recently undergone major political and economic changes.

19. Has only about 50 people per square mile but lots of trees; timber and fish exporter.

20. Sliver of a country on Europe's Atlantic coast; by far the world's largest exporter of cork.

    A. Argentina
    B. Australia
    C. Barbados
    D. Canada
    E. China
    F. Costa Rica
    G. Egypt
    H. France
    I. Germany
    J. India
    K. Italy
    L. Japan
    M. Portugal
    N. Russia
    O. Saudi Arabia
    P. South Africa
    Q. Spain
    R. Sweden
    S. United States
    T. Democratic Republic of the Congo

Answers: 1–C, 2–O, 3–B, 4–A, 5–F, 6–E, 7–H, 8–T, 9–K, 10–S, 11–L, 12–I, 13–D, 14–Q, 15–G, 16–P, 17–J, 18–N, 19–R, 20–M.

Fluctuations in world trade are also explained in part by trade restrictions that countries have imposed from time to time. For example, decreases in world income during the Depression caused a large decrease in trade, but that decrease was exacerbated by a worldwide increase in trade restrictions during the 1930s.

Differences in the Importance of Trade The importance of international trade to countries' economies differs widely, as we can see in the table below, which presents the importance of the shares of **exports**—*the value of goods sold abroad*—and **imports**—*the value of goods purchased abroad*—for various countries.

	GDP*	Export Ratio	Import Ratio
United States	$10 486	11%	14%
Canada	703	43	40
Netherlands	382	66	59
Germany	1 858	29	27
United Kingdom	1 417	26	27
Italy	1 097	28	22
France	1 314	26	23
Japan	4 177	9	8

*Numbers in billions of U.S. dollars.
Source: *The World Development Report*, The World Bank, 2001 (http://www.worldbank.org) and individual country Web pages.

Canada's major trading partner is the United States.

Q.6 Among the countries listed in the table, which has the lowest exports and imports as a percentage of GDP?

Among the countries listed, the Netherlands has the highest amount of exports compared to GDP; the United States and Japan have the lowest.

The Netherlands' imports are also the highest as a percentage of GDP. Japan has the lowest. The relationship between a country's imports and its exports is no coincidence. For most countries, imports and exports roughly equal one another, though in any particular year that equality can be rough indeed. For Canada in recent years, exports have generally significantly exceeded imports. But that situation can't continue forever, as we'll discuss.

Total trade figures provide us with only part of the international trade picture. We must also look at what types of goods are traded and with whom that trade is conducted.

What Canada Trades and with Whom The majority of Canadian exports and imports involve significant amounts of manufactured goods. This isn't unusual, since much of international trade is in manufactured goods.

Figure 3-5 shows the regions with which Canada trades. Exports to the United States and the European Union made up the largest percentage of total Canadian exports to individual countries in 2001. Countries from which Canada imports major quantities include the United States and the regions of the European Union and the Pacific Rim. Thus, the countries we export to are also the countries we import from.

One reason a Canadian economics course must consider international issues early on is the Canadian **balance of trade**—the difference between the value of goods and services Canada exports and the value of goods and services it imports. When *imports exceed exports* the country is running a balance of **trade deficit**; when it *exports more than it imports*, it runs a balance of **trade surplus**. A large share of Canadian production is destined for foreign markets so the balance of trade is an important measure in Canada.

We have to be careful about terminology when we look at Canada's international position because the balance of trade contains two components. The first is the

Figure 3-5 (a and b)   **CANADIAN EXPORTS AND IMPORTS BY REGION, 2000**

Major regions that trade with Canada include the United States, the European Union, and the Pacific Rim.

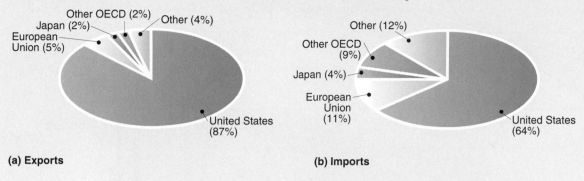

(a) Exports   **(b) Imports**

merchandise trade balance—it *measures the difference between exports and imports of goods.* The second component is the **services balance**, which *measures trade in services.* Canada has been a net exporter of goods since the early 1970s but we've been a net importer of services since the 1950s. It may sound funny, but when your cousin Fred goes to Florida on vacation, he's importing the services the Florida vacation provides. The Canadian goods and services trade balance has cycled up and down as the balance of trade and the services balance have changed over time. Figure 3-6 (on the next page) shows how this looks for the last 30 years or so.

Debtor and Creditor Nations Running a trade surplus isn't necessarily a bad thing, nor is running a trade deficit. In fact, if you were a country, running a trade deficit would be rather nice. It would probably mean that you are consuming (importing) more than you're producing (exporting). How can you do that? By living off past savings, getting support from your parents or spouse, or borrowing.

Countries have the same options. They can live off foreign aid, past savings, or loans. The **current account balance** *measures trade in goods and services and includes the interest payments we make to foreigners for the use of their savings.* From 1986 until 1998, Canada ran a current account deficit (with the exception of a small surplus in 1996), which meant it was borrowing from abroad and selling off assets—financial assets such as stocks and bonds, or real assets such as real estate and corporations. Since the assets of Canada total many billions of dollars, we could run trade deficits for many years. The problem with doing so is that it requires that we continually borrow from abroad, and the interest payments we make to foreigners for the use of their funds don't contribute to Canadian incomes.

In 1999 and 2000, Canada had a current account surplus, which means we were exporting more than we were importing. As we go to press, figures for 2001 suggest we also ran a surplus, but since the figures are subject to sometimes substantial revisions, they are preliminary. We don't need to borrow as much, or look for friendly support. If we look south, we'll see that the United States is the world's largest debtor. It has a huge trade deficit — it has borrowed more from abroad than it has lent abroad.

Q-7 Will a debtor nation necessarily be running a trade deficit?

Figure 3-6   THE CANADIAN BALANCE OF TRADE

The balance of trade is composed of the merchandise trade balance and the services balance. The Canadian services balance has been negative for the past 30 years, but we export more goods than we import, leading to a trade surplus for most of this period.

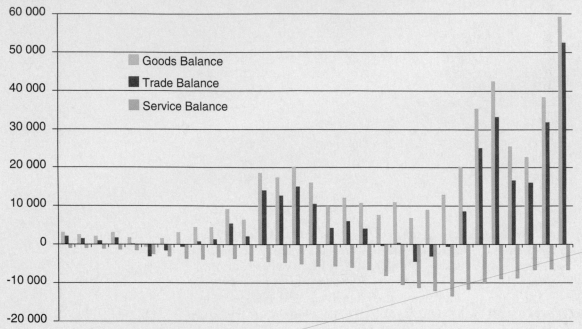

Legend:
- Goods Balance
- Trade Balance
- Service Balance

Source: Statistics Canada, Cansim II Table 380–0027.

Let's consider an example from history. In the Middle Ages, Greek ideas and philosophy were lost to Europe when hordes of barbarians swept over the continent. These ideas and that philosophy were only reddiscovered in the Renaissance as a byproduct of trade between the Italian merchant cities and the Middle East. (The Greek ideas that had spread to the Middle East were protected from European upheavals.) *Renaissance* means rebirth; a rebirth in Europe of Greek learning. Many of our traditions and sensibilities are based on those of the Renaissance, and that Renaissance was caused, or at least significantly influenced, by international trade. Had there been no trade, our entire philosophy of life might have been different.

Fernand Braudel, a French historian, has provided wonderful examples of the broader implications for trade. For instance, he argued that the effects of international trade, specifically Sir Walter Raleigh's introduction of the potato into England from South America in 1588, had more long-term consequences than the celebrated 1588 battle between the English navy and Spanish Armada.

Another example, which Braudel did not live to see, is the major change in socialist countries in the 1990s.

BEYOND THE TOOLS

International Issues in Perspective

Through the 1960s China, the Soviet Union, and the Eastern European countries were relatively closed societies—behind the Iron Curtain. That changed in the 1970s and 1980s as these socialist countries opened up trade with the West as a way to speed up their own economic development. That trade, and the resulting increased contact with the West, gave the people of those countries a better sense of the material goods to be had in the West. That trade also spread Western ideas of the proper organization of government and the economy to these societies. A strong argument can be made that along with trade came the seeds of discontent that changed those societies and their economies forever.

In economics courses we do not focus on these broader cultural issues but instead focus on relatively technical issues such as the reasons for trade and the implications of tariffs. But keep in the back of your mind these broader implications as you go through the various components of international economics. They add a dimension to the story that otherwise might be forgotten.

The world economy is often divided into three main areas or trading blocs: The Americas, Europe and Africa, and East Asia. These trading blocs are shown in the map below.

KNOWING THE TOOLS

Our International Competitors

The table below gives you a sense of the similarities and differences in the economies of the United States, Japan, and Europe.

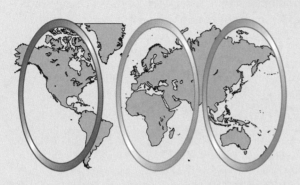

	Canada	United States	Japan	Europe
Area (square km)	9,976,140	9,629,091	377,835	2,371,321
Population (million)	31.6	278	126.8	292
GDP (billion US$)	774.7	9,963	3,150	€6,430
GDP per capita	$24,500	$35,800	$24,800	€22,000
Natural resources	Timber, fish, metal ore, natural gas	Coal, copper, lead, and others	Very few	Coal, iron ore, natural gas, fish, and others
Exports/GDP	35%	8%	14%	33%
Imports/GDP	31%	12%	11%	28%
Currency value ($C per foreign currency unit, January 25, 2002)	1.00	1.61	0.01196	1.39

Source: CIA World Factbook (www.cia.gov/cia/publication/factbook), European Central Bank. All values are in U.S. dollars unless otherwise noted.

The three dominant economies in these trading blocs are the Unites States, Germany, and Japan. Each area has a major currency. In the Americas, it is the U.S. dollar; in Europe it is the euro, a new currency recently created by the European Union; and in East Asia it is the Japanese yen.

HOW INTERNATIONAL TRADE DIFFERS FROM DOMESTIC TRADE

International trade differs from *intranational* (domestic) trade in two ways. First, international trade involves potential barriers to the flow of imports and exports. Before they can be sold in Canada, international goods must be sent through customs; that is, when they enter Canada they are inspected by Canadian officials and usually charged fees, known as *customs*. A company in Toronto can produce output to sell in any province without worrying that its right to sell will be limited; a producer outside the Canadian boundary cannot. At any time, a foreign producer's right to sell in Canada can be limited by government-imposed **quotas** (*limitations on how much of a good can be shipped into a country*), **tariffs** (*taxes on imports*), and **nontariff barriers** (*indirect regulatory restrictions on imports and exports*).

The last category, indirect regulatory restrictions on imports and exports, may be unfamiliar to you, so let's consider an example. U.S. building codes require that plywood have fewer than, say, three flaws per sheet. Canadian building codes require that plywood have fewer than, say, five flaws per sheet. The different building codes are a nontariff barrier, making trade in building materials between the United States and Canada difficult.

Two ways in which *international* trade differs from *intranational* (domestic) trade are:

1. International trade involves potential barriers to trade; and
2. International trade involves multiple currencies.

Q-8 What is the difference between a quota and a tariff?

The second way international trade differs from domestic or intranational trade is countries' use of different currencies. When people in one country sell something to people in another, they must find a way to exchange currencies as well as goods. **Foreign exchange markets** (*markets where one currency can be exchanged for another*) have developed to provide this service.

How many dollars will a Canadian have to pay to get a given amount of the currency of another country? That depends on the supply of and demand for that currency. To find out what you'd have to pay, you look in the newspaper for the **exchange rate**—*the rate at which one currency is traded for another*—such as in the following table:

A foreign exchange market is a market in which one currency can be exchanged for another.

A Foreign Exchange Rate Table

3.4

see page 77

From the exchange rate table, you learn how much a dollar is worth in other countries. For example, on this day, Feb. 28, 2002, the table tells you how many dollars other currencies can buy. For example, one Euro could buy 1.3896 dollars.

FOREIGN EXCHANGE BY COUNTRY

Supplied BMO Nesbitt Burns Capital Markets – indicative noon rates

Currency	in C$	in US$	Daily % chg	Currency	in C$	in US$	Daily % chg
Antigua, Gr. EC $	0.6010	0.3745	nil	Kuwait (Dinar)	5.2118	3.2478	nil
Argentina (Peso)	0.74464	0.46404	-0.70	Lebanon (Pound)	0.001060	0.000661	-0.02
Austria (Euro)	1.3896	0.8660	0.19	Luxemb. Euro	1.38960	0.86596	0.19
Bahamas (Dollar)	1.6047	1.0000	nil	Malaysia (Ringgit)	0.4223	0.2632	-0.01
Bahrain (Dinar)	4.2565	2.6525	nil	Malta (Lira)	3.4817	2.1697	0.07
Barbados (Dollar)	0.8064	0.5025	nil	Netherlands (Euro)	1.3896	0.5460	0.19
Belgium (Euro)	1.3896	0.8660	0.19	Neth. Ant. Guilder	0.9015	0.5618	nil
Bermuda (Dollar)	1.6047	1.0000	nil	New Zealand $	8.6767	0.4217	0.52
Brazil (Real)	0.6802	0.4239	0.25	Norway (Krone)	0.1801	0.1122	0.07
Bulgaria (Lev)	0.713835	0.4448	0.29	Pakistan (Rupee)	0.02677	0.01668	-0.08
Chile (Peso)	0.002388	0.001488	0.31	Panama (Balloa)	1.6047	1.0000	nil
Colombia (Peso)	0.000697	0.000434	0.22	Philippines (Peso)	0.03137	0.01955	0.23
Costa Rica Colon	0.004624	0.002881	-0.04	Poland (Zloty)	0.3798	0.2367	-0.73
Cuba (Peso)	0.0764	0.0476	nil	Portugal (Euro)	1.3896	0.8660	0.19
Cyprus (Pound)	2.4145	1.5047	0.32	Peru (New Sol)	0.46265	0.28831	0.07
Czech (Koruna)	0.0440	0.0274	0.56	Romania (Leu)	0.000049	0.000031	-0.23
Denmark (Krone)	0.1870	0.1165	0.19	Russia (Ruble)	0.051836	0.032303	nil
Dominican Rep Peso	0.0973	0.0606	nil	Saudi Arabia Riyal	0.4279	0.2667	nil
Egypt (Pound)	0.3473	0.2165	-0.22	Slovakia (Koruna)	0.0334	0.0208	0.49
Finland (Euro)	1.3896	0.8660	0.19	Slovenia (Tolar)	0.0062	0.0039	0.23
Greece (Euro)	1.3896	0.8660	0.19	S. Africa (Rand)	0.1415	0.0882	0.45
Guyana (Dollar)	0.00889	0.00554	nil	S. Korea (Won)	0.001221	0.000761	0.27
Hong Kong (Dollar)	0.2058	0.1282	nil	Spain (Euro)	1.3896	0.8660	0.19
Hungary (Forint)	0.00567	0.00354	0.09	Sri Lanka (Rupee)	0.01717	0.01070	nil
India (Rupee)	0.03298	0.02055	nil	Sweden (Krona)	0.1533	0.0956	0.14
Indonesia Rupiah	0.000158	0.000099	0.39	Taiwan (Dollar)	0.04584	0.0286	nil
Ireland (Euro)	1.3896	0.8660	0.19	Thailand (Baht)	0.03674	0.0229	0.23
Israel (N Shekel)	0.3444	0.2146	-1.16	Trinidad & Tob: $	0.2626	0.1637	nil
Italy (Euro)	1.3896	0.8660	0.19	Turkey (Lira)	0.0000012	0.0000007	1.08
Jamaica (Dollar)	0.03385	0.02110	-0.11	Venezuela Bolivar	0.001581	0.00099	3.94
Jordan (Dinar)	2.2665	1.4124	nil	Spec Draw Right SDR	1.9924	1.2416	0.06

Source: Reprinted by permission of *The National Post,* March 1, 2002.

If you want shekels, you'll have to pay about 34¢ apiece. If you want punt, one rand will cost you $0.1415. (If you're wondering what shekels and rand are, look at the table above.)

Unless you collect currencies, the reason you want the currency of another country is that you want to buy something that country produces or an existing asset of that country. Say you want to buy a Hyundai car that costs 13,476,000 South Korean won. Looking at the table, you see that the exchange rate is $1 for 819 won. Dividing 819 into 13,476,000 won tells you that you need $16,454 to buy the car. So before you can

By looking at an exchange rate table, you can determine how much various goods will likely cost in different countries.

buy the Hyundai, somebody must go to a foreign exchange market with $16,454 and exchange those dollars for 13.476 million won. Only then can the car be bought in Canada. Most final buyers don't do this; the importer does it for them. But whenever a foreign good is bought, someone must trade currencies.

Q.9 You are going to Chile and plan to exchange $100. Based on the foreign exchange rate table in the text, how many Chilean pesos will you receive?

INSTITUTIONS SUPPORTING FREE TRADE

As we stated in Chapter 2, economists generally like markets and favour trade being as free as possible. They argue that trade allows specialization and the division of labour. When each country follows its comparative advantage, production is more efficient, and the production possibility curve shifts out. These views mean that most economists, liberal and conservative alike, generally oppose international trade restrictions.

Free Trade Organizations

Despite political pressures to restrict trade, governments have generally tried to follow economists' advice and have entered into a variety of international agreements and organizations. The most important is the **World Trade Organization (WTO),** which is *an organization committed to getting countries to agree not to impose new tariffs or other trade restrictions except under certain limited conditions*. The WTO is the successor to the **General Agreement on Tariffs and Trade (GATT),** *an agreement among many subscribing countries on certain conditions of international trade*, to which you will still occasionally see references, even though the WTO has taken its place. One of the differences between the WTO and GATT is that the WTO includes some enforcement mechanisms.

Important international economic organizations include the WTO, GATT, the EU, and NAFTA.

The push for free trade has a geographic dimension, which includes **free trade associations**—*groups of countries that have reduced or eliminated trade barriers among themselves*. For example, the **European Union** is *a free trade association of 15 western European countries*, 12 of which have adopted a single currency called the euro. Other groups have loose trading relationships because of cultural or historical reasons. These loose trading relationships are sometimes called trading zones. For example, many European countries maintain close trading ties with many of their former colonies in Africa, where they fit into a number of overlapping trading zones. European companies tend to see that area as their turf. Similarly, the United States, Canada, and Mexico have created the **North American Free Trade Agreement (NAFTA),** *a U.S.–Canada–Mexico free trade zone that is phasing in reductions in tariffs*. Canada has entered into a free trade agreement with Chile, and continues to build close ties in South America, making the Western hemisphere another trading zone. Another example of a trading zone is that of Japan and its economic ties with other Far East countries; Japanese companies often see that area as their commercial domain.

These trading zones overlap, sometimes on many levels. For instance, Australia and England, Portugal and Brazil, and the United States and Saudi Arabia are tied together for historical or political reasons, and those ties lead to increased trade between them that seems to deviate from the above trading zones. Similarly, as companies become more and more global, it is harder and harder to associate companies with particular countries. Let us give an example: Do you know who the largest exporters of cars from the United States are? The answer is: Japanese automobile companies!

Thus, there is no hard-and-fast specification of trading zones, and knowing history and politics is important to understanding many of the relationships.

International Economic Policy Organizations

Just as international trade differs from domestic trade, so does international economic policy differ from domestic economic policy. When economists talk about Canadian economic policy, they generally refer to what the Canadian federal government can do to achieve certain goals. In theory, at least, the Canadian federal government has both the power and the legal right of compulsion to make Canadian citizens do what it says. It can tax, it can redistribute income, it can regulate, and it can enforce property rights.

There is no international counterpart to a nation's federal government. Any meeting of a group of countries to discuss trade policies is voluntary. No international body has powers of compulsion. Hence, international problems must be dealt with through negotiation, consensus, bullying, and concessions.

3.5

see page 77

To discourage bullying and to encourage negotiation and consensus, governments have developed a variety of international institutions to promote negotiations and co-ordinate economic relations among countries. These include the United Nations (UN), the World Bank, the World Court, and the International Monetary Fund (IMF). These organizations have a variety of goals. For example, the **World Bank** is *a multinational, international financial institution that works with developing countries to secure low-interest loans,* channelling such loans to them to foster economic growth. The **International Monetary Fund (IMF)** is *a multinational, international financial institution concerned primarily with monetary issues.* It deals with international financial arrangements. When developing countries encountered financial problems in the 1980s and had large international debts that they could not pay, the IMF helped work out repayment plans.

In addition to these formal institutions, there are informal meetings of various countries. These include the **Group of Five,** which *meets to promote negotiations and coordinate economic relations among countries.* The Five are Japan, Germany, Britain, France, and the United States. The **Group of Eight** also *meets to promote negotiations and coordinate economic relations among countries.* The Eight are the five countries just named plus Canada, Italy, and Russia.

Since governmental membership in international organizations is voluntary, their power is limited.

Since governmental membership in international organizations is voluntary, their power is limited. When Canada doesn't like a World Court ruling, it simply states that it isn't going to follow the ruling. When the United States is unhappy with what the United Nations is doing, it withholds some of its dues. Other countries do the same from time to time. Other member countries complain, but can do little to force compliance. It doesn't work that way domestically. If you decide you don't like Canadian policy and refuse to pay your taxes, you'll wind up in jail.

Q-10 If Canada chooses not to follow a World Court decision, what are the consequences?

What keeps nations somewhat in line when it comes to international rules is a moral tradition: Countries want to (or at least want to look as if they want to) do what's "right." Countries will sometimes follow international rules to keep international opinion favourable to them. But perceived national self-interest often overrides international scruples.

CONCLUSION

This has been a whirlwind tour of the Canadian economy and its global setting. The Canadian economy in the 21st century is a global economy with links through both its trade sector and its financial sector. To understand it, you must understand its components—business, households, and government—and their interrelationship.

The economy is undergoing significant changes because of technological change. E-commerce is growing exponentially and is making markets more global. On the

Internet the location of a trade doesn't matter. Countries, however, pose barriers to trade, and there will likely be much conflict as the push for free trade comes up against national boundaries.

Chapter Summary

- A diagram of the Canadian market economy shows the connections among businesses, households, and government. It also shows the Canadian economic connection to other countries.

- In Canada, businesses make the *what, how much,* and *for whom* decisions.

- Although businesses decide what to produce, they succeed or fail depending on their ability to meet consumers' desires. That's consumer sovereignty.

- The three main forms of business are corporations, sole proprietorships, and partnerships. Each has its advantages and disadvantages.

- Government plays two general roles in the economy: (1) as a referee, and (2) as an actor.

- Although households are the most powerful economic institution, they have assigned much of their power to government and business. Economics focusses on households' role as the supplier of labour.

- To understand the Canadian economy, one must understand its role in the world economy.

- Global corporations are corporations with significant operations in more than one country. They are increasing in importance.

- The areas with which Canada trades include the United States, the Pacific Rim countries, and the European Union.

- Canadian exports of goods and services have significantly exceeded imports for many years.

- International trade differs from domestic trade because (1) there are potential barriers to trade and (2) countries use different currencies.

- The rate at which one currency trades for another is that currency's exchange rate.

- Governments of many countries have formed free trade associations that agree to reduce barriers to trade among members. Three well-known free trade organizations are the WTO, NAFTA, and the European Union.

- International policy coordination must be achieved through consensus among nations.

Key Terms

balance of trade   (68)

business   (57)

consumer sovereignty   (57)

corporations   (58)

current account balance   (69)

entrepreneurship   (57)

European Union   (73)

exchange rate   (72)

exports   (68)

foreign exchange markets   (72)

free trade associations   (73)

General Agreement on Tariffs and Trade (GATT)   (73)

global corporations   (66)

Group of Five   (74)

Group of Eight   (74)

households   (61)

imports   (68)

International Monetary Fund (IMF)   (74)

limited liability   (59)

merchandise trade balance   (69)

nontariff barriers   (71)

North American Free Trade Agreement (NAFTA)   (73)

partnerships   (58)

profit   (57)

quotas   (71)

services balance   (69)

sole proprietorships   (58)

stock   (58)

tariffs   (71)

trade deficit   (68)

trade surplus   (68)

World Bank   (74)

World Trade Organization (WTO)   (73)

Questions for Thought and Review

1. Why does an economy's strength ultimately reside in its people?

2. A market system is often said to be based on consumer sovereignty—the consumer determines what's to be produced. Yet business decides what's to be produced. Can these two views be reconciled? How? If not, why?

3. Why is entrepreneurship a central part of any business?

4. You're starting a software company in which you plan to sell software to your fellow students. What form of business organization would you choose? Why?

5. What are the two largest categories of federal government expenditures?

6. A good measure of a country's importance to the world economy is its area and population. True or false? Why?

7. What are the two ways in which international trade differs from domestic trade?

8. If one Canadian dollar will buy .67 Swiss francs, how many Canadian dollars will one Swiss franc buy?

9. The U.S. economy is falling apart because the United States is the biggest debtor nation in the world. Discuss.

10. Why do most economists oppose trade restrictions?

11. What is the relationship between GATT and the WTO?

12. Look up a recent foreign currency exchange rate table from *The National Post*.
   a. How many Egyptian pounds will you receive for $100?
   b. Say you want to buy a Volvo directly from Sweden. The foreign car dealer quotes a price of 235,794 Swedish krona. How many dollars will you have to exchange to purchase the Volvo?

Problems and Exercises

1. Go to a store in your community.
   a. Ask what limitations the owners faced in starting their business.
   b. Were these limitations necessary?
   c. Should there have been more or fewer limitations?
   d. Under what heading of reasons for government intervention would you put each of the limitations?
   e. Ask what kinds of taxes the business pays and what benefits it believes it gets for those taxes.
   f. Is it satisfied with the existing situation? Why? What would it change?

2. You've been appointed to a county counterterrorist squad. Your assignment is to work up a set of plans to stop a group of 10 terrorists the government believes are going to disrupt the economy as much as possible with explosives.
   a. List their five most likely targets in your county, city, or town.
   b. What counterterrorist action would you take?
   c. How would you advise the economy to adjust to a successful attack on each of the targets?

3. Tom Rollins heads a new venture called Teaching Co. He has taped lectures at the top universities, packaged the lectures on audio- and videocassettes, and sells them for $90 and $150 per eight-hour series.
   a. Discuss whether such an idea could be expanded to include college courses that one could take at home.
   b. What are the technical, social, and economic issues involved?
   c. If it is technically possible and cost-effective, will the new venture be a success?

4. This is a library research question.
   a. What are the primary exports of Brazil, Honduras, Italy, Pakistan, and Nigeria?
   b. Which countries produce most of the world's tin, rubber, potatoes, wheat, marble, and refrigerators?

5. This is an entrepreneurial research question. You'd be amazed what information is out there if you use a bit of initiative.
   a. Does the largest company in your relevant geographic area (town, city, whatever) have an export division? Why or why not?
   b. If you were an adviser to the company, would you suggest expanding or contracting its export division? Why or why not?
   c. Go to a store and look at 10 products at random. How many were made in Canada? Give a probable explanation of why they were produced where they were.

6. Exchange rates can be found in a variety of sources including the Internet.
   a. Using the exchange rate table on page 72, determine the Canadian dollar equivalent of the:
      (1) Euro
      (2) Zloty
      (3) Rand
      (4) Forint
   b. Determine the most recent dollar equivalent of those same currencies. (Use the Web or a recent newspaper.)
   c. Using the information in *a* or *b*, calculate the number of dollars you could get from one unit of each of the above currencies.

Web Questions

1. Go to the Nortel home page (www.nortelnetworks.com) and answer the following questions:
   a. Is Nortel a sole proprietorship, partnership, or corporation? For what reasons do you suspect it has chosen that form of business?
   b. Is Nortel a global corporation? Explain your answer.
   c. Are the shares of Nortel publicly traded?

2. Visit the Toronto Stock Exchange Web site (www.tse.com) and answer the following questions:
   a. How many IPOs were there last year on the TSE?
   b. How many firms' shares are included in the TSE 300?
   c. Find the area of the Web site that lists job openings. What kinds of qualifications are required for a position at the TSE?

3. Visit the Federal Department of Finance Web site (www.fin.gc.ca) and find the section on transfer payments. Answer the following questions:
   a. Which provinces have most recently been recipients of equalization payments?
   b. How are equalization payments calculated?
   c. Have Canadian Health and Social Transfers (CHST) risen recently? Why?

   d. What changes do the provinces want made to the CHST?

4. Visit the Bank of Canada's Web site (www.bankofcanada.ca) and answer the following questions:
   a. What is the value of the Canadian dollar against the Euro?
   b. What is the exchange rate between the Canadian and the U.S. dollars?
   c. Using your answers to *a* and *b*, what should be the exchange rate between the U.S. dollar and the Euro? Is the actual rate (check another Web site or a local newspaper) close to this figure? Can you explain why?

5. Go to the World Bank's home page (www.worldbank.org) to answer the following questions:
   a. What is the World Bank?
   b. What goals has the World Bank set for the new millennium?
   c. How does the World Bank finance its activities?
   d. Which two regions of the world get the largest loans from the World Bank?

Answers to Margin Questions

1. Market economies are generally broken up into businesses, households, and government. *(56)*

2. False. In Canada individuals are free to start any type of business they want, provided it doesn't violate the law. The invisible hand sees to it that only those businesses that customers want earn a profit. The others lose money and eventually go out of business, so in that sense only businesses that customers want stay in business. *(57)*

3. In Canada "Ltd." denotes limited liability—in the United States "Inc." is short for incorporated. Although it is also possible to create a limited liability corporation in the U.S. the two forms of business differ in the way their activities are taxed. Check out www.4inc.com/choices.htm for more. *(59)*

4. While profits are important to business, because of internal monitoring problems it is not clear that managers maximize profit. They may waste profit potential in high-priced benefits for themselves and in inefficiency generally. The market, however, provides a limit on

   inefficiency, and firms that exceed that limit and have losses go out of business. *(59)*

5. The largest percentage of federal expenditure is for social services. *(63)*

6. Japan has the lowest exports and imports as a percentage of GDP, followed closely by the United States. *(68)*

7. A debtor nation will not necessarily be running a trade deficit. *Debt* refers to accumulated past deficits. If a country had accumulated large deficits in the past, it could run a surplus now but still be a debtor nation. *(69)*

8. A quota is a quantitative limitation on trade. A tariff is a type of tax on imports. *(71)*

9. You will receive 41,876 pesos. *(73)*

10. The World Court has no enforcement mechanism. Thus, when a country refuses to follow the Court's decisions, the country cannot be directly punished except through indirect international pressures. *(74)*

APPENDIX A

Valuing Stocks and Bonds

A financial asset's worth comes from the stream of income it will pay in the future. With financial assets like bonds, that stream of income can be calculated rather precisely. With stocks, where the stream of income is a percentage of the firm's profits, which fluctuate significantly, the stream of future income is uncertain and valuations depends significantly on expectations.

Let's start by considering some generally held beliefs among economists and financial experts. The first is that an average share of stock in a company in a mature industry sells for somewhere between 15 and 20 times its normal profits. The second is that bond prices rise as market interest rates fall, and fall as market interest rates rise. The first step in understanding where the beliefs come from is to recognize that $1 today is not equal to $1 next year. Why? Because if you have $1 today you can invest it and earn interest (say 10 percent per year), and next year you will have $1.10, not $1. So if the annual interest rate is 10 percent, $1.10 next year is worth $1 today; alternatively, $1 next year is worth roughly 91 cents today. A dollar two years in the future is worth even less today, and dollars 30 years in the future are worth very little today.

Present value is *a method of translating a flow of future income or savings into its current worth.* For example, say a smooth-talking, high-pressure salesperson is wining and dining you. "Isn't that amazing?" the salesman says. "My company will pay $10 a year not only to you, but also to your great-great-great-grandchildren, and more, for 500 years—thousands of dollars in all. And I will sell this annuity—this promise to pay money at periodic intervals in the future—to you for a payment to me now of only $800, but you must act fast. After tonight the price will rise to $2,000."

Do you buy it? Our rhetoric suggests that the answer should be no—but can you explain why? And what price *would* you be willing to pay?

To decide how much an annuity is worth, you need some way of valuing that $10 per year. *You can't simply add up the $10 five hundred times.* Doing so is wrong. Instead you must *discount* all future dollars by the interest rate in the economy. Discounting is required because a dollar in the future is not worth a dollar now.

If you have $1 now, you can take that dollar, put it in the bank, and in a year you will have that dollar plus interest. If the interest rate you can get from the bank is 5

percent, that dollar will grow to $1.05 a year from now. That means also that if the interest rate in the economy is 5 percent, if you have 95 cents now, in a year it will be worth $.9975 (5% × $.95 = $.0475). Reversing the reasoning, $1 one year in the future is worth 95 cents today. So the present value of $1 one year in the future at a 5 percent interest rate is 95 cents.

A dollar *two* years from now is worth even less today. Carry out that same reasoning and you'll find that if the interest rate is 5 percent, $1 two years from now is worth approximately 90 cents today. Why? Because you could take 90 cents now, put it in the bank at 5 percent interest, and in two years have $1.

THE PRESENT VALUE FORMULA

Carrying out such reasoning for every case would be a real pain. But luckily, there's a formula and a table that can be used to determine the present value (PV) of future income. The formula is:

$$PV = A_1/(1 + i) + A_2/(1 + i)^2 + A_3/(1 + i)^3 + \ldots + A_n/(1 + i)^n$$

where

A_n = the amount of money received n periods in the future

i = the interest rate in the economy (assumed constant)

Solving this formula for any time period longer than one or two years is complicated. To deal with it, people either use a business calculator or a present value table like that in Table A3-1.

Table A3-1(a) gives the present value of a single dollar at some time in the future at various interest rates. Notice a couple of things about the chart. First, the further into the future one goes, the lower the present value. Second, the higher the interest rate, the lower the present value. At a 12 percent interest rate, $1 fifty years from now has a present value of essentially zero.

Table A3-1(b) is an annuity table; it tells us how much a constant stream of income for a specific number of years is worth. Notice that as the interest rate rises, the value of an annuity falls. At an 18 percent interest rate, $1 per year for 50 years has a present value of $5.55. To get the value of amounts other than $1, one simply multiplies the entry in the table by the amount. For example, $10 per year for 50 years at 18 percent interest is 10 × $5.55, or $55.50.

As you can see, the interest rate in the economy is a key to present value. *You must know the interest rate to know the value of money over time.* The higher the current (and assumed constant) interest rate, the more a given amount of money in the present will be worth in the future. Or, alternatively, the higher the current interest rate, the less a given amount of money in the future will be worth in the present.

SOME RULES OF THUMB FOR DETERMINING PRESENT VALUE

Sometimes you don't have a present value table or a business calculator handy. For those times, there are a few rules of thumb and simplified formulas for which you don't need either a present value table or a calculator. Let's consider two of them: the infinite annuity rule and the rule of 72.

The Annuity Rule

To find the present value of an annuity that will pay $1 for an infinite number of years in the future when the interest rate is 5 percent, we simply divide $1 by 5 percent (.05). Doing so gives us $20. So at 5 percent, $1 a year paid to you forever has a present value of $20. The **annuity rule** is that *the present value of any annuity is the annual income it*

yields divided by the interest rate. Our general annuity rule for any annuity is expressed as:

$$PV = X/i$$

That is, the present value of an infinite flow of income, X, is that income divided by the interest rate, i.

Most of the time, people don't offer to sell you annuities for the infinite future. A typical annuity runs for 30, 40, or 50 years. However, the annuity rule is still useful. As you can see from the present value table, in 30 years at a 9 percent interest rate, the present value of $1 isn't much (it's 8 cents), so we can use this infinite flow formula as an approximation of long-lasting, but less than infinite, flows of future income. We simply subtract a little bit from what we get with our formula. The longer the time period, the less we subtract. For example, say you are wondering what $200 a year for 40 years is worth when the interest rate is 8 percent. Dividing $200 by .08 gives $2,500, so we know the annuity must be worth a bit less than $2,500. (It's actually worth $2,411.)

The annuity rule allows us to answer the question posed at the beginning of this section: How much is $10 a year for 500 years worth right now? The answer is that it depends on the interest rate you could earn on a specified amount of money now. If the interest rate is 10 percent, the maximum you should be willing to pay for that 500-year $10 annuity is $100:

$$\$10/.10 = \$100$$

If the interest rate is 5 percent, the most you should pay is $200 ($10/.05 = $200). So now you know why you

TABLE A3-1 (a and b)   **Sample Present Value and Annuity Tables**

Year	Interest Rate						
	3%	4%	6%	9%	12%	15%	18%
1	$0.97	$0.96	$0.94	$0.92	$0.89	$0.87	$0.85
2	0.94	0.92	0.89	0.84	0.80	0.76	0.72
3	0.92	0.89	0.84	0.77	0.71	0.66	0.61
4	0.89	0.85	0.79	0.71	0.64	0.57	0.52
5	0.86	0.82	0.75	0.65	0.57	0.50	0.44
6	0.84	0.79	0.70	0.60	0.51	0.43	0.37
7	0.81	0.76	0.67	0.55	0.45	0.38	0.31
8	0.79	0.73	0.63	0.50	0.40	0.33	0.27
9	0.77	0.70	0.59	0.46	0.36	0.28	0.23
10	0.74	0.68	0.56	0.42	0.32	0.25	0.19
15	0.64	0.56	0.42	0.27	0.18	0.12	0.08
20	0.55	0.46	0.31	0.18	0.10	0.06	0.04
30	0.41	0.31	0.17	0.08	0.03	0.02	0.01
40	0.31	0.21	0.10	0.03	0.01	0.00	0.00
50	0.23	0.14	0.05	0.01	0.00	0.00	0.00

Number of years	Interest Rate						
	3%	4%	6%	9%	12%	15%	18%
1	$0.97	$0.96	$0.94	$0.92	$0.89	$0.87	$0.85
2	1.91	1.89	1.83	1.76	1.69	1.63	1.57
3	2.83	2.78	2.67	2.53	2.40	2.28	2.17
4	3.72	3.63	3.47	3.24	3.04	2.85	2.69
5	4.58	4.45	4.21	3.89	3.60	3.35	3.13
6	5.42	5.24	4.92	4.49	4.11	3.78	3.50
7	6.23	6.00	5.58	5.03	4.56	4.16	3.81
8	7.02	6.73	6.21	5.53	4.97	4.49	4.08
9	7.79	7.44	6.80	6.00	5.33	4.77	4.30
10	8.53	8.11	7.36	6.42	5.65	5.02	4.49
15	11.94	11.12	9.71	8.06	6.81	5.85	5.09
20	14.88	13.59	11.47	9.13	7.47	6.26	5.35
30	19.60	17.29	13.76	10.27	8.06	6.57	5.52
40	23.11	19.79	15.05	10.76	8.24	6.64	5.55
50	25.73	21.48	15.76	10.96	8.30	6.66	5.55

(a) Present value table (value now of $1 to be received *x* years in the future)
The present value table converts a future amount into a present amount.

(b) Annuity table (value now of $1 per year to be received for *x* years)
The annuity table converts a known stream of income into a present amount.

APPLYING THE TOOLS

The Press and
Present Value

The failure to understand the concept of present value often shows up in the popular press. Here are three examples.

Headline: **COURT SETTLEMENT IS $40,000,000**

Inside story: The money will be paid out over a 40-year period.

Actual value: $11,925,000 (8 percent interest rate).

Headline: **DISABLED WIDOW WINS $25 MILLION LOTTERY**

Inside story: The money will be paid over 20 years.

Actual value: $13,254,499 (8 percent interest rate).

Headline: **BOND ISSUE TO COST CITY TAXPAYERS $68 MILLION**

Inside story: The $68 million is the total of interest and principal payments. The interest is paid yearly; the principal won't be paid back to the bond purchasers until 30 years from now.

Actual cost: $20,000,000 (8 percent interest rate).

Such stories are common. Be on the lookout for them as you read the newspaper or watch the evening news.

---

should have said no to that supersalesman who offered it to you for $800.

The Rule of 72

A second rule of thumb for determining present values of shorter time periods is the **rule of 72,** which states:

The number of years it takes for a certain amount to double in value is equal to 72 divided by the rate of interest.

Say, for example, that the interest rate is 4 percent. How long will it take for your $100 to become $200? Dividing 72 by 4 gives 18, so the answer is 18 years. Conversely, the present value of $200 at a 4 percent interest rate 18 years in the future is about $100. (Actually it's $102.67.)

Alternatively, say that you will receive $1,000 in 10 years. Is it worth paying $500 for that amount now if the interest rate is 9 percent? Using the rule of 72, we know that at a 9 percent interest rate it will take about eight years for $500 to double:

$$72/9 = 8$$

so the future value of $500 in 10 years is more than $1,000. It's probably about $1,200. (Actually it's $1,184.) So if the interest rate in the economy is 9 percent, it's not worth paying $500 now in order to get that $1,000 in 10 years. By investing that same $500 today at 9 percent, you can have $1,184 in 10 years.

THE IMPORTANCE OF PRESENT VALUE

Many business decisions require such present value calculations. In almost any business, you'll be looking at flows of income in the future and comparing them to present costs or to other flows of money in the future.

Generally, however, when most people calculate present value they don't use any of the formulas. They pull out a handy business calculator, press in the numbers to calculate the present value, and watch while the calculator graphically displays the results.

Let's now use our knowledge of present value to explain the two observations at the beginning of the appendix. Since all financial assets can be broken down into promises to pay certain amounts at certain times in the future, we can determine their value with the present value formula. If the asset is a bond, it consists of a stream of income payments over a number of years and the repayment of the face value of the bond. Each year's interest payment and the eventual repayment of the face value must be calculated separately, and then the results must be added together. If the financial asset is a share of stock, the valuation is a bit less clear since a stock does not guarantee the payment of anything definite—just a share of the profits. No profits, no payment. So, with stocks, expectations of profits are of central importance. Let's consider an example: Say a share of stock is earning $1 per share per year and is expected to continue to earn that long into the future. Using the annuity rule and an interest rate of 6.5 percent, the present value of that future stream of expected earnings is about 1/.065, or a bit more than $15. Assuming profits are expected to grow slightly, that would mean that the stock should sell for somewhere around $20, or 20 times its profit per share, which is the explanation to the first observation in the appendix.

To see the answer to the second, say the interest rate rises to 10 percent. Then the value of the stock or bond that is earning a fixed amount—in this case $1 per share—

will go down to $10. Interest rate up, value of stock or bond down. This is the explanation of the second observation.

There is nothing immutable in the above reasoning. For example, if promises to pay aren't trustworthy, you don't put the amount that's promised into your calculation; you put in the amount you actually expect to receive. That's why when a company or a country looks as if it's going to default on loans or stop paying dividends, the value of its bonds and stock will fall considerably. For example, in the late 1980s many people thought Brazil would default on its bonds. That expectation caused the price of Brazilian bonds to fall to about 30 percent on the dollar. Then in the 1990s, when people believed total default was less likely, the value rose.

Of course, the expectations could go in the opposite direction. Say that the interest rate is 10 percent, and that you expect a company's profit, which is now $1 per share, to grow by 10 percent per year. In that case, since expected profit growth is as high as the interest rate, the current value of the stock is infinite. It is such expectations of future profit growth that have fueled the Internet stock craze

and have caused the valuation of firms with no current profits (indeed, many are experiencing significant losses) at multiples of sales of 300 or more. Financial valuations based on such optimistic expectations are the reason most economists considered the stock market in Internet stocks to be overvalued in the late 1990s.

ASSET PRICES, INTEREST RATES, AND THE ECONOMY

This appendix isn't meant to cover the intricacies of valuation over time. That's done in a finance course. The point is to help you understand the relationship between interest rates and asset prices. Central to valuing stocks or bonds is the present value formula. From that we know that increases in interest rates (because they make future flows of income coming from an asset worth less now) make financial asset prices fall, and that decreases in interest rates (because they make the future flow of income coming from an asset worth more now) make financial asset prices rise.

Key Terms

annuity rule   *(79)*   present value   *(78)*   rule of 72   *(80)*

Questions for Thought and Review

1. How much is $50 to be received 50 years from now worth if the interest rate is 5 percent? (Use Figure A3-1).

2. How much is $50 to be received 50 years from now worth if the interest rate is 10 percent? (Use Figure A3-1).

3. Your employer offers you a choice of two bonus packages: $1,400 today or $2,000 five years from now. Assuming a 5 percent rate of interest, which is the better value? Assuming an interest rate of 10 percent, which is the better value?

4. Suppose the price of a one-year 10 percent coupon bond with a $100 face value is $98.
   a. Are market interest rates likely to be above or below 10 percent? Explain.
   b. What is the bond's yield or return?
   c. If market interest rates fell, what would happen to the price of the bond?

5. Explain in words why the present value of $100 to be received in 10 years would decline as the interest rate rises.

6. A 6 percent bond will pay you $1,060 one year from now. The interest rate in the economy is 10 percent. How much is that bond worth now?

7. You are to receive $100 a year for the next 40 years. How much is it worth now if the current interest rate in the economy is 6 percent? (Use annuity table.)

8. You are to receive $200, thirty years from now. About how much is it worth now? (The interest rate is 3 percent.)

9. A salesperson calls you up and offers you $200 a year for life. If the interest rate is 7 percent, how much should you be willing to pay for that annuity?

10. The same salesperson offers you a lump sum of $20,000 in 10 years. How much should you be willing to pay? (The interest rate is still 7 percent.)

11. What is the present value of a cash flow of $100 per year forever (a perpetuity), assuming:

    The interest rate is 10 percent.

    The interest rate is 5 percent.

    The interest rate is 20 percent.

    a. Working with those same three interest rates, what are the future values of $100 today in one year? How about in two years?
    b. Working with those same three interest rates, how long will it take you to double your money?

Supply and Demand

4

After reading this chapter, you should be able to:

- State the law of demand.

- Explain the importance of substitution to the laws of supply and demand.

- Distinguish a shift in demand from a movement along the demand curve.

- Draw a demand curve from a demand table.

- State the law of supply.

- Distinguish a shift in supply from a movement along the supply curve.

- Draw a supply curve from a supply table.

- Explain how the law of demand and the law of supply interact to bring about equilibrium.

- Show how equilibrium maximizes consumer and producer surplus.

Teach a parrot the terms supply *and* demand
and you've got an economist.

Thomas Carlyle

Supply and demand. Supply and demand. Roll the phrase around in your mouth, savour it like a good wine. *Supply* and *demand* are the most-used words in economics. And for good reason. They provide a good off-the-cuff answer for any economic question. Try it. Why are bacon and oranges so expensive this winter? *Supply and demand.*

Why are interest rates falling? *Supply and demand.*

Why can't I find decent wool socks anymore? *Supply and demand.*

The importance of the interplay of supply and demand makes it only natural that, early in any economics course, you must learn about supply and demand. Let's start with demand.

DEMAND

People want lots of things; they "demand" much less than they want because demand means a willingness and capacity to pay. Unless you are willing and able to pay for it, you may *want* it, but you don't *demand* it. For example, we want to own fancy cars. But, we must admit, we're not willing to do what's necessary to own one. If we really wanted one, we'd mortgage everything we own, increase our income by doubling the number of hours we work, not buy anything else, and get that car. But we don't do any of those things, so at the going price, $360,000, we do not demand a Maserati. Sure, we'd buy one if it cost $10,000, but from our actions it's clear that, at $360,000, we don't demand it. This points to an important aspect of demand: The quantity you demand at a low price differs from the quantity you demand at a high price. Specifically, the quantity you demand varies inversely—in the opposite direction—with price.

Prices are the tool by which the market coordinates individuals' desires and limits how much people are willing to buy—how much they demand. When goods become scarce, the market reduces the quantity of those scarce goods people demand; as their prices go up, people buy fewer goods. As goods become abundant, their prices go down, and people want more of them. The invisible hand—the price mechanism—sees to it that what people demand (do what's necessary to get) matches what's available. In doing so, the invisible hand coordinates individuals' demands.

Prices are the tool by which the market coordinates individual desires.

The Law of Demand

The ideas expressed above are the foundation of the **law of demand:**

> *Quantity demanded rises as price falls, other things constant.*

Or alternatively:

> *Quantity demanded falls as price rises, other things constant.*

This law is fundamental to the invisible hand's ability to coordinate individuals' desires: as prices change, people change how much of a particular good they're willing to buy.

What accounts for the law of demand? Individuals' tendency to substitute other goods for goods whose price has gone up. If the price of CDs rises from $15 to $20 but the price of cassette tapes stays at $9.99, you're more likely to buy that new Christina Aguilera recording on cassette than on CD.

The law of demand states that the quantity of a good demanded is inversely related to the good's price. When price goes up, quantity demanded goes down. When price goes down, quantity demanded goes up.

To see that the law of demand makes intuitive sense, just think of something you'd really like but can't afford. If the price is cut in half, you—and other consumers—will become more likely to buy it. Quantity demanded goes up as price goes down.

Just to be sure you've got it, let's consider a real world example: scalpers and the demand for hockey tickets. Standing outside a sold-out game between Montreal and Pittsburgh in Montreal, we saw scalpers trying to sell tickets for $100 a seat. There were few takers — that is, there was little demand at that price. The sellers saw that they had set too high a price and they started calling out lower prices. As the price dropped to $60, then $50, quantity demanded increased; when the price dropped to $35, quantity demanded soared. That's the law of demand in action.

Figure 4-1   A SAMPLE DEMAND CURVE

The law of demand states that the quantity demanded of a good is inversely related to the price of that good, other things constant. As the price of a good goes up, the quantity demanded goes down, so the demand curve is downward sloping.

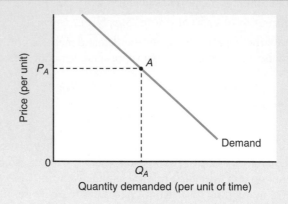

The Demand Curve

A **demand curve** is *the graphic representation of the relationship between price and quantity demanded*. Figure 4-1 shows a demand curve.

As you can see, in graphical terms, the law of demand states that as the price goes up, the quantity demanded goes down, other things constant. An alternative way of saying the same thing is that price and quantity demanded are inversely related, so the demand curve slopes downward to the right.

Notice that in stating the law of demand, we put in the qualification "other things constant." That's three extra words, and unless they were important we wouldn't have put them in. But what does "other things constant" mean? Say that over a period of two years, the price of cars rises as the number of cars purchased likewise rises. That seems to violate the law of demand, since the number of cars purchased should have fallen in response to the rise in price. Looking at the data more closely, however, we see that a third factor has also changed: individuals' income has increased. As income increases, people buy more cars, increasing the demand for cars.

The increase in price works as the law of demand states—it decreases the number of cars bought. But in this case, income doesn't remain constant; it increases. That rise in income increases the demand for cars. That increase in demand outweighs the decrease in quantity demanded that results from a rise in price, so ultimately more cars are sold. If you want to study the effect of price alone—which is what the law of demand refers to—you must make adjustments to hold income constant when you make your study. That's why the qualifying phrase "other things constant" is an important part of the law of demand.

The other things that are held constant include individuals' tastes, prices of other goods, and even the weather. Those other factors must remain constant if you're to make a valid study of the effect of an increase in the price of a good on the quantity demanded. In practice, it's impossible to keep all other things constant, so you have to be careful when you say that when price goes up, quantity demanded goes down. Quantity demanded is likely to go down, but it's always possible that something besides price has changed.

Shifts in Demand versus Movements along a Demand Curve

To distinguish between the effects of changes in a good's price and the effects of other factors on how much of a good is demanded, economists have developed the following precise terminology—terminology that inevitably shows up on exams. The first distinction to make is between demand and quantity demanded.

Q-1 Why does the demand curve slope downward?

"Other things constant" places a limitation on the application of the law of demand.

- **Demand** refers to *a schedule of quantities of a good that will be bought per unit of time at various prices, other things constant.*
- **Quantity demanded** refers to *a specific amount that will be demanded per unit of time at a specific price, other things constant.*

In graphical terms, the term *demand* refers to the entire demand curve. Demand tells how much of a good will be bought *at various prices. Quantity demanded* refers to a point on a demand curve, such as point A in Figure 4-1. This terminology allows us to distinguish between *changes in quantity demanded* and *shifts in demand.* A change in the quantity demanded refers to the effect of a price change on the quantity demanded. It refers to a **movement along a demand curve**—*the graphical representation of the effect of a change in price on the quantity demanded.* A **shift in demand** refers to *the effect of anything other than price on demand.*

Shift Factors of Demand

Shift factors of demand are factors that cause shifts in the demand curve. A change in anything besides a good's price causes a shift of the entire demand curve.

Important shift factors of demand include:

1. Society's income.
2. The prices of other goods.
3. Tastes.
4. Expectations.
5. Population.

Income From our example above of "the other things constant" qualification, we saw that a rise in income increases the demand for goods. For most goods this is true. As individuals' income rises, they can afford more of the goods they want.

Price of Other Goods Because people make their buying decisions based on the price of related goods, demand will be affected by the prices of other goods. Suppose the price of jeans rose from $25 to $35, but the price of khakis remained at $25. Next time you need pants, you're apt to try khakis instead of jeans. They are substitutes. When two goods are substitutes, if the price of one of the goods falls while the other price remains unchanged, there will be an increase in the quantity demanded of the good whose price fell, and a reduction in the demand for the good whose price remained fixed.

Tastes An old saying goes: "There's no accounting for taste." Of course, many advertisers believe otherwise. Changes in taste can affect the demand for a good without a change in price. As you become older, you may find that your taste for rock concerts has changed to a taste for an evening at the opera or local philharmonic.

Expectations Expectations will also affect demand. Expectations can cover a lot. If you expect your income to rise in the future, you're bound to start spending some of it today. If you expect the price of computers to fall soon, you may put off buying one until later.

These aren't the only shift factors. In fact anything—except the price of the good itself—that affects demand (and many things do) is a shift factor. While economists agree these shift factors are important, they believe that no shift factor influences how much is demanded as consistently as does price of the specific item. That's what makes economists focus first on price as they try to understand the world. That's why economists make the law of demand central to their analysis.

Q-2 In the 1980s and early 1990s, as animal rights activists made wearing fur coats déclassé, the _____ decreased. Should the missing words be "demand for furs" or "quantity of furs demanded"?

Q-3 Explain the effect of each of the following on the demand for new computers:
1. The price of computers falls by 30 percent.
2. Total income in the economy rises.

Figure 4-2   SHIFT IN DEMAND VERSUS A CHANGE IN QUANTITY DEMANDED

A rise in a good's price results in a reduction in quantity demanded and is shown by a movement up along a demand curve from point A to point B in (a). A change in any other factor besides price that affects demand leads to a shift in the entire demand curve as shown in (b).

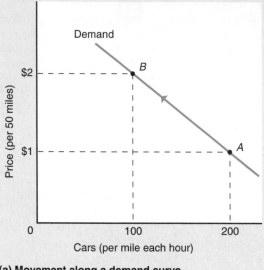

(a) Movement along a demand curve

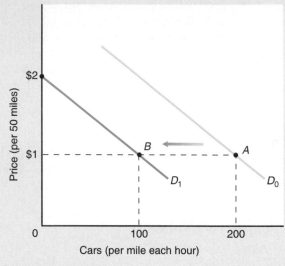

(b) Shift in demand

Population Finally, population will also affect demand. If there is an increase in population, there will be a higher quantity demanded at every price. If population falls, as it did in Newfoundland's outports in the mid-1900s, demand falls. It's that simple.

Change in price causes a movement along a demand curve; a change in a shift factor causes a shift in demand.

To make sure you understand the difference between a movement along a demand curve and a shift in demand, let's consider an example. Singapore has one of the highest numbers of cars per mile of road. This means that congestion is considerable. Singapore has adopted two policies to reduce road use: It increased the fee charged to use roads, and it provided an expanded public transportation system. Both policies reduced congestion. Figure 4-2(a) shows that increasing the toll charged to use roads from $1 to $2 per 50 miles of road reduces quantity demanded from 200 to 100 cars per mile every hour (a movement along the demand curve). Figure 4-2(b) shows that providing alternative methods of transportation such as buses and subways will shift the demand curve for roads. Demand for road use shifts to the left so that at the $1 fee, demand drops from 200 to 100 cars per mile every hour (a shift in the demand curve).

A Review

Let's test your understanding by having you specify what happens to your demand curve for videocassettes in the following examples: First, let's say you buy a DVD player. Next, let's say that the price of videocassettes falls; and finally, say that you won $1 million in a lottery. What happens to the demand for videocassettes in each case? If you answered: It shifts in; it remains unchanged; and it shifts out—you've got it.

**Figure 4-3 (a and b)   FROM A DEMAND TABLE TO
                          A DEMAND CURVE**

The demand table in (a) is translated into a demand curve in (b).
Each combination of price and quantity in the table corresponds
to a point on the curve. For example, point A on the graph represents row A in the table: Marie demands 9 videocassette rentals at
a price of 50 cents. A demand curve is constructed by plotting all
points from the demand table and connecting the points by a line.

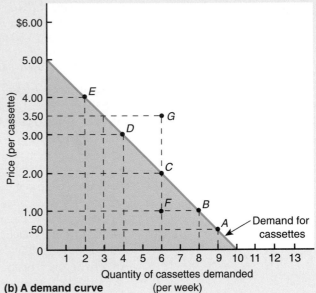

	Price per cassette	Cassette rentals demanded per week
A	$0.50	9
B	1.00	8
C	2.00	6
D	3.00	4
E	4.00	2

(a) A demand table

(b) A demand curve

The Demand Table

As we emphasized in Chapter 1, introductory economics depends heavily on graphs and
graphical analysis—translating ideas into graphs and back into words. So let's graph the
demand curve.

Figure 4-3(a), a demand table, describes Marie's demand for renting videocassettes.
For example, at a price of $2, Marie will rent (buy the use of) 6 cassettes per week and
at a price of 50 cents she will rent 9.

There are four points about the relationship between the number of videos Marie
rents and the price of renting them that are worth mentioning. First, the relationship
follows the law of demand: as the rental price rises, quantity demanded decreases. Second, quantity demanded has a specific *time dimension* to it. In this example demand
refers to the number of cassette rentals per week. Without the time dimension, the table
wouldn't provide us with any useful information. Nine cassette rentals per year is quite
a different concept from 9 cassette rentals per week. Third, Marie's cassette rentals are
interchangeable—the 9th cassette rental doesn't significantly differ from the 1st, 3rd, or
any other cassette rental. The fourth point is already familiar to you: The schedule assumes that everything else is held constant.

From a Demand Table to a Demand Curve

Figure 4-3(b) translates the demand table in Figure 4-3(a) into a graph. Point A (quantity = 9, price = $.50) is graphed first at the (9, $.50) coordinates. Next we plot points
B, C, D, and E in the same manner and connect the resulting dots with a solid line.
The result is the demand curve, which graphically conveys the same information that's
in the demand table. Notice that the demand curve is downward sloping (from left to
right), indicating that the law of demand holds in the example.

The demand curve represents the *maximum price* that an individual will pay for various quantities of a good; the individual will happily pay less. For example, say someone

The demand curve represents the
maximum price that an individual
will pay.

offers Marie 6 cassette rentals at a price of $1 each (point F of Figure 4-3(b)). Will she accept? Sure; she'll pay any price within the shaded area to the left of the demand curve. But if someone offers her 6 rentals at $3.50 each (point G), she won't accept. At a rental price of $3.50 apiece, she's willing to buy only 3 cassette rentals.

Individual and Market Demand Curves

Normally, economists talk about market demand curves rather than individual demand curves. A **market demand curve** is *the horizontal sum of all individual demand curves.* Market demand curves are what most firms are interested in. Firms don't care whether individual A or individual B buys their goods; they only care that *someone* buys their goods.

It's a good graphical exercise to add individual demand curves together to create a market demand curve. We do that in Figure 4-4. In it we assume that the market consists of three buyers, Marie, Pierre, and Cathy, whose demand tables are given in Figure 4-4(a). Marie and Pierre have demand tables similar to the demand tables discussed previously. At a price of $3 each, Marie rents 4 cassettes; at a price of $2, she rents 6. Cathy is an all-or-nothing individual. She rents 1 cassette as long as the price is equal to or below $1; otherwise she rents nothing. If you plot Cathy's demand curve, it's a vertical line. However, the law of demand still holds: as price increases, quantity demanded decreases.

The quantity demanded by each consumer is listed in columns 2, 3, and 4 of Figure 4-4(a). Column 5 shows total market demand; each entry is the horizontal sum of the entries in columns 2, 3, and 4. For example, at a price of $3 apiece (row F), Marie

Q.4

Derive a market demand curve from the following two individual demand curves:

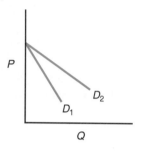

Figure 4-4 (a and b)   FROM INDIVIDUAL DEMANDS TO A MARKET DEMAND CURVE

The table (**a**) shows the demand schedules for Marie, Pierre, and Cathy. Together they make up the market for videocassette rentals. Their total quantity demanded (market demand) for videocassette rentals at each price is given in column 5. As you can see in (**b**), Marie's, Pierre's, and Cathy's demand curves can be added together to get the total market demand curve. For example, at a price of $2, Cathy demands 0, Pierre demands 3, and Marie demands 6, for a market demand of 9 (point D).

	(1)	(2)	(3)	(4)	(5)
	Price (per cassette)	Marie's demand	Pierre 's demand	Cathy's demand	Market demand
A	$0.50	9	6	1	16
B	1.00	8	5	1	14
C	1.50	7	4	0	11
D	2.00	6	3	0	9
E	2.50	5	2	0	7
F	3.00	4	1	0	5
G	3.50	3	0	0	3
H	4.00	2	0	0	2

(a) A demand table

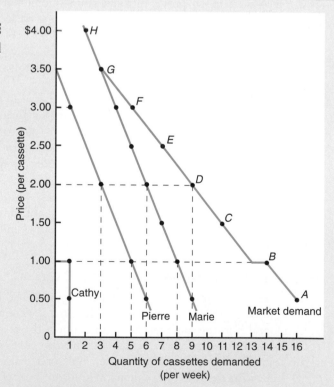

(b) Adding demand curves

demands 4 cassette rentals, Pierre demands 1, and Cathy demands 0, for a total market demand of 5 cassette rentals.

Figure 4-4(b) shows three demand curves: one each for Marie, Pierre, and Cathy. The market, or total, demand curve is the horizontal sum of the individual demand curves. To see that this is the case, notice that if we take the quantity demanded at $1 by Marie (8), Pierre (5), and Cathy (1), they sum to 14, which is point B (14, $1) on the market demand curve. We can do that for each price. Alternatively, we can simply add the individual quantities demanded, given in the demand tables, prior to graphing (which we do in column 5 of Figure 4-4(a)), and graph that total in relation to price. Not surprisingly, we get the same total market demand curve.

In practice, of course, firms don't measure individual demand curves, so they don't sum them up in this fashion. Instead, they estimate total demand. Still, summing up individual demand curves is a useful exercise because it shows you how the market demand curve is the sum (the horizontal sum, graphically speaking) of the individual demand curves, and it gives you a good sense of where market demand curves come from. It also shows you that, even if individuals don't respond to small changes in price, the market demand curve can still be smooth and downward sloping. That's because, for the market, the law of demand is based on two phenomena:

1. At lower prices, existing demanders buy more.
2. At lower prices, new demanders (some all-or-nothing demanders like Cathy) enter the market.

For the market, the law of demand is based on two phenomena:
1. *At lower prices, existing demanders buy more.*
2. *At lower prices, new demanders enter the market.*

SUPPLY

In one sense, supply is the mirror image of demand. Individuals control the factors of production—inputs, or resources, necessary to produce goods. Individuals' supply of these factors to the market mirrors other individuals' demand for those factors. For example, say you decide you want to rest rather than weed your garden. You hire someone to do the weeding; you demand labour. Someone else decides she would prefer more income instead of more rest; she supplies labour to you. You trade money for labour; she trades labour for money. Her supply is the mirror image of your demand.

For a large number of goods and services, however, the supply process is more complicated than demand. For many goods there's an intermediate step in supply: individuals supply factors of production to firms.

Let's consider a simple example. Say you're a taco technician. You supply your labour to the factor market. The taco company demands your labour (hires you). The taco company combines your labour with other inputs like meat, cheese, beans, and tables, and produces many tacos (production), which it supplies to customers in the goods market. For produced goods, supply depends not only on individuals' decisions to supply factors of production but also on firms' ability to produce—to transform those factors of production into usable goods.

The supply process of produced goods is generally complicated. Often there are many layers of firms—production firms, wholesale firms, distribution firms, and retailing firms—each of which passes on in-process goods to the next layer of firms. Real-world production and supply of produced goods is a multistage process.

The supply of nonproduced goods is more direct. Individuals supply their labour in the form of services directly to the goods market. For example, an independent contractor may repair your washing machine. That contractor supplies his labour directly to you.

Thus, the analysis of the supply of produced goods has two parts: an analysis of the supply of factors of production to households and to firms, and an analysis of one process by which firms transform those factors of production into usable goods and services.

> Supply of produced goods involves a much more complicated process than demand and is divided into analysis of factors of production and the transformation of those factors into goods.

The Law of Supply

In talking about supply, the same convention exists that we used for demand. Supply refers to the various quantities offered for sale at various prices. Quantity supplied refers to a specific quantity offered for sale at a specific price.

There's a law of supply that corresponds to the law of demand. The **law of supply** states:

Quantity supplied rises as price rises, other things constant.

Or alternatively:

Quantity supplied falls as price falls, other things constant.

Price regulates quantity supplied just as it regulates quantity demanded. Like the law of demand, the law of supply is fundamental to the invisible hand's (the market's) ability to coordinate individuals' actions.

What accounts for the law of supply? When the price of a good rises, individuals and firms can rearrange their activities in order to supply more of that good to the market. The law of supply is based on a firm's ability to substitute production of one good for another, or vice versa. If the price of corn rises and the price of wheat has not changed, farmers will grow less wheat and more corn, other things constant.

With firms, there's a second explanation of the law of supply. Assuming firms' costs are constant, a higher price means higher profits (the difference between a firm's revenues and its costs). The expectation of those higher profits leads it to increased output as price rises, which is what the law of supply states.

The Supply Curve

A **supply curve** is *the graphical representation of the relationship between price and quantity supplied.* A supply curve is shown graphically in Figure 4-5.

Notice how the supply curve slopes upward to the right. That upward slope captures the law of supply. It tells us that the quantity supplied varies *directly*—in the same direction—with the price.

As with the law of demand, the law of supply assumes other things are held constant. Thus, if the price of wheat rises and quantity supplied falls, you'll look for something else that changed—for example, a drought might have caused a drop in supply. Your explanation would go as follows: Had there been no drought, the quantity supplied would have increased in response to the rise in price, but because there was a drought, the supply decreased, which caused prices to rise.

As crude oil prices rise, the incentive to produce more oil rises.

Figure 4-5 A SAMPLE SUPPLY CURVE

The supply curve demonstrates graphically the law of supply, which states that the quantity supplied of a good is directly related to that good's price, other things constant. As the price of a good goes up, the quantity supplied also goes up, so the supply curve is upward sloping.

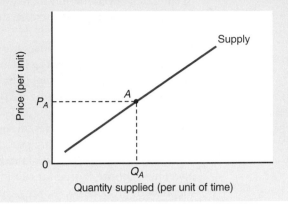

As with the law of demand, the law of supply represents economists' off-the-cuff response to the question "What happens to quantity supplied if price rises?" If the law seems to be violated, economists search for some other variable that has changed. As was the case with demand, these other variables that might change are called shift factors.

Shifts in Supply versus Movements along a Supply Curve

The same distinctions in terms made for demand apply to supply.

Supply refers to *a schedule of quantities a seller is willing to sell per unit of time at various prices, other things constant.*

Quantity supplied refers to *a specific amount that will be supplied at a specific price.*

In graphical terms, supply refers to the entire supply curve because a supply curve tells us how much will be offered for sale at various prices. "Quantity supplied" refers to a point on a supply curve, such as point A in Figure 4-5.

The second distinction that is important to make is between the effects of a change in a good's price and the effects of shift factors on how much of a good is supplied. Changes in price cause changes in quantity supplied; such changes are represented by a **movement along a supply curve**—*the graphic representation of the effect of a change in a good's price on the quantity supplied.* If the amount supplied is affected by anything other than that good's price, that is, by a shift factor of supply, there will be a **shift in supply**—*the graphic representation of the effect of a change in a factor other than price on supply.*

Shift Factors of Supply

Other factors besides a good's price that affect how much will be supplied include the price of inputs used in production, technology, expectations, and taxes and subsidies. Let's see how.

Price of Inputs Firms produce to earn a profit. Since their profit is tied to costs, it's no surprise that costs will affect how much a firm is willing to supply. If costs rise, profits will decline, and a firm has less incentive to supply. Supply falls when the price of inputs rises. If costs rise substantially, a firm might even shut down.

Technology Advances in technology change the production process, reducing the number of inputs needed to produce a given supply of goods. Thus, a technological advance that reduces the number of workers will reduce costs of production. A reduction

Q.5 In the 1980s and 1990s, as animal activists caused a decrease in the demand for fur coats, the prices of furs fell. This made _____ decline. Should the missing words be "the supply" or "the quantity supplied"?

in the costs of production increases profits and leads suppliers to increase production. Advances in technology increase supply.

Expectations Supplier expectations are an important factor in the production decision. If a supplier expects the price of her good to rise at some time in the future, she may store some of today's supply in order to sell it later and reap higher profits, decreasing supply now and increasing it later.

Taxes and Subsidies Taxes on supplies increase the cost of production by requiring a firm to pay the government a portion of the income from products or services sold. Because taxes increase the cost of production, profit declines and suppliers will reduce supply. The opposite is true for subsidies. Subsidies are payments by the government to suppliers to produce goods; thus, they reduce the cost of production. Subsidies increase supply. Taxes on suppliers reduce supply.

These aren't the only shift factors. As was the case with demand, a shift factor of supply is anything that affects supply, other than its price.

Shift in Supply versus a Movement along a Supply Curve

The same "movement along" and "shift of" distinction that we developed for demand exists for supply. To make that distinction clear, let's consider an example: the supply of oil. In 1990 and 1991, world oil prices in U.S. dollars rose from $15 to $36 a barrel when oil production in the Persian Gulf was disrupted by the Iraqi invasion of Kuwait. Oil producers, seeing that they could sell their oil at a higher price, increased oil production. As the price of oil rose, domestic producers increased the quantity of oil supplied. The change in domestic quantity supplied in response to the rise in world oil prices is illustrated in Figure 4-6(a) as a movement up along the domestic supply curve

Q-6 Explain the effect of each of the following on the supply of romance novels:

1. The price of paper rises by 20 percent.
2. Government increases the sales tax on all books by 5 percentage points.

Figure 4-6   SHIFT IN SUPPLY VERSUS CHANGE IN QUANTITY SUPPLIED

A change in quantity supplied results from a change in price and is shown by a movement along a supply curve like the movement from point A to point B in (a). A shift in supply—a shift in the entire supply curve—brought about by a change in a nonprice factor is shown in (b).

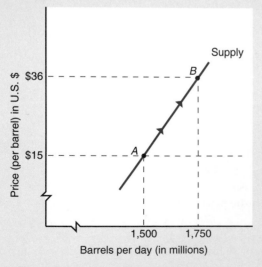

(a) Movement along a supply curve

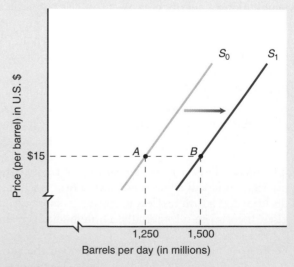

(b) Shift in supply

from point A to point B. At $15 a barrel, producers supplied 1,500 million barrels of oil a day, and at $36 a barrel they supplied 1,750 million barrels per day.

Earlier, in the 1980s, technological advances in horizontal drilling more than doubled the amount of oil that could be extracted from some oil fields. Technological innovations such as this reduced the cost of supplying oil and shifted the supply of oil to the right as shown in Figure 4-6(b). Before the innovation, suppliers were willing to provide 1,250 million barrels of oil per day at U.S. $15 a barrel. After the innovation, suppliers were willing to supply 1,500 million barrels of oil per day at U.S. $15 a barrel.

A Review

To be sure you understand shifts in supply, explain what is likely to happen to your supply curve for labour in the following cases: (1) You suddenly decide that you absolutely need a new car. (2) You suddenly won a million dollars in the lottery. And finally, (3) the wage you could earn doubled. If you came up with the answers: shift out, shift in, and no change—you've got it down. If not, it's time for a review.

Do we see such shifts in the supply curve often? Yes. A good example is computers. For the past 30 years, technological changes have continually shifted the supply curve for computers out.

The Supply Table

Remember Figure 4-4(a)'s demand table for cassette rentals. In Figure 4-7(a), columns 2 (Ann), 3 (Barry), and 4 (Charlie), we follow the same reasoning to construct a supply

Figure 4-7 (a and b) FROM INDIVIDUAL SUPPLIES TO A MARKET SUPPLY

As with market demand, market supply is determined by adding all quantities supplied at a given price. Three suppliers—Ann, Barry, and Charlie—make up the market of videocassette suppliers. The total market supply is the sum of their individual supplies at each price, shown in column 5 of (a).

Each of the individual supply curves and the market supply curve have been plotted in (b). Notice how the market supply curve is the horizontal sum of the individual supply curves.

	(1)	(2)	(3)	(4)	(5)
Quantities supplied	Price (per cassette)	Ann's supply	Barry's supply	Charlie's supply	Market supply
A	$0.00	0	0	0	0
B	0.50	1	0	0	1
C	1.00	2	1	0	3
D	1.50	3	2	0	5
E	2.00	4	3	0	7
F	2.50	5	4	0	9
G	3.00	6	5	0	11
H	3.50	7	5	2	14
I	4.00	8	5	2	15

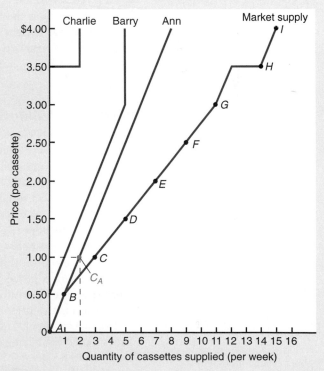

(a) A supply table

(b) Adding supply curves

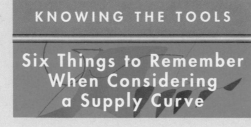

- A supply curve follows the law of supply. When price rises, quantity supplied increases, and vice versa.
- The horizontal axis—quantity—has a time dimension.
- The quantities are of the same quality.

KNOWING THE TOOLS

Six Things to Remember When Considering a Supply Curve

- The vertical axis—price—assumes all other prices remain constant.
- The curve assumes everything else is constant.
- Effects of price changes are shown by movements along the supply curve. Effects of nonprice determinants of supply are shown by shifts of the entire supply curve.

table for three hypothetical cassette suppliers. Each supplier follows the law of supply: When price rises, each supplies more, or at least as much as each did at a lower price.

From a Supply Table to a Supply Curve

Q-7 Derive the market supply curve from the following two individual supply curves.

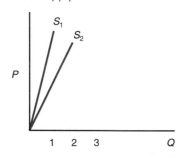

Figure 4-7(b) takes the information in Figure 4-7(a)'s supply table and translates it into a graph of each supplier's supply curve. For instance, point C_A on Ann's supply curve corresponds to the information in columns 1 and 2, row C. Point C_A is at a price of $1 per cassette and a quantity of 2 cassettes per week. Notice that Ann's supply curve is upward sloping, meaning that price is positively related to quantity. Charlie's and Barry's supply curves are similarly derived.

The supply curve represents the set of *minimum* prices an individual seller will accept for various quantities of a good. The market's invisible hand stops suppliers from charging more than the market price. If suppliers could escape the market's invisible hand and charge a higher price, they would gladly do so. Unfortunately for them, and fortunately for consumers, a higher price encourages other suppliers to begin selling cassettes. Competing suppliers' entry into the market sets a limit on the price any supplier can charge.

Individual and Market Supply Curves

The market supply curve is derived from individual supply curves in precisely the same way that the market demand curve was. To emphasize the symmetry, we've made the three suppliers quite similar to the three demanders. Ann (column 2) will supply 2 at $1; if price goes up to $2, she increases her supply to 4. Barry (column 3) begins supplying at $1, and at $3 supplies 5, the most he'll supply regardless of how high price rises. Charlie (column 4) has only two units to supply. At a price of $3.50 he'll supply that quantity, but higher prices won't get him to supply any more.

The **market supply curve** is *the horizontal sum of all individual supply curves*. In Figure 4-7(a) (column 5), we add together Ann's, Barry's, and Charlie's supply to arrive at the market supply curve, which is graphed in Figure 4-7(b). Notice that each point on it corresponds to the information in columns 1 and 5 for each row. For example, point H corresponds to a price of $3.50 and a quantity of 14.

The law of supply is based on two phenomena:
1. At higher prices, existing suppliers supply more.
2. At higher prices, new suppliers enter the market.

The market supply curve's upward slope is determined by two different sources: by existing suppliers supplying more and by new suppliers entering the market. Sometimes existing suppliers may not be willing to increase their quantity supplied in response to an increase in prices, but a rise in price often brings brand-new suppliers into the market. For example, a rise in teachers' salaries will have little effect on the amount of teaching current teachers do, but it will increase the number of people choosing to be teachers.

THE MARRIAGE OF SUPPLY AND DEMAND

Thomas Carlyle, the English historian who dubbed economics "the dismal science," also wrote this chapter's introductory tidbit. "Teach a parrot the words *supply* and *demand* and you've got an economist." In earlier chapters, we tried to convince you that economics is *not* dismal. In the rest of this chapter, we hope to convince you that, while supply and demand are important to economics, parrots don't make good economists. If students think that when they've learned the terms *supply* and *demand* they've learned economics, they're mistaken. Those terms are just labels for the ideas behind supply and demand, and it's the ideas that are important. What matters about supply and demand isn't the labels but how the concepts interact. For instance, what happens if a freeze kills the blossoms on the orange trees? The quantity of oranges supplied isn't expected to equal the quantity demanded. It's in understanding the interaction of supply and demand that economics becomes interesting and relevant.

During the 1990s, an overproduction of wheat led to excess supply and downward pressure on glodal wheat prices.

Excess Supply

When you have a market in which neither suppliers nor consumers can collude and in which prices are free to adjust, economists have a good answer for the question: What happens if quantity supplied doesn't equal quantity demanded? If there is **excess supply** (a surplus), *quantity supplied is greater than quantity demanded*, and some suppliers won't be able to sell all their goods. Each supplier will think: "Gee, if I offer to sell it for a bit less, I'll be the lucky one who sells my goods; someone else will be stuck with not selling their goods." But because all suppliers with excess goods will be thinking the same thing, the price in the market will fall. As that happens, consumers will increase their quantity demanded. So the movement toward equilibrium created initially by excess supply will be on both the supply and demand sides.

Excess Demand

The reverse is also true. Say that instead of excess supply, there's **excess demand** (a shortage)—*quantity demanded is greater than quantity supplied*. There are more consumers who want the good than there are suppliers selling the good. Let's consider what's likely to go through demanders' minds. They'll likely call long-lost friends who just happen to be sellers of that good and tell them it's good to talk to them and, by the way, don't they want to sell that . . . ? Suppliers will be rather pleased that so many of their old friends have remembered them, but they'll also likely see the connection between excess demand and their friends' thoughtfulness. To stop their phones from ringing all the time, they'll likely raise their price. The reverse is true for excess supply. It's amazing how friendly suppliers become to potential consumers when there's excess supply.

Q-8 Explain what a sudden popularity of "Economics Professor" brand casual wear would likely do to prices of that brand.

Price Adjusts

This tendency for prices to rise when the quantity demanded exceeds the quantity supplied and for prices to fall when the quantity supplied exceeds the quantity demanded is a central element to understanding supply and demand. So remember:

 4.1
see page 102

When quantity demanded is greater than quantity supplied, prices tend to rise.
When quantity supplied is greater than quantity demanded, prices tend to fall.

Two other things to note about supply and demand are (1) the greater the difference between quantity supplied and quantity demanded, the more pressure there is for prices to rise or fall, and (2) when quantity demanded equals quantity supplied, the market is in equilibrium.

People's tendencies to change prices exist as long as there's some difference between quantity supplied and quantity demanded. But the change in price brings the laws of supply and demand into play. As price falls, quantity supplied decreases as some suppliers leave the business (the law of supply). And as some people who originally weren't really interested in buying the good think, "Well, at this low price, maybe I do want to buy," quantity demanded increases (the law of demand). Similarly, when price rises, quantity supplied will increase (the law of supply) and quantity demanded will decrease (the law of demand).

Whenever quantity supplied and quantity demanded are unequal, price tends to change. If, however, quantity supplied and quantity demanded are equal, price will stay the same because no one will have an incentive to change.

The Graphical Marriage of Supply and Demand

Figure 4-8 shows supply and demand curves for cassette rentals and demonstrates the force of the invisible hand. Let's consider what will happen to the price of cassettes in three cases:

1. When the price is $3.50 each;
2. When the price is $1.50 each; and
3. When the price is $2.50 each.

1. When price is $3.50, quantity supplied is 7 and quantity demanded is only 3. Excess supply is 4. Individual consumers can get all they want, but most suppliers can't sell all they wish; they'll be stuck with cassettes that they'd like to rent. Suppliers will tend to offer their goods at a lower price and demanders, who see plenty of suppliers out there, will bargain harder for an even lower price. Both these forces will push the price as indicated by the A arrows in Figure 4-8.

Now let's start from the other side.

2. Say price is $1.50. The situation is now reversed. Quantity supplied is 3 and quantity demanded is 7. Excess demand is 4. Now it's consumers who can't get

Q.9 In a flood, it is ironic that usable water supplies tend to decline because the pumps and water lines are damaged. What will a flood likely do to the prices of bottled water?

Figure 4-8 **THE MARRIAGE OF SUPPLY AND DEMAND**

Combining Ann's supply from Figure 4-7 and Marie's demand from Figure 4-4, let's see the force of the invisible hand. When there is excess demand there is upward pressure on price. When there is excess supply there is downward pressure on price. Understanding these pressures is essential to understanding how to apply economics to reality.

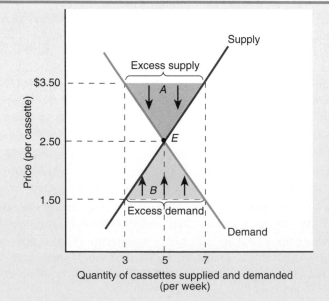

what they want and suppliers who are in the strong bargaining position. The pressures will be on price to rise in the direction of the *B* arrows in Figure 4-8.

3. At $2.50, price is at its equilibrium: quantity supplied equals quantity demanded. Suppliers offer to sell 5 and consumers want to buy 5, so there's no pressure on price to rise or fall. Price will tend to remain where it is (point *E* in Figure 4-8). Notice that the equilibrium price is where the supply and demand curves intersect.

EQUILIBRIUM

The concept of equilibrium appears often throughout this text. You need to understand what equilibrium is and what it isn't.

What Equilibrium Is

The concept itself comes from physics—classical mechanics. **Equilibrium** is *a concept in which opposing dynamic forces cancel each other out.* For example, a hot-air balloon is in equilibrium when the upward force exerted by the hot air in the balloon equals the downward pressure exerted on the balloon by gravity. In supply and demand analysis, equilibrium means that the upward pressure on price is exactly offset by the downward pressure on price. **Equilibrium price** is *the price toward which the invisible hand drives the market.* **Equilibrium quantity** is *the amount bought and sold at the equilibrium price.*

4.2

see page 102

So much for what equilibrium is. Now let's consider what it isn't.

What Equilibrium Isn't

First, equilibrium isn't a state of the world. It's a characteristic of the model—the framework you use to look at the world. The same situation could be seen as an equilibrium in one framework and as a disequilibrium in another. Say you're describing a car that's speeding along at 100 kilometres an hour. That car is changing position relative to objects on the ground. Its movement could be, and generally is, described as if it were in disequilibrium. However, if you consider this car relative to another car going 100 kilometres an hour, the cars could be modelled as being in equilibrium because their positions relative to each other aren't changing.

Second, equilibrium isn't inherently good or bad. It's simply a state in which dynamic pressures offset each other. Some equilibria are awful. Say two countries are engaged in a nuclear war against each other and both sides are blown away. An equilibrium will have been reached, but there's nothing good about it.

Equilibrium is not inherently good or bad.

Desirable Characteristics of Supply/Demand Equilibrium

While there is nothing necessarily good about equilibrium, the supply/demand equilibrium has certain desirable characteristics that are very important when applying economic analysis. To see those desirable characteristics, let's consider what the demand curve and supply curve are telling us. Each of these curves tells us how much individuals would be willing to pay (in the case of demand) or accept (in the case of supply) for a good. Thus, in Figure 4-9(a) (on the next page) a consumer at quantity 2 would be willing to pay $8 for a good, and the supplier would be willing to sell it for $2.

If the consumer pays less than what he's willing to pay, he walks away better off. Thus, the distance between the demand curve and the price he pays is a net gain for the consumer. Economists call this net benefit **consumer surplus**—*the value the consumer*

Figure 4-9 (a and b)   CONSUMER AND PRODUCER SURPLUS

Market equilibrium price and quantity maximizes the combination of consumer surplus (shown in blue) and producer surplus (shown in red) as demonstrated in **(a).** When price deviates from its equilibrium as in **(b),** combined consumer and producer surplus falls. The grey shaded region shows the loss of total surplus when price is $1 higher than equilibrium price.

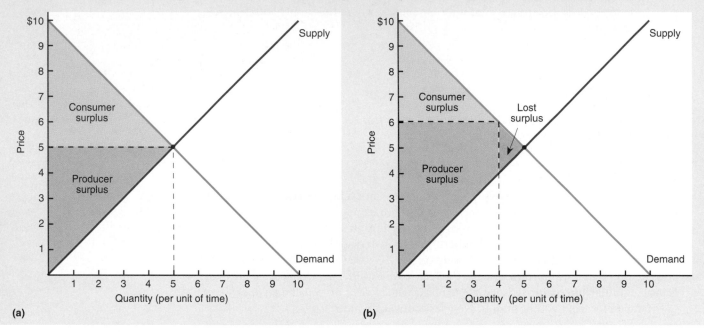

(a)   **(b)**

---

gets from buying a product, less its price. It is represented by the area underneath the demand curve and above the price that an individual pays. Thus, with the price at equilibrium ($5), consumer surplus is represented by the blue area.

Similarly, if a producer receives more than the price she would be willing to sell it for, she too receives a net benefit. Economists call this gain **producer surplus**—*the price the producer sells a product for, less the cost of producing it.* We use this cost information to construct a supply curve, so producer surplus is represented by the area above the supply curve but below the price the producer receives. Thus, with the price at equilibrium ($5), producer surplus is represented by the red area.

What's good about equilibrium is that it makes the combination of consumer and producer surpluses as large as it can be. To see this, say that for some reason the equilibrium price is held at $6. Consumers will demand only 4 units of the good, and some suppliers are not able to sell all the goods they would like. The combined producer and consumer surplus will decrease, as shown in Figure 4-9(b). The grey triangle represents lost consumer and producer surplus. In general, a deviation of price from equilibrium lowers the combination of producer and consumer surplus. This is one of the reasons economists support markets and why we teach the supply/demand model. It gives us a visual sense of what is good about markets: By allowing trade, markets maximize the combination of consumer and producer surplus. How the government might intervene in a market to alter the distribution of consumer surplus and producer surplus takes us into the realm of normative economics.

Q-10 If price moves from disequilibrium to equilibrium, what happens to the combination of producer and consumer surplus in the market?

APPLYING THE TOOLS

The Supply and Demand for Children

In Chapter 1, we distinguished between an economic force and a market force. Economic forces are operative in all aspects of our lives; market forces are economic forces that are allowed to be expressed through a market. Our examples in this chapter are of market forces—of goods sold in a market—but supply and demand can also be used to analyze situations in which economic, but not market, forces operate. An economist who is adept at this is Gary Becker of the University of Chicago. He has applied supply and demand analysis to a wide range of issues, even the supply and demand for children.

Becker doesn't argue that children should be bought and sold. But he does argue that economic considerations play a large role in people's decisions on how many children to have. In farming communities, children can be productive early in life; by age six or seven, they can work on a farm. In an advanced industrial community, children provide pleasure but generally don't contribute productively to family income. Even getting them to help around the house can be difficult.

Becker argues that since the price of having children is lower for a farming society than for an industrial society, farming societies will have more children per family. Quantity of children demanded will be larger. And that's what we find. Developing countries that rely primarily on farming often have three, four, or more children per family. Industrial societies average fewer than two children per family.

To fix the ideas of consumer and producer surplus in your mind, let's consider a couple of real-world examples. Think about the water you drink. What does it cost? Almost nothing. Given that water is readily available, it has a low price. But since you'd die from thirst if you had no water, you are getting an enormous amount of consumer surplus from that water. Next, consider a ballet dancer who loves the ballet so much he'd dance for free. But he finds that people are willing to pay to see him and that he can receive $400 a performance. He is receiving producer surplus.

CONCLUSION

Throughout the book we'll be presenting examples of supply and demand. So we'll end this chapter here because its intended purposes have been served. What were those intended purposes? First, we exposed you to enough economic terminology and economic thinking to allow you to proceed to our more complicated examples. Second, we have set your mind to work putting the events around you into a supply/demand framework. Doing that will give you new insights into the events that shape all our lives. Once you incorporate the supply/demand framework into your way of looking at the world, you will have made an important step toward thinking like an economist.

4.3

see page 102

Chapter Summary

- The law of demand states that quantity demanded rises as price falls, other things constant.

- The law of supply states that quantity supplied rises as price rises, other things constant.

- Factors that affect supply and demand other than price are called shift factors. Shift factors of demand include income, prices of other goods, tastes, population, and expectations. Shift factors of supply include the price of inputs, technology, expectations, and taxes and subsidies.

- A change in quantity demanded (supplied) is a movement along the demand (supply) curve. A change in demand (supply) is a shift of the entire demand (supply) curve.

- The laws of supply and demand hold true because individuals can substitute.

- A market demand (supply) curve is the horizontal sum of all individual demand (supply) curves.

- When quantity demanded is greater than quantity supplied, prices tend to rise. When quantity supplied is greater than quantity demanded, prices tend to fall.

- When quantity supplied equals quantity demanded, prices have no tendency to change. This is equilibrium.

- Equilibrium maximizes the combination of consumer surplus and producer surplus. Consumer surplus is the net benefit a consumer gets from purchasing a good, while producer surplus is the net benefit a producer gets from selling a good.

Key Terms

consumer surplus (97)

demand (85)

demand curve (84)

equilibrium (97)

equilibrium price (97)

equilibrium quantity (97)

excess demand (95)

excess supply (95)

law of demand (83)

law of supply (90)

market demand curve (88)

market supply curve (94)

movement along a demand curve (85)

movement along a supply curve (91)

producer surplus (98)

quantity demanded (85)

quantity supplied (91)

shift in demand (85)

shift in supply (91)

supply (91)

supply curve (90)

Questions for Thought and Review

1. State the law of demand. Why is price inversely related to quantity demanded?

2. State the law of supply. Why is price directly related to quantity supplied?

3. List four shift factors of demand and explain how each affects demand.

4. Distinguish the effect of a shift factor of demand on the demand curve from the effect of a change in price on the demand curve.

5. Draw a market demand curve from the following demand table.

P	Q
37	20
47	15
57	10
67	5

6. Draw a demand curve from the following demand table.

P	D_1	D_2	D_3
37	20	4	8
47	15	2	7
57	10	0	6
67	5	0	5

7. Danielle has just stated that normally, as price rises, supply will increase. Her teacher grimaces. Why?

8. List four shift factors of supply and explain how each affects supply.

9. Draw a market supply curve from the following supply table.

P	S_1	S_2	S_3
37	0	4	14
47	0	8	16
57	10	12	18
67	10	16	20

10. It has just been reported that eating meat is bad for your health. Using supply and demand curves, demonstrate the report's likely effect on the price and quantity of steak sold in the market.

11. Explain why the combination of consumer and producer surplus is not maximized if there is either excess demand or supply.

12. Use economic reasoning to explain why nearly every purchase you make provides you with consumer surplus.

Problems and Exercises

1. You're given the following individual demand tables for comic books.

Price	Jean	Liz	Connie
$ 2	4	36	24
4	4	32	20
6	0	28	16
8	0	24	12
10	0	20	8
12	0	16	4
14	0	12	0
16	0	8	0

   a. Determine the market demand table.
   b. Graph the individual and market demand curves.
   c. If the current market price is $4, what's the total market demand? What happens to total market demand if price rises to $8?
   d. Say that an advertising campaign increases demand by 50 percent. Illustrate graphically what will happen to the individual and market demand curves.

2. Draw hypothetical supply and demand curves for tea. Show how the equilibrium price and quantity will be affected by each of the following occurrences:
   a. Bad weather wreaks havoc with the tea crop.
   b. A medical report implying tea is bad for your health is published.
   c. A technological innovation lowers the cost of producing tea.
   d. Consumers' income falls.

3. This is a question concerning what economists call the *identification problem*. Say you go out and find figures on the quantity bought of various products. You will find something like the following:

Product	Year	Quantity	Average Price
VCRs	1998	100,000	$210
	1999	110,000	220
	2000	125,000	225
	2001	140,000	215
	2002	135,000	215
	2003	160,000	220

   Plot these figures on a graph.
   a. Have you plotted a supply curve, a demand curve, or what?

   b. If we assume that the market for VCRs is competitive, what information must you know to determine whether these are points on a supply curve or on a demand curve?
   c. Say you know that the market is one in which suppliers set the price and allow the quantity to vary. Could you then say anything more about the curves you have plotted?
   d. What information about shift factors would you expect to find to make these points reflect the law of demand?

4. You're a commodity trader and you've just heard a report that the winter wheat harvest will be 2.09 billion bushels, a 44 percent jump, rather than an expected 35 percent jump to 1.96 billion bushels.
   a. What would you expect would happen to wheat prices?
   b. Demonstrate graphically the effect you suggested in *a*.

5. In Canada, gasoline costs consumers about $0.80 per litre. In Italy it costs consumers about $2 per litre. What effect does this price differential likely have on:
   a. The size of cars in Canada and in Italy?
   b. The use of public transportation in Canada and in Italy?
   c. The fuel efficiency of cars in Canada and in Italy? What would be the effect of raising the price of gasoline in Canada to $2 per litre?

6. Use the graph below to answer the following questions:

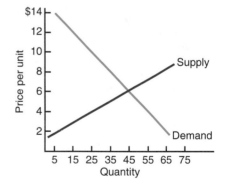

   a. What is equilibrium price and quantity?
   b. What is producer surplus when the market is in equilibrium?
   c. What is consumer surplus when the market is in equilibrium?
   d. If price were held at $10 a unit, what is consumer and producer surplus?

7. The following graph shows the market for apples.

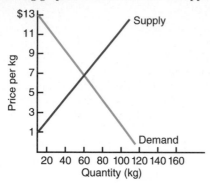

a. What are equilibrium price and quantity?
b. Determine producer surplus and consumer surplus at the equilibrium price.
c. If the government places a price floor at $9, what is the quantity traded in the market?
d. What are producer and consumer surplus at this controlled price?
e. What is the lost surplus resulting from the price floor?

Web Questions

1. Go to the World Bank's Health, Nutrition and Population home page (devdata.worldbank.org/hnpstats/) and find data about Canada's population in 2000 and projections for 2010, 2020, and 2035. What do you expect to happen to the proportion of the population over 65? Report your findings. Other things constant, what do you expect will happen in the next 50 years to the relative demand and supply for each of the following, being careful to distinguish between shifts of and a movement along a curve:
   a. Nursing homes.
   b. Prescription medication.
   c. Baby high chairs.
   d. Postsecondary education.

2. Go to Natural Resources Canada's Energy Policy Branch home page (www.nrcan.gc.ca/es/epb/eng/enghome.htm)and answer the following questions:
   a. List the factors that are expected to affect demand and supply for energy in the near term. How will each factor affect demand? Supply?

   b. What is the Energy Policy Branch's forecast for world oil prices? Show graphically how the factors listed in your answer to (a) are consistent with the Energy Policy Branch's forecast. Label all shifts in demand and supply.
   c. Describe and explain the Energy Policy Branch's forecast for the price of gasoline, heating oil and natural gas. Be sure to mention the factors that are affecting the forecast.

3. Go to the Canadian Taxpayers Federation home page (www.taxpayer.com) and look up sales tax rates for the 10 provinces.
   a. Which province(s) have no sales tax? Which province(s) have the highest sales tax?
   b. Show graphically the effect of sales tax on supply, demand, equilibrium quantity, and equilibrium price.
   c. Name two neighbouring provinces that have significantly different sales tax rates. How does that affect the supply or demand for goods in those provinces?

Answers to Margin Questions Q

1. The demand curve slopes downward because price and quantity demanded are inversely related. As the price of a good rises, people switch to purchasing other goods whose prices have not risen as much.   (84)

2. *Demand for furs*. The other possibility, *quantity demanded*, is used to refer to movements along (not shifts of) the demand curve.   (85)

3. (1) The decline in price will increase the quantity of computers demanded (movement down along the demand curve); (2) With more income, demand for computers will rise (shift of the demand curve to the right).   (85)

4. When adding two demand curves, you sum them horizontally, as in the accompanying diagram.   (88)

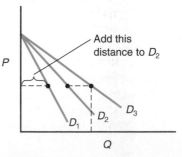

5. "The quantity supplied" declined because there was a movement along the supply curve. The supply curve itself remained unchanged. *(91)*

6. (1) The supply of romance novels declines since paper is an input to production (supply shifts to the left); (2) the supply of romance novels declines since the tax increases the cost to the producer (supply shifts to the left). *(92)*

7. When adding two supply curves, sum horizontally the two individual supply curves, as in the diagram below. *(94)*

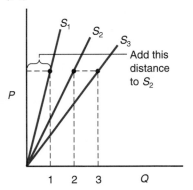

8. Customers will flock to stores demanding that funky "Economics Professor" look, creating excess demand. This excess demand will soon catch the attention of suppliers, and prices will be pushed upward. *(95)*

9. As substitutes—tap water—decrease, demand for bottled water increases enormously, and there will be upward pressure on prices. Social and political forces will, however, likely work in the opposite direction—against "profiteering" in people's misery. *(96)*

10. The combination of consumer and producer surplus will increase since there will be no lost surplus at the equilibrium price. *(98)*

Using Supply and Demand

5

After reading this chapter, you should be able to:

- Show the effect of a shift in demand and supply on equilibrium price and quantity.

- Explain real-world events using supply and demand.

- Demonstrate the effect of a price ceiling and a price floor on a market.

- Explain the effect of taxes, tariffs, and quotas on equilibrium price and quantity.

- State the limitations of demand and supply analysis.

- State six roles of government.

*It is by invisible hands that we are bent
and tortured worst.*

Nietzsche

In the last chapter we introduced you to the concepts of supply and demand. In this chapter we will (1) show you the power of supply and demand, (2) show you how the invisible hand interacts with social and political forces to change the outcome of supply and demand analysis; and (3) discuss how one must adjust supply and demand analysis with other issues kept at the back of one's mind.

THE POWER OF SUPPLY AND DEMAND

To ensure that you understand the supply and demand graphs throughout the book, and can apply them, let's go through an example. Figure 5-1(a) deals with an increase in demand. Figure 5-1(b) deals with a decrease in supply.

Figure 5-1 (a and b)   SHIFTS IN SUPPLY AND DEMAND

When there is an increase in demand (the demand curve shifts outward), there is upward pressure on the price, as shown in (a). If demand increases from D_0 to D_1, the quantity of cassette rentals that was demanded at a price of $2.25, 8, increases to 10, but the quantity supplied remains at 8. This excess demand tends to cause prices to rise. Eventually, a new equilibrium is reached at the price of $2.50, where the quantity supplied and the quantity demanded is 9 (point B).

If supply of cassette rentals decreases, then the entire supply curve shifts inward to the left, as shown in (b), from S_0 to S_1. At the price of $2.25, the quantity supplied has now decreased to 6 cassettes, but the quantity demanded has remained at 8 cassettes. The excess demand tends to force the price upward. Eventually, an equilibrium is reached at the price of $2.50 and quantity 7 (point C).

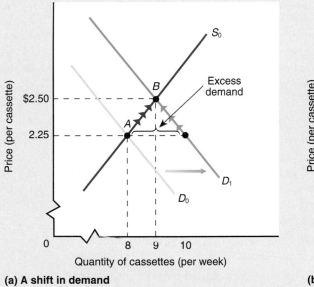

(a) A shift in demand

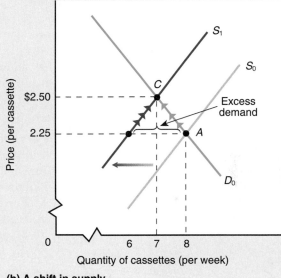

(b) A shift in supply

Let's consider again the supply and demand for videocassette rentals from Chapter 4. In Figure 5-1(a), the supply is S_0 and initial demand is D_0. They meet at an equilibrium price of $2.25 per cassette and an equilibrium quantity of 8 cassettes per week (point A). Now say that the demand for cassette rentals increases from D_0 to D_1. At a price of $2.25, the quantity of cassette rentals supplied will be 8 and the quantity demanded will be 10; excess demand of 2 exists.

The excess demand pushes prices upward in the direction of the small arrows, decreasing the quantity demanded and increasing the quantity supplied. As it does so, movement takes place along both the supply curve and the demand curve.

The upward push on price decreases the gap between the quantity supplied and the quantity demanded. As the gap decreases, the upward pressure decreases, but as long as that gap exists at all, price will be pushed upward until the new equilibrium price ($2.50) and new quantity (9) are reached (point B). At point B, quantity supplied equals quantity demanded. So the market is in equilibrium. Notice that the adjustment is twofold: The higher price brings about equilibrium by both increasing the quantity supplied (from 8 to 9) and decreasing the quantity demanded (from 10 to 9).

Figure 5-1(b) begins with the same situation that we started with in Figure 5-1(a); the initial equilibrium quantity and price are 8 cassettes per week and $2.25 per cassette (point A). In this example, however, instead of demand increasing, let's assume supply decreases—say because some suppliers change what they like to do, and decide they will

Q-1 Demonstrate graphically the effect of a heavy frost in Nova Scotia on the equilibrium quantity and price of apples.

Q-2 Say a hormone has been discovered that increases cows' milk production by 20 percent. Demonstrate graphically what effect this discovery would have on the price and quantity of milk sold in a market.

Q.3 Demonstrate graphically the likely effect of an increase in the price of gas on the equilibrium quantity and price of compact cars.

no longer supply cassettes. That means that the entire supply curve shifts inward to the left (from S_0 to S_1). At the initial equilibrium price of $2.25, the quantity demanded is greater than the quantity supplied. Two more cassettes are demanded than are supplied. (Excess demand = 2.)

This excess demand exerts upward pressure on price. Price is pushed in the direction of the small arrows. As the price rises, the upward pressure on price is reduced but will still exist until the new equilibrium price, $2.50, and new quantity, 7, are reached. At $2.50, the quantity supplied equals the quantity demanded. The adjustment has involved a movement along the demand curve and the new supply curve. As price rises, quantity supplied is adjusted upward and quantity demanded is adjusted downward until quantity supplied equals quantity demanded where the new supply curve intersects the demand curve at point C, an equilibrium of 7 and $2.50.

Here is an exercise for you to try. Demonstrate graphically how the price of computers could have fallen dramatically in the past 10 years, even as demand increased. (Hint: Supply has shifted even more, so even at lower prices, far more computers have been supplied than were being supplied 10 years ago.)

Six Real-World Examples

Now that we've been through a generic example of shifts in supply and demand, let's consider some real-world examples. Below are six events. After reading each, try your hand at explaining what happened, using supply and demand curves. To help you in the process, Figure 5-2 provides some diagrams. *Before* reading our explanation, try to match the shifts to the examples. In each, be careful to explain which curve, or curves, shifted and how those shifts affected equilibrium price and quantity.

If this orange orchard was damaged, supply would be reduced, thereby putting upward pressure on orange prices.

1. Brazil is the world's largest sugar producer. Inclement weather reduced production in 2000 by 15%. Market: Sugar.

2. In the mid-1990s baby boomers started to put away more and more savings for retirement. This saving was directed toward the purchase of financial assets, driving up the price of stocks. Market: Financial assets.

3. The majority of golfers in Korea prefer to use the newest American-made golf clubs. The Korean government, in an effort to protect domestic golf club producers, imposed a 20 percent luxury tax on imported American clubs. Market: American-made golf clubs in Korea.

4. Rice is crucial to Indonesia's nutritional needs and its rituals. In 1997, drought, pestilence, and a financial crash led to disruptions in the availability of rice. Its price rose so high that in 1998 more than a quarter of all Indonesians could not buy enough market-priced rice to meet their daily needs. Government programs to deliver subsidized rice were insufficient to bring the price of rice back to affordable levels. Market: Rice in Indonesia.

5. In late summer 1998, U.S. farmers were hard pressed to find enough seasonal farmhands. Why? El Niño's weather patterns compressed the harvest season. Grape, apple, and peach growers, who usually harvested at different times, were competing for the same workers. In addition, stronger efforts by authorities had reduced the flow of illegal workers to the United States. Market: Farm labourers.

6. Every Christmas a new toy becomes the craze. In 1997 it was Tickle Me Elmo and in 1998 it was Furby. Before Christmas Day, these toys were hard to find and sold for as much as 10 times their retail price on what is called the black market. Here we use the Furby as the example. Toymaker Tiger, along with retailers, worked up initial interest in Furby in late November, advertising the

Figure 5-2 (a–f)

In this exhibit, six shifts of supply and demand are shown. Your task is to match them with the events listed in the chapter.

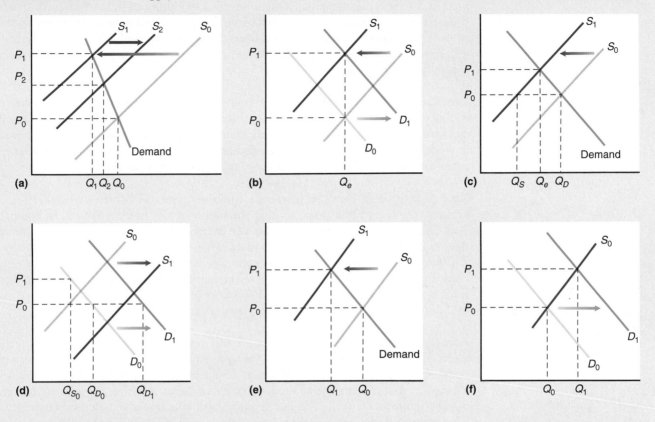

(a)   (b)   (c)   (d)   (e)   (f)

Answers: 1:c; 2:f; 3:e; 4:a; 5:b; 6:d.

limited supply. As early as 2:00 A.M., lines formed at the stores carrying Furbies. Some shoppers (including "toy scouts") were able to buy Furbies then resell them the same afternoon for as much as $300 apiece. Even with the shortage, retailers kept the price at its preset advertised price and producers continued to limit distribution. Newspapers carried stories about the lines and black market prices, intensifying demand for Furbies, which became even harder to come by. Days before Christmas, the supplier increased shipments of Furbies to meet the increased demand. Customers felt "lucky" when they were able to find Furbies with so few days left before Christmas, and for only $30 instead of $300 on the black market. Market: Furbies in 1998.

Sugar Shock The weather is invariably uncooperative. Nearly every year, some market is hit with a crop-damaging freeze, too little precipitation, or even too much rain. This is a shift factor of supply because it raises the cost of supplying sugar. The bad weather in 2000 shifted the supply curve for Brazilian sugar in, as shown in Figure 5-2(c). At the original price, quantity demanded exceeded quantity supplied and the invisible hand of the market pressured the price to rise until quantity demanded equalled quantity supplied.

Financial Assets and the Baby Boomers The postwar population swell we call the baby boom resulted in increased demand for all sorts of products as the boomers graduated, then bought houses, and now are demanding more health care and financial assets. In this case, demographic changes have led to a shift out in the demand curve for financial assets, resulting in a rise in stock market prices and an increase in the quantity of stocks and mutual funds supplied. This is depicted in Figure 5-2(f). This figure could also be used to describe the huge rise in housing prices in the 1980s as baby boomers began to purchase houses.

Excise Taxes In Chapter 4's discussion of shift factors, we explained that taxes levied on the supplier will reduce supply. The 20 percent luxury tax will shift the supply curve in. That some golfers use their old clubs and others look elsewhere to buy clubs is substitution at work, and a movement up along the demand curve. Figure 5-2(e) shows this scenario. After the tax, price rises to P_1 and quantity of clubs sold declines to Q_1.

Rice in Indonesia Drought, pestilence, and the financial crash all increased the cost of supplying rice in Indonesia, shifting the supply of rice in from S_0 to S_1 in Figure 5-2(a). Since rice is so important to the well-being of Indonesians, quantity demanded doesn't change much with changes in price. This is shown by the steep demand curve. The price rose to levels unaffordable to many people. In response, the government purchased imported rice and distributed it to the market. This shifted the supply curve out from S_1 to S_2. Since the price was still above its previous level, we know that this second shift in supply is smaller than the first.

Farm Labourers In this case both supply and demand shift, but this time in opposite directions. The previous year's demand is represented in Figure 5-2(b) by D_0 and supply is shown by S_0. Q_e labourers were hired at a wage of P_0. The compressed harvesting season meant that more farmers were looking for labourers, shifting the demand for farm workers out from D_0 to D_1. This put upward pressure on wages and increased quantity of labour supplied. Simultaneously, however, the supply of farm workers shifted in from S_0 to S_1 as the authorities increased border patrols. This put further upward pressure on wages and reduced the quantity of labour demanded. Wages are clearly bid up, in this case to P_1. The effect on the number of labourers hired, however, depends on the relative size of the demand and supply shifts. As we have drawn it, the quantity of labourers hired returns to the quantity of the previous year, Q_e. If the supply shift were greater than the shift in demand, the number of labourers would have declined. If it were smaller, the number of labourers would have risen.

Christmas Toys In this example, both supply and demand shift in the same direction. The initial market is shown by D_0 and S_0 in Figure 5-2(d). The price of $30 (shown by P_0) was below the equilibrium price and a shortage of $Q_{D_0} - Q_{S_0}$ existed. The black market price of $300 (shown by P_1) is shown by the amount that consumers are willing to pay for the quantity supplied, Q_{S_0}. As the craze for the toy intensified following the free newspaper publicity of the lines and black market prices, demand shifted out to D_1. Price was kept at $30 and the shortage became even greater, $Q_{D_1} - Q_{S_0}$. When Tiger made more Furbies available, supply shifted to S_1, eliminating most, but not all, of the shortage. At least one Walmart employee was injured in the mad rush to obtain a Furby.

Sorting out the effects of the shifts of supply or demand or both can be confusing. Here are some helpful hints to keep things straight:

- Draw the initial demand and supply curves and label them. The equilibrium price and quantity is where these curves intersect. Label them.
- If only price has changed, no curves will shift and a shortage or surplus will result.

KNOWING THE TOOLS

Supply and Demand in Action

- If a nonprice factor affects demand, determine the direction demand has shifted and add the new demand curve. Do the same for supply.
- Equilibrium price and quantity is where the new demand and supply curves intersect. Label them.
- Compare the initial equilibrium price and quantity to the new equilibrium price and quantity.

See if you can describe what happened in the three graphs below.

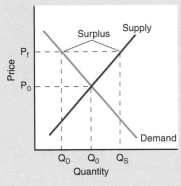

A change in price

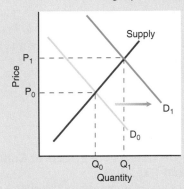

A shift in demand

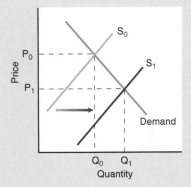

A shift in supply

A Review

As you can see, supply and demand analysis can get quite complicated. That is why you must separate shifts in demand and supply from movements along the supply and demand curves. Remember: Anything that affects demand and supply other than price of the good under consideration will shift the curves. Changes in the price of the good under consideration result in movements along the curves. Another thing to recognize is that when both curves are shifting you can get a change in price but little change in quantity, or a change in quantity but little change in price.

To test your understanding, we'll now give you six generic results from the interaction of supply and demand. Your job is to decide what shifts produced those results. This exercise is a variation of the first. It goes over the same issues, but this time without the graphs. On the left-hand side of the table below, we list combinations of movements of observed prices and quantities, labeling them 1–6. On the right we give six shifts in supply and demand, labeling them *a–f*.

Anything other than price that affects demand or supply will shift the curves.

Price and Quantity Changes		
1.	P↑	Q↑
2.	P↑	Q↓
3.	P↑	Q?
4.	P↓	Q?
5.	P?	Q↑
6.	P↓	Q↓

Shifts in Supply and Demand

a. Supply shifts in. No change in demand.
b. Demand shifts out. Supply shifts in.
c. Demand shifts in. No change in supply.
d. Demand shifts out. Supply shifts out.
e. Demand shifts out. No change in supply.
f. Demand shifts in. Supply shifts out.

If you don't confuse your "shifts of" with your "movements along," supply and demand provide good off-the-cuff answers for many economic questions.

You are to match the shifts with the price and quantity movements that best fit each described shift, using each shift and movement only once. Our recommendation to you

Q-4   If both demand and supply shift in, what happens to price and quantity?

is to draw the graphs that are described in *a–f*, decide what happens to price and quantity, and then find the match in 1–6.

Now that you've worked them, let us give you the answers we came up with. They are: 1:*e*; 2:*a*; 3:*b*; 4:*f*; 5:*d*; 6:*c*. How did we come up with the answers? We did what we suggested you do—took each of the scenarios on the right and predicted what happens to price and quantity. For case *a*, supply shifts in and there is a movement up along the demand curve. Since the demand curve is downward sloping, the price rises and quantity declines. This matches number *2* on the left. For case *b*, demand shifts out. Along the original supply curve, price and quantity would rise. But supply shifts in, leading to even higher prices, but lower quantity. What happens to quantity is unclear, so the match must be number *3*. For case *c*, demand shifts in. There is movement down along the supply curve with lower price and lower quantity. This matches number 6. For case *d*, demand shifts out and supply shifts out. As demand shifts out, we move along the supply curve to the right and price and quantity rise. But supply shifts out too, and we move out along the new demand curve. Price declines, erasing some or all of the previous rise, and the quantity rises even more. This matches number 5.

We'll leave it up to you to confirm our answers to *e* and *f*. Notice that when supply and demand both shift, the change in either price or quantity is uncertain—it depends on the direction and the relative size of the shifts. As a summary, we present a diagrammatic of the combinations in Table 5-1.

TABLE 5-1   Diagram of Effects of Shifts of Demand and Supply on Price and Quantity
This table provides a summary of the effects of shifts in supply and demand on price and quantity. Notice that when both curves shift, the effect on either price or quantity depends on the relative size of the shifts.

	No change in supply.	Supply shifts out.	Supply shifts in.
No change in demand.	No change.	P↓ Q↑ Price declines and quantity rises.	P↑ Q↓ Price rises. Quantity declines.
Demand shifts out.	P↑ Q↑ Price rises. Quantity rises.	P? Q↑ Quantity rises. Price could be higher or lower depending upon relative size of shifts.	P↑ Q? Price rises. Quantity could rise or fall depending upon relative size of shifts.
Demand shifts in.	P↓ Q↓ Price declines. Quantity declines.	P↓ Q? Price declines. Quantity could rise or fall depending upon relative size of shifts.	P? Q↓ Quantity declines. Price rises or falls depending upon relative size of shifts.

GOVERNMENT INTERVENTIONS: PRICE CEILINGS AND PRICE FLOORS

People don't always like the market-determined price. When prices fall, sellers look to government for ways to hold prices up; when prices rise, buyers look to government for ways to hold prices down. Let's now consider the effect of such actions. Let's start with an example of the price being held down.

Price Ceilings

When government wants to hold prices down, it imposes a **price ceiling**—*a government-imposed limit on how high a price can be charged*. Rent control is an example of a price ceiling. (For the price ceiling to be effective, it must be below the equilibrium price, and throughout this discussion we shall assume that it is.)

Specifically, let's consider rent control in Paris in 1948. **Rent control** is *a price ceiling on rents set by government*. During the First World War, to stabilize housing prices and help out those fighting for France, rents were frozen. Upon the return of veterans, the freeze was held in the interest of society. In 1926, rent control was reviewed but by that time, lifting the controls would have resulted in huge increases in rents. Rents were allowed to rise only slightly. Again, during the Second World War, rents were frozen. Right after the end of the Second World War rent was capped at $2.50 a month. Without rent control, rent would have been $17 a month.

5.1

see page 126

This was a good situation for those occupying apartments, but it had drawbacks. For instance, there was an enormous shortage of apartments. The situation is shown in Figure 5-3.

What were the results of the rent control besides the shortage of apartments? More than 80 percent of Parisians had no private bathrooms and 20 percent had no running water. Since rental properties weren't profitable, no new buildings were being constructed and existing buildings weren't kept in repair. From 1914 (before the First World War) to 1948, the housing stock increased by only 10 percent. Many couldn't find housing in Paris. Couples lived with their in-laws. Existing apartments had to be rationed in some way. To get into a rent-controlled apartment, individuals paid bribes of up to

Figure 5-3 RENT CONTROL IN PARIS

A price ceiling imposed on housing rent in Paris during the First World War created a shortage of housing when the war ended and veterans returned home. The shortage would have been eliminated if rents had been allowed to rise to $17 per month.

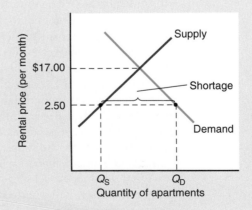

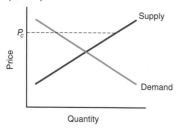

Q.5 What is the effect of the price ceiling, P_c, shown in the graph below on price and quantity?

With price ceilings, existing goods are no longer rationed entirely by price. Other methods of rationing existing goods arise called nonprice rationing.

$1,500 per room or watched the obituaries and then simply moved in their furniture before anyone else did. Eventually the situation got so bad that rent controls were lifted.

The system of rent controls is not only of historical interest. Below we list some phenomena that existed recently.

1. A couple pays $350 a month for a two-bedroom downtown apartment with a solarium and two terraces, while another individual pays $1,200 a month for a studio apartment shared with two roommates.

2. The vacancy rate for apartments in Montreal was 1.5 percent in 2000. Anything under 5 percent is considered a housing emergency.

3. Would-be tenants make payments, called key money, to current tenants or landlords to get apartments.

Your assignment is to explain how these phenomena might have come about, and to demonstrate, with supply and demand, the situation that likely caused them.

Now that you have done your assignment (you have, haven't you?), let us give you our answers so that you can check them with your answers.

The situation is identical with that presented above in Figure 5-3. Take the first item. The couple lives in a rent-controlled apartment while the individual with roommates does not. If rent control were eliminated, rent on the downtown apartment would rise and rent on the studio would most likely decline. Item 2: The housing emergency is a result of rent control. Below-market rent results in excess demand and little vacancy. Item 3: New residents must search for a long time to find apartments to rent, and many discover that illegal payments to landlords are the only way to obtain a rent-controlled apartment. Key money is a side payment for a rent-controlled apartment. Because of the limited supply of apartments, individuals are willing to pay far more than the controlled price. Landlords can use other methods of rationing the limited supply of apartments—instituting first-come, first-served policies, and, in practice, selecting tenants based on gender, race, or other personal characteristics, even though such discriminatory selection is illegal.

Before we move away from our discussion of rent controls, there's a dynamic issue we need to explicitly consider. In the long run an increase in rents should increase the quantity of apartments supplied as building owners convert commercial properties to residential use and erect new buildings, but since it takes time to construct a new apartment building or convert existing structures to apartment use, in the short run the supply of apartments is relatively fixed. This suggests we should use two supply curves to examine how rent controls differ in their impacts in the short-run and the long-run. You can see this in Figure 5–4. The short run supply curve is vertical to illustrate that the supply of apartments is fixed at a point in time, while the long run supply curve slopes upward to show that higher rents will increase the quantity of units supplied in the long run.

Suppose the market is in equilibrium at point A at a price of $750 per month for a one bedroom apartment. The introduction of rent controls at the initial price creates excess demand in the short run since the quantity demanded at the controlled price of $500 per month is higher than the fixed quantity supplied. Over time, landlords will have little incentive to maintain existing properties and may decide to convert their apartment buildings to commercial use structures that are not subject to rent controls. Over the long term, the supply of apartments will fall to S_S' in Figure 5–4, leading to a permanent excess demand for housing.

What does our model suggest will happen if rent controls are relaxed? In the short-term, rents will rise to what people are willing to pay, given the existing stock of apartments: point B in Figure 5–4. Over time, as landlords adjust to the new higher rents by building new units, the shortages will be eliminated. This is what is happening today in

Figure 5-4 RENT CONTROLS OVER TIME

In the short run the supply of rental units is relatively fixed and given by S_S. The long-run supply curve demonstrates that landowners will increase the quantity of apartments supplied if rents rise, over time. The initial equilibrium is at A.

Rent controls will set the price below the equilibrium, leading to excess demand in the short run. The shortages will grow over time as landlords decide to convert existing apartments to commercial use or refuse to maintain their current units. The short-run supply curve will shift left to S_S'. If rent controls are removed, in the short run rents will rise to what the market will bear at point B. Landlords respond by increasing supply over time, shifting the short-run supply curve back to its initial position.

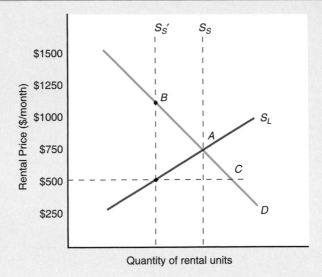

Ontario. Rent controls were introduced there in 1975. In 1998 the Ontario government passed the *Ontario Tenants Act*, which, among other things, relaxed rent controls. In the first three months rents rose by over 7 percent; in 1999 they rose by over 5 percent; and they just keep rising. The *Act* provides a guideline for rent increases for 2001 of 2.9 percent and in 2002 of 3.9 percent. Actual increases depend on how long you've been in your apartment. For new tenants, landlords can charge "what the market will bear." If you rent an apartment in Ontario, has your rent risen by the amount suggested by the guideline this year? Check out the Ontario Rental Housing Tribunal Web site for more on some Ontario evidence (http://www.orht.gov.on.ca/home.html).

If rent controls create a wedge between quantity demanded and quantity supplied, why would a government ever introduce them? Well, consider Toronto's bid for the 2008 Olympics. The demand for housing was expected to swell in anticipation of the games, and remain high until shortly after the closing ceremony. Figure 5–5 demonstrates that there would be a temporary increase in the demand for rental units with demand shifting to D'. Given the existing supply of rental units and the fact that landlords weren't expected to construct a large number of new buildings (since after the games, demand for rental units was expected to fall back to its initial level), rents would rise from R_0 to R_1, and then fall back to R_0 after the games. Landlords would earn a temporary windfall of the shaded area. The authorities might have viewed this as an undesirable distribution of income and a negative consequence of holding the games in Toronto. People already living in Toronto would face the higher rents, as would those temporarily trying to find accommodations in the area. To stop this from happening, the authorities could put in place a system of rent controls. If the price ceiling were set at the initial price, landlords wouldn't gain, existing renters wouldn't lose, and the controls would create a temporary shortage of housing. Those wishing to rent units in the area might have to commute from other areas (like Buffalo) or seek alternative accommodations (such as living at campsites in their RV).

Figure 5-5   **WHEN RENT CONTROLS WORK**

A temporary increase in demand transfers the shaded area from tenants to landlords. The government can stop this by placing rent controls at the initial price R_0, creating a temporary shortage of AB.

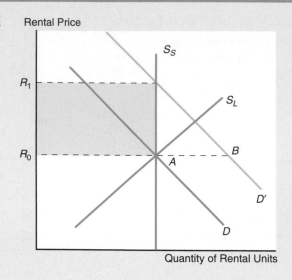

Price Floors

Sometimes political forces favour suppliers, sometimes consumers. So let us now go briefly through a case when the government is trying to favour suppliers by attempting to prevent the price from falling below a certain level. **Price floors**—*government-imposed limits on how low a price can be charged*—do just this. An example of a price floor is the minimum wage. Both individual provinces and the federal government impose **minimum wage laws**—*laws specifying the lowest wage a firm can legally pay an employee*. These price floors were initially set to provide a level of income that would allow a worker to cover their basic necessities. British Columbia was the first province to enact minimum wage legislation (in 1925), with the federal minimum wage set at the provincial level. In late 2001 these wages ranged from $5.50 per hour in Newfoundland to $8.00 per hour in British Columbia. (In 1965 the B.C. minimum wage was $1 per hour; with inflation, that's a much smaller increase than it looks). At an average of 2000 hours worked a year, many believe these wage are too low to provide for the basic necessities of life. The minimum wage affects thousands of workers who are mostly unskilled. The market-determined equilibrium wage for skilled workers is generally above the minimum wage.

The effect of a minimum wage on the unskilled labour market is shown in Figure 5-6. The government-set minimum wage is above equilibrium, as shown by W_{min}. At the market-determined equilibrium wage W_e, the quantity of labour supplied and demanded equals Q_e. At the higher minimum wage, the quantity of labour supplied rises to Q_1 and the quantity of labour demanded declines to Q_2. There is an excess supply of workers (a shortage of jobs) represented by the difference $Q_2 - Q_1$. This represents people who are looking for work but cannot find it.

Who wins and who loses from a minimum wage? The minimum wage improves the wages of the Q_2 workers who are able to find work. Without the minimum wage, they would have earned W_e per hour. The minimum wage hurts those, however, who cannot find work at the minimum wage but who are willing to work, and would have been hired, at the market-determined wage. These workers are represented by the distance

Q-6 What is the effect of the price floor, P_f, shown in the graph below on price and quantity?

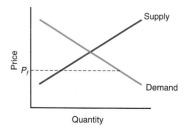

The minimum wage helps some people and hurts others.

Figure 5-6   A MINIMUM WAGE

A minimum wage, W_{min}, set above equilibrium wage, W_e, helps those who are able to find work, shown by Q_2, but hurts those who would have been employed at the equilibrium wage but can no longer find employment, shown by $Q_e - Q_2$. A minimum wage also hurts producers who have higher costs of production and consumers who may face higher product prices.

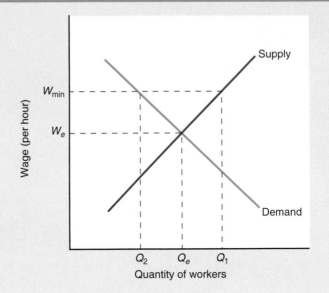

$Q_e - Q_2$ in Figure 5-6. The minimum wage also hurts firms who now must pay their workers more, increasing the cost of production. The minimum wage also hurts consumers to the extent that firms are able to pass that increase in production cost on in the form of higher product prices.

Late in 2001 the government of British Columbia introduced new legislation to create two different minimum wages in the province. It raised the general minimum wage to $8.00 an hour and introduced a "first-job rate" of $6.00 an hour for the first 500 hours. After the first 500 hours, workers would then be entitled to the general minimum wage of $8.00 an hour. This was an attempt to encourage employers to hire and train new workers, recognizing that it may take several months to fully train a new employee. Those people already earning the minimum wage would continue to earn $8.00 an hour; only new hires would face the $6.00 wage floor.

5.2
see page 126

Some commentators suggested that the introduction of a $6.00 first-job rate would stimulate employment, particularly of youth, while others argued that after 500 hours, many young workers will receive their layoff notice, only to be replaced by new entrants into the labour force. Other provinces are watching closely to see whether they should follow suit.

All economists agree that the above analysis is logical and correct. But they disagree about whether governments should have minimum wage laws. One reason is that the empirical effects of minimum wage laws are difficult to determine, since "other things" are never remaining constant. A second reason is that some real-world labour markets are not sufficiently competitive to fit the supply/demand model. The third reason is that the minimum wage affects the economy in ways that some economists see as desirable and others see as undesirable. We point this out to remind you that the supply/demand framework is a tool to be used to analyze issues. It does not provide final answers about policy. That's where the art of economics—blending positive economic analysis with normative issues—comes into play. (In microeconomics, economists explore the policy issues of interventions in markets much more carefully.)

Figure 5-7   **THE EFFECT OF AN EXCISE TAX**

An excise tax on suppliers shifts the entire supply curve up by the amount of the tax. Since at a price equal to the original price plus the tax there is excess supply, the price of the good rises by less than the tax.

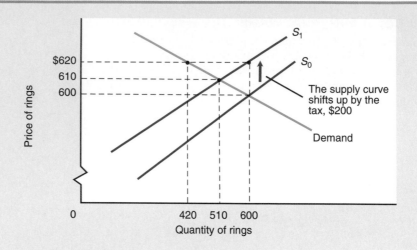

GOVERNMENT INTERVENTIONS: TAXES, TARIFFS, AND QUOTAS

Let's now consider an example of the government entering into a market and modifying the results of supply/demand analysis in the form of a tax. An **excise tax** is *a tax that is levied on a specific good.* The luxury tax on expensive cars that the United States imposed in 1991 is an example. A **tariff** is *an excise tax on an imported good.* What effect will excise taxes and tariffs have on the price and quantity in a market?

Excise Taxes and Tariffs

To lend some sense of reality, let's take the example of the only luxury tax in Canada still in existence—that on jewellery manufactured in Canada. This tax was paid by the supplier. Say the price of a ring before the luxury tax was $600, and 600 rings were sold at that price. Now the government places a tax of $20 on such rings. What will the new price of the ring be, and how many will be sold?

If you were about to answer "The new price will be $620," be careful. Ask yourself whether we would have given you that question if the answer were that easy. By looking at supply and demand curves in Figure 5-7 you can see why $620 is the wrong answer.

To supply 600 rings, suppliers must be fully compensated for the tax. So the tax of $20 on the supplier shifts the supply curve up from S_0 to S_1. However, at $620, consumers are not willing to purchase 600 rings. They are willing to purchase only 420 rings. Quantity supplied exceeds quantity demanded at $620. Suppliers lower their prices until quantity supplied equals quantity demanded at $610, the new equilibrium price. Consumers increase the quantity of rings they are willing to purchase to 510, still less than the original 600 at $600. Why? At the higher price of $610 some people choose not to buy rings and others purchase their rings manufactured outside Canada.

Notice that at the new equilibrium the new price is $610, not $620. The reason is that at the higher price, the quantity of rings people demand is less. This is a movement up along a demand curve to the left. Excise taxes reduce the quantity of goods demanded. That's why jewellers remain up in arms that the tax has not been repealed and why the revenue generated from the tax was less than expected. Instead of collecting $20 × 600 ($12,000), revenue collected was only $10 × 510 ($5100).

A tax on suppliers shifts the supply curve up by the amount of the tax.

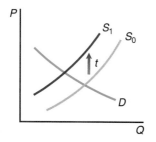

Q.7   Your study partner, Umar, has just stated that a tax on demanders of $2 per unit will raise the equilibrium price from $4 to $6. How do you respond?

Figure 5-8 (a and b)   THE RELATIONSHIP BETWEEN A QUOTA AND A TARIFF

Figure (a) shows the effect of a quota of 5 million cars on the price of Japanese cars sold. Price rises from $20,000 to $27,000. Figure (b) demonstrates that a tax of $11,000 on each Japanese car sold in Canada has the same effect as the quota shown in (a). The difference between a quota and a tariff lies in who gets the revenue. With a quota, the firm selling the good gets the revenue as additional profits. With a tariff, the government gets the revenue shown by the shaded box in (b).

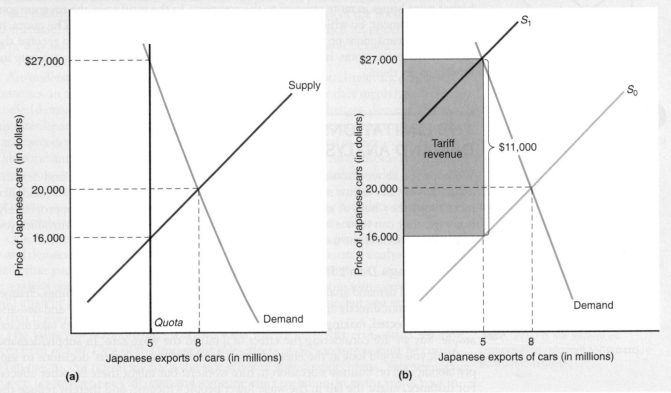

(a)   (b)

Quotas

The next example we want to consider is the imposition of a quantity control—a legal restriction on the quantity that can be bought or sold. The most common type of quantity control is the international **quota**—*a quantitative restriction on the amount that one country can export to another.* Suppose Canada wanted to restrict imports of Japanese cars. We show the effect in Figure 5-8(a).

The market price of a Japanese car is $20,000. At that price, Canadian consumers demand, and Japanese car makers are willing to supply, 8 million cars. But, when Canada places an import quota of, say, 5 million cars into Canada, Canadian consumers are willing to pay $27,000 a car even though Japanese firms are willing to sell them for $16,000 apiece. Of course, sellers will accept what consumers are willing to pay, and the price of Japanese cars rises to $27,000. Notice what the effect of the quota is. It raises the price of Japanese cars in Canada.

The Relationship between a Quota and a Tariff

Above we considered the effect of both quotas and taxes, and we noted that a tariff is a type of excise tax. Both devices increase price and reduce quantity. Let's now compare

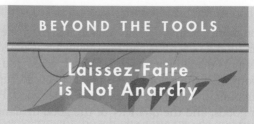

Laissez-Faire is Not Anarchy

Most reasons for government intervention discussed in this chapter are debatable.

There is, however, one governmental role that even the strongest laissez-faire advocates generally accept. That role is for government to set up an appropriate institutional and legal structure within which markets can operate.

The reason there's little debate about this role is that all economists recognize that markets do not operate when there is anarchy. They require institutional structures that determine the rules of ownership, what types of trade are allowable, how contracts will be enforced, and what productive institutions are most desirable.

Before anyone conducts business, he or she needs to know the rules of the game and must have a reasonable expectation that those rules will not be changed. The operation of the modern economy requires that contractual arrangements be made among individuals. These con-tractual arrangements must be enforced if the economy is to operate effectively.

Economists differ significantly as to what the rules for such a system should be and whether any rules that already exist should be modified. Even if the rules are currently perceived as unfair, it can be argued that they should be kept in place. Individuals have already made decisions based on those rules, and it's unfair to them to change the rules in the middle of the game.

Stability of rules is a benefit to society. When the rules are perceived as unfair and changing them is also perceived as unfair, the government must find a balance between these two degrees of unfairness. Government often finds itself in that difficult position. Thus, while there's little debate about government's role in providing some institutional framework, there's heated debate about which framework is most appropriate.

Roles of government in a market economy are:

1. providing a stable set of institutions and rules;
2. promoting effective and workable competition;
3. correcting for externalities;
4. ensuring economic stability and growth;
5. providing public goods; and
6. adjusting for undesired market results.

Provide a Stable Set of Institutions and Rules

A basic role of government is to provide a stable institutional framework that includes the set of laws specifying what can and cannot be done as well as a mechanism to enforce those laws. Before people conduct business, they need to know the rules of the game and have a reasonable belief about what those rules will be in the future. These rules can initially develop spontaneously, but as society becomes more complex, the rules must be codified; enforcement mechanisms must be established. The modern market economy requires enforceable complex contractual arrangements among individuals. Where governments don't provide a stable institutional framework, as often happens in developing and transitional countries, economic activity is difficult; usually such economies are stagnant. Russia in the late 1990s is an example. As various groups fought for political control, the Russian economy stagnated.

Promote Effective and Workable Competition

In a market economy the forces of monopoly and competition are always in conflict, and the government must decide what role it is to play in protecting or promoting competition. Historically, consumer sentiment runs against monopoly power. **Monopoly power** is *the ability of individuals or firms currently in business to prevent other individuals or firms from entering the same kind of business.* Monopoly power gives existing firms and individuals the ability to raise their prices. Similarly, individuals' or firms' ability to enter freely into business activities is generally seen as good. Government's job is to promote policies that prevent excess monopoly power from limiting competition. It needs competition policies that work.

What makes this a difficult function for government is that most individuals and firms believe that competition is far better for the other guy than it is for themselves, that their own monopolies are necessary monopolies, and that competition facing them is unfair competition. For example, most farmers support competition, but these same farmers also support government farm subsidies (payments by government to producers based on production levels) some marketing boards (which set price floors), and import restrictions. Likewise, most firms support competition, but these same firms also support tariffs, which protect them from foreign competition. Most professionals, such as architects and engineers, support competition, but they also support professional licensing, which limits the number of competitors who can enter their field. Now, as you will see in reading the newspapers, there are always arguments for limiting entry into fields. The job of the government is to determine whether these arguments are strong enough to overcome the negative effects those limitations have on competition.

This isn't an easy task. Take the recent merger of Canadian Airlines and Air Canada. It gave Air Canada a monopoly on some domestic routes. Was this fair to the other air carriers? The government believed so, partly because the Canadian market is relatively small and geographically distinct from many others. Air Canada needed the benefits accruing to a monopolist to remain a viable business. Other air carriers responded by searching for niche markets—leisure travel, short-notice travel—to compete against Air Canada. The events of September 11, 2001 notwithstanding, Air Canada reacted by creating its own no-frills carrier, Air Canada Tango. Whether Tango will be capable of competing against Westjet and other carriers remains to be seen, but this example highlights the complexity of designing competition policies that work.

Correct for Externalities

When two people freely enter into a trade agreement, they both believe that they will benefit from the trade. But unless they're required to do so, traders are unlikely to take into account any effect that an action may have on a third party. Economists call *the effect of a decision on a third party not taken into account by the decision maker* an **externality.** An externality can be positive (in which case society as a whole benefits from the trade between the two parties) or negative (in which case society as a whole is harmed by the trade between the two parties).

An example of a positive externality is education. When people educate themselves, all of society benefits, since better-educated people usually make better citizens and are better equipped to figure out new approaches to solving problems—approaches that benefit society as a whole. An example of a negative externality is pollution. Air conditioners emit a small amount of chlorofluorocarbons into the earth's atmosphere and contribute to the destruction of the ozone layer. Since the ozone layer protects all living things by filtering out some of the sun's harmful ultraviolet light rays, having a thinner layer of ozone can contribute to cancer and other harmful or fatal conditions. Neither the firms that produce the air conditioners nor the consumers who buy them take those effects into account. This means that the destruction of the ozone layer is an externality—the result of an effect that is not taken into account by market participants.

When there are externalities, there is a potential role for government to adjust the market result. If one's goal is to benefit society as much as possible, actions with positive externalities should be encouraged and actions with negative externalities should be restricted. Governments can step in and change the rules so that the actors must take into account the effect of their actions on society as a whole. We emphasize that the role is a potential one for two reasons. The first is that government often has difficulty dealing with externalities in such a way that society gains. For example, even if the government totally banned products that emit chlorofluorocarbons, other countries might not do the same and the ozone layer would continue to be destroyed. The second reason is that government is an institution that reflects, and is often guided by, politics and vested interests. It's not clear that, given the political realities, government intervention to correct externalities would improve the situation. In later chapters we'll have a lot more to say about government's role in correcting for externalities.

When there are externalities, there is a potential role for government.

Environmental damage is a negative externality.

Ensure Economic Stability and Growth

In addition to providing general stability, government has the potential role of providing economic stability. If it's possible, most people would agree that government should prevent large fluctuations in the level of economic activity, maintain a relatively constant price level, and provide an economic environment conducive to economic growth. These aims are generally considered macroeconomic goals. They're justified as appropriate aims for government to pursue because they involve **macroeconomic externalities** (*externalities that affect the levels of unemployment, inflation, or growth in the economy as a whole*).

Here's how a macro externality could occur. When individuals decide how much to spend, they don't take into account the effects of their decision on others; thus, there may be too much or too little spending. Too little spending often leads to unemployment. But in making their spending decisions, people don't take into account the fact that spending less might create unemployment. So their spending decisions can involve a macro externality. Similarly, when people raise their price and don't consider the effect on inflation, they too might be creating a macro externality.

> A macroeconomic externality is the effect of an individual decision that affects the levels of unemployment, inflation, or growth in an economy as a whole, but is not taken into account by the individual decision maker.

Provide for Public Goods

A **public good** is *a good that if supplied to one person must be supplied to all and whose consumption by one individual does not prevent its consumption by another individual*. In contrast, a **private good** is *a good that, when consumed by one individual, cannot be consumed by another individual*. An example of a private good is an apple; once you eat that apple, no one else can consume it. National defense is generally considered a public good.

There are very few pure public goods, but many goods have public good aspects to them, and in general economists use the term *public good* to describe goods that are most efficiently provided collectively rather than privately. Parks, playgrounds, roads, and national defense are examples. Let's consider national defense more closely. For technological reasons national defense must protect all individuals in an area; a missile system cannot protect some houses in an area without protecting others nearby.

Everyone agrees that national defense is needed, but not everyone takes part in it. If someone else defends the country, you're defended for free; you can be a **free rider**—*a person who participates in something for free because others have paid for it*. Because self-interested people would like to enjoy the benefits of national defense while letting someone else pay for it, everyone has an incentive to be a free rider. But if everyone tries to be a free rider, there won't be any national defense. In such cases government can step in and require that everyone pay part of the cost of national defense, reducing the free rider problem.

Adjust for Undesired Market Results

A controversial role for government is to adjust the results of the market when those market results are seen as socially undesirable. An example is income distribution. Many people believe the government should see to it that income is "fairly" distributed. Determining what's fair is a difficult philosophical question. Let's consider two of the many manifestations of the fairness problem. Should the government use a **progressive tax** (*a tax whose rates increase as a person's income increases*) to redistribute money from the rich to the poor? (A progressive income tax schedule might tax individuals at a rate of 15 percent for income up to $20,000; at 25 percent for income between $20,000 and $40,000; and at 35 percent for every dollar earned over $40,000.) Or should government impose a **regressive tax** (*a tax whose rates decrease as income rises*) to redistribute money from the poor to the rich? Or should government impose a flat or **proportional tax** (*a tax whose rates are constant at all income levels, no matter what a taxpayer's total* *annual income is*)? Such a tax might be, say, 25 percent of every dollar of income. Canada has chosen a progressive income tax, while contributions for employment insurance and the Canada Pension Plan are a proportional tax up to a specified earned income. Economists can tell government the effects of various types of taxes and forms of taxation, but we can't tell government what's fair. That is for the people, through the government, to decide.

Another example of this role involves having government decide what's best for people, independently of their desires. The market allows individuals to decide. But what if people don't know what's best for themselves? Or what if they do know but don't act on that knowledge? For example, people might know that addictive drugs are bad for them, but because of peer pressure, or because they just don't care, they may take drugs anyway. Government action prohibiting such activities through laws or high taxes may then be warranted. *Goods or activities that government believes are bad for people even though they choose to use the goods or engage in the activities* are called **demerit goods or activities.** Illegal drugs are demerit goods and using addictive drugs is a demerit activity.

Alternatively, there are some activities that government believes are good for people, even if people may not choose to engage in them. For example, government may believe that going to the opera or contributing to charity is a good activity. But in Canada only a small percentage of people go to the opera, and not everyone in Canada contributes to charity. Similarly, government may believe that whole-wheat bread is more nutritious than white bread. But many consumers prefer white bread. Goods like whole-wheat bread and activities like contributing to charity are known as **merit goods or activities**—*goods and activities that government believes are good for you even though you may not choose to engage in the activities or consume the goods*. Government sometimes provides support for them through subsidies or tax benefits.

> With merit and demerit goods, individuals are assumed not to be doing what is in their self-interest.

Market Failures and Government Failures

The reasons for government intervention are often summed up in the phrase *market failure*. **Market failures** are *situations in which the market does not lead to a desired result*. In the real world, market failures are pervasive—the market is always failing in one way or another. But the fact that there are market failures does not mean that government intervention will improve the situation. There are also **government failures**—*situations in which the government intervenes and makes things worse*. Government failures are pervasive in the government—the government is always failing in one way or another. So real-world policy makers usually end up choosing which failure—market failure or government failure—will be least problematic.

CONCLUSION

We will conclude the chapter here. We will talk much more about these roles of government in later chapters. For now, we simply want you to understand the general policy framework. When you combine that general policy framework with the supply/demand framework that we presented in Chapter 4 and the first part of this chapter, you have a good foundation for understanding the economic way of thinking about policy issues.

Chapter Summary

- When the demand curve shifts to the right (left), equilibrium price rises (declines) and equilibrium quantity rises (falls).

- When the supply curve shifts to the right (left), equilibrium price declines (rises) and equilibrium quantity rises (falls).

- By minding your Ps and Qs—the shifts of and movements along curves—you can describe almost all events in terms of supply and demand.

- A price ceiling is a government-imposed limit on how high a price can be charged. Price ceilings below market price create shortages.

- A price floor is a government-imposed limit on how low a price can be charged. Price floors above market price create surpluses.

- Taxes and tariffs paid by suppliers shift the supply curve up by the amount of the tax or tariff. They raise the equilibrium price (inclusive of tax) and decrease the equilibrium quantity.

- Quotas restrict the quantity of goods that one country can export to another. They increase equilibrium price and reduce equilibrium quantity. The effect of a quota on equilibrium price and quantity is the same as a tariff. The difference between the two is who gets the additional revenue.

- In macro, small side effects that can be assumed away in micro are multiplied enormously. Thus, they can significantly change the results and cannot be ignored. To ignore them is to fall into the fallacy of composition.

- Six roles of government are (1) to provide a stable set of institutions and rules, (2) to promote effective and workable competition, (3) to correct for externalities, (4) to ensure economic stability and growth, (5) to provide public goods, and (6) to adjust for undesired market results.

Key Terms

demerit goods or activities *(123)*

excise tax   *(116)*

externality   *(121)*

fallacy of composition   *(118)*

free rider   *(122)*

government failure   *(123)*

macroeconomic externality   *(122)*

market failure   *(123)*

merit goods or activities *(123)*

minimum wage laws   *(114)*

monopoly power   *(120)*

price ceiling   *(111)*

price floor   *(114)*

private good   *(122)*

progressive tax   *(122)*

proportional tax   *(122)*

public good   *(122)*

quota   *(117)*

regressive tax   *(122)*

rent control   *(111)*

tariff   *(116)*

Questions for Thought and Review

1. Say that price and quantity both fell. What would you say was the most likely cause?

2. Say that price fell and quantity remained constant. What would you say was the most likely cause?

3. Demonstrate graphically the effect of a price ceiling.

4. Demonstrate graphically why rent controls might increase the total payment that new renters pay for an apartment.

5. Demonstrate graphically the effect of a price floor.

6. Graphically show the effects of a minimum wage on the number of unemployed.

7. Oftentimes, to be considered for a job, you have to know someone in the firm. What does this observation tell you about the wage paid for that job?

8. In most developing countries, there are long lines of taxis at airports, and these taxis often wait two or three hours. What does this tell you about the price in that market? Demonstrate with supply and demand analysis.

9. Supply/demand analysis states that equilibrium occurs where quantity supplied equals quantity demanded, but in Canadian agricultural markets quantity supplied almost always exceeds quantity demanded. How can this be?

10. Demonstrate graphically the effect of a tax of $4 per unit on equilibrium price and quantity.

11. Using a graph like the one you drew for question 10 above, show graphically a quota that leads to the same price and quantity.

12. You've set up the rules for a game and started the game, but now realize that the rules are unfair. Should you change the rules?

13. Say the government establishes rights to pollute so that without a pollution permit you aren't allowed to emit pollutants into the air, water, or soil. Firms are allowed to buy and sell these rights. In what way will this correct for an externality?

14. What are six roles of government?

Problems and Exercises

1. The Canadian government has supported the price of sugar produced by Canadian sugar producers by placing a tariff on sugar imported into Canada. The tariff is effective because Canada consumes more sugar than it produces.
   a. Using supply/demand analysis, demonstrate how the tariff increases the price of domestic sugar.
   b. What other import policy could the government implement to have the same effect as the tariff?
   c. If Canada were to eliminate the tariff, how would this affect the Canadian sugar market?

2. "Scalping" is the name given to the buying of tickets at a low price and reselling them at a high price. The following information about a Grey Cup game appeared in your local newspaper. At the beginning of the season:
   a. Tickets sell for $27 and are sold out in preseason.
   b. Halfway through the season, both front-runners have maintained unbeaten records. Resale price of tickets rises to $200.
   c. One week before the game, both conference finalists have remained unbeaten and are ranked 1 and 2. Ticket price rises to $600.
   d. Three days before the game, price falls to $400.

   Demonstrate, using supply/demand analysis and words, what might have happened to cause these fluctuations in price.

3. In some localities "scalping" is against the law, although enforcement of these laws is spotty (difficult).
   a. Using supply/demand analysis and words, demonstrate what a weakly enforced antiscalping law would likely do to the price of tickets.
   b. Using supply/demand analysis and words, demonstrate what a strongly enforced antiscalping law would likely do to the price of tickets.

4. Apartments in large Canadian cities like Toronto are often hard to find. One of the major reasons is that there are, or were, rent controls.
   a. Demonstrate graphically how rent controls could make apartments hard to find.
   b. Often one can get an apartment if one makes a side payment to the current tenant. Can you explain why?
   c. What would be the likely effect of eliminating rent controls?
   d. What is the political appeal of rent controls?

5. Until recently, angora goat wool (mohair) has been designated as a strategic commodity (it used to be utilized in some military clothing). Because of that, in 1992 for every dollar's worth of mohair sold to manufacturers, ranchers received $3.60.
   a. Demonstrate graphically the effect of the elimination of this designation and subsidy.
   b. Explain why the program was likely kept in existence for so long.
   c. Say that a politician has suggested that the government should pass a law that requires all consumers to pay a price for angora goat wool high enough so that the sellers of that wool would receive $3.60 more than the market price. Demonstrate the effect of the law graphically. Would consumers support it? How about suppliers?

6. The technology is now developing so that road use can be priced by computer. A computer in the surface of the road picks up a signal from your car and automatically charges you for the use of the road.
   a. How could this technological change contribute to ending bottlenecks and rush hour congestion?
   b. What are some of the problems that might develop with such a system?
   c. How would your transportation habits likely change if you had to pay to use roads?

7. Suppose your province established a licensing requirement for all beauticians last year, and your neighbour continued to operate her salon out of her basement, without obtaining a license. After a particularly bad visit, one of her clients reports her to the authorities, and she is fined and forced to close her home business.
   a. Why would the province have created the licensing requirement in the first place?
   b. What options might you propose to change the system?
   c. What will be the political difficulties of implementing those options?

A per capita growth rate of 1 percent per year means on average people will be able to consume 1 percent more per year. Most of you, we suspect, are hoping to do better than that, and most of you will do better, both because you're studying economics (so you'll do better than average) and because most individuals in their working years can expect to consume slightly more each year than they did the previous year. Since income also tends to increase with age up to retirement, and ends completely at death, a specific individual's income, and hence his or her consumption, will generally increase by more than the per capita growth in income.

So, if the future is like the past, the average person can look forward to a rate of increase in consumption significantly above average.

Canadian economic output has grown at an annual 2.5 to 3.5 percent rate.

Q-2 Output in Canada in 2001 was about $1.1 trillion, and there were about 31 million people living in Canada. What was per capita output?

last 130 years, but more recently it has been more like 2.5 to 3.5 percent. Explaining why this average annual growth rate has fallen recently is one of the challenges facing macroeconomists today. This 2.5 to 3.5 percent average annual growth rate is sometimes called the *secular trend growth rate*. The rate at which the actual output grows in any one year fluctuates, but on average, the Canadian economy has been growing at that long-term trend. Since population has also been growing, per capita economic growth (growth per person) has been less than 2.5 to 3.5 percent.

This brings us to another measure of growth—changes in per capita real output. **Per capita real output** is *real output divided by the total population*. Output per person is an important measure of growth because, while total output may be increasing, the population could be growing so fast that per capita real output is falling.

Global Experiences with Growth

Table 6-1 shows per capita growth for various areas of the world from 1820 to 2000. It tells us a number of important facts about growth:

1. Growth rates today are high by historical standards. For 130 years beginning in 1820, world output grew by only 0.9 percent per year. At that rate it took 82 years for world income to double. From 1950 to 2000, the world economy grew

TABLE 6-1 Average Annual Per Capita Income, Various Regions: 1820 to 2000

	Growth Rates			Income Levels (1990 International Dollars)		
	1820–1950	1950–2000*	1820–2000*	1820	1950	2000*
The world	0.9	1.8	1.1	$ 675	$2,108	$ 5,672
Western Europe	1.1	2.5	1.5	1,269	6,546	19,846
North America	1.6	1.8	1.6	1,233	9,463	26,224
Japan	0.8	4.8	1.9	675	1,927	20,438
Eastern Europe	1.1	1.0	1.0	803	3,162	5,967
Latin America	1.0	1.4	1.1	671	2,478	6,797
China	−0.2	3.4	0.8	600	439	3,442
Other Asia	0.3	2.4	0.9	560	848	3,269
Africa	0.6	0.8	0.6	400	1,307	1,291

*Authors' estimates.

Source: Angus Maddison, *Monitoring the World Economy* (1995) and *Chinese Economic Performance in the Long Run* (1998), OECD Development Center, Paris.

at a much faster rate, 1.8 percent per year, cutting the number of years it took income to double from 80 to 40.

2. The range in growth rates among countries is wide. From 1820 to 1950, North America led, with 1.6 percent annual growth. From 1950 to 2000, however, Japan and Western Europe were among the fastest growing, partially due to the opportunities for growth lost during the Second World War and the replacement of productive capital destroyed in the war. Japan's growth acceleration is the most pronounced. Japan turned from investing in military might before the Second World War to investing in capital destroyed by the war. This acceleration meant that these countries were catching up to other high-growth areas of the world. Japan's average income in 1950 was around one-fifth of the average income in North America. By 2000 it had grown close to equal. Another country that has been catching up is China. While income in China was actually lower in 1950 than in 1820, beginning in the last part of the 20th century and continuing into the 21st century China's income has become one of the fastest growing in the world.

3. African countries have consistently grown below the average for the world. In 1820, Africa's per capita income was 40 percent less than the world average. The gap remained around 40 percent in 1950 but by 2000 it had widened to almost 80 percent.

This 180-year perspective of growth is useful, but by historical standards even 180 years is relatively short. Looking back even further shows us how high our current growth rates are. Before 1820 world income per capita grew about 0.03 percent a year. The growth trend that we now take for granted started only at the end of the 18th century, about the time that markets and democracies became the primary organizing structures of the economy and society. Thus, growth seems to be associated with the development of markets and democracy. Significant growth took off only as the market system developed, and it increased as markets increased in importance.

The growth trend we now take for granted started only at the end of the 18th century.

The Benefits and Costs of Growth

Economic growth (per capita) allows everyone in society, on average, to have more. Thus, it isn't surprising that most governments are generally searching for policies that will allow their economies to grow. Indeed, one reason market economies have been so successful is that they have consistently channelled individual efforts toward production and growth. Individuals feel a sense of accomplishment in making things grow and, if sufficient economic incentives and resources exist, individuals' actions can lead to a continually growing economy.

Politically, growth, or predictions of growth, allows governments to avoid hard distributional questions of who should get what part of our existing output: With growth there is more to go around for everyone. A growing economy generates jobs, so politicians who want to claim that their policies will create jobs generally predict those policies will create growth.

Politically, growth, or predictions of growth, allows governments to avoid hard questions.

Of course, there are also costs to material growth—pollution, resource exhaustion, and destruction of natural habitat. These costs lead some people to believe that we would be better off in a society that de-emphasized material growth. (That doesn't mean we shouldn't grow emotionally, spiritually, and intellectually; it simply means we should grow out of our material goods fetish.) Many people believe these environmental costs are important, and the result is often an environmental–economic growth stalemate.

To reconcile the two goals, some have argued that spending on the environment can create growth and jobs, so the two need not be incompatible. Unfortunately, there's a problem with this argument. It confuses growth and jobs with increased material consumption—what most people are worried about. As more material goods made available by growth are used for pollution control equipment, less is available for the growth of an average individual's personal consumption, since the added material goods created by growth have already been used. What society gets, at best, from these expenditures is a better physical environment, not more of everything. Getting more of everything would violate the TANSTAAFL law (see Chapter 1).

BUSINESS CYCLES

A business cycle is the upward or downward movement of economic activity that occurs around the growth trend.

While the secular, or long-term, trend is a 2.5 to 3.5 percent per year increase in output, there are numerous fluctuations around that trend. Sometimes real output is above the trend; at other times output is below the trend. This phenomenon has given rise to the term *business cycle*. A **business cycle** is *the upward or downward movement of economic activity, or real output, that occurs around the growth trend*. Figure 6-1 graphs the fluctuations in output for the Canadian and U.S. economies since the late 1800s. You can see that Canadian business cycles are closely tied to cycles in the United States.

Until the late 1930s, economists took such cycles as facts of life. They had no convincing theory to explain why business cycles occurred, nor did they have policy suggestions to smooth them out. In fact, they felt that any attempt to smooth them through government intervention would make the situation worse.

Since the 1940s, however, many economists have not taken business cycles as facts of life. They have hotly debated the nature and causes of business cycles and of the underlying growth. In this book we distinguish two groups of macroeconomists: **Keynesians** (who *generally favour activist government policies*) and **Classicals** (who *generally favour laissez-faire or nonactivist policies*). Classical economists argue that fluctuations in economic activity are to be expected in a market economy. Indeed, they say, it would be strange if fluctuations did not occur when individuals are free to decide what they want to do. We should simply accept these fluctuations as we do the seasons of the year. Keynesian economists argue that fluctuations can and should be controlled. They argue that *expansions* (the part of the business cycle above the long-term trend) and *contractions* (the part of the cycle below the long-term trend) are symptoms of underlying problems of the economy, which should be dealt with by government actions. Classical economists respond that individuals will anticipate government's reaction, thereby undermining government's attempts to control cycles. Which of these two views is correct is still a matter of debate.

The Phases of the Business Cycle

Much research has gone into measuring business cycles and setting official reference dates for the beginnings and ends of contractions and expansions. As a result of this research, business cycles have been divided into phases, and an explicit terminology has been developed. Statistics Canada announces the government's official dates of contractions and expansions. In the postwar era (since 1945), the average business expansion has lasted 51 months. A major expansion occurred from 1982 until April 1990, when the Canadian economy fell into a recession. In April 1992 it slowly came out of the recession, and began the longest expansion in Canadian history (as of February 2002 the expansion has lasted 122 months, but the events of September 11, 2001, have led many to expect the economy will remain sluggish into 2003).

Business cycles have varying durations and intensities, but economists have developed a terminology to describe all business cycles and just about any position on a given business cycle. Since this terminology is often used by the press it is helpful to go over it. We do so in reference to Figure 6-2 (on the next page), which gives a visual representation of a business cycle.

Let's start at the top. The top of a cycle is called the *peak*. A *boom* is a very high peak, representing a big jump in output. (That's when the economy is doing great. Most everyone who wants a job has one.) Eventually an expansion peaks. (At least, in the past, they always have.) A *downturn* describes the phenomenon of economic activity

The four phases of the business cycle are:

1. The peak.
2. The downturn.
3. The trough.
4. The upturn.

Figure 6-1 CANADIAN BUSINESS CYCLES

Business cycles have always been a part of the Canadian economic scene. They are closely linked to business cycles in the United States.

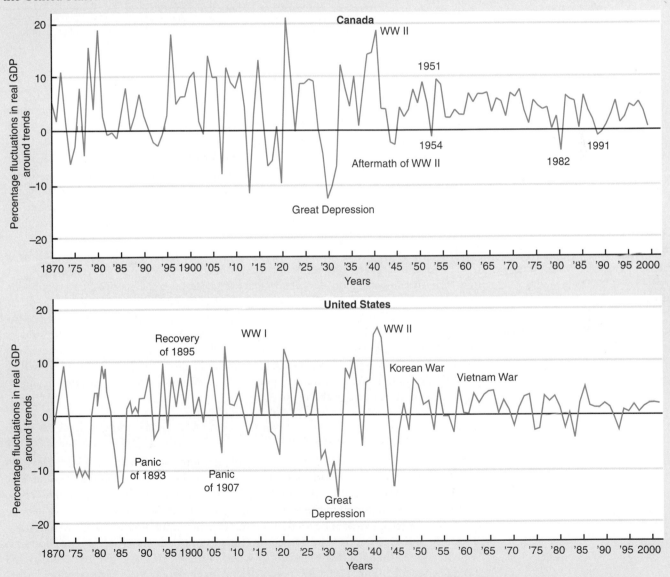

Source: Statistics Canada, *Historical Statistics of Canada*, Series F33, F55; Statistics Canada, CANSIM II, Table 380-0002; authors' calculations. *Historical Statistics of the United States, Colonial Times to 1970*, and U.S. Department of Commerce (http://www.doc.gov).

Figure 6-2   BUSINESS CYCLE PHASES

Economists have many terms that describe the position of the economy on the business cycle. Some of them are given in this graph.

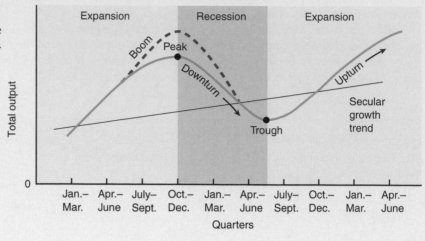

starting to fall from a peak. In a recession the economy isn't doing so great and many people are unemployed. Formally, a **recession** is *a decline in real output that persists for more than two consecutive quarters of a year.*

.A **depression** is *a large recession.* There is no formal line indicating when a recession becomes a depression. In general, a depression is much longer and more severe than a recession. This ambiguity allows some economists to joke, "When your neighbour is unemployed, it's a recession; when you're unemployed, it's a depression." If pushed for something more specific, we'd say that if unemployment exceeds 12 percent for more than a year, the economy is in a depression.

The bottom of a recession or depression is called the *trough.* As total output begins to expand, the economy comes out of the trough; economists say it's in an *upturn,* which may turn into an **expansion**—*an upturn that lasts at least two consecutive quarters of a year.* An expansion leads us back up to the peak. And so it goes.

This terminology is important because if you're going to talk about the state of the economy, you need the words to do it. Why are businesses so interested in the state of the economy? They want to be able to predict whether it's going into a contraction or an expansion. Making the right prediction can determine whether the business will be profitable or not. That's why a large amount of economists' activity goes into trying to predict the future course of the economy.

Q.3 True or false? During the quarter before the start of a recession, the economy is at a peak.

6.1

see page 158

Why Do Business Cycles Occur?

Why do business cycles occur? Are they simply random events, a bit like static on a radio, or do they have some fundamental causes that make them predictable? And if they have causes, are those causes on the supply side or demand side of the economy? These questions will be addressed in the short-run chapters on business cycles. What we will see is that the consensus view believes that fluctuations of output around the growth trend—recessions and expansions—are caused by changes in the demand side of the economy. We will also see that a debate exists about whether these economic fluctuations can and should be reduced. There is far less policy debate about depressions. Most economists believe that potential depressions should be offset by economic policy. Thus, when in 1998 the Southeast Asian economies went into what people believed could lead to a depression, there were substantial calls for government to institute policies that might help off-set it. (There was debate, however, about precisely what those policies should be.)

The general view that something must be done to offset depressions was built into economics in the Great Depression of the 1930s. Production of goods and services fell by 30 percent from 1929 to 1933, leading to changes in the Canadian economy's structure. The new structure included a more active role for government in reducing the severity of cyclical fluctuations. Look back at Figure 6-1 and compare the periods before and after the Second World War. (The Second World War began in 1939 and ended in 1945.) Notice that the downturns and panics since 1945 have generally been less severe than before.

If prolonged contractions are a type of cold the economy catches, the Great Depression of the 1930s was double pneumonia.

Leading Indicators

Economists have developed a set of signs that indicate when a recession is about to oc-cur and when the economy is in one. These signs are called *leading indicators*—indica-tors that tell us what's likely to happen 12 to 15 months from now, much as a barometer gives us a clue about tomorrow's weather. The variables that make up this composite leading indicator include:

1. Average workweek for production workers in manufacturing.
2. An index of housing starts.
3. The U.S. composite leading index.
4. The money supply, M1, divided by a price index.
5. New orders for durable goods.
6. Retail trade in furniture and appliances.
7. Durable goods sales excluding furniture and appliances.
8. The ratio of shipments to inventories of finished products.
9. The TSE 300 stock price index.
10. Employment in business and personal services sectors.

Q.4 List three leading indicators.

These are combined into an index of leading economic indicators that is frequently re-ported in the popular press. (You can find the most recent index at the Statistics Canada Web site, www.statcan.ca.) Economists use leading indicators to make forecasts about the economy. They are called indicators, not predictors, because they're only rough approximations of what's likely to happen in the future. For example, before building a house, you must apply for a building permit. Usually this occurs six to nine months before the actual start of construction. By looking at the housing index, you can predict how much building is likely to begin in six months or so. But the prediction might be wrong, since getting a building permit does not require someone to actually build. Business economists—who spend much of their time and effort delving deeper into these indicators, trying to see what they are really telling us, as opposed to what they seem to be telling us—joke that the leading indicators have predicted six of the past two recessions.

6.2

see page 158

UNEMPLOYMENT

Both business cycles and growth are directly related to unemployment in the Canadian economy. Unemployment occurs when people are looking for a job and cannot find one. The **unemployment rate** is *the percentage of people in the economy who are willing and*

For most people, unemployment means being out of work. For economists, however, there are three different types of unemployment – frictional, structural, and cyclical – each of which needs different policy prescriptions.

able to work but who are not working. When an economy is growing and is in an expansion, unemployment is usually falling; when an economy is in a recession, unemployment is usually rising, although often with a lag.

The relationship between the business cycle and unemployment is obvious to most people, but often the seemingly obvious hides important insights. Just why are the business cycle and growth related to unemployment? True, aggregate income must fall in a recession, but, logically, unemployment need not result. A different result could be that everyone's income falls. Looking at the problem historically, we see that unemployment has not always been a problem associated with business cycles.

In preindustrial farming societies, unemployment wasn't a problem because preindustrial farmers didn't receive wages—they received net revenue (the income left after all costs had been paid). That means the average amount they netted per hour (the equivalent of a wage) was variable. In good years they had a high income per hour; in bad years they had a low income per hour.

The variability in people's net income per hour meant that when there were fluctuations in economic activity, people's income rose or fell, but they kept on working. Low income was a problem, but since people didn't become unemployed **cyclical unemployment** *(unemployment resulting from fluctuations in economic activity)* was not a problem.

While cyclical unemployment did not exist in preindustrial society, **structural unemployment** *(unemployment caused by economic restructuring making some skills obsolete)* did. For example, the demand for scribes in Europe fell after the invention of the printing press in 1438. Some unemployment would likely result; that unemployment would be called *structural unemployment*. But structural unemployment wasn't much of a problem for government, or at least people did not consider it government's problem. The reason is that those in the family with income would share it with unemployed family members.

Unemployment as a Social Problem

Structural unemployment arises when changes in consumer demand, technology, and the need to become more competitive make some skills and jobs obsolete.

The Industrial Revolution changed the nature of work and introduced unemployment as a problem for society. This is because the Industrial Revolution was accompanied by a shift to wage labour and to a division of responsibilities. Some individuals (capitalists) took on ownership of the means of production and *hired* others to work for them, paying them a wage per hour. This change in the nature of production marked a significant change in the nature of the unemployment problem.

First, it created the possibility of cyclical unemployment. With wages set at a certain level, when economic activity fell, workers' income per hour did not fall. Instead, factories would lay off or fire some workers. That isn't what happened on the farm; when a slack period occurred on the farm, the income per hour of all workers fell and few were laid off.

Second, the Industrial Revolution was accompanied by a change in how families dealt with unemployment. Whereas in preindustrial farm economies individuals or families took responsibility for their own slack periods, in a capitalist industrial society factory owners didn't take responsibility for their workers in slack periods. The pink slip (a common name for the notice workers get telling them they are laid off) and the problem of unemployment were born in the Industrial Revolution.

Without wage income, unemployed workers were in a pickle. They couldn't pay their rent, they couldn't eat, they couldn't put clothes on their backs. What was previously a family problem became a social problem. Not surprisingly, it was at that time— the late 1700s—that economists began paying more attention to the problem of unemployment.

Initially, economists and society still did not view unemployment as a social problem. It was the individual's problem. If people were unemployed, it was their own fault;

hunger, or at least the fear of hunger, and people's desire to maintain their lifestyle would drive them to find other jobs relatively quickly. Thus, early capitalism had an unemployment solution: the fear of hunger.

Unemployment as Government's Problem

As capitalism evolved, the fear-of-hunger solution to unemployment decreased in importance. The government developed social welfare programs such as employment insurance and assistance to the poor. During the Great Depression, Prime Minister R.B. Bennett introduced the Federal Employment and Social Insurance Act to assuage fears of rioting, unemployed workers. It was later found to be unconstitutional and was replaced by the Federal Unemployment Insurance Act of 1940, which assigned government the responsibility for providing assistance to the unemployed. The government had already committed itself to creating an economic climate in which just about everybody who wanted a job could have one—a situation that economists call *full employment*. It was government's responsibility to offset cyclical fluctuations and thereby prevent cyclical unemployment, and to somehow deal with structural unemployment.

Initially government regarded 3 percent unemployment as a condition of full employment. The 3 percent was made up of **frictional unemployment** (*unemployment caused by new entrants into the job market and people quitting a job just long enough to look for and find another one*) and of a few "unemployables," such as alcoholics and drug addicts, along with a certain amount of necessary structural and seasonal unemployment resulting when the structure of the economy changed. Thus, any unemployment higher than 3 percent was considered either unnecessary structural or cyclical unemployment and was now government's responsibility; frictional and necessary structural unemployment were still the individual's problem.

By the 1950s, government had given up its view that low unemployment was consistent with full employment. Since then the government has continually revised its target for unemployment, having given up the goal of attaining a zero rate of unemployment. The term we will use in this book is *target rate of unemployment*, although you should note that it is sometimes called the *natural rate of unemployment*. The **target rate of unemployment** is *the lowest sustainable rate of unemployment that policymakers believe is achievable under existing conditions*. Since the late 1980s the appropriate target rate of unemployment has been a matter of debate, but most economists place it at somewhere between 6 and 8 percent unemployment.

Why the Target Rate of Unemployment Changed

Why has the target rate of unemployment changed over time? One reason is that, in the 1970s and early 1980s, a low inflation rate, which also was a government goal, seemed to be incompatible with a low unemployment rate. We'll talk about this incompatibility later when we discuss the problem of simultaneous inflation and unemployment. A second reason is demographics: Different age groups have different unemployment rates, and as the population's age structure changes, so does the target rate of unemployment.

A third reason is our economy's changing social and institutional structure. These social and institutional changes affected the nature of the unemployment problem. For example, women's role in the workforce has changed significantly in the past 40 years. In the 1950s, the traditional view that "woman's place is in the home" remained strong. Usually only one family member—the man—had a job. If he lost his job, no money came in. In the 1970s to 1990s, more and more women entered the workforce so that today over 60 percent of all married-couple families are two-earner families. In a

As capitalism evolved, capitalist societies no longer saw the fear of hunger as an acceptable answer to unemployment.

The target rate of unemployment is the lowest sustainable rate of unemployment that policymakers believe is achievable under existing conditions.

Q.5 Why has the target rate of unemployment changed over time?

As we emphasized in Chapter 1, good economists attempt to remain neutral and objective. It isn't always easy, especially since the language we use is often biased.

This problem has proved to be a difficult one for economists in their attempt to find an alternative to the concept of full employment. An early contender was the natural rate of unemployment. Economists have often used the word *natural* to describe economic concepts. For example, they've talked about "natural" rights and a "natural" rate of interest. The problem with this usage is that what's natural to one person isn't necessarily natural to another. The word *natural* often conveys a sense of "that's the way it should be." However, in describing as "natural" the rate of unemployment that an economy can achieve, economists weren't making any value judgments about whether 7 percent unemployment

BEYOND THE TOOLS

From Full Employment to the Target Rate of Unemployment

is what should, or should not, be. They simply were saying that, given the institutions in the economy, that is what is achievable. So a number of economists objected to the use of the word *natural*.

As an alternative, a number of economists started to use the term *nonaccelerating inflation rate of unemployment (NAIRU)*, but even they agreed it was a horrendous term. So many avoided its use and shifted to the relatively neutral term *target rate of unemployment*.

The target rate of unemployment is the rate that one believes is attainable without causing accelerating inflation. It is not determined theoretically; it is determined empirically. Economists look at what seems to be achievable and is historically normal, adjust that for structural and demographic changes they believe are occurring, and come up with the target rate of unemployment.

two-earner family, if one person loses a job, the family doesn't face immediate starvation. The other person's income carries the family over.

Government institutions also changed. As programs like employment insurance and public welfare were created to reduce suffering associated with unemployment, people's responses to unemployment changed. People today are more picky about what jobs they take than they were in the 1920s and 1930s. People don't just want any job, they want a *fulfilling* job with a decent wage. As people have become choosier about jobs, a debate has raged over the extent of government's responsibility for unemployment. Many economists argue that employment insurance programs have raised the level of structural unemployment, particularly outside central regions of Canada.

Whose Responsibility Is Unemployment?

Differing views of individuals' responsibility and society's responsibility affect people's views on whether somebody is actually unemployed. Classical economists take the position that, generally, individuals should be responsible for finding jobs. They emphasize that an individual can always find *some* job at *some* wage rate, even if it's only selling apples on the street for 40 cents apiece. Given this view of individual responsibility, unemployment is impossible. If a person isn't working, that's his or her choice; the person simply isn't looking hard enough for a job. For an economist with this view, almost all unemployment is actually frictional unemployment.

Keynesian economists tend to say society owes people jobs commensurate with their training or past job experience. They further argue that the jobs should be close enough to home so people don't have to move. Given this view, frictional unemployment is only a small part of total unemployment. Structural and cyclical unemployment are far more common.

In the 1960s the average rate of unemployment in Europe was considerably below the average rate of unemployment in Canada. In the 1990s that reversed and the average

A good sense of the differing types of unemployment and the differing social views that unemployment embodies can be conveyed through three examples of unemployed individuals. As you read the following stories, ask yourself which category of unemployment each individual falls into.

Example 1   Joe is listed as unemployed and collects employment insurance. He's had various jobs in the past and was laid off from his last one. He spent a few weeks on household projects, believing he would be called back by his most recent employer—but he wasn't. He's grown to like being on his own schedule. He's living on his employment insurance (while it lasts, which usually isn't long), his savings, and money he picks up by being paid cash under the table working a few hours now and then at construction sites.

The Employment Insurance Office requires him to make at least an attempt to find work, and he's turned up a few prospects. However, some were back-breaking labouring jobs and one would have required him to move to a distant city, so he's avoiding accepting regular work. Joe knows the employment insurance payments won't last forever. When they're used up, he plans to increase his under-the-table activity. Then, when he gets good and ready, he'll really look for a job.

Example 2   Flo is a middle-aged, small-town housewife. She worked before her marriage, but when she and her husband started their family she quit her job to be a full-time housewife and mother. She never questioned her family values of hard work, independence, belief in free enterprise, and scorn of government handouts. When her youngest child left the nest, she decided to finish the college education she'd only just started when she married.

After getting her degree, she looked for a job, but found the market for middle-aged women with no recent experience to be depressed—and depressing. The employment office where she sought listings recognized her abilities and gave her a temporary job in that very office. Because she was a "temp," however, she was the first to be laid off when the government cut its spending—but she'd worked long enough to be eligible for employment insurance.

She hesitated about applying, since handouts were against her principles. But while working there she'd seen plenty of people, including her friends, applying for benefits after work histories even slimmer than hers. She decided to take the benefits. While they lasted, she found family finances on almost as sound a footing as when she was working. Although she was bringing in less money, net family income didn't suffer much since she didn't have taxes withheld nor did she have the commuting and clothing expenses of going to a daily job.

Example 3   Tom had a good job at a manufacturing plant where he'd worked up to a wage of $450 a week. Occasionally he was laid off, but only for a few weeks, and then he'd be called back. But then the plant was bought by another corporation that laid off half the workforce and put in automated equipment. Tom, an older worker with comparatively high wages, was one of the first to go, and he wasn't called back.

Tom had a wife, three children, a car payment, and a mortgage. He looked for other work but couldn't find anything paying close to what he'd been getting. Tom used up his employment insurance and his savings. He sold the house and moved his family into a trailer. Finally he heard that there were a lot of jobs in Alberta, 800 kilometres away. He moved there, found a job, and began sending money home every week. Then the Alberta economy faltered. Tom was laid off again, and his employment insurance ran out again. Relying on his $100,000 life insurance policy, he figured he was worth more to his family dead than alive, so he killed himself.

As these three examples suggest, unemployment encompasses a wide range of cases. Unemployment is anything but a one-dimensional problem, so it's not surprising that people's views of how to deal with it differ.

unemployment rate in Europe has now significantly exceeded that in Canada (in 2001 the average European unemployment rate was 8.5 percent compared to Canada's 7.2 percent). One of the reasons for this reversal is that Europe tried to create high-paying jobs, while it left a variety of taxes and social programs in place that discouraged the creation of low-paying jobs.

Canada, in contrast, actively promoted the creation of jobs of any type. The result has been a large growth of jobs in Canada, many of which are low-paying jobs. An unemployed engineer, had he been in Canada, might well have given up engineering and become a restaurant manager.

Figure 6-3 **UNEMPLOYMENT RATE SINCE 1946**

The unemployment rate has always fluctuated, with an average of about 6.7 percent since 1946. You can see that from the 1960s to the 1980s the unemployment rate seems to have trended upward. The average unemployment rate from 1980 to 2001 was about 9 percent. In 2001 the rate of unemployment in Canada was 7.2 percent.

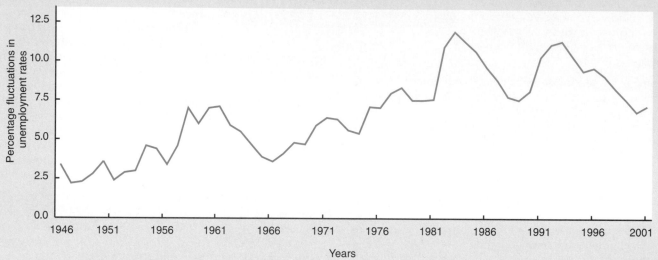

Source: Statistics Canada, *Historical Statistics of Canada*, Series D491; and CANSIM II, Table 279-0001.

How Is Unemployment Measured?

When there's debate about what the unemployment problem is, it isn't surprising that there's also a debate about how to measure it. When talking about unemployment, economists usually refer to the "unemployment rate" published by Statistics Canada. Fluctuations in the official unemployment rate since 1946 appear in Figure 6-3. In it you can see that while the rate started to rise in the 1950s, reaching 7 percent, it remained low until the 1970s, when the rate began gradually to rise again. After peaking in the early 1980s it began to descend again. In 1989 it was about 7.6 percent; then in 1991 the economy fell into recession and unemployment rates rose to over 11.4 percent in 1993. During the expansion that followed the unemployment rate returned to slightly below 7 percent in 2000 but rose to 7.2 percent in 2001.

Calculating the Unemployment Rate The Canadian unemployment rate is determined by dividing the number of unemployed individuals by the number of people in the **labour force**—*those people in an economy who are willing and able to work*—and multiplying by 100. For example, if the total unemployed stands at 1.17 million and the labour force stands at 16.25 million, the unemployment rate is:

$$\frac{1.17 \text{ million}}{16.25 \text{ million}} = 0.072 \times 100 = 7.2\%$$

> The unemployment rate is measured by dividing the number of unemployed individuals by the number of people in the labour force and multiplying by 100.

To determine the labour force, start with the total civilian population and subtract all persons incapable of working, such as inmates of institutions and people under 15 years of age. (The civilian population excludes individuals who are in the military as well as residents of Indian reserves.) From that figure subtract the number of people not in the labour force, including homemakers, students, retirees, the voluntarily idle, and the dis-

Figure 6-4 UNEMPLOYMENT/EMPLOYMENT FIGURES (IN MILLIONS)

This exhibit shows you how the unemployment rate is calculated. Notice that the labour force is not the entire population.

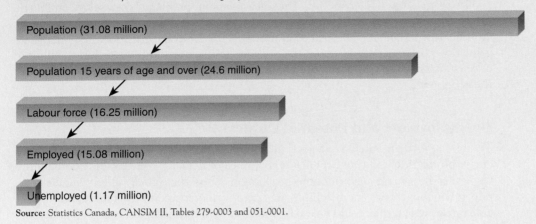

Population (31.08 million)

Population 15 years of age and over (24.6 million)

Labour force (16.25 million)

Employed (15.08 million)

Unemployed (1.17 million)

Source: Statistics Canada, CANSIM II, Tables 279-0003 and 051-0001.

abled. The result is the potential workforce, which is about 16.25 million people, or about 66 percent of the civilian population over the age of 15 (see Figure 6-4).

The civilian labour force can be divided into employed and unemployed. Statistics Canada defines people as *employed* if they work at a paid job (including part-time jobs). The definition of *employed* includes all those who were temporarily absent from their jobs that week because of illness, bad weather, vacation, labour–management dispute, or personal reasons, whether or not they were paid by their employers for the time off.

In 2001 the number of unemployed individuals was about 1.17 million. Dividing this number by the labour force (16.25 million) gives us an unemployment rate of 7.2 percent.

Q.6 During some months, the unemployment rate declines, but the number of unemployed rises. How can this happen?

How Accurate Is the Official Unemployment Rate? Statistics Canada measures unemployment using a number of assumptions that have been the source of debate. For example, should *discouraged workers*—people who do not look for a job because they feel they don't have a chance of finding one—be counted as unemployed? Some Keynesian economists believe these individuals should be considered unemployed. Moreover they question whether part-time workers who would prefer full-time work, the *underemployed*, should be classified as employed.

6.3

see page 158

The Keynesian argument is that there is such a lack of decent jobs and of affordable transportation to get to the jobs that do exist that many people become very discouraged and have simply stopped trying. Because statisticians define these people as voluntarily idle, and do not count them as unemployed, Keynesians argue that Statistics Canada undercounts unemployment significantly.

The Classical argument about unemployment is that being without a job often is voluntary. People may say they are looking for a job when they're not really looking. Many are working "off the books"; others are simply vacationing. Some Classicals contend that the way Statistics Canada measures unemployment exaggerates the number of those who are truly unemployed. A person is defined as unemployed if he or she is not employed and is actively seeking work.

To help overcome these problems, economists use supplemental measures to give them insight into the state of the labour market; these include the **labour force participation rate**, which *measures the labour force as a percentage of the total population at least*

Q.7 In what way is the very concept of unemployment dependent on the value judgments made by the individual?

15 years old, and the **employment rate**—*the number of people who are working as a percentage of the labour force*.

Despite problems, the unemployment rate statistic still gives us useful information about changes in the economy. The measurement problems themselves are little changed from year to year, so in comparing one year to another, those problems are not an issue. Keynesian and Classical economists agree that a changing unemployment rate generally tells us something about the economy, especially if interpreted in the light of other statistics. That's why the unemployment rate is used as a measure of the state of the economy.

Unemployment and Potential Output

The unemployment rate gives a good indication of how much labour is available to increase production and thus provides a good idea of how fast the economy could grow. Capital is the second major input to production. Thus, the *capacity utilization rate*—the rate at which factories and machines are operating compared to the maximum sustainable rate at which they could be used—indicates how much capital is available for economic growth.

Table 6-2 shows the unemployment rates and the capacity utilization rates for selected countries over the last 25 years. Generally Canadian economists today feel that unemployment rates of about 7 percent and capacity utilization rates between 80 and 85 percent are about as much as we should expect from the economy. To push the economy beyond that would be like driving your car 130 kilometres an hour. True, the marks on your speedometer might go up to 160 kilometres, but 130 is a more realistic top speed. Beyond 130 (assuming that's where your car is red-lined), the engine is likely to blow up (unless you have a Maserati).

Economists translate the target unemployment rate and target capacity utilization rate into the target level of potential output, or simply potential output (or *potential income*, because output creates income). **Potential output** is *the output that would materialize at the target rate of unemployment and the target rate of capacity utilization*. It is the rate of output beyond which the economy would experience accelerating inflation. Potential output grows at the secular (long-term) trend rate of 2.5 to 3.5 percent per year. When the economy is in a downturn or recession, actual output is below potential output. As you will see throughout the rest of the book, there is much debate about what

TABLE 6-2   **Unemployment and Capacity Utilization Rates for Selected Countries (percentages)**

	Capacity Utilization			Unemployment			Annual Growth in Real Output
	1975	1985	2000**	1975	1985	2000	1975–2000
Canada	83.1	82.5	85.8	6.9	10.5	6.6	2.5
United States	74.6	79.8	80.4	8.5	7.2	4.0	2.9
Japan	81.4	82.5	74.6	1.9	2.6	4.4	2.5
Germany	76.9	79.6	85.1	3.4	8.2	10.0	3.0
United Kingdom	81.9	81.1	81.8	4.6	11.2	5.7	2.2
Mexico	85.0	92.0	85.7	*	*	2.0	1.6
Republic of Korea	86.4	74.6	83.3	*	10.9	4.8	7.7

*Unavailable.

**Capacity utilization rates are for most recent year available.

Source: Organization for Economic Cooperation and Development (http://www.oecd.org) and authors' estimates for 2000.

the appropriate target rates of unemployment, capacity utilization, and potential output actually are.

To determine what effect changes in the unemployment rate will have on output we use **Okun's rule of thumb,** which states that *a 1 percentage point change in the unemployment rate will cause output to change in the opposite direction by 2 percent.* For example, if unemployment rises from 5 percent to 6 percent, total output of $1.1 trillion will fall by 2 percent, or $22 billion, to $1.078 trillion. In terms of number of workers, a 1 percent increase in the unemployment rate means about 160,000 additional people are out of work (assuming the labour force is held constant).

These figures are rough, but they give you a sense of the implications of a change. For example, say unemployment falls 0.2 percentage point, from 7 to 6.8 percent. That means about 32,000 more people have jobs and that output will be $4.4 billion higher than otherwise would have occurred if the increase holds for the entire year.

Notice we said "will be $4.4 billion higher than otherwise would have occurred" rather than simply saying "will increase by $4.4 billion." That's because generally the economy is growing as a result of increases in productivity or increases in the number of people choosing to work. Changes in either of these can cause output and employment to grow, even if there's no change in the unemployment rate. We must point this out because in the 1980s the number of people choosing to work increased substantially, significantly increasing the labour participation rate. Then, in the mid-1990s, as many large firms structurally adjusted their production methods to increase their productivity, unemployment sometimes rose even as output rose. Thus, when the labour participation rate and productivity change, an increase in unemployment doesn't necessarily mean a decrease in employment or a decrease in output.

> Okun's rule of thumb states that a 1 percentage point change in the unemployment rate will cause output in the economy to change in the opposite direction by 2.0 percent.

Microeconomic Categories of Unemployment

In the post–Second World War period, unemployment was seen primarily as cyclical unemployment, and the focus of macroeconomic policy was on how to eliminate that unemployment through a specific set of macroeconomic policies.

Understanding macroeconomic policies is important, but today it's not enough. Unemployment has many dimensions, so different types of unemployment are susceptible to different types of policies. Today's view is that you don't use a sledgehammer to pound in finishing nails, and you don't use macro policies to deal with certain types of unemployment; instead you use micro policies. To determine where microeconomic policies are appropriate as a supplement to macroeconomic policies, economists break unemployment down into a number of categories and analyze each category separately. For example, Figure 6-5 (on the next page) gives you a view of unemployment in Canada. Nearly 13 percent of people between 15 and 24 were unemployed in 2001, while only 3.3 percent of people over 65 were unemployed. Why? What do you think is the proportion of people aged 15–24 in the labour force? How about those over 65? As you can see, unemployment is particularly high among young people in Canada.

> Some microeconomic categories of unemployment are demographic unemployment and unemployment by age group.

INFLATION

Inflation is *a continual rise in the price level.* The price level is an index of all prices in the economy. Even when inflation itself isn't a problem, the fear of inflation guides macroeconomic policy. Fear of inflation prevents governments from expanding the economy and reducing unemployment. It prevents governments from using macroeconomic policies to lower interest rates. It gets some political parties booted out of office.

> Inflation is a continual rise in the price level.

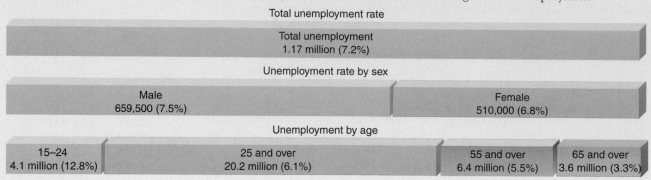

Figure 6-5   UNEMPLOYMENT BY MICROECONOMIC SUBCATEGORIES, 2001

Unemployment isn't all the same. This figure gives you a sense of some of the subcategories of unemployment.

Total unemployment rate

| Total unemployment 1.17 million (7.2%) |

Unemployment rate by sex

| Male 659,500 (7.5%) | Female 510,000 (6.8%) |

Unemployment by age

| 15–24 4.1 million (12.8%) | 25 and over 20.2 million (6.1%) | 55 and over 6.4 million (5.5%) | 65 and over 3.6 million (3.3%) |

Source: Statistics Canada, CANSIM II, Table 279-0003.

A one-time rise in the price level is not inflation. Unfortunately, it's often hard to tell if a one-time rise in the price level is going to stop, so the distinction blurs in practice, but we must understand the distinction. If the price level goes up 10 percent in a month, but then remains constant, the economy doesn't have an inflation problem. Inflation is an *ongoing rise* in the price level.

From 1800 until the Second World War the Canadian inflation rate and price level fluctuated; sometimes the price level would rise, and sometimes the price level would fall—there would be deflation. Since the Second World War the price level has nearly always risen, which means the inflation rate (the measure of the change in prices over time) has been positive, as can be seen in Figure 6-6. The rate fluctuates, but the movement of the price level has been consistently upward.

Measurement of Inflation

Since inflation is a sustained rise in the general price level, we must first determine what the general price level was at a given time by creating a **price index,** *a number that summarizes what happens to a weighted composite of prices of a selection of goods (often called a market basket of goods) over time.* An index converts prices relative to a base year. Price indexes are important. Many people lament the high cost of goods and services today. They complain, for example, that an automobile that costs $20,000 today cost only $3,000 in the "good old days." But that comparison is meaningless, because the price level has changed. Today, the average wage is more than five times what it was when cars cost only $3,000. To relate the two prices, we need a price index. There are a number of different measures of the price level. The most often used are the raw materials price index, the GDP deflator, and the consumer price index. Each has certain advantages and disadvantages.

Creating a Price Index Before introducing the official price indexes, let's work through the creation of a fictitious price index—the CSR price index—and calculate the associated inflation. We'll do so for 2001 and 2002, using 2001 as the base year. A price index is calculated by dividing the current price of a basket of goods by the base price of a basket of goods. Table 6-3 lists a market basket of goods we consume in a base

Figure 6-6   INFLATION IN CANADA SINCE 1915

Since the early 1960s the inflation rate in Canada has almost always been positive. This means that the price level has been continually rising.

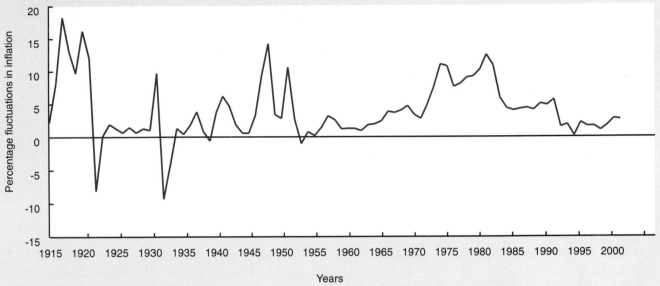

Source: Statistics Canada, CANSIM II, Table 326-0001.

year and their associated prices in 2001 and 2002. The market basket of goods is listed in column 1 and represents the quantity of each item purchased in the base year.

The price of the market basket in each year is the sum of the expenditures on each item—the quantity of each good purchased times its market price. The market basket remains the same in each year; only the prices change. The price of the market basket in 2001 is $540 and in 2002 is $675. To calculate the CSR price index, divide the price of the market basket by the price of the market basket in the base year and multiply it by 100. In this case 2001 is the base year, so the price index in 2002 is

$675/$540 × 100 = 125

To make sure you are following this example, calculate the CSR price index in 2001.

Q-8 Health care costs make up 15 percent of total expenditures. Say they rise by 10 percent, while the other components of the price index remain constant. By how much does the price index rise?

TABLE 6-3   A Simple Year-to-Year Market Basket Comparison

(1)	(2)	(3)	(4)	(5)
	Prices		**Expenditures**	
Basket of Goods	2001	2002	2001	2002
10 pairs jeans	$20.00/pr.	$25.00/pr.	$200	$250
12 flannel shirts	15.00/shirt	20.00/shirt	180	240
100 kg apples	0.80/kg	1.05/kg	80	105
80 kg oranges	1.00/kg	1.00/kg	80	80
Total expenditures			$540	$675

You may have wondered about the fixed basket of goods used to calculate our fictitious price index and the CPI. The basket of goods was fixed in the base year. But buying habits change. The further in time that fixed basket is from the current basket, the worse any fixed-basket price index is at measuring inflation. Four biases that stem from this problem are the substitution bias, the quality improvement bias, the new product bias, and the discounting bias.

- **Substitution bias.** First of all, changes in prices will change consumption patterns. In our fictitious price index example, the price of apples rose, but the price of oranges did not. It is likely that the basket of goods in 2002 included more oranges and fewer apples than in the base year basket, in which case total expenditures in 2002 would have been less and measured inflation would have been less. Any fixed-basket price index has a substitution bias because it does not take into account the fact that when the price of one good rises, consumers substitute a cheaper item.

- **Quality improvement bias.** The fixed basket of goods is assumed to accurately represent similar products in later years. For example, a car in 1982 is assumed to be the same as a car in 1992. But in 1992 many cars had airbags as a standard feature. Some of the price increase for cars reflected this quality improvement, but the CPI treated it as if it were a price increase for a comparable product sold in 1982. The CPI does not reflect quality improvements.

- **New product bias.** A fixed basket of goods leaves no room for the introduction of new products. This would not be a problem if the prices of new products changed at about the same rate as prices of other goods in the basket, but in the 1970s this was not true. For years, the CPI did not include the price of computers, whose prices were declining at a 17 percent annual rate! This resulted in the CPI overstating inflation during this period.

- **Discounting bias.** With the advent of shopping at discount stores, consumers can change their spending patterns. If prices rise, consumers have an incentive to move to factory outlet stores. The survey data on which the CPI is constructed do not take these changes in spending patterns into account, so changes in the CPI may overstate the actual rate of inflation.

These and other problems arise because of the choices we must make when constructing a price index. The choices are what to name as the base year, what products to include in the basket, the relative importance to assign each product, and how to account for changes in the quality and for the introduction of new products. In the 1990s a Bank of Canada report suggested that because of these biases, the CPI may overstate inflation by about 0.5 percentage points per year.

The answer is 100. The base year index is always 100 since you are dividing base years by the base year prices and multiplying by 100.

Inflation in 2002, then, is the percent change in the price index. This is calculated in 2002 as

$$(125/100 - 1) \times 100 = 25\%$$

But enough on price indexes in general. Let's now discuss the price indexes most commonly used when talking about inflation.

Real-World Price Indexes The **raw materials price index** *measures the prices of a number of important raw materials, such as steel.* It does not correctly measure the inflation that most consumers are interested in (people are more interested in final goods). But it does give an early indication of which way inflation will likely head since many of the prices that make it up are the prices of raw materials used as inputs in the production of consumer goods.

The total output deflator, or **GDP deflator** (gross domestic product deflator), is *an index of the price level of aggregate output, or the average price of the components in total output (or GDP), relative to a base year.* (Recently, another price index, the chain-type price index for GDP, has become more popular; it is a GDP deflator with a constantly moving base year.) GDP is a measure of the total market value of aggregate production of goods and services produced in an economy in a year. (We'll discuss the calculation of GDP in more detail in Chapter 7.) A deflator is an adjustment for "too much air." In this context, it is an adjustment for inflation—so that we know how much total output would have risen if there were no inflation.

The GDP deflator is one of the inflation indexes economists generally favour because it includes the widest number of goods. Unfortunately, since it's difficult to compute, it's published only quarterly and with a fairly substantial lag. That is, by the time the figures come out, the period the figures measure has been over for quite a while.

Published monthly, the **consumer price index (CPI)** *measures the prices of a fixed basket of consumer goods, weighted according to each component's share of an average consumer's expenditures.* It measures the price of a fixed basket of goods rather than measuring the prices of all goods. It is the index of inflation most often used in news reports about the economy and is the index most relevant to consumers. Figure 6-7 shows the relative percentages of the basket's components. As you see, shelter, transportation, and food make up the largest percentages of the CPI. To give you an idea of what effect the rise in price of a component of the CPI will have on the CPI as a whole, let's say food prices rise 10 percent in a year and all other prices remain constant. Since food is about 18 percent of the total, the CPI will rise 18% × 10% = 1.8%. The CPI and GDP deflator indexes roughly equal each other when averaged over an entire year.

In the mid-1990s some economists believed that the CPI overstated inflation by as much as 1 percentage point a year. Statistics Canada revises the representative household's basket used to construct the CPI about every 10 years in an effort to measure prices properly. However, indexes are not perfect measures of inflation (see the Knowing the Tools box).

The *GDP deflator* is an index of the price level of aggregate output or the average price of the components in GDP relative to a base year.

The *consumer price index (CPI)* is an index of inflation measuring prices of a fixed basket of consumer goods, weighted according to each component's share of an average consumer's expenditures.

| Figure 6-7 | **COMPOSITION OF CPI, 1992** |

The consumer price index is determined by looking at the prices of goods in the categories listed in this exhibit. These categories represent the rough percentages of people's expenditures.

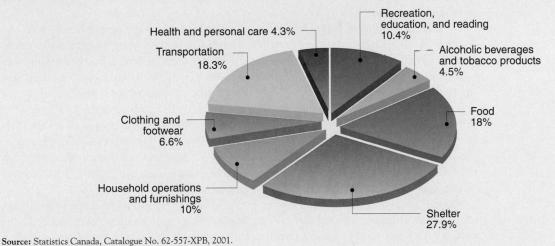

Source: Statistics Canada, Catalogue No. 62-557-XPB, 2001.

Real and Nominal Concepts

One important way in which inflation indexes are used is to separate changes in real output from changes in nominal output. Economists use the term *real* when talking about concepts that are adjusted for inflation. **Real output** is *the total amount of goods and services produced, adjusted for price-level changes*. It is the measure of output that would exist if the price level had remained constant. **Nominal output** is *the total amount of goods and services measured at current prices*. For example, say total output rises from $1.0 trillion to $1.2 trillion. Nominal output has risen by

$$\frac{\$1.2 \text{ trillion} - \$1.0 \text{ trillion}}{\$1.0 \text{ trillion}} = \frac{\$0.2 \text{ trillion}}{\$1.0 \text{ trillion}} \times 100 = 20\%$$

Let's say, however, the price index has risen 10 percent, from 100 to 110. The price index is 110. Because the price index has increased, real output (nominal output adjusted for inflation) hasn't risen by 20 percent; it has risen by less than the increase in nominal output. To determine how much less, we use a formula to adjust the nominal figures to account for inflation. This is called *deflating* the nominal figures. To deflate we divide the most recent nominal figure, $1.2 trillion, by the price index of 110 (or 1.1):

$$\text{Real output} = \frac{\text{Nominal output}}{\text{Price index}} \times 100 = \frac{\$1.2 \text{ trillion}}{1.1} = \$1.09 \text{ trillion}$$

That $1.09 trillion is the measure of output that would have existed if the price level had not changed, that is, the measure of real output. Real output has increased from $1.0 trillion to $1.09 trillion, or by $90 billion.

When you consider price indexes, you mustn't lose sight of the forest for the trees. Keep in mind the general distinction between real and nominal output. The concepts *real* and *nominal* and the process of adjusting from nominal to real by dividing the nominal amount by a price index will come up again and again. So whenever you see the word *real*, remember:

> The "real" amount is the nominal amount divided by the price index. It is the nominal amount adjusted for inflation.

Q.9 Nominal output has increased from $1.5 trillion to $1.8 trillion. The GDP deflator has risen by 15 percent. By how much has real output risen?

The "real" amount is the nominal amount divided by the price index. It is the nominal amount adjusted for inflation.

Expected and Unexpected Inflation

An important distinction to make when talking about inflation is between expected and unexpected inflation. **Expected inflation** is *inflation people expect to occur*. **Unexpected inflation** is *inflation that surprises people*.

When an individual sets a price (for goods or labour) he or she is actually setting a relative price—relative to other prices in the economy. The money price is the good's nominal price. The laws of supply and demand affect relative prices, not nominal prices.

Now let's say that everyone suddenly expects the price level to rise 10 percent. Let's also say that all individual sellers want a 0.5 percent raise in their relative price. They're not greedy; they just want a little bit more than what they're currently getting. The relative price increase people want must be tacked onto the inflation they expect. In this case, they have to raise their money price by 10.5 percent—10 percent to keep up and 0.5 percent to get ahead. Ten percent of the inflation is caused by expectations of inflation; 0.5 percent of the inflation is caused by pressures from suppliers wanting to increase profits. Thus, whether or not inflation is expected makes a big difference in individuals' behaviour.

Since prices and wages are often set for periods of two months to three years ahead, whether inflation is expected can play an important role in the inflation process. In the early 1970s people didn't expect the high inflation rates that did occur. When inflation hit, people just tried to keep up with it. By the end of the 1970s, people expected more inflation than actually occurred and raised their prices—and, in doing so, caused the inflation rate to increase.

Expectations of inflation play an important role in any ongoing inflation. They can snowball a small inflationary pressure into an accelerating large inflation. Individuals keep raising their prices because they expect inflation, and inflation keeps on growing because individuals keep raising their prices. That's why expectations of inflation are of central concern to economic policymakers.

Costs of Inflation

Inflation has costs, but not the costs that noneconomists often associate with it. Specifically, inflation doesn't make the nation poorer. True, whenever prices go up somebody (the person paying the higher price) is worse off, but the person to whom the higher price is paid is better off. The two offset each other. So inflation does not make society on average any poorer. Inflation does, however, redistribute income from people who cannot or do not raise their prices to people who can and do raise their prices. This often creates feelings of injustice about the economic system. Thus, inflation can have significant distributional or equity effects.

A second cost of inflation is its effect on the information prices convey to people. Consider an individual who laments the high cost of housing, pointing out that it has doubled in 10 years. But if inflation averaged 7 percent a year over the past 10 years, a doubling of housing prices should be expected. In fact, with 7 percent inflation, on average *all* prices double every 10 years. That means the individual's wages have probably also doubled, so he or she is no better off and no worse off than 10 years ago. The price of housing relative to other goods, which is the relevant price for making decisions, hasn't changed. When there's inflation it's hard for people to know what is and what isn't a relative price. People's minds aren't computers, so inflation reduces the amount of information that prices can convey and causes people to make choices that do not reflect relative prices.

Despite these costs, inflation is usually accepted by governments as long as it stays at a low rate. Economists become alarmed when inflationary pressures rise above and beyond expectations of inflation. In that case, expectations of higher inflation can cause inflation to build and compound itself. A 3 percent inflation becomes a 6 percent inflation, which in turn becomes a 12 percent inflation. Once inflation hits 5 percent or 6 percent, it's definitely no longer a little thing. Inflation of 10 percent or more is significant. While there is no precise definition, we may reasonably say that inflation has become **hyperinflation** *when inflation hits triple digits—100 percent or more per year.*

Canada has been either relatively lucky or wise because it has not experienced hyperinflation. Other countries, such as Brazil, Israel, and Argentina, have not been so lucky (or have not followed the same policies Canada has). These countries have frequently had hyperinflation. But even with inflation at these levels, economies have continued to operate and, in many cases, continued to do well.

In hyperinflation people try to spend their money quickly, but they still use the money. Let's say the Canadian price level is increasing 1 percent a day, which is a yearly inflation rate of about 4,000 percent.[3] Is an expected decrease in value of 1 percent per

While inflation may not make the nation poorer, it does cause income to be redistributed, and it can reduce the amount of information that prices are supposed to convey.

Q.10 True or false? Inflation makes everyone in an economy worse off because everyone is paying higher prices.

Hyperinflation is exceptionally high inflation of, say, 100 percent or more per year.

---

[3]Why about 4,000 percent and not 365 percent? Because of compounding. In the second day the increase is on the initial price level *and* the 1 percent rise in price level that occurred the first day. When you carry out this compounding for all 365 days, you get almost 4,000 percent.

day going to cause you to stop using dollars? Probably not, unless you have a good alternative. You will, however, avoid putting your money into a savings account unless that savings account somehow compensates you for the expected inflation (the expected fall in the purchasing power of the dollar), and you will try to ensure that your wage is adjusted for inflation. In hyperinflation, wages, the prices firms receive, and individual savings are all in some way adjusted for inflation. Hyperinflation leads to economic institutions with built-in expectations of inflation. For example, usually in a hyperinflation the government issues indexed bonds whose value keeps pace with inflation.

6.4

see page 158

Once these adjustments have been made, substantial inflation will not destroy an economy, but it certainly is not good for it. Such inflation tends to break down confidence in the monetary system, the economy, and the government.

CONCLUSION

This chapter has talked about growth, inflation, and unemployment. The interrelationship among these three concepts centres on trade-offs between inflation on the one hand and growth and unemployment on the other. If the government could attack inflation without worrying about unemployment or growth, it probably would have solved the problem of inflation by now. Unfortunately, when the government tries to stop inflation, it often causes a recession—increasing unemployment and slowing growth. Similarly, reducing unemployment by stimulating growth tends to increase inflation. To the degree that inflation and unemployment are opposite sides of the coin, the opportunity cost of reducing unemployment is inflation. The government must make a trade-off between low unemployment and slow growth on the one hand and inflation on the other. Opportunity costs must be faced in macro as well as in micro. The models you will learn in later chapters will help clarify the choices policymakers face.

Chapter Summary

- Economists use two frameworks to analyze macroeconomic problems. The long-run growth framework focuses on supply, while the short-run business-cycle framework focuses on demand.

- Growth is measured by the change in real gross domestic product (real GDP) and by the change in per capita real GDP. Per capita real GDP is real GDP divided by the total population.

- The secular trend growth rate of the economy is 2.5 to 3.5 percent per year. Fluctuations of real output around the secular trend growth rate are called *business cycles*.

- Phases of the business cycle include peak, trough, upturn, and downturn.

- Unemployment is calculated as the number of unemployed individuals divided by the labour force. Unemployment rises during a recession and falls during an expansion.

- The target rate of unemployment is the lowest sustainable rate of unemployment possible under existing institutions. It's associated with an economy's potential output. The lower the target rate of unemployment, the higher an economy's potential output.

- The microeconomic approach to unemployment subdivides unemployment into categories and looks at those individual components.

- A real concept is a nominal concept adjusted for inflation. Real output equals nominal output divided by the price index.

- Inflation is a continual rise in the price level. The CPI, the raw materials price index, and the GDP deflator are all price indexes used to measure inflation.

- The GDP deflator is the broadest price index. It is used to measure inflation of all goods produced in an economy. The CPI measures inflation faced by consumers. The raw materials price index tells us what is happening to producers' prices.

- Expectations of inflation can provide pressure for an inflation to continue even when other causes don't exist.

- Inflation redistributes income from people who do not raise their prices to people who do raise their prices. Inflation also reduces the information that prices convey.

Key Terms

business cycle   *(138)*

Classicals   *(138)*

consumer price index (CPI)
  (153)

cyclical unemployment
  (142)

depression   *(140)*

employment rate   *(148)*

expansion   *(140)*

expected inflation   *(154)*

frictional unemployment
  (143)

GDP deflator   *(153)*

hyperinflation   *(155)*

inflation   *(149)*

Keynesians   *(138)*

labour force   *(146)*

labour force participation
  rate   *(147)*

nominal output   *(154)*

Okun's rule of thumb
  (149)

per capita real output
  (136)

potential output   *(148)*

price index   *(150)*

raw materials price index
  (152)

real gross domestic product
  (real GDP)   *(135)*

real output   *(154)*

recession   *(140)*

structural unemployment
  (142)

target rate of unemployment
  (143)

unemployment rate   *(141)*

unexpected inflation
  (154)

Questions for Thought and Review

1. What are two ways in which long-term economic growth is measured?

2. How does the Canadian per capita growth rate compare to growth rates in other areas around the world?

3. What is the difference between real output and potential output?

4. Draw a representative business cycle, and label each of the four phases.

5. The index of leading indicators has predicted all past recessions. Nonetheless it's not especially useful for predicting recessions. Explain.

6. If unemployment fell to 1.2 percent in the Second World War, why couldn't it be reduced to 1.2 percent today?

7. Distinguish between structural unemployment and cyclical unemployment.

8. What type of unemployment is best studied within the long-run framework? What type is best studied under the short-run framework?

9. Does the unemployment rate underestimate or overestimate the unemployment problem? Explain.

10. If unemployment rises by 2 percentage points, what will likely happen to output in Canada?

11. Why are expectations central to understanding inflation?

12. Inflation, on average, makes people neither richer nor poorer. Therefore it has no cost. True or false? Explain.

13. Would you expect that inflation would generally be associated with low unemployment? Why?

Problems and Exercises

1. Statistics Canada reported that in 2000 the total labour force aged 20–24 was 1,568,900 of a possible 2,038,900 individuals. The total number of unemployed in that age group was 159,700. From this information calculate the following for 2000:
   a. Labour force participation rate.
   b. Unemployment rate.
   c. Employment rate.

2. Answer the following questions about real output, nominal output, and inflation:
   a. The price level of a basket of goods in 2002 was $64. The price level of that same basket of goods in 2003 was $68. If 2002 is the base year, what was the price index in 2003?
   b. If nominal output is $300 billion and the price index is 115, what is real output?

   c. Inflation is 5 percent; real output rises 2 percent. What would you expect to happen to nominal output?
   d. Real output rose 3 percent and nominal output rose 7 percent. What happened to inflation?

3. In H.G. Wells' *Time Machine*, a late-Victorian time traveller arrives in England in AD 802700 to find a new race of people, the Eloi, in their idleness. Their idleness is, however, supported by another race, the Morlocks, underground slaves who produce the output. If technology were such that the Elois' lifestyle could be sustained by machines, not slaves, is it a lifestyle that would be desirable? What implications does the above discussion have for unemployment?

4. In 1991, Japanese workers' average tenure with a firm was 10.9 years; in 1991 in North America the average tenure of workers was 6.7 years.

a. What are two possible explanations for these differences?

b. Which system is better?

c. In the mid-1990s Japan experienced a recession while the North American economy grew. What effect did this likely have on these ratios?

5. Assume that nominal output rises from $1.5 billion in 2004 to $1.8 billion in 2005. Assume also that the GDP deflator rises from 100 to 105.

a. What is the percentage increase in nominal output?

b. What is the percentage increase in the price index?

c. How much has real output increased?

d. What is the percentage increase in real output?

e. By how much would the price index have had to rise for real income to remain constant?

6. The table below contains information on the consumer price index and nominal GDP for Canada:

Year	Nominal GDP ($millions)	Consumer Price Index (1992=100)
1980	315245	52.4
1981	361355	58.9
1982	380793	65.3
1983	412386	69.1
1984	450731	72.1
1985	486847	75.0
1986	513805	78.1
1987	560390	81.5
1988	614530	84.8
1989	659270	89.0
1990	681657	93.3
1991	686971	98.5
1992	702393	100.0
1993	729580	101.8
1994	772827	102.0
1995	812460	104.2
1996	839064	105.8
1997	885022	107.6
1998	915865	108.6
1999	975263	110.5
2000	1056010	113.5

a. Calculate the year over year growth rate of nominal GDP and the consumer price index. Use the formula $\left(\dfrac{\text{current number}}{\text{previous number}} - 1\right) \times 100$.

b. Calculate the average growth rate in nominal GDP from 1981 to 1991. Compare this average to the average from 1992 to 2000.

c. Plot the inflation rate against the growth rate of GDP, with inflation on the vertical axis. Is inflation low when nominal growth is low? Why?

d. How much larger is nominal GDP in 2000 relative to 1980? Do you think the growth rate of real output was as large as this over this period? Why?

7. Using the data provided in the previous question, answer the following:

a. There was a recession in Canada in the early 1990s. How could there have been a recession if nominal output was growing?

b. How much higher were consumer prices in 1990 than in 1980? To buy the same bundle of goods in 1990 as in 1980, what increase in income would have been required? Why?

Web Questions

1. Use the Statistics Canada Web site (www.statcan.ca) to answer the following questions:

a. What are the current unemployment rate and inflation rate?

b. What was real output growth last year?

c. Did the leading index rise last month? What was its change from a year ago?

2. Use the Statistics Canada Web site (www.statcan.ca) to answer the following questions:

a. Graph quarterly real GDP since 1980. Mark a peak and a trough of a business cycle.

b. What phase of the business cycle is the economy currently in?

c. For how many quarters has the economy been in this phase?

d. How long ago was the last recession?

3. Using data at the Statistics Canada Web site (www.statcan.ca) as well as information at the OECD Web site (www.oecd.org), answer the following:

a. What was Canadian unemployment last year? What was it in France? In Germany?

b. Compare the participation rates in Canada and Spain.

c. Is the Canadian labour force similar in size to that in the United Kingdom? Are their unemployment rates similar?

4. Use information at the IMF Web site (www.imf.org) to find recent inflation rates for Brazil, Israel, and Argentina. Are these nations experiencing hyperinflation now?

Answers to Margin Questions

1. This is both a long-run and a short-run issue. It is a short-run issue because the Japanese economy was in a severe recession and aggregate expenditures had declined. It is a long-run issue because the recession put in motion institutional changes that will make it easier for Japanese firms to lay off workers so that the average unemployment rate may be higher during times of expansion too. *(135)*

2. To calculate per capita output, divide real output ($1.1 trillion) by the total population (31 million). This equals $35,484. *(136)*

3. True. A recession is a decline in real output that persists for more than two consecutive quarters of a year. Output must peak just before it begins declining. *(140)*

4. Three leading indicators are the average workweek, new orders for durable goods, and changes in the money supply. There are others. *(141)*

5. The target rate of unemployment changed over time because (1) low inflation was incompatible with what people thought was the target rate of unemployment, and (2) demographics—the age structure of the population—changed, and people of different ages have different rates of unemployment. *(143)*

6. The unemployment rate is the number of unemployed divided by the labour force. The unemployment rate can fall while the number of unemployed rises if the labour force rises by a proportionately greater amount than the rise in the number of unemployed. *(147)*

7. Unemployment is a hypothetical concept, and what unemployment means is dependent on a value judgment as to what types of possibilities society owes individuals. *(147)*

8. The price index will rise by $0.15 \times 0.1 = 0.015 = 1.5\%$. *(151)*

9. Real output equals the nominal amount divided by the price index. Since the price index has risen by 15%, real output equals $1.565 trillion ($1.8 trillion divided by 1.15). Real output has risen by $65 billion. *(154)*

10. False. Inflation does not make everyone worse off because, although some people are paying higher prices, others are receiving higher prices. *(155)*

APPENDIX A

Nonmainstream Approaches to Macro

An introductory book necessarily focuses on mainstream views, leaving out many of the other views of economists. But you should be aware that there are many more views of macroeconomics out there than those of the Classicals and Keynesians. Not only are there many subdivisions of Classicals and Keynesians, but many economists don't fit into either group. They're called nonmainstream or heterodox economists.

A characteristic of nonmainstream, or heterodox, economists is that they are far more open to discuss major institutional changes than are mainstream economists. More specifically, a **heterodox economist,** or nonmainstream economist, is *one who doesn't accept the basic underlying model used by a majority of economists as the most useful model for analyzing the economy.* Economists who do accept that model are called **mainstream economists.**

In this appendix we will briefly introduce four heterodox macroeconomists' approaches to give you a sense of how their analyses differ from the mainstream analysis presented in this book. The four heterodox approaches are Austrian, Post-Keynesian, Institutionalist, and Radical.

AUSTRIANS

Austrian economists are *economists who believe in the liberty of all individuals first and social goals second.* They oppose state intrusion into private property and private activities. They are not all economists from Austria; rather, they are economists from anywhere who follow the ideas of Ludwig von Mises and Friedrich von Hayek, two economists who were from Austria. Austrian economists are sometimes classified as conservative, but they are more appropriately classified as **libertarians,** who *believe in liberty of individuals first and in other social goals second.* Consistent with their views, they are often willing to support what are sometimes considered radical ideas, such as legalizing addictive drugs or eliminating our current monetary system—ideas that conservative economists would oppose.

In macroeconomics, Austrian economists emphasize the uncertainty in the economy and the inability of a government controlled by self-interested politicians to undertake socially beneficial policy. Well-known Austrian macroeconomists include Murray Rothbard, Peter Boettke, and Mario Rizzo.

One proposal of Austrian economists will give you a flavour of their approach. That proposal is to eliminate the central bank and to establish a **free market in money**—*a policy that would leave people free to use any money they want, and would significantly reduce banking regulation.* In a sense, their proposal carries the Classical argument in favour of laissez-faire to its logical conclusions. Why should the government have a monopoly of the money supply? Why shouldn't people be free to use whatever money they desire, denominated in whatever unit they want? Why don't we rely upon competition to prevent inflation? Why don't we have a free market in money?

A sub-group of Austrian economists is *public choice* economists. They use the mainstream supply and demand approach, but apply it much more broadly than do mainstream economists. Specifically, they see government decisions as reflecting economic forces rather than attempts by government to do good. Well-known public choice economists include Gordon Tullock, James Buchanan, and Robert Tollison.

POST-KEYNESIANS

Post-Keynesian macroeconomists are *economists who believe that uncertainty is a central issue in macroeconomics.* They follow Keynes's approach more so than do mainstream economists. They agree with Austrians about the importance of uncertainty in understanding the macro economy, but their policy response to that uncertainty is not to have government get out of the macro economy; it is for the government to take a larger role in guiding the economy.

One of their policy proposals that gives you a flavour of their approach is **tax-based incomes policies**—*policies in which the government tries to directly affect the nominal wage- and price-setting institutions.* Under a tax-based incomes policy, any firm raising its wage or price would be subject to a tax, and any firm lowering its wage or price would get a subsidy. Such a plan, they argue, would reduce the upward pressure on the nominal price level, and reduce the rate of unemployment necessary to hold down inflation.

Well-known Post-Keynesian economists include Paul Davidson, Barkley Rosser, and John Cornwall.

INSTITUTIONALISTS

Institutionalist economists are *economists who argue that any economic analysis must involve specific considerations of institutions.* Institutionalists have a long history in economics; their lineage goes back to the early 1930s and the writings of Thorstein Veblen, J.M. Clarke, and John R. Commons. Institutionalists were early supporters of welfare capitalism, and they helped set up many of the institutions of welfare capitalism (such as social insurance) we now take for granted. Institutionalists are very close to Post-Keynesians in their approach to macroeconomics, but they give stronger emphasis to the role of institutions, and to the role of government in establishing new institutions, than do Post-Keynesians.

You can get a sense of their policy approach from one of the policies many Institutionalists support: **indicative planning**—*a macroeconomic policy in which the government sets up an overall plan for various industries and selectively directs credit to certain industries.* Thus for Institutionalists political forces direct the invisible hand. Well-known Institutionalists include James Peach, Ronnie Phillips, and Anne Mayhew.

RADICALS

Radical economists are *economists who believe substantial equality-preferring institutional changes should be implemented to our economic system.* Radical economists evolved out of Marxian economics. Compared to mainstream economists, Radicals are far more willing to consider major institutional changes in our macro economy. They focus on the lack of equity in our current economic system, and their political discussions focus on institutional changes that might bring about a more equitable system. Specifically, they see the current economic system as one in which a few people—capitalists and high-level managers—benefit enormously, while others—minority groups such as African-Americans and Hispanics—are left out, without jobs. To incorporate such issues, Radical economists often use a class-oriented analysis and are much more willing to talk about social conflict and tensions in our society than are mainstream economists.

Compared to mainstream economists, Radical economists' analysis focuses much more on distributional fights between capitalists and workers and their different savings propensities. According to one important branch of radical theory, when profits are high, because capitalists save a large portion of their income, aggregate demand will be too low, and the economy goes into a recession; then government must run a deficit to bail out the economy. Mainstream economists agree that such distributional effects exist, but they consider them too small to worry about. Mainstream economists focus on fluctuations in business investment and consumers' spending decisions, not on differences in people's consumption.

Policy proposals some Radicals favour and that give you a sense of their approach are policies to establish worker cooperatives to replace the corporation. Radicals argue that such worker cooperatives would see that the income of the firm was more equitably allocated. Well-known Radical economists include Samuel Bowles, Herbert Gintis, and Howard Sherman.

CONSISTENCY OF THE VARIOUS APPROACHES

A characteristic of almost all heterodox economists of all types is that their analyses tend to be less formal than mainstream analysis. *Less formal* doesn't mean better or worse. There are advantages and disadvantages to formality, but *less formal* does mean that there's more potential for ambiguity in interpretation. It's easy to say whether the logic in a formal model is right or wrong. It's much harder to say whether the logic in an informal model is right or wrong because it's often hard to see precisely what the logic is. The advantage of an informal model is that it can

include many more variables and can be made more realistic, so you can discuss real-world problems more easily with that model. Nonmainstream economists often want to talk about the real world, which is why they use informal models.

Often, after we discuss the mainstream and nonmainstream approaches, some student asks which is right. We respond with a story told by a former colleague, Abba Lerner; the story goes as follows:

"But look," the rabbi's wife remonstrated, "when one party to the dispute presented their case to you, you said, 'You are quite right,' and then when the other party presented their case you again said, 'You are quite right.' Surely they cannot both be right?" To which the rabbi answered, "My dear, you are quite right!"

The moral of the story is that there's nothing necessarily inconsistent among mainstream and heterodox economists' approaches. They are simply different ways of looking at the same event. Which approach is most useful depends on what issues and events you are analyzing. The class analysis used by radicals is often more appropriate to developing countries than it is to Canada, and, in analyzing developing countries, many mainstream economists also include class fights in their approach. Similarly, Austrian analysis provides more insight into the role of the entrepreneur and individual in the economy than does mainstream analysis, while Post-Keynesian and Institutionalist analyses are useful when considering major institutional changes.

The distinctions between nonmainstream and mainstream economists can be overdone. One economist may well fall into two or three different groupings and use a combination of various analyses.

Key Terms

Austrian economists *(159)*

free market in money *(160)*

heterodox economists *(159)*

indicative planning *(160)*

Institutionalist economists *(160)*

libertarian *(159)*

mainstream economists *(159)*

Post-Keynesian macroeconomists *(160)*

Radical economists *(160)*

tax-based incomes policy *(160)*

National Income Accounting

7

After reading this chapter, you should be able to:

- State why national income accounting is important.

- Define GDP and calculate it in a simple example, avoiding double counting.

- Explain why GDP can be calculated using either the income approach or the expenditures approach.

- List the four expenditure components of GDP.

- Distinguish between real GDP and nominal GDP.

- State some limitations of national income accounting.

- Describe the shortcomings of using GDP to compare standards of living among countries.

> *The government is very keen on amassing statistics . . . They collect them, add them, raise them to the nth power, take the cube root and prepare wonderful diagrams. But you must never forget that every one of these figures comes in the first instance from the village watchman, who just puts down what he damn pleases.*

> Sir Josiah Stamp (head of Britain's revenue department in the late 19th century)

Before you can talk about macroeconomics in depth, you need to be introduced to some terminology used in macroeconomics. That terminology can be divided into two parts. The first part deals with the macroeconomic statistics you are likely to see in the newspaper—GDP and its components. The second part discusses problems of using

GDP figures. Among other things it distinguishes between real and nominal (or money) concepts, which are used to differentiate and compare goods and services over time. These concepts play a central role in interpreting the movement in components of the national income accounts.

NATIONAL INCOME ACCOUNTING

In the 1930s, it was impossible for macroeconomics to exist in the form we know it today because many aggregate concepts we now take for granted either had not yet been formulated or were so poorly formulated that it was useless to talk rigorously about them. This lack of aggregate terminology was consistent with the Classical economists' lack of interest in the aggregate approach to studying the economy in the 1930s; they preferred to focus on microeconomics.

With the advent of Keynesian macroeconomics in the mid-1930s, development of a terminology to describe macroeconomic aggregates became crucial. Measurement is a necessary step toward rigour. A group of Keynesian economists set out to develop an aggregate terminology and to measure the aggregate concepts they defined so that people would have concrete terms to use when talking about macroeconomic problems. Their work (for which two of them, Simon Kuznets and Richard Stone, received the Nobel Prize) is called **national income accounting**—*a set of rules and definitions for measuring economic activity in the aggregate economy*—*that is, in the economy as a whole*.

National income accounting provides a way of measuring total, or aggregate, production. In national income accounting, aggregate economic production is broken down into subaggregates (such as consumption, investment, and personal income); national income accounting defines the relationship among these subaggregates. In short, national income accounting enables us to measure and analyze how much the nation is producing and consuming.

National income accounting enables us to measure and analyze how much a nation is producing and consuming.

Measuring Total Economic Output of Goods and Services

The previous chapter introduced economists' primary measure of domestic output: real gross domestic product (real GDP). **Gross domestic product (GDP)** is *the total market value of all final goods and services produced in an economy in a one-year period*. GDP is probably the single most-used economic measure. When economists, journalists, and other analysts talk about the economy, they continually discuss GDP, how much it has increased or decreased, and what it's likely to do.

Gross domestic product (GDP) is the aggregate final output of residents and businesses in an economy in a one-year period.

Whereas gross domestic product measures the economic activity that occurs within a country, the economic activity of the citizens and businesses of a country is measured by **gross national product (GNP)**—*the aggregate final output of citizens and businesses of an economy in a one-year period*. So the economic activity of Canadian citizens working abroad is counted in Canadian GNP but isn't counted in Canadian GDP. Similarly for the foreign economic activity of Canadian companies. However, the income of an American or German person or business working in Canada isn't counted in Canadian GNP but is counted in Canadian GDP. Thus, GDP describes the economic output within the physical borders of a country while GNP describes the economic output produced by the citizens of a country, regardless of where they are located. To move from GDP to GNP we must add *net foreign factor income* to GDP. **Net foreign factor income** is defined as *the income from foreign domestic factor sources minus foreign factor income earned domestically*. Put another way, we must add the foreign income of our citizens and subtract the income of residents who are not citizens.

GDP is output produced within a country's borders; GNP is output produced by a country's citizens.

Q.1 Which is higher: Kuwait's GDP or its GNP? Why?

For many countries there's a significant difference between GNP and GDP. For example, consider Kuwait. Its citizens have significant foreign income—income that far exceeds the income of the foreigners in Kuwait. This means that Kuwait's GNP (the income of its citizens) far exceeds its GDP (the income of its residents). For Canada, however, foreign output of Canadian businesses and people is much smaller than the output of foreign businesses and people within Canada. Kuwait's net foreign factor income has been large and positive, while that of Canada has been negative. This chapter focuses on GDP, since it has been the primary measure presented in government statistics since 1986.

Calculating GDP

7.1

see page 184

Aggregate final output (GDP) consists of millions of different services and products: apples, oranges, computers, haircuts, financial advice, and so on. To arrive at total output, somehow we've got to add them all together into a composite measure. Say we produced 7 oranges plus 6 apples plus 12 computers. We have not produced 25 comapplorgs. You can't add apples and oranges and computers. You can only add like things (things that are measured in the same units). For example, 2 apples + 4 apples = 6 apples. If we want to add unlike things, we must convert them into like things. We do that by multiplying each good by its *price*. Economists call this *weighting the importance of each good by its price*. For example, if you have 4 pigs and 4 horses and you price pigs at $200 each and horses at $400 each, the horses are weighted as being twice as important as the pigs.

Multiplying the quantity of each good by its market price changes the terms in which we discuss each good from a quantity of a specific product to a *value* measure of that good. For example, when we multiply 6 apples by their price, 25 cents each, we get $1.50; $1.50 is a value measure. Once all goods are expressed in that value measure, they can be added together.

Take the example of 7 oranges and 6 apples. (For simplicity let's forget the computers, haircuts, and financial advice.) If the oranges cost 50 cents each, their total value is $3.50; if the apples cost 25 cents each, their total value is $1.50. Their values are expressed in identical measures, so we can add them together. When we do so, we don't get 13 orples; we get $5 worth of apples and oranges.

If we follow that same procedure with all the final goods and services produced in the economy in the entire year, multiplying the quantity produced by the market price per unit, we have all the economy's outputs expressed in units of value. If we then add up all these units of value, we have that year's gross domestic product.

There are two important aspects to remember about GDP. First, GDP represents a flow (an amount per year), not a stock (an amount at a particular moment of time). Second, GDP refers to the market value of *final* output. Let's consider these statements separately.

Two important aspects to remember about GDP are:

1. GDP represents a flow.
2. GDP represents the market value of final output.

GDP Is a Flow Concept In economics it's important to distinguish between flows and stocks. Say a student just out of high school tells you she earns $8,000. You'd probably think, "Wow! She's got a low-paying job!" That's because you implicitly assume she means $8,000 per year. If you later learned that she earns $8,000 per week, you'd quickly change your mind. The confusion occurred because how much you earn is a *flow* concept; it has meaning only when a time period is associated with it: so much per week, per month, per year. A *stock* concept is the amount of something at a given point in time. No time interval is associated with it. Your weight is a stock concept. You weigh 75 kilograms; you don't weigh 75 kilograms per week.

GDP is a flow concept, the amount of total final output a country produces per year. The *per year* is often left unstated, but it is important to keep in your mind that it's es-

Figure 7-1 **CANADIAN FINANCIAL FLOWS ($MILLIONS)**

Canada's net wealth has increased enormously over the past 40 years.

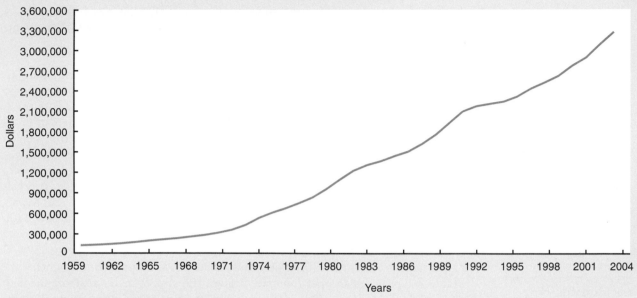

Source: Statistics Canada, CANSIM II, Table 378-0004.

sential. GDP is usually reported quarterly or every three months, but it is reported on an *annualized basis*, meaning Statistics Canada, which compiles GDP figures, uses quarterly figures to estimate total output for the whole year.

The store of wealth, in contrast, is a stock concept. The stock equivalent to national income accounts is the **national balance sheet**—*a balance sheet of an economy's stock of assets and liabilities.* Figure 7-1 shows that Canadian net wealth has risen 25-fold over the last 40 years. Remember that these are stock measures; they exist at a moment in time. For example, on December 31, 2000, the accounting date for these accounts, Canadian net wealth was $3.26 trillion. That's $106,000 per person in Canada.

Q-2 How does the national balance sheet differ from national income accounts?

GDP Measures Final Output As a student in his first economics class, one of us was asked how to calculate GDP. He said, "Add up the value of the goods and services produced by all the companies in the country to arrive at GDP." He was wrong (which is why he remembers it). Many goods produced by one firm are sold to other firms, which use those goods to make other goods. GDP doesn't measure total transactions in an economy; it measures **final output**—*goods and services purchased for final use.* When one firm sells products to another firm for use in production of yet another good, the first firm's products aren't considered final output. They're **intermediate products**—*products used as input in the production of some other product.* To count intermediate goods as well as final goods as part of GDP would be to double-count them. An example of an intermediate good would be wheat sold to a cereal company. If we counted both the wheat (the intermediate good) and the cereal (the final good) made from that wheat, the wheat would be double-counted. Double counting would significantly overestimate final output.

If we did not eliminate intermediate goods, a change in organization would look like a change in output. Say a firm that produced steel merged with a firm that produced cars. Both together then produce exactly what each did separately before the merger. Final output hasn't changed, nor has intermediate output. The only difference is that the intermediate output of steel is now internal to the firm. Using only each firm's sales of goods to final consumers (and not sales to other firms) as the measure of GDP prevents mere changes in organization from affecting the measure of output.

Two Ways of Eliminating Intermediate Goods There are two ways to eliminate intermediate goods from the measure of GDP. One is to calculate only final sales. To do so, firms would have to separate goods they sold to consumers from intermediate goods used to produce other goods. For example, each firm would report how much of its product it sold to consumers and how much it sold to other producers for use that year in production of other goods; we would eliminate the latter to exclude double counting.

A second way to eliminate double counting is to follow the value added approach. **Value added** is *the increase in value that a firm contributes to a product or service.* It is calculated by subtracting intermediate goods (the cost of materials that a firm uses to produce a good or service) from the value of its sales. For instance, if a firm buys $100 worth of thread and $10,000 worth of cloth and uses them in making a thousand pairs of jeans that are sold for $20,000, the firm's value added is not $20,000; it is $9,900 ($20,000 in sales minus the $10,100 in intermediate goods that the firm bought).

To avoid double counting, you must eliminate intermediate goods, either by calculating only final output (expenditures approach), or by calculating only final income (income approach) by using the value added approach.

For all manufactured goods that go through various and extensive stages of production, the final market value of the goods is equivalent to the sum of the values added at each stage of the production process.

Table 7-1 provides another example. It gives the cost of materials (intermediate goods) and the value of sales in the following scenario: Say we want to measure the contribution to GDP made by a vendor who sells 200 ice cream cones at $2.50 each for total sales of $500. The vendor bought his cones and ice cream at a cost of $400 from an intermediary, who in turn paid the cone factory and ice cream maker a total of $250. The farmer who sold the cream to the factory got $100. Adding up all these transactions, we get $1,250, but that includes intermediate goods. Either by counting only the final value of the vendor's sales, $500, or by adding the value added at each stage of production (column III), we eliminate intermediate sales and arrive at the vendor's contribution to GDP of $500.

Value added is calculated by subtracting the cost of materials from the value of sales at each stage of production. The aggregate value added at each stage of production is, by definition, precisely equal to the value of final sales, since it excludes all intermediate products. In Table 7-1, the equality of the value added approach and the final sales approach can be seen by comparing the vendor's final sales of $500 (row 4, column II) with the $500 value added (row 5, column III).

TABLE 7-1   Value Added Approach Eliminates Double Counting

Participants	I Cost of Materials	II Value of Sales	III Value Added	Row
Farmer	$ 0	$ 100	$100	1
Cone factory and ice cream maker	100	250	150	2
Intermediary (final sales)	250	400	150	3
Vendor	400	500	100	4
Totals	$750	$1,250	$500	5

Calculating GDP: Some Examples To make sure you understand what value added is and what makes up GDP, let's consider some sample transactions and determine what value they add and whether they should be included in GDP. Let's first consider secondhand sales: When you sell your two-year-old car, how much value has been added? The answer is none. The sale involves no current output, so there's no value added. If, however, you sold the car to a used-car dealer for $2,000 and he or she resold it for $2,500, $500 of value has been added—the used-car dealer's efforts transferred the car from someone who didn't want it to someone who did. We point this out to remind you that GDP is not only a measure of the production of goods; it is a measure of the production of goods *and services*.

Now let's consider a financial transaction. Say you sell a bond (with a face value of $1,000) that you bought last year. You sell it for $1,200 and pay $100 commission to the dealer through whom you sell it. What value is added to final output? You might be tempted to say that $200 of value has been added, since the value of the bond has increased by $200. GDP, however, refers only to value that is added as the result of production or services, not to changes in the values of financial assets. Therefore, the price at which you buy or sell the bond is irrelevant to the question at hand. The only value that is added by the sale is the transfer of that bond from someone who doesn't want it to someone who does. Thus, the only value added as a result of economic activity is the dealer's commission, $100. The remaining $1,100 (the $1,200 you got from the bond minus the $100 commission you paid) is a transfer of an asset from one individual to another but such transfers do not enter into GDP calculations. Only production of goods and services enters into GDP.

Let's consider a different type of financial transaction: The government pays an individual pension benefits. What value is added? Clearly no production has taken place, but money has been transferred. As in the case of the bond, only the cost of transferring it—not the amount that gets transferred—is included in GDP. This is accomplished by including in GDP government expenditures on goods and services, but not the value of government transfer payments. Thus, pension payments, welfare payments, and employment insurance benefits do not enter into calculations of GDP. That's why the federal government could have a $270 billion budget but only $220 billion ($270 billion minus $50 billion of transfer payments) would be included in GDP.

Finally, let's consider the work of a housespouse. (See the Beyond the Tools box for further discussion of this issue.) How much value does it add to economic activity in a year? Clearly if the housespouse is any good at what he or she does, a lot of value is added. Taking care of the house and children is hard work. Estimates of the yearly value of a housespouse's services often range from $25,000 to $40,000. Even though much value is added and hence, in principle, housespouse services should be part of GDP, by convention a housespouse contributes nothing to GDP. GDP measures only *market activities*; since housespouses are not paid, their value added is not included in GDP. This leads to some problems in measurement. For example, suppose a woman divorces her housespouse and then hires him to continue cleaning her house for $20,000 per year. Then he will be contributing $20,000 value added. That, since it is a market transaction, is included in GDP.

The housespouse example shows that the GDP measure has some problems. There are other areas in which it also has problems, but these are best left for intermediate courses. What's important for an introductory economics student to remember is that numerous decisions about how to handle various types of transactions had to be made to get a workable measure. Overall, the terminology of national income accounting is a model of consistency. It focuses on measuring final market output for the entire economy.

Q.3 If a used-car dealer buys a car for $2,000 and resells it for $2,500, how much has been added to GDP?

Mowing your lawn and painting your fence are economic activities, but because there is no exchange of money for these activities they are not included in the measure of GDP.

Q.4 How can the government have a $270 billion budget but only have $220 billion of that included in GDP?

BEYOND THE TOOLS

Is GDP Biased against Women?

Although in the example in the book the housespouse is a man, the reality is that most housespouses are women. The fact that GDP doesn't include the work of housespouses is seen, by some, as a type of discrimination against women who work at home since their work is not counted as part of the domestic product. One answer for why it is not counted is that housework does not involve a market transaction and hence cannot be measured. That makes some sense, but why can't the value of housework be estimated?

The answer is that it can be estimated, and our suspicion is that not including housespouses' services in GDP does represent the latent discrimination against women that was built into the culture in the 1930s. That latent dis-

crimination against women was so deep that it wasn't even noticed.

In thinking about whether GDP is biased against women it is important to remember that the concepts we use are culturally determined and, over time, as cultural views change, the concepts can no longer match our changed views. There is no escaping the fact that language is value-loaded. But so, too, is our attempt to point out the values in language. There are many other ways in which GDP makes arbitrary choices and discriminates against groups. The major discussion of the fact that latent discrimination against women was embodied in GDP accounting itself reflects our current values, just as not including housespouses' work reflected earlier values.

TWO METHODS OF CALCULATING GDP

GDP can be calculated in two ways: the expenditures method and the factor incomes method. This is because of the national income accounting identity.

The National Income Accounting Identity

National income accounting is a form of accounting. Accounting is a way of keeping track of things. It is based on certain identities; for a firm, cost plus profit equals revenues because cost plus profit is identical to revenues. National income accounting is no different. It too is based on an identity. By definition, whenever a good or service (output) is produced, somebody receives an income for producing it. The equality of output and income is an accounting identity in the national income accounts. The identity can be seen in Figure 7-2, which illustrates the circular flow of income in an economy.[1]

Figure 7-2 shows the overall flows of income and expenditures in the economy. The top half of the flows (flow 1) shows the income households receive for supplying their factor services. The bottom half shows the outflow of expenditures individuals make to firms for the goods and services they buy. The two sides of the flow suggest that there might be two approaches to calculating GDP, and there are; there is the *expenditures approach* and the *factor incomes approach*. In the expenditures approach, we look at the bottom flow. In the income approach, we look at the top flow.

The Expenditures Approach

$GDP = C + I + G + (X - IM)$ is an accounting identity because it is defined as true.

The bottom half of Figure 7-2 gives us a picture (flows 2–5) of the components of expenditures. Specifically, gross domestic product is equal to the sum of four expenditure categories: consumption (C), investment (I), government expenditures (G), and net

---

[1]An *identity* is a statement of equality that's true by definition. In algebra, an identity is sometimes written as a triple equal sign ($\equiv$). It is more equal than simply equal.

Figure 7-2   THE CIRCULAR FLOW

One of the most important insights about the aggregate economy is that it is a circular flow in which output and input are interrelated. Households' expenditures (consumption and saving) are firms' income; firms' expenditures (wages, rent, etc.) are households' income.

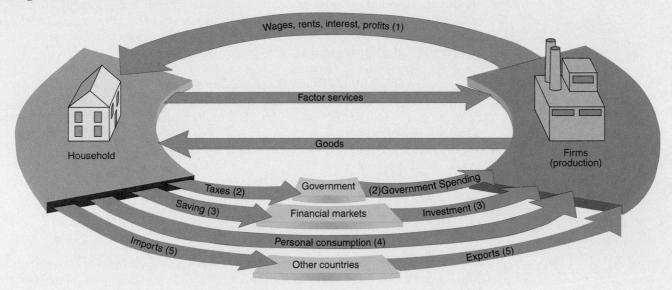

exports $(X - IM)$. A shorthand way of saying this is: GDP = $C + I + G + (X - IM)$. Let's consider each of these categories in relation to the flows in Figure 7-2.

Consumption When individuals receive income, they can either spend it on domestic goods, save it, pay taxes, or spend it on foreign goods. These four alternatives are the channels through which income is brought back into the spending stream. The largest and most important of the flows is **personal consumption expenditures**—*payments by households for goods and services* (flow 4). It is also the most obvious way in which income received is returned to firms. The other three flows are slightly more complicated.

Investment The saving/investment flow through the financial sector (flow 3) is the portion of income that individuals save. This money leaves the spending stream and goes into financial markets. If the financial markets are working properly, they translate that saving back into the spending flow by lending it to individuals who want to spend. *Business spending on equipment, structures, and inventories and household spending on new owner-occupied housing* are counted as part of **gross private investment.**

Housing, tractors, steel mills, and wine barrels are examples of gross private investment. Thus, when economists speak of investment they don't mean the kind of activity taking place when individuals buy stocks or bonds—economists consider that saving, not investing.

Sooner or later, assets such as plants and equipment wear out or become technologically obsolete. Economists call this wearing out process **depreciation**—*the decrease in an asset's value.* Depreciation is part of the cost of producing a good; it is the amount by which plants and equipment decrease in value as they grow older. Much of each year's private investment involves expenditures to replace assets that have worn out. For

This 17th-century engraving "The Money Lender" shows that careful bookkeeping and accounting have been around for a long time.

example, as you drive your car, it wears out. A car with 80,000 kilometres on it is worth less than the same type of car with only 1,000 kilometres on it. The difference in value is attributed to depreciation.

To differentiate between total or gross private domestic investment and the new investment that's above and beyond replacement investment, economists use the term **net private investment**—*gross private domestic investment minus depreciation*. In 2001, gross investment was $188.3 billion and depreciation was $142.5 billion, so net investment was $45.8 billion. Economists pay close attention to net private investment because it gives an estimate of the increase in the country's productive capacity.

Q.5 What are the four components of expenditures in national income?

Government Expenditures Let's next consider the taxes/transfer flow through government (flow 2). When individuals pay taxes, those taxes are either spent by government on goods and services or are returned to individuals in the form of transfer payments. *Government payments for goods and services and investment in equipment and structures* are referred to as **government expenditures.** The transfer payments are spent and included in consumption or saved and channelled to investment. Notice also that there is a connection drawn between the government and financial markets. That's there because if the amount government takes in does not match the amount government spends (i.e., if it runs a deficit), it must borrow from financial markets to make up the difference.

Net Exports Finally, individuals' spending on foreign goods escapes the system and does not add to domestic production. Spending on foreign goods, imports, is subtracted from total expenditures. That flow out is offset by a flow in—foreign demand for Canadian goods; that is, Canadian exports (flow 5). Exports are added in to total expenditures. Usually these flows are combined and we talk about **net exports**—*exports minus imports*.

All expenditures fall into one or another of these four divisions—consumption, investment, government spending, or net exports—so by adding up these four categories, we get total expenditures on Canadian goods and services minus Canadian residents' expenditures on foreign goods. By definition, in national income accounting, those total expenditures on Canadian goods and services equal (with some adjustments for taxes and such) the total amount of production of goods and services (GDP). Table 7-2 gives the breakdown for GDP of selected countries. Notice that personal consumption expenditures is the largest component of expenditures in all countries and that there is a rough similarity of the other components in percentage terms.

GDP and NDP In the discussion of investment, we differentiated gross investment from net investment. Gross investment minus depreciation equals net investment. Economists have created another aggregate term, *net domestic product*, to reflect the adjustment to investment because of depreciation. **Net domestic product (NDP)** is *the sum of consumption expenditures, government expenditures, net foreign expenditures, and investment less depreciation*. Thus,

$$GDP = C + I + G + (X - IM)$$

$$NDP = [C + I + G + (X - IM)] - \text{Depreciation}$$

NDP takes depreciation into account, and depreciation is a cost of producing goods; so NDP is actually preferable to GDP as the expression of a country's domestic output. However, measuring true depreciation (the actual decrease in an asset's value) is difficult because asset values fluctuate. In fact, it's so difficult that in the real world accountants don't try to measure true depreciation, but instead use a number of conventional rules of

TABLE 7-2   **Expenditure Breakdown of GDP for Selected Countries**

Country	Nominal GDP (US$ in billions)	Personal Consumption (% of GDP)	Gross Private Investment (% of GDP)	Government Expenditures (% of GDP)	Exports (% of GDP)	Imports (−% of GDP)
Canada	750	58%	18%	19%	42%	-37%
United States	10,198	69	16	18	10	-13
Brazil	760	64	21	16	10	-11
Germany	2,081	58	21	19	27	-25
Japan	4,395	60	29	10	11	-10
Pakistan	60	78	15	11	15	-19
Tunisia	21	63	28	12	42	-45
Tanzania	9	72	18	13	20	-23

Source: *World Development Report 2000/2001,* The World Bank; *Survey of Current Business,* Bureau of Economic Analysis; *OECD Main Economic Indicators,* OECD. (Data for Canada and the United States are for 2001; data for other countries are for 1999.)

thumb. In recognition of this reality, economists call the adjustment made to GDP to arrive at NDP the *capital consumption allowance* rather than *depreciation.* Since estimating depreciation is difficult, GDP rather than NDP is generally used in discussions.

The Factor Incomes Approach

Now look back at the top portion of Figure 7-2. The factor incomes approach to measuring GDP adds up payments by firms to households, called *factor payments,* to arrive at **national income (NI),** or *total income earned by citizens and businesses of a country.* Firms make payments to households for supplying their services as factors of production (flow 1). These payments are broken up into employee compensation, rent, interest, and profits. When we add indirect taxes (less subsidies) and depreciation to national income, we have GDP.[2]

    Payments are broken up into employee compensation, rent, interest, and profits. Table 7-3 (on the next page) presents some recent data for Canada.

Wages, Salaries, and Supplementary Labour Income Payments by firms to households for their labour services is the largest component of gross domestic product. These payments include all wages and salaries and all fringe benefits (such as pension contributions) that firms pay to workers.

Profits Before Taxes Corporate profits before taxes are paid out to shareholders—households—as dividends, or they are plowed back into the firm in the form of retained earnings. The federal and provincial governments own shares in corporations (called government business enterprises and Crown corporations—examples include your provincial power corporation, unless it has been sold to the private sector, or privatized; the Bank of Canada; and Canada Post) that generate profits and these, too, before taxes, are included in incomes.

Q.6 What is the largest factor payments component of national income for Canada?

[2]Sometimes you'll see these figures referred to as calculated at factor cost. Valuation at factor cost is meant to capture the producer's expenses rather than the purchaser's costs. Thus, estimates based at factor cost do not include indirect taxes, customs duties, or property taxes. We add these components (indirect taxes less subsidies) into our measures of income, calculated at factor cost, to arrive at GDP at market prices.

TABLE 7-3   **GDP Using the Factor Incomes Approach**

Canadian GDP can be measured using the factor incomes approach, which sums incomes paid to factors of production. You can see that wages, salaries, and supplementary labour income is the largest component in the calculation.

Component	($1,000)
Wages, salaries, and supplementary labour income	$559,102
Corporate profits before taxes	119,922
Government business enterprise profits before taxes	9,678
Interest and miscellaneous investment income	53,463
Accrued net income of farm operators from farm production	2,963
Net income of nonfarm unincorporated business, including rent	65,719
Inventory valuation adjustment	−458
Taxes less subsidies on factors of production	56,253
Taxes less subsidies on products	75,269
Capital consumption allowances	142,498
Statistical discrepancy	−290
GDP	1,084,120

Source: Statistics Canada, CANSIM II, Table 380-0016.

Interest and Miscellaneous Interest Income   Table 7-3 shows that interest and investment income was about $53 billion in 2001. It measures the difference between total interest payments that households receive (on loans they have made) and total interest payments that households make (on funds they have borrowed).

Farm and Nonincorporated Nonfarm Income   These components measure income from activities where the operator is actually the owner of the factors employed in the business. Trying to separate out payments on a detailed basis would be too difficult, so we simply add them together to measure incomes accruing to owner-operators. Rental income is included in this category.

Inventory Valuation Adjustment   Gains and losses from holding inventories are included in corporate profits before taxes—when prices change, changes in the inventory book value and the value of the physical changes in inventories won't be equal. These effects need to be removed to measure current production.

Taxes Less Subsidies   So far, we haven't adjusted the figures for the effects of indirect taxes (such as sales taxes) and subsidies the government provides to certain producers (such as those paid to some dairy farmers). These adjustments are made for both factors of production and final goods and services.

Capital Consumption Allowance   As we have already noted, capital wears out over time. An adjustment to the capital stock for the effects of depreciation is the last component to consider in constructing an incomes-based measure of GDP (aside from that pesky statistical discrepancy, which is usually small and captures measurement errors).

Equality of Income and Expenditure

The value of the employee compensation, rents, interest, and profits (the flow along the top in Figure 7-2) equals the value of goods bought (the flow along the bottom). How are these values kept exactly equal? That's the secret of double-entry bookkeeping: output must always equal income.

The definition of profit is the key to the equality. Recall that *profit* is defined as what remains after all the firm's other income (employee compensation, rent, and interest) is paid out. For example, say a firm has a total output of $800 and that it paid $400 in wages, $200 in rent, and $100 in interest. The firm's profit is total output less these payments. Profit equals $800 − $700 = $100.

The accounting identity works even if a firm incurs a loss. Say that instead of paying $400 in wages, the firm paid $700, along with its other payments of $200 in rent and $100 in interest. Total output is still $800, but total payments are $1,000. Profits, still defined as total output minus payments, are negative: $800 − $1,000 = (−$200). There's a loss of $200. Adding that loss to other income [$1,000 + (−$200)] gives total income of $800—which is identical to the firm's total output of $800. It is no surprise that total output and total income, defined in this way, are equal.

The national income accounting identity (Total output ≡ Total income) allows us to calculate GDP either by adding up all values of final outputs (the *expenditures approach*) or by adding up the values of all earnings or income (the *income approach*).

The income accounting identity as presented so far has skipped over three qualifications. We've already discussed two of the adjustments. The first concerns the words *national* and *domestic*. National income is all income earned by citizens of a country and is equivalent to GNP. To move from domestic to national, we add net foreign factor income. We've also introduced the second adjustment when talking about net domestic product (NDP). NDP is GDP less depreciation. Depreciation, though a cost of production and included in expenditures, is not paid out as income. Thus, depreciation is subtracted from GDP. The third adjustment is similar. Indirect business taxes (less subsidies) are reflected in all prices and, thus, in the value of total expenditures (GDP). They are not, however, paid out to owners of production as income and are not part of national income. To move from GDP to national income, we must also subtract indirect business taxes (less subsidies) from GDP. Figure 7-3 (on the next page) shows these adjustments. As you can see, total expenditures (consumption, investment, government expenditures, and net exports) equals GDP (column 1). GDP plus net foreign factor income equals GNP (column 2). GNP less depreciation and indirect business taxes (less subsidies) equals national income (employee compensation, rents, interest, profit) shown in column 3.

Other Income Terms

Two other often-used concepts deserving mention are *personal income* and *disposable personal income*. (These can be either national or domestic concepts.)

Personal Income National income measures the income individuals receive for doing productive work, whereas personal income measures all income actually received by individuals. Individuals receive other income that they do not directly earn (for example, pension payments, welfare payments, and employment insurance benefits). These payments from government to individuals are not part of national income, but they are available to spend.

Similarly, in national income accounting, individuals are attributed income that they do not actually receive. This income includes undistributed corporate profits (retained

Figure 7-3 EQUALITY OF EXPENDITURE AND INCOME

These bars show just how total output equals total income in the national accounts. Bar 1 shows that GDP is the sum of consumption, investment, government expenditures, and net exports. National income is the bracketed portion of bar 3. It equals employee compensation, rents, interest, and profit. To go from GDP to national income, we must first add net foreign factor income. This equals GNP. To get national income, then subtract depreciation and indirect business taxes (less subsidies) (the top two items on the right-hand bar).

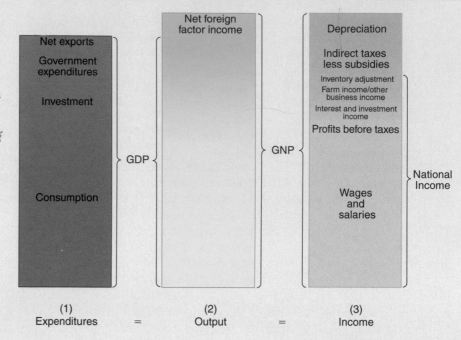

earnings), employers' contributions to Canada Pension Plan and Employment Insurance, and corporate income taxes.

If we add to national income the amounts of such payments that households receive, and subtract from national income the amounts attributed to households but not actually received by them, we arrive at **personal income (PI)**—*national income plus net transfer payments from government minus amounts attributed but not received.* Personal income can be set forth as follows:

PI = NI + Transfer payments from government

  − Corporate retained earnings

  − Corporate income taxes

  − Employment (CPP, EI) taxes

Disposable Personal Income Personal income has accounted for some taxes, but not all. There are still personal income taxes and other personal taxes, which are subtracted from individuals' paycheques or paid directly by self-employed individuals. Personal income taxes and payroll taxes show up on employees' paycheque stubs, but employees don't actually get the money; the government does. Subtracting these personal income taxes from personal income, we arrive at **disposable personal income**—*personal income minus personal income taxes and other personal taxes:*

  Disposable personal income = PI − Personal taxes

Disposable personal income is what people have readily available to spend. Thus, economists follow disposable personal income carefully.

We've covered a lot of definitions quickly, so a review is in order. GDP (the total output of the residents of a society) can be measured two ways: the expenditures approach and the factor incomes approach.

Under the expenditures approach,

$$GDP = C + I + G + (X - IM)$$

Since much investment is replacement investment meant to cover depreciation, net domestic product is

$$NDP = GDP - Depreciation$$

Under the factor incomes approach, net domestic income at factor cost is the sum of several components:

NDI = wages and salaries plus supplementary labour income
+ corporate profits before taxes
+ interest and miscellaneous investment income
+ farm and nonincorporated nonfarm income
+ inventory adjustment

GDP is obtained by adding indirect taxes less subsidies, and depreciation

GDP at market prices = NDI + indirect taxes less subsidies + depreciation

Net national income takes net domestic product at factor cost and adjusts for the difference between investment income from and to nonresidents. GNP at market prices adds indirect taxes (less subsidies) and depreciation to NNI. Personal income (PI) adjusts net national income for earned and unearned components of income. Personal disposable income subtracts personal taxes.

USING GDP FIGURES

The most important way GDP figures are used is to make comparisons of one country's production with another country's and of one year's production with another year's.

Comparing GDP among Countries

Most countries use somewhat similar measures to calculate GDP. Thus, we can compare various countries' GDP levels and get a sense of their economic size and power.

Per capita GDP is another measure often used to compare various nations' income. To arrive at per capita GDP, we divide GDP by the country's total population. Doing so gives us a sense of the relative standards of living of the people in various countries.

If you look up some of these measures, some of the comparisons should give you cause to wonder. For example, Bangladesh has per capita GDP of only about US$270, compared to Canadian per capita GDP of about US$23,000. How do people in Bangladesh live? In answering that question, remember that GDP measures market transactions. In poor countries, individuals often grow their own food (subsistence farming), build their own shelter, and make their own clothes. None of those activities are market activities, and while they're sometimes estimated and included in GDP, they often aren't estimated accurately. They certainly aren't estimated at the value of what these activities would cost in Canada. Also, remember that GDP is an aggregate measure that values activities at the market price in a society. The relative prices of the products and services a consumer buys often differ substantially among countries. In Toronto, $1,500 a month will get you a two-bedroom apartment in a nice area of town. In Haiti, $1,500 a month might get you a mansion with four servants, while in New York City, after converting to U.S. dollars, you wouldn't even be able to afford a small

7.2

see page 184

Q-7 Why are national income statistics not especially good for discussing the income of developing countries?

studio apartment. Thus, GDP can be a poor measure of the relative living standards in various countries.

To avoid this problem in comparing per capita GDP, economists often calculate a different concept, *purchasing power parity (PPP)*, which adjusts for the different relative prices among countries before making comparisons. That's why you'll see us use U.S. dollars when we're comparing GDP across countries: The International Monetary Fund (IMF), World Bank, and OECD construct PPPs using the American dollar for comparison purposes.

Just how much of a difference the two approaches can make can be seen in the case of China. In May 1992, the IMF changed from calculating China's GDP using the exchange rate approach to calculating it using the purchasing power parity approach. Upon doing so, the IMF calculated that China's GDP grew over 400 percent in one year. Per capita income rose from about US$300 to well over US$1,000. When methods of calculation can make that much difference, one must use statistics very carefully.

Economic Welfare over Time

A second way in which the GDP concept is used is to compare one year with another. Using GDP figures to compare the economy's performance over time is much better than relying merely on our perceptions. Most of us have heard the phrase *the good old days*. Generally we hear it from our parents or grandparents, who are lamenting the state of the nation or economy. In comparing today to yesterday, they always seem to picture the past with greener grass, an easier life, and happier times. Compared to the good old days, today always comes out a poor second.

Our parents and grandparents may be right when they look back at particular events in their own lives, but if society were to follow such reasoning, it would conclude that all of history has been just one long downhill slide, worsening every year. In actuality, perceptions of the good old days are likely to be biased. It's easy to remember the nice things of yesterday while forgetting its harsh realities. Relying on past perception is not an especially helpful way of making accurate comparisons.

A preferable way is to rely on data that are not changed by emotion or anything else. Looking at GDP over time provides a way of using data to make comparisons over time. For example, say we compare Canadian GDP in 1961 ($41.3 billion) to GDP in 2001 ($1.08 trillion). Would it be correct to conclude the economy had grown 25 times larger? No. As we discussed earlier, GDP figures aren't affected by emotions, but they are affected by inflation. To make comparisons over time, we can't confine ourselves to a simple look at what has happened to nominal GDP. We must also look at what has happened to prices.

Suppose prices of all goods and hence the price level go up 25 percent in one year, but outputs of all goods remain constant. GDP will have risen 25 percent, but will society be any better off? No. To compare GDP over time, you must distinguish between increases in GDP due to inflation and increases in GDP that represent real increases in production and income.

Real and Nominal GDP

As stated earlier, to separate increases in GDP caused by inflation from increases in GDP that represent real increases in production and income, economists distinguish between **nominal GDP** (*GDP calculated at existing prices*) and **real GDP** (*nominal GDP adjusted for inflation*). This distinction is sufficiently important to warrant repetition in this chapter.

Using GDP figures to compare the economy's performance over time is much better than relying merely on our perceptions.

A real concept is a nominal concept adjusted for inflation.

Real GDP is nominal GDP adjusted for inflation.

To adjust nominal output for inflation we create a price index (a measure of how much the price level has risen from one year to the next) and divide nominal GDP by that price index. That price index is the GDP deflator, introduced in the previous chapter.[3]

For example, say the price level rises 4 percent (from a GDP deflator of 1 to a GDP deflator of 1.1) and nominal GDP rises from $950 billion to $1 trillion. Part of that rise in nominal GDP represents the 4 percent rise in the price level. If you divide nominal GDP, $1 trillion, by the new GDP deflator, 1.04, you get $961.5 billion (the amount GDP would have been if the price level had not risen). That $961.5 billion is called real GDP. To decide whether production has increased or decreased over time, we simply compare the real incomes. In this example, real income has risen from $950 billion to $961.5 billion, so we can conclude that the real economy has grown by 11.5/950, or 1.2 percent.

Real GDP is what is important to a society because it measures what is *really* produced. Considering nominal GDP instead of real GDP can distort what's really happening. Let's say the Canadian price level doubled tomorrow. Nominal GDP would also double, but would Canada be better off? No.

We'll use the distinction between real and nominal continually in this course, so to firm up the concepts in your mind, let's go through another example. Consider Indonesia in 1997 and 1998, when nominal GDP rose from 673 trillion to 943 trillion rupiah (their local currency unit) while the GDP deflator rose from 100 percent to 161 percent. Dividing nominal GDP in 1998 by the GDP deflator, we see that *real GDP* fell by over 12 percent. So not only did Indonesia's economy not grow; it actually shrank.

Q.8 If real income has risen from $1 trillion to $1.1 trillion and the price level went up by 3 percent, by how much has nominal income risen?

SOME LIMITATIONS OF NATIONAL INCOME ACCOUNTING

The quotation at this chapter's start pointed out that statistics can be misleading. We want to reiterate that here. Before you can work with statistics, you need to know how they are collected and the problems they have. If you don't, the results can be disastrous.

Here's a possible scenario: A student who isn't careful looks at the data and discovers an almost perfect relationship between imports and investment occurring in a Latin American country. Whenever capital goods imports go up, investment of capital goods goes up by an equal proportion. The student develops a thesis based on that insight, only to learn after submitting the thesis that no data on investment are available for that country. Instead of gathering actual data, the foreign country's statisticians estimate investment by assuming it to be a constant percentage of imports. Since many investment goods are imported, this is reasonable, but the estimate is not a reasonable basis for an economic policy. It would be back to the drawing board for the student, whose thesis would be useless because the student didn't know how the country's statistics had been collected.

If you ever work in business as an economist, statistics will be your life's blood. Much of what economists do is based on knowing, interpreting, and drawing inferences from statistics. Statistics must be treated carefully. They don't always measure what they seem to measure. Though Canadian national income accounting statistics are among the most accurate in the world, they still have serious limitations.

Limitations of national income accounting include the following:

1. Measurement problems exist.
2. GDP measures economic activity, not welfare.
3. Subcategories are often interdependent.

---

[3]Now you know why the total output deflator is called the *GDP deflator*. It is an index of the rise in prices of the goods and services that make up GDP.

The only way economists can determine how happy people are is to ask them if they're happy and then develop a happiness index. We've done so in some of our classes by giving students a numerical measure for degrees of happiness:

Ecstatic	5
Very happy	4
Happy	3
Somewhat unhappy	2
Depressed	1

Each student writes down the number that most closely represents his or her average state of happiness for the past year. The average of those calculations forms the "happiness index" for the class—usually between 3 and 3.2. Our students are essentially reasonably happy.

In fact, when other economists have taken a type of happiness poll elsewhere, results have been fairly consistent—even in poor countries. Except in times of crisis, people on average are reasonably happy, regardless of their income level, their wealth, or the state of the economy where they live.* We interpret this as meaning

there's some level of income below which we'll be unhappy because we're starving, but above that level more output for a society doesn't mean more happiness for a society.

Now this stability of happiness could mean that economics, economic progress, and growth don't matter, that they're irrelevant to happiness. But we economists are naturally loath to give it such an interpretation. Instead, economists slide over such problems and poll people as to how many prefer a higher income to a lower income. We've also conducted these polls and have yet to find an individual who says he or she prefers less income to more income. (If we found one, of course, we'd volunteer to relieve that person of some income, which would make us all happier.)

The fact that everyone, or almost everyone, prefers more output, but that more output or an increase in income doesn't make everyone happier, is not really a contradiction. We know from watching *Star Trek* (and from reading Lord Tennyson) that it's in striving that human beings acquire happiness. Without striving, the human being is but an empty shell. But enough; if this discussion continues, it will, heaven forbid, turn from economics to philosophy.

---

*We've given the test to students in Vermont, New York, New Brunswick, and Great Britain, and each time the results have been similar. However, when the test was given to students in Florida at the University of Miami and to students in Bulgaria, the results were different. In Miami they came up consistently higher for each category. Four students actually checked "ecstatic." We're not sure precisely what this Florida factor signifies. In Bulgaria, the results were lower (a 2.8 average). Bulgaria was undergoing a wrenching economic change and many incomes had been cut by two-thirds, so this low result was explainable.

While an economy's GDP may rise as a result of increased military spending, the economic welfare or standard of living of most of its citizens could remain unchanged as the benefits from increased economic activity does not trickle down through the economy.

GDP Measures Market Activity, Not Welfare

The first, and most important, limitation to remember is that GDP measures neither happiness nor economic welfare. GDP measures economic (market) activity. Real GDP could rise and economic welfare could fall. For example, say some Martians came down and let loose a million Martian burglars in Canada just to see what would happen. GDP would be likely to rise as individuals bought guns and locks and spent millions of dollars on protecting their property and replacing stolen items. At the same time, however, welfare would fall.

Welfare is a complicated concept. The economy's goal should not be to increase output for the sake of increasing output, but to make people better off or at least happier. But a pure happiness measure is impossible. Economists have struggled with the concept of welfare and have decided that the best they can do is to concentrate their analysis on economic activity, leaving others to consider how economic activity relates to happiness. We should warn you, however, that there is no neat correlation between increases in GDP and increases in happiness. You can see that in the accompanying Applying the Tools box. Some spending may not contribute to welfare—observers point to advertising and packaging as prime examples—so this is another problem we face in linking national income accounting to welfare. Similarly, nonmarket activities such as the production of goods by households for their own use enhance welfare, but are difficult to measure, as is the value placed on leisure (some people place a high value on an extra hour of leisure, while others value it much less).

Measurement Errors

GDP figures are supposed to measure all market economic activity, but they do not. Illegal drug sales, under-the-counter sales of goods to avoid income and sales taxes, work performed and paid for in cash to avoid income tax, nonreported sales, and prostitution are all market activities, yet none of them is included in GDP figures. Estimates of the underground, nonmeasured economy range from 1.5 to 20 percent of GDP in Canada and as high as 70 percent in Nigeria. That is, if measured Canadian GDP is $1 trillion, inclusion of the underground, nonmeasured activity would raise it to between $1.015 trillion and $1.2 trillion. If we were able to halt underground activity and direct those efforts to the above-ground economy, GDP would rise significantly. For instance, if we legalized prostitution and marijuana sales and quadrupled tax-collection mechanisms, GDP would rise. But that rise in GDP wouldn't necessarily make us better off.

> **Q.9** How can measurement errors occur in adjusting GDP figures for inflation?

A second type of measurement error occurs in adjusting GDP figures for inflation. Earlier we discussed problems using indexes. Measurement of inflation involves numerous arbitrary decisions including what base year to use, how to weight various prices, and how to adjust for changes in the quality of products. Let's take, for example, changes in the quality of products. If the price of a Toyota went up 5 percent from 2003 ($20,000) to 2004 ($21,000), that's certainly a 5 percent rise in price. But what if the 2004 Toyota had a "new, improved" 16-valve engine? Can you say that the price of cars rose 5 percent, or should you adjust for the improvement in quality? And if you adjust, how do you adjust? The people who keep track of the price indexes used to measure inflation will be the first to tell you there's no one right answer to any one of these choices. How that question, and a million other similar questions involved in measuring inflation, is answered can lead to significant differences in estimates of inflation and hence in estimates of real GDP growth.

> Measurements of inflation can involve significant measurement errors.

One study for Canada argued inflation could be either 5.4 or 15 percent, depending on how the inflation index was calculated. Which inflation figure you chose would make a big difference in your estimate of how the economy was doing. Canada used to switch base years and update its price weights every few years, resulting in the recalculation of history every five years. In 2001, however, it began to use a new measure that updates price weights and the reference year every year. The Appendix to this chapter contains an example of how the new system compares to the old one.

 7.3

see page 184

Misinterpretation of Subcategories

A third limitation of national income accounting concerns possible misinterpretation of the components. In setting up the accounts, a large number of arbitrary decisions had to be made: What to include in "investment"? What to include in "consumption"? How to treat government expenditures? The decisions made were, for the most part, reasonable, but they weren't the only ones that could have been made. Once made, however, they influence our interpretations of events. For example, when we see that investment rises, we normally think that our future productive capacity is rising, but remember that investment includes housing investment, which does not increase our future productive capacity. In fact, some types of consumption (say, purchases of personal computers by people who will become computer-literate and use their knowledge and skills to be

> **Q.10** How can some types of consumption increase our productive capacity by more than some types of investment?

The Bank of Canada has issued over $35 billion worth of cash. That's about $1,100 for every man, woman, and child. Now ask yourself how much cash you're carrying on you. Add to that the amounts banks and businesses keep, and divide that by the number of people in Canada. The number economists get when they do that calculation is way below the total amount of cash the Bank of Canada has issued. So what happens to the extra cash?

Let's switch for a minute to a Montreal safehouse being raided by drug enforcement officers. They find $5 million in cash. That's what most economists believe happens to much of the extra cash: It goes underground. An underground economy lurks below the real economy.

The underground economy consists of two components: (1) the production and distribution of illegal goods and services; and (2) the nonreporting of legal economic activity.

Illegal activity, such as selling illegal drugs and prostitution, generates huge amounts of cash. (Most people who buy an illegal good or service would prefer not to have the transaction appear on their monthly credit card statements.) This presents a problem for a big-time illegal business. It must explain to the government where all that money came from. That's where money laundering comes in. Money laundering is simply making illegally gained income look as if it came from a legal business. Any business through which lots of cash moves is a good front for money laundering. Laundromats move lots of cash, which is where the term *money laundering* came from. The mob bought laundromats and claimed a much higher income from the laundromats than it actually received. The mob thus "laundered" the excess money. Today money laundering is much more sophisticated. It involves billions of dollars and international transactions in many different countries, but the purpose is the same: making illegally earned money look legal. In 2000 the RCMP and the Bank of Canada withdrew $1,000 bills from circulation in Canada. Why? That was the "bill of choice" in illegal transactions. The authorities figured this change would make it more difficult to engage in illegal activities.

The second part of the illegal economy involves deliberately failing to report income in order to escape paying taxes on it. When people work "off the books," when restaurants don't ring up cash sales, when waiters forget to declare tips on their tax returns, they reduce their tax payments and make it look as if they have less income and as if the economy has less production than it actually does.

How important is the underground economy? That's tough to say; it is, after all, underground. Early in 2002 estimates were as high as $130 billion, about 15 percent of GDP. A Statistics Canada economist estimated it to be in the range of 1 to 5 percent of GDP. Some economists estimate it to be as high as 30 percent of GDP. Some countries have significant underground economies. For example, it is estimated that Nigeria's underground economy is as much as 70 percent of its above-ground economy. In other countries, more like Canada but which have higher tax rates, such as Italy, Belgium, and Spain, estimates of the underground economy range as high as 30 percent of the above-ground economy.

more productive than they were before they owned computers) increase our productive capacity more than some types of investment.

Genuine Progress Indicator

7.4

see page 184

The problems of national income accounting have led to a variety of measures of economic activity. One of the most interesting of these is the *genuine progress indicator (GPI)*, which makes a variety of adjustments to GDP so that it better measures the progress of society rather than simply economic activity. The GPI makes adjustments to GDP for changes in other social goals. For example, if pollution worsens, the GPI falls even though the GDP remains constant. Each of these adjustments requires someone to value these other social goals, and there is significant debate about how social goals should be valued. Advocates of the GPI agree that such valuations are difficult, but they argue that avoiding any such valuation, as is done with the GDP, implicitly values other social goals, such as having no pollution, at zero. Since some index will be used as an in-

Measurement is necessary, and the GDP measurements and categories have made it possible to think and talk about the aggregate economy.

dicator of the progress of the economy, it is better to have an index that includes all social goals rather than an index of only economic activity.

By pointing out these problems, economists are not suggesting that national income accounting statistics should be thrown out. Far from it; measurement is necessary, and the GDP measurements and categories have made it possible to think and talk about the aggregate economy. We wouldn't have devoted an entire chapter of this book to national income accounting if we didn't believe it was important. We are simply arguing that national income accounting concepts should be used with sophistication, that is, with an awareness of their weaknesses as well as their strengths.

CONCLUSION

Used with that awareness, national income accounting is a powerful tool; you wouldn't want to be an economist without it. For those of you who aren't planning to be economists, it's still a good idea for you to understand the concepts of national income accounting. If you do, the business section of the newspaper will seem less like Greek to you. You'll be a more informed citizen and will be better able to make up your own mind about macroeconomic debates.

Chapter Summary

- National income accounting is a set of rules and definitions for measuring activity in the aggregate economy.

- GDP is the total market value of all final goods produced in an economy in one year. It's a flow, not a stock, measure of market activity.

- GDP describes the economic output produced within the physical borders of an economy, while GNP describes the economic output produced by the citizens of a country.

- Intermediate goods can be eliminated from GDP in two ways:

    1. By measuring only final sales.
    2. By measuring only value added.

- National income is directly related to national output. Whenever there's output, there's income.

- GDP is divided up into four types of expenditures:
    $$GDP = C + I + G + (X - IM)$$

- NI = Compensation to employees + Rent + Interest + Profit.

- GDP plus net foreign factor income less depreciation less indirect business taxes equals national income.

- Personal income is all income received by individuals, and personal disposable income is personal income less personal taxes.

- Because GDP measures only market activities, GDP can be a poor measure of relative living standards among countries.

- To compare income over time, we must adjust for price-level changes. After adjusting for inflation, nominal measures are changed to "real" measures.

- Real GDP is the nominal GDP divided by the GDP deflator.

- National income accounting concepts are powerful tools for understanding macroeconomics, but we must recognize their limitations.

- GDP has its problems: GDP does not measure economic welfare; it does not include transactions in the underground economy; the price index used to calculate real GDP is problematic; subcategories of GDP are often interdependent.

Key Terms

depreciation *(169)*	intermediate products *(165)*	net private investment *(170)*
disposable personal income *(174)*	national balance sheet *(165)*	nominal GDP *(176)*
final output *(165)*	national income (NI) *(171)*	personal consumption expenditures *(169)*
government expenditures *(170)*	national income accounting *(163)*	
gross domestic product (GDP) *(163)*	net domestic product (NDP) *(170)*	personal income (PI) *(174)*
gross national product (GNP) *(163)*	net exports *(170)*	real GDP *(176)*
gross private investment *(169)*	net foreign factor income *(163)*	value added *(166)*

Questions for Thought and Review

1. Which will be larger, gross domestic product or gross national product?

2. If you add up all the transactions in an economy, do you arrive at GDP, GNP, or something else?

3. What's the relationship between a stock concept and a flow concept? Give an example that hasn't already been given in this chapter.

4. Many countries are considering introducing a value added tax. What tax rate on value added is needed to get the same increase in revenue as is gotten from an income tax with a rate of 15 percent? Why?

5. If Canada introduces universal child care, what will likely happen to GDP? What are the welfare implications of that rise?

6. Economists normally talk about GDP even though they know NDP is a better measure of economic activity. Why?

7. What is the largest component of national income for most countries?

8. If the government increases transfer payments, what will happen to national income?

9. How does personal income differ from national income?

10. What is the difference between national personal income and domestic personal income?

11. If society's goal is to make people happier, and higher GDP isn't closely associated with being happier, why do economists even talk about GDP?

Problems and Exercises

1. There are three firms in an economy: A, B, and C. Firm A buys $250 worth of goods from firm B and $200 worth of goods from firm C, and produces 200 units of output, which it sells at $5 per unit. Firm B buys $100 worth of goods from firm A and $150 worth of goods from firm C, and produces 300 units of output, which it sells at $7 per unit. Firm C buys $50 worth of goods from firm A and nothing from firm B. It produces output worth $1,000. All other products are sold to consumers.
   a. Calculate GDP.
   b. If a value added tax (a tax on the total value added of each firm) of 10 percent is introduced, how much revenue will the government get?
   c. How much would government get if it introduced a 10 percent income tax?
   d. How much would government get if it introduced a 10 percent sales tax on final output?

2. State whether the following actions will increase or decrease GDP:
   a. The federal government decriminalizes prostitution.
   b. An individual sells her house on her own.
   c. An individual sells his house through a broker.
   d. Government increases pension payments.
   e. Stock prices rise by 20 percent.
   f. An unemployed worker gets a job.

3. Find personal consumption expenditures (as a percent of GDP) for the following countries. (Requires research.)
   a. Mexico
   b. Thailand
   c. Poland
   d. Nigeria
   e. Kuwait

4. You've been given the following data:

Transfer payments	$ 72
Interest paid by consumers	4
Net exports	4
Indirect business taxes (less subsidies)	47
Net foreign factor income	2
Corporate income tax	64
Contribution for Employment Insurance (EI) and Canada Pension Plan (CPP)	35
Personal tax and nontax payments	91
Undistributed corporate profits	51
Gross private investment	185
Government purchases	195
Personal consumption	500
Depreciation	59

On the basis of these data calculate GDP, GNP, NDP, NI, personal income, and disposable personal income.

5. Given the following data about the economy:

Personal consumption	$700
Investment	500
Corporate income tax	215
Government purchases	300
Profits	500
Wages	972
Net exports	275
Rents	25
Depreciation	25
Indirect business taxes (less subsidies)	100
Undistributed corporate profits	60
Net foreign factor income	−3
Interest	150
CPP and EI contribution	0
Transfer payments	0
Personal taxes	165

a. Calculate GDP and GNP with both the expenditures approach and the income approach.
b. Calculate NDP and NI.
c. Calculate PI.
d. Calculate disposable personal income.

6. You have been hired as a research assistant and are given the following data.

Compensation	$329
Consumption	370
Exports	55
Net foreign factor income	3
Government purchases	43
Gross investment	80
Imports	63
Indirect business taxes (less subsidies)	27
Net interest	49
Profits	69
Rental income	1

a. Calculate GNP, GDP, NDP, and NI.
b. What is depreciation in this year?
c. Right after you finish, your boss comes running to you and tells you that she made a mistake. Imports were really $68 and compensation was $340. She tells you to get her the corrected answers to *a* and *b* immediately.

7. Below are nominal GDP and GDP deflators for four years.

Year	Nominal GDP	GDP Deflator
2001	$7,813	100.0
2002	8,301	101.9
2003	8,760	103.1
2004	9,256	104.6

a. Calculate real GDP in each year.
b. Did the percentage change in nominal GDP exceed the percentage change in real GDP in any of the last three years listed?
c. In which year did society's welfare increase the most?

8. Congratulations! You've been hired by a political party to comment on its economic policy proposals. The document you are reviewing assumes that each component of real GDP (consumption, investment, government spending, and net exports) will rise by 2.5 percent under the party's plan. It further indicates that real GDP is expected to rise by 9 percent.
   a. Should you question the GDP forecast? If so, should the estimate of real GDP growth be revised? Why?
   b. Can the political party argue that society is better off under its proposals? What additional information would it need to provide?
   c. Should forecasts of real GDP using the factor incomes approach lead to the same estimate as the forecast using the expenditures approach? Why?

9. Suppose nominal GDP is $1.2 billion and the underground economy is estimated to be 3 percent of nominal GDP. The government is trying to decide whether it makes sense to be more vigilant about tax evasion.
   a. If tax revenue on the income generated in the underground economy is estimated to be $20 million, what would be the average tax rate on the income generated in the underground economy?
   b. If the government had to spend $14 million to collect the tax revenue on underground activities, would it make sense to do so?
   c. If the government spent $36 million to collect the tax on the underground economy, what would the tax rate on underground activities have to be for the government to break even on enforcing the tax laws?

Web Questions

1. Find GDP for the most recent quarter from the Statistics Canada home page at www.statcan.ca.
   a. What were consumption, investment, government expenditures, and net exports?
   b. What was nominal GDP? Real GDP?
   c. By how much did nominal GDP increase? How much of the increase was due to an increase in the aggregate price level?
   d. Which of the components listed in *a* contributed the most to the change in GDP? Did any of the components move in opposite directions?

2. Visit the CIA's World Fact Book home page (www.cia.gov) and answer the following questions:
   a. What was GDP in Norway last year? Compare that value to GDP in Oman.
   b. What is the major economic activity in the Pitcairn Islands? How large is its labour force?
   c. How many airports are there in Andorra? What is its major economic activity?

3. Visit the Statistics Canada home page (www.statcan.ca) and search for information on the Chain Fisher Index:
   a. Why did Statistics Canada decide to update price weights and the reference year every year?
   b. Are there any drawbacks to making the change?
   c. How do we construct the GDP deflator?

4. Some economists have proposed that we use the genuine progress indicator (GPI) rather than GDP as an indication of economic well-being. Using the information you find at the home page of Redefining Progress at www.rprogress.org answer the following questions:
   a. What is one category included in the GPI that suggests that GDP understates economic well-being?
   b. Name four categories included in the GPI that suggest that GDP overstates economic well-being. What is the largest of these categories?
   c. Has the GPI gone up or down during the most recent year for which there are data? What happened to GDP during that year?

Answers to Margin Questions

1. GDP measures the output of the residents of a country—the output within its geographical borders. GNP measures the output of the citizens and businesses of a country. Kuwait is a very rich country whose residents have a high income, much of it from investments overseas. Thus their GNP will be high. However, Kuwait also has large numbers of foreign workers who are not citizens and whose incomes would be included in GDP but not in GNP. In reality, Kuwait citizens' and businesses' foreign income exceeds foreign workers' and foreign companies' income within Kuwait, so Kuwait's GNP is greater than its GDP. *(164)*

2. The national balance sheet measures stocks—a country's assets and liabilities at a point in time. Income accounts measure flows—a country's income and expenditures over a period of time. *(165)*

3. Only the value added by the sale would be added to GDP. In this case the value added is the difference between the purchase price and the sale price, or $500. *(167)*

4. The government budget includes transfer payments, which are not included in GDP. Only those government expenditures that are for goods and services are included in GDP. *(167)*

5. The four components of expenditures in national income are personal consumption, gross private investment, net exports, and government purchases. *(170)*

6. The largest factor payments component of national income for Canada is wages, salaries, and supplementary labour income. *(171)*

7. In developing countries, individuals often grow their own food and take part in many activities that are not measured by the GDP statistics. The income figures that one gets from the GDP statistics of developing countries do not include such activities and, thus, can be quite misleading. *(175)*

8. Nominal income must have risen $133 billion to $1.133 trillion so that, when it is adjusted for inflation, real income will have risen to $1.1 trillion. *(177)*

9. Measurement errors occur in adjusting GDP figures for inflation because measuring inflation involves numerous arbitrary decisions such as choosing a base year, adjusting for quality changes in products, and weighting prices. *(179)*

10. Dividing goods into consumption and investment does not always capture the effect of the spending on productive capacity. For example, housing "investment" does little to expand the productive capacity. However, "consumption" of computers or books could expand the productive capacity significantly. *(179)*

APPENDIX A

Calculating Real GDP

In the text, we briefly mentioned that Statistics Canada recently changed the way it calculates real GDP. In this appendix, we'll tell you a bit more about how the new figures are constructed.

First we'll need to define some variables. Let P_1 be the price level in the first year and P_2 be the price level in the second year. Q_1 denotes the quantity of output produced in the first year and Q_2 represents the quantity of output produced in the second year.

NOMINAL GDP

Nominal GDP values current production at current prices, so in the first year this is given by $P_1 \times Q_1$; in the second year, this is $P_2 \times Q_2$.

The Old Method of Calculating Real GDP

Real GDP values current production at base period prices, so if we take first period prices as the base period, in the first year real GDP is the same as nominal GDP, $P_1 \times Q_1$. This is always true: Real and nominal GDP are the same in the base year. In the second year, the old method of estimating real GDP takes physical production in year two and values that output at prices in the base year, so real GDP would be $P_1 \times Q_2$.

The New Method of Calculating Real GDP

Statistics Canada has found that prices have been changing so quickly over time for some goods that trying to value production at those base period prices provides a biased view of the real value of those goods (mostly these prices are on high-tech goods and services). To try to eliminate some of this bias, Statistics Canada uses a new method to create real GDP.

The first step is to value production in year one at period two prices; this gives us $P_2 \times Q_1$.

Now calculate two growth rates. The first is based on using prices in the first year to value production in years one and two.

$$\text{Growth rate one} = \frac{P_1 \times Q_2 - P_1 \times Q_1}{P_1 \times Q_1} \times 100$$

The second growth rate uses prices in the second year to value production in both years:

$$\text{Growth rate two} = \frac{P_2 \times Q_2 - P_2 \times Q_1}{P_2 \times Q_1} \times 100$$

Now take the geometric average (multiply the numbers together and then take the square root) of the two growth rates (denoted by g) and apply this growth rate to the estimate of real GDP in the base period:

Real GDP in second year
= Real GDP in first year $\times (1 + g)$
= $P_1 \times Q_1 \times (1 + g)$

This process is repeated, year after year, so that successive estimates of real GDP are chain-linked to real GDP in the first period. As of 2002, Statistics Canada uses 1997 as the reference year.

AN EXAMPLE

The "Old" Method

Let's suppose you live in a country that produces four products: apples (A), beets (B), cotton (C), and denim (D). The following table lists prices and quantities for the two years.

Commodity	2002 Price Per Unit	2002 Quantity Units	2003 Price Per Unit	2003 Quantity Units
Apples	$5	100	$6	40
Beets	$3	200	$4	150
Cotton	$2	500	$3	400
Denim	$8	100	$10	200

Nominal GDP values current production at current prices, so for 2002:

Nominal GDP = Price of apples in 2002 × Quantity of apples in 2002 + Price of beets in 2002 × Quantity of beets in 2002 + Price of cotton in 2002 × Quantity of cotton in 2002 + Price of denim in 2002 × Quantity of denim in 2002
= 5 × 100 + 3 × 200 + 2 × 500 + 8 × 100
= $2,900

Repeating the calculation for 2003 yields a nominal GDP of $4,040 (obtained as $6 \times 40 + 4 \times 150 + 3 \times 400 + 10 \times 200$).

Real GDP values current production at base period prices, so nominal and real GDP are the same in the base year. What about 2003? The old way of measuring real GDP would calculate real GDP as 2003 physical production valued at 2002 prices. So:

Real GDP = Price of apples in 2002 × Quantity of apples in 2003 + Price of beets in 2002 × Quantity of beets in 2003 + Price of cotton in 2002 × Quantity of cotton in 2003 + Price of denim in 2002 × Quantity of denim in 2003
= $5 \times 40 + 3 \times 150 + 2 \times 400 + 8 \times 200$
= \$3,050

Real GDP in 2003, measured the old way, was $3,050. Our old measure of real GDP suggests that aggregate economic activity was higher than in 2002 (when real GDP was $2,900)—even though the production of three out of four goods fell.

The "New" Method

The new method of calculating real GDP allows prices in both years to influence our calculation. There are two steps we need to add to the "old" method.

Step 1 Calculate the Value of the Quantities Produced in 2002 at Prices in 2003 The first step in the construction of our new measure of real GDP takes the quantities produced in 2002 and values them at prices that existed in 2003:

   Value of 2002 output at 2003 prices
= Price of apples in 2003 × Quantity of apples in 2002 + Price of beets in 2003 × Quantity of beets in 2002 + Price of cotton in 2003 × Quantity of cotton in 2002 + Price of denim in 2003 × Quantity of denim in 2002

$= 6 \times 100 + 4 \times 200 + 3 \times 500 + 10 \times 100$
= \$3,900

Step 2 Average the Growth Rates Now we have two different measures of the change in the value of output between 2002 and 2003. Using the old method of calculating real GDP we said real GDP went from $2,900 to $3,050. This results from holding the prices at their 2002 levels and comparing the change in the value of what was produced given that only quantities were changing. In this case we obtain a growth rate of 5.17 percent, calculated as:

$$\frac{3{,}050 - 2{,}900}{2{,}900} \times 100 = 5.17$$

The value of output produced in 2002 and valued at 2003 prices was $3,900. The output produced in 2003 and valued at 2003 prices was $4,040. The growth rate we calculate based on holding prices at their 2003 level and considering changes in physical production is 3.59 percent, calculated as:

$$\frac{4{,}040 - 3{,}900}{3{,}900} \times 100 = 3.59$$

Take the geometric average of these two growth rates and you'll get 4.31 percent. This is an estimate of the change in real GDP from the base period, 2002. We know real (and nominal) GDP in 2002 was $2,900, so real GDP in 2003 under the new method of calculating real GDP is $2,900 × (1.0431) = $3,025. That's a bit below the "old" estimate of $3,050, acknowledging that while prices rose, physical production for some goods fell. Taking both of those factors into account, real GDP in 2003 was $3,025.

It's that simple! If you want to learn more about the nitty-gritty details, check out the Statistics Canada Web site at http://www.statcan.ca/english/concepts/chainfisher/index.htm.

Growth, Productivity, and the Wealth of Nations

8

After reading this chapter, you should be able to:

- Define growth and relate it to living standards.

- List five sources of growth.

- Distinguish diminishing marginal productivity from decreasing returns to scale.

- Distinguish Classical growth theory from new growth theory.

- List and discuss six government policies to promote growth.

Queen Elizabeth owned silk stockings. The capitalist achievement does not typically consist in providing more silk stockings for queens but in bringing them within the reach of factory girls in return for steadily decreasing amounts of effort.

Joseph Schumpeter

Growth matters. In the long run, growth matters a lot. Thus, it is not surprising that modern economics began with a study of growth. In *The Wealth of Nations*, Adam Smith noted that what was good about market economies was that they raised society's standard of living. He argued that people's natural tendency to exchange and specialize allowed economies to grow.

As we discussed above, growth remained an important focus of economics through the 1920s as economists took a long-run perspective. The long-run perspective refers to the average rise in real output over a long period of time, which for Canada has been between 2.5 and 3.5 percent a year. Then, in the 1930s, the world economy fell into a

Macroeconomics includes both
the study of long-run growth and
business cycles.

serious depression. It was at that time that modern macroeconomics developed as a separate subject with a significant focus on short-run business cycles. It asked the questions "What causes depressions?" and "How does an economy get out of one?" Short-run macroeconomics became known as Keynesian economics, and remained the standard macroeconomics through the 1960s. Keynesian economics focuses on fluctuations around the growth trend and on whether those fluctuations influence that trend.

In the 1970s, as the memories of the Great Depression faded, the pendulum started to swing back again, and now, at the start of the 21st century, macroeconomists are taking a more balanced position, including both long-run growth and short-run business cycles as the core content of macro. In this chapter we consider long-run growth, and in later chapters, we examine business cycles and policies to deal with them.

GENERAL OBSERVATIONS ABOUT GROWTH

Before discussing the sources of growth, we want to make a number of general observations about growth.

Growth and the Economy's Potential Output

Growth is *an increase in the amount of goods and services an economy produces*. The study of growth is the study of why that increase comes about, assuming that both labour and capital are fully employed. Using the terminology from an earlier chapter, growth is an increase in potential output. (Recall that *potential output* can also be called *potential income* because, in the aggregate, income and output are identical.) One way to think about growth and potential output is to relate them to the production possibility curve, presented in Chapter 2. That curve gave us a picture of the choices an economy faces given available resources. When an economy is at its potential output, it is operating on its production possibility curve. When an economy is below its potential output, it is operating inside its production possibility curve. The analysis of growth focuses on the forces that shift out the production possibility curve.

Why do we use potential output in macro rather than the production possibility curve? Because macro focuses on aggregate output—GDP—and does not focus on the choices of dividing up GDP among alternative products as does micro and the production possibility curve. But the concept is the same. Potential output is a barrier beyond which an economy cannot expand without either increasing available factors of production (land, labour, resources) or increasing **productivity** (*output per unit of input*).

Long-run growth analysis focuses on supply; it assumes demand is sufficient to buy whatever is supplied. That assumption is called **Say's law** (*supply creates its own demand*), named after a French economist, Jean Baptiste Say, who first pointed it out. The reasoning behind Say's law is as follows: People work and supply goods to the market because they want other goods. The very fact that they supply goods means that they demand goods of equal value. According to Say's law, aggregate demand will always equal aggregate supply.

In the short run economists consider potential output fixed; they focus on how to get the economy operating at its potential if, for some reason, it is not. In the long run, economists consider an economy's potential output changeable. Growth analysis is a consideration of why an economy's potential shifts out, and growth policy is aimed at increasing an economy's potential output.

The Importance of Growth for Living Standards

Growth makes an enormous difference for living standards. Take France and Argentina as examples. In the 1950s per capita income was about US$5,000 in each country, but

Q-1
How does long-run growth
analysis justify its focus on supply?

BEYOND THE TOOLS

Is Growth Good?

The discussion in the chapter emphasizes the generally held view among economists that growth is inherently good. It increases our incomes, thereby improving our standard of living. But that does not mean that all economists support unlimited growth. Growth has costs, and economics requires us to look at both costs and benefits. For example, growth may contribute to increased pollution—reducing the quality of the air we breathe and the water we drink, and endangering the variety of species in the world. In short, the wrong type of growth may produce undesirable side effects including global warming and polluted rivers, land, and air.

New technology, upon which growth depends, also raises serious moral questions: Do we want to replace sexual reproduction with cloning? Will a brain implant be an improvement over 12 years of education? Will selecting your baby's genetic makeup be better than relying on nature? Just because growth *can* continue does not mean that it *should* continue. Moral judgments can be made against growth. For example, some argue that growth changes traditional cultures, with beautiful handiwork,

music and dance, into cultures of gadgets where people have lost touch with what is important. They argue that we have enough gadgets cluttering our lives and that it is time to start focusing on noneconomic priorities.

This moral argument against growth carries the most weight in highly developed countries—countries with per capita incomes of US$30,000 a year. For developing countries, where per capita income can be as low as US$150 per year, the reality is the choice between growth or poverty or even between growth or starvation. In these countries it is difficult to argue against growth.

One final comment: The benefits of growth do not have to be just higher incomes and more gadgets. They could also include more leisure activities and improved working conditions. In the 19th century a 12-hour workday was common. Today the workday is eight hours, but had we been content with a lower income the workday could now be two hours, with the remainder left for free time. We'd have less growth in GDP, but we'd have a lot more time to play.

their growth rates differed. From 1950 to 2000, France's income grew at an average rate of 3 percent per year while Argentina's grew at an average rate of 1 percent per year. Because of the differences in growth rates, France's per capita income is now over US$24,000 and Argentina's per capita income is about US$7,000. The difference in income levels translates into very real differences in the quality of life. For example, in France 100 percent of the people have access to safe water; in Argentina only 64 percent have such access. In France there are 546 phones per 1,000 people; in Argentina there are 174 phones per 1,000 people.

Other examples are Korea and the Congo. In the 1950s their incomes were also nearly identical, at US$150 per person. Because of differing growth rates, Korea's per capita income has multiplied more than 60 times, to about US$10,000, while the Congo's per capita income is still US$150. Why? Because the Congo has a zero growth rate while Korea has averaged a 9 percent annual growth rate. The moral of these stories: In the long run growth rates matter a lot.

Small differences in growth rates can mean huge differences in income levels because of *compounding*. Compounding means that growth is based not only on the original level of income but also on the accumulation of previous-year increases in income. For example, say you start at $100 and your income grows at a rate of 10 percent each year; the first year your income grows by $10, to $110. The second year the same growth rate increases income by $11, to $121. Then, the third year income grows by $12.10, which is still 10 percent but is a larger total increase. After 50 years that same 10 percent means an increase of over $70 a year.

Another way to see the effects of the difference in growth rates is to see how long it would take income to double at different growth rates. The Rule of 72 tells you that. The **Rule of 72** states. *divide 72 by the annual growth rate of income (or any variable) to get the number of years over which income (or any variable) will double.* For example, if

Growth in income improves lives by fulfilling basic needs and making more goods available to more people.

Q.2 If an economy is growing at 4 percent a year, how long will it take for its income to double?

Argentina's income grows at a 1 percent annual rate, it will double in 72 years (72/1). If France's income grows at a 3 percent annual rate, it will double in only 24 years (72/3).

Markets, Specialization, and Growth

One of the facts about growth mentioned in a previous chapter is that growth began when markets developed, and then, as markets expanded, growth accelerated. Why are markets so important to growth? To answer that question let's go back to Adam Smith's argument for markets. Smith argued that markets allow **specialization** (*the concentration of individuals in certain aspects of production*) and **division of labour** (*the splitting up of a task to allow for specialization of production*). According to Smith, markets create an interdependent economy in which individuals can take advantage of the benefits of specialization and trade for their other needs. In doing so markets increase productivity—and, in turn, improve the standard of living.

You saw in Chapter 2 how comparative advantage and specialization increase productivity. If individuals concentrate on the production of goods for which their skills and other resources are suited, and trade for those goods for which they do not have a comparative advantage, the economy's combined production possibility curve shifts out. To see this even more clearly, consider what your life would be like without markets, trade, and specialization. You would have to grow all your food, build your own living space, and provide all your own transportation. Simply to exist under these conditions, you'd need a lot of skills, and it is unlikely that you'd become sufficiently adept in any one of them to provide yourself with anything other than the basics. You'd have all you could do to keep up.

Now consider your life today with specialization. Someone who specializes in dairy farming produces the milk you need. You don't need to know how it is produced, just where to buy it. How about transportation? You buy, not build, your car. It runs somehow—you're not quite sure how—but if it breaks down, you take it to a garage. And consider your education: are you learning how to grow food or build a house? No, you are probably learning a specific skill that has little relevance to the production of most goods. But you'll most likely provide some good or service that will benefit the dairy farmer and auto mechanic. You get the picture—for most of the things you consume you don't have the faintest idea who makes them or how they are made, nor do you need to know.

Economic Growth, Distribution, and Markets

Markets and growth are often seen as unfair with regard to the distribution of income. Is it fair that markets give some individuals so much (billions to Bill Gates), and others so little ($6.85 an hour to Joe Wall, who has a minimum wage job and two kids)? Such questions are legitimate and need to be asked. But in answering them we should also remember the quotation from Joseph Schumpeter that opened this chapter: Even if markets and growth do not provide equality, they tend to make the poor better off. The relevant question is: Would the poor be better off with or without markets and growth?

Based on historical evidence, there are strong arguments that people are better off with markets. Consider the number of hours an average person must work to buy certain goods at various periods in history. A century ago it took a worker 1 hour and 41 minutes to earn enough to buy a pair of stockings; today it takes only 18 minutes of work. Figure 8-1 gives a number of other examples. As you can see from the figure, growth has made average workers significantly better off; to get the same amount, they have to work far less now than they did in the past. Growth has also made new products available. For example, before 1952 air conditioners were not available at any price.

Specialization and the division of labour that accompany markets increase productivity and growth.

Even though growth isn't evenly distributed, it generally raises the incomes of the poor.

Figure 8-1 | COST OF GOODS IN HOURS OF WORK

Growth in the economy in the past century has reduced the number of hours the average person needs to work to buy consumer goods.

Source: Federal Reserve Bank of Dallas, *Time Well Spent* (*1997 annual report*).

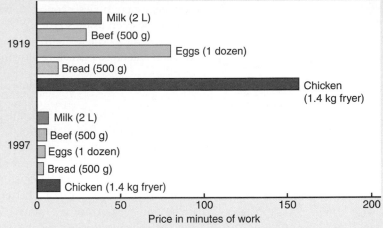

The reality is that, judged from an *absolute* standard, the poor benefit enormously from the growth that markets foster. Markets, through competition, make the factors of production more productive and lower the cost of goods, making more goods available to everyone.

The above argument does not mean that the poor always benefit from growth; many of us judge our well-being by relative, not absolute, standards. By reducing the share of income earned by the poorest proportion of society, growth often makes the poor *relatively* worse off. So, if one uses relative standards, one could say that the poor have become worse off over certain periods. Moreover, it is not at all clear that markets require the large differentials in pay that have accompanied growth in market economies. If such large differentials did not exist, and growth had been at the same rate, the poor would be even better off than they are.

> Just because the poor benefit from growth does not mean they might not be better off if income were distributed more in their favour.

Per Capita Growth

So far the discussion of growth has focused on increases in total output. Another important measure to consider is per capita output, or total output divided by the total population. Let's look at an example. But before we do, remember we need to add apples with apples. Each nation has its own currency and measures its output in terms of that currency. To compare output levels across countries, we need to convert figures to a common base. International agencies (such as the IMF) use the U.S. dollar as the standard, so let's frame our discussion in U.S. dollars. In China 1.3 billion people produce US$5.1 trillion worth of goods and services. Per capita output is US$3,900 (US$5.1 trillion divided by 1.3 billion). Production in Canada was about US$750 billion in 2001, so with our population of about 31 million, Canada's per capita output is US$24,200, or over six times that of China. In comparison, the U.S. economy produces about US$9.2 trillion of output, nearly twice as large as China's economy. The United States, however, has only 275 million people. Its per capita output is just over US$35,000, nearly 9 times that of China and about 1.4 times that of Canada. **Per capita growth** means *producing more goods and services per person.* For example, say the real output of the economy is $4 billion and that there are 1 million people. Each person, on average, has $4,000 to spend. Now say output increases by 50 percent but population also increases by 50 percent. There has been growth in output, but not in per capita

Q.3 Which country has experienced higher growth per capita: country A, whose economy is growing at a 4 percent rate and whose population is growing at a 3 percent rate, or country B, whose economy is growing at a 3 percent rate and whose population is growing at a 1 percent rate?

output; each person still has only $4,000 to spend. The reality is that even though many developing countries' economies have grown faster than that of Canada, their populations grew even faster so their per capita output growth has been lower.

If you know the percentage change in output and percentage change in population, you can calculate per capita growth:

Per capita growth = % change in output − % change in population

Let's try an example. In 1996, the Syrian economy grew 2 percent but the population grew 2.9 percent. Per capita growth equalled −0.9 percent (2 − 2.9). In that same year in Kazakhstan, output grew 1.3 percent and the population declined 0.4 percent. Per capita growth equalled 1.7 percent [1.3 − (−0.4)].

Some economists have argued that per capita output is not what we should be focusing on; they suggest that a better measure would be median income. (Remember, income and output are the same.) Per capita output measures the average, or *mean*, income. The *median* income, in contrast, is the income level that divides the population in equal halves. Half the people earn more and half the people earn less than the median income. Information from the 1996 Census indicates that median income per household in Canada was $33,326. Half of all households earned less than $33,326, and half earned more.

Q.4 How would changes in income have to be distributed for the mean and median to remain unchanged from their initial values?

Why focus on median income? Because it takes into account how income is distributed. If the growth in income goes to a small minority of individuals who already receive the majority of income, the mean will rise but the median will not. Let's consider an example where there is a large difference between the two measures. Say that the incomes of five people in a five-person economy are $20,000; $20,000; $30,000; $120,000; and $450,000. The median income is $30,000 (the middle income with two above and two below); the mean income is $128,000. Now say that the economy grows but that the two richest people get all the benefits, raising their incomes to $150,000 and $500,000, respectively. The median income remains $30,000; the mean income rises to $144,000. Unfortunately statistics on median income are generally not collected, so we will follow convention and focus on the mean, or per capita, income.

THE SOURCES OF GROWTH

Five sources of growth are:

1. Capital accumulation.
2. Available resources.
3. Growth-compatible institutions.
4. Technological development.
5. Entrepreneurship.

Economists have determined five important sources of growth:

1. Capital accumulation—investment in productive capacity.
2. Available resources.
3. Growth-compatible institutions.
4. Technological development.
5. Entrepreneurship.

Let's consider each in turn.

Investment and Accumulated Capital

At one point, capital accumulation (where capital was thought of as just *physical capital*—the buildings and machines available for production) and investment were seen as the key elements in growth. The *flow* of investment leads to the growth of the *stock* of capital. While physical capital is still considered a key element in growth, it is now generally recognized that the growth recipe is far more complicated. One of the reasons for the de-emphasis on capital accumulation is that empirical evidence has suggested that capital accumulation doesn't necessarily lead to growth. For instance, the former Soviet Union invested a lot and accumulated lots of capital goods, but its economy didn't grow much because its capital was often internationally obsolete. Another reason is that products change, and buildings and machines useful in one time period may be useless in another (e.g., a six-year-old computer often is worthless). The value of the capital stock depends on its future expected earnings, which are very uncertain. Capital's role in growth is extraordinarily difficult to measure with accuracy.

A third reason for this de-emphasis on capital accumulation is that it has become clear that capital includes much more than machines. In addition to physical capital, modern economics includes **human capital** (*the skills that are embodied in workers through experience, education, and on-the-job training, or more simply, people's knowledge*) and **social capital** (*the habitual way of doing things that guides people in how they approach production*) as types of capital. The importance of human capital is obvious; consider how money and a well-developed financial market make many investment projects possible that otherwise wouldn't be possible. Social capital is embodied in institutions such as the government, the legal system, and the fabric of society. In a way, anything that contributes to growth can be called a type of capital, and anything that slows growth can be called a destroyer of capital. With the concept of capital including such a wide range of things, it is difficult to say what is not capital, which makes the concept of capital less useful.

Despite this modern de-emphasis on investment and physical capital, all economists agree that the right kind of investment at the right time is a central element of growth. If an economy is to grow it must invest. The debate is about what kinds and what times are the right ones.

Available Resources

If an economy is to grow it will need resources. England grew in the late 1700s because it had iron and coal; Canada grew in the 20th century because it had a major supply of many resources, and it imported people, a resource it needed.

Of course, you have to be careful in thinking about what is considered a resource. A resource in one time period may not be a resource in another. For example, at one time oil was simply black gooey stuff that made land unusable. When people learned that the black gooey stuff could be burned as fuel, oil became a resource. What's considered a resource depends on technology. If solar technology is ever perfected, oil will go back to being black gooey stuff. So creativity can replace resources, and if you develop new technology fast enough, you can overcome almost any lack of existing resources. Even if a country doesn't have the physical resources it needs for growth, it can import them—as did Japan following the Second World War.

Greater participation in the market is another means by which to increase available resources. In China, for example, at the end of the 20th century many individuals migrated into the southern provinces, where there is a free trade sector. Before they migrated they were only marginally involved in the market economy. After they migrated they became employed in the market economy. This increased the labour available to the market, helping push up China's growth rate. In Canada beginning in the 1950s, the percentage of women entering the workforce increased, contributing to economic growth.

Increasing the labour force participation rate is not a totally costless way of increasing growth. What we lose is whatever it was people were doing before they went into the labour force (which was, presumably, something of value to society). Our national income accounting figures, which are measures of market activity, simply do not measure such losses.

A key determinant of an economy's economic well-being is the extent to which it has a well-educated, skilled labour force.

There are three types of capital:
1. Physical capital.
2. Social capital.
3. Human capital.

 8.1

see page 209

What is a resource depends on the production processes of an economy and technology.

The development of physical capital enhances an economy's capacity to produce, creates employment, and is a key element of long-term economic growth.

Growth-Compatible Institutions

Throughout this book we have emphasized the importance of economic institutions, which are vital for growth. Growth-compatible institutions—institutions that foster growth—must have incentives built into them that lead people to put forth effort and that discourage people from spending a lot of their time in leisure pursuits or creating impediments for others to gain income for themselves.

Q.5 Why is private property a source of growth?

When individuals get much of the gains of growth themselves, they have incentives to work harder. That's why markets and private ownership of property play an important role in growth. In the former Soviet Union, individuals didn't get much of the gain from their own initiative and, hence, often spent their time in pursuits other than those that would foster measured economic growth. Another growth-compatible institution is the corporation, a legal institution that gives owners limited liability and thereby encourages large enterprises (because people are more willing to invest their savings when their potential losses are limited).

Many developing countries follow a type of mercantilist policy in which government must approve any new economic activity. Some government officials get a large portion of their income from bribes offered to them by individuals who want to undertake economic activity. Such policies inhibit economic growth. Many regulations, even reasonable ones, also tend to inhibit economic growth because they inhibit entrepreneurial activities. But we should recall that some regulation is necessary to ensure that the growth is of a socially desirable type. The policy problem is in deciding between necessary and unnecessary regulation.

Technological Development

Growth isn't just getting more of the same thing. It's also getting some things that are different.

To think of growth as getting more of the same things is to take an incomplete view. While in some ways growth involves more of the same, a much larger aspect of growth involves changes in **technology**—changes in *the way we make goods and supply services* and changes in the goods and services we buy. Think of what this generation spends its income on—CDs, cars, computers, fast food—and compare that to what the preceding generation spent money on—LP records, cars that would now be considered obsolete, and tube and transistor radios. Technological change does more than cause economic growth; it changes social and political dimensions of society.

Contrast today's goods with the goods the next generation might spend its income on: video brain implants (little gadgets in your head to receive sound and full-vision broadcasts—you simply close your eyes and tune in whatever you want, if you've paid your cellular fee for that month); fuel-cell-powered cars (gas cars will be considered quaint but polluting); and instant food (little pills that fulfil all your nutritional needs, letting your brain implant gadget supply all the ambiance). Just imagine! You probably can get the picture even without a video brain implant.

How does society get people to work on developments that may change the very nature of what we do and how we think? One way is through economic incentives; another is with institutions that foster creativity and bold thinking—like this book; a third is through institutions that foster hard work. There are, of course, trade-offs. For example, the Japanese educational system, which fosters hard work and discipline, doesn't do as good a job at fostering creativity as the Canadian educational system, and vice versa. Thus, many of the new technologies of the 1980s were thought up in Canada and the United States but translated into workable products in Japan. For example, the transistor was developed in the United States, but Japan integrated it into competitive electronic products. Canadian inventors came up with a design for the electric light bulb—but sold out to Thomes Edison when they couldn't get funding for their new invention.

Still, Canada has done well on the technology front. Important developments in biotechnology, computers, and communications have occurred, and those developments helped fuel growth in the 1990s. Those new industries were much slower to develop in another important Canadian competitor, the European Union, which is one key reason why EU countries have grown far more slowly than has Canada in recent years.

Entrepreneurship

Entrepreneurship is the ability to get things done. That ability involves creativity, vision, and a talent for translating that vision into reality. When a country's population demonstrates entrepreneurship, it can overcome deficiencies in other ingredients that contribute to growth.

Turning the Sources of Growth into Growth

The five sources of growth cannot be taken as givens. Even if all five ingredients exist, they may not exist in the right proportions. For example, economic growth depends upon people's saving and investing rather than consuming their income. Investing now helps create machines that in the future can be used to produce more output with less effort. Growth also depends upon technological change—finding new, better ways to do things. For instance, when Nicolas Appert discovered canning (storing food in a sealed container in such a way that it wouldn't spoil) in the early 19th century, the economic possibilities of society expanded enormously. But if, when technological developments occur, the savings aren't there to finance the investment, the result will not be growth. It is finding the right combination of the sources of growth that plays a central role in the growth of any economy.

THE PRODUCTION FUNCTION AND THEORIES OF GROWTH

To try to get a better handle on the sources of growth, economists have developed a number of theories of growth. These have centred around the **production function,** an abstraction that shows *the relationship between the quantity of inputs used in production and the quantity of output resulting from production*. The production function we shall use is the following:

Output = A · f(Labour, Capital, Land)

This production function has land, labour, and capital as factors of production, and an adjustment factor A to capture the effect of changes in technology. The adjustment factor is outside the production function since it can affect the production of all factors. (The f stands for "function of.") The production function emphasizes the sources of growth: entrepreneurship is captured by labour, available resources by land, capital accumulation by capital, and technology and institutions by the production function itself.

In talking about production functions economists use a couple of important terms. The first describes what happens when all inputs increase equally—this is called *scale economies*. Scale economies describe what happens to output if all inputs increase by the same percentage. Say the amount of labour, land, and capital is doubled. What happens to output? If output also doubles, economists say that the production function exhibits **constant returns to scale,** which means that *output will rise by the same proportionate increase as all inputs*. With constant returns to scale, if all inputs rise by, say, 10 percent,

The production function shows the relationship between the quantity of inputs used in production and the quantity of output resulting from production.

Q-6 True or false? If you can increase production by 10 percent, by increasing all inputs by 20 percent the production process exhibits diminishing marginal productivity.

output will also rise by 10 percent. When *output rises by a greater proportionate increase than all inputs*, there are **increasing returns to scale;** and, when *output rises by a smaller proportionate increase than all inputs*, there are **decreasing returns to scale.**

The second term describes what happens when more of one input is added without increasing any other inputs. This case follows the **law of diminishing marginal productivity** (*increasing one input, keeping all others constant, will lead to smaller and smaller gains in output*). You were introduced to the law of diminishing marginal productivity in Chapter 2 when we discussed the production possibility curve. It is also known as the principle of increasing opportunity cost, or the flowerpot law. (If you keep adding seeds to a flowerpot, you will, past a certain point, get fewer and fewer flowers. See page 35 for a review.)

The law of diminishing marginal productivity applies to increases in any input, holding the others constant. As you put more and more labourers on a fixed plot of land, the increase in output contributed by each additional worker falls; eventually workers will get into each other's way and not only will the output per worker decline but so too will total output. The same goes for capital. The first computer will help a secretary prepare documents more quickly. A second might help, too, but less so than the first. A third would clutter the office.

The Standard Theory of Growth—the Classical Growth Model

Classical economists recognized that all the above factors contributed to growth, but (as mentioned earlier in this chapter) their models of growth focused on capital accumulation. The **Classical growth model** is *a model of growth that focuses on the role of capital accumulation in the growth process.* The Classical economists' major policy conclusion was: The more capital an economy has, the faster it will grow. This focus on capital is what caused our economic system to be called *capitalism*.

Since investment leads to the increase in capital, Classical economists focused their analysis, and their policy advice, on how to increase investment. The way to do that was for people to save:

Saving → Investment → Increase in capital → Growth

According to the Classical growth model, if an economy wants to grow, it has to save; the more saving, the better. Saving was good for both private individuals and governments. Thus, Classical economists objected to government deficits, which occur when government spends more than it collects in taxes. (This view of deficits and saving was directly challenged by Keynes in the 1930s, as we will see in the next chapter.)

Saving, investment, and capital are central to the Classical growth model.

Focus on Diminishing Marginal Productivity of Labour The early economists also focused on the law of diminishing marginal productivity. In the 1800s, when farming was the major activity of the economy, economists such as Thomas Malthus emphasized the limitations land placed on growth. They predicted that since land was relatively fixed, as the population grew diminishing marginal productivity would set in. Figure 8-2 shows a production function exhibiting diminishing marginal productivity.

Since each additional worker adds less output to production than the individual before, the production function is bowed downward. Output rises as the number of labourers increases, but it does not keep pace with increases in labour. Because of diminishing marginal productivity, per capita income declines as the labour supply increases. As output per person declines, at some point output available is no longer sufficient to feed the population.

In Figure 8-2 the straight line, labelled *subsistence level of output*, shows the minimum amount of output necessary to feed the labour force L. For example, at L_1, output is Q_2 and the minimum level of income for subsistence is Q_1. There is a surplus of $Q_2 - Q_1$. At L^* output is at its subsistence level. There is no surplus. Beyond L^* income falls below subsistence. If the population grows beyond L^*, some people would starve to death and the population would decline. Classical economists argued that the economy would be driven to point L^* in the long run, because whenever there was a surplus, workers would have more children, increasing the labour supply. This belief, called the *iron law of wages*, combined with the diminishing marginal productivity, led to the conclusion that in the long run there was no surplus and no growth. They called the long run the *stationary state*.

Focus on Diminishing Marginal Productivity of Capital The Classical economists' predictions were wrong. Per capita output did grow because of technological progress and increases in capital. Increases in technology and capital overwhelmed the law of diminishing marginal productivity and eventually economists no longer saw land as a constraint. Modern economists, such as Robert Solow, then changed the focus of the law of diminishing marginal productivity from labour to capital. They argued that as capital grew faster than labour, capital would become less productive and lead to slower and slower growth; eventually the per capita growth of our economy would stagnate. The economy could still grow if labour increased at the same rate as capital, but output would not grow any faster than the growth of the population. That is, per capita income would not grow.

The Classical growth model also predicted that as countries get more capital and become richer, their growth rates would slow down. Thus, poorer countries with little capital (such as the Latin American countries) should grow faster than richer countries with lots of capital (such as Canada). Why? Because diminishing marginal productivity would be stronger for richer countries with lots of capital than for poorer countries with little capital. Eventually per capita incomes among countries should converge.

These predictions have not come true either. As we saw in an earlier chapter, growth rates have increased, not decreased, and relative income levels of rich and poor countries have in many cases diverged, not converged. This difference between the observed reality and the predictions of the model caused economists to study the growth process empirically.

Q.7 If individuals suddenly needed less food to subsist, what would happen, according to the Classical growth model?

Technological progress and increases in capital have overwhelmed diminishing marginal productivity of labour.

Figure 8-2   DIMINISHING RETURNS AND POPULATION GROWTH

This production function exhibits diminishing marginal productivity of labour. Because of diminishing marginal productivity, per capita income declines as the labour supply increases. As output per person declines, at some point output available per person is no longer sufficient to feed the population. If the minimum level of income needed to survive is shown by the straight line, a population that exceeds L^* will experience starvation.

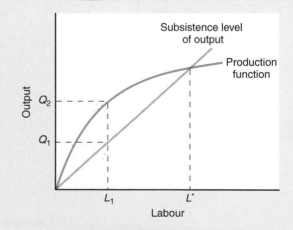

Sometimes newspapers write as if the importance of technology to the economy in the 21st century is a new phenomenon. It is not. Technology has been changing our society for the last two centuries, and it is not at all clear that the technological changes we are currently experiencing are any more revolutionary than those experienced by other generations in the last 200 years. For example, in terms of its impact on people's lives and communications in general, the Internet is small potatoes compared to the phone system.

One economist who recognized the importance of technology was Joseph Schumpeter. Schumpeter emphasized the role of the entrepreneur. He argued that entrepreneurs

APPLYING THE TOOLS

Is the 21st Century the Age of Technology or One of Many Ages of Technology?

create major technological changes that drive the economy forward.

According to Schumpeter, the economy's growth depends on these entrepreneurs, and the industries they are in will be the leading industries, pulling the rest of the economy along after them. The accompanying figure lists five waves of technological innovation that have driven our economy. As you can see, in the late 1700s steam power and iron manufacturing were the driving forces. In the 1860s, railroads were the dynamic industry. Later, electronics, automobiles, and chemicals drove our economy. In the 1980s through the early 21st century, computers and biotechnology have been the leading industries.

First wave 1785–1835	Second wave 1835–1885	Third wave 1885–1935	Fourth wave 1935–1985	Fifth wave 1985–?
Steam power Iron manufacturing	Railroad construction Mobile steam power Steam shipping	Chemicals Electricity Telegraph Telephone Automobiles	Electronics Drugs Oil Air transport Computers Nuclear power	Genetic engineering Telecommunications Biotechnology

Time

Why doesn't the theory match the reality? Economists came up with two answers: ambiguity in the definition of the factors of production, and technological progress.

Ambiguities in the Definition of the Factors of Production On the surface the terms in the production function seem relatively straightforward, but in reality they involve enormous ambiguity. We will focus on one important ambiguity—precisely what we mean by *labour*. As an input in production, labour may seem rather simple—it is the hours of work that go into production. As a first approximation that is what economists use as their measure of labour input. But labour is much more than the number of hours worked or the number of people working. The measure of labour needs adjustments to capture the skills, education, experience, and effort that labourers bring to production. These adjustments mean that measuring labour, and comparing the measurements among different countries, is difficult.

Here's an example of the type of problem that develops: Both Bangladesh and Japan have populations of about 125 million, but the average worker in Japan has more education than the average worker in Bangladesh. Do we increase the labour measured in Japan to account for that country's higher education? Generally, economists do so by separating labour into two components: standard labour (the actual number of workers or hours worked) and human capital (the skills that are embodied in workers through experience, education, and on-the-job training). Human capital gives us a measure for comparing the relative productivity of different workers. Thus, for example, when a society increases the amount of education it provides its workers, the country's human capital increases, even though labour hours may not increase.

Figure 8-3 **SOURCES OF REAL GDP GROWTH, 1928–1998**

Technology accounts for the majority of growth in many nations, followed closely by increases in labour.

Source: Edward F. Denison, *Trends in Economic Growth, 1928–82* (Washington, D.C.: The Brookings Institution, 1985), and authors' estimates.

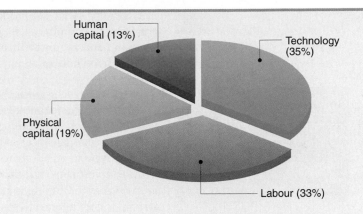

Notice how modifying the definition of *labour* to emphasize human capital provides a possible answer for the Classical growth model's incorrect predictions. If labour skills can be continually increasing, there is no need for physical capital to exhibit diminishing marginal productivity. The labour force might be growing at 5 percent, and capital at 7 percent, but the human capital measure of labour may be also increasing at 2 percent, so no diminishing marginal productivity should be expected and per capita output will rise by 2 percent. A variation of this argument can be used to explain why incomes between poor and rich countries have not converged. If skills in rich countries are increasing at a faster rate than skills in poor countries, incomes would not be expected to converge.

> Increases in human capital have allowed labour to keep pace with capital, allowing economies to avoid the diminishing productivity of capital.

Technology An additional explanation for the failure of the Classical growth model to accurately predict our growth experience is that we are continually finding new and better ways of doing things. Technology has developed, and is growing, faster in rich countries than in poor countries. If technology grows, it increases the productivity of all inputs and allows growth to continue. If technology grows faster than the diminishing marginal productivity of new capital, and grows faster over time, growth for all practical purposes has no limit. Technology overwhelms diminishing marginal productivity and growth rates increase over time: the economy gets richer and richer. The Classical model does not focus on technology but rather takes it as given.

Empirical Estimates of Factor Contribution to Growth To determine which of these explanations was most probable, economist Edward Denison estimated the importance of each of the sources of growth for many countries.

These estimates, shown in Figure 8-3, suggest that increases in labour account for 33 percent, increases in physical capital account for 19 percent, increases in human capital account for 13 percent, and advances in technology account for the remaining 35 percent of growth. (Land does not appear in Denison's estimates; countries are assumed to be endowed with a given amount of land and natural resources.) While the specific percentages are at best rough, the importance of technology to growth is not. It is for that reason that modern economic thinking about growth has focused more and more on technology.

New Growth Theory

Modern growth theory goes under the name *new growth theory*. **New growth theory** is *a theory that emphasizes the role of technology rather than capital in the growth process.* Increases

> New growth theory emphasizes technology as the primary source of growth.

8.2
see page 209

in technology shift the production possibility curve out, and thus make the choices an economy faces a bit easier to make—they allow the society to get more of everything. Unlike Classical growth theory, which left technology outside of economic analysis, new growth theory focuses its analysis on technology.

Technological advances are a primary source of economic growth and an enhancement to an economy's standard of living.

Technology New growth theory's central argument is that increases in technology do not just happen. Technological advance is the result of what the economy does—it invests in research and development (e.g., drug companies researching new ways to fight disease); makes advances in pure science (e.g., the human genome project); and works out new ways to organize production (e.g., just-in-time inventory techniques). Thus, in a sense, investment in technology increases the technological stock of an economy just as investment in capital increases the capital stock of an economy. Investment in technology is called research and development; firms hire researchers to explore options. Some of those options pay off and others do not, but the net return of that investment in technology is an increase in technology.

If investment in technology is similar to investment in capital, why does new growth theory separate the two? The reason is twofold. First, increases in technology are not as directly linked to investment as capital is. Increases in investment require increases in saving, that is, building the capital. Increases in technology can occur with little investment and saving if the proverbial light bulb goes off in someone's head and that person sees a new way of doing something.

The common knowledge aspect of technology creates positive externalities, which new growth theory sees as the key to growth.

Second, increases in technology often have enormous positive spillover effects, especially if the new technology involves common knowledge and is freely available to all. A technological gain in one sector of production gives other sectors of production new ideas on how to change what they are doing, which gives other people new ideas. Ideas spread like pool balls after the break. One hits another, and soon all the nearby balls have moved. Put in technical economic terms, technological change often has significant **positive externalities**—*positive effects on others not taken into account by the decision maker.* Through those externalities, what is called general purpose technological change can have a much larger effect on growth than can an increase in capital.

The positive externalities result from the *common knowledge* aspect of technology because the idea behind the technology can often be used by others without payment to the developer. Using the same assembly line for different car models is just one example of a technological advance that has become incorporated into common knowledge. Any car manufacturer can use it.

8.3
see page 209

Basic research is not always freely available; it is often protected by **patents**—*legal ownership of a technological innovation that gives the owner of the patent sole rights to its use and distribution for a limited time.* (If the development is an idea rather than a good, it can be copyrighted rather than patented, but the general concept is the same.) Patents turn innovations into private property. The Windows operating system is an example of a technology that is owned, and hence is not common knowledge. The ideas in technologies that are covered by patents, however, often have common knowledge elements. Once people have seen the new technology, they figure out sufficiently different ways of achieving the same end.

Learning by doing overcomes the law of diminishing marginal productivity because learning by doing increases the productivity of workers.

Learning by Doing As the new growth theory has analyzed technology, it has focused economic thinking on another aspect of economic processes—an individual's tendency to **learn by doing,** or *to improve the methods of production through experience.* As people do something, they become better and better at it, sometimes because of new technologies, and sometimes simply because they learned better ways to do it just from practice.

Figure 8-4　INCREASING RETURNS TO SCALE

With increasing returns, increases in inputs lead to proportionately greater increases in output. New growth theory focuses on increasing returns to scale. With increasing returns, output per person can rise forever.

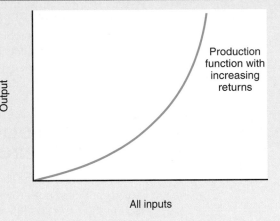

Thus, as production increases, costs of production tend to decrease over time. The introduction of new technology is sometimes the result of learning by doing.

Learning by doing changes the laws of economics enormously. It suggests that production has positive externalities in learning. If these positive externalities overwhelm diminishing marginal productivity, as new growth theory suggests they do, the predictions about growth change. In the Classical theory, growth is limited by diminishing marginal productivity; in the new theory, growth potential is unlimited and can accelerate over time. It's a whole new world out there—one in which, holding wants constant, scarcity decreases over time.

We can see in Figure 8-4 new growth theory's predictions for future growth. All inputs are on the horizontal axis, and the production function exhibits increasing returns to scale. (As more inputs are added, the additional output per combination of inputs increases.) With this curve, per capita income can grow forever and the dismal science of economics becomes the optimistic science.

Technological Lock-In One of the questions new growth theory raises is: Does the economy always use the "best" technology available? Some say no and point to examples of technologies that have become entrenched in the market, or locked in to new products despite the availability of more efficient technologies. This is known as *technological lock-in*.

One proposed example of technological lock-in goes under the name QWERTY, which is the upper left six keys on the standard computer keyboard. Economist Paul David argues that the design of this keyboard was chosen to slow people's typing down so that the keys in old-style mechanical typewriters would not lock up. He further argues that developments in word processing have since eliminated the problem the QWERTY keyboard was designed to solve (we don't use mechanical typewriters any more). But once people started choosing this keyboard, it was too costly for them to develop another.

This interpretation of history has been disputed by other economists, who argue that the QWERTY keyboard is not significantly less efficient than other keyboard arrangements and that, if it were, competition would have eliminated it. Sometimes this counterargument almost seems to state that the very fact that a technology exists means that it is the most efficient. Most economists do not go that far; they argue that even if the QWERTY keyboard is not a highly inefficient technology, other examples of lock-in exist—beta format videos were preferable to VHS, the Windows operating

Q-8　In what way does the Internet demonstrate network externalities?

system is inferior to many alternatives, the English language doesn't compare to Esperanto, and English measurement systems are quite inefficient compared to metric.

One reason for technological lock-in is *network externalities*—an externality in which the use of a good by one individual makes that technology more valuable to other people. Network externalities make switching to a superior technology expensive or nearly impossible. The Windows operating system exhibits network externalities.

ECONOMIC POLICIES TO ENCOURAGE PER CAPITA GROWTH

General pronouncements about growth are nice, but society is most interested in growth policies, not growth theories. What policies lead to higher growth rates? This section discusses six different policy options that have been used to increase an economy's per capita growth rate.

Policies to Encourage Saving and Investment

Although new growth theory has downplayed the central role of capital in the growth process, new growth theorists agree that capital and investment are still important. So policymakers interested in increasing growth are always looking for ways to encourage both saving and investment. One of the plans they have used in Canada is tax incentives for saving. Thus, our income tax laws have registered retirement savings plans (RSPs) that allow individuals to save without incurring taxes on contributions until they are withdrawn. Some economists have even proposed switching from an income tax to a consumption tax, which taxes individuals only when they consume and therefore exempts all saving from taxation.

Developed countries can generate saving and investment far more easily than can developing countries. The problem in poorer countries is that the poor don't have much discretionary income, and hence can't save much, and the rich are concerned about confiscation of their wealth, and hence save abroad, either legally or illegally. Moreover, the small middle class that does exist can find few financial instruments to effectively channel saving into investment. For developing countries, generating saving and investment often requires creating new financial institutions. Let's consider a case study that gives some insight into a success story.

Developing countries have a much harder time designing saving policies than do developed countries.

A Case Study: The Borrowing Circle Our case study considers the development of a financial institution in one of the poorest countries of the world—Bangladesh. There, Mohammed Yunus, a U.S.-trained economist, created a bank—the Grameen Bank—that made loans to poor village women at market interest rates. According to reports, the loans had a 97 percent payback rate, and Yunus made a profit.

How did he do it? Most banks in developing countries are internationally oriented. They use the same structure that Western banks use. This leaves the traditional part of many developing countries' economies without an effective way to translate saving into investment, stranding many entrepreneurial individuals without ways to develop their ideas. Yunus reconsidered the fundamental role of banking in an economy—to make it possible for people with good ideas to develop those ideas by providing them with funds and to devise a structure that allowed such lending to take place.

He saw that Western banking institutions did not provide the answer for Bangladesh. By basing their lending decisions on the amount of collateral a borrower had, they essentially made it impossible for most people in Bangladesh to get loans. But Yunus also recognized that the collateral function served a useful purpose: it forced people to make the difficult decision about whether they really needed the loans, and to work hard to see that they could pay the loans back, even if the going got tough. If you eliminate collateral, something else must replace it.

Yunus' ingenious solution was the *borrowing circle*—a credit system that replaces traditional collateral with guarantees by friends of the borrower. Recognizing that social pressures were extremely strong in Bangladesh, Yunus offered to make loans to any woman who could find four friends who would agree to help her pay the loan back if necessary. If the borrower defaulted, the others could not borrow until the loan was repaid.

This simple concept worked. Today the Grameen Bank has more than 2.3 million borrowers and lends US$35 million every month. The loans are taken out to buy such things as a cow or material to make a fishing net—not large items, but items to use in the types of activity that generate bottom-up growth.

Yunus' work has received numerous accolades, and even developed countries are looking into the borrowing circle concept as a way of getting credit to the poor. While the concept is extraordinarily simple, it made use of economic insights that simultaneously reflected an understanding of the cultural and social dimensions of the economy. It is the type of macro policy most needed to promote growth in developing countries.

Growth through Foreign Investment If developing countries don't generate sufficient saving domestically, they must turn to foreign sources for saving. They can borrow from either the International Monetary Fund, the World Bank, or private sources. All have their problems. IMF and World Bank loans usually come with strict requirements on the country's fiscal and monetary policy, and private investment can leave the country exposed to capital flight and exchange rate problems. (We'll consider these issues in more detail in later chapters.)

Policies to Control Population Growth

Population control policies in developing countries have played an important role in discussions of increasing per capita growth rates. Population among low-income countries has grown an average 2.3 percent a year since 1980, compared to 0.7 percent for high-income countries. The reason high population growth presents a problem for economic growth is that it makes providing sufficient capital and education for everyone difficult. The factors of production have to be shared among more people and the law of diminishing productivity sets in. Workers cannot produce as much as before and per capita growth falls. For some low-income countries, population growth has meant an increase in the relative number of dependents (people too old or too young to work). For these countries, each worker must support a larger number of people.

Policies that reduce population growth include setting up free family-planning services, increasing the availability of contraceptives, and allowing only one child per family. China, which has one-fifth of the world's population, adopted the latter policy in 1980 and enforced it by harsh penalties, such as job loss, for those who did not comply. It reduced population growth from over 2 percent in the 1970s to just over 1 percent today.

In contrast, some economists argue that to reduce population growth, a country needs to grow first. They argue that as income and work opportunities, especially for women, rise, the opportunity cost of having children rises and families will choose to have fewer children. In most industrialized countries, population growth has not been a problem. Economic growth has led many people to have fewer children and to want other things instead—more income, more vacations, more cars, and so on.

In Canada, where the birth rate is below replacement levels, immigration has provided one source of growth in population and total output. Immigration in Canada was substantial in the 1990s. This has increased the labour force and output. However, there is a debate about whether greater immigration has increased output per capita or not.

Developing countries whose populations are rapidly growing have difficulty providing enough capital and education for everyone. Consequently, income per capita is low.

Policies to Increase the Level of Education

Another way to increase output per capita is to increase human capital. Increasing the educational level of the workforce increases labour productivity. In Canada, government policies to increase education include free mandatory education for students through high school, financial support for students going on to higher education, and direct subsidies of teaching institutions to help keep tuition down.

In developing countries, basic skills—reading, writing, and arithmetic—are very important for economic growth. For these countries, the return on investment in education is much higher than it is for Canada, where the level of human capital is already high. In Canada, an additional year of education increases a worker's wages by an average of 10 percent, whereas in developing countries, an additional year of education will increase wages by 15 to 20 percent.

Of course by *education*, we mean the right kind of education. For developing countries the majority of jobs require only a primary education, so spending on general education is important. Technical training in improved farming methods or construction is also important; studying movements in postmodern philosophy is significantly less relevant to growth. Unfortunately, politics often guides developing countries' education policies to place more emphasis on higher education than on basic education.

Policies to Create Institutions That Encourage Technological Innovation

As we saw in Figure 8-3, the largest source of growth is technology. Thus, it is not surprising that economic policies focus on technology. The policy problem is that while all agree that technology is important, no one is sure what the best technological growth policies are.

The reason is that technological development is inherently uncertain. New technologies could result intentionally from research and development, or unintentionally from some other activity, or simply from a wondering mind. (Is your mind wondering now—are you developing the next new big idea that will reshape the world?) No one really knows when another innovation will be discovered. Some investments take years to pay off. For example, drug companies have been working for the past 30 years to find a drug to target diabetes affecting kidneys and nerves. A number of times they thought they had found it but were proved wrong. However, a new drug is currently being tested and, if it passes the tests, will reach the market early in this century.

Not only is the nature of research uncertain, but so is its application. Individuals have not been especially good at deciding which technologies will work and which will not. Consider some famous examples of poor guesses. In 1877, Western Union turned down the opportunity to buy the patent on Alexander Graham Bell's telephone for US$100,000 because it believed that the telegraph was superior. In the 1940s, the chairman of IBM, Thomas Watson Sr., could see no commercial demand for computers and felt that the IBM computer at the company's New York headquarters "could solve all the important scientific problems in the world involving scientific calculations." Perhaps the poorest guess came in 1899 from the commissioner of patents, who argued that the U.S. Patent Office should be closed because "everything that can be invented has been invented." We could list many more examples, but the idea is clear: When it comes to technology, few have done well in predicting what would succeed and what would fail.

Create Patents and Protect Property Rights Government can reduce the risks faced by innovators and entrepreneurs by creating and protecting property rights, creating in-

Q.9 Why would increases in education likely have a greater return in terms of increased output in developing countries than in developed countries?

Unlike capital, technological innovation can occur without investment; conversely, investment in technology can also result in no technological innovation.

stitutions that limit the risk to investing in R&D, and providing a stable government. Consider patents. By holding a patent, a firm can be the sole supplier, and charge higher prices for its product than it could otherwise. The promise of higher profit that comes with a patent provides an incentive to innovate.

Patents, however, are not costless to society. While patents provide an incentive to innovators, patented innovations will be priced high and thus fewer people will benefit from them. As we noted earlier, it is the common knowledge aspect of technology that leads to positive externalities and, thus, to the highest payoff in terms of growth. Our decimal number system is an example of a nonpatented idea. The Arabians developed a system of counting based on the decimal system; it was far more efficient than the Roman numeral system. (Have you ever tried multiplying IV times VI?) Had that idea been copyrighted (and if that copyright could be enforced), every time you multiply using the Arabic numeral system, you would have to make a small payment to the holder of the copyright. Currently Canada is struggling with questions such as: Should general Internet business methods, such as providing a virtual shopping cart to purchase items over the Internet, be patentable?

In assigning copyrights, patents, and property rights all agree that societies must find a middle ground between giving individuals appropriate incentives to create new technologies by giving them monopoly rights to those developments and allowing everyone to take advantage of the benefits of technology. There is far less agreement on what the appropriate middle ground is.

Pharmaceuticals provide an example of the type of debate that develops. Since pharmaceutical products save lives, an argument can be made that any patent that causes higher prices and thereby limits their use is immoral. The problem is that without the patent, fewer drugs will be developed. What happens in practice is that drugs are given a patent for a limited period, after which the drugs become "generically reproducible," and their price goes down considerably. The policy debate is over what the length of that period should be.

Patents and Developing Countries Developing countries face an even more complicated issue. Should they accept our patent laws, or should they allow much freer use of new technological developments? Canada naturally wants them to accept and enforce our patents and copyrights, and has made that acceptance a requirement for open trade relations. This puts great pressure on the other countries to comply in theory, but to enforce the laws as weakly as possible in practice. For example, the United States and China have been engaged in an ongoing fight on the enforcement of U.S. copyrights on computer software. You can buy a Windows 98 CD in many of the open markets in China for under $2; that's below the copyright cost, so it is a good bet that those CDs are "bootlegged"—produced out of copyright.

The Corporation and Financial Institutions Along with providing incentives for investment through patents, governments have also developed institutions that limit the risk to investors. As noted earlier in this chapter the corporation was developed to limit liability to investors. In a corporation, an investor's only risk is his or her investment in that corporation. This encourages investors to pool their funds. The corporate form of organization is important to the growth of technology because bringing technological innovation to market often requires large amounts of investment over a number of years. Consider railroads or telephones, which both required huge investments to make them available.

Well-developed financial institutions such as the stock market also help drive technological development. The stock market allows initial investors to sell their investment

Q-10 Which has the possibility for a greater payoff to growth—an idea that is patented or common knowledge? Which does an individual have a greater incentive to discover?

Finding a middle ground between allowing patents which create incentives for developing countries' new technologies and exploiting the common knowledge aspect of technology is a difficult policy problem.

to others so that they are not tied into one company alone. Consider whether you would invest in Amazon.com if you couldn't sell the shares to someone else. Put in technical terms, the stock market makes investments more liquid (changeable into other types of assets) and thereby encourages investment in general.

Policies to Provide Funding for Basic Research

Canadian government agencies provide the lion's share of all research and development funds for basic research.

As we discussed above it is technology's "common knowledge" aspect that has the greatest positive effect on growth but that gives firms little incentive to do research. By funding basic research the government can create the seeds for growth. The Canadian government funds the lion's share of basic research in Canada. Much of this funding is channelled through universities. Thus, it is not surprising that many of the high-tech businesses that have led the recent growth spurt are clustered around universities. Because basic research creates spin-offs and leads to pockets of growth, communities are willing to subsidize universities in their area and give tax relief to new-technology firms.

Many professors doing basic research for universities are also working for for-profit start-up companies. Their dual roles create a conflict of allegiances. Wearing their university hat, they want to make their discoveries widely available; wearing the for-profit hat, they want to keep their discoveries proprietary.

Policies to Increase the Economy's Openness to Trade

At the beginning of this chapter we emphasized that growth is associated with the development of markets. Markets allow individuals and firms to specialize, and specialization allows firms and workers to become more productive. In specialization, the bigger the market, the better. You have to be able to sell your specialized product to large numbers of people—that is, you need a large market.

Stating a policy rule is easy; applying it to specific cases is difficult.

Large markets allow firms to take advantage of economies of scale. The effect of markets on growth is an important reason economists generally support policies that encourage international free trade. Most economists believe that policies allowing free trade increase growth by increasing competition. (For example, relaxation of import tariffs on Japanese automobile imports made North American producers change their production methods and improve the quality of North American–made cars.) That's why they generally support the creation of free trade areas such as NAFTA and the EU, as well as the World Trade Organization.

Domestically, being open to trade means opposing regulations whose primary function is to protect vested interests. The problem is that most regulations have multiple functions—some preventing trade, and some providing necessary protections.

CONCLUSION

This chapter has presented economists' thinking about the nature and causes of growth. That thinking has evolved from a view that in the long run our growth prospects are limited because of diminishing marginal productivity to a view that technological change creates unlimited growth potential.

This new optimism needs to be tempered. The majority of you reading this book were born in the 1980s. Your memories started around the late 1980s, and your knowledge of the economy is shaped by those memories. For you, growth is probably just something that happens, and a growing economy seems natural. Focusing the analysis on long-run growth seems the reasonable thing to do. But the focus can change suddenly. In October 1998, the world economy almost experienced a meltdown. The situation originated in Asia in 1997. The "Asian tiger" economies—including countries such as Singapore, South Korea, and Thailand, which had grown the fastest of any economies in the 1980s and early 1990s—collapsed and fell into a serious recession. Many feared that the Canadian economy would enter recession too.

Luckily, the Canadian economy kept growing, but the possibility of a recession still exists. Should the possibility become a threat, the focus of policy would quickly change from growth, and from the long run to the short run. The question would become how to prevent, or get out of, the recession. In the next two chapters, we'll present the short-run framework that economists use to analyze such issues.

Chapter Summary

- Growth is an increase in the amount of goods and services an economy can produce when both labour and capital are fully employed.

- Growth increases potential output and shifts the production possibility curve out, allowing an economy to produce more goods.

- Growth in income improves lives by fulfilling basic needs and making more goods available to more people.

- Per capita growth means producing more goods and services per person. It can be calculated by subtracting the percentage change in the population from the percentage change in output.

- Five sources of growth are (1) investment in accumulated capital, (2) available resources, (3) growth-compatible institutions, (4) technological development, and (5) entrepreneurship.

- The production function shows the relationship between the quantity of labour, capital, and land used in production and the quantity of output resulting from production.

- The law of diminishing marginal productivity states that increasing one input, keeping all others constant, will lead to smaller and smaller gains in output.

- Returns to scale describes what happens to output when all inputs increase equally.

- The Classical growth model focuses on the role of capital accumulation in the growth process. The law of diminishing productivity limits growth of per capita income.

- New growth theory emphasizes the role of technology in the growth process. Increasing returns to scale means output per person can rise forever.

- Advances in technology, which account for 35 percent of growth, have overwhelmed the effects of diminishing returns.

- Six government policies to promote growth are (1) encourage saving and investment, (2) control population growth, (3) increase the level of education, (4) create institutions that encourage technological innovation, (5) fund basic research, and (6) increase openness to trade.

Key Terms

Classical growth model (196)

constant returns to scale (195)

decreasing returns to scale (196)

division of labour (190)

growth (188)

human capital (193)

increasing returns to scale (196)

law of diminishing marginal productivity (196)

learn by doing (200)

new growth theory (199)

patents (200)

per capita growth (191)

positive externality (200)

production function (195)

productivity (188)

Rule of 72 (189)

Say's law (188)

social capital (193)

specialization (190)

technology (194)

Questions for Thought and Review

1. a. If you suddenly found yourself living as a poor person in a developing country, what are some things that you now do that you would no longer be able to do? What new things would you have to do?

   b. Answer the questions again assuming that you are living in Canada 100 years ago.

2. Who most likely worked longer to buy a dozen eggs: a person living in 1990 or a person living in 1910? Why?

3. What roles do specialization and division of labour play in economists' support of free trade?

4. How can an increase in the Canadian saving rate lead to higher living standards? What problem would a

politician face when promoting policies to encourage saving?

5. Name three types of capital and explain the differences among them.

6. Name two ways in which growth through technology differs from growth through the accumulation of physical capital.

7. What are two actions government can take to promote the development of new technologies?

8. On what law of production did Thomas Malthus base his prediction that population growth would exceed growth in goods and services? Why hasn't his prediction come true?

9. If individuals suddenly needed more food to subsist, what would the Classical growth model predict would happen to labour and output? Demonstrate graphically.

10. What are network externalities and how do they lead to growth?

11. List three ways in which growth can be undesirable. Can growth itself address those problems?

12. *Credentialism* occurs when a person's degrees become more important than his or her actual knowledge. How can credentialism hurt economic growth?

13. In what ways can competition promote technological advance? In what ways can competition harm technological advance?

14. If you were designing a development plan for Pakistan, would you suggest the country accept or reject Western copyright and patent law? Why?

15. Explain why communities are willing to give tax relief to new-technology firms that locate in their community.

Problems and Exercises

1. Income in the world economy grew an average of 2 percent per year since 1950. If this growth continues, how many years will it take for income to double?

2. If output increases by 20 percent when one of two inputs increases by 20 percent, are there constant returns to scale? Why or why not?

3. Per capita income is growing at different rates in the following countries: Nepal, 1.1 percent; Kenya, 1.7 percent; Singapore, 7.2 percent; Egypt, 3.9 percent. How long will it take for each country to double its income per person?

4. Calculate growth per capita from 1996 to 1997 in the following countries:
   a. Democratic Republic of Congo: population growth = 3.2 percent; output growth = 0.5 percent.
   b. Estonia: population growth = −1.2 percent; output growth = 6.4 percent.
   c. India: population growth = 3.2 percent; output growth = 5 percent.
   d. Canada: population growth = 1.0 percent; output growth = 3.8 percent.

5. Say that you have been hired to design an education system for a developing country.
   a. What skills will you want it to emphasize?
   b. How might it differ from an ideal educational system here in Canada?

6. Could the borrowing circle concept be adopted for use in Canada?
   a. Why or why not?

b. What modifications would you suggest if it were to be adopted?

c. Minorities in Canada often do not use banks. In what ways are Canadian minorities' problems similar to those of people in developing countries?

7. The graph below shows a production function and the subsistence level of output.
   a. Does the production function exhibit increasing or decreasing marginal productivity?
   b. Label a level of population at which the population is expected to grow. What is the surplus output at that population level?
   c. Label a level of population at which the population is expected to decline. Why is the population declining at this point?
   d. Label the population at which the economy is in a steady state. Why is this a steady state?

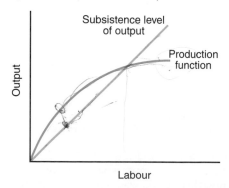

Web Questions

1. Go to the World Bank's home page (www.worldbank.org) and look up Kenya, Mexico, Canada, and Japan.
   a. What is the per capita growth rate of income for each country over the past 20 years?
   b. What is the population growth for each country over the past 20 years?
   c. What is the investment share for each country over the past 20 years?

2. The Heritage Foundation and *The Wall Street Journal* co-publish an Index of Economic Freedom designed to measure the extent to which markets are allowed to operate freely in a country. Go to the home page of the Heritage Foundation (www.heritage.org) and look up the index for two of the top-rated countries and two of the bottom-rated countries.

   a. What are the reasons for their ratings?
   b. Compare the recent per capita growth rates of each country. Is economic freedom related to growth? If so, how?

3. Go to the Canadian Intellectual Property Office Web site (strategis.ic.gc.ca) and find out for how long patents are granted in Canada. Now go to the U.S. patent office Web site (www.uspto.gov) and find out for how long patents are granted in the United States.
   a. What are the advantages of shortening the length of patents?
   b. What are the disadvantages of shortening the length of patents?
   c. Is there a difference in the time granted to patents in the U.S. and Canada? Why?

Answers to Margin Questions

1. The long-run growth analysis justifies its focus on supply by assuming that aggregate supply will create an equal level of aggregate demand. This is known as Say's law. *(188)*

2. Using the Rule of 72 (divide 72 by the growth rate of income) we can calculate that it will take 18 years for income to double when its growth rate is 4 percent a year. *(189)*

3. Country B is experiencing the higher growth in income per capita. To calculate this, subtract the population growth rates from the income growth rates for each country. Country A's per capita growth rate is 1 percent $(4 - 3)$ and country B's per capita growth rate is 2 percent $(3 - 1)$. *(192)*

4. If the mean is unchanged, those who gained income would have to receive exactly what those who lost income gave up. For the median to remain fixed, the gains and losses would have to be symmetrically distributed around the initial median. *(192)*

5. Private property provides an incentive for people to produce by creating the possibility of benefiting from their efforts. *(194)*

6. False. A 20 percent increase in production that results from a 10 percent increase in all inputs means the production process exhibits decreasing returns to scale. A key part of the statement is that all inputs are changing.

If one input were being kept fixed, the production function would be exhibiting diminishing marginal productivity. *(196)*

7. If individuals suddenly needed less food, the subsistence level line would rotate down. The number of labourers the economy could sustain would rise, and output would rise as well. *(197)*

8. The Internet connects hundreds of millions of people around the globe and reduces communication costs. The benefit of one person using the Internet is virtually nonexistent. The benefit of the Internet rises as more people use it, because the higher usage increases the amount of information available on the Internet and increases the ability of each user to communicate. *(201)*

9. Because the level of education is higher in Canada compared to developing countries, the law of diminishing marginal productivity of education is stronger in Canada. The benefit of additional education in Canada is lower compared to that in developing countries. *(204)*

10. Because common knowledge has greater positive externalities, common knowledge has a greater possibility of payoff in terms of growth. People have a greater incentive to discover an idea that can be patented because a patent gives the innovator the sole right to sell the idea. *(205)*

Aggregate Demand, Aggregate Supply, and Modern Macroeconomics

9

After reading this chapter, you should be able to:

- Discuss the historical development of modern macroeconomics.

- Explain the shape of the aggregate demand curve and what factors shift the curve.

- Explain the shape of the short-run aggregate supply curve and what factors shift the curve.

- Explain the shape of the long-run aggregate supply curve.

- Show the effects of shifts of the aggregate demand and aggregate supply curves on price level and output in both the short run and long run.

- Discuss the limitations of the macro policy model.

The Theory of Economics . . . is a method rather than a doctrine, an apparatus of the mind, a technique of thinking which helps its possessor to draw correct conclusions.

J. M. Keynes

In the last chapter's discussion of growth and markets we focused on the positive side of markets; we saw that markets unleash individual incentives, increase supply, and bring about growth. But markets can run into serious problems—markets can create recessions, inflation, and unemployment. Japan in the late 1990s is a good example. After a number of years of substantial growth, Japan's economy fell into recession.

Policymakers had to decide whether to intervene in the market or simply hope the recession would end on its own.

The macro intervention tools—monetary and fiscal policy—are tools governments use on the aggregate demand side of the economy to deal with recessions, inflation, and unemployment. Thus, whereas the last chapter's policy focus was on production (the supply side) and individual incentives, this chapter and the next focus on expenditures (the demand side).

Economists debate the effectiveness of monetary and fiscal policy. Some favour intervention; some don't. While the problems of a recession are serious, so too are the problems with government policies. The debate among economists is about whether the cure (intervention) is worse than the disease.

Even if the noninterventionist economists were to convince all other economists that government should not intervene with monetary and fiscal policy, the odds are that government would still intervene. As we've said before, the reality is that politicians make policy; they listen to economists only when they want to. And whenever the economy faces the threat of a recession, politicians' focus inevitably changes from long-run supply issues and growth to short-run demand issues and stabilization.

Consider 2001 as an example. After a number of years of steady growth, world output began to fall. A severe recession that had begun in Asia in 1997 was spreading. The U.S. and Canadian economies began to grow at a much slower pace than in the late 1990s. In response, both the Bank of Canada and the Federal Reserve Board, the central banks in Canada and the United States, respectively, began running expansionary policies to try to offset the effects of the slowdown. The events of September 11, 2001, and the already weak outlook led to a reduction in real GDP in Canada in the third quarter. By the end of the year it appeared Canada would probably sidestep a full-blown recession, but the outlook for the economy remained guarded. Early in 2002 government officials expressed confidence that the Canadian economy was strong and that it would return to its previous levels of growth, but that it may take a year or more for the economy to gain "its second wind."

> The short-run macro intervention tools are monetary and fiscal policy. We'll be discussing these in detail later, but it pays to learn them now.

> Politicians listen to economists only when they want to; politics, not economics, generally guide policy.

THE HISTORICAL DEVELOPMENT OF MODERN MACRO

An important reason for politicians' initial interest in short-run stabilization is the Great Depression of the 1930s, a deep recession that lasted for many years. It was that experience that led to the development of macroeconomics as a separate course, and to the development of aggregate demand tools to deal with recurring recessions.

Most of you only think of the Great Depression as something your grandparents and great-grandparents experienced. But it was a defining event that undermined people's faith in markets and was the beginning of modern macro's focus on the demand side of the economy. It is also where our story of modern macroeconomics begins.

During the Depression, output fell by 30 percent and unemployment rose to nearly 20 percent. Not only was the deadbeat up the street unemployed, so were your brother, your mother, your uncle—the hardworking backbone of the country. These people wanted to work, and eventually decided that if the market wasn't creating jobs for them, the market system was at fault.

 9.1

see page 233

From Classical to Keynesian Economics

As we discussed in an earlier chapter, economists before the Depression focused on the long run and the problem of growth. Their policy recommendations were designed to lead to long-run growth, and they avoided discussing policies that would affect the economy in the short run. In the 1930s macroeconomists started focusing their discussion of macroeconomic policy on short-run issues. To distinguish the two types of economics, the earlier economists who focused on long-run issues such as growth were called *Classical economists* and economists who focused on the short run were called *Keynesian economists*. Keynesian economists were named because a leading advocate of the short-run focus was John Maynard Keynes, the author of *The General Theory of Employment, Interest and Money*, and the originator of modern macroeconomics.

Classical Economists

Classical economists believed in the market's ability to be self-regulating through the invisible hand (the pricing mechanism of the market). Short-run problems were seen as temporary glitches; the Classical framework said that the economy would always return to its potential output and its target (or natural) rate of unemployment in the long run. Thus, the essence of Classical economists' approach to problems was laissez-faire (leave the market alone).

As long as the economy was operating smoothly, the Classical analysis of the aggregate economy met no serious opposition. But when the Great Depression hit and unemployment became a problem, most Classical economists avoided the issue (as most people tend to do when they don't have a good answer). When pushed by curious students to explain how the invisible hand, if it was so wonderful, could have allowed the Depression, Classical economists used microeconomic supply and demand arguments. They argued that labour unions and government policies kept prices and wages from falling. The problem, they said, was that the invisible hand was not being allowed to coordinate economic activity.

Their laissez-faire policy prescription followed from their analysis: Eliminate labour unions and change government policies that held wages too high. If government did so, the wage rate would fall, unemployment would be eliminated, and the Depression would end.

The Layperson's Explanation for Unemployment

Laypeople (average citizens) weren't pleased with this argument. (Remember, economists don't try to present pleasing arguments—only arguments they believe are correct.) But laypeople couldn't point to anything wrong with it. It made sense, but it wasn't satisfying. People thought, "Gee, Uncle Maurice, who's unemployed, would take a job at half the going wage. But he can't find one—there just aren't enough jobs to go around at any wage." So most laypeople developed different explanations. One popular explanation of the Depression was that an oversupply of goods had glutted the market. All that was needed to eliminate unemployment was for government to hire the unemployed, even if only to dig ditches and fill them back up. The people who got the new jobs would spend their money, creating even more jobs. Pretty soon, Canada would be out of the Depression.

Classical economists argued against this lay view. They felt that money to hire people would have to be borrowed. Such borrowing would use money that would have financed private economic activity and jobs, and would thus reduce private economic activity even further. The net effect would be essentially zero. Their advice was simply to have faith in markets.

Q-1 Distinguish a Classical economist from a Keynesian economist.

Classical economists support laissez-faire policies.

When Keynes said, "In the long run, we're all dead," he didn't mean that we can forget the long run. What he meant was that if the long run is so long that short-run forces do not let it come about, then for all practical purposes there is no long run. In that case, the short-run problem must be focused on.

Keynes believed that voters would not be satisfied waiting for market forces to bring about full employment. If something were not done in the short run to alleviate unemployment, he felt, voters would opt for fascism (as had the Germans) or communism (as had the Russians). He saw both alternatives as undesirable. For him, what would happen in the long run was academic.

Classicals, in contrast, argued that the short-run problems were not as bad as Keynes made them out to be and therefore should not be focused on to the exclusion of long-run problems.

Modern-day Classicals argued that while Keynes was dead, we were not, and the results of his short-run focus created long-run problems—specifically an inflationary bias in the economy. It is only by giving up Keynesian policies that we eliminated that bias.

The Essence of Keynesian Economics

As the Depression deepened, the Classical "have-faith" solution lost its support. Everyone was interested in the short run, not the long run. John Maynard Keynes put the concern most eloquently: "In the long run, we're all dead."

Keynes stopped asking whether the economy would eventually get out of the Depression on its own, and started asking what short-run forces were causing the Depression and what society could do to counteract them. By taking this approach he created the macroeconomic framework that focuses on stabilization.

While Keynes's ideas had many dimensions, the essence was that as wages and the price level adjusted to sudden changes in expenditures (such as an unexpected decrease in investment demand), the economy could get stuck in a rut.

If, for some reason, people stopped buying—decreased their demand in the aggregate—firms would decrease production, causing people to be laid off; these people would, in turn, buy less—causing other firms to further decrease production, which would cause more workers to be laid off, and so on. The cumulative circle of declining production would end with the economy stuck at a low level of income. In developing this line of reasoning Keynes provided the theoretical foundation for the view that unemployment was caused by too little spending.

Equilibrium Income Fluctuates The key idea is that, in the short run, equilibrium income is not fixed at the economy's long-run potential income; it fluctuates. Thus, for Keynes, there was a difference between **equilibrium income** (*the level of income toward which the economy gravitates in the short run because of the cumulative circles of declining or increasing production*) and **potential income** (*the level of income that the economy technically is capable of producing without generating accelerating inflation*). Keynes believed that at certain times the economy needed some help in reaching its potential income.

He argued that market forces that are supposed to bring the economy back to long-run potential income don't work fast, and at times will not be strong enough to get the economy out of a recession; the economy could get stuck in a low-income, high-unemployment rut. As the economy adjusts to fluctuations of supply and demand in the aggregate, the equilibrium income toward which the economy would gravitate would change. The economy would not naturally gravitate to potential income in the short run.

Keynes focused on the short run, not the long run.

 9.2

see page 233

The key idea in Keynesian economics is that equilibrium income fluctuates and can differ from potential income.

The Paradox of Thrift Let's say that a large portion of the people in the economy suddenly decide to save more and consume less. Expenditures would decrease and saving would increase. If that saving is not immediately transferred into investment, and hence back into expenditures (as the Classicals assumed it would be), investment demand will not increase by enough to offset the fall in consumption demand, and total demand will fall. There will be excess supply. Faced with this excess supply, firms will likely cut back production, which will decrease income. People will be laid off. As people's incomes fall, both their consumption and saving will decrease. (When you're laid off, you don't save.) Eventually income will fall far enough so that once again saving and investment will be in equilibrium, but then the economy could be at an almost permanent recession, with ongoing unemployment. Keynesians believed that in this case the economy would need government's help to hold up aggregate expenditures. That is the essence of macro demand-side expansionary policy.

Notice that the Keynesian framework gives a quite different view of saving than did the growth framework in the last chapter. There, saving was seen as something good; more saving leads to more investment, which leads to more growth. In the Keynesian framework there is a *paradox of thrift*—an increase in saving can lead to a decrease in expenditures, decreasing output and causing a recession.

By the 1950s Keynesian economics had been accepted by most of the profession. It was taught almost everywhere in Canada. The terminology of national income accounting developed, which is closely tied to Keynesian concepts. The model that eventually developed from these early debates is called the *aggregate demand/aggregate supply* (AS/AD) *model*. Aggregate supply captures production and pricing decisions by firms, and aggregate demand captures aggregate spending decisions. Even though economists still debate how fluctuations in an economy arise, this model, which focuses on aggregate expenditures as the primary determinant of short-run income, is used by most real-world economists to discuss short-run fluctuations in output and unemployment.

THE AS/AD MODEL

The *AS/AD* model consists of three curves. The curve describing the short-run supply side of the aggregate economy is the short-run aggregate supply curve, the curve describing the demand side of the economy is the aggregate demand curve, and the curve describing the highest sustainable level of output is the long-run aggregate supply curve.

The first thing to note about the *AS/AD* model is that it is fundamentally different from the microeconomic supply/demand model. In microeconomics the price of a single good is on the vertical axis and the quantity of a single good on the horizontal axis. The reasoning for the shapes of the micro supply and demand curves is based on the concepts of substitution and opportunity cost. In the macro *AS/AD* model, the price level of all goods, as measured by the GDP deflator, not just the price of one good, is on the vertical axis and aggregate output, not a single good, is on the horizontal axis. The shapes of the curves have nothing to do with opportunity cost or substitution.

The second thing to note about the *AS/AD* model is that it is a *historical model*. A historical model is a model that starts at a point in time and says what will likely happen when changes affect the economy. It does not try to explain how the economy got to its starting point; the macroeconomy is too complicated for that. Instead, the model starts from a historically given price and output levels and, given the institutional structure of the economy, considers how changes in the economy are likely to affect those levels. What this means is that much of the discussion in this chapter is based on the economy's institutional realities and observed empirical regularities.

Keynesian economists advocated an activist demand management policy.

Q.2 How does the short-run view of saving differ from the long-run view?

Knowing the difference between microeconomic supply and demand curves and macroeconomic aggregate demand and supply curves is very important.

Figure 9-1   THE AD CURVE

The *AD* curve is a downward-sloping curve that looks like a typical demand curve, but it is important to remember that it is quite a different curve. The reason it slopes downward is not the substitution effect, but instead the wealth effect, the interest rate effect, and the international effect. The multiplier effect strengthens each of these effects.

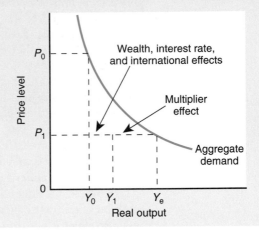

Let's now consider the three central components of the *AS/AD* model—the aggregate demand (*AD*) curve, the short-run aggregate supply (*SAS*) curve, and the long-run aggregate supply (*LAS*) curve.

THE AGGREGATE DEMAND CURVE

The **aggregate demand (AD) curve** is *a curve that shows how a change in the price level will change aggregate expenditures on all goods and services in an economy.* A standard *AD* curve is shown in Figure 9-1. Although the curve is called an aggregate demand curve, let us repeat that it is not the same as a microeconomic demand curve. The *AD* curve is more of an equilibrium curve.[1] It shows the level of expenditures at every price level, taking into account interactions among all producers and consumers in an economy.

Take the time to draw an *AD* curve, making sure to label the axes correctly.

The Slope of the AD Curve

As you can see, the *AD* curve is downward-sloping. A good place to begin understanding why it is downward-sloping is to remember what aggregate demand is composed of. As we discussed in an earlier chapter, aggregate expenditures (demand) is the sum of consumption, investment, government, and net exports:

$$\text{Expenditures} = C + I + G + (X - IM)$$

The slope of the *AD* curve depends on how these components respond to changes in the price level. In particular, expenditures on consumption, investment, and net exports rise when the price level falls. A number of explanations have been suggested for why a falling price level increases aggregate expenditures. We'll discuss three of them: the wealth effect, the interest rate effect, and the international effect.

The Wealth Effect Let's start at price P_0 and output Y_0 in Figure 9-1. (Remember, as we said above, in a historical model we start at a given price and output and determine what would happen if the price level rises or falls from that level.) Now, say that the

---

[1]In a number of articles and in previous editions we tried to change the terminology, so that students would not be misled into thinking that the *AD* curve was a normal demand curve. But our changes did not catch on. In this edition we follow standard terminology. Students who want to consider the issue more deeply should see the Web site (www.mhhe.com/economics/colander).

price level falls to P_1. How will this affect the total amount of goods and services that people demand? Let's first consider what is called the **wealth effect,** which tells us that *a fall in the price level will make the holders of money and of other financial assets richer, so they buy more*. In other words, if the price level falls, the loonie in your pocket will buy more than before; as you get richer, you will buy more goods and services. Since consumption expenditures are a component of aggregate demand, the quantity of aggregate demand will increase. Most economists do not see the wealth effect as strong; they do, however, accept the logic of the argument.

The Interest Rate Effect A second explanation for why the aggregate demand curve slopes downward is called the **interest rate effect**—*the effect that a lower price level has on investment expenditures through the effect that a change in the price level has on interest rates*. The interest rate effect works as follows: a decrease in the price level will increase real cash on hand (called *money balances*), as in the wealth effect. But the path of the interest rate effect is not through making holders of cash richer. The interest rate effect focuses on the effect that changes in real money balances have on interest rates. The increase in the real money supply will give banks more money to loan out. As they make more loans, interest rates will fall, which, in turn, will increase investment expenditures. Why? Because at lower interest rates businesses will undertake more investment projects. Since investment is one component of aggregate demand, the quantity of aggregate demand will increase when the price level falls.

The International Effect A third reason why aggregate quantity demanded increases with a fall in the price level is the **international effect,** which tells us that *as the price level falls (assuming the exchange rate does not change), net exports will rise*. As the price level in Canada falls, the price of Canadian goods relative to foreign goods goes down and Canadian goods become more competitive than foreign goods; thus, Canadian exports increase and Canadian imports decrease. Let's consider an example. In the mid-1990s the Bulgarian currency was fixed to the German mark. Bulgaria's price level rose enormously, increasing the demand for German imports and reducing the quantity of aggregate demand in Bulgaria.

So, in Figure 9-1 when we include the international effect, the interest rate effect, and the wealth effect, a fall in the price level from P_0 to P_1 causes the quantity of aggregate demand to increase to Y_1.

The slope of the *AD* curve is determined by the wealth effect, the interest rate effect, the international effect, and the multiplier effect.

In micro other things can be assumed to remain constant, whereas in macro other things change.

The Multiplier Effect The wealth effect, the interest rate effect, and the international effect tell us that the quantity of aggregate demand will increase with a fall in the price level, and will decrease with an increase in the price level. But the story about the slope of the aggregate demand curve doesn't end there. It also takes into account the **multiplier effect**—*the amplification of initial changes in expenditures*. It is important to recognize that when considering the demand curve in micro, we can reasonably assume that other things remain constant; in macro, other things change. Whereas the demand curve in micro only includes the initial change, the aggregate demand curve includes the repercussions that these initial changes have throughout the economy. What we mean by *repercussions* is that the initial changes in expenditures set in motion a process in the economy that amplifies these initial effects.

To see how these repercussions will likely work in the real world, imagine that the price level in Canada rises. Canadian citizens will reduce their purchases of Canadian goods, and increase their purchases of foreign goods. (That's the international effect.) Canadian firms will see the demand for their goods and services fall and will decrease their output. Profits will fall and people will be laid off. Both these effects will cause income to fall, and as income falls, people will demand still fewer goods and services. (If you're unemployed, you cut back your purchases.) Again production and income fall, which again leads to a drop in expenditures. This secondary cutback is an example of a repercussion. These repercussions *multiply* the initial effect that a change in the price level has on expenditures.

The multiplier effect amplifies the initial wealth, interest rate, and international effects, thereby making the slope of the AD curve flatter than it would have been. You can see this in Figure 9-1. The three effects discussed above increase output from Y_0 to Y_1. The repercussions multiply that effect so that output increases to Y_e.

Economists have suggested other reasons why changes in the price level affect the quantity of aggregate demand, but these four should be sufficient to give you an initial understanding. Going through the same exercise that we did above for the wealth, interest rate, international, and multiplier effects for a fall (rather than a rise) in the price level is a useful exercise.

Let's conclude this section with an example that brings out the importance of the multiplier effect in determining the slope of the AD curve. Say that the multiplier effect amplifies the wealth, interest rate, and international effects by a factor of 2 and that the international, wealth, and interest rate effects reduce output by 2 percent when the price level rises by 10 percent. What will be the slope of the AD curve? Since the multiplier effect is 2, the total decline in output will be $2 \times 2 = 4$ percent, so the slope will be -2.5 ($10\%/-4\%$).

The multiplier effect of an investment in physical capital has profound effects on an economy through its demand for labour and services in the construction and operational phases and its subsequent effect on personal income, consumption, and the level of real output.

Shifts in the AD Curve

Next, let's consider what causes the AD curve to shift. A shift in the AD curve means that at every price level, total expenditures have changed. Anything other than the price level that changes the components of aggregate demand will shift the AD curve. Five important shift factors of aggregate demand are foreign income, expectations, exchange rate fluctuations, the distribution of income, and government policies.

Q.3 True or false? As the price level falls by 10 percent, the international effect increases output by 1 percent. Therefore, the slope of the AD curve will be -10.

Foreign Income A country is not an island unto itself. Canadian economic output is closely tied to the income of its major world trading partners. When our trading partners go into a recession, the demand for Canadian goods, and hence Canadian exports, will fall, causing the Canadian AD curve to shift to the left. Similarly, a rise in foreign income leads to an increase in Canadian exports and a rightward shift of the Canadian AD curve.

Exchange Rates The currencies of various countries are connected through exchange rates. When a country's currency loses value relative to other currencies, its goods become more competitive compared to foreign goods. Foreign demand for domestic goods increases and domestic demand for foreign goods decreases as individuals shift their spending to domestic goods at home. Both these effects increase net exports and shift the AD curve to the right. By the same reasoning, when a country's currency gains value, the AD curve shifts in the opposite direction. You can see these effects on the U.S.–Canadian border. In the early 1990s the Canadian dollar had a high value relative to the U.S. dollar. This caused many Canadians near the border to make buying trips to the United States. Then in the mid-1990s, when the Canadian dollar fell in value, those buying trips decreased and the Canadian AD curve shifted to the right.

Q.4 If the value of a country's currency rises, what happens to its AD curve?

Expectations Another important shift factor of aggregate demand is expectations. Many different types of expectations can affect the AD curve. To give you an idea of the role of expectations, let's consider two expectational shift factors—expectations of future output and future prices. When businesspeople expect demand to be high in the future,

Expectations of higher future income increase expenditures and shift the AD curve out.

they will want to increase their production capacity; their investment demand, a component of aggregate demand, will increase. Thus, positive expectations about future demand will shift the AD curve to the right.

Similarly, when consumers expect the economy to do well, they will be less worried about saving for the future, and they will spend more now—the AD curve will shift to the right. Alternatively, if consumers expect the future to be gloomy, they will likely try to save for the future, and will decrease the consumption expenditures. The AD curve will shift to the left.

Another type of expectation that shifts the AD curve concerns expectations of future prices. If you expect the prices of goods to rise in the future, it pays to buy goods now that you might want in the future—before their prices rise. The current price level hasn't changed, but aggregate quantity demanded at that price level has increased, indicating a shift of the AD curve to the right.

The effect of expectations of future price levels is seen more clearly in hyperinflation. In most cases of hyperinflation, people rush out to spend their money quickly—to buy whatever they can to beat the price increase. So even though prices are rising, aggregate demand stays high because the rise in price creates an expectation of even higher prices, and thus the current high price is seen as a low price relative to the future. We said that an increase in expectations of inflation will "have a tendency to" rather than "definitely" shift the AD curve to the right because those expectations of inflation are interrelated with a variety of other expectations. For example, an expectation of a rise in the price of goods you buy could be accompanied by an expectation of a fall in income, and that fall in income would work in the opposite direction, decreasing aggregate demand.

This interrelation of various types of expectations makes it very difficult to specify precisely what effect certain types of expectations have on the AD curve. But it does not eliminate the importance of expectations as shift factors. It simply means that we often aren't sure what the net effect of a change in expectations on aggregate demand will be.

Distribution of Income Some people save more than others, and everyone's spending habits differ. Thus, as income distribution changes, so too will aggregate demand. One of the most important of these distributional effects concerns the distribution of income between wages and profits. Workers receive wage income and are more likely to spend the income they receive; firms' profits are distributed to stockholders or are retained by the firm. Since stockholders in Canada tend to be wealthy, and the wealthy save a greater portion of their income than the poor do, a higher portion of income received as profits will likely be saved. Assuming all saving is not translated into investment, as the real wage decreases but total income remains constant, it is likely that consumption expenditures will fall and the aggregate demand will shift to the left. Similarly, as the real wage increases, it is likely that aggregate demand will shift to the right.

Monetary and Fiscal Policies One of the most important reasons why the aggregate demand curve has been so important in macro policy analysis is that often macro policymakers think that they can control it, at least to some degree. For example, if the government goes out and spends lots of money without increases in taxes, it shifts the AD curve to the right; if the government raises taxes significantly and holds spending constant, consumers will have less disposable income and will reduce their expenditures, shifting the AD curve to the left. Similarly, when the Bank of Canada, the Canadian economy's central bank, expands the money supply it can often lower interest rates, making it easier for both consumers and investors to borrow, increasing their spending, and thereby shifting the AD curve to the right. This deliberate increase in aggregate demand to influence the level of income in the economy is what most policymakers

---

Expectations of a rising price level in the future increase expenditures and shift the AD curve to the right.

Five important shift factors of AD are:

1. *Foreign income.*
2. *Expectations.*
3. *Exchange rates.*
4. *The distribution of income.*
5. *Monetary and fiscal policies.*

Deliberate shifting of the AD curve is what most policymakers mean by macro policy.

Figure 9-2   EFFECT OF A SHIFT FACTOR ON THE AD CURVE

The *AD* curve shifts out by more than the initial change in expenditures. In this example, exports increase by 100. The multiplier magnifies this shift, and the *AD* curve shifts to the right by a multiple of 100, in this case by 300.

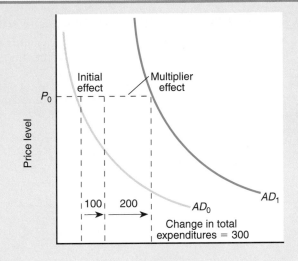

mean by the term *macro policy*. Expansionary macro policy shifts the *AD* curve to the right; contractionary macro policy shifts it to the left.

Multiplier Effects of Shift Factors As we emphasized when we introduced the *AD* curve, you cannot treat the *AD* curve like a micro demand curve. This comes out most clearly when considering shifts in the curve caused by shift factors. The aggregate demand curve may shift by more than the amount of the initial shift factor because of the multiplier effect. The explanation is the same as when we introduced the multiplier effect. When government increases its spending, firms increase production, which leads to higher income. A fraction of that increase in income is spent on more goods and services, shifting the *AD* curve even further to the right. This leads firms to increase production again; income and expenditures also rise. Each round, the increase gets smaller and smaller until the increase becomes negligible. In the end the *AD* curve will have shifted by a multiple of the initial shift. Just how large that multiple is depends on how much of the change in income affects spending in each round. Thus, in Figure 9-2, when an initial shift factor of aggregate demand is 100 and the multiplier effect is 3, the *AD* curve will shift to the right by 300, three times the initial shift. The extra 200 shift is the multiplier effect.

To see that you are following the argument, consider the following two shifts: (1) a fall in the value of the Canadian dollar, increasing net exports by 50; and (2) an increase in government spending of 100. Explain how the *AD* curve will shift in each of these cases, and why that shift will be larger than the initial shift. If you are not sure about these explanations, review the multiplier effect discussion above.

Q.5   If government spending increases by 20, by how much does the *AD* curve shift out?

The *AD* curve holds all shift factors constant, so the slope of the *AD* curve reflects only the effects of a change in the price level (including multiplier effects).

THE AGGREGATE SUPPLY CURVE

The second component of the *AS/AD* model is the **short-run aggregate supply (SAS) curve**—*a curve that shows how firms adjust the quantity of real output they will supply when the price level changes, holding all input prices fixed.* A standard SAS curve is shown in Figure 9-3(a).

Figure 9-3 (a and b)   THE SHORT-RUN AGGREGATE SUPPLY CURVE

The *SAS* curve shows how changes in aggregate demand affect output and the price level. As you can see in (**a**), the *SAS* curve is generally thought to be upward sloping in the short run; (**b**) shows an upward shift in the *SAS* curve caused by an increase in wages.

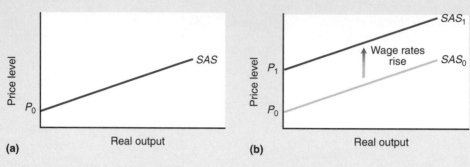

The Slope of the SAS Curve

An upward-sloping short-run aggregate supply curve tells us that the price level and real output will change in response to changes in aggregate demand.

Notice that in Figure 9-3(a) we have drawn the *SAS* curve as an upward-sloping line. We do this for several reasons. The first is that it fits the reality of recent times reasonably well. The upward-sloping *SAS* curve tells us that a large majority of Canadian goods markets are both **quantity-adjusting and price-adjusting markets**—*markets in which firms respond to changes in demand by modifying both their output and their prices.* While many retail markets in Canada are posted-price markets—markets in which stores post their prices and agree to sell as much as people want at that posted price, these prices can change fairly quickly in response to economic conditions.

Of course, some markets exhibit a greater degree of price adjustment than others. Natural resource and agricultural markets are prime examples of markets where prices move quickly, while service industries may see much more variation in quantity than price.

There are several other reasons why the *SAS* curve has a positive slope, all of which are related to deviations of the actual price level from what it was expected to be during the period. Suppose a firm sees the economy-wide price level rising faster than it expected. The managers of the firm have to determine whether this signals an increase in the demand for *their* product. If so, they may want to increase output to maximize their profits. A higher-than-expected price level could lead firms to expand capacity, increasing output and employment.

Similarly, many firms encounter *menu costs*—the costs associated with changing prices. Think about your local grocery store before the advent of bar codes and scanners. Each item was individually priced, so changing prices involved reticketing everything on the shelves. That was expensive, so firms wouldn't change prices until it was worth the effort (this is one reason why your favourite restaurant doesn't put a price on its menu for lobster dinners—the menu usually reads "market price"—if demand is high, so is the price). If the economy-wide price level rises, and firms don't raise their prices because they don't want to incur the costs of changing those prices, the demand for their products will rise, leading to an expansion of production and employment.

Finally, many firms sign agreements with their workers that set wage rates for multiple periods. If the actual price level is higher than it was expected to be, and workers signed contracts that set their nominal wages during the contract period, a higher-than-expected price level will reduce the real cost of hiring workers. Employment will rise and firms will expand production.

All of these explanations offer compelling reasons to suspect that the SAS curve would be upward-sloping. To recap: The SAS curve is upward-sloping because:

1. Firms adjust both price and quantity in response to changes in aggregate demand.

2. Differences between the actual price level and its expected value cause firms to (a) misinterpret changes in the price level to be changes in relative prices, leading them to adjust output; (b) adjust quantities when it is costly to change prices; and (c) change employment and production plans when the real wage—the nominal wage adjusted for the price level—is different from what it was expected to be.

Shifts in the SAS Curve

Firms change their quantity and pricing decisions when aggregate demand changes, as well as in response to changes in their costs of production. These costs include wage rates, interest rates, energy prices, and changes in the prices of other factors of production, such as land. In the extreme case in which all firms are quantity adjusting (so the SAS curve would be horizontal), firms would still change their prices if input costs changed. The rule of thumb used by most firms is that prices adjust by the change in wages and other factor prices minus changes in productivity. If input costs rise by 7 percent but productivity rises by 5 percent, firms would limit their price increases to 2 percent. If wages and productivity rise by the same proportion, the price level could remain constant.

If productivity remains unchanged, increases in input prices shift the SAS curve to the left. The same quantity will be supplied at a higher price—the higher price required to offset the increase in costs. If input prices fall, the SAS curve shifts to the right so a lower price level is associated with the same level of output as before input prices declined.

When productivity and input prices change the SAS curve shifts left or right depending on the net effect of the productivity and factor price changes. Looking at the rule of thumb, you can see there are two factors that shift the SAS curve:

% change in price level = % change in input prices − % change in productivity

We show a leftward shift in the SAS curve in Figure 9-3(b). Let's consider an example: If wages increase 6 percent and productivity rises by 2 percent, then the price level rises by 4 percent. It's that simple!

In the real world we see many shifts in the SAS curve. In the 1970s, for example, oil prices shot up enormously. That led to a sharp increase in all producer prices, and the SAS curve shifted to the left. Another example occurred in Thailand in 1998 when the value of its currency, the bhat, fell drastically. That caused the price of imports measured in bhat to increase substantially, which shifted the SAS curve to the left.

Higher wage settlements lead to higher cost of production and the aggregate supply curve shifting leftward.

% change in the price level = % change in input prices − % change in productivity

THE LONG-RUN AGGREGATE SUPPLY CURVE

The final curve that makes up the AS/AD model is the **long-run aggregate supply (LAS) curve,** which shows *the amount of goods and services an economy can produce when both labour and capital are fully employed*. It is determined by the supply conditions in the economy and the maximum sustainable amount of output that can be produced from the factors of production available to the economy. Figure 9-4 (on the next page) shows the LAS curve.

Notice that the LAS curve is vertical. That is because a higher price level will not bring about higher potential output. Since at potential output all resources are fully utilized, a rise in the price level means the prices of all goods and factors of production, including wages, rise. Consider it this way. If all prices doubled, including your wage, your real income would not change. You would have no reason to work more than you are,

The long-run aggregate supply (LAS) curve shows the amount of goods and services an economy can produce when both labour and capital are fully employed.

THE LONG-RUN AGGREGATE SUPPLY CURVE

The long-run aggregate supply curve shows the output that an economy can produce when both labour and capital are fully employed. It is vertical because at potential output a rise in the price level means that all prices, including input prices, rise. Available resources do not rise and thus neither does potential output.

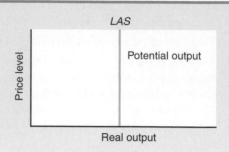

so output does not change. Since potential output is unaffected by the price level, the *LAS* curve is vertical. This curve plays an important role in determining long-run equilibrium and in determining whether policy should focus on long-run or short-run issues.

EQUILIBRIUM IN THE AGGREGATE ECONOMY

Now that we have introduced the *SAS*, *AD*, and *LAS* curves, we'll consider short-run and long-run equilibrium and how changes in the curves affect those equilibria. We start with the short run because it requires only the *SAS* and *AD* curves.

Short-Run Equilibrium

In the short run the price level and output are variable.

In the short run the intersection of the short-run aggregate supply curve and the aggregate demand curve determines equilibrium of the economy. Thus, short-run equilibrium is shown by point *E* in Figure 9-5(a). If the *AD* curve shifts to the right, from AD_0 to AD_1, equilibrium will shift from point *E* to point *F*. The price level will rise to P_1 and output will increase to Y_1. A decrease in aggregate demand will shift output and the price level in the other direction.

Figure 9-5 (a and b) **SHORT-RUN EQUILIBRIUM**

Short-run equilibrium is where the short-run aggregate supply and aggregate demand curves intersect. Point *E* in (a) is equilibrium; (a) also shows how a shift in the aggregate demand curve to the right changes equilibrium from *E* to *F*, increasing output from Y_0 to Y_1 and the price level from P_0 to P_1. In (b) you can see how a shift left in the short-run aggregate supply curve changes equilibrium from *E* to *G*, reducing output from Y_0 to Y_2 and increasing the price level from P_0 to P_2.

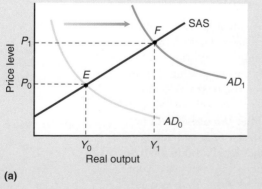
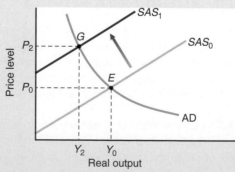

(a)   (b)

Figure 9-6 (a and b)   **LONG-RUN EQUILIBRIUM**

Long-run equilibrium is where the *LAS* curve and *AD* curves intersect. Point *E* in (a) is long-run equilibrium. In (b) you can see how a shift in the aggregate demand curve changes equilibrium from *E* to *H*, increasing the price level from P_0 to P_1 but leaving output unchanged.

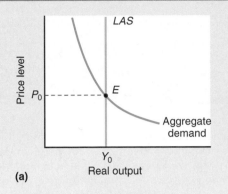

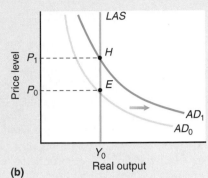

(a)

(b)

Figure 9-5(b) shows the effect on equilibrium of a leftward shift in the *SAS* curve. Initially equilibrium is at point *E*. An upward shift in the *SAS* curve from SAS_0 to SAS_1 increases the price level from P_0 to P_2 and reduces equilibrium output from Y_0 to Y_2.

Long-Run Equilibrium

Long-run equilibrium is determined by the intersection of the *AD* curve and the long-run aggregate supply curve, as shown by point *E* in Figure 9-6(a). Since the output level is fixed at Y_0, the aggregate demand curve can determine only the price level; it does not affect the level of real output. Thus, as shown in Figure 9-6(b), when aggregate demand increases from AD_0 to AD_1, the price level rises (from P_0 to P_1) but output does not change. When aggregate demand decreases, the price level falls and output remains at potential. In the long run, output is fixed and the price level is variable, so aggregate output is determined not by aggregate demand but by potential output. Aggregate demand determines the price level.

> Long-run equilibrium is determined by the intersection of the *AD* curve and the *LAS* curve.

Integrating the Short-Run and Long-Run Frameworks

To complete our analysis we have to relate the long run and short run. We start with the economy in both long-run and short-run equilibrium, as in Figure 9-7(a) on page 225. As you can see at point *E*, with output, Y_0, and price level, P_0, the economy is in both a long-run equilibrium and a short-run equilibrium, since at point *E* the *AD* curve and *SAS* curve intersect the *LAS* at the economy's potential output. That is the situation economists hope for—that aggregate demand grows at just the same rate as potential output, so that growth and unemployment are at their target rates, with no, or minimal, inflation. In the late 1990s the Canadian economy was in just such a position—potential output was increasing at the same rate that aggregate demand was increasing; unemployment was low, as was inflation.

The Recessionary Gap Alas, the economy is not always at that point *E*. An economy at point A in Figure 9-7(b) is in a situation where the quantity of aggregate demand is below potential output and not all the resources in the economy are being fully used. The distance $Y_0 - Y_1$ shows the amount of output that is not being produced but could be. This distance is often referred to as a **recessionary gap**, *the amount by which equilibrium output is below potential output.*

Q-6 If the *SAS* and *AD* curves intersect at potential output and wages are constant, what is likely to happen to output and the price level?

Why do some firms adjust production instead of price? A number of reasons have been put forward by economists, and recently a group of economists, led by Princeton economist Alan Blinder, surveyed firms to find out which reasons firms believed were most important. The survey choices were coordination failure, cost-based pricing rules, the use of variables other than prices to clear markets, and implicit contracts. In this box we'll briefly consider these and one other reason—menu costs.

Coordination Failure and Strategic Pricing

About 90 percent of final goods markets are oligopolistic with cost-determined prices. These are markets in which there are a few major firms that take each other's reactions into account in their decisions. Oligopolistic markets can be highly competitive, but the competition is strategic. Strategic competition has a number of implications for pricing. Under Canadian law, firms cannot directly collude—get together and decide on a pricing strategy for the industry—but they can informally coordinate their pricing procedures. You probably have seen advertisements in which a store offers to match a competitor's price or makes a price guarantee. If all firms can implicitly agree to act in a coordinated fashion and hold their prices up when faced with generalized decreased demand, they are not violating the law and will be better off than they would be if they acted in an uncoordinated fashion.

But it isn't only when firms experience a decrease in demand that they feel strategic pricing leads to holding price constant. They also follow that strategy when they experience an increase in demand. In Blinder's survey, firms stated that they are also hesitant to raise prices on the up side when demand increases. They fear that if they increase their price they will undermine the coordinated pricing strategy with other firms, or that other firms will not follow their move and they will lose market share.

To say that the economy is oligopolistic is not to say that it is not competitive. Ask any businessperson and he or she will tell you that it is highly competitive. But firms now often compete on fronts other than price.

Cost-Based Pricing Rules

The pricing coordination strategy discussed above is maintained by firms' tendency to use cost-based pricing rules. In a cost-plus-markup pricing procedure, firms determine their direct costs and then set price in relation to those costs. Costs play a central role in determining price, and for most firms the most important costs are labour costs, which tend to be fixed by long-term wage contracts between workers and employers. (Unions, for example, typically negotiate wage contracts for three-year periods.)

Thus, costs do not change with changes in demand, and, following a cost-plus-markup strategy, neither do prices.

Other Methods to Clear Markets

The use of cost-plus or markup pricing rules does not mean that markets do not clear. If firms set the price in the market too high, and therefore don't sell all they were planning to sell, they will hold that price and, initially, build up inventory before changing the quantity of goods they are producing. If inventory gets too high, firms may run sales, temporarily lowering price to eliminate excess inventory, but they will also tie production to sales. Alternatively, firms may increase their advertising when sales fall, or they may provide higher bonuses for salespeople. So when demand changes, output changes to match demand at the price determined in the firm's long-run pricing strategy. Markets clear when firms vary production more than price.

Implicit Contracts

Most firms have ongoing relationships with their customers. That means they don't want to antagonize them. They have found that one way to avoid antagonizing customers is not to take advantage of them even when they could. In the Blinder survey firms felt that they had implicit contracts with their customers to raise prices only when their costs changed, or when market conditions changed substantially.

Menu Costs

Another explanation economists have put forward for why firms don't change prices in response to changes in demand is that changing prices can be costly. They argue that the cost involved in pricing goods and distributing new catalogues, menus, and price tags can lead firms to change prices infrequently. While this sounds like a reasonable explanation, the firms surveyed by Blinder did not think it very important. They felt that changing production also had costs. (The decision to change price had to be based on the relative importance of the two costs.)

The combination of these reasons leads to our having a large segment of the economy in which the prices do not significantly change as demand changes. For that reason, as demand increased in the 1990s, there was little pressure on prices. Of course, if costs, especially labour costs, start rising, then prices will rise. To the degree that demand changes affect costs, prices will respond, but as a first approximation it is generally acceptable to say that the price level does not significantly move in response to demand. It is for that reason that economists use a relatively flat, yet upward-sloping *SAS* curve.

Figure 9-7 (a, b, and c)   **SHORT-RUN AND LONG-RUN FRAMEWORKS**

The economy is in both short-run and long-run equilibrium when all three curves intersect in the same location. When the economy is in short-run equilibrium but not long-run equilibrium, the position of the SAS curve is determined by the relationship between output and potential output. If output is below potential, the SAS is pulled down by falling input prices, as shown in (b). If output is above potential, the SAS curve is pulled up by rising input prices, as shown in (c).

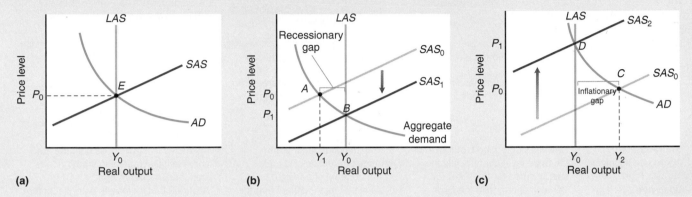

If the economy remains at this level of output for a long time, costs and wages would tend to fall because there would be an excess supply of factors of production. As costs and wages fall, the price level also falls. The short-run aggregate supply curve would shift down (from SAS_0 to SAS_1) until eventually the long-run and short-run equilibrium would be reached at point B. But generally in our economy that does not happen.[2] Long before costs fall, either the economy picks up on its own or the government introduces policies to expand output. That's why we seldom see declines in the price level. If the government expands aggregate demand, or some other shift factor expands aggregate demand, the AD curve shifts to the right, eliminating the recessionary gap and keeping the price level constant.

Late in 2001, with the North American economies floundering, both the U.S. and Canadian governments adopted expansionary policies to try to stimulate aggregate demand. As we write this, there is considerable uncertainty in markets. As confidence returns and aggregate demand responds to macro policies, the recessionary gap may disappear, but few economists were forecasting a recovery to the growth rates of the late 1990s.

Q.7 Demonstrate graphically both the short-run and long-run AS/AD equilibrium with a recessionary gap.

The Inflationary Gap An economy at point C in Figure 9-7(c) demonstrates a case where the short-run equilibrium is at a higher income than the economy's potential output. In this case economists say that the economy has an **inflationary gap** shown by $Y_2 - Y_0$—*aggregate expenditures above potential output that exist at the current price level.* Output cannot remain at Y_2 for long because the economy's resources are being used beyond their potential. Factor prices will rise and the SAS curve will shift up from SAS_0 to SAS_2; the new equilibrium is at point D.

The Economy beyond Potential How can resources be used beyond potential? By overutilizing resources. Consider the resources you put into classwork. Suppose that your potential is a B+. If you stay up all night studying and cram in extra reading during

---

[2]If, as happened in the Great Depression in the 1930s and in Japan in the late 1990s, the economy stays below its potential output curve long enough, we would see the price level fall.

The *AS/AD* model is composed of three curves: the aggregate demand curve, the short-run aggregate supply curve, and the long-run aggregate supply curve. The following table summarizes those three curves.

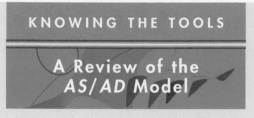

KNOWING THE TOOLS

A Review of the AS/AD Model

The economy is in short-run and long-run equilibrium when all three curves intersect at the same location. Short-run equilibrium is where the *AD* and *SAS* curves intersect. Long-run equilibrium is where the *AD* and *LAS* curves intersect.

	What Shape Is It?	What Determines Its Shape?	What Shifts the Curve?
Aggregate demand	• Downward sloping: As the price level declines expenditures rise.	• The wealth effect, the interest rate effect, the international effect, and the multiplier effect.	• Sudden changes in *C, I, (X − IM)*, or G caused by changes in foreign income, expectations about future income or prices, exchange rates, monetary policy, fiscal policy.
Short-run aggregate supply	• Upward sloping: both output and the price level change. It is the supply curve for the short run.	• Firm behaviour. Most firms change production and price when demand changes.	• Increases in input prices shift the *SAS* curve left. Decreases in input prices shift the *SAS* curve right.
Long-run aggregate supply	• Vertical: changes in the price level have no effect on output. It is the supply curve for the long run.	• Potential output is output that the economy can produce when labour and capital are fully utilized. It is not affected by prices.	• Anything that increases potential output, such as increases in available resources and technological innovation.

mealtimes, you could earn an A. But eventually you'll get tired. You can't keep up that amount of effort for long. The same is true for production. Extra shifts can be added and machinery can be run for longer periods, but eventually the workers will become exhausted and the machinery will wear out. Output will have to return to its potential.

The result of this inflationary gap will be a bidding up of factor prices and a rise in costs for firms. Explanations of a fixed price level are based on firms' constant production costs. When an economy is below potential, firms can hire additional factors of production to increase production without increasing production costs. Once the economy reaches its potential output, however, that is no longer possible. If a firm is to increase its factors of production, it must lure resources away from other firms. It will do so by offering higher wages and prices. But the firm facing a loss of its resources will likely respond by increasing its wages and other prices it pays to its employees and other suppliers.

As firms compete for resources, their costs rise beyond increases in productivity, shifting up the short-run *AS* curve. This means that once an economy's potential output is reached, the price level tends to rise. In fact, economists sometimes look to see whether the price level has begun to rise before deciding where potential output is. Thus, in the 1990s economists kept increasing their estimates of potential output because the price level did not rise even as the economy approached, and exceeded, what they previously thought was its potential output.

If the economy *is* operating above potential, the short-run aggregate supply curve will shift up until the inflationary gap is eliminated. Again, that is usually not what happens. Either the economy slows down on its own or the government introduces aggregate demand policy to contract output and eliminate the inflationary gap. As we will see in later chapters, the government tries to keep short-run aggregate demand in both short-run and long-run equilibrium.

If aggregate expenditures are above potential output, then increased demand for labour would put upward pressure on wages and subsequently the overall level of prices.

That's the end of our presentation of the AS/AD model of income and price-level determination. It gives us a simple framework for considering short-run macro policy and for forecasting what will happen in the economy. Let's now move on to apply the model to some policy examples.

Some Additional Policy Examples

To begin, let's make you an adviser to the prime minister. He comes to you for some advice. The economy initially has 12 percent unemployment and no inflation. Based on history you believe that the economy is well below its potential output, so there is no need to worry about increasing factor prices. You are told that consumers have just become more optimistic, which initially increases aggregate demand by 30. What do you predict will happen to the economy? Demonstrate your analysis graphically.

The answer is that aggregate demand will increase by some multiple of 30 (because we must take into account multiplier effects), and the price level rises. Figure 9-8(a) demonstrates this prediction. The economy begins at point A, and the AD curve shifts to the right by 90 because the multiplier effect is estimated to be 3. Equilibrium output increases from Y_0 to Y_1, point B. If the AD curve had shifted to the right further, the economy might be in an inflationary gap and the price level might have risen further.

Alternatively, say that, by reducing government expenditures, politicians suddenly cut the government budget deficit to zero, and even achieve a large surplus. What effect will you expect that action to have on the economy in the short run? The answer is that the AD curve shifts to the left by three times the cut, and the economy goes into a recession.

Now let's try a different scenario. The economy initially has 7 percent unemployment and it is believed that 7 percent is the *target rate of unemployment*—the rate of unemployment that is consistent with potential output. Again consumer optimism leads to an increase in expenditures. What do you predict will be the result? Demonstrate your analysis graphically.

The answer is that the AD curve will shift to the right by a multiple of the initial shift as before, but, because the economy is at its potential output, the effect of that shift will be a rise in the price level, and a temporary increase in real output. That prediction is demonstrated in Figure 9-8(b). The economy is initially at point C, where the price level is P_0 and output is Y_0. The increase in expenditures along with the multiplier initially moves the economy to point D at a level of output (Y_1) above potential. If left alone, factor prices will rise, shifting the short-run aggregate supply curve up until it reaches SAS_1. The price level rises to P_2 and the real output returns to Y_0, point E.

As a final example, let's say that you are asked to recommend policy. What policy should the government follow in the previous example? If you answered "Try to cut government spending or raise taxes so that the AD curve shifts to the left and the economy avoids the rise in prices," you've got the analysis down pat.

WHY MACRO POLICY IS MORE COMPLICATED THAN THE AS/AD MODEL MAKES IT LOOK

The AS/AD model makes the analysis of the aggregate economy look easy. All you have to do is determine where the economy is relative to its potential output and, based on that, choose the appropriate policy to shift the AD curve. The problem is that we have no way of determining exactly where potential output is, so we can't determine whether the SAS curve will be shifting up or not when we increase aggregate demand. Thus, the key to applying the policy is to know where the potential output curve is.

Q-8 If politicians suddenly raise government expenditures, and the economy is well below potential output, what would happen to prices and real income?

Figure 9-8 (a and b)   SHIFTING AD AND SAS CURVES

In (a) you can see what happens when the economy is below potential and aggregate demand increases just enough to bring output to its potential. The AD curve shifts by 90, three times the initial increase in aggregate expenditures. Output increases by 90 and the price level rises to P_1. In (b) you can see what happens when the economy begins at potential and aggregate expenditures rise. The AD curve shifts to the right by a multiple of the initial shift and output increases beyond potential output. Since the economy is above potential, input prices begin to rise and the SAS curve shifts left. Input prices continue to rise and output falls until output returns to its potential. The price level rises to P_2.

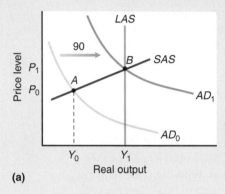

(a)

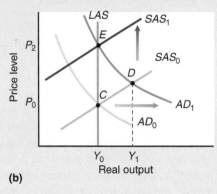

(b)

Three Policy Ranges

The three ranges of an economy are:

1. The Keynesian range, where prices are fixed.
2. The Classical range, where prices are flexible.
3. The intermediate range, where prices are somewhat flexible.

Policymakers usually divide the economy into three ranges based on what they believe the effect of an expansion of aggregate demand will have on the price level. These three ranges are shown in Figure 9-9. When the economy is far from potential income, and there is little fear that an increase in aggregate demand will cause the SAS curve to shift up and cause inflationary pressures, economists say that the economy is in the *Keynesian range*. In that range an increase in aggregate demand will increase income and have no effect on the price level. In other words, the SAS curve will be horizontal because all firms are quantity-adjusters. The price/output path of the economy is horizontal. This range corresponds to the recessionary gap position discussed earlier. That is why Keynesian economics is sometimes called depression or recession economics.

When the economy is thought to be at the level of potential output and there is a belief that any increase in aggregate demand will increase factor prices, pushing up the SAS curve by the full amount that aggregate demand increases, economists say that the economy is in the *Classical range*. In that range an increase in aggregate demand will only

Figure 9-9   THREE RANGES OF THE ECONOMY

When output is far below potential, it is in the Keynesian range, where prices do not change. When output is in the intermediate range, the price/output path becomes upward sloping. Wages begin to rise by more than productivity rises and prices begin to rise. When the economy is at potential, it is in the Classical range, where prices rise to bring the economy back to potential.

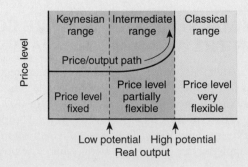

push up the price level; it will not affect real output. The price/output path of the economy is vertical. This range corresponds to the inflationary gap position discussed earlier.

As we have emphasized earlier, there is much debate about where potential output is; potential output is really a range of output rather than a single level of output. We can capture this debate by specifying a low level of potential output and a high level of potential output and having a range for potential output between the low and high levels of potential output as an intermediate range. In this range the price/output path is upward sloping; the price level will shift up some as wages increase because of tight labour markets, and real output will increase some. The relative increases will be determined by whether the economy is closer to the low level of potential output or the high level. A key to policy is determining what range we are in, which requires us to determine whether low or high potential output is the more reasonable estimate.

The Problem of Estimating Potential Output

Because inflation accelerates when an economy is operating at potential, one way of estimating potential output is to estimate the rate of unemployment below which inflation has begun to accelerate in the past. This is the target rate of unemployment. We can then calculate output at the target rate of unemployment, adjust for productivity growth, and estimate potential output. Unfortunately the target rate of unemployment fluctuates and is difficult to predict.

The problem can be made clearer by relating it to an earlier chapter's discussion of cyclical and structural unemployment. There we stated that cyclical unemployment occurs when output is below potential output. Workers have been laid off, and it is relatively easy to call them back to work to increase production. Structural unemployment is unemployment that remains when the economy is at its potential output. The problem isn't layoffs; it's lack of appropriate jobs for the existing skills. That sounds easy, but in reality it is difficult.

Another way to determine potential output is to take the economy's previous income level and add the normal growth factor of 3 percent (the secular trend rate of growth). This gives us a very rough estimate. Regulations, technology, institutions, available resources, and expectations are always changing. Estimating potential income from past growth rates can be problematic if these shift factors are changing quickly or dramatically.

In some cases, the economy can be undergoing significant structural readjustment, in which it is not trying to repeat what it did in the past but trying to change from what it has been doing to something new. If that is true, potential output may have declined and what looks like cyclical unemployment is actually structural unemployment.

Some Real-World Examples

To see the problem of applying the AS/AD model, let's consider some real-world examples.

Canada in the Mid-1990s In Canada in the mid-1990s, unemployment was 9 percent—high by normal standards—and inflation was 2 percent. But most economists felt that Canada had significant structural unemployment. They believed that output was close to, or at, its potential (in the intermediate range) and if the economy expanded, the result would be inflation, not strong growth. This was the majority view. Some economists argued that the Canadian economy's potential output was much higher, and that an increase in aggregate demand would lead to higher output and no inflation. (They were right.)

Japan in the Late 1990s In the late 1990s, Japan had an unemployment rate of 4.6 percent and inflation was below 1 percent. It would seem that most economists would

Q.9 How does the Keynesian range of the AS/AD model differ from the Classical range?

 9.3

see page 233

Q.10 If politicians suddenly raise government expenditures and the economy is above potential income, what would happen to prices and real income?

believe that, with such a low unemployment rate, the Japanese economy was at potential output in the Classical range. But that was not the case; most economists felt that the Japanese economy had room for expansion and was far below potential compared to the other major industrial countries.

The European Union in the Mid-1990s Another example is Europe in the mid-1990s. Unemployment was over 10 percent, so it would seem the economy was operating in the Keynesian range, far below potential. It didn't have to worry about inflation. But wait—Europe was undergoing a restructuring of its economy, and social welfare programs significantly reduced people's incentive to work. Because of this, some economists felt that Europe in the mid-1990s was close to potential in the intermediate range, and called for a "no expansionary demand" policy. Others disagreed, and called for significant tax cuts to stimulate the economy. What range was Europe actually in? Economic theory doesn't tell us.

The United States in the Mid-1990s In the mid-1990s the U.S. economy expanded slowly, but that expansion was accompanied by major structural changes. This meant that firms expanded and increased output, but they often simultaneously laid off workers. Before these workers could be re-employed, they had to structurally change their professions rather than simply be hired back by their former companies. That takes a lot longer—first to realize that one must redefine one's profession, and then to actually do it.

So there was debate about what the target rate of unemployment was. Initially, most economists seemed united in saying that anything below 6.5 percent unemployment would generate inflation. Then in 1996 unemployment fell to 5 percent, without generating inflation. In the early 2000s it fell to 4 percent and still did not generate inflation. Faced with this empirical evidence, economists changed their estimates of the target rate (and lost some credibility about being able to estimate the U.S. economy's potential output). Some argued the U.S. economy could expand still further without generating inflation. Others argued that the inflation had already started and was simply taking time to show itself.

The Formerly Socialist Countries in the Early 1990s The problem of structural change is even more real for the formerly socialist economies. Even though their output had fallen by 40 to 50 percent, many of them still found themselves close to their potential outputs—they didn't want to produce what, or how, they did before. They are trying to develop whole new institutional structures, which means that neither their previous incomes nor their unemployment rates are especially relevant in determining their potential output. When there is major structural change, normal is no longer normal.

Debates about Potential Output

Making adjustments for real-world factors is complicated, and the resulting estimates of potential output leave much room for debate. There's usually a composite estimate, but actual potential output could be higher, or lower, than that composite, leaving room for disagreement about what the appropriate macro policy is.

Knowing potential output is crucial to knowing what policy to advocate, and it is tough to know where potential output is.

The problems of estimating potential output have led some modern economists, called *real-business-cycle economists*, to argue that the best estimate of potential output that we have is the actual income in the economy. These economists believe the fluctuations in the economy are not caused primarily by fluctuations in aggregate demand but rather by short-run fluctuations in potential output. Expansions in aggregate demand beyond what the economy provides will always cause inflation. Their Classical supply-side explanation is called *real-business-cycle* theory, and they see all changes in the economy as real shifts—changes in potential output—that reflect real causes such as technological changes or shifting tastes. It should not be a surprise when we tell you that real-business-cycle economists are Classical economists.

CONCLUSION

Let's conclude the chapter with a brief summary. In the 1930s modern macroeconomics developed as Classical economists' interest in growth and supply-side issues shifted to Keynesian economists' interest in business cycles and demand-side issues. To capture the issues about the effect of aggregate demand on the economy, economists have developed an *AS/AD* model. When talking about policy, it is useful to distinguish a Classical and Keynesian range in this model.

When the economy is in the Classical range, it is at or above its potential income; in this range policy focuses on supply issues such as those discussed in the previous chapter on long-run growth. Such supply policies ask "How can we increase potential output?" That is why the Classical range is sometimes called the supply-side range.

When the economy is in the Keynesian range, the economy is significantly below its potential income. There is little fear that factor prices will rise in response to an increase in aggregate demand, so the *SAS* curve can be considered relatively flat. Aggregate demand increases have most of their influence on real output. That is why the Keynesian range is sometimes called the demand-side range.

The Keynesian and Classical ranges give us the extremes. Most of the time the economy is in the intermediate range, where an increase in aggregate demand will result in some upward push in the price level as the *SAS* curve shifts up, and some increase in real income. Knowing potential output is crucial to knowing what policy to advocate.

Chapter Summary

- The Depression marked a significant change in Canadian economic institutions. Keynesian economics developed.

- Classical economists focus on the long run and use a laissez-faire approach.

- Keynesian economists focus on short-run fluctuations and use an activist government approach.

- The *AS/AD* model consists of the aggregate demand curve, the short-run aggregate supply curve, and the long-run aggregate supply curve.

- The aggregate demand curve slopes downward because of the wealth effect, the interest rate effect, the international effect, and the multiplier effect.

- The short-run aggregate supply curve is upward sloping because, for the most part, firms in Canada adjust production and prices to meet demand.

- The long-run aggregate supply curve is vertical at potential output.

- Short-run equilibrium is where the *SAS* and *AD* curves intersect. Long-run equilibrium is where the *AD* and potential output curves intersect.

- When the economy is in a short-run equilibrium but not long-run equilibrium, the *SAS* curve will shift up or down to bring the economy back to long-run equilibrium unless government policy shifts the *AD* curve first.

- When output exceeds potential, there is an inflationary gap and the *SAS* curve will shift up to eliminate the gap. When output is below potential, there is a recessionary gap and the *SAS* curve will shift down to eliminate the gap.

- Macroeconomic policy is difficult to conduct because we don't really know where potential output is.

- We must estimate potential output by looking at past levels of potential output and by looking at where the price level begins to rise.

- Economists separate the economy into three ranges: the Keynesian range, which is far below potential output; the intermediate range, which is closer to potential output; and the Classical range, which is above potential.

Key Terms

aggregate demand (*AD*) curve   *(215)*

equilibrium income   *(213)*

inflationary gap   *(225)*

interest rate effect   *(216)*

international effect   *(216)*

long-run aggregate supply (*LAS*)
  curve   *(221)*

multiplier effect   *(216)*

potential income   *(213)*

quantity-adjusting and price-adjusting
  markets   *(220)*

recessionary gap   *(223)*

short-run aggregate supply (*SAS*)
  curve   *(219)*

wealth effect   *(216)*

Questions for Thought and Review

1. Distinguish between a laissez-faire economist and an activist economist.

2. Classicals saw the Depression as a political problem, not an economic problem. Why?

3. What are five factors that cause the *AD* curve to shift?

4. Use the wealth, interest rate, international, and multiplier effects to explain how a rise in the price level affects aggregate quantity demanded.

5. What are two factors that cause the *SAS* curve to shift?

6. If an economy is in short-run equilibrium that is below potential, what forces will bring the economy to long-run equilibrium?

7. Moore's law states that every 18 months, the computing speed of a microchip doubles. What effect does this likely have on the economy? Explain your answer using the *AS/AD* model.

8. If the economy were at a point in the intermediate range close to high potential output, would policymakers present their policy prescriptions to increase real output any differently than if the economy were at a point far from potential output? Why?

9. In the late 1990s a growing number of economists argued that world policymakers were focusing too much on fighting inflation. The economists also argued that the technical level of potential output had risen. Show their argument using the *AS/AD* model. Assume the price level is fixed.

10. Explain why macro policy is more difficult than the simple model suggests.

Problems and Exercises

1. Explain what will likely happen to the *SAS* curve in each of the following instances:
   a. Productivity rises 3 percent; wages rise 4 percent.
   b. Productivity rises 3 percent; wages rise 1 percent.
   c. Productivity declines 1 percent; wages rise 1 percent.
   d. Productivity rises 2 percent; wages rise 2 percent.

2. The opening quotation of the chapter refers to Keynes's view of theory.
   a. What do you think he meant by it?
   b. How does it relate to the emphasis on the "other things constant" assumption?
   c. Do you think Keynes's interest was mainly in positive economics, the art of economics, or normative economics? Why?

3. Explain what will likely happen to the slope or position of the *AD* curve in the following circumstances:
   a. The exchange rate changes from fixed to flexible.
   b. A fall in the price level doesn't make people feel richer.
   c. A fall in the price level creates expectations of a further-falling price level.
   d. Income is redistributed from rich people to poor people.
   e. Autonomous exports increase by 20.
   f. Government spending decreases by 10.

4. Explain what will happen to the position of the *SAS* curve and/or the *LAS* curve in the following circumstances:
   a. Available factors of production increase.
   b. A civil war occurs.
   c. The price of oil quadruples.
   d. Wages that were fixed become flexible, and aggregate demand increases.

5. Congratulations! You have been appointed an economic policy adviser to Canada. You are told that the economy is significantly below its potential output, and that the following will happen next year: World income will fall significantly; and the price of oil will rise significantly. (Suppose that Canada is an oil importer.)
   a. Using the *AS/AD* model, demonstrate your predictions graphically, assuming the price level is fixed.
   b. What policy might you suggest to the government?
   c. How would a real business cycle economist likely criticize the policy you suggest?

6. Late in 2001 the Canadian economy experienced a decline in aggregate demand. Using the *AD/AS* model, describe how the economy will behave in the short run and what might be expected to take place as time passes (in the absence of government intervention).

7. Critics of the federal government called for significant tax cuts late in 2001 in an effort to hold off a recession. At the same time, the United States placed a significant duty on Canadian softwood lumber exports to the U.S. from Canada.
   a. What would each of these factors have done to the economy in the short run if taken in isolation?

   b. How will the softwood lumber duty affect the Canadian economy in the long run? What assumptions did you make to get this answer?
   c. Taken together, will a tax cut offset the impacts of the softwood lumber duty? Why?

Web Questions

1. Go to Statistics Canada's home page (www.statcan.ca) and look up the recent changes in the consumer price index. Using that information, what range do you think the Canadian economy is in now—the Keynesian range, the intermediate range, or the Classical range? How does your answer to that determine what policy you would suggest the government should follow?

2. Go to the Statistics Canada home page (www.statcan.ca).
   a. Find the price level and the level of real output (GDP) over the last 10 years.

   b. Graph the data with price level on the vertical axis and the level of real GDP on the horizontal axis.
   c. Is the curve you have drawn a supply curve, a demand curve, or neither? Why?

3. Go to the Conference Board's home page (www.conferenceboard.ca) and search for information on consumer confidence in Canada and the United States. Based on what you've found, what do you think will happen to the AD curve? How will this affect the price level and equilibrium output? Demonstrate your answer graphically, assuming the price level is fixed.

Answers to Margin Questions

1. A Classical economist takes a laissez-faire approach. Classical economists believe the economy is self-regulating. A Keynesian economist takes an interventionist approach. Keynesian economists believe that equilibrium output can remain below potential output. *(212)*

2. In the short run, saving can lead to a decrease in expenditures and reduce equilibrium output. In the long run saving leads to the accumulation of capital and an increase in potential output. In the long run saving increases equilibrium output. *(214)*

3. False. The multiplier magnifies the initial effect. The rise in expenditures will be greater than 1 percent, making the AD curve flatter than a slope of −10. *(217)*

4. A rise in the value of a country's currency will make domestic goods more expensive to foreigners and foreign goods less expensive to domestic residents. It will shift the AD curve to the left because net exports will fall. *(217)*

5. The AD curve will shift out by more than 20 because of the multiplier. *(219)*

6. If the AD and SAS curves intersect at potential output, the economy is in both long-run and short-run equilibrium. Nothing will happen to the price level and output. *(223)*

7. If there is a recessionary gap, the AS/AD curves intersect to the left of potential output at a point such as A in the following figure. At that level of output there will be pressure for factor prices to fall, pushing the SAS

curve down. Unless the AD curve shifts out (as it usually does) the SAS curve will shift down and output will rise until output equals potential output and the economy is in both long-run and short-run equilibrium at a point such as B. *(225)*

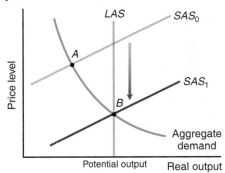

8. If the economy is well below potential, we would predict that output will rise and the price level will too. *(227)*

9. In the Keynesian range the price level remains fixed. In the Classical range, the price level will change as factor prices change. *(229)*

10. If the economy is above potential output, we would predict that factor prices will rise, shifting the SAS curve up. The expansion in government expenditures will shift the AD curve out further, putting even more pressure on factor prices to rise. Our answer, therefore, is that the price level will rise very quickly and output will fall until it equals potential output. *(229)*

The Multiplier Model

10

After reading this chapter, you should be able to:

● Explain the difference between induced and autonomous expenditures.

● Show how the level of income is graphically determined in the multiplier model.

● Use the multiplier equation to determine equilibrium income.

● Explain how the multiplier process amplifies shifts in autonomous expenditures.

● List six reasons why the multiplier model might be misleading.

*Keynes stirred the stale economic
frog pond to its depth.*

Gottfried Haberler

Some of our kids' favourite books are in the Magic Schoolbus series. The kids in those books can go just about anywhere with their teacher, Ms. Frizzle, in their schoolbus—inside the human body, through ant hills, to outer space. Let's borrow that bus and go to a pretend policy meeting of the Japanese government. Some background: The Japanese economy has just fallen into recession, and the Japanese government is trying to determine why, and what to do about it. As we arrive, a man stands up. He tells the prime minister that the decrease in exports that resulted from the rise in the value of the yen, combined with the effects of the enormous fall in the Japanese stock market, cut consumer expenditures, causing unemployment, and that unemployment caused further cuts, and those further cuts caused further cuts, and a downward spiral was in process. He suggests that to stimulate the economy the government should significantly increase its expenditures without raising taxes and that that policy will start a cumulative spiral

The models presented in this chapter are a major simplification of econometric models. In econometric models, economists find standard relationships among aspects of the macroeconomy and use those relationships to predict what will happen to inflation, unemployment, and growth under certain conditions. In the 2000 election, when Prime Minister Chrétien wanted to know the effect his policy proposals would have on the economy, he went to economists who entered the tax cut into their econometric model and estimated the effect.

While econometric models are much more complicated than the models presented here, they have the same structure—a short-run aggregate supply component with flexible prices, an aggregate demand component, and a potential output component.

going in the opposite direction. The prime minister agrees and, based on that reasoning, the Japanese government increases its expenditures significantly.

The magic schoolbus transports us back into the text. What have we learned from the trip? We learned that some people think that increasing expenditures can expand the economy and that those expenditures can start the economy on a cumulative expansion path.

THE MULTIPLIER MODEL

Policymakers want numbers. The *AS/AD* model of the last chapter didn't give them numbers; it talked about the multiplier and about how an initial shift in aggregate expenditures (other things equal) would have a multiplied effect on income. In this chapter we present a model—the multiplier model—that provides the numbers. Even though it is a highly simplified model, it forms an important element of most modern econometric models (computer models that economists use to make forecasts about the economy) of the economy, which are used to guide economic policymakers. (See the Beyond the Tools box.)

The multiplier model in this chapter assumes that the price level remains constant, and then explores what happens when aggregate expenditures expand by a certain number, say, 20. In terms of the *AS/AD* model, the question it explores (shown in Figure 10-1 on the next page) is: When a shift factor of aggregate demand increases by 20, how much will the *AD* curve shift out if the price level is fixed? Whereas the *AS/AD* model gives us insights into the general *qualitative* effects of these shifts, the multiplier model tells about their *quantitative* effects. For example, say that the economists at the Bank of Canada have determined that the multiplier effect of a shift in expenditures will be 3. Their research department informs them that investment and consumption have suddenly fallen by 1 percent of GDP because a stock market bubble has burst. The Bank of Canada's economists would then predict that output would fall by 3 percent.

It was just such a precipitous fall in income that the multiplier model was initially designed to explain. As we discussed in the previous chapter, in the 1930s income fell enormously and the economy fell into a depression. The multiplier model was designed to show how an initial drop in investment could have led to such a large drop in income.

We'll start our discussion of the multiplier model by looking separately at production decisions and expenditure decisions.

The *AS/AD* model gives insight into qualitative effects of aggregate demand shifts; the multiplier model gives insight into quantitative effects of aggregate demand shifts.

Policy fights in economics occur on many levels. Keynes fought on most of them. But it wasn't Keynes who got Canadian policymakers to accept his ideas. Instead it was a small group of powerful civil servants, including R.B. Bryce (a former student of Keynes), W. Clifford Clark (a deputy minister of finance), and W.A. MacKintosh (the director general of economic research in the Department of Reconstruction and Supply). MacKintosh wrote a policy paper that adapted the salient features of Keynesian economics to the Canadian environment—strong-willed federal and provincial governments in a small open economy. The Liberal government of the day used the paper in its 1945 election campaign, but it soon became apparent that the policies would be difficult to implement. They required a significant redistribution of powers between the federal and provincial governments, and the provinces were unwilling to hand over control to the federal authorities.

What made these mandarins switch to Keynesian economics? It was the Depression; the Keynesian story explained it much better than did the Classical real-wage story of the Depression.

At the same time that Canadian policy was being pushed toward Keynesian theories, influential American economists were advising the U.S. government to adopt similar economic policies. These economists, along with Canadian economist Laurie Tarshis, developed what is now called the textbook model of Keynesian economics. That model gave the Keynesian ideas a structure embodied in the specific models that policymakers demanded. While all of this was taking place, Dutch and Norwegian economists developed an empirically determined macro model that policymakers could use. For their contributions, many in this group won Nobel prizes.

Aggregate Production

Aggregate production (AP) is *the total amount of goods and services produced in every industry in an economy.* It is at the centre of the multiplier model. As we noted in an earlier chapter, production creates an equal amount of income, so actual income and actual production are always equal: the terms can be used interchangeably.

Graphically, aggregate production in the multiplier model is represented by a 45° line on a graph, with real income in dollars measured on the horizontal axis and real production measured in dollars on the vertical axis, as in Figure 10-2. Given the definition of the

Graphically, aggregate production in the multiplier model is represented by a 45° line through the origin.

Figure 10-1   THE AS/AD MODEL WHEN PRICES ARE FIXED

The multiplier model was designed to explain how an initial shift in expenditures changes equilibrium output when the price level is fixed. It is designed to fill in the question mark in this figure. When an expenditure shift of 20 hits the economy, that shift causes additional induced effects. These shifts are called multiplier effects.

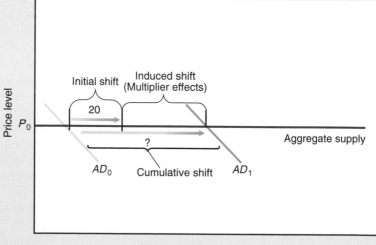

Figure 10-2 THE AGGREGATE PRODUCTION CURVE

Since, by definition, real output equals real income, on each point of the aggregate production curve income must equal production. This equality holds true only on the 45° line.

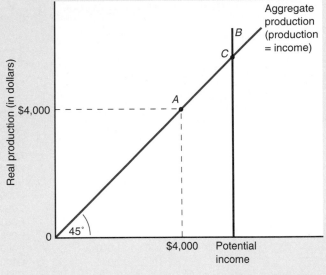

axes, connecting all the points at which real production equals real income produces a 45° line through the origin. Since, by definition, production creates an amount of income equal to the amount of production or output, this 45° line is the *aggregate production curve*, or alternatively the *aggregate income curve*. At all points on the aggregate production curve, income equals production, so it describes an equilibrium relationship where income equals production. For example, consider point A in Figure 10-2, where real income (measured on the horizontal axis) is $4,000 and real production (measured on the vertical axis) is also $4,000. That identity between real production and real income is true only on the 45° line. Output and income, however, cannot expand without limit. The model is relevant only when output is below its potential. Once production expands to the capacity constraint of the existing institutional structure—to potential income (line B)—any increase beyond that can only be temporary.

Q.1 What is true about the relationship between income and production on the aggregate production curve?

Aggregate Expenditures

Aggregate expenditures (AE) in the multiplier model consist of *consumption (spending by consumers), investment (spending by business), spending by government, and net foreign spending on Canadian goods (the difference between Canadian exports and Canadian imports)*. These four components were presented in our earlier discussion of national income accounting, which isn't surprising since the national income accounts were designed around the multiplier model. In that earlier discussion you saw that consumption was the largest component of expenditures. In this chapter we assume that consumption is the only component of aggregate expenditures that varies with income. (An algebraic model in which other components are dependent on income is presented in Appendix A of this chapter.)

Total level of expenditures in an economy (AE) equals $C + I + G + (X - IM)$.

Autonomous and Induced Expenditures While expenditures are determined by many things, one of the most important is income. When income in society rises, expenditures rise. The multiplier model is based on this relationship being relatively

TABLE 10-1   Aggregate Expenditures Related to Income

(1)	(2)	(3)	(4)	
Income (Y)	Change in Income (ΔY)	Aggregate Expenditures (AE)	Change in Aggregate Expenditures (ΔAE)	Row
$ 0	—	$ 1,000	—	A
1,000	$ 1,000	1,800	$ 800	B
2,000	1,000	2,600	800	C
3,000	1,000	3,400	800	D
4,000	1,000	4,200	800	E
5,000	1,000	5,000	800	F
6,000	1,000	5,800	800	G
7,000	1,000	6,600	800	H
8,000	1,000	7,400	800	I
9,000	1,000	8,200	800	J
10,000	1,000	9,000	800	K
11,000	1,000	9,800	800	L
12,000	1,000	10,600	800	M
13,000	1,000	11,400	800	N
14,000	1,000	12,200	800	O
15,000	1,000	13,000	800	P

stable and taking a specific nature: Specifically, as income changes, expenditures change, but not by as much as the change in income.

Table 10-1 shows a hypothesized relationship between possible income and expenditure levels for an economy. Notice that when income is zero, we still assume there is spending. How does that happen? By the economy borrowing or dipping into previous savings. Expenditures that would exist even at a zero level of income are called **autonomous expenditures**—*expenditures that are independent of income*. They may change because something other than income changes. For example, if bad weather stops people from buying, *autonomous* expenditures would fall.

Notice that as income rises, expenditures also rise, but not by as much as the rise in income. The relationship between changes in income and changes in expenditures is shown in columns 2 and 4. The numbers in these columns can be derived from columns 1 and 3. Each entry in column 2 represents the difference between the corresponding entry in column 1 and the entry in the previous row of column 1. Similarly, each entry in column 4 is the difference between the corresponding entry in column 3 and the entry in the previous row of column 3. For example, as income rises from $10,000 to $11,000 (column 1, row K to L), the change in income is $1,000 (column 2, row L). Similarly, as expenditures rise from $9,000 to $9,800 (column 3, row K to L), the change in expenditures is $800 (column 4, row L).

Since much of the multiplier model focuses on changes in expenditures that occur in response to changes in income, it is important to distinguish the portion of expenditures that changes in response to changes in income from the portion that does not. As previously stated, expenditures that do not change when income changes are called *autonomous expenditures*. **Induced expenditures** are *expenditures that change as income changes*.

The relationship between expenditures and income—as in Table 10-1—can be expressed more concisely as an **expenditures function**—*a representation of the relationship*

Autonomous expenditures are expenditures that change because something other than income changes.

Autonomous expenditures are unrelated to income; induced expenditures are directly related to income.

between aggregate expenditures (which include both induced and autonomous expenditures) and income as a mathematical function:

$$AE = AE_0 + mpcY$$

where:

AE = Aggregate expenditures

AE_0 = Autonomous expenditures

mpc = Marginal propensity to consume

Y = Income

The expenditures function corresponding to Table 10-1 is

$$AE = \$1,000 + 0.8Y$$

Notice that if you substitute the data from any row in Table 10-1, both sides of the expenditures function are equal. For example, in row C of Table 10-1, we see that aggregate expenditures $(AE) = \$2,600$. So $\$2,600 = \$1,000 + 0.8Y$. Since income $(Y) = \$2,000$, we can calculate $(0.8)(\$2,000) = \$1,600$ and add it to $\$1,000$, giving us $\$2,600$. So the two sides are equal.

The Marginal Propensity to Consume There is one part of the expenditures function we haven't talked about yet: the letters mpc (0.8 in the numerical example). The **marginal propensity to consume (mpc)** is *the ratio of a change in consumption,* ΔC, *to a change in income,* ΔY. (The Greek letter Δ, or delta, which corresponds to the letter D in our alphabet, is commonly used to designate *a change in.*) The mpc is the fraction spent from an additional dollar of income.

$$mpc = \frac{\text{Change in consumption}}{\text{Change in income}} = \frac{\Delta C}{\Delta Y}$$

The mpc captures a rule of thumb that individuals in aggregate tend to follow: Their consumption varies with their income, but not by as much as their income varies. So if income goes up by 100, and the mpc is 0.8, they increase their consumption by 80, not 100. We can determine the mpc by looking at consumption and income data.

Recall that we assumed that only consumption expenditures depend on income. Hence in our simple model,

$$\frac{\Delta C}{\Delta Y} = \frac{\Delta AE}{\Delta Y}$$

This equality is not true if the other components of aggregate expenditures change as income changes. (For the more complicated model, see Appendix A.)

Using the data in Table 10-1, we can determine the mpc by dividing a change in expenditures by a corresponding change in income:

$$mpc = \frac{\Delta AE}{\Delta Y} = \frac{\$800}{\$1,000} = 0.8$$

Graphing the Expenditures Function Now that we're familiar with the terminology used in the expenditures function, let's see how to graph it. Figure 10-3 (on the next page) graphs the expenditures function represented by

$$AE = \$1,000 + 0.8Y$$

Notice that at zero income, expenditures are $\$1,000$. This is the autonomous portion of expenditures.

Q-2 What is the difference between induced expenditures and autonomous expenditures?

$$mpc = \frac{\text{Change in consumption}}{\text{Change in income}}$$

Q-3 If expenditures change by $\$60$ when income changes by $\$100$, what is the mpc?

Figure 10-3 **GRAPH OF EXPENDITURES FUNCTION**

The expenditures function graphed here represents the function derived from the information in Table 10-1. It has a slope of 0.8, the *mpc*, and an intercept of $1,000, the level of autonomous expenditures. The shaded area is the difference between production and expenditures. Thus, when real income is $14,000, expenditures are $12,200.

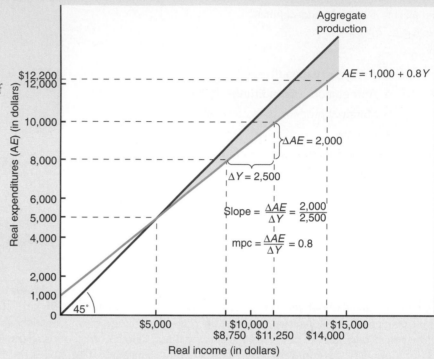

The expenditures function's slope tells us how much expenditures change with a particular change in income. In other words, the slope of an expenditures function graphically represents the marginal propensity to consume for an expenditures function. *The graphical representation of the expenditures function* is called the **aggregate expenditures (AE) curve.**

In thinking about the relationship between aggregate expenditures and income, remember that we have assumed that only the largest component of expenditures, consumption, changes with income; the other components—*I*, *G*, and (*X* − *IM*)—are all autonomous (independent of income).

10.1

Shifts in the Expenditures Function A key element of the expenditures function for our purposes concerns shifts in the autonomous components. To consider those shifts it is good to break up autonomous expenditures into its four autonomous components (consumption, investment, government spending, and net exports).

$$AE = C + I + G + (X - IM)$$

Each of these can shift suddenly, and when they do the *AE* curve shifts up or down.

Imagine that consumer confidence suddenly decreases, perhaps because some economist gave a gloomy prediction about the future. Consumers figure they had better save more to prepare themselves for the upcoming recession, so they cut back expenditures; autonomous consumption falls and the expenditures function shifts down. Alternatively, imagine that businesses come to believe that the economy will grow faster than they expected. To prepare, they will increase investment, increasing autonomous investment and shifting the aggregate expenditures curve up.

We'll let you work the final two examples by yourself. The first is that the government enters into a major war, and the second is that the country's currency suddenly loses value, causing the price of the country's exports to fall and the price of imports to rise. If you answered that they both shift the expenditures function up, you've got the reasoning down.

The reason these shifts are so important is that the multiplier model is a historical model. It can be used to analyze shifts in aggregate expenditures from a historically given income level, but not to determine income independent of the economy's historical position. Notice how we discussed the model in the examples—some shift in autonomous expenditures occurred and that shift led to a change in income from its existing level.

While economists speak of what expenditures would be at zero income, or while we say the *mpc* is constant over all ranges of income, that is done simply to make the geometric portrayal of the model easier. What is actually assumed is that within the relevant range around existing income—say a 5 percent increase or decrease—the *mpc* remains constant, and the autonomous portion of the expenditures is the intercept that would occur if we extended the expenditures function.

DETERMINING THE EQUILIBRIUM LEVEL OF AGGREGATE INCOME

Now that we've developed the graphical framework for the multiplier model, we can put the aggregate production and aggregate expenditures together and see how the level of aggregate income is determined. We begin by considering the relationship between the aggregate expenditures curve and the aggregate production curve more carefully. We do so in Figure 10-4.

The aggregate production (*AP*) curve is a 45° line up until the economy reaches potential income. Its slope is 1, so at all points on it, aggregate expenditures equal aggregate

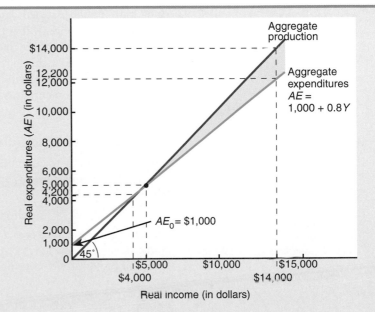

Figure 10-4 **COMPARING *AE* TO *AP* AND SOLVING FOR EQUILIBRIUM GRAPHICALLY**

Equilibrium in the multiplier model is determined where the *AE* and *AP* curves intersect. That equilibrium is at $5,000. At income levels higher or lower than that, planned production will not equal planned expenditures.

For those of you who are mathematically inclined, the multiplier equation can be derived by combining the equations presented in the text algebraically to arrive at the equation for income. Rewriting the expenditures relationship, we have:

$$AE = AE_0 + mpcY$$

Aggregate production, by definition, equals aggregate income (Y) and, in equilibrium, aggregate income must equal the four components of aggregate expenditures. Beginning with the national income accounting identity, we have

$$Y = AE$$

Substituting the terms from the first equation, we have

$$Y = AE_0 + mpcY$$

Subtracting $mpcY$ from both sides,

$$Y - mpcY = AE_0$$

To arrive at the multiplier equation we factor out Y:

$$Y(1 - mpc) = AE_0$$

Now solve for Y by dividing both sides by $(1 - mpc)$:

$$Y = \left[\frac{1}{(1 - mpc)}\right] \times [AE_0]$$

This is the multiplier equation.

income. It tells you the level of aggregate production and also the level of aggregate income since, by definition, real income equals real production when the price level does not change. Expenditures are shown by the AE curve. Planned expenditures do not necessarily equal production or income. In equilibrium, however, planned expenditures must equal production. Why is that the case?

Let's first say that production, and hence income, is $14,000. As you can see, at income of $14,000, planned expenditures are $12,200. Aggregate production exceeds planned aggregate expenditures. This is true for any income level above $5,000. Similarly, at all income levels below $5,000, aggregate production is less than planned aggregate expenditures. For example, at a production level of $4,000, planned aggregate expenditures are $4,200.

The only income level at which aggregate production equals planned aggregate expenditures is $5,000. Since we know that, in equilibrium, planned aggregate expenditures must equal planned aggregate production, $5,000 is the equilibrium level of income in the economy. It is the level of income at which neither producers nor consumers have any reason to change what they are doing. At any other level of income, since there is either a shortage or a surplus of goods, or firms' inventory is greater than or less than desired, there will be incentive to change production. Thus, you can use the aggregate production curve and the aggregate expenditures curve to determine the level of income at which the economy will be in equilibrium.

The Multiplier Equation

Another useful way to determine the level of income in the multiplier model is through the **multiplier equation,** *an equation that tells us that income equals the multiplier times autonomous expenditures.*[1]

$$Y = \text{Multiplier} \times \text{Autonomous expenditures}$$

The **multiplier** is *a number that tells us how much income will change in response to a change in autonomous expenditures.* To calculate the multiplier, you divide 1 by (1 minus the marginal propensity to consume). Thus:

To determine income graphically in the multiplier model, you find the income level at which aggregate expenditures equals planned aggregate production.

The multiplier equation is an equation showing the relationship between autonomous expenditures and the equilibrium level of income: $Y = $ *(Multiplier) (Autonomous expenditures).*

[1]The multiplier equation does not come out of thin air. It comes from combining the set of equations underlying the graphical presentation of the multiplier model into the two brackets. The multiplier equation is derived in the Knowing the Tools box.

$$\text{Multiplier} = \frac{1}{(1 - mpc)}$$

Once you know the value of the marginal propensity to consume, you can calculate the multiplier by reducing $\left(\dfrac{1}{(1 - mpc)}\right)$ to a simple number. For example, if $mpc = 0.8$, the multiplier is

$$\frac{1}{(1 - 0.8)} = \frac{1}{0.2} = 5$$

Since the multiplier tells you the relationship between autonomous expenditures and income, once you know the multiplier, calculating the equilibrium level of income is easy. All you do is multiply autonomous expenditures by the multiplier. For example, using the autonomous expenditures of $1,000 and a multiplier of 5, from Figure 10-4, we can calculate equilibrium income in the economy to be $5,000. This is the same equilibrium income we got from the graphical exercise.

Let's see how the equation works by considering another example. Say the mpc is 0.75. Subtracting 0.75 from 1 gives 0.25. Dividing 1 by 0.25 gives 4. Say, also, that autonomous expenditures (AE_0) are $750. The multiplier equation tells us to calculate income multiply autonomous expenditures, $750, by 4. Doing so gives $4 \times \$750 = \$3,000$.

The multiplier equation gives you a simple way to determine equilibrium income in the multiplier model. Five different marginal propensities to consume and the multiplier associated with each are shown in the table below.

mpc	$\text{Multiplier} = \dfrac{1}{1 - mpc}$
0.5	2
0.75	4
0.8	5
0.9	10
0.95	20

Notice as mpc increases, the multiplier increases. The reason is that as the mpc gets larger, the induced effects of any initial shift in income also get larger. Knowing the multiplier associated with each marginal propensity to consume gives you an easy way to determine equilibrium income in the economy.

Let's look at one more example of the multiplier. Say that the mpc is 0.75 but that autonomous expenditures are $1,000 instead of $750. What is the level of equilibrium income? Multiplying autonomous expenditures, $1,000, by 4 tells us that equilibrium income is $4,000. With a multiplier of 4, income rises by $1,000 because of the $250 increase in autonomous expenditures.

The Multiplier Process

Let's now look more carefully at the forces that are pushing the economy toward equilibrium. What happens when the macroeconomy is in disequilibrium—when the amount being injected into the economy does not equal the amount leaking from the economy? Put another way, what happens when aggregate production does not equal aggregate expenditures? Figure 10-5 (on the next page) shows us.

The multiplier is a number that tells us how much income will change in response to a change in autonomous expenditures: $[1/(1 - mpc)]$.

Q.4 If the $mpc = 0.5$, what is the multiplier?

To determine equilibrium income using the multiplier equation, you determine the multiplier and multiply it by the level of autonomous expenditures.

Q.5 If autonomous expenditures are $2,000 and the $mpc = 0.75$, what is the level of equilibrium income in the economy?

Figure 10-5 THE MULTIPLIER PROCESS

At income levels A and B, the economy is in disequilibrium. Depending on which direction the disequilibrium goes, it generates increases or decreases in planned production and expenditures until the economy reaches income level C, where aggregate expenditures equal planned aggregate production.

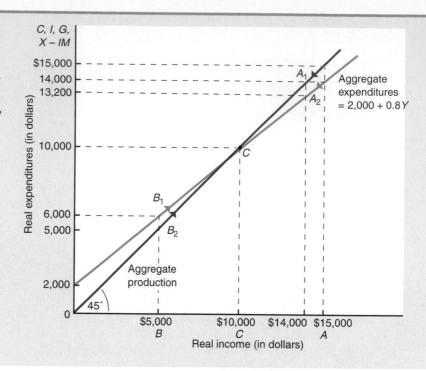

Let's first consider the economy at income level A, where aggregate production equals $15,000 and planned aggregate expenditures equal $14,000. Since production exceeds planned expenditures by $1,000 at income level A, firms can't sell all they produce; inventories pile up. In response, firms make an adjustment. They decrease aggregate production and hence income. As businesses slow production, the economy moves inward along the aggregate production curve, as shown by arrow A_1. As income falls, people's expenditures fall, and the gap between aggregate production and aggregate expenditures decreases. For example, say businesses decrease aggregate production to $14,000. Aggregate income also falls to $14,000, which causes aggregate expenditures to fall, as indicated by arrow A_2, to $13,200. Production still exceeds planned expenditures, but the gap has been reduced by $200, from $1,000 to $800.

Since a gap still remains, production and income keep falling. A good exercise is to go through two more steps. With each step, the economy moves closer to equilibrium.

Now let's consider the economy at income level B ($5,000) and expenditures level $6,000. Here production is less than planned expenditures. Firms find their inventory is running down. (Their investment in inventory is far less than they'd planned.) In response, they increase aggregate production and hence income. The economy starts to expand as aggregate production moves along arrow B_2 and aggregate expenditures move along arrow B_1. As individuals' income increases, their expenditures also increase, but by less than the increase in income, so the gap between aggregate expenditures and aggregate production decreases. But as long as expenditures exceed production, production and hence income keep rising.

Finally, let's consider the economy at income level C, $10,000. At point C, production is $10,000 and planned expenditures are $10,000. Firms are selling all they produce, so they have no reason to change their production levels. The aggregate economy is in equilibrium. This discussion should give you insight into what's behind the arithmetic of those earlier models.

Q-6 When inventories fall below planned inventories, what is likely happening to the economy?

The Circular Flow Model and the Intuition behind the Multiplier Process

Now let's think about the intuition behind the multiplier. You know from the circular flow diagram that when all individuals spend all their income (which they derive from production), the aggregate economy is in equilibrium. The circular flow diagram shown in the margin expresses the national income identity: aggregate income equals aggregate output. The flow of expenditures equals the flow of income (production). How, if not all income is spent (the *mpc* is less than 1), can expenditures equal income? The answer is that the withdrawals through saving (income that is not spent) are offset by injections of autonomous expenditures. We've already discussed autonomous expenditures, but let us briefly review them, concentrating here on investment.

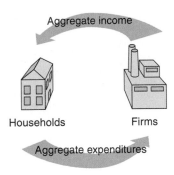

Aggregate income

Households   Firms

Aggregate expenditures

Autonomous investment by businesses is an injection of spending back into the economy; it offsets the saving withdrawal. So, for the circular flow to be constant, leakages through saving must be offset by injections through investment. To keep the analysis simple in this discussion we focus on injections and withdrawals associated with saving and investment, but you should be aware that there are other injections into, and withdrawals from, the spending stream associated with the other components of expenditures. For example, taxes are a withdrawal from the spending stream and government expenditures are an injection. Imports are a withdrawal from the spending stream (the income goes abroad), but exports are an injection. Net exports $(X - IM)$ are the net effect of the combination of these two.

In the multiplier model the *mpc* measures the percentage of expenditures that remains in the economy in each round of the circular flow. For example, if the *mpc* = 0.8, 80 percent of the income flow is retained in the system. The other 20 percent is saved. Saving represents a withdrawal from the system and is assumed not to lead to an injection into the system.

 10.2

see page 255

To focus on that withdrawal, some economists find it helpful to define a term that represents the withdrawals in each round: **marginal propensity to save (*mps*)**—*the percentage of income flow that is withdrawn from the income/expenditure flow of the economy in each round.* By definition:

$$mpc + mps = 1$$

Alternatively expressed:

$$mps = 1 - mpc$$

This means that the multiplier can also be written as:

$$\text{Multiplier} = \frac{1}{mps}$$

Q.7 If the marginal propensity to save is 0.4, what is the size of the multiplier?

When thinking about the multiplier process, we picture a leaking bathtub. Saving or withdrawals are leaks out of the bathtub. Investment or injections are businesspeople dumping buckets of water into the tub. When the water leaking out of the bathtub just equals the water being poured in, the level of water in the tub will remain constant; the bathtub will be in equilibrium. If the amount being poured in is either more or less than the amount leaking out, the level of the water in the bathtub will be either increasing or decreasing. Thus, equilibrium in the economy requires the withdrawals from the spending stream to equal injections into the spending stream. If they don't, the economy will not be in equilibrium and will be either expanding or contracting.

To see this let's consider what happens if saving and investment are not equal. Say that saving exceeds investment (more water is leaking out than is being poured in). In that case, the income in the economy (the level of water in the bathtub) will be declining. As income declines, so will saving. Income will continue to decline until the autonomous investment flowing in (the buckets of water) just equals the saving flowing out (the water leaks).

THE MULTIPLIER MODEL IN ACTION

Determining the equilibrium level of income using the multiplier is an important first step in understanding the multiplier analysis. The second step is to modify that analysis to answer a question that is of much more interest to policymakers: How much would a change in autonomous expenditures change the equilibrium level of income? This second step is important since it is precisely those sudden changes in autonomous expenditures that can cause a recession. That is why we discuss shifts in autonomous expenditures in Figure 10-6.

It is because autonomous expenditures are subject to sudden shifts that we were careful to point out *autonomous* means "determined outside the model and not affected

---

Figure 10-6 (a and b)   SHIFTS IN THE AGGREGATE EXPENDITURES CURVE

Graph (a) shows the effect of a shift of the aggregate expenditures curve. When expenditures decrease by $20, the aggregate expenditures curve shifts downward from AE_0 to AE_1. In response, income falls by a multiple of the shift, in this case by $100.

Graph (b) shows the multiplier process under a microscope. In it the adjustment process is broken into discrete steps. For example, when income falls by $20 (shift B), expenditure falls by $16 (shift C). In response to that fall of expenditures, producers reduce output by $16, which decreases income by $16 (shift D). The lower income causes expenditures to fall further (shift E) and the process continues.

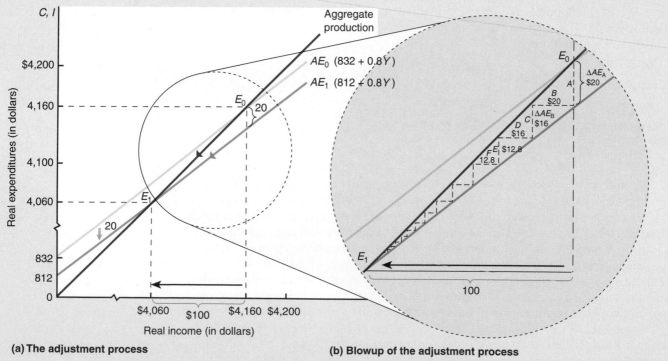

(a) The adjustment process

(b) Blowup of the adjustment process

Figure 10-7 THE FIRST FIVE STEPS OF FOUR MULTIPLIERS

The larger the marginal propensity to consume, the more steps are required before the shifts become small.

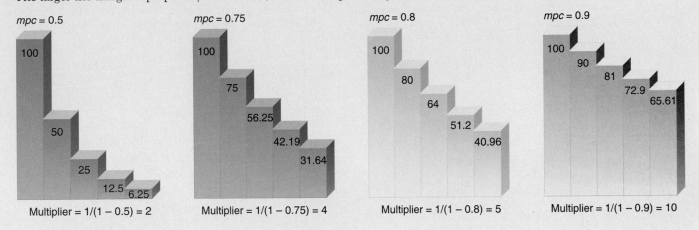

by income." Autonomous expenditures can, and do, shift for a variety of reasons. When they do, the multiplier process is continually being called into play.

The Steps of the Multiplier Process

Any initial change in autonomous aggregate expenditures is amplified in the multiplier process. Let's see how this works in the example in Figure 10-6, which will also serve as a review. Assume that trade negotiations between Canada and other countries have fallen apart and Canadian exports decrease by $20. This is shown in the AE curve's downward shift from AE_0 to AE_1.

How far must income fall until equilibrium is reached? To answer that question, we need to know the initial change $\Delta AE = -\$20$, and the size of the multiplier, $[1/(1 - mpc)]$. In this example, $mpc = 0.8$, so the multiplier is 5. That means the final decrease in income that brings about equilibrium is $100 (five times as large as the initial shift of $20).

Figure 10-6(b), a blowup of the circled area in Figure 10-6(a), shows the detailed steps of the multiplier process so you can see how it works. Initially, autonomous expenditures fall by $20 (shift A), causing firms to decrease production by $20 (shift B). But that decrease in income causes expenditures to decrease by another $16 (0.8 × $20) (shift C). Again firms respond by cutting production, this time by $16 (shift D). Again income falls (shift E), causing production to fall (shift F). The process continues again and again (the remaining steps) until equilibrium income falls by $100, five times the amount of the initial change. The mpc tells how much closer at each step aggregate expenditures will be to aggregate production. You can see this adjustment process in Figure 10-7, which shows the first steps with multipliers of various sizes.

Examples of the Effects of Shifts in Aggregate Expenditures

There are many reasons for shifts in autonomous expenditures that can affect the economy: natural disasters, changes in investment caused by technological developments, shifts in government expenditures, large changes in the exchange rate, and so on. As we

Q.8 If exports fall by $30 and the mpc = 0.9, what happens to equilibrium income?

-30 = ΔAE
(1/1-.9) = mult. = 10
-$30 × 10 = -$300 drop

Figure 10-8 (a and b) **TWO DIFFERENT EXPENDITURES FUNCTIONS AND TWO DIFFERENT SHIFTS IN AUTONOMOUS EXPENDITURES**

The steeper the slope of the AE curve, the greater the effect of a shift in the AE curve on equilibrium income. In (a) the slope of the AE curve is 0.75 and a shift of $30 causes a shift in income of $120. In (b), the slope of the AE curve is 0.66 and a shift of $30 causes a shift in income of $90.

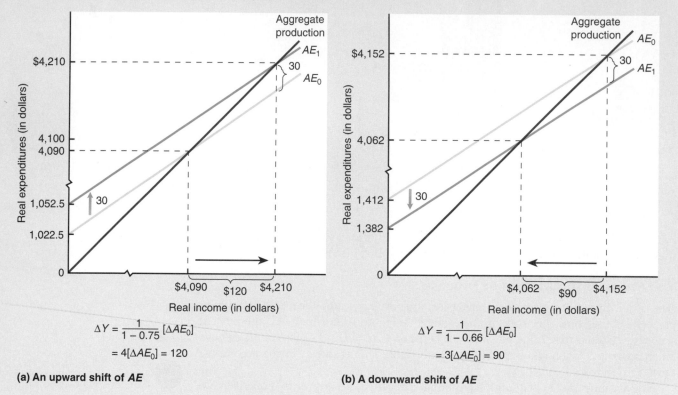

$$\Delta Y = \frac{1}{1 - 0.75} [\Delta AE_0]$$

$$= 4[\Delta AE_0] = 120$$

(a) An upward shift of AE

$$\Delta Y = \frac{1}{1 - 0.66} [\Delta AE_0]$$

$$= 3[\Delta AE_0] = 90$$

(b) A downward shift of AE

discussed above, in order to focus on these shift factors the expenditures function is often broken up into its component parts—consumption (C), investment (I), government spending (G), and net exports (X−IM) (the difference between exports and imports). Thus:

Aggregate expenditures (AE) = C + I + G + (X−IM)

Changes in consumer sentiment affect C; major technological breakthroughs affect I, changes in government's spending decisions affect G, and changes in foreign income and exchange rates affect (X−IM).

Learning to work with the multiplier model requires practice, so in Figure 10-8 (a and b) we present two different expenditures functions and two different shifts in autonomous expenditures. Below each model is the equation representing how much aggregate income changes in terms of the multiplier and autonomous expenditures. As you see, the multiplier equation calculates the shift, while the graph determines it in a visual way. Now let's turn to some real-world examples.

Canada in 2000 In Canada in 2000, consumer confidence rose substantially, causing autonomous consumption expenditures to increase by about $15 billion more than

The *AE* curve is an upward-sloping curve whose slope is equal to the *mpc* and whose *y*-intercept is equal to the level of autonomous expenditures.

Shifts of the *AE* Curve
Anything that affects the level of autonomous expenditures will shift the *AE* curve. That is, anything that *lowers* (raises) autonomous

- consumption
- investment
- government spending
- net exports

will shift the *AE* curve *down* (up) by the amount of the change in autonomous expenditures.

economists had predicted. Assuming a multiplier of 2, that increase meant that income was $30 billion higher than expected. Economists had expected the economy to grow slowly; instead it boomed.

Japan in the 1990s A dramatic rise in the value of the yen in 1995 cut Japanese exports, decreasing aggregate expenditures so that aggregate production was greater than planned aggregate expenditures. Suppliers could not sell all that they produced. Their reaction was to lay off workers and decrease output. That response would have solved the problem if only one firm had been affected. But since all firms (or at least a large majority) were affected the fallacy of composition came into play. As all producers responded in this fashion, aggregate income, and hence aggregate expenditures, also fell. The suppliers' cutback started what is sometimes called a vicious circle. Aggregate expenditures and production spiralled downward, which is what the multiplier process explains.

The 1930s Depression In 1929 there was a financial crash that continued into the 1930s. Financial markets were a mess. Businesspeople became scared, so they decreased investment; consumers became scared, so they decreased autonomous consumption and increased saving, thereby increasing withdrawals from the system. Governments cut spending in an attempt to balance their budgets in the face of declining tax revenues. The result was a sudden large shift downward in the aggregate expenditures curve.

Businesspeople responded by decreasing output, which decreased income and started a downward spiral. This downward spiral confirmed business's fears. The decreased output further decreased income and expenditures. The process continued until eventually the economy settled at an equilibrium far below the potential, or full-employment, level of income.

Recall from an earlier chapter that a process that played an important role in bringing about the Depression is the *paradox of thrift*. Individuals attempted to save more, but in doing so spent less and caused income to decrease, and they ended up saving no more, or even less.

Q.9 Your study partner has just said that *autonomous* means "unchanging." How do you respond?

The paradox of thrift occurs when individuals attempting to save more cause income to decrease; thereby they end up saving no more, or even less.

LIMITATIONS OF THE MULTIPLIER MODEL

On the surface the multiplier model makes a lot of intuitive sense. However, surface sense can often be misleading. Some of the model's limitations are discussed below.

The Multiplier Model Is Not a Complete Model of the Economy

The multiplier model provides a technical method of determining equilibrium income. But in reality the model doesn't do what it purports to do—determine equilibrium income from scratch. Why? Because it doesn't tell us where those autonomous expenditures come from or how we would go about measuring them.

At best, what we can estimate are directions and rough sizes of autonomous demand or supply shifts.

At best, what we can measure, or at least estimate, are directions and rough sizes of autonomous demand or supply shifts, and we can determine the direction and possible overadjustment the economy might make in response to those changes. If you think back to our initial discussion of the multiplier model, this is how we introduced it—as an explanation of forces affecting the adjustment process, not as a determinant of the final equilibrium independent of where the economy started. It is a historical, not an analytical, model. Without some additional information about where the economy started from, or what is the desired level of output, the multiplier model is incomplete.

Shifts Are Not as Great as Intuition Suggests

A second problem with the multiplier model is that it leads people to overemphasize the shifts that would occur in aggregate expenditures in response to a shift in autonomous expenditures. Say people decide to save some more. You might think that it would lead to a fall in expenditures. But wait, that saving will go into the financial sector and be translated back into the expenditures sector as loans to other consumers or as loans to businesses funding investment. So if you take a broad view of aggregate expenditures, many of the shifts in expenditures are simply rearrangements from one group of expenditures to another.

The Price Level Will Often Change in Response to Shifts in Demand

One of the assumptions of the multiplier model was that the price level was fixed—the short-run aggregate supply curve was horizontal. Figure 10-9 illustrates how an upward-sloping *SAS* curve affects the analysis. An increase in aggregate expenditures shifts the aggregate expenditures curve up, and the level of aggregate demand in the economy rises. If the price level were fixed, the red *SAS* curve illustrates that the economy would move from point A to point B. However, with a flexible price level the blue curve describes the short-run aggregate supply curve. At the initial price level an increase in aggregate demand places upward pressure on the price level, since the quantity of output demanded is greater than that supplied. As the price level rises, the quantity of output demanded falls from point B, and the economy settles at point C. Note that the aggregate expenditures curve shifts back somewhat as the price level rises, since higher prices reduce desired spending.

If the same expansion in aggregate expenditures were to take place from a situation of full employment, the multiplier story would change once again, as shown in Figure 10-10. The increase in aggregate expenditures and aggregate demand leads to excess demand at the initial price level. Since the economy is already operating at potential, wages rise in response to the excess demand, shifting the short-run aggregate supply curve left until equilibrium is restored at point B. Again, you can see that the higher price level shifts the aggregate expenditures curve back, in this case, to its initial location. The multiplier in this example is zero.

The degree of flexibility in the price level is an important determinant of the size and strength of the multiplier in the real world.

Figure 10-9 (a and b) THE MULTIPLIER WITH A FLEXIBLE PRICE LEVEL

An increase in autonomous expenditures shifts the AE and AD curves to AE_1 and AD_1. If the price level were fixed, the red short-run aggregate supply curve suggests the economy would move to point B. With flexible prices the blue short-run aggregate supply curve describes the supply side of the economy. At the initial price level the increase in aggregate expenditures would create excess demand, putting pressure on the price level to rise to P_1. As this takes place the quantity of aggregate output demanded would fall from Y_1 to Y_2 since higher prices reduce desired spending and shift the AE curve back somewhat to AE_2.

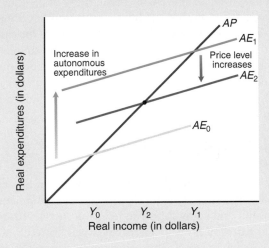
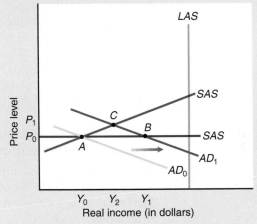

Figure 10-10 (a and b) THE MULTIPLIER WITH OUTPUT FIXED

When the economy begins at potential output an increase in aggregate expenditures shifts the AE and AD curves to AE_1 and AD_1. Since the economy is already operating at potential, excess demand puts upward pressure on all wages and prices. With wage rates rising the short-run aggregate supply curve shifts left and the system settles at point B with a higher price level. Notice that the higher price level has shifted the aggregate expenditures curve back to its initial position.

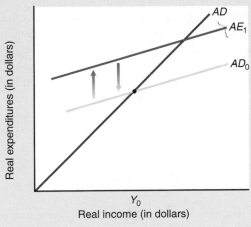
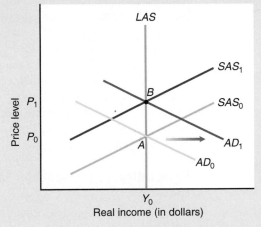

People's Forward-Looking Expectations Make the Adjustment Process Much More Complicated

People's forward-looking expectations make the adjustment process much more complicated. The multiplier model presented here assumes that people respond to current changes in income. Most people, however, act on the basis of expectations of the future. Consider the assumed response of businesses to changes in expenditures. They lay off workers and cut production at the slightest fall in demand. In reality, their response is far more complicated. They may well see the fall as a temporary blip. They will allow their inventory to rise in the expectation that the next month another temporary blip will offset the previous fall. Business decisions about production are forward looking, and do not respond simply to current changes. As a contrast to the simple multiplier model, some modern economists have put forward a **rational expectations model** of the macroeconomy in which *all decisions are based on the expected equilibrium in the economy.* They argue that since people rationally expect the economy to achieve its potential income, it will do so.

Shifts in Expenditures Might Reflect Desired Shifts in Supply and Demand

There is an implicit assumption in the multiplier model that shifts in demand are not reflections of shifts in desired production or supply. Reality is much more complicated. Shifts can occur for many reasons, and many shifts can reflect desired shifts in aggregate production, which are accompanied by shifts in aggregate expenditures. Say, for example, that technology changes. Production will shift from one sector of the economy to another and there could be significant dislocation of firms and workers. People's expenditures might decrease as they try to adjust their lives to the new technology. In the 21st century, the Internet is expected to replace functions of the personal computer and the Windows operating system, displacing PC makers and possibly Microsoft.

These shifts may be simultaneous shifts in supply and demand and need not reflect suppliers' responses to changes in demand. Suppliers operate in the future—shifting supply, not to existing demand, but to expected demand, making the relationship between aggregate production and current demand far more complicated than it seems in the multiplier model. Expansion of this line of thought has led some economists (in an earlier chapter called *real-business-cycle economists*) to develop the **real-business-cycle theory** of the economy: *the theory that fluctuations in the economy reflect real phenomena—simultaneous shifts in supply and demand, not simply supply responses to demand shifts.* Let's consider an example—the expansion of the Canadian economy in the late 1990s. The *AS/AD* model would attribute that to a shift of the *AD* curve to the right, combined with a relatively fixed *AS* curve that does not shift up as output expands. The real-business-cycle theory would attribute that shift in income to businesses' decision to increase supply due to technological developments, and a subsequent increase in demand via Say's law.

Expenditures Depend on Much More Than Current Income

Q.10 What effect would expenditures being dependent on permanent income have on the size of the multiplier?

Let's say your income goes down 10 percent. The multiplier model says that your expenditures will go down by some specific percentage of that. But will they? If you are rational, it seems reasonable to base your consumption on more than one year's income—say, instead, on your permanent or lifetime income. What happens to your income in a particular year has little effect on your lifetime income. If it is true that people base their spending primarily on lifetime income, not yearly income, the marginal propensity to consume out of changes in current income could be very low, approaching zero. In that case, the expenditures function would essentially be a flat line, and the multiplier would be 1. There would be no secondary effects of an initial shift in expenditures. This set of arguments is called the **permanent income hypothesis**—*the hypothesis that expenditures are determined by permanent or lifetime income*. It undermines the reasoning of much of the specific results of the simple multiplier model.

CONCLUSION

While each of the above criticisms has some validity, most economists still use some variation of the multiplier model as the basis for their policy decisions. They don't see it as a *mechanistic model*—a model that pictures the economy as representable by a mechanically determined, timeless model with a determinant equilibrium. Modern economists have come to the conclusion that there is no simple way to understand the aggregate economy. Any mechanistic interpretation of an aggregate model is doomed to fail. The hope of economists to have a model that would give them a specific numeric guide to policy has not been met.

The model is still useful if it is seen as an *interpretive model* or an aid in understanding complicated disequilibrium dynamics. The specific results of the multiplier model are a guide to common sense, enabling us to emphasize a particular important dynamic interdependency while keeping others in mind. With that addendum—that it is not meant to be taken literally but only as an aid to intuition—the simple multiplier model deals with the issues that concern today's highest-level macro theorists.

Chapter Summary

- The multiplier model focuses on the induced effect that a change in production has on expenditures, which affects production, and so on.

- The multiplier model is made up of the aggregate production and aggregate expenditures curves. In equilibrium, aggregate production must equal planned aggregate expenditures.

- The aggregate production curve is a line along which real income equals real production. It is a 45° line.

- Aggregate expenditures (AE) are made up of consumption, investment, government spending, and net exports:

  $AE = C + I + G + (X - IM)$

- Expenditure depends on the level of income; the *mpc* tells us the change in expenditure that occurs with a change in income.

- The AE curve shows aggregate expenditures graphically. Its slope is the *mpc* and its y-intercept equals autonomous expenditures.

- Equilibrium output, or income, is where the AP and AE curves intersect.

- Equilibrium output can be calculated using the multiplier equation. It is:

  Y = Multiplier × Autonomous expenditures

- The multiplier tells us how much a change in autonomous expenditures will change equilibrium income. The multiplier equals $1/(1 - mpc)$.

- When an economy is in equilibrium, withdrawals from the spending stream (saving) equal injections into the spending stream (autonomous expenditures).

- Shifts in autonomous expenditures can be the initial change that begins the multiplier process. The multiplier process expands that initial shift to a much larger decrease or increase in production and income.

- The multiplier model has limitations: (1) it is incomplete without information about where the economy started and what is the desired level of output, (2) it overemphasizes shifts that occur in aggregate expenditures, (3) it assumes that the price level is fixed when in reality it isn't, (4) it doesn't take expectations into account, (5) it ignores the possibility that shifts in expenditures are desired, and (6) it ignores the possibility that consumption is based on lifetime income, not annual income.

● Macroeconomic models cannot be applied mechanistically; they are only guides to common sense.

Key Terms

aggregate expenditures (AE)   *(237)*

aggregate expenditures (AE) curve   *(240)*

aggregate production (AP)   *(236)*

autonomous expenditures   *(238)*

expenditures function   *(238)*

induced expenditures   *(238)*

marginal propensity to consume (*mpc*)   *(239)*

marginal propensity to save (*mps*)   *(245)*

multiplier   *(242)*

multiplier equation   *(242)*

permanent income hypothesis   *(253)*

rational expectations model   *(252)*

real-business-cycle theory   *(252)*

Questions for Thought and Review

1. If planned expenditures are below actual production, what will happen to income? Explain the process by which this happens.

2. Are inventories building up at levels of output above or below equilibrium output? Explain your answer.

3. What happens to the aggregate expenditures curve when autonomous expenditures fall?

4. What happens to equilibrium income when the marginal propensity to consume rises?

5. If saving were instantaneously translated into investment, what would be the multiplier's size? What would be the level of autonomous expenditures?

6. Name some forces that might cause shocks to aggregate expenditures.

7. Mr. Whammo has just invented a magic pill. Take it and it transports you anywhere. Explain his invention's effects on the economy.

8. Why is the circular flow diagram of the economy an only partially correct conception of the multiplier model?

9. How do mechanistic models differ from interpretive models?

10. A political pundit was quoted in a newspaper article as stating, "I can't tell you why this happens, but there's a lag time (before people tune into good economic news)." What is the effect of this delay in the adjustment of expectations by consumers on the dynamics of the multiplier model?

Problems and Exercises

1. The marginal propensity to consume is 0.8. Autonomous expenditures are $4,200. What is the level of equilibrium income in the economy? Demonstrate graphically.

2. The marginal propensity to consume is 0.66 and autonomous expenditures have just fallen by $20.
   a. What will likely happen to equilibrium income?
   b. Demonstrate graphically.

3. Congratulations. You've been appointed economic adviser to Happyland. Your research assistant says the country's *mpc* is 0.8 and autonomous expenditures have just risen by $20.
   a. What will happen to income?
   b. Your research assistant comes in and says he's sorry but the *mpc* wasn't 0.8; it was 0.5. How does your answer change?

   c. He runs in again and says exports have fallen by $10 and investment has risen by $10. How does your answer change?
   d. You now have to present your analysis to the premier, who wants to see it all graphically. Naturally you oblige.

4. Congratulations again. You've just been appointed economic adviser to Examland. The *mpc* is 0.6; investment is $1,000; government spending is $8,000; consumption is $10,000; and net exports are $1,000.
   a. What is the level of income in the country?
   b. Net exports increase by $2,000. What will happen to income?
   c. What will happen to unemployment? (Remember Okun's rule of thumb.)

d. You've just learned the *mpc* changed from 0.6 to 0.5. How will this information change your answers in *a*, *b*, and *c*?

5. In 1993, as Prime Minister Kim Campbell was running (unsuccessfully) for re-election, the economy slowed down; then in late 1993, after Prime Minister Chrétien's election, the economy picked up steam.
   a. Demonstrate graphically with the multiplier model a shift in the *AE* curve that would have caused the slowdown. Which component of aggregate expenditures was the likely culprit?
   b. Demonstrate graphically with the multiplier model a shift in the *AE* curve that would have caused the improvement. Which component of aggregate expenditures was likely responsible?
   c. What policies do you think Prime Minister Campbell could have used to stop the slowdown?
   d. What policies do you think Prime Minister Chrétien used to try to speed up the economy?

Web Questions

1. The Conference Board publishes a report detailing consumer attitudes and buying plans and compiles the consumer confidence index. It also reports on business executives' expectations. Go to the Conference Board's home page (www.conferenceboard.ca) and read the most recent reports on consumer confidence and business executives' expectations to answer the following questions:
   a. What has happened to the consumer confidence index in the past few months?
   b. Using the multiplier model show the likely effect of the change in consumer confidence on equilibrium output.
   c. What has happened to expectations of business executives over the past few months?
   d. Do the consumer confidence and business executives' expectations match? If not, what do you expect to happen to inventories in the coming months?

2. Statistics Canada reports data about recent economic events. Go to its home page (www.statcan.ca) and find the data to answer the following questions:
   a. What has happened to inventories during the past six months?
   b. What does the change in inventories suggest about the direction of the economy in the coming months? Explain your answer using the multiplier model.

Answers to Margin Questions

1. Income equals production on the aggregate production curve. *(237)*
2. Induced expenditures change as income changes. Autonomous expenditures are independent of income. *(239)*
3. The *mpc* is 0.6. *(239)*
4. The multiplier is 2 when the *mpc* = 0.5. *(243)*
5. The level of income is $8,000. *(243)*
6. When inventories fall below planned inventories the economy is probably expanding; firms will likely increase production, which will cause expenditures to increase, which will further draw down inventories. *(244)*
7. If the *mps* equals 0.4, the *mpc* equals 0.6, which means that the multiplier equals 2.5. *(245)*
8. Equilibrium income falls by $300. *(247)*
9. We respond by saying that *autonomous* means "determined outside the model." That is, autonomous expenditures do not change in a predetermined way with income. Autonomous expenditures can, and do, change, and as they change, equilibrium income in the economy changes. *(249)*
10. If expenditures are dependent on permanent income, not current income, expenditures would not change as much with a change in current income and the multiplier would get smaller. *(252)*

APPENDIX A

An Algebraic Presentation
of the Expanded Multiplier Model

In the chapter we developed the basic multiplier model with only consumption being related to income. In this appendix we briefly outline a fuller presentation in which consumption, taxes, and imports are related to income. That means there is a marginal propensity to consume (mpc), specified as c in the equations, a marginal propensity to import, specified as m in the equations, and a marginal tax rate, specified as t in the equations.

The basic multiplier model consists of the following equations:

(1) $C = C_0 + cY_d$

(2) $Y_d = Y - T + R$

(3) $I = I_0$

(4) $G = G_0$

(5) $R = R_0$

(6) $T = T_0 + tY$

(7) $X = X_0$

(8) $IM = IM_0 + mY$

(9) $C + I + G + (X - IM) = Y$

Equation (1) is the consumption function. C_0 is autonomous consumption; cY_d is the mpc multiplied by disposable income.

Equation (2) defines disposable income as a function of income minus taxes plus government transfers.

Equation (3) is the investment function. I_0 is autonomous investment.

Equation (4) is the government expenditures function. G_0 is autonomous spending.

Equation (5) is the government transfer function. R_0 is autonomous transfer payments.

Equation (6) is the tax function. Taxes are composed of two parts. The autonomous component, T_0, is unaffected by income. The induced portion of taxes is tY. The tax rate is represented by t.

Equation (7) is the exogenous export function.

Equation (8) is the import function. Imports are composed of two parts. IM_0 is the autonomous portion. The induced portion is mY. The marginal propensity to import is represented by m.

Equation (9) is the national income accounting identity: Total expenditures = income.

To use this model meaningfully, we must combine all these equations into a single equation, called a *reduced-form equation,* which will neatly show the effect of various shifts on the equilibrium level of income. To do so we first substitute Equation (2) into Equation (1) giving us:

(1a) $C = C_0 + c(Y - T + R)$

We then substitute (1a), (3), (4), (5), (6), (7), and (8) into Equation (9), giving:

$C_0 + c[Y - (T_0 + tY) + R_0] + I_0 + G_0 + [X_0 - (IM_0 + mY)] = Y$

Removing the parentheses:

$C_0 + cY - cT_0 - ctY + cR_0 + I_0 + G_0 + X_0 - IM_0 - mY = Y$

Moving all of the Y terms to the right side:

$C_0 - cT_0 + cR_0 + I_0 + G_0 + X_0 - IM_0 = Y - cY + ctY + mY$

Factoring out Y on the right side:

$C_0 - cT_0 + cR_0 + I_0 + G_0 + X_0 - IM_0 = Y(1 - c + ct + m)$

Dividing by $(1 - c + ct + m)$ gives:

$$(C_0 - cT_0 + cR_0 + I_0 + G_0 + X_0 - IM_0)$$
$$\left[\frac{1}{(1 - c + ct + m)}\right] = Y$$

$1/(1 - c + ct + m)$ is the multiplier for a simple multiplier model with endogenous taxes and endogenous imports.

If t and m are both zero (the assumption we made in the chapter), this equation reduces to the multiplier, $1/(1 - c)$ where c is the mpc. The additional terms adjust the multiplier for the other induced expenditures that the simple model did not consider. Notice that they both make the multiplier smaller. For example, if the mpc is 0.8, $t = 0.25$, and $m = 0.1$, the multiplier using only the mpc would be $1/(1 - 0.8) = 5$. Taking into account other induced expenditures the denominator changes to $0.8 - 0.8(0.25) - 0.1 = 0.5$. Substituting 0.5 into our generalized multiplier formula, $1/(1 - 0.5)$ we see that the multiplier becomes $[1/(0.5)] = 2$.

To see whether you follow the math, let's try another numerical example. Say you want to increase income (Y) by 100. Assume $c = 0.8$, $t = 0.2$, and $m = 0.04$. Substituting in these numbers you find that the multiplier is 2.5. (The approximate multiplier for Canada is usually considered to be somewhere between 1.5 and 2.0; the additional terms play an important role in making it this small.)

Having calculated the multiplier we can now determine how much to change autonomous expenditures to affect income. For example, to increase income by 100, we must increase autonomous expenditures by (100/2.5) = 40.

Questions for Thought and Review

1. You have just been made our nation's adviser. The prime minister wants output to increase by 400 by decreasing taxes. Your research assistant tells you that the *mpc* is 0.8, and all other components of aggregate expenditures are determined outside the model. What policy would you suggest?

2. The prime minister returns to you and tells you that instead of changing taxes, he wants to achieve the same result by increasing government expenditures. What policy would you recommend?

3. Your research assistant has a worried look on her face. "What's the problem?" you ask. "I goofed," she confesses. "I thought taxes were exogenous when actually there's a marginal tax rate of 0.1." Before she can utter another word, you say, "No problem. I'll simply recalculate my answers to questions 1 and 2 and change them before I send them in." What are your corrected answers?

4. She still has a pained expression. "What's wrong?" you ask. "You didn't let me finish," she says. "Not only was there a marginal tax rate of 0.1; there's also a marginal propensity to import of 0.2." Again you interrupt to make sure she doesn't feel guilty. Again you say, "No problem. I'll simply recalculate my answers to questions 1 and 2 to account for the new information." What are your new answers?

5. Explain, using the words "expenditures" and "leakages," why making taxes and imports endogenous reduces the multiplier.

6. Suppose imports were a function of disposable income instead of income. What would be the new multiplier? How does it compare with the multiplier when imports were a function of income?

APPENDIX B

The Multiplier Model and the AS/AD Model

In an earlier chapter we emphasized that the *AD* curve was quite different from a micro demand curve; it was an equilibrium curve—a curve that told us the relationship between different price levels and different equilibria in the goods market. It has traditionally been derived from the multiplier model, and thus it has implicitly accepted the dynamics of that model. To see how it is derived from the multiplier model we must first recall how the *AE* curve shifts as the price level rises and falls.

In Figure B10-1(a) we draw three *AE* curves—one for each of the price levels P_0, P_1, and P_2, where $P_0 > P_1 > P_2$. How a change in the price level affects the *AE* curve can be explained by the wealth, interest rate, and international effects. A rise in the price level will shift the *AE* curve down. Similarly, a fall in the price level will shift the *AE* curve up. (A much more detailed discussion of the re-

lationship between the price level and expenditures can be found in the previous chapter.)

The initial equilibrium is at point A. Notice that as the price level falls, aggregate expenditures rise. This initial increase causes induced expenditures to change. Production shifts because of these induced effects, increasing output further than the initial shift in aggregate expenditures and the initial increase in output to Y_1'. The new equilibrium output at P_1 is Y_1 (point B), and at P_2 the new equilibrium output is Y_2 (point C).

In Figure B10-1(b) we show the equilibrium price levels and outputs on a graph, with price level on the vertical axis and real income on the horizontal axis. That gives us points A, B, and C, which correspond to points A, B, and C in Figure B10-1(a). Drawing a line through these points gives us the aggregate demand curve: a curve that shows

Figure B10-1 (a – d)   RELATIONSHIP BETWEEN THE MACRO POLICY MODEL AND THE AP/AE MODEL

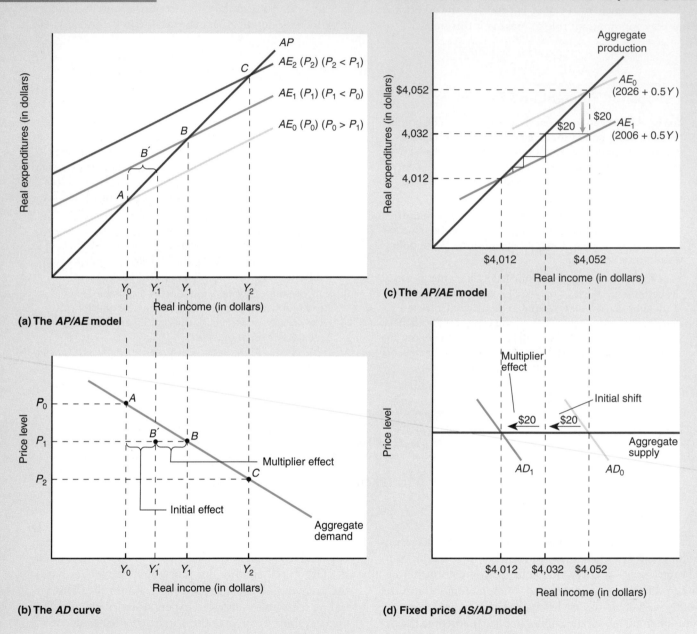

(a) The *AP/AE* model

(b) The *AD* curve

(c) The *AP/AE* model

(d) Fixed price *AS/AD* model

how a change in the price level will affect quantity of aggregate demand. Notice that the *AD* curve includes both the effect of the initial shift in aggregate expenditures from a change in the price level and the multiplier effects as production and expenditures move to equilibrium. The initial shift in aggregate expenditures is shown by point *B'*.

If there were no multiplier effects, the *AD* curve would go through points *A* and *B'*.

The first thing to note when considering the two models is that the multiplier model assumes that the price level is constant, so it assumes that the aggregate supply curve is flat. This means that the multiplier model tells us precisely how much the *AD* curve will shift when autonomous expenditures shift by a specified amount. The difference between the shift in autonomous expenditures and the *AD* curve shift is due to the multiplier.

The relationship between a shift in autonomous expenditures in the *AS/AD* model and the multiplier model can be seen in Figure B10-1(c) and (d). These consider a fall in autonomous expenditures of $20 when the multiplier is 2. In Figure B10-1(c) you can see that, in the multiplier model, a fall in expenditures of $20 will cause income to fall by $40, from $4,052, to $4,012.

Figure B10-1(d) shows that same adjustment in the *AS/AD* model. Initially expenditures fall by $20, but the *AD* curve shifts back not by $20, but by $40—the initial shift multiplied by the multiplier. That's because the *AD* curves take into account the interdependent shifts between supply and demand decisions that are set in motion by the initial shift. Thus we need the multiplier model, or some alternative model of induced effects, before we can draw an *AD* curve. (We make the qualification "or some other model" to emphasize that the interdependent shifts assumed in the multiplier model are not the only interdependent shifts that could occur. Had we assumed a different dynamic adjustment process, we would have had a different *AD* curve.)

A good test of your understanding here is to ask yourself what happens in the long run if the economy is operating above its potential where prices are perfectly flexible. (In that case, the rise in aggregate demand is fully offset by a rise in the price level, and the *AE* curve shifts right back where it started.)

Much of the modern debate in macro concerns the dynamic adjustment process that the multiplier model is meant to describe. We won't go into that debate here since it quickly becomes very complicated, but we do want to point out to you that the multiplier model is not the end of the analysis; it is simply the beginning—one of the simplest cases of dynamic adjustment. The real-world dynamic adjustment is more complicated, which is one of the reasons why there is so much debate about macroeconomic issues.

Questions for Thought and Review

1. Demonstrate graphically the effect of an increase in autonomous expenditures when the *mpc* = 0.5 and the price level is fixed:
   a. In the multiplier model.
   b. In the *AS/AD* model.
   c. Do the same thing as in *a* and *b*, only this time assume prices are somewhat flexible and the economy begins close to its potential.

2. State how the following information changes the slope of the *AD* curve discussed in the previous chapter.
   a. The effect of price level changes on autonomous expenditures is reduced.
   b. The size of the multiplier increases.
   c. Autonomous expenditures increase by $20.
   d. Falls in the price level disrupt financial markets, which offset the normally assumed effects of a change in the price level.

Demand Management Policy: The Fiscal Approach

11

After reading this chapter, you should be able to:

- Demonstrate expansionary and contractionary fiscal policies using words and graphs.

- List three alternatives to fiscal policy.

- Discuss two real-world examples of fiscal policy.

- List six problems with fiscal policy and explain how those problems limit its use.

- Define *crowding out* and explain how it can undermine the Keynesian view of fiscal policy.

- Describe how automatic stabilizers work.

An economist's lag may be a politician's catastrophe.

George Schultz

The multiplier model presented in the last chapter highlights the role of aggregate demand management policies. These include monetary policy, to which we'll return in Chapters 13 and 14, and fiscal policy, which we cover in this chapter. **Fiscal policy** is *the deliberate change in either government spending or taxes to stimulate or slow down the economy.* If aggregate income is too low (actual income is below target income), the appropriate fiscal policy is **expansionary fiscal policy:** *decrease taxes or increase government spending.* If aggregate income is too high (actual income is above target income), the appropriate fiscal policy is **contractionary fiscal policy:** *increase taxes or decrease government spending.*

Expansionary fiscal policy involves decreasing taxes or increasing government spending. Contractionary fiscal policy involves increasing taxes or decreasing government spending.

THE STORY OF FISCAL POLICY

Let's start this discussion with the story of fiscal policy for an economy in a recession. What caused that recession? As we saw in an earlier chapter, when people got scared and cut back their spending, the multiplier took over and expanded that small decline in spending into a full-blown recession. In a recession, the economy is at a level of income and production below the potential level of income—below full employment of all productive resources.

Seeing this low level of income, and understanding the multiplier model of the previous chapter, you should be led to the following insight: If somehow you can generate a countershock (a jolt in the opposite direction of the shift in aggregate demand that started the recession), you can get the multiplier working in reverse, expanding the economy in the same way the initial decline in spending and multiplier effect had contracted it. You need a countershock to motivate people to spend, and as they increase their spending, society will be better off. But each individual, acting in her own interest, has no incentive to spend more. Each individual would reason: If I spend more, I'll be worse off. Theoretically, my additional spending might help society, but the positive effect would be so diluted that, in terms of my own situation, I don't see how my increased spending is going to benefit me.

For example, if a grocery store clerk increased her shopping expenditures by $100, only about $25 of that expenditure would go into food, so if her store is one of five stores selling various articles in the area where she shops, only $5 would go to her store. If she were one of 20 employees, her $5 represents only an additional 25 cents of spending per employee at the store. If she were about to lose her job, her $100 spending wouldn't save it. However, if *all* individuals, or a large proportion of all individuals, increased their spending by $100 each, spending at her store would rise considerably and her job would likely be saved.

How do you simultaneously get all or most individuals to spend more than they want to? In the Depression of the 1930s, government found it wasn't easy to encourage people to spend to create more jobs.

According to the multiplier model, these encouragements could have worked if they had generated a sufficient increase in spending; that initial increase would have generated some more spending, which in turn would have generated even more spending. But these admonitions didn't work. The multiplier model offered expansionary fiscal policy as an alternative.

With fiscal policy, government could provide the needed increased spending by decreasing taxes, increasing government spending, or both. Fiscal policy would provide the initial expansionary spending, increasing individuals' incomes. As individuals' incomes increased, they would spend more. As they spent more, the multiplier process would take over and expand the effect of the initial spending.

Aggregate Demand Management

There is nothing special about government's ability to stimulate the economy with additional spending. If a group of individuals wanted to—and had spending power large enough to make a difference—they could do so, but private individuals don't have the incentive to do so. The expansionary effect of their spending helps other people mainly and themselves only a little. Unless they're altruistic, they don't take into account the effect of their spending on the aggregate spending stream and hence on aggregate income.

Think of fiscal policy as a countershock designed to stabilize income.

Expansionary fiscal policy stimulates autonomous expenditures, which increases people's income, which increases people's spending even more.

Q-1 If spending in the economy is too low, why don't individuals simply increase their spending?

BEYOND THE TOOLS

Keynes and Fiscal Policy

One of the themes of this book is that economic thought and policy are more complicated than an introductory book must necessarily make them seem. Fiscal policy is a good case in point. In the early 1930s, before Keynes wrote *The General Theory,* he was advocating public works programs and deficits (government spending in excess of tax revenue) as a way to get the British economy out of the Depression. He came upon what we now call the *Keynesian theory* as he tried to explain to Classical economists why he supported deficits. After arriving at his new theory, however, he spent little time advocating fiscal policy and, in fact, never mentions fiscal policy in *The General Theory.* The book's primary policy recommendation is the need to socialize investments—for the government to take over the investment decisions from private individuals. When one of his followers, Abba Lerner, advocated expansionary fiscal policy at a seminar Keynes attended, Keynes strongly objected, leading Evsey Domar, another Keynesian follower, to whisper to a friend, "Keynes should read *The General Theory.*"

What's going on here? There are many interpretations, but the one we find most convincing is the one presented by historian Peter Clarke. He argues that, while working on *The General Theory,* Keynes turned his interest from a policy revolution to a theoretical revolution. He believed he had found a serious flaw in Classical economic theory. The Classicals assumed that an economy in equilibrium was at full employment, but did not show how the economy could move to that equilibrium from a disequilibrium. That's when Keynes' interest changed from a policy to a theoretical revolution.

His followers, such as Lerner, carried out the policy implications of his theory. Why did Keynes sometimes oppose these policy implications? Because he was also a student of politics and he recognized that economic theory can often lead to politically unacceptable policies. In a letter to a friend he later said Lerner was right in his logic, but he hoped the opposition didn't discover what Lerner was saying. Keynes was more than an economist; he was a politician as well.

Keynesians argued that, in times of recession, spending is a public good that benefits everyone.

Government spending on defence and infrastructure is one way to assist in expanding economic activity.

Q.2 Demonstrate graphically the effect of expansionary fiscal policy.

The fact that the effects are significantly different when everyone does something rather than when only one person does it plays an important role in economics. This difference has a number of names: the public goods problem, the tragedy of the commons, the fallacy of composition, and the multiperson dilemma.

The problem is neatly seen by considering an analogy to a football game. If everyone is standing, and you sit down, you can't see. Everyone is better off standing. No one has an incentive to sit down. However, if somehow all individuals could be enticed to sit down, all individuals would be even better off. Sitting down is a public good—a good that benefits others; but one that nobody on his or her own will do. Keynesians argued that, in times of recession, spending is a public good because it benefits everyone, so government should spend or find ways of inducing private individuals to spend. This difference between individual and economywide reactions to spending decisions creates a possibility for government to exercise control over aggregate expenditures and thereby over aggregate output and income. *Government's attempt to control the aggregate level of spending in the economy* is called **aggregate demand management.** It involves the government's influence of a shift factor of aggregate expenditures, and then relying on the multiplier effect to multiply that initial effect into a larger effect on aggregate demand and thus on income.

Fighting Recession: Expansionary Fiscal Policy

Let's consider a numerical case of how government policy can get an economy out of a recession. We consider this case in Figure 11-1. For simplicity of exposition we assume that the price level remains constant until potential income is reached (so the *SAS* curve is flat). Later we'll extend the analysis to an upward-sloping *SAS* curve.

Figure 11-1 FIGHTING A RECESSION

If the economy is below its potential income level, the government can increase its expenditures to stimulate the economy. Doing so shifts the AD curve to the right. The shift in the AD curve is greater than the initial shift in expenditures because the multiplier process takes over and expands the initial shock of the additional spending. If the government has chosen the right fiscal policy, income increases until actual income equals potential income.

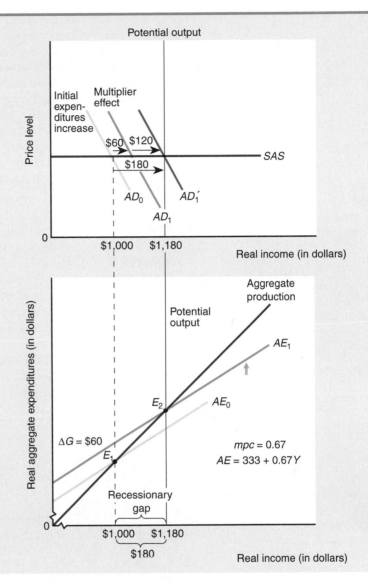

The top panel shows the AS/AD model; the bottom part shows the multiplier model. Initially the economy is at equilibrium at income level $1,000, which is below potential income ($1,180). The economy is in a recessionary gap. This is what happens: The government recognizes this recessionary gap in aggregate income of, say, $180 and responds with expansionary fiscal policy by increasing government expenditures by $60. This shifts the AD curve to the right by three times that amount, or by $180. The initial shock shifts the AD curve to the right by $60; the $120 shift is due to the multiplier effects that the initial shift brings about.

The same effects are shown in the multiplier model in the bottom part of Figure 11-1. There the increased government spending shifts the AE curve from AE_0 upward to AE_1. Businesses that receive government contracts hire the workers who have been laid off by other firms and open new plants; output increases by the initial expenditure of $60. But the process doesn't stop there. At this point, the multiplier process sets in. As the newly employed workers spend more, other businesses find that their demand increases. They hire more workers, who spend an additional $40 (since their $mpc = 0.67$). This increases income further. The same process occurs again and again. By the time the process has ended, income has risen by $180 to $1,180, the potential level of income.

How did the government economists know to increase spending by $60? By backward induction. They empirically estimated that the mpc—the slope of the aggregate expenditures curve—was 0.67, which meant that the multiplier was $1/(1 - 0.67) = 1/0.33 = 3$. They divided the multiplier, 3, into the recessionary gap, $180, and determined that if they increased spending by $60, income would increase by $180.

Fighting Inflation: Contractionary Fiscal Policy

Q.3 Demonstrate graphically the effect of contractionary fiscal policy.

Fiscal policy can also work in reverse, decreasing expenditures that are too high. Expenditures are "too high" when the economy temporarily exceeds its potential output. An economy operating above potential will generate accelerating inflation.

Figure 11-2(a) shows the situation in the AS/AD model; Figure 11-2(b) shows it in the multiplier model. Initially the economy is at point A—real output is $5,000 and the price level is P_0. Notice that equilibrium income is at $5,000, while the economy's potential income is $4,000. Given this assumption, the economy is not in long-run equilibrium in either model unless the price level increases, bringing real income back to $4,000.

What would likely happen in reality is that the initial expansion in aggregate demand to AD_0 will be met by an increase in output above potential output. Input prices would begin to rise, and the SAS curve would shift from SAS_0 to SAS_1. Output would decline to, say, $4,700. But even at that level, output exceeds potential output; workers and firms will continue to adjust their pricing strategies, causing the rise in the price level to accelerate. This continuing increase in the price level would cause the SAS curve to continue to shift left and drive the economy back to its potential income at point B. To prevent inflation from occurring, the government must reduce aggregate demand by $1,000, from $5,000 to $4,000, before the price level rises from P_0 to P_1 (before the SAS curve shifts upward from SAS_0 to SAS_1). Contractionary fiscal policy can be used to shift the AD curve to the left from AD_0 to AD_1.

Q.4 The marginal propensity to consume is 0.33 and there is an inflationary gap of $100. What fiscal policy would you recommend?

To bring about that shift in the AD curve the government does not decrease its expenditures by $1,000. It decreases them by an amount less than that. How much less? To determine that, it had to calculate the multiplier. In this example the marginal propensity to consume is assumed to be 0.8, which means that the multiplier would be 5. So a cut in expenditures of $200 would cause the AD curve to shift to the left by $1,000.

Figure 11-2(b) shows contractionary fiscal policy in the multiplier model. Potential income is $4,000, but the equilibrium level of income is $5,000. The difference between the two, $1,000, is the inflationary gap. This inflationary gap causes upward pressure on wages and prices with no additional lasting increase in output. If the government wants to avoid inflation, it can use contractionary fiscal policy. For example, a decrease in government spending of $200 shifts the AE curve down by $200 and decreases the equilibrium income by $1,000.

The Questionable Effectiveness of Fiscal Policy

There are two ways to think about the effectiveness of fiscal policy—in the model, and in reality. Models are great, and simple models, like the one we've presented in this book, that you can understand intuitively are even greater. You put in the numbers, and out comes the answer. Questions based on such models make great exam questions. But don't think that policies that work in a model will necessarily work in the real world.

Figure 11-2 (a and b)   FIGHTING INFLATION

Once the economy reaches its potential output, any further increase will lead to accelerating inflation. If the quantity of aggregate demand exceeds potential income at that price level, there will be excess demand and pressures for inflation. Temporarily, output may exceed potential output as firms and workers are slow to raise their prices and wages. But soon, shortages and accelerating inflation will drive the economy back to its potential income (at a point like B). To prevent this the government must use contractionary fiscal policy shifting the AD curve back from AD_0 to AD_1. This case is shown in (a). In (b), the same situation is shown in the multiplier model. Again, contractionary fiscal policy, shifting the AE curve downward, from AE_0 to AE_1 is called for.

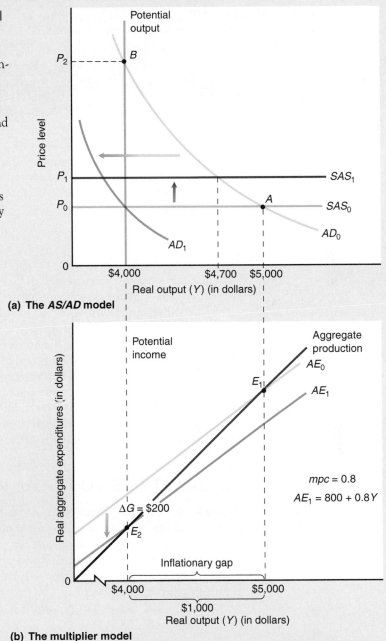

(a) The *AS/AD* model

$mpc = 0.8$

$AE_1 = 800 + 0.8Y$

(b) The multiplier model

The effectiveness of fiscal policy in reality depends on the government's ability to perceive a problem and to react appropriately to it. The essence of fiscal policy is government changing its taxes and its spending to offset any fluctuation that would occur in other autonomous expenditures, thereby keeping the economy at its potential level of income. If the model is a correct description of the economy, and if the government can act fast enough and change its taxes and spending in a *countercyclical* way, recessions can be prevented. This type of management of the economy is called **countercyclical**

A countercyclical fiscal policy designed to keep the economy always at its target or potential level of income is called fine tuning.

As a brain teaser you might try to figure out what you would have advised the government to do if it had wanted to increase taxes rather than decrease expenditures to get the economy out of the inflationary gap in Figure 11-2. By how much should it increase taxes? If you said by $200 since the multiplier is 5, you're on the right wave length, but not quite right. True, the multiplier, $1/(1 - mpc)$, is 5, but taxes affect total expenditures in a slightly different way than does the initial change in expenditures. Specifically, expenditures will not decrease by the full amount of the tax increase. The reason why is that people will likely reduce their saving in order to hold up their expenditures. Expenditures will initially fall by the mpc multiplied by the increased taxes, or $(0.8 \times \$200) = \$160$, rather than by $200. To get the initial shift of $200 from increasing taxes, the government must increase taxes by $250. Then when people reduce spending by 0.8 of that, their expenditures will fall by $200.

fiscal policy—*fiscal policy in which the government offsets any change in aggregate expenditures that would create a business cycle.* The term **fine tuning** is used to describe such *fiscal policy designed to keep the economy always at its target or potential level of income.*

As we will discuss below, today almost all economists, whether Keynesian or Classical, agree the government is not up to fine-tuning the economy. The modern debate is whether it is up to any tuning of the economy at all. The reason is that the dynamic adjustment in the economy is extraordinarily complicated and that, once you take into account reasonable expectations of future policy, the formal model becomes hopelessly complex. Graduate students in economics get Ph.D.s for worrying about such hopeless complexities. At the introductory level, all we require is that you (1) know this simple multiplier model and (2) remember that, in the real world, it cannot be used in a mechanistic manner; it must be used with judgment.

Almost all economists, whether Keynesian or Classical, agree the government is not up to fine-tuning the economy.

11.1

see page 282

ALTERNATIVES TO FISCAL POLICY

As questions about the effectiveness of fiscal policy have developed, policy discussions have moved toward alternatives to fiscal policy. To understand how these alternatives work, you must simply remember that any change in autonomous expenditures, ΔAE, not just changes in the government taxes and expenditures, will affect the level of income. You can see the alternatives to fiscal policy by breaking down autonomous expenditures into its components:

$$\Delta Y = \text{Multiplier} \times \begin{pmatrix} \Delta \text{ Autonomous consumption} \\ + \\ \Delta \text{ Autonomous investment} \\ + \\ \Delta \text{ Autonomous government spending} \\ + \\ \Delta \text{ Autonomous net exports} \end{pmatrix}$$

Three alternatives to fiscal policy are directed investment policies, trade policies, and autonomous consumption policies.

Any policy that affects any of these four components of autonomous expenditures can achieve the same results as fiscal policy. So three alternatives to fiscal policy are directed investment policies, trade policies, and autonomous consumption policies. The above requires one addendum: any policy that can influence *autonomous* expenditures *without having offsetting effects on other expenditures* can be used to influence the direction and movement of aggregate income. That addendum in italics is important because, in reality, no expenditure is totally autonomous. If you push on one type of expenditure, you pull on another, and the net effect is often far more ambiguous than assumed.

We considered government spending policy before when we talked about fiscal policy. Let us briefly consider some of the other policies that could be used to influence income. We discuss investment first, then net exports, and, finally, consumption.

Directed Investment Policies: Policy Affecting Expectations

Early macro economists thought that the Depression was caused by some type of collective psychological fear on the part of investors who, because they predicted that the economy was going into a recession, decided not to invest. If somehow government could have supported investment, it could have avoided the Depression.

A Numerical Example To give you some practice with the model, let's consider a numerical example. Say that income is $400 less than desired and that the marginal propensity to consume is 0.5. How much will government policy have to increase autonomous investment in order to achieve the desired level of income? Working backward, we see that the multiplier is 2, so autonomous investment must be increased by $200.

Rosy Scenario: Talking the Economy into Fiscal Health Numerical examples like the one above are a bit far-fetched since it is difficult to relate a specific policy to a specific numerical result or investment. But the relationship is there, and you can see examples of government trying to exploit it every day. For example, listen to government officials on the radio or television. Almost inevitably you will hear rosy scenarios from them—the **rosy scenario policy**—*government policy of making optimistic predictions and never making gloomy predictions*. You almost never hear a policy-level government economist telling the newspapers how bad the economy is going to be. Why? Because a gloomy prediction could affect expectations and decrease investment and consumption spending. If you're a high-level government policy economist and you have a gloomy forecast, you're told to keep quiet or quit.

A good example comes from the aftermath of the September 11, 2001, attacks in the United States. Every government official—every single one—said what they needed was for people to go out and spend. That would lead to recovery. There was no talk of economic gloom and doom. Positive thoughts; positive results.

Financial Guarantees Another way to influence investment is to protect the financial system by government guarantees or promises of guarantees. Nothing can decrease business confidence quite like a large number of bank and financial institution failures.

Let's consider how such investment-expectations policies work in practice. Say the economy is in a slight recession and, because of that, banks are in financial trouble. The government recognizes that if the public decides that banks are in trouble, they will try to get their money out of the banks, in which case banks will have to close. As banks close, loans will dry up, investment will decrease, and the economy will fall into a deep recession. To prevent that, the government comes along and tells everyone that it will bail out the banks so that people's money is safe. If the government is believed, everything stays fine and the recession doesn't happen (and, hopefully, the banks get themselves out of their financial trouble).

Japan used such a "save the financial institutions" policy in the 1990s. When the Japanese stock and real estate markets collapsed in the early 1990s, the Japanese government loosened bank accounting rules in order to prevent banks from failing. In

Q.5 How is it possible to "talk" the economy into a boom?

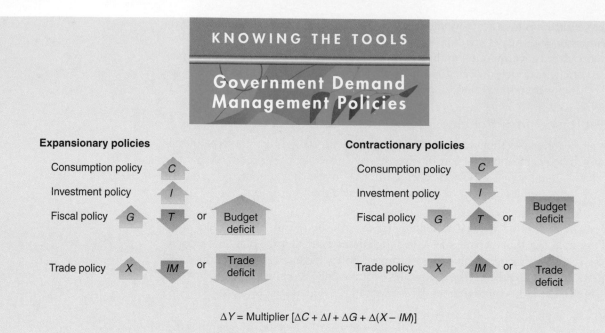

KNOWING THE TOOLS

Government Demand Management Policies

$$\Delta Y = \text{Multiplier } [\Delta C + \Delta I + \Delta G + \Delta(X - IM)]$$

the late 1990s, the U.S. central bank, the Fed, arranged a $3.6 billion bailout of a private U.S. investment firm, Long-Term Capital Management (LTCM), which had lost billions of dollars when the Russian ruble (Russia's currency) collapsed in 1998. Guaranteeing LTCM's solvency worked. The Asian crisis that had spread to Russia did not pull the U.S. economy into a recession. Since Canadian exports are heavily dependent on demand from the United States, the continued U.S. expansion was good for Canadian exporters.

11.2

see page 282

Another way in which the government can influence investment is through influencing the interest rate. We will discuss this policy in detail in a later chapter, on monetary policy.

The answer to the question "When do such policies affecting investment (through changing expectations or interest rates) make sense?" doesn't come from the models; it is a matter of judgment. In the 1930s, Keynes didn't see any of these policies affecting investment as being sufficient; in his book *The General Theory*, he advocated the government taking over the investment decisions—nationalizing investment. That policy didn't receive high marks. Instead, Keynesian policy quickly came to mean fiscal policy. Why? Because politically, Keynesians quickly saw that fiscal policy could be sold to the public, whereas the more radical Keynesian nationalizing investment policies couldn't be.

Trade Policy and Export-Led Growth

Any policy that increases autonomous exports or decreases autonomous imports (and thereby increases autonomous expenditures) will also have multiplied effects on income. Examples of such policies abound. The Department of Foreign Affairs and International Trade has entire subdepartments assisting firms to develop their export markets. Similarly, Canadian trade delegations visit other nations, pushing to get the other nations' trade restrictions on Canadian goods lowered. Those policies are called **export-led growth policies**—*policies designed to stimulate Canadian exports and increase*

Export-led growth policies are policies designed to stimulate exports and hence have a multiplied effect on Canadian income.

aggregate expenditures on Canadian goods, and hence to have a multiplied effect on Canadian income.

Notice that it is the trade balance (exports minus imports) that affects aggregate expenditures, so any policy that will reduce imports, such as tariffs, will have the same expansionary effect on income.[1] That's why you hear so much about trade restrictions. They're a way of protecting Canadian jobs and of stimulating the Canadian economy in the short run. (In the long run most economists believe that tariff policies have serious problems.) Of course, policies that expand Canadian exports also raise Canadian income, but the protectionist policies of our trading partners (such as the softwood lumber dispute) sometimes ration us out of foreign markets.

A Numerical Example Let's start with a numerical example of a small country with a large percentage of imports. Say the country's income is $300 million too low and its marginal propensity to consume is 0.33. How must it affect net exports to achieve its desired income? Since the *mpc* is low, the multiplier is small (1.5), which means that net exports must be increased by approximately $200 million (either by decreasing imports or increasing exports by that amount).

Interdependencies in the Global Economy We'll discuss these trade policies in much more detail in later chapters, but for now let us remind you that one country's exports are another country's imports, so that every time Canada is out pushing its exports in an attempt to follow an export-led growth policy, it is the equivalent to getting another country to follow an *import-led decline* for its economy. Similarly, every trade restriction on foreign goods has an offsetting effect on another country's economy, an effect that will often lead to retaliation. So a policy of trying to restrict imports can often end up simultaneously restricting exports as other countries retaliate. Expectations of such retaliation is one of the reasons many economists support free trade agreements, such as the North American Free Trade Agreement (NAFTA), in which member countries agree not to engage in restrictive trade policies on imports.

11.3
see page 282

Exchange Rate Policies A final way in which the trade balance can be affected is through **exchange rate policy**—*a policy of deliberately affecting a country's exchange rate in order to affect its trade balance.* You were introduced to this policy when we presented the shift factors of aggregate demand. A low value of a country's currency relative to currencies of other countries encourages exports and discourages imports; a high value of a country's currency relative to other countries' currency discourages exports and encourages imports.

The effect of such exchange rates can be seen in the automobile industry. In the 1970s and 1980s, Japanese exports of cars were increasing enormously. An important reason for that was the relative value of the Japanese yen (somewhere around 300 to the dollar in 1970). In the 1990s, the value of the dollar fell relative to the yen, so that it was about one-third the value (around 100 to the dollar) of what it was in the 1970s. With this change, Japanese cars no longer seemed the good buy that they had been, and the Canadian automobile industry made a comeback. Again, we'll discuss such policies in more detail in a later chapter.

Q.6 In the 1990s, the value of the Canadian dollar fell. What effect would that have had on income in Canada?

---

[1]You'll notice that the Knowing the Tools box describes how expansionary and contractionary policies affect the *trade deficit*. We could have used the *trade surplus*, and then the direction of the arrows would be reversed so that, for example, an expansionary policy raises the trade surplus rather than reducing the trade deficit. We had to pick one way to measure the trade balance, so we chose the trade deficit. Make sure you know what happens to the trade surplus when policy changes—it's a good test of your understanding!

Q-7 By how much do autonomous expenditures need to change to decrease income by $60 if the *mpc* is 2/3?

Autonomous Consumption Policy

A third alternative to fiscal policy is autonomous consumption policy. Any policy designed to encourage autonomous consumption can hold autonomous expenditures up and have the same effect as fiscal policy. Increasing the availability of consumer credit to individuals by making the institutional environment conducive to credit is one way of achieving this. Remember, consumption makes up about 60 percent of Canadian GDP.

The growth of the Canadian economy from the 1950s through the 1980s was marked by significant institutional changes that made credit available to a larger and larger group of people. This increase in consumer credit allowed significant expansion in income of the Canadian economy. In the early 1990s, some consumers cut back as they tried to consolidate their financial obligations, and that played a major role in the slow growth of the Canadian economy at that time. Similarly the resolution of those problems played a major role in the rise in growth through the early 2000s.

REAL-WORLD EXAMPLES

To give you an idea of how fiscal and other expenditures policies work in the real world, we'll look at two examples—the effect of wartime spending in the 1930s and 1940s and the prolonged expansion of the mid-1990s to early 2000s.

Fiscal Policy in the Second World War

By the end of the 1930s the Depression was no longer the focus of Canadian policy; that was when Canada entered the Second World War.

Fighting a war requires transferring civilian production to war production, so economists' attention turned to how to do so. Taxes went up enormously, but government expenditures rose far more. The result can be seen in Figure 11-3(a), which tabulates real GNP, the deficit, and unemployment data for the wartime time span 1937–1946. As you can see, the deficit increased greatly and real income rose by more than the increase in the deficit. Figure 11-3(b) shows the effect in the AS/AD model. The AD curve shifts to the right by more than the increase in the deficit. As predicted, the economy expanded enormously in response to the expansionary fiscal policy that accompanied the war. One thing should bother you about this episode: If the economy exceeded its potential output, shouldn't the price level have risen? It didn't because the wartime expansion was accompanied by wage and price controls, which prevented price-level increases, and by rationing.

During the war, economic output was expanded as far as anyone dared hope it could be. This expansion was also accompanied by an expansionary monetary policy, so we must be careful about drawing too strong an inference about the effect of fiscal policy from the episode. (The importance of monetary policy will be discussed in a later chapter.)

It might seem from the example of the Second World War, when the economy expanded sharply, that wars are good for the economy. They certainly do bring about expansionary policy, increase GNP, and decrease unemployment. But remember, GNP is *not* welfare and a decrease in unemployment is not necessarily good. In the Second World War people went without many goods; production of guns and bombs increased but production of butter decreased. Many people were killed or permanently disabled, which decreases unemployment but can hardly be called a good way to expand the economy and lower unemployment.

Figure 11-3 (a and b)   WAR FINANCE: EXPANSIONARY FISCAL POLICY

During wars, government budget deficits have risen significantly. As they have, unemployment has fallen and GNP has risen enormously. You can see the effect in the table in (a), which presents the Canadian government budget deficit and unemployment rate during the Second World War. The graph in (b) shows that this is what would be predicted in the multiplier model.

Year	GNP (billions of 1971 dollars)	Federal deficit (millions of dollars)	Unemployment rate
1937	16.4	17	9.0
1938	16.6	51	11.4
1939	17.8	119	11.4
1940	20.3	378	9.2
1941	23.2	396	4.4
1942	27.5	2137	3.0
1943	28.6	2557	1.7
1944	29.8	2559	1.4
1945	29.1	2123	1.6
1946	28.3	374	2.6

(a)

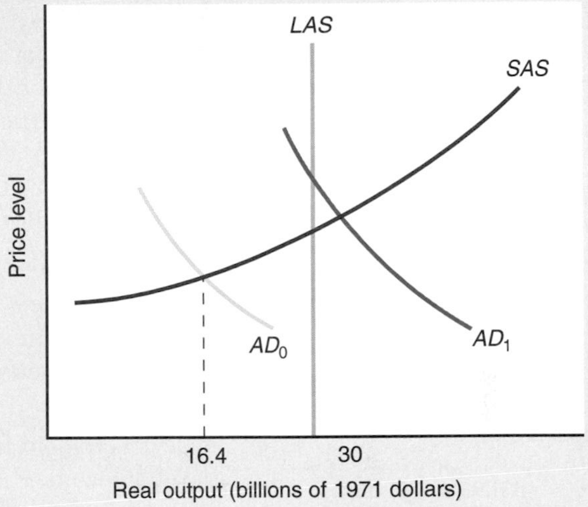

(b)

Source: Statistics Canada, Historical Statistics of Canada, Series D132, D129, F55, H18, H34.

Recent Fiscal Policy

As a second example, let's consider the government budget picture in the early 2000s. In the late 1990s and early 2000s the budget went from a large deficit to a large surplus, so it would seem as if government fiscal policy was slowing the economy down. But the economy was booming. There are two explanations for this seeming paradox. The first is that, yes, the surplus was slowing the economy, but the contractionary effect of the surplus was offset by significant increases in consumer and investment spending. The private saving rate actually fell to zero at times, making the marginal propensity to consume 100 percent. Had the government budget not been in surplus, the economy would have likely exceeded potential output and inflation would have accelerated.

The second explanation for the paradox is that much of the surplus was the result of the booming economy, not contractionary fiscal policy. In fact, much of the deficit reduction, and movement into budget surplus, resulted from unexpected increases in income. When an economy is booming, as income rises, tax revenues rise and expenditures on income-support programs decline automatically. Most of the unexpected decline in the deficit was a result of tax revenue surprises.

Normally, such a surplus would have been expected to be temporary. Whether the budget surplus will continue depends on where the economy is relative to potential output. In the early 2000s the economy exceeded economists' estimate of potential output, without generating accelerating inflation, by far more than economists thought possible. As the economy exceeded economists' estimate of potential output, their estimates of potential output and future surpluses rose.

PROBLEMS WITH FISCAL AND OTHER ACTIVIST POLICIES

Fiscal policy, and activist government policy in general, sounds so easy—and in the model it is. If there's a contraction in the economy, the government runs an expansionary fiscal policy; if there's inflation, the government runs a contractionary fiscal policy, keeping the economy at the desired level of income.

In reality, that's not the way it is. A number of important problems arise that make the actual practice of fiscal policy difficult. These problems don't mean that the model is wrong; they simply mean that for fiscal policy to work, the policy conclusions drawn from the model must be modified to reflect the real-world problems. Let's consider how the reality might not fit the model. The model assumes:

Six assumptions of the model that could lead to problems with fiscal policy are:
1. Financing the deficit doesn't have any offsetting effects.
2. The government knows what the situation is.
3. The government knows the economy's potential income level.
4. The government has flexibility in changing spending and taxes.
5. The size of the government debt doesn't matter.
6. Fiscal policy doesn't negatively affect other government goals.

1. Financing the deficit doesn't have any offsetting effect. (In reality, it often does.)
2. The government knows what the situation is—for instance, the size of the *mpc*, and other exogenous variables. (In reality, the government must estimate them.)
3. The government knows the economy's potential income level—the highest level of income that doesn't cause inflation. (In reality, the government may not know what this level is.)
4. The government has flexibility in changing spending and taxes. (In reality, government cannot change them quickly.)
5. The size of the government debt doesn't matter. (In reality, the size of the government debt often does matter.)
6. Fiscal policy doesn't negatively affect other government goals. (In reality, it often does.)

Let's consider each assumption a bit further.

1. Financing the Deficit Doesn't Have Offsetting Effects

One of the most important limitations of the multiplier model is that it assumes that financing the deficit has no offsetting effects on income. Some economists argue that that is not the case, that the government financing of deficit spending will offset the deficit's expansionary effect.

The multiplier model assumes saving and investment are unequal, and that the government can increase its expenditures without at the same time causing a decrease in private expenditures. Some economists object to that assumption. They believe the interest rate equilibrates saving and investment. They argue that when the government borrows to finance the deficit, that borrowing will increase interest rates and crowd out private investment.

Interest rate crowding out reduces the effect of increases in government expenditures.

Interest rate **crowding out**—*the offsetting of a change in government expenditures by a change in private expenditures in the opposite direction*—occurs as follows: When the government runs a deficit, it must sell bonds (that is, it must borrow) to finance that deficit. To get people to buy and hold the bonds, the government must make them attractive. That means the interest rate the bonds pay must be higher than it otherwise would have been. This tends to push up the interest rate in the economy, which makes it more expensive for private businesses to borrow, so they reduce their borrowing and their investment. That private investment is "crowded out" by expansionary fiscal policy. Hence the name "crowding out." Increased government spending crowds out private spending.

Figure 11-4 (a and b)   A SCHEMATIC REPRESENTATION OF CROWDING OUT AND PARTIAL CROWDING OUT

An increase in government spending will expand income through the multiplier. However, it will also cause interest rates to rise and thereby cause investment to decrease, which will tend to decrease income. This is called *interest rate crowding out*. The net effect of fiscal policy depends on the degree of crowding out that takes place. When there is complete crowding out, the effect of fiscal policy will be totally offset. Where there is partial crowding out, as in this figure, an increase in government spending will still have an expansionary effect, but the effect will be smaller than it otherwise would have been. The *AD* curve will shift back to the left as shown in (**a**) and the *AE* curve will shift back down as shown in (**b**) due to the rise in interest rates.

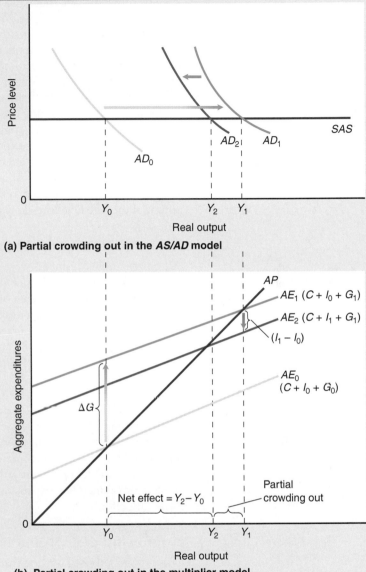

(a) **Partial crowding out in the *AS/AD* model**

(b) **Partial crowding out in the multiplier model**

Crowding out is shown in Figure 11-4 (a and b). Income in the economy is Y_0 and government has decided to expand that income to Y_1 by increasing its spending by ΔG (from G_0 to G_1). Note that we've retained the assumption that the price level is fixed.

If financing were not an issue, expansionary fiscal policy would shift the *AD* curve to the right by a multiple of the increase in government spending, increasing income from Y_0 to Y_1. Financing the deficit, however, increases interest rates and decreases investment by ΔI, which shifts the *AD* curve to the left to AD_2. Income falls back to Y_2.

Because of crowding out, the net expansionary effect of fiscal policy is much smaller than it otherwise would have been. Some economists argue that crowding out can totally offset the expansionary effect of fiscal policy, so the net effect is zero, or even negative, since they consider private spending more productive than government spending.

Crowding out is the offsetting effect on private expenditures caused by the government's sale of bonds to finance expansionary fiscal policy.

Q.8 Demonstrate graphically what would happen if government expenditures policy stimulated private investment.

The crowding out effect also works in reverse with contractionary fiscal policy. Say the government runs a surplus. That surplus will slow the economy through the multiplier effect. But it also means the government can buy back some of its outstanding bonds, which will have a tendency to push bond prices up and interest rates down. Lower interest rates will stimulate investment which, in turn, will have an offsetting expansionary effect on the economy. So when we include financing the deficit in our consideration of fiscal policy, the net multiplier effect is reduced.

How large this financing offset to fiscal policy will be is a matter of debate. Some economists see the crowding out effect as relatively large, in many cases almost completely negating the effect of expansionary fiscal policy. Others see it as relatively small, as long as the economy is in a recession or operating below its potential income level.

The empirical evidence is mixed and has not resolved the debate. Both sides see some crowding out occurring as the debt is financed by selling bonds. The closer to the potential income level the economy is, the more crowding out is likely to occur.

2. Knowing What the Situation Is

All our examples' numbers were chosen arbitrarily. In reality, the numbers used in the model must be estimated since data upon which estimates can be made aren't always available. Most economic data are published quarterly, and it usually takes six to nine months of data to indicate, with any degree of confidence, the state of the economy and which way it is heading. Thus, we could be halfway into a recession before we even knew it was happening. (Data are already three months old when published; then we need two or three quarters of such data before they compose a useful body of information to work with.)

In an attempt to deal with this problem, the government relies on large macroeconomic models and leading indicators to predict what the economy will be like six months or a year from now. As part of the input to these complex models, the government must predict economic factors that determine the size of the multiplier. These predictions are imprecise so the forecasts are imprecise. Economic forecasting is still an art, not a science.

Economists' data problems limit the use of fiscal policy for fine tuning. There's little sense in recommending expansionary or contractionary policy until you know what policy is called for.

3. Knowing the Level of Potential Income

This problem of not knowing the level of potential income is related to the problem we just discussed. The target rate of unemployment and the potential level of income are not easy concepts to define. At one time it was thought 3 percent unemployment meant full employment. Some time later it was generally thought 7 percent unemployment meant full employment. About that time economists stopped calling the potential level of income the *full-employment* level of income.

Any variation in potential income can make an enormous difference in the policy prescription that could be recommended. To see how big a difference, let's translate a 1 percent change in unemployment into a change in income. According to *Okun's rule of thumb* (defined in an earlier chapter as the general rule of thumb economists use to translate changes in the unemployment rate into changes in income), a 1 percentage point fall in the unemployment rate is associated with a 2 percent increase in income. Thus, in 2002 with income at about $1.4 trillion, a 1 percentage point fall in the unemployment rate would have increased income $28 billion.

Now let's say one economist believes 7 percent is the long-run achievable target rate of unemployment, while another believes it's 5.5 percent. That's a 1.5 percentage point difference. Since a 1 percent decrease in the unemployment rate means an increase of about $28 billion in national income, their views of the income level we should target differ by over $42 billion ($1.5 \times \$28 = \$42$). Yet both views are reasonable. Looking at the same economy (the same data), one economist may call for expansionary fiscal policy while the other may call for contractionary fiscal policy.

In practice, differences in estimates of potential income often lead to different policy recommendations. Empirical estimates suggest that the size of the multiplier is somewhere between 1.5 and 2.0. Let's say it's 2.0. That means autonomous expenditures must be predicted to increase or decrease by more than $21 billion before an economist who believes the target rate of unemployment is 5.5 percent would agree in policy recommendation with an economist who believes the rate is 7 percent. Since almost all fluctuations in autonomous investment and autonomous consumption are less than this amount, there's no generally agreed-on policy prescription for most fluctuations. Some economists will call for expansionary policy; some will call for contractionary policy; and the government decision makers won't have any clear-cut policy to follow.

You might wonder why the range of potential income estimates is so large. Why not simply see whether the economy has inflation at the existing rate of unemployment and income level? Would that it were so easy. Inflation is a complicated process. Seeds of inflation are often sown years before inflation results. The main problem is that establishing a close link between the level of economic activity and inflation is a complicated statistical challenge to economists, one that has not yet been satisfactorily met. That leads to enormous debate as to what the causes are.

Almost all economists believe that outside some range (perhaps 5 percent unemployment on the low side and 10 percent on the high side), too much spending causes inflation and too little spending causes a recession. That 5 to 10 percentage point range is so large that in most cases the Canadian economy is in an ambiguous state where some economists are calling for expansionary policy and others are calling for contractionary policy.

Once the economy reaches the edge of the range of potential income or falls outside it, the economists' policy prescription becomes clearer. For example, in the Depression, when this multiplier model was developed, unemployment was about 20 percent—well outside the range. Should the economy ever go into such a depression again, economists' policy prescriptions will be clear. The call will be for expansionary fiscal policy. Most times the economy is within the ambiguous range so there are disagreements among economists.

4. The Government's Flexibility in Changing Taxes and Spending

For argument's sake, let's say economists agree that contractionary policy is needed and that's what they advise the government. Will the government implement it? And, if so, will it implement contractionary fiscal policy at the right time? The answer to both questions is: probably not. There are also problems with implementing economists' calls for expansionary fiscal policy. Even if economists are unanimous in calling for expansionary fiscal policy, putting fiscal policy in place takes time and has serious implementation problems.

Numerous political and institutional realities in Canada today make it a difficult task to implement fiscal policy. Government spending and taxes cannot be changed instantaneously. New taxes and new spending must be legislated. It takes time for the government to pass a bill. Politicians face intense political pressures; their other goals may conflict with the goals of fiscal policy. For example, few members of Parliament who hope to be re-elected would vote to raise taxes in an election year. Similarly, few members would vote

Differences in estimates of potential income often lead to different policy recommendations.

In most cases the economy is in an ambiguous state where some economists are calling for expansionary policy and others are calling for contractionary policy.

Q.9 Why don't economists have an accurate measure of potential income?

Early in the 21st century the federal government reduced tax rates on lower- and middle-income earners, but it refused to reduce tax rates for high-income earners. Why? Government economists knew that people with modest incomes had a higher marginal propensity to consume than those with high incomes, so they decided to target the tax cut to make it as expansionary as possible. High-income earners were expected to save a larger proportion of their income than those with lower incomes, so the tax cuts were given to those who would spend rather than save.

to slash defence spending when a large military base is a major source of employment in their ridings, even when there's little to defend against. Squabbles in the Commons and the Senate may delay initiating appropriate fiscal policy for months, even years. By the time the fiscal policy is implemented, what may have once been the right fiscal policy may have ceased to be right, and some other policy may have become right.

Imagine trying to steer a car at 100 kilometres an hour when there's a five-second delay between the time you turn the steering wheel and the time the car's wheels turn. Imagining that situation will give you a good sense of how fiscal policy works in the real world.

5. Size of the Government Debt Doesn't Matter

There is no inherent reason why the adoption of activist policies should have caused the government to run deficits year after year and hence to incur ever-increasing debt—accumulated deficits less accumulated surpluses. Activist policy is consistent with running deficits some years and surpluses other years. In practice, the introduction of activist policy has been accompanied by many deficits and few surpluses, and by a large increase in government debt. If that increase in government debt hurts the economy, one can oppose policies of deficit spending, even if one believes that policy might otherwise be beneficial.

There are two reasons why activist government policies have led to an increase in government debt. First, early activist economists favoured large increases in government spending as well as favouring the government's using fiscal policy. These early activist economists employed the multiplier model to justify increasing spending without increasing taxes. A second reason is political. Politically it's much easier for government to increase spending and decrease taxes than to decrease spending and increase taxes. Due to political pressure, expansionary fiscal policy has predominated over contractionary fiscal policy.

Whether debt is a problem is an important and complicated issue, as we'll see in a later chapter devoted entirely to the question. For now, all you need remember is that if one believes that the debt is harmful, then there might be a reason not to conduct expansionary fiscal policy, even when the model calls for it.

6. Fiscal Policy Doesn't Negatively Affect Other Government Goals

A society has many goals; achieving potential income is only one of those goals. So it's not surprising that those goals often conflict. When the government runs expansionary fiscal policy, the balance of trade deficit grows. As the economy expands and income rises, exports remain constant but imports rise. If a nation's international considerations do not allow a balance of trade deficit to become larger, as is true in many countries, those governments cannot run expansionary fiscal policies—unless they can somehow prevent this balance of trade deficit from becoming larger.

Summary of the Problems

So where do these six problems leave fiscal policy? While they don't eliminate its use-fulness, they severely restrict it. Fiscal policy is a sledgehammer, not an instrument for fine tuning. When the economy goes into a depression, the appropriate fiscal policy is clear. Similarly when the economy has a hyperinflation, the appropriate policy is clear. But in less extreme cases, there will be debate on what the appropriate fiscal policy is— a debate economic theory can't answer conclusively.

Fiscal policy is a sledgehammer, not an instrument for fine tuning.

FISCAL POLICY WHEN THE PRICE LEVEL IS FLEXIBLE

Previously we considered how fiscal policy works when the short-run aggregate supply curve is horizontal. Now it's time to examine how a flexible price level affects our analysis.

Figure 11-5(a) presents the flexible price AS/AD model with a recessionary gap of $180, as was the case in our initial example. How does a flexible price level affect our multiplier? Well, as in the case of crowding out, a change in fiscal policy is not going to multiply fully into a change in output. When we considered crowding out, this resulted from higher interest rates that reduced the level of investment in the economy, and the aggregate expenditures (and aggregate demand) curve shifted back somewhat from where it initially was. The same effects are at play when the price level rises in response to

Figure 11-5 (a and b)   ELIMINATING A RECESSIONARY GAP WHEN PRICES ARE FLEXIBLE

When the price level is flexible, the multiplier is smaller than when the price level is fixed. This is because an increase in spending leads to higher prices, which reduce the level of desired spending in the economy. To close a $180 recessionary gap when the multiplier is 2, the government would need to raise its spending by $90. This shifts the aggregate expenditures curve to $AE_1(P_0)$, holding the price level constant. Excess demand at the old price level will put upward pressure on prices, shifting the aggregate expenditures curve down to $AE_1(P_1)$. The recessionary gap is closed once the price level adjusts to P_1.

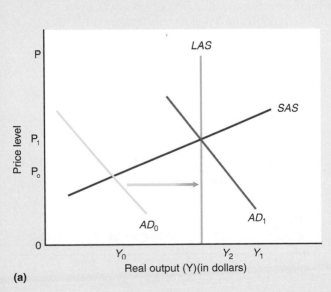

(a)

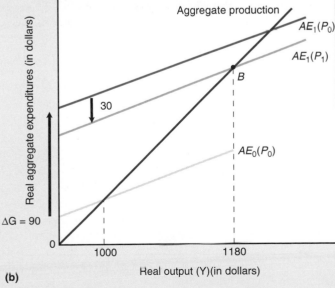

(b)

higher levels of government spending. A higher price level tends to reduce the level of aggregate expenditures below what they would have been if the price level had remained constant. This means the multiplier is now smaller than in the fixed-price case, since the higher price level leads to less of an increase in aggregate demand and expenditures.

In Figure 11-5(b) the recessionary gap of $180 requires an increase in government spending greater than $60 to close the difference. If we assume that the introduction of flexible prices reduces the multiplier from 3 to 2, then to eliminate the recessionary gap, the government must raise spending by $90. This shifts the aggregate expenditures curve to $AE_1(P_0)$, where the index (P_0) explicitly notes we are holding the price level constant. As the price level rises to P_1 in response to excess demand in the economy, the aggregate expenditures curve shifts back somewhat until the recessionary gap is closed at point B. The aggregate demand curve shifts initially as a result of higher government spending, with the multiplier process taking it to AD_1 in Figure 11-5(a).

The same analysis can be used to demonstrate the appropriate government response to an inflationary gap. The authorities need to cut spending by an amount that is higher than when the price level is fixed. In our previous example of an inflationary gap, the multiplier was assumed to be 5. A $1,000 inflationary gap required that the government reduce its spending by $200. With a flexible price level, the reduction in government spending will lead to a fall in the price level, stimulating aggregate demand. To reduce income by $1,000 the authorities might need to cut spending by $250 if we assume the multiplier drops from 5 when the price level is fixed to 4 when the price level is flexible. The extra reduction in spending is required to offset the induced increases in aggregate expenditures that result from the lower price level. You can see this in both panels of Figure 11-6.

Previously we saw that crowding out has the potential to frustrate fiscal objectives. So will changes in the price level. Knowing how sensitive the price level is to shifts in aggregate spending is an important determinant of fiscal policies in the real world.

Figure 11-6 (a and b)   ELIMINATING AN INFLATIONARY GAP WHEN PRICES ARE FLEXIBLE

When the price level is flexible, the multiplier is smaller than when the price level is fixed. An inflationary gap of $1,000 can be eliminated by a $250 reduction in government spending when the multiplier is 4. A reduction in government spending shifts the aggregate expenditures curve initially to $AE_1(P_0)$. As the price level falls, the aggregate expenditures curve shifts back somewhat to $AE_1(P_1)$. The economy moves from point A to point B. If you compare these figures to those in Figure 11-2, you will see that the degree of price level flexibility affects the appropriate setting of fiscal policy variables.

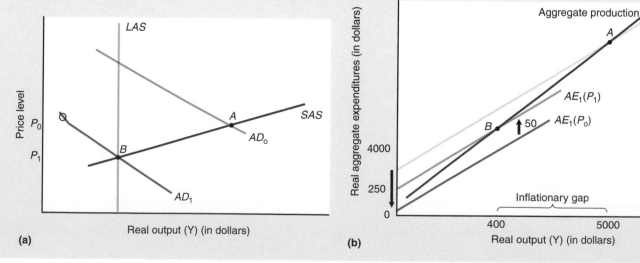

BUILDING FISCAL POLICIES INTO INSTITUTIONS

Economists quickly recognized the political problems with instituting direct counter-cyclical fiscal policy. To avoid these problems they suggested policies that built fiscal policy into Canadian institutions so that it would be put into effect without any political decisions being necessary. They called a built-in fiscal policy an **automatic stabilizer,** which is *any government program or policy that will counteract the business cycle without any new government action.* Automatic stabilizers include welfare payments, employment insurance, and the income tax system.

To see how automatic stabilizers work, consider the employment insurance system. When the economy is slowing down or is in a recession, the unemployment rate will rise. When people lose their jobs, they will reduce their consumption, starting the multiplier process, which decreases income. Employment insurance immediately helps offset the decrease in individuals' incomes as the government pays benefits to the unemployed. Thus, the budget deficit increases, and part of the fall in income is stopped without any explicit act by the government. Automatic stabilizers also work in reverse. When income increases, they decrease the size of the deficit.

Another automatic stabilizer is our income tax system. Tax revenue fluctuates as income fluctuates, which makes the deficit hard to predict. When the economy expands unexpectedly, the budget deficit is lower than originally expected; when the economy contracts unexpectedly, the budget deficit is higher than expected. Let's go through the reasoning why. When the economy is strong, people have more income and thus pay higher taxes. This increase in tax revenue reduces consumption expenditures from what they would have been, and moderates the economy's growth. When the economy goes into a recession, the opposite occurs.

Automatic stabilizers may seem like the solution to the economic woes we have discussed, but they, too, have their shortcomings. One problem is that when the economy is first starting to climb out of a recession, automatic stabilizers will slow the process, rather than help it along, for the same reason they slow the contractionary process. As income increases, automatic stabilizers increase government taxes and decrease government spending, and as they do, the discretionary policy's expansionary effects are decreased.

Despite these problems, most economists believe automatic stabilizers have played an important role in reducing fluctuations in our economy. They point to the kind of data we see in Figure 11-7 (on the next page), which they say show a significant decrease in fluctuations in the economy. Other economists aren't so sure; they argue the apparent decrease in fluctuations is an optical illusion. As usual, economic data are sufficiently ambiguous to give both sides strong arguments. The jury is still out.

An automatic stabilizer is any government program or policy that will counteract the business cycle without any new government action.

Q.10 What effect do automatic stabilizers have on the size of the multiplier?

CONCLUSION

By now you should be able to think in terms of the multiplier model and see how a disequilibrium between aggregate production and aggregate expenditures can be resolved by adjustments in aggregate income. But beware. The multiplier model is only a model. It's a tool, a crutch, to help you see certain relationships. It does so by obscuring others, including interest rate adjustment, price level adjustment, and supply incentive effects.

Consideration of these aspects led to significant changes in macroeconomic thinking over the years. In the 1970s Classical economic ideas, focusing on the long run and growth, rose like a phoenix from the ashes and re-emerged. Modern Classical econo-

Figure 11-7   DECREASE IN FLUCTUATIONS IN THE ECONOMY

One of the arguments in favour of activist economics is that since it was introduced into the Canadian economy, fluctuations in the economy have decreased.

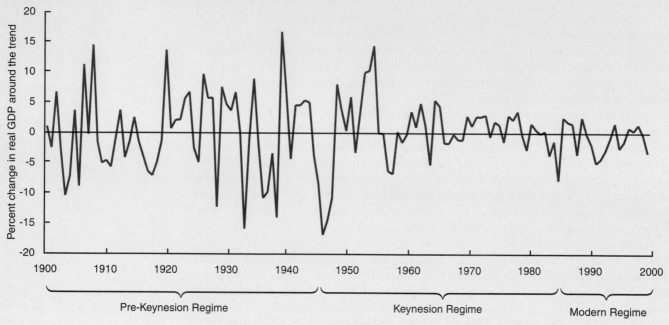

Source: Statistics Canada, Historical Statistics of Canada, Series F33, F55; CANSIM II, Table 380-0002; authors' calculations.

mists challenged the way Keynesian economists thought about expansionary effects of fiscal policy. They won many converts and modified the presentation of Keynesian economics so that it focuses on dynamic adjustment and is no longer presented mechanistically. The modern Classical economists argue that expectations of policy can change the dynamic adjustment process, and that any simple dynamic adjustment models are unlikely to describe the aggregate economy.

Most economists agree with that, but they still use the multiplier model as the basis of their short-run analysis. But they use it as a guide to their thinking, not in a mechanistic way. This agreement among economists means that today far less emphasis is placed on the Classical/Keynesian distinction. Although there are still differences, the mainstream of macroeconomists have blended into one school reflecting a combination of its Classical and Keynesian roots.

Chapter Summary

- Aggregate demand management policy attempts to influence the level of output in the economy by influencing aggregate demand and relying on the multiplier to expand any policy-induced change in aggregate demand.

- Fiscal policy—the change in government spending or taxes—works by providing a deliberate countershock to offset unexpected shocks to the economy.

- Expansionary fiscal policy, increasing government expenditures or decreasing taxes, is represented graphically as an upward shift of the aggregate expenditures curve or a rightward shift in the *AD* curve.
- Contractionary fiscal policy, decreasing government expenditures or increasing taxes, is represented graphically as a downward shift of the aggregate expenditures curve or a leftward shift in the *AD* curve.
- The effect of fiscal policy can be determined by using the multiplier model.
- Three alternatives to fiscal policy are directed investment policies, trade policies, and autonomous consumption policies.

- Fiscal policy is affected by the following problems, among others:
    1. Lack of knowledge of what policy is called for.
    2. Government's inability to respond quickly enough.
    3. Government debt.
    4. Interest rate crowding out.
    5. Conflicting goals
- Activist fiscal policy is now built into economic institutions through automatic stabilizers.
- Aggregate demand management policies are most effective in the Keynesian range of the economy—when the economy is significantly below its potential income.

Key Terms

aggregate demand management (262)
automatic stabilizer (279)
contractionary fiscal policy (260)
countercyclical fiscal policy (265)
crowding out (272)
exchange rate policy (269)
expansionary fiscal policy (260)
export-led growth policies (268)
fine tuning (266)
fiscal policy (260)
rosy scenario policy (267)

Questions for Thought and Review

1. Explain how the statement "We have nothing to fear but fear itself" pertains to macroeconomic policy.
2. What is the current state of Canadian fiscal policy? Would you advise Canada to change its fiscal policy? Why?
3. The marginal propensity to consume is 0.5 and there is a recessionary gap of $200. What fiscal policy would you recommend?
4. What two trade policies would you recommend if an economy has a recessionary gap?
5. Why does cutting taxes by $100 have a smaller effect on GDP than increasing expenditures by $100?
6. If government cuts taxes and wants a neutral fiscal policy, what should it do with its trade policy?
7. Why is countercyclical fiscal policy difficult to implement?
8. If interest rates have no effect on investment, how much crowding out will occur?
9. Why is knowing the level of potential income important to designing an appropriate fiscal policy?
10. Use the *AS/AD* model to explain why most politicians increase government spending programs when running for re-election.
11. Use the *AS/AD* model to explain the maxim in politics that if you are going to increase taxes, the time to do it is right after your election, when re-election is far off.
12. Why in the late 1990s, when unemployment in Europe exceeded 10 percent, were few economists pushing for an increase in European governments' budget deficits?

Problems and Exercises

1. Congratulations! You've just been appointed Minister of Economics in Textland. The *mpc* is 0.8. There is a recessionary gap of $400.
    a. The government wants to eliminate the gap by changing expenditures. What policy would you suggest?
    b. Your research assistant comes running in and tells you that instead of changing expenditures, the government wants to achieve the same result by decreasing taxes. What policy would you recommend now? (Requires reading and using the math in Appendix A of Chapter 10.)
    c. Your research assistant has a worried look on her face. "What's the problem?" you ask. "I goofed," she confesses. "I thought taxes were exogenous when actually

there's a marginal tax rate of 0.2." Before she can utter another word, you say, "No problem, I'll simply recalculate my answers to parts *a* and *b* and change them before I send them in." What are your corrected answers? (Requires reading Appendix A of Chapter 10.)

d. She still has a pained expression, "What's wrong?" you ask. "You didn't let me finish," she says. "Not only was there a marginal tax rate of 0.2; there's also a marginal propensity to import of 0.1." Again you interrupt to make sure she doesn't feel guilty. Again you say, "No problem," and recalculate your answers to parts *a* and *b* to account for the new information. What are your new answers? (Requires reading Appendix A of Chapter 10.)

e. That pained look is still there, but this time you don't interrupt. You let her finish. She says, "And they want to see the answers graphically." You do the right thing.

2. Condolences. You've been fired from your job in Textland, but you found another job in neighbouring Fantasyland. You must rely on your research assistant for the specific numbers. He says income is $50,000, *mpc* is 0.75, and the prime minister wants to lower unemployment from 8 to 6 percent.
   a. Advise him.
   b. Your research assistant comes in and says "Sorry, I meant that the *mpc* is 0.67." You redo your calculations.
   c. You're just about to see the prime minister when your research assistant comes running, saying "Sorry, sorry, I meant that the *mpc* is 0.5." Redo your calculations.

3. Your first job involved working for the Minister of Finance in Niferland. One day the minister ran into your office and told you that he lowered his estimate of the natural, or target, unemployment rate from 6 percent to 5.5 percent and that he just created 600,000 jobs.

a. What events most likely motivated his revision of the target unemployment rate?
b. Show the effect this revision would have on the *AS/AD* model.
c. The unemployment rate at the time of the revision was 5.5 percent. Income was $7.3 trillion. Within 18 months the unemployment rate had fallen to 5 percent without signs of accelerating inflation. How much higher would the level of potential income have been if the target rate of unemployment were 5 percent rather than 5.5 percent?

4. Prime Minister Chrétien's policy in 2001 was designed to reduce the deficit but increase employment.
   a. Why would such a policy not fit well in the multiplier model?
   b. Explain in words how such a policy might achieve the desired effect.
   c. Graphically demonstrate your answer in *b*.
   d. What data would you look at to see if your explanation in *b* and *c* is appropriate?

5. Congratulations. You are appointed as the Economic Adviser in Fantasyland. Income is currently $600,000, unemployment is 5 percent, and there are signs of coming inflation. You rely on your research assistant for specific numbers. He tells you that potential income is $564,000 and the *mpc* is 0.5.
   a. The government wants to eliminate the inflationary gap by changing expenditures. What policy do you suggest?
   b. By how much will unemployment change after your policy has taken effect?
   c. Your research assistant comes in and says "Sorry, I meant that the *mpc* is 0.8." Redo your calculations to parts *a* and *b*.

Web Questions

1. The Virtual Economy Home Page provides a model of the British economy where you can play the role of Chancellor, the person who helps determine levels of taxation and spending in Britain. Go to its home page at ve.ifs.org.uk and answer the following questions:
   a. Visit the Chancellor's office on the ground floor. What are the four key economic targets?
   b. What are the main policy tools at the Chancellor's disposal? Provide a brief description of each.
   c. Find the economic model on the fourth floor. Use the model to predict what will happen to each of the policy targets within the first 3–4 years if income taxes are raised 9 percentage points. Report your results.

d. What does the model predict will happen within the first 3–4 years if government spending is increased 10 percent?

2. Visit the NOVA Web site (http://www.pbs.org/wgbh/nova/stockmarket) and answer the following questions:
   a. Can you say whether day traders have increased or decreased market volatility?
   b. Early in 1997 LTCM's returns fell dramatically. How high had they been, and how far did they fall?
   c. What events precipitated the decline of LTCM?

3. The Department of Foreign Affairs and International Trade Web site (http://www.dfait.gc.ca) provides a wealth of information on issues relating to Canadian trade.
   a. Go to the section of the Web site devoted to the North American Free Trade Agreement (NAFTA).

Has NAFTA benefited Canadian firms? Use an example to illustrate how and why.

b. What is a "trade mission"? When was the most recent trade mission, and to which nation was it made? What was the mission's objective?

c. Find the section of the Web site devoted to trade sanctions. What are they? Does Canada currently sanction trade with any countries? If so, give an example and explain why the sanctions are in place.

Answers to Margin Questions

1. Each individual's spending primarily affects others' income, not their own. The feedback effects on their own income are so small that they do not take them into account. Only coordinated effort, in which many people increase their spending simultaneously, will create a significant multiplier effect. Thus, people's spending decision is a type of externality. *(261)*

2. As you can see, expansionary fiscal policy shifts the *AD* curve to the right. The multiplier then takes over to shift the *AD* curve to the right by a multiple of the initial shift. Income rises by a multiple of the increase in government expenditures. *(262)*

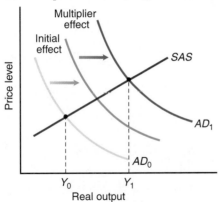

3. As you can see, contractionary fiscal policy shifts the *AD* curve to the left. The multiplier then takes over to shift the *AD* curve to the left by a multiple of the initial decline in aggregate expenditures. Income falls by a multiple of the initial shift. *(264)*

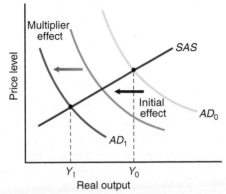

4. Since there is an inflationary gap, we would recommend contractionary fiscal policy. Since the multiplier is 1.5 (given the marginal propensity to consume of 0.33), we would recommend decreasing government spending by $66. *(264)*

5. Expectations play a central role in both spending and production decisions. If positive talk about the economy can influence expectations, it may be possible to "talk" an economy into a boom by increasing expenditures, or productivity, or both. *(267)*

6. According to the multiplier model, a fall in the value of the dollar should increase exports, which would have had a multiplied positive effect on income. *(269)*

7. Since the *mpc* is 2/3, the multiplier is 3. Autonomous expenditures need to fall by 20. *(270)*

8. If government spending stimulated private spending, the phenomenon of what might be called *crowding in* might occur. The increase in government spending would shift the *AE* curve up from AE_0 to AE_1 as in the diagram below. The resulting shift in income would cause a further shift up in investment, shifting the aggregate expenditure curve up further to AE_2. Income would increase from Y_0 to Y_2—by more than what the simple multiplier model would predict. *(274)*

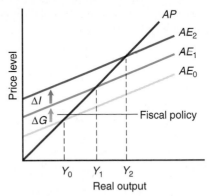

9. Potential income is not a measurable number. It is a conceptual number that must be estimated based on observable information about such phenomena as inflation, productivity, and unemployment. Estimating potential income is a challenge. *(275)*

10. Automatic stabilizers tend to decrease the size of the multiplier, decreasing the fluctuations in the economy. *(279)*

Politics, Surpluses, Deficits, and Debt

12

After reading this chapter, you should be able to:

- Define the terms *deficit, surplus,* and *debt*.

- Differentiate between real and nominal deficits and surpluses.

- Distinguish between a passive deficit and a structural deficit.

- Explain why the debt needs to be judged relative to assets.

- Describe the historical record for the Canadian deficit, surplus, and debt.

- Explain how the surplus of the late 1990s came about and what policymakers decided to do with the surplus.

Safeguarding our financial health at home is the sine qua non of riding out the global storm we are now in. Turbulence abroad mandates vigilance at home. Make no mistake. We will do what we can. But we will only do what we can afford.

Paul Martin

After having run budget deficits for many decades, in 1997 the federal government started to run budget surpluses. Early in 2001 economists predicted that the surpluses would continue as long as the government held the line on its program spending and the economy continued to grow. By late 2001 these projections fell by the wayside as increased spending on national security made it nearly impossible to predict the budget balance over the near term. This was quite a change from the billion-dollar deficit predictions of the early 1990s. This chapter considers budget surpluses and deficits from an economist's perspective in order to give you some deeper insight into policy debates that you will likely hear about in the newspapers.

In the long-run framework, surpluses are good because they provide additional saving for an economy and deficits are bad because they reduce saving, growth, and income. In the short-run framework, the view of surpluses and deficits depends on the state of the economy relative to its potential. If the economy is operating below its potential output, deficits are good and surpluses are bad because deficits increase expenditures, moving output closer to potential.

Combining the two frameworks gives us the following policy directive: Whenever possible, run surpluses, or at least a balanced budget, to help stimulate long-run growth. That recommendation is made even stronger when the economy is booming; that is, when it is above its level of potential income. Should the economy fall into a recession, however, policymakers must choose between the different policies suggested by the long-run and short-run frameworks.

At the beginning of 2000, the Canadian economy was booming, unemployment was at historic lows, and there was general agreement that the economy was closing in on potential output. If ever there was a time to let government build up a surplus and cut debt, it was then; that was the policy both the short-run and long-run economic frameworks recommended. What policy did the government explore? The Liberal government of the day decided it would use half of the surplus to pay down the national debt, and allocated the other half to spending and transfer payments.

At least, that was the plan. When economic growth began to fall across North America late in 2000 and throughout 2001, governments began to re-evaluate their budget projections. Forecasts of budget surpluses had been based on the assumption that both the U.S. and Canadian economies would continue to grow at robust rates. Lower growth rates implied lower tax revenues, and perhaps even greater spending as more and more Canadians required social assistance. When economists revisited their models, the outlook for continual surpluses was somewhat weaker than previously expected. The terrorist attacks in the United States in September 2001 contributed to greater economic uncertainty and caused a further decline in economic growth and tax revenues, as well as an increase in government spending.

Late in 2001 the federal government brought in a new budget to outline its approach to managing the economy in the "new era." Increased spending on national security and the economic uncertainty of 2001/2002 took the budget surplus off its previously forecast track. The government decided to postpone its debt-reduction strategy for the near term, arguing that economic growth would continue to reduce the debt-to-GDP ratio (for more on this point see the Appendix to this chapter). The Minister of Finance announced that the government budget balance was not expected to return to deficit even though he was planning to raise government spending by more than $10 billion.

How could the government increase its spending, postpone its debt retirement strategy, and remain deficit-free? It's the result of several years of budgets containing billions of dollars in "fiscal prudence"—funds the Minister of Finance puts in the budget to deal with unforeseen events. These dollars hadn't been spent for several years, and they helped generate the large budget surpluses of the late 1990s and allowed the government to retire some of its outstanding debt. Late in 2001 the government was able to use this "mad money"[1] to respond to increased calls for national security and stimulative fiscal policy.

Surpluses are good for an economy in the long-run framework because they provide saving for investment, which will lead to growth. Whether surpluses are good or bad for an economy in the short-run framework depends on whether the economy is above or below potential income.

Q-1 How can deficits be both good and bad for an economy?

---

[1]Mad money, as was pointed out to one of us by a student in her seventies taking one of our courses for interest's sake, was money given to a young woman by her parents when she went out on a date. If she got mad at her date, the "mad money" would get her home safely!

So what's going on here? The answer is complicated. To explain it we need some background on accounting issues that pertain to deficits, some specifics about the demography and institutions of Canada, and some knowledge of politics as it relates to surpluses, deficits, and debt. This chapter is intended to provide you with that background.

The definitions of *surplus*, *deficit*, and *debt* are simple, but this simplicity hides important aspects that will help you understand current debates about deficits and debt. Thus, it's necessary to look carefully at some ambiguities in the definitions.

DEFINING SURPLUSES AND DEFICITS

A *deficit* is a shortfall of incoming revenues under payments. A *surplus* is an excess of revenues over payments.

A **surplus** is *an excess of revenues over payments.* A **deficit** is *a shortfall of revenues under payments;* both are flow concepts. If your income (revenue) is $20,000 per year and your expenditures (payments) are $30,000 per year, you are running a deficit. This definition tells us that a government budget deficit occurs when government expenditures exceed government revenues. Table 12-1 shows federal government total expenditures, total revenue, and the difference between the two from 1994 to 2001. As you can see, the federal government ran deficits through 1996 and began to run surpluses in 1997.

Financing the Deficit

The government finances its deficits by selling bonds to private individuals and to the central bank.

Just like private individuals, the government must pay for the goods and services it buys. This means that whenever the government runs a deficit, it has to finance that deficit. It does so by selling *bonds*—promises to pay back the money in the future—to private individuals and to the central bank.

Canada is fortunate to have people who want to buy its bonds. Some countries, such as Russia, have few people who want to buy their bonds (lend them money) and therefore have trouble financing their deficits. However, countries have an option that individuals don't have. Their central banks can loan them the money (buy their bonds). Since the central bank's IOUs are money, the loans can be made simply by printing money; in principle, therefore, the central bank has a potentially unlimited source of funds. But, as we shall see in later chapters, printing too much money can lead to serious inflation problems, which have negative effects on the economy. So, whenever possible, governments try not to use the "print money" option to finance their deficits.

Arbitrariness of Defining Surpluses and Deficits

Whether or not you have a surplus or deficit depends on what you count as a revenue and what you count as an expenditure. These decisions can make an enormous difference in whether you have a surplus or deficit. For example, consider the problem of a firm with annual revenues of $8,000 but no expenses except a $10,000 machine expected to last five years. Should the firm charge the $10,000 to this year's expenditures?

TABLE 12-1 Revenue, Expenditures, and Budget Balance (in millions of dollars)

	1994	1995	1996	1997	1998	1999	2000	2001
Revenue	131,911	140,313	147,954	162,556	167,864	176,045	194,327	194,304
Expenditures	165,888	172,390	166,086	160,069	163,149	171,536	178,857	184,795
(−) Deficit/(+) surplus	−35,088	−31,700	−16,957	6,476	9,026	8,321	19,371	12,661

Source: Statistics Canada, CANSIM II, Table 380-0007.

Should it split the $10,000 evenly among the five years? Or should it use some other approach? Which method the firm chooses makes a big difference in whether its current budget will be in surplus or deficit.

Accounting is central to the debate about whether we should be concerned about a deficit. Say, for example, that the government promises to pay an individual $1,000 ten years from now. How should government treat that promise? Since the obligation is incurred now, should government count as a current expense an amount that, if saved, would allow it to pay that $1,000 later? Or should government not count the amount as an expenditure until it actually pays out the money? Canada's **Retirement Income system**—*social insurance programs that provide financial benefits to the elderly and disabled and to their eligible dependants and/or survivors*—is based on promises to pay, and thus the accounting procedures used for these programs play an important role in whether the government budget has a deficit or surplus.

Surpluses and Deficits as Summary Measures

The point of the previous discussion is that deficits are simply a summary measure of a budget. As a summary, a surplus or deficit figure reduces a complicated set of accounting relationships to one figure. To understand what that summary measure is telling us, you need to understand the accounting procedures used to calculate it. Only then can you make an informed judgment about whether a deficit is something to worry about. What's important is not whether a budget is in surplus or deficit but whether the economy is healthy.

> Deficit and surplus figures are simply summary measures of the financial health of the economy. To understand the summary, you must understand the methods that were used to calculate it.

NOMINAL AND REAL SURPLUSES AND DEFICITS

Another ambiguity important in understanding the budget deficit and surplus picture is the real/nominal ambiguity. A **nominal deficit** is *the deficit determined by looking at the difference between expenditures and receipts.*[2] It's what most people think of when they think of the budget deficit; it's the value that is generally reported. The **real deficit** is *the nominal deficit adjusted for inflation.* To understand this distinction it is important to recognize that inflation wipes out debt (accumulated deficits less accumulated surpluses). How much does it wipe out? Consider an example: If a country has a $500 billion debt and inflation is 4 percent per year, the real value of all assets denominated in dollars is declining by 4 percent each year. If you had $100 and there's 4 percent inflation in a year, that $100 will be worth 4 percent less at the end of the year—the equivalent of $96 without inflation. By the same reasoning, when there's 4 percent inflation, the value of the debt is declining 4 percent each year. Four percent of $500 billion is $20 billion, so with an outstanding debt of $500 billion, 4 percent inflation will eliminate $20 billion of the debt each year.

The larger the debt and the larger the inflation, the more debt will be eliminated by inflation. For example, with 10 percent inflation and a $500 billion debt, $50 billion of the debt will be eliminated by inflation each year. With 4 percent inflation and a $1 trillion debt, $40 billion of the debt would be eliminated.

If inflation is wiping out debt, and the deficit is equal to the increases in debt from one year to the next,[3] inflation also affects the deficit. Economists take this into account by differentiating nominal deficits from real deficits.

> **Q-2** Explain how inflation can wipe out debt.

> Inflation reduces the value of the debt. That reduction is taken into account when the real deficit is calculated.

---

[2]In this section we will discuss deficits only. Since a surplus is a negative deficit, the discussion can be easily translated into a discussion of surpluses.

[3]The Appendix to this chapter provides additional detail on the relationship between the deficit and the debt.

Real deficit = Nominal deficit −
(Inflation × Total debt)

Q.3 The nominal deficit is $40 billion, inflation is 2 percent, and the total debt is $4 trillion. What is the real deficit?

We can calculate the real deficit by subtracting the decrease in the value of the government's total outstanding debts due to inflation. Specifically:[4]

Real deficit = Nominal deficit − (Inflation × Total debt).

Let's consider an example. Say that the nominal deficit is $15 billion, inflation is 6 percent, and total debt is $700 billion. Substituting into the formula gives us a real surplus of $27 billion [$15 billion − (0.06 × $700 billion) = $15 billion − $42 billion = −$27 billion]. (This follows because a surplus is a negative deficit and hence is written here as a negative number.)

This insight into debt is directly relevant to the budget situation in Canada. For example, back in 1980 the nominal federal deficit was about $13 billion, while the real deficit was about half of that—$5 billion; in 2001 the federal government surplus was about $12.6 billion; there was 3 percent inflation and a total debt of about $545 billion. That means the real surplus was even larger—$29 billion.[5] Table 12-2 shows the federal nominal and real deficits and surpluses for selected years. Because Canada has had both debt and inflation during these periods, the real deficits are smaller than the nominal deficits and the real surpluses are greater than the nominal surpluses.

The lowering of the real deficit by inflation is not costless to the government. Persistent inflation becomes built into expectations and causes higher interest rates. When inflationary expectations were low, as they were in the 1950s, the federal government paid low interest rates on its bonds. In 1991, when inflationary expectations were high, the government paid about 10 percent interest, which is about 5 percent more than it paid in 2001, when inflationary expectations were low. In 1991, with its $400 billion debt, this meant that Canada was paying about $20 billion more in interest than it would have had to pay if no inflation had been expected and the nominal interest rate had been 5 rather than 10 percent. That reduced the amount it could spend on current services by $20 billion. In other words, $20 billion of the 1991 nominal federal deficit existed because of the rise in interest payments necessary to compensate bondholders for the expected inflation. As inflationary expectations and nominal interest rates fell through the 1990s, the difference between the real and nominal deficit (surplus) decreased, but the fear that inflation would reignite left bondholders requiring a small inflation premium, meaning interest rates paid by government were higher than they otherwise would have been.

---

[4]This is an approximation for low rates of inflation. When inflation becomes large, total debt is multiplied by $1/(1 + \text{inflation})$.

[5]Because a surplus is a negative deficit, you must add inflation times total debt to the nominal surplus to arrive at the real surplus.

TABLE 12-2   Real and Nominal Deficits (in millions of dollars)

	1975	1980	1985	1990	1995	2000
Nominal (−)deficit/(+)surplus	−5,215	−12,545	−37,998	−33,309	−31,700	19,371
Plus Inflation × Total debt	2,650	7,400	8,395	17,420	12,115	15,249
Government debt	27,769	72,555	209,891	362,920	550,685	564,793
CPI inflation	10.7	10.2	4.0	4.8	2.2	2.7
Equals Real (−)deficit/(+)surplus	−7,865	−19,945	−46,393	−50,729	−43,815	34,620

Source: Statistics Canada, CANSIM II, Tables 380-0007, 326-0001, and 385-0010.

STRUCTURAL AND PASSIVE SURPLUSES AND DEFICITS

Another important distinction to be made when discussing deficits and surpluses is between a structural deficit and a passive deficit. The discussion of fiscal policy in the previous chapter emphasized the effect of the deficit on total income. But in thinking about such policies, it is important to remember that many government revenues and expenditures depend on the level of income in the economy. For example, say that the multiplier is 2 and the government is running expansionary policy. Say that that policy increases government spending by $100 (increasing the budget deficit by $100), which causes income to rise by $200. If the tax rate is 20 percent, tax revenues will increase by $40 and the net effect of the policy will be to increase the budget deficit by $60, not $100.

To differentiate between a budget deficit being used as a policy instrument to affect the economy and a budget deficit that is the result of income deviating from its potential, economists ask the question "Would the economy have a budget deficit or surplus if it were at its potential level of income?" If it would, that portion of the budget deficit or surplus is said to be a **structural deficit or surplus**—*the part of a budget deficit or surplus that would exist even if the economy were at its potential level of income.* In contrast, if an economy is operating below its potential, the actual deficit will be larger than the structural deficit. In such an economy, that part of the total budget deficit or surplus is a **passive deficit or surplus**—*the part of the deficit or surplus that exists because the economy is operating below or above its potential level of output.* The passive deficit is also known as the *cyclical deficit.* When an economy is operating above its potential, it has a passive surplus. Economists believe that an economy can eliminate a passive budget deficit through growth in income, whereas it can't grow out of a structural deficit. Because the economy can't grow out of them, structural budget deficits are of more concern to policymakers than are passive budget deficits.

Let us give an example. Say potential income is $1.2 trillion and actual income is $1.0 trillion, a shortfall of $200 billion. The actual budget deficit is $25 billion and the marginal tax rate is 25 percent. If the economy were at its potential income, tax revenue would be $50 billion higher and the deficit would actually be a surplus of $25 billion. That $25 billion is the structural surplus. The $50 billion (25 percent multiplied by the $200 million shortfall) is the passive portion of the deficit. Table 12-3 (on the next page) shows the actual, structural, and passive budget deficits and surpluses for selected years. You can see that Canada ran passive surpluses throughout the late 1980s but that these quickly turned into deficits throughout most of the 1990s. This led to belt-tightening and a review of government programs that have created passive surpluses in the early 21st century.

In reality there is significant debate about what an economy's potential income level is, and hence there is disagreement about what percentage of a deficit is structural and what percentage is passive. Nonetheless, the distinction is often used and is important to remember.

The structural deficit is the deficit that remains when the cyclical elements of the deficit have been removed.

Q.4   An economy's actual income is $1 trillion; its potential income is also $1 trillion. Its actual deficit is $100 billion. What is its passive deficit?

THE DEFINITION OF DEBT AND ASSETS

Debt is *accumulated deficits minus accumulated surpluses.* Whereas deficits and surpluses are flow measures (they are defined for a period of time), debt is a stock measure (it is defined at a point in time). For example, say you've spent $30,000 a year for 10 years and have had annual income of $20,000 for 10 years. So you've had a deficit of $10,000

Debt is accumulated deficits minus accumulated surpluses. Whereas *deficit* is a flow concept, *debt* is a stock concept.

TABLE 12-3   Budget Deficits and Surpluses: Actual, Passive, and Structural

Year	Actual (–) deficit/ (+) surplus	Structural (–) deficit/ (+) surplus	Passive (–) deficit/ (+) surplus
1976	–4,835	–5,574	739
1977	–9,505	–10,245	740
1978	–13,526	–14,372	846
1979	–11,162	–12,490	1,328
1980	–12,545	–12,714	169
1981	–10,001	–9,630	–371
1982	–21,341	–15,651	–5,690
1983	–27,880	–22,200	–5,680
1984	–33,677	–31,310	–2,367
1985	–37,998	–38,190	192
1986	–28,933	–29,679	746
1987	–25,990	–29,901	3,911
1988	–26,292	–33,854	7,562
1989	–27,697	–35,113	7,416
1990	–33,309	–36,135	2,826
1991	–37,214	–31,007	–6,207
1992	–35,787	–27,102	–8,685
1993	–39,696	–31,777	–7,919
1994	–35,088	–31,593	–3,495
1995	–31,700	–28,117	–3,583
1996	–16,957	–11,190	–5,767
1997	6,476	9,994	–3,518
1998	9,026	11,816	–2,790
1999	8,321	8,394	–73
2000	19,371	18,200	1,171

Source: Finance Canada, Fiscal Reference Tables, 2000, Table 54, September 2001, www.fin.gc.ca/afr/2001/frt01e.pdf

per year—a flow. At the end of 10 years, you will have accumulated a debt of $100,000 (10 × $10,000 = $100,000)—a stock. (Spending more than you have in income means that you need to borrow the extra $10,000 per year from someone, so in later years much of your expenditure will be for interest on your previous debt.) If a country has been running more surpluses than deficits, the accumulated surpluses minus accumulated deficits are counted as part of its assets.

Q.5 Distinguish between *deficit* and *debt*.

Debt Management

The Canadian government must continually refinance the bonds that are coming due by selling new bonds, as well as sell new bonds when running a deficit. This makes for a very active market in Canadian government bonds, and the interest rate paid on government bonds is a closely watched statistic in the economy. If the government runs a surplus, it can either retire some of its previously issued bonds by buying them back, or simply not replace the previously issued bonds when they come due. In the early 2000s, the federal government did both.

To judge a country's debt, we must view its debt in relation to its assets.

The Need to Judge Debt Relative to Assets Debt is also a summary measure of a country's financial situation. As a summary measure, debt has even more problems than deficit. Unlike a deficit, which is the difference between outflows and inflows, and hence provides both sides of the ledger, debt by itself is only half of a picture. The other half of the picture is assets. For a country, assets include its skilled workforce, its natural resources, its factories, its housing stock, and its holdings of foreign assets. For a government, assets include not only the buildings and land it owns but also, and more importantly, a portion of the assets of the people in the country, since government gets a portion of all earnings of those assets in tax revenue.

To get an idea of why the addition of assets is necessary to complete the debt picture, consider two governments: one has debt of $3 trillion and assets of $50 trillion; the other has only $1 trillion in debt but only $1 trillion in assets. Which is in a better position? The government with the $3 trillion debt is, because its debt is significantly exceeded by its assets. The example's point is simple: To judge a country's debt, we must view its debt in relation to all its assets.

This need to judge debt relative to assets adds an important caveat to the long-run position that government budget deficits are bad. When the government runs a deficit, it might be spending on projects that increase its assets. If the assets are valued at more than their costs, then the deficit is making the society better off. Government investment can be as productive as private investment or even more productive.

Arbitrariness in Defining Debt and Assets Like income and revenues, assets and debt are subject to varying definitions. Say, for example, that an 18-year-old is due to inherit $1 million at age 21. Should that expected future asset be counted as an asset now? Or say that the government buys an aircraft for $1 billion and discovers that it doesn't fly. What value should the government place on that aircraft? Or say that a country owes $1 billion, due to be paid 10 years from now, but inflation is ongoing at 100 percent per year. The inflation will reduce the value of the debt when it comes due by so much that its current real value will be $1 million—the approximate present value of $1 billion in 10 years with 100 percent inflation. It will be like paying $1 million today. Should the country list the debt as a $1 billion debt or a $1 million debt?

As was the case with income, revenues, and deficits, there's no single answer to how assets and debts should be valued. So even after you take assets into account, you still have to be careful when deciding whether or not to be concerned about debt.

In addition, the total stock of outstanding federal debt (gross debt) can be broken down into *market debt* and *nonmarket debt*. Market debt in 2000 was about $440 billion and included marketable bonds, treasury bills, Canada Savings Bonds, and other marketable securities that government issues when it borrows. Nonmarket debt includes federal public sector pension liabilities as well as other federal liabilities; in 2000 this amounted to just over $173 billion, bringing the gross debt to $613 billion. When we subtract from this the value of federal government financial assets such as cash, reserves, and loans, we arrive at an estimate of net debt in Canada. This is the figure we usually see reported in the popular press. In 2001 net federal debt in Canada was just over $545 billion.

Who holds this debt? Aside from the central bank, pension funds, chartered banks, life insurance companies, and other intermediaries, some of the federal debt is held by nonresidents. In 2000 and 2001 this amounted to about 20 percent of total market debt.

Difference between Individual and Government Debt

The final point we want to make concerns who is issuing the debt. Not all debt is the same. In particular, government debt is different from an individual's debt. There are three reasons for this.

First, government is ongoing. Government never has to pay back its debt. An individual's life span is limited; when a person dies, there's inevitably an accounting of

Q.6 Why is debt only half the picture of a country's financial situation?

12.1
see page 303

Incurring budgetary deficits as a result of increased infrastructure spending may be justified if it yields benefits for future generations and if the revenue generated over the long term pays for the investment.

Three reasons government debt is different from individual debt are:

1. The government lives forever; people don't.
2. The government can print money to pay its debt; people can't.
3. Government owes much of its debt to itself—to its own citizens.

12.2

see page 303

assets and debt to determine whether anything is left to go to heirs. Before any part of a person's estate is passed on, all debts must be paid. The government, however, doesn't ever have to settle its accounts.

Second, government has an option that individuals don't have for paying off a debt. Specifically, it can pay off a debt by creating money. As long as people will accept a country's currency, a country can always exchange money (non-interest-bearing debt) for bonds (interest-bearing debt).

Third, about 80 percent of government debt is **internal debt** (*government debt owed to other governmental agencies or to its own citizens*). Paying interest on the internal debt involves a redistribution among citizens of the country, but it does not involve a net reduction in income of the average citizen. For example, say that a country has $500 billion in internal debt. Say also that the government pays $40 billion in interest on its debt each year. That means the government must collect $40 billion in taxes, so people are $40 billion poorer; but it pays out $40 billion in interest to them, so on average, people in the country are neither richer nor poorer because of the debt. **External debt** (*government debt owed to individuals in foreign countries*) is more like an individual's debt. Paying interest on external debt involves a net reduction in domestic income. Canadian taxpayers will be poorer; foreign holders of Canadian bonds will be richer.

CANADIAN GOVERNMENT DEFICITS AND DEBT: THE HISTORICAL RECORD

Now that we have been through the basics of deficits and debt, let's look at the historical record. From the Second World War until the early 1970s, the Canadian government budget balance fluctuated between small surpluses and small deficits. Beginning in the mid-1970s, deficits grew considerably, from $5 billion in 1975 to nearly $40 billion in 1993, before declining in the mid-1990s and disappearing by 1997. Over most of that time total debt has increased. It more than doubled in the 30 years from 1945 to 1975 and grew more quickly beginning in the mid-1970s, rising by a multiple of 22 to $545 billion in 2001. Most economists, however, are much more concerned with deficits and debt relative to GDP than with the absolute figures.

Figure 12-1 graphs the federal budget deficit and debt as a percentage of GDP. From this perspective, as you can see in Figure 12-1(a), deficits as a percentage of GDP rose significantly in the 1970s and the 1980s, as they did when we considered them in absolute terms. And it's the same with debt. As you can see in Figure 12-1(b) debt, relative to GDP, rose substantially from 1975 until the late 1990s when it started to fall.

Deficits and debt relative to GDP provide a measure of a country's ability to pay off a deficit and service its debt.

Economists prefer the "relative to GDP" measurement because it better measures the government's ability to handle the deficit; a nation's ability to pay off a debt depends on its productive capacity (the asset side of the picture). GDP serves the same function for government as income does for an individual. It provides a measure of how much debt, and how large a deficit, government can handle. So when GDP grows, so does the debt the government can reasonably carry.

The Debt Burden

Most of the decrease in the debt-to-GDP ratio in Canadian history occurred through growth in GDP. There are two ways in which growth in GDP can occur—through inflation (a rise in nominal but not real GDP) or through real growth. Both ways reduce the problem of the debt. As we discussed above, inflation wipes out the value of existing

Figure 12-1 (a and b)   CANADIAN BUDGET DEFICITS AND DEBT RELATIVE TO GDP

The size of the deficits and the size of the debt look somewhat different when considered relative to GDP. Notice how the net debt-to-GDP ratio rose substantially from the 1970s to the 1990s and how it declined in the late 1990s.

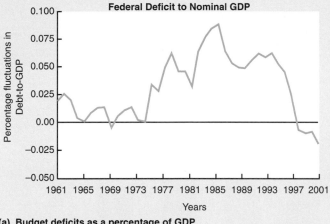

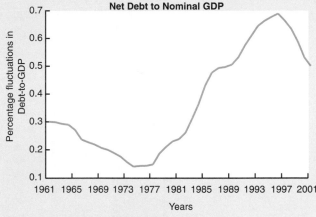

(a) Budget deficits as a percentage of GDP

(b) Net debt as a percentage of GDP

Source: Statistics Canada, CANSIM II, Tables 385-0010 and 380-0002.

debt; when there is inflation, there can be large nominal budget deficits but a small real deficit.

When an economy experiences real growth, the ability of the government to incur debt is increased; the economy becomes richer and, being richer, can handle more debt. As noted in an earlier chapter, real growth in Canada has averaged about 2.5 to 3.5 percent per year, which means that Canadian debt can grow at a rate of 2.5 to 3.5 percent without increasing the debt-to-GDP ratio. But for debt to grow, government must run a deficit, so a constant debt-to-GDP ratio in a growing economy is consistent with a continual deficit.

How much of a deficit are we talking about? Canadian federal government debt in 2001 was about $545 billion and GDP was about $1.1 trillion, so the government debt-to-GDP ratio was about 50 percent. A real growth rate of 2.5 percent means that real GDP is growing at about $28 billion per year. That means that government can run a deficit of $10 billion a year without increasing the debt-to-GDP ratio. Of course, for those who believe that the total federal government debt is already too large relative to GDP, this argument (that the debt-to-GDP ratio is remaining constant) is unsatisfying. They'd prefer the debt-to-GDP ratio to fall.

Q-7 What annual deficit could a $5 billion economy growing at a real annual rate of 5 percent have without changing its debt burden?

Canadian Debt Relative to Other Countries

When judged relative to other advanced countries, early in the new millennium Canada had a relatively large debt burden, as can be seen in Figure 12-2 (on the next page). At 66 percent of Canadian GDP, the debt ratio was second only to Italy, and well above the level enjoyed by the United Kingdom. This might make you think Canadian fiscal policy is out of control, but we need to view the Canadian figures in historical perspective. In 1995 the ratio of net debt to GDP was nearly 89 percent! In 1996 the ratio had fallen marginally to just under 88 percent. It fell again in 1997 to just over 84 percent. The following year the debt-to-GDP ratio was around 81 percent.

Figure 12-2 **CANADIAN DEBT COMPARED TO FOREIGN COUNTRIES' DEBT (NET DEBT AS % OF GDP, YEAR-END)**

Canada's debt-to-GDP ratio was among the highest of the major advanced economies early in the 21st century.

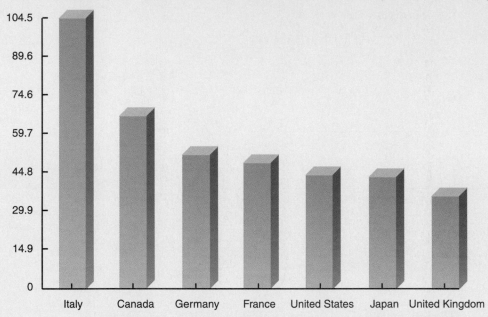

Source: *World Economic Outlook*, International Monetary Fund, 2001.

Economic growth and relatively tight fiscal policies caused this turnaround. In 1999 the debt-to-GDP ratio had fallen to 75 percent, and in 2000 the ratio fell further to 66 percent. Viewed in this light, the Canadian fiscal house appears to be back on track. Indeed, one of the reasons the government adopted changes to its spending and taxation policies in the mid-1990s was its realization that, without change, the debt-to-GDP ratio would continue to rise. There was a structural deficit: Even at full employment, spending exceeded revenues. To move off this unsustainable path, the authorities realized they had to revamp their policies and programs. That's what happened throughout the late 1990s. Structural deficits became surpluses—you can see this if you revisit Table 12-3.

While Canada's debt-to-GDP ratio is still relatively high, it is much lower than it was in the mid-1990s. As we write this chapter, the interesting question is whether the economic slowdown in 2001/2002 and the war against terrorism will take the government off its desired debt-to-GDP path. At this point it's not clear whether the federal government will be able to achieve its targets for revenues and expenditures.

Interest Rates and Debt Burden

Considering debt relative to GDP is still not quite sufficient to give an accurate picture of the debt burden. How much of a burden a given amount of debt imposes depends on the interest rate that must be paid on that debt. The annual **debt service** is *the interest rate on debt times the total debt.*

Figure 12-3　FEDERAL INTEREST PAYMENTS RELATIVE TO GDP

Interest payments as a percentage of GDP remained relatively constant until the 1970s, after which they rose significantly due to high interest rates and large increases in debt. In the 1990s they fell as interest rates fell and surpluses reduced the total debt.

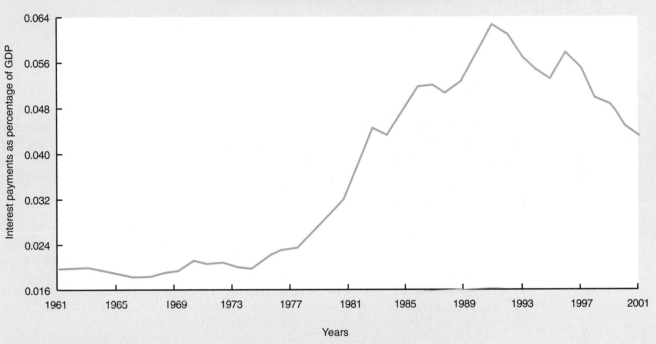

Interest on Federal Debt as Percentage of Nominal GDP

Source: Statistics Canada, CANSIM II, Tables 380-0002 and 385-0001.

In 2001, the federal government paid out approximately $43 billion in interest. A larger debt would require even higher interest payments. The interest payment is government revenue that can't be spent on defence or welfare; it's a payment for past expenditures. Ultimately, the interest payments are the burden of the debt. That's what people mean when they say a deficit is burdening future generations.

Over the past 40 years, the interest rate has fluctuated considerably; when it has risen, the debt service has increased; when it has fallen, debt service has decreased. Figure 12-3 shows the federal interest rate payments relative to GDP. This ratio increased substantially in the 1970s and 1980s. In the early 1990s it fell, and by 2001 it had fallen to 4 percent of GDP. If growth remains high and tax rates and spending are not changed, in 20 years the debt could be totally eliminated.

Canada can afford its current debt in the sense that it can afford to pay the interest on that debt. In fact, as we discussed above, it could afford a higher debt-to-GDP ratio, since Canadian government bonds are still considered one of the safest assets in the world. No one is worried about the Canadian government's defaulting.

THE MODERN DEBATE ABOUT THE SURPLUS

With these preliminaries, let us return to the current situation. What should government do—figure out ways to spend the surplus, or use the surplus to lower the debt? And, if we expect to continue to see a federal budget surplus, have we solved our fiscal problems? To answer these questions, let's start with a consideration of why the surplus came about.

Why Did the Surplus Come About?

The adoption of Keynesian policy—using deficits to stimulate the economy—in the 1940s has led to nearly continual budget deficits ever since the end of the Second World War.

Until the 1940s, economists and laypeople shared the same view of deficits—they are bad. Then Keynesian economics made clear that that view was too simplistic and that, when the economy was significantly below its potential output, deficits could serve a positive function. The view that all government debt should be paid off as quickly as possible did not follow from economic theory. The more enlightened view of deficits lessened the pressure to eliminate them and contributed to the almost continual deficits that the federal government ran after the Second World War.

That Keynesian view of deficits was never fully accepted by politicians, or by the public. Both had a deep-seated fear of deficits. They equated government deficits with individual deficits, when in fact the two are quite different. So, even when the government was running large deficits, most politicians were saying that the deficits should be eliminated. However, they did not act on their statements.

In the 1980s the political landscape changed. Politicians, who opposed large government spending programs, developed a political strategy that focused on cutting taxes. They saw most government spending as unproductive, but saw political forces driving toward higher and higher spending. Their solution was to cut taxes, and to allow the deficits to expand. Some justified this by arguing that the tax cuts would increase incentives to work and expand the economy so much that no deficits would result. The majority of economists, while they agreed that the incentives could play a positive role in the long run, felt that they were too small to play a significant role in expanding the economy in the short run.

By the mid-1990s the federal government realized it had increased its spending to the point where it was running a structural deficit. Even if the economy were operating at potential output, the budget would be in deficit. To rectify this, the authorities raised taxes, cut many social programs, and redesigned existing programs. For example, unemployment insurance became employment insurance, and the program was redesigned to reduce repeat use of the system. All of these changes were aimed at shifting government spending and taxes closer to the point of a structural budget surplus.

The surpluses of the late 1990s were brought about by the unexpected growth of the economy, fiscal restraint, and a low and stable rate of inflation. As estimates of the level of potential output increased, the predicted future tax revenue increased; and, as it did, the deficit projections moved in the opposite direction. Because inflation remained low, interest rates remained low, holding down government interest payments. It was that combination of economic growth and low inflation that was primarily responsible for turning the budget deficit predictions into the budget surplus predictions.

The Federal Deficit and Debt Are Only Part of the Picture

So far we've only discussed the *federal* deficit and the *federal* debt. Provinces and municipalities also run deficits by borrowing to spend in excess of their revenues, and when they do they raise the total amount of government debt in the economy. Indeed, throughout the 1990s, as the federal government eliminated and/or reduced spending on many of its programs, provincial, territorial and local governments were forced to fill the gap. You can see this in Figure 12-4(a): Net provincial and territorial debt rose significantly during the 1990s.

Until the early 1980s many provinces alternated between periods of budget surplus and deficit. The recession of 1981–82 led to provincial deficits as governments weathered the economic downturn. The traditional Keynesian approach to fiscal policy suggests that during the recovery phase of the business cycle we could expect provincial (and federal) governments to adopt less expansionary policies in an attempt to build a surplus out of which to fund programs during the next recession. Unfortunately, the political will to raise taxes and cut spending from 1982 to 1990 didn't materialize, as you can see in Figure 12-4(b). The recession of 1990–91 saw a shift in provincial and territorial budget balances back into larger deficits, and the federal deficit rose significantly, with a return to surplus budget balances only by the late 1990s.

Many provincial governments argued they were forced to undertake higher levels of spending because the federal government "off-loaded" programs in its attempt to reduce the federal deficit and debt. This, in conjunction with a revision to the process through which the federal government provides transfer payments to the provinces for services such as health care and education, led to a breakdown in federal–provincial relations.

It didn't take long for the provinces to realize they could not afford to fund every project they deemed worthy of government support. Many provinces enacted balanced budget legislation that included hefty fines on finance ministers whose balanced budget projections were off the mark. A "common sense" revolution in the political arena along with the promise of future tax cuts led to the election of a number of new political leaders intent on adopting "fiscally responsible" programs. The difficulty, of course, was in identifying those programs deemed to be fiscally responsible. Reasonable people often failed to find common ground and frequently disagreed over which policies the government should have implemented. That's because they entered the realm of normative economics (if you don't remember the difference between positive economics and normative economics, take another look at Chapter 1).

A Different Type of Crowding Out

In mid-1994 the inflation rate hovered around zero, yet interest rates rose almost continuously over the year. Media accounts attributed these anomalies to (1) uncertainty regarding the Quebec election and the chance that Quebec would separate from Canada, and (2) the rising deficits and debts of the Canadian economy.

Higher and higher government deficits require an ever-increasing amount of borrowing, and this reduces the pool of capital available to government and private enterprise. Firms that wish to fund expansion by issuing debt (such as bonds) are forced to pay higher rates of return. In many cases the internal rate of return on the project the firm wants to fund just can't match the kinds of rates the government offers when it issues bonds and treasury bills. Thus, private sector investment is **crowded out**—*higher levels of government spending raise interest rates, which in turn reduce the level of private investment.*

Figure 12-4 (a and b)   FEDERAL AND PROVINCIAL/TERRITORIAL DEBT AND DEFICITS

(a) As net federal debt fell in the 1990s, net debt at other levels of government rose. Many feel this was the result of the federal government off-loading its spending to the provinces. This figure contains data up to 1999 for local government net debt and up to 2000 for provincial and territorial net debt. This is because the calculations of provincial/territorial net debt are subject to substantial delay.

(b) Deficits were high at all levels of government in Canada in the 1990s. Changes in spending and tax programs at all levels of government eliminated the federal deficit and most provincial and territorial deficits by the late 1990s. The war on terrorism has caused concerns over a return to deficit spending.

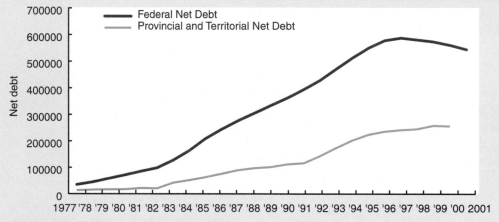

(a) Net debt: Federal and provincial/territorial

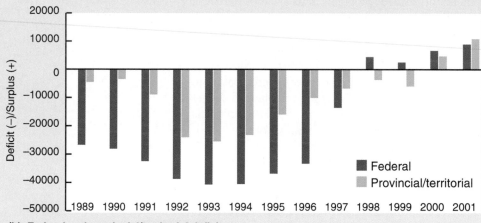

(b) Federal and provincial/territorial deficits

Source: Statistics Canada, CANSIM II, Tables 385-0017, 385-0001, and 385-0002.

However, there's another form of crowding out that comes from the appreciation of the domestic currency that follows an expansion of government spending. As the dollar gains value, it becomes more expensive for foreigners to buy Canadian goods and services, and Canadian exports fall. Canadian imports rise since Canadians can buy goods from the rest of the world more cheaply than before the dollar gained value. Thus, higher levels of government spending lead to higher deficits and debt levels and to an appreciated currency, and private sector spending takes "two hits"—one directly to investment through higher interest rates, and one directly to net exports as the dollar gains value.

Most bonds are fixed-interest bonds. They pay back a stated number of dollars in a given period. For example, at 10 percent interest a $1,000 five-year bond pays $100 interest each year for five years, and pays back another $1,000 at the end of the five years.

BEYOND THE TOOLS

Inflation and Indexed Bonds

Some economists have proposed the following: Make the amount that is to be paid back, the $1,000, indexed to inflation. Thus, if the price level rises 40 percent, the amount paid back would be $1,400 rather than $1,000. Bonds that pay back an amount dependent on inflation are called *indexed bonds.*

Let's now ask: What would happen if Canada were to issue indexed bonds? Since bondholders are compensated for inflation, the interest on bonds would fall. If 5 percent inflation were the expected rate and the nominal interest rate were 8 percent, the real interest rate would be 3 percent—so the interest rate on bonds would be 3 percent instead of 8 percent, and Canadian debt service would fall from about $40 billion to somewhere around $15 billion.

Most economists oppose having the government issue indexed bonds. Yes, they agree, it would lower the measured deficit, but it would not change real Canadian debt. At the same time, indexing would introduce new complexities of government finance as the inflation index came under even more scrutiny because so much money would be riding on it.

Whether or not you favour the proposal, it is a superb proposal from an academic perspective. It helps us recognize the difference between real and nominal deficits. What's so interesting about the proposal is that is has already been in effect since 1991! Real-return bonds are long-term bonds whose nominal yield is indexed to the Consumer Price Index. Institutional investors and portfolio managers have shown great interest in this bond program, and as of 2001 there were over $13 billion outstanding real-return bonds.

How does the return on a real-return bond compare to the return on an instrument that is not indexed? The following table lists the yield on real-return bonds and the yield on long-term Government of Canada bonds, along with the inflation rate. Which would you prefer?

Month	Long-Term Government Bond Yield	Inflation Rate	Real Return Bond Yield	Real Return + Inflation Bond Yield
2000:07	5.83	2.97	3.65	6.62
2000:08	5.79	2.52	3.67	6.19
2000:09	5.83	2.69	3.60	6.29
2000:10	5.79	2.78	3.52	6.30
2000:11	5.63	3.23	3.51	6.74
2000:12	5.59	3.22	3.42	6.64
2001:01	5.71	2.96	3.36	6.32
2001:02	5.63	2.85	3.39	6.24
2001:03	5.74	2.48	3.45	5.93
2001:04	5.94	3.55	3.61	7.16
2001:05	6.08	3.89	3.58	7.47
2001:06	5.97	3.34	3.53	6.87
2001:07	6.01	2.62	3.66	6.28

Source: Statistics Canada, CANSIM II, Tables 326-0001 and 176-0043.

Late in 2001 interest rates were at forty-year lows and inflation was low and stable. The Canadian dollar had lost much of its value against the U.S. dollar, with markets settling at a new low nearly every day in November. Some pundits argued the value of the dollar would continue to fall, while others forecast a substantial increase in the value of the dollar by 2003. Low interest rates and the low value of the dollar should encourage investment as well as net exports, and expand aggregate demand. Our analysis suggests we might reasonably expect to see the opposite of crowding out—*crowding in*—throughout 2002 and beyond. The difficulty in providing an accurate assessment is that the slowdown of 2001/2002 and the heightened sense of uncertainty arising from the war on terrorism have left substantial room for error in economic forecasting. As we write this chapter, it's just not clear when confidence will return to markets.

Is the Deficit a Good Measure of the Stance of Fiscal Policy?

We've spent a lot of time looking at the deficit and the debt. Now we want to ask whether we can use the deficit to tell us if fiscal policies are becoming more or less expansionary—

Figure 12-5 (a and b)   THE BUDGET SURPLUS FUNCTION

(a) Reduction in income from Y_0 to Y_1 could change a budget surplus to a budget deficit, but fiscal policy variables T_0, G_0 and t have not changed. The budget surplus is a bad measure of the stance of fiscal policy.

(b) Holding income at potential, Y_P, we can see how changes in fiscal policy affect the budget surplus. If BS_0 shifts to BS_1, when autonomous taxes rise, the budget surplus rises, signalling contractionary fiscal policy.

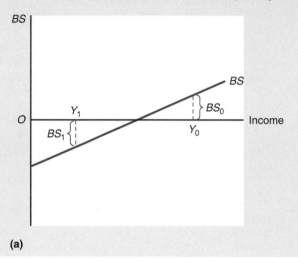

(a)

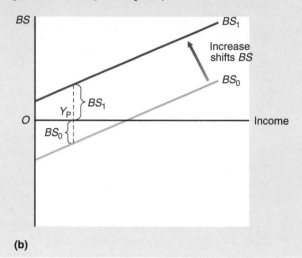

(b)

that is, we want to know the *stance* of fiscal policy. For example, let's say your campus radio station wants you to comment—live—on the next federal budget. Going over the documents, would you be able to say that fiscal policy has become more expansionary if the deficit figures went up?

If you said no, then kudos to you—you read the chapter on fiscal policy and it stuck with you. If you said yes, you need to review tax and fiscal policies. The basic reason is that the government deficit can change as a result of a shift in an autonomous component of demand. For example, say autonomous investment fell. This would reduce income and tax revenues, and the deficit would rise. If you said that fiscal policy had become more expansionary, you'd be wrong, since government spending and taxation variables hadn't changed. A good measure of the stance of fiscal policy is the structural deficit—the deficit we'd get if we adjusted the figures for the business cycle.

To cement this in your mind, consider Figure 12-5(a). It shows the government budget surplus as a function of income, using our tax and expenditure functions from Chapter 11:

Government spending	G	=	G_0		
Taxes	T	=	T_0	+	tY
Budget surplus:	BS	=	T	−	G
	BS	=	$[T_0$	−	$G_0]$ + tY

Clearly, a change in equilibrium income (due to a reduction in autonomous investment, for example) will change the budget surplus independently of changes in fiscal policy variables T_0, G_0, or t (the tax rate). A better measure of the stance of fiscal policy would be to control for changes in income over the business cycle and look at how the budget surplus changes as fiscal policy variables change. Figure 12-5(b) provides a view to how this would be done, holding income fixed at potential income. Then, the budget surplus measured at that estimate of potential income would tell us whether fiscal policy has become more expansionary (reducing the budget surplus) or less expansionary (raising the budget surplus).

Another aspect of the demographic changes brought about by the baby boom relates to stock market prices. Stock prices were soaring in the late 1990s as the baby boomers moved into their peak earning periods and, through pension systems, saved for the future—by buying stock. In 2014, when the boomers start anticipating retiring and selling stock, the effect of the baby boom on the stock market will be in the opposite direction. Many elderly will be redeeming their stocks as they retire, hoping to live off the proceeds of their savings. (These forces are the reverse of those that were pushing the stock market prices up at the turn of the century.) As the expectations of that happening develop, stock prices will likely fall precipitously and there will be much less there than people thought. Contrary to the experience of those of you born in the mid-1980s, the stock market does not only go up.

CONCLUSION

This has been a relatively short chapter, but the points in it are important. Deficits, debts, and surpluses are all accounting measures. Whether a budget is in surplus or deficit is not especially important. What is important is the health of the economy. The economic framework tells us that if the economy is in a recession, you shouldn't worry much about deficits—they can actually be good for the economy. If you are in an expansion, surpluses make much more sense. It is the state of the economy that we need to consider when making decisions about whether deficits or surpluses are good.

Economics also tells us that there are limits to how much real output one can transfer with financial assets over time. In each time period the real aggregate demand must equal the real aggregate supply; otherwise inflation or deflation will result. When demographic changes cause real supply and demand to differ substantially, as they will beginning in the 2020s, there will be a real problem that financial transfers cannot solve. The AS/AD model tells us that that a "real" problem must have a "real" solution. Politically we are unlikely to hear much discussion of such solutions, which is why the future economic health of Canada is precarious despite the movement from deficits to surpluses in the government budget.

This lithograph, titled "Legislative assault (on the budget)," appeared in a French newspaper in 1835.

Chapter Summary

- A deficit is a shortfall of revenues over payments. A surplus is the excess of revenues over payments. Debt is accumulated deficits minus accumulated surpluses.

- Budget deficits and surpluses should be judged in light of economic and political conditions.

- Deficits and surpluses are summary measures of a budget. Whether a budget is a problem depends on the budgeting procedures that measure it.

- A real deficit is a nominal deficit adjusted for the effect of inflation:

    Real deficit = Nominal deficit − (Inflation × Debt)

- A structural deficit or surplus is that part of a budget deficit or surplus that would exist even if the economy were at its potential level of income. A passive deficit or surplus is that part of the deficit or surplus that exists because the economy is below or above potential:

    Structural deficit = Actual deficit − Passive deficit

- A country's debt must be judged in relation to its assets. What is counted as a debt and as an asset can be arbitrary.

- Government debt and individual debt differ in three major ways: (1) government is ongoing and never needs to repay its debt, (2) government can pay off its debt by printing money, and (3) most of government debt is internal—owed to its own citizens.

- Deficits, surpluses, and debt should be viewed relative to GDP because this ratio better measures the government's ability to handle the deficit and pay off the debt. Compared to many countries, Canada has a low debt-to-GDP ratio.

Key Terms

crowded out   (297)

debt   (289)

debt service   (294)

deficit   (286)

external debt   (292)

internal debt   (292)

nominal deficit   (287)

passive deficit or surplus
   (289)

real deficit   (287)

Retirement Income system
   (287)

structural deficit or surplus
   (289)

surplus   (286)

Questions for Thought and Review

1. "Budget deficits should be avoided, even if the economy is below potential, because they reduce saving and lead to lower growth." Does this policy directive follow from the short-run or the long-run framework? Explain your answer.

2. What are the two ways government can finance a budget deficit?

3. Your income is $40,000 per year; your expenditures are $45,000. You spend $10,000 of that $45,000 for tuition. Is your budget in deficit or surplus? Why?

4. "The deficit should be of concern." What additional information do you need to undertake a reasonable discussion of this statement?

5. Inflation is 20 percent. Debt is $2 trillion. The nominal deficit is $300 billion. What is the real deficit?

6. How would your answer to question 5 differ if you knew that expected inflation was 15 percent?

7. If the actual budget deficit is $100 billion, the economy is operating $250 billion above its potential, and the marginal tax rate is 20 percent, what is the structural deficit and the passive deficit?

8. Two economists are debating whether the target rate of unemployment is 4 percent or 6 percent. Mr. A believes it's 4 percent; Ms. B. believes it's 6 percent. One says the structural deficit is $40 billion; the other says it's $20 billion. Which one says which? Why?

9. "The debt should be of concern." What additional information do you need to undertake a reasonable discussion of this statement?

10. List three ways in which individual debt differs from government debt.

11. If all of the government's debt were internal, would financing that debt make the nation poorer?

12. How can a government that isn't running a deficit still get itself into financial trouble?

13. Why is debt service an important measure of whether debt is a problem?

14. Economist Paul W. McCracken stated, "A decision to go with budgets that involve deficits is a decision to have a future economy delivering lower incomes." Do you agree or disagree? Why?

Problems and Exercises

1. Calculate the real deficit or surplus in the following cases:
   a. Inflation is 10 percent. Debt is $3 trillion. Nominal deficit is $220 billion.
   b. Inflation is 2 percent. Debt is $1 trillion. Nominal deficit is $50 billion.
   c. Inflation is −4 percent. (Price levels are falling.) Debt is $500 billion. Nominal deficit is $30 billion.
   d. Inflation is 3 percent. Debt is $2 trillion. Nominal surplus is $100 billion.

2. Assume a country's nominal GDP is $600 billion, government expenditures less debt service are $145 billion, and revenue is $160 billion. The nominal debt is $360 billion. Inflation is 3 percent and interest rates are 6 percent.
   a. Calculate debt service payments.
   b. Calculate the nominal deficit.
   c. Calculate the real deficit.

3. Assume that a country's real growth is 2 percent per year, while its real deficit is rising 5 percent per year. Can the country continue to afford such deficits indefinitely? What problems might it face in the future?

4. You've been hired by Creative Accountants, economic consultants. Your assignment is to make suggestions about how to structure a government's accounts so that the current deficit looks as small as possible. Specifically, they want to know how to treat the following:
   a. Government pensions.
   b. Sale of land.
   c. Canada Pension Plan contributions.
   d. Proceeds of a program to allow people to prepay taxes for a 10 percent discount.
   e. Expenditures on water bombers.

Web Questions

1. Go to the Department of Finance Web site (www.fin.gc.ca) and find the most recent Fiscal Reference Tables. Answer the following questions:
   a. What were gross and net debt in the last fiscal year?
   b. Look for the most recent Debt Management Strategy. What are its objectives? How does the structure of the debt matter?
   c. What are Foreign Exchange Reserve Assets, and how do they influence fiscal policy?

2. Find the tax calculator at the Department of Finance Web site (www.fin.gc.ca) and answer the following questions:
   a. How much will a single parent with one child whose income is $20,000 save in taxes based on the January 2001 tax savings?
   b. How much would this same person save if his or her income were $125,000?
   c. How about a typical elderly couple earning $35,000? Comment on this result relative to those in parts *a* and *b*.

Answers to Margin Questions

1. Deficits can be good when an economy is operating below its potential because they increase aggregate demand and total output. Deficits can be bad in the long run if they lead to lower investment, because lower investment will lead to lower growth. *(285)*

2. Inflation reduces the value of the dollars with which the debt will be repaid and hence, in real terms, wipes out a portion of the debt. *(287)*

3. The real deficit equals the nominal deficit minus inflation times the total debt. Inflation times the total debt in this case equals $80 billion (0.02 × $4 trillion). Since the nominal deficit is $40 billion, the real deficit is actually a surplus of $40 billion. ($40 billion − $80 billion = −$40 billion). *(288)*

4. Since the economy is at its potential income, its passive deficit is zero. All of its budget deficit is a structural deficit. *(289)*

5. Deficit is a flow concept, the difference between income and expenditures. Debt—accumulated deficits minus accumulated surpluses—is a stock concept. *(290)*

6. To get a full picture of a country's financial situation, you have to look at assets as well as debt, since a large debt for a country with large assets poses no problem. *(291)*

7. A $5 billion economy growing at a real annual rate of 5 percent could have an annual deficit of $250 million (0.05 × $5 billion) and not increase its debt burden. *(293)*

APPENDIX A

Changes in the Debt-to-GDP Ratio

We know that governments sometimes spend more than they receive in tax revenues, and that this is possible because they can borrow the difference by increasing their debt. While it's also possible for the government to sell some of its assets (such as gold, land, or buildings) to finance a budget deficit, we'll assume any shortfall in revenues will be augmented by an increase in the outstanding stock of IOUs the government has issued. In this appendix we want to examine the relationship between government deficits, debt, and borrowing more closely.

The basic accounting relationship is described by equating the government's total spending to its revenues and borrowing. The federal government purchases goods and services, provides transfer payments to other levels of governments and individuals, and pays interest on the national debt. This must equal total tax revenues plus borrowing. The following equation illustrates that total spending, G* (all spending on goods and services as well as transfer payments made by the federal government), and interest on the national debt (the interest rate, *i*, multiplied by the total debt, *D*) must equal total tax revenues, *T*, and borrowing:

$$\text{Expenditures} + \text{Interest on Debt} = \text{Revenues} + \text{Borrowing}$$
$$G^* \quad + \quad iD \quad = \quad T \quad + \quad \text{Borrowing}$$

Hence, the government's budget deficit, including interest on the debt ($G^* + iD - T$) must equal its borrowing.

Borrowing adds to the stock of outstanding debt, which we'll denote by ΔD (you'll recall that the Greek letter delta, Δ, denotes "the change in"). If the government spends less than it receives in revenues, its borrowing falls (it retires some of its debt, so D falls). Hence,

$$G^* + iD - T = \Delta D$$

The debt changes over time because of changes in the government's budget balance, inclusive of transfer payments and debt service costs.

Previously we argued that we must compare a nation's debt to its ability to repay its debt, or the ratio of debt to nominal GDP. Figure 12-1(b) contains a plot of the ratio of debt to GDP, which we denote here by the Greek letter delta in lower case ($\delta = D/\text{GDP}$). It might be interesting to ask what determines the proportionate rate of change of this debt-to-GDP ratio. Some interesting policy implications might develop, so let's see if we can work through the math to find an answer.

The ratio of debt to GDP is given by D/GDP. The proportionate rate of change of this ratio is given by

$$\Delta(D/\text{GDP}) / (D/\text{GDP})$$

Now, you might recall from an old math class that when you look at the proportionate rate of change of a ratio of variables, you can construct this as the proportionate rate of change of the term in the numerator less the proportionate rate of change of the term in the denominator (i.e., $\Delta(X/Y)/(X/Y) = (\Delta X/X) - (\Delta Y/Y)$; if you don't remember this, then believe us—it's true!). So, we can write the proportionate rate of change of the debt-to-GDP ratio (which we'll denote as $\Delta\delta/\delta$) as:

$$\Delta\delta/\delta = \Delta D/D - \Delta\text{GDP}/\text{GDP}$$

We know that the change in the debt is given by $G^* + iD - T$, so we have

$$\delta = (G^* + iD - T)/D - \Delta\text{GDP}/\text{GDP}$$

We also know that nominal GDP can change because real GDP changes or the price level changes, so the proportionate change in GDP is simply the sum of the proportionate growth in real output (denoted by α) and the proportionate change in the price level (the inflation rate, denoted by π):

$$\Delta\delta/\delta = (G^* + iD - T) / D - (\alpha + \pi)$$

We can rearrange terms to obtain:

$$\Delta\delta = [(G^* - T) / \text{GDP}] + i\delta - \delta(\alpha + \pi)$$

where we've used the fact that $\delta = D/\text{GDP}$. If we group terms involving δ we obtain:

$$\Delta\delta = [(G^* - T) / \text{GDP}] + (i - \pi - \alpha)\delta$$

What does this expression tell us? Well, the left-hand side is the change in the debt-to-GDP ratio. It's equal to the government's budget deficit as a proportion of GDP (excluding debt service costs) and some terms related to the level of the debt-to-GDP ratio. Let's look at those terms more closely.

The first term is the nominal interest rate, the second is the inflation rate, and the third is the rate of growth of real output. Since we're subtracting the inflation rate from the nominal interest rate, we could think of this as the inflation-adjusted interest rate. Later we'll give this a name: the real interest rate. So, if the inflation-adjusted interest rate is above the rate of growth in real GDP, an increase in the debt-to-GDP ratio will further increase the debt-to-GDP ratio. This means that real output isn't growing quickly enough relative to the stock of debt to allow the ratio to fall. In the opposite case, the inflation-adjusted interest rate is below the growth rate of real GDP, so an increase in the debt-to-GDP ratio will actually lead to a decline in that ratio over time.

What are the policy implications? There are two factors affecting the stability of the debt-to-GDP ratio. The first is the ratio of the budget balance (net of interest payments on the debt) to GDP; the second is the inflation-adjusted interest rate relative to the rate of real economic growth. If the authorities can set their spending and tax policies to fully offset the effects of real interest rates and economic growth on the debt-to-GDP ratio, there's no need for the debt-to-GDP ratio to change.

Since the mid-1990s we've seen a substantial reduction in the debt-to-GDP ratio in Canada. Why? Economic growth was far above the inflation-adjusted nominal interest rate and the federal government revised its program spending and tax policies. What will happen in the future? Like any good economist, we'll answer with "it depends." As long as real interest rates remain low and economic growth stabilizes at its historical average of about 2 to 3 percent, the government can afford to increase its spending on items such as national security without substantially raising taxes. It may even be able to offer a tax cut in conjunction with an increase in spending as long as it keeps a watchful eye on the simple relationships we identified above.

Money, Banking, and the Financial Sector

After reading this chapter, you should be able to:

- Explain why the financial sector is central to almost all macroeconomic debates.

- Explain what money is.

- Enumerate the three functions of money.

- State the alternative measures of money and their primary components.

- Explain how banks create money.

- Calculate both the simple and the approximate real-world money multiplier.

- Explain how a financial panic can occur and the potential problem with government guarantees to prevent such panics.

The process by which banks create money is so simple that the mind is repelled.

John Kenneth Galbraith

Financial institutions are central to almost all macroeconomic debates. This central role is often not immediately obvious to students. In thinking about the economy, they often focus on the *real sector*—the market for the production and exchange of goods and services. In the real sector, real goods or services such as shoes, operas, automobiles, and textbooks are exchanged. That's an incomplete view of the economy. The *financial sector*—the market for the creation and exchange of financial assets such as money, stocks, and bonds—plays a central role in organizing and coordinating our economy; it makes

For every real transaction there is a financial transaction that mirrors it.

modern economic society possible. A car won't run without oil; a modern economy won't operate without a financial sector.

As we've noted throughout this book, markets make specialization and trade possible and thereby make the economy far more efficient than it otherwise would be. But the efficient use of markets requires a financial sector that facilitates and lubricates those trades. Let's consider an example of how the financial sector facilitates trade. Say you walk into a store and buy a CD. You shell out a 20-dollar bill and the salesperson hands you the CD. Easy, right? Right—but why did the salesperson give you a CD for a little piece of paper? The answer to that question is: Because the economy has a financial system that has convinced him that that piece of paper has value. To convince him (and you) of that requires an enormous structural system, called the financial sector, underlying the CD transaction and all other transactions. That financial system makes the transaction possible; without it the economy as we know it would not exist.

As long as the financial system is operating smoothly, you hardly know it's there; but should that system break down, the entire economy would be disrupted, and would either stagnate or go into a recession. That's why it is necessary to give you an overview of the financial sector as part of your foundation of macroeconomics.

In thinking about the financial sector's role, remember the following insight: *For every real transaction there is a financial transaction that mirrors it.* For example, when you buy an apple, the person selling the apple is buying 35 cents from you by spending his apple. The financial transaction is the transfer of 35 cents; the real transaction is the transfer of the apple.

For larger items, the financial transaction behind the real transaction can be somewhat complicated. When you buy a house, you'll probably pay for part of that house with a mortgage, which requires that you borrow money from a bank. The bank, in turn, borrows from individuals the money it lends to you. There's a similar financial transaction when you buy a car, or even a book, on credit.

Because there's a financial transaction reflecting every real transaction, the financial sector is important for the real sector. If you think back to the circular flow diagram, you can see the importance of the financial sector. Every time there is a flow of either goods and services or factors from one sector to another, there is financial flow in the opposite direction. If the financial sector doesn't work, the real sector doesn't work. All trade involves both the real sector and the financial sector. Thus, in this book we don't have a separate section on the steel sector or even the computer sector of the economy, but we do have a separate section on money, banking, and the financial sector of the economy.

WHY IS THE FINANCIAL SECTOR IMPORTANT TO MACRO?

The financial sector is important in macroeconomics because of its role in channelling flows out of the circular flow—such as saving—back into the circular flow, either in the form of consumer loans (such as you get when you buy something with your credit card), business loans (loans that finance business investment), or loans to government. Think of the financial sector as a gigantic channelling device, something like that shown in Figure 13-1.

The financial sector—financial markets and institutions—channels or transfers saving—outflows from the spending stream in hundreds of different forms—back into spending. This channelling device is extraordinarily complicated and requires years of study to understand fully. However, you don't need that extensive study to understand that what's interesting for macro involves the aggregates—the total amount of flows

Figure 13-1 THE FINANCIAL SECTOR AS A CONDUIT FOR SAVINGS

Financial institutions channel saving—outflows from the spending stream from various entities (government, households, and corporations)—back into the spending stream as loans to various entities (government, households, and corporations). To emphasize the fact that savings take many forms, a breakdown of the type of savings for one entity, households, is shown on the left. The same is done for loans on the right, but for corporations. Each of these loans can itself be broken down again and again until each particular loan is identified individually. The lending process is an individualistic process, and each loan is different in some way from each other loan.

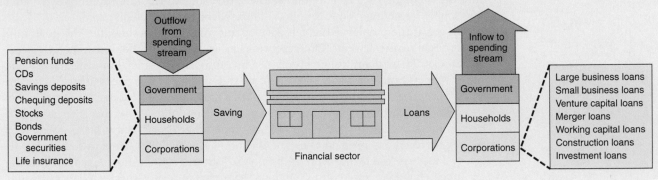

coming out of, and the total amount of flows returning to, the spending stream—and how well the financial sector does at keeping these aggregate flows matched, or expanding sufficiently to allow for real growth. If the financial sector expands the flow too much, you get inflationary pressures. If it contracts the flow too much, you get a recession. And if it transfers just the right amount, you get a smoothly running economy.

Flow from the spending stream is channelled into the financial sector as saving when individuals buy **financial assets**—*assets such as stocks or bonds, whose benefit to the owner depends on the issuer of the asset meeting certain obligations.* These obligations by the issuer of the financial asset are called financial liabilities. For every financial asset there is a corresponding financial liability. (Financial assets and liabilities are discussed in detail in Appendix A to this chapter.)

For every financial asset there is a financial liability.

The Role of Interest Rates in the Financial Sector

Price is the mechanism that equilibrates supply and demand in the real sector. Interest rates are the mechanism that equilibrates supply and demand in the financial sector. The channelling of saving into financial assets and the willingness of individuals to incur financial liabilities is strongly influenced by the interest rate on those financial assets and liabilities. In simple terms, the **interest rate** is the *price paid for the use of a financial asset.* When you deposit cash into an account, the bank pays you interest for the use of your financial asset. When the interest rate rises, people are less likely to borrow (sell a financial asset) and more likely to save (buy a financial asset). Thus, when interest rates fall, you often see more borrowing. The funds acquired from the sale of a financial asset re-enter the spending stream as consumption and investment.

When financial assets make fixed interest payments, as do most **bonds**—*promises to pay a certain amount plus interest in the future*—the price of the financial asset is determined by the market interest rate. As the market interest rate goes up, the price of the bond goes down. When the market interest rate goes down, the price of the bond goes up. Why does this relationship exist? Because when the interest rate rises, the value of the flow of payments from fixed interest rate bonds goes down since you can earn more

see page 325

The price of bonds varies inversely with the interest rate.

on new bonds that pay the new, higher interest. The only way anyone will buy the old, lower interest rate bonds is if their price falls. (For a further discussion of this inverse relationship between bond prices and current interest rates, see the present value discussion in the Appendix to Chapter 3.)

Saving That Escapes the Circular Flow

Some economists argue that the interest rate does not perfectly translate saving back into the spending stream. They don't believe that the interest rate equilibrates demand and supply for saving. When it does not, macroeconomic problems can arise.

To get at the problems that can develop, macroeconomics simplifies the flows into two types of financial assets. One type works its way back into the system: bonds, loans, and stocks. These are translated back into investment by financial intermediaries. The other type of financial asset, when held by individuals, is not necessarily assumed to work its way back into the flow—we'll call this financial asset "money."

What's important about money from a macroeconomic perspective is that, when a person holds money as opposed to holding some other financial asset, the saving that money represents is assumed to escape the circular flow. Saving held in some other financial asset is assumed to work its way back into the circular flow. Compared to the complicated maze of interconnected flows that exists in reality, this is an enormous simplification, but it captures a potentially serious problem and possible cause of fluctuations in the economy.

So let's now turn our attention to money.

THE DEFINITION AND FUNCTIONS OF MONEY

At this point you're probably saying, "I know what money is; it's currency—the dollar bills I carry around." In one sense you're right: currency is money. But in another sense you're wrong. In fact, a number of short-term financial assets are included as money. To see why, let's consider the definition of money: **Money** is *a highly liquid financial asset that's generally accepted in exchange for other goods, is used as a reference in valuing other goods, and can be stored as wealth.*

Money is a financial asset that makes the real economy function smoothly by serving as a medium of exchange, a unit of account, and a store of wealth.

To be *liquid* means to be easily changeable into another asset or good. When you buy something with money you are exchanging money for another asset. So any of your assets that are easily spendable are money. Social customs and standard practices are central to the liquidity of money. The reason you are willing to hold money is that you know someone else will accept it in trade for something else. Its value is determined by its general acceptability to others. If you don't believe that, try spending yuan (Chinese money) in Canada. If you try to buy dinner with 100 yuan, you will be told, "No way—give me money."

The Canadian Central Bank: The Bank of Canada

So is there any characteristic other than general acceptability that gives value to money? Consider the five-dollar bill that you know is money. Look at it. It states right on the bill that it is legal tender, which means that it is an IOU (a liability) of the **Bank of Canada**—*the Canadian central bank whose liabilities (bank notes) serve as cash in Canada.* Individuals are willing to accept the Bank of Canada's IOUs in return for real goods and services, which means that Bank of Canada notes are money.

What, you ask, is a central bank? To answer that question we had better first consider what a bank is. A **bank** is *a financial institution whose primary function is holding* *money for, and lending money to, individuals and firms*. (There are more complicated definitions and many types of banks, but that will do for now; the issues are discussed more fully in Appendix A to this chapter.) You have extra currency? Take it to the bank and it will "hold" the extra for you, giving you a piece of paper (or a computer entry) that says you have that much currency held here ("hold" is in quotation marks because the bank does not actually hold the currency). What the bank used to give you was a bank note, and what you used to bring in to the bank was gold, but those days are gone forever. These days what you bring is that Bank of Canada note described above, and what you get is a paper receipt and a computer entry in your chequing or savings account. Individuals' deposits in these accounts serve the same purpose as does currency and are also considered money.

Which brings us back to the Bank of Canada, the Canadian central bank. It is a bank that has the right to issue notes (IOUs). By law these notes are acceptable payment for people's taxes, and by convention these notes are acceptable payment to all people in Canada, and to many people outside Canada. IOUs of the Bank of Canada are what most of you think of as cash.

To understand why money is more than just cash, it is helpful to consider the functions of money in more detail. Having done so, we will consider which financial assets are included in various measures of money.

Functions of Money

As we stated above, money is an asset that can be quickly exchanged for any other asset or good. This definition says money serves three functions:

1. It serves as a medium of exchange.
2. It serves as a unit of account.
3. It serves as a store of wealth.

To get a better understanding of what money is, let's consider each of its functions in turn.

Money as a Medium of Exchange The easiest way to understand money's medium-of-exchange use is to imagine what an economy would be like without money. Say you want something to eat at a restaurant. Without money you'd have to barter with the restaurant owner for your meal. *Barter* is a direct exchange of goods and/or services. You might suggest bartering one of your papers or the shirt in the sack that you'd be forced to carry with you to trade for things you want. Not liking to carry big sacks around, you'd probably decide to fix your own meal and forgo eating out. Bartering is simply too difficult. Money makes many more trades possible because it does not require a double coincidence of wants by two individuals, as simple barter does.

The use of money as a medium of exchange makes it possible to trade real goods and services without bartering. It facilitates exchange by reducing the cost of trading. Instead of carrying around a sack full of diverse goods, all you need to carry around is a billfold full of money. You go into the restaurant and pay for your meal with money; the restaurant owner can spend (trade) that money for anything she wants.

Money doesn't have to have any inherent value to function as a medium of exchange. All that's necessary is that everyone believes that other people will accept it in exchange for their goods. This neat social convention makes the economy more efficient.

That social convention depends on there not being too much or too little money. If there's too much money compared to the goods and services offered at existing prices, the goods and services will sell out, and money won't buy you anything. The social convention will break down, or prices will rise. If there's too little money compared to the goods and services offered at the existing prices, there will be a shortage of money and

The three functions of money are:

1. Medium of exchange;
2. Unit of account; and
3. Store of wealth.

13.2

see page 325

Money doesn't have to have any inherent value to function as a medium of exchange.

Q.2 Since the cost of printing money is low compared to its value, why doesn't the Bank of Canada print up lots of money?

people will have to resort to barter, or prices will fall. Since the Bank of Canada controls the supply of money, it also controls the value of money as a medium of exchange.

People accept money in payment and agree to hold money because they believe the Bank of Canada, and the banks the Bank of Canada regulates, will issue neither too little nor too much money. This explains why the Bank of Canada doesn't freely issue large amounts of money and why it controls (or at least tries to control) the amount of money banks issue. To issue money without restraint would destroy the social convention that gives money its value.

Money as a Unit of Account A second use of money is as a unit of account. Money prices are actually relative prices. A nominal price, say 25 cents, for a pencil conveys the information of a relative price: 1 pencil = ¼ of 1 dollar or ⅙ of a hamburger because money is both our unit of account and our medium of exchange. When you think of 25 cents you think of ¼ of a dollar and of what a dollar will buy. The 25 cents a pencil costs only has meaning relative to the information you've stored in your mind about what it can buy. If a hamburger costs $1.50, you can compare hamburgers and pencils (1 pencil = ⅙ of a hamburger) without making the relative price calculations explicitly.

Having a unit of account makes life much easier. For example, say we had no unit of account and you had to remember the relative prices of all goods. For instance, with three goods you'd have to memorize that an airplane ticket to Fredericton costs 6 lobster dinners in Halifax or 4 pairs of running shoes, which makes a pair of shoes worth 1½ lobster dinners.

Memorizing even a few relationships is hard enough, so it isn't surprising that societies began using a single unit of account. If you don't have a single unit of account, all combinations of 100 goods will require that you remember almost 5,000 relative prices. If you have a single unit of account, you need know only 100 prices. A single unit of account saves our limited memories and helps us make reasonable decisions based on relative costs.

Money is a useful unit of account only as long as its value relative to other prices doesn't change too quickly.

Money is a useful unit of account only as long as its value relative to the average of all other prices doesn't change too quickly. That's because it's not only used as a unit of account at a point in time, it's also a unit of account *over time*. Money is a standard of deferred payment. The value of payments that will be made in the future (such as the loan payments many of you will be making in the future) is determined by the future value of money. Again, the Bank of Canada plays a central role in money's usefulness as a unit of account. If the Bank of Canada printed excessive currency to pay all the government's expenses, money's relative price would fall quickly (an increase in supply lowers price), which is another way of saying that the price level would explode and the unit-of-account function of money would be seriously undermined.

Maintaining the unit-of-account usefulness of money is a second reason the Bank of Canada doesn't pay all the government's bills by printing money. Consider a loan. Hyperinflation would significantly reduce the value of what you have to pay back. So hyperinflation would help you, right? Actually, probably not—because hyperinflation would also rapidly destroy money's usefulness as a store of value and unit of account, thereby destroying the Canadian economy.

In hyperinflation, all prices rise so much that our frame of reference is lost.

As described in an earlier chapter, in hyperinflation, all prices rise so much that our frame of reference for making relative price comparisons is lost. Is 25 cents for a pencil high or low? If the price level increased 33,000 percent (as it did in 1988 in Nicaragua) or over 100,000 percent (as it did in 1993 in Serbia), 25 cents for a pencil would definitely be low, but would $100 be low? Without a lot of calculations we can't answer that question. A relatively stable unit of account makes it easy to answer.

Given the advantages to society of having a unit of account, it's not surprising that a monetary unit of account develops even in societies with no central bank or government. For example, in a prisoner of war camp during the Second World War, prisoners had no money, so they used cigarettes as their unit of account. Everything traded was given a price in cigarettes. The exchange rates on December 1, 1944, were:

    1 bar of soap: 2 cigarettes

    1 candy bar: 4 cigarettes

    1 razor blade: 6 cigarettes

    1 can of fruit: 8 cigarettes

    1 can of cookies: 20 cigarettes

As you can see, all prices were in cigarettes. If candy bars rose to 6 cigarettes and the normal price was 4 cigarettes, you'd know the price of candy bars was high.

Money as a Store of Wealth When you save, you forgo consumption now so that you can consume in the future. To bridge the gap between now and the future, you must acquire a financial asset. This is true even if you squirrel away currency under the mattress. In that case, the financial asset you've acquired is simply the currency itself. Money is a financial asset. (It's simply a bond that pays no interest.) So a third use of money is as a store of wealth. As long as money is serving as a medium of exchange, it automatically also serves as a store of wealth. The restaurant owner can accept your money and hold it for as long as she wants before she spends it. (But had you paid her in fish, she'd be wise not to hold it more than a few hours.)

Money's usefulness as a store of wealth also depends on how well it maintains its value. If prices are going up 100,000 percent per year, the value of a stated amount of money is shrinking fast. People want to spend their money as quickly as possible before prices rise any more. Thus, once again, money's usefulness as a social convention depends on the Bank of Canada not issuing too much money.

Even if prices aren't rising, you might wonder why people would hold money that pays no interest. Put another way: Why do people hold a government bond that pays no interest? The reason is that money, by definition, is highly liquid—it is more easily translated into other goods than are other financial assets. Since money is also the medium of exchange, it can be spent instantaneously (as long as there's a shop open nearby). Our ability to spend money for goods makes money worthwhile to hold even if it doesn't pay interest.

Canada's first paper money was issued in 1685 in Quebec, then called New France. Playing cards, signed by the king of France, were used as the medium of exchange. The cards were given to soldiers who accepted them as legal tender. Sometimes, corners of the cards were cut off to indicate smaller denominations. This is strong testimony that money is what people accept as money.

> As long as money is serving as a medium of exchange, it automatically also serves as a store of wealth.

Q.3 Why do people hold money rather than bonds when bonds pay higher interest than money?

ALTERNATIVE MEASURES OF MONEY

According to the definition of *money*, what people believe is money and what people will accept as money are determining factors in deciding whether a financial asset is money. Consequently, it's difficult to measure *money* unambiguously. A number of different financial assets serve some of the functions of money and thus have claims to being called *money*. To handle this ambiguity, economists have developed different measures of money and have called them M_1, M_2, M_3, M_1+, M_2+, and M_2++. Each is a reasonable concept of money. Let's consider their components.[1]

M_1

M_1 consists of *currency in circulation and chequing account balances at chartered banks.* Clearly, currency in circulation (the bills and coins you carry around with you) are

> M_1 is the component of the money supply that consists of currency in circulation plus chequing accounts at chartered banks.

---

[1]There are many measures of money. We'll discuss some of them here. To learn everything you've ever wanted to know about measuring money, see Web Question 13.3.

The characteristics of a good money are that its supply be relatively constant, that it be limited in supply (sand wouldn't make good money), that it be difficult to counterfeit, that it be divisible (have you ever tried to spend half a horse?), that it be durable (raspberries wouldn't make good money), and that it be relatively small and light compared to its value (watermelon wouldn't make good money either). All these characteristics were reasonably (but not perfectly) embodied in gold. Many other goods have served as units of account (shells, wampum, rocks, cattle, horses, silver), but gold historically became the most important money, and in the 17th and 18th centuries gold was synonymous with money.

But gold has flaws as money. It's relatively heavy, easy to counterfeit with coins made only partly of gold, and, when new gold fields are discovered, subject to fluctuations in supply. These flaws led to gold's replacement by paper currency backed only by trust that the government would keep its commitment to limit its supply.

Paper money can be a good money if somehow people can trust the government to limit its supply and guarantee that its supply will be limited in the future. That trust has not always been well placed.

money, but how about your chequing account deposits? The reason they're included in this measure of money is that just about anything you can do with currency, you can do with a cheque. You can store your wealth in your chequing account; you can use a cheque as a medium of exchange (indeed, for some transactions you have no choice but to use a cheque), and your chequing account balance is denominated in the same unit of account (dollars) as is currency. If it looks like money, acts like money, and functions as money, it's a good bet it's money. Indeed, chequing account deposits are included in all measures of money.

Figure 13-2 presents the relative sizes of M_1's components.

M_2

M_2 is the component of the money supply that consists of M_1 plus other relatively liquid assets at chartered banks.

M_2 is made up of M_1 *plus personal savings deposits and nonpersonal notice deposits (deposits that can be withdrawn only after prior notice) held at chartered banks*. The relative sizes of the components of M_2 are given in Figure 13-2.

The money in savings accounts (savings deposits) is counted as money because it is readily spendable—all you need do is go to the bank and draw it out. Some time deposits are also called *certificates of deposit (CDs)*, or term deposits.

Q.4 Which would be a larger number, M_1 or M_2? Why?

M_2's components include more financial assets than M_1. All its components are highly liquid and play an important role in providing reserves and lending capacity for chartered banks. What makes the M_2 measure important is that economic research has shown that M_2 is one of the measures of money often most closely correlated with the price level and economic activity.

Beyond M_2: "The Pluses"

The broadest definition of the money supply is M_2++.

An even wider variety of financial assets also have some of the attributes of money. They're liquid and can be "spent" relatively easily. For that reason they're included in some measures of money. There are measures for M_3, M_1+, M_2+, and beyond. Most economists concern themselves with relatively broad measures of money, the broadest of which is M_2++. M_2++ includes almost all assets that can be turned into cash on short notice. In the 1980s and 1990s the frequent introduction of new types of bank accounts made it difficult to come up with an unchanging measure of money. Because of that dif-

Figure 13-2   COMPONENTS OF M₂ AND M₁

Two measures of the money supply are M_1 and M_2. The two primary components of M_1 are currency in circulation and chequing accounts at chartered banks. M_2 includes all of M_1, plus personal savings deposits and nonpersonal notice deposits at chartered banks.

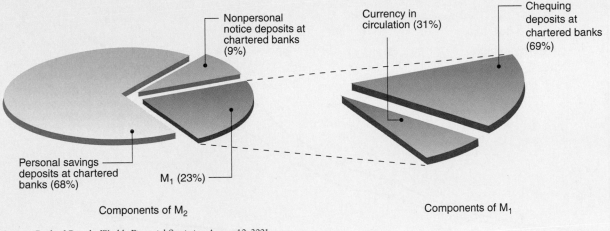

Nonpersonal notice deposits at chartered banks (9%)

Currency in circulation (31%)

Chequing deposits at chartered banks (69%)

Personal savings deposits at chartered banks (68%)

M_1 (23%)

Components of M_2

Components of M_1

Source: Bank of Canada, Weekly Financial Statistics, August 10, 2001.

ficulty, measures of money have lost some of their appeal, and broader concepts of asset liquidity have gained greater appeal.

No doubt you'll have noticed the plus ("+") signs on some of the definitions of money. Measures of money such as M_1, M_2, and M_3 only include deposits held at *chartered banks*. These are financial institutions that meet all of the legal conditions to be called a *bank* in Canada. There are a host of other institutions that offer deposits similar to banks but these intermediaries cannot legally call themselves banks. These *near banks* offer savings and chequing accounts too, so the measures of money that include "+" signs add these near bank deposits to give a more accurate measure of money in Canada. Indeed, M_2+ is the most widely analyzed measure of money in Canada.

Various measures of the Canadian money supply are plotted in Figure 13-3. Notice that as the definition is expanded to include savings deposits and deposits at near banks, the measured money supply changes by a large amount. In mid-2001, the Canadian money supply was either $114 billion or $724 billion. This makes monetary policy a bit difficult to implement in practice, since there are so many different ways to measure money.

Distinguishing between Money and Credit

You might have thought that credit cards would be included in one of the measures of *money*. But we didn't include them. In fact, credit cards are nowhere to be seen in a list of financial assets. Credit cards aren't a financial liability of the bank that issues them. Instead credit cards create a liability for their users (money owed to the company or bank that issued the card) and the banks have a financial asset as a result.

Let's consider how a credit card works. You go into a store and buy something with your credit card. You have a real asset—the item you bought. The store has a financial asset—an account receivable. The store sells that financial asset at a slight discount to

13.3

see page 325

Credit card balances cannot be money since they are assets of a bank. In a sense, they are the opposite of money.

Figure 13-3   **MEASURES OF MONEY IN CANADA: M_1, M_2, AND M_2+**

Financial innovation has led to large differences in our measures of money. M_2+ is one of the widest definitions and includes M_2 as well as deposits in near banks. M_2++ is the broadest definition of money in Canada (see Web Question 13.3 to see how it differs from M_2+).

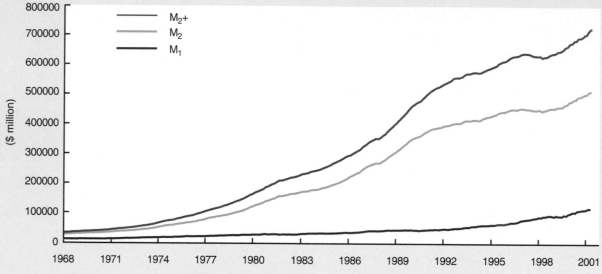

Source: Statistics Canada, CANSIM II, Table 176-0025.

the bank and gets cash in return. Either the bank collects cash when you pay off your financial liability or, if you don't pay it off, the bank earns interest on its financial asset (usually at a high rate, about 18 percent per year). Credit cards are essentially prearranged loans.

This distinction between credit and money should be kept in mind. Money is a financial asset of individuals and a financial liability of banks. Credit is savings made available to be borrowed. Credit is not an asset of the borrowing public.

Credit cards and credit affect the amount of money people hold. When preapproved loan credit is instantly available (as it is with a credit card) there's less need to hold money. (If you didn't have a credit card, you'd carry a lot more currency.) With credit immediately available, liquidity is less valuable to people. So credit and credit cards do make a difference in how much money people hold, but because they are not financial assets, they are not money.

Now that we've considered what money is, both in theory and in practice, let's consider the banking system's role in creating money, and what happens if individuals start holding their assets as some form of money rather than as bonds or some other financial asset.

BANKS AND THE CREATION OF MONEY

Banks are financial institutions that borrow from people (take in deposits) and use the money they borrow to make loans to other individuals. Banks make a profit by charging a higher interest on the money they lend out than they pay for the money they borrow.

APPLYING THE TOOLS

Financial Innovation

At one time the only chequing accounts were those of chartered banks. You put your money in a chartered bank and wrote a cheque. Then banks started allowing individuals to write cheques on their savings accounts. So if you held $10,000 in a savings account you could write an IOU to someone and the bank promised to pay it. That IOU looked like a cheque, and for all practical purposes it was a cheque. But unlike a chequing account, these new accounts paid interest on depositors' balances. Many people started shifting from chequing accounts to chequable savings accounts.

Mutual funds saw how nicely these accounts worked and decided to imitate them. The mutual fund invested depositors' money in the money market (short-term bills, commercial paper, and CDs) and allowed individuals to write cheques on these accounts. These brokerage accounts pay slightly higher interest than chequing accounts but have cheque-writing restrictions and do not have the same guarantees.

So today people have a choice of depository institutions, which is nice for people, but tough for textbook writers and students who have to learn more divisions.

Individuals keep their money in banks, accepting lower interest rates, because doing so is safer and more convenient than the alternatives.

Banking is generally analyzed from the perspective of **asset management** (*how a bank handles its loans and other assets*) and **liability management** (*how a bank attracts deposits and what it pays for them*). When banks offer people "free chequing" and special accounts paying 4 percent, they do so after carefully considering the costs of those liabilities to them.

To think of banks as borrowers as well as lenders may seem a bit unusual, but borrowing is what they do. When you own a savings account or a chequing account, the bank is borrowing from you, paying you a zero (or low) interest rate. It then lends your money to other people at a high interest rate.

> It is important to think of banks as both borrowers and lenders.

How Banks Create Money

Banks are centrally important to macroeconomics because they create money. How do banks create money? As John Kenneth Galbraith's epigram at the start of this chapter suggests, the process is simple—so simple it seems almost magical to many.

The key to understanding how banks create money is to remember the nature of financial assets: Financial assets can be created from nothing as long as an offsetting financial liability is simultaneously created. Since money is any financial asset that can be used as a medium of exchange, unit of account, and store of value, money can be created rather easily. The asset just needs to serve the functions of money. Seeing how bank notes are created is the easiest way to begin examining the process. Whenever the Bank of Canada issues an IOU, it creates money. Similarly, other banks create money by creating financial assets that serve the functions of money. As we saw when we considered the measures of *money*, bank chequing accounts serve those functions, so they are money, just as currency is money. When a bank places the proceeds of a loan it makes to you in your chequing account, it is creating money. You have a financial asset that did not previously exist.

> Banks "create" money because a bank's liabilities are defined as money. So when a bank incurs liabilities it creates money.

The First Step in the Creation of Money To see how banks create money, let's consider what would happen if you were given a freshly printed $100 bill. Remember, the central bank created that $100 bill simply by printing it. The $100 bill is a $100 financial asset of yours and a financial liability of the Bank of Canada, which issued it.

If the process of creating money stopped there, it wouldn't be particularly mysterious. But it doesn't stop there. Let's consider what happens next as you use that money.

The Second Step in the Creation of Money The second step in the creation of money involves the transfer of money from one form to another—from currency to a bank deposit. Say you decide to put the $100 bill in your chequing account. To make the analysis easier, let's assume that your bank is a branch of the country's only bank, Big Bank. All money deposited in branch banks goes into Big Bank. After you make your deposit, Big Bank is holding $100 currency for you, and you have $100 more in your chequing account. You can spend it whenever you want simply by writing a cheque. So Big Bank is performing a service for you (holding your money and keeping track of your expenditures) for free. Neat, huh? Big Bank must be run by a bunch of nice people.

But wait. You and we know that bankers, while they may be nice, aren't as nice as all that. There's no such thing as a free lunch. Let's see why the bank is being so nice.

Banking and Goldsmiths To see why banks are so nice, let's go way back in history to when banks first developed.[2] At that time, gold was used for money and people carried around gold to make their payments. But gold is rather heavy, so if they had to make a big purchase, it was difficult to pay for the purchase. Moreover, carrying around a lot of gold left them vulnerable to being robbed by the likes of Robin Hood. So they looked for a place to store their gold until they needed some of it.

From Gold to Gold Receipts The natural place to store gold was the goldsmith shop, which already had a vault. For a small fee, the goldsmith shop would hold your gold, giving you a receipt for it. Whenever you needed your gold, you'd go to the goldsmith and exchange the receipt for gold.

Pretty soon most people kept their gold at the goldsmith's, and they began to wonder: Why go through the bother of getting my gold out to buy something when all that happens is that the seller takes the gold I pay and puts it right back into the goldsmith's vault. That's two extra trips.

Consequently, people began using the receipts the goldsmith gave them to certify that they had deposited $100 worth (or whatever) of gold in his vault. At that point gold was no longer the only money—gold receipts were also money since they were accepted in exchange for goods. However, as long as the total amount in the gold receipts directly represented the total amount of gold, it was still reasonable to say, since the receipts were 100 percent backed by gold, that gold was the money supply.

Q.5 Most banks prefer to have many depositors rather than one big depositor. Why?

Gold Receipts Become Money Once this process of using the receipts rather than the gold became generally accepted, the goldsmith found that he had substantial amounts of gold in his vault. All that gold, just sitting there! On a normal day only 1 percent of the gold was claimed by "depositors" and had to be given out. Usually on the same day an amount at least equal to that 1 percent came in from other depositors. What a waste! Gold sitting around doing nothing! So when a good friend came in, needing a loan, the goldsmith said, "Sure, I'll lend you some gold receipts as long as you pay me some interest." When the goldsmith made this loan, he created more gold receipts than he had covered in gold in his vault. He created money.

---

[2]The banking history reported here is, according to historians, apocryphal (more myth than reality). But it so nicely makes the point that we repeat it anyhow.

Pretty soon the goldsmith realized he could earn more from the interest he received on loans than he could earn from goldsmithing. So he stopped goldsmithing and went full-time into making loans of gold receipts. At that point the number of gold receipts outstanding significantly exceeded the amount of gold in the goldsmith's vaults. But not to worry; since everyone was willing to accept gold receipts rather than gold, the goldsmith had plenty of gold for those few who wanted actual gold.

It was, however, no longer accurate to say that gold was the country's money or currency. Gold receipts were the money. They met the definition of *money*. These gold receipts were backed partially by gold and partially by people's trust that the goldsmiths would pay off their deposits on demand. The goldsmith shops had become banks.

Banking Is Profitable The banking business was very profitable for goldsmiths. Soon other people started competing with them, offering to hold gold for free. After all, if they could store gold, they could make a profit on the loans to other people (with the first people's money). Some even offered to pay people to store their gold.

The goldsmith story is directly relevant to banks. People store their currency in banks and the banks issue receipts—chequing accounts—that become a second form of money. When people place their currency in banks and use their receipts from the bank as money, those receipts also become money because they meet the definition of *money*: They serve as a medium of exchange, a unit of account, and a store of wealth. So money includes both currency that people hold and their deposits in the bank.

Which brings us back to why banks hold your currency for free. They do it not because they're nice, but because when you deposit currency in the bank, your deposit allows banks to make profitable loans they otherwise couldn't make.

The Money Multiplier

With that background, let's go back to your $100, which the bank is now holding for you. You have a chequing account balance of $100 and the bank has $100 currency. As long as other people are willing to accept your cheque in payment for $100 worth of goods, your cheque is as good as money. In fact it *is* money in the same way gold receipts were money. But when you deposit $100, no additional money has been created yet. The form of the money has simply been changed from currency to a chequing account or demand deposit.

Now let's say Big Bank lends out 90 percent of the currency you deposit, keeping only 10 percent as **reserves**—*currency and deposits a bank keeps on hand or at the central bank, enough to manage the normal cash inflows and outflows*. This 10 percent is the **desired reserve ratio** (*the ratio of reserves to total deposits*). Banks used to be required by the Bank of Canada to hold a percentage of deposits; that percentage was called the required reserve ratio. Banks could also choose to hold an additional percentage, called the excess reserve ratio. Today, Canadian banks are no longer required by law to hold reserves against their deposits, although in practice banks do hold desired reserves to meet the demand for currency, to settle cheques with one another, and to facilitate the day-to-day transactions the banks' customers make. The reserve ratio is the sum of the desired reserve ratio and the excess reserve ratio. Thus, it is at least as large as the desired reserved ratio, but it can be larger.

So, like the goldsmith, Big Bank lends out $90 to someone who qualifies for a loan. That person the bank loaned the money to now has $90 currency and you have $100 in a demand deposit, so now there's $190 of money, rather than just $100 of money. The $10 in currency the bank holds in reserve isn't counted as money since the bank holds it as reserves and will not use it as long as it's backing loans. Only currency held by the

Money is whatever meets the definition of money.

The desired reserve ratio is the ratio of currency (or deposits at the central bank) to deposits a bank keeps as a reserve against currency withdrawals.

public, not currency held by banks, is counted as money. By making the loan, the bank has created $90 in money.

Of course, no one borrows money just to hold it. The borrower spends the money, say on a new sweater, and the sweater store owner now has the $90 in currency. The store owner doesn't want to hold it either. She'll deposit it back into the bank. Since there's only one bank, Big Bank discovers that the $90 it has loaned out is once again in its coffers. The money operates like a boomerang: Big Bank loans $90 out and gets the $90 back again.

The same process occurs again. The bank doesn't earn interest income by holding $90, so if the bank can find additional credible borrowers, it lends out $81, keeping $9 (10 percent of $90) in reserve. The story repeats and repeats itself, with a slightly smaller amount coming back to the bank each time. At each step in the process, money (in the form of chequing account deposits) is being created.

Determining How Many Demand Deposits Will Be Created What's the total amount of demand deposits that will ultimately be created from your $100 when individuals hold no currency? To answer that question, we continue the process over and over: $100 + 90 + 81 + 72.9 + 65.6 + 59 + 53.1 + 47.8 + 43.0 + 38.7 + 34.9$. Adding up these numbers gives us $686. Adding up $686 plus the numbers from the next 20 rounds gives us $961.08. As we add more and more rounds, the number eventually converges to $1,000.

As you can see, that's a lot of adding. Luckily there's an easier way. Economists have shown that you can determine the amount of money that will eventually be created by such a process by multiplying the initial $100 in money that was printed by the Bank of Canada and deposited by $1/r$, where r is the desired reserve ratio (the percentage banks keep out of each round). In this case the desired reserve ratio is 10 percent.

Dividing,

$$\frac{1}{r} = \frac{1}{0.10} = 10$$

so the amount of demand deposits that will ultimately exist at the end of the process is

$$(10 \times \$100) = \$1,000$$

The $1,000 is in the form of chequing account deposits (demand deposits). The entire $100 in currency that you were given, and that started the whole process, is in the bank as reserves, which means that $900 ($1,000 − $100) of money has been created by the process.

The money multiplier is the measure of the amount of money ultimately created per dollar deposited by the banking system. When people hold no currency it equals $1/r$.

Calculating the Money Multiplier The ratio $1/r$ is called the **simple money multiplier**—*the measure of the amount of money ultimately created per dollar deposited in the banking system, when people hold no currency*. It tells us how much money will ultimately be created by the banking system from an initial inflow of money. In our example, $1/0.10 = 10$. Had the bank kept out 20 percent each time, the money multiplier would have been $1/0.20 = 5$. If the reserve ratio were 5 percent, the money multiplier would have been $1/0.05 = 20$. The higher the reserve ratio, the smaller the money multiplier, and the less money will be created.

An Example of the Creation of Money[3] To make sure you understand the process, let's consider an example. Say that the desired reserve ratio is 20 percent and that Jean Finder finds $10,000 in currency, which he deposits in the bank. Thus, he has $10,000

---

[3]The first three rounds of this example are shown in Appendix B, using T-accounts.

TABLE 13-1   The Money-Creating Process

In the money-creating process, the currency keeps coming back to the banking system like a boomerang. With a 20 percent desired reserve ratio ultimately ($\frac{1}{0.2}$) × $10,000 = $50,000 will be created. In this example you can see that after 10 rounds, most of the creation of deposits will have taken place. As you carry out the analysis further, the money creation will approach the $50,000 shown in the last line.

Bank Gets	Bank Keeps (Desired Reserve Ratio: 20%)	Bank Loans (80%) = Person Borrows
$10,000	$2,000	$ 8,000
8,000	1,600	6,400
6,400	1,280	5,120
5,120	1,024	4,096
4,096	819	3,277
3,277	656	2,621
2,621	524	2,097
2,097	419	1,678
1,678	336	1,342
1,342	268	1,074
$44,631 (total deposits)	$8,926	+	$35,705

Total money existing (after 10 rounds) = $44,631
Eventual total money creation (after infinite rounds)

| $50,000 (total deposits) | $10,000 | + | $40,000 |

in his chequing account and the bank has $8,000 ($10,000 − $2,000 in reserves) to lend out. Once it lends that money to Fred Baker, there is $8,000 of additional money in the economy. Fred Baker uses the money to buy a new oven from Mary Builder, who, in turn, deposits the money back into the banking system. Big Bank lends out $6,400 (8,000 − $1,600 in reserves).

Now the process occurs again. Table 13-1 shows the effects of the process for 10 rounds, starting with the initial $10,000. Each time it lends the money out, the money returns like a boomerang and serves as reserves for more loans. After 10 rounds we reach a point where total demand deposits are $44,631, and the bank has $8,926 in reserves. This is approaching the $50,000 we'd arrive at using the money multiplier:

$$\frac{1}{r}(\$10,000) = \frac{1}{0.2}(\$10,000) = 5(\$10,000) = \$50,000$$

If we carried it out for more rounds, we'd actually reach what the formula predicted.

Note that the process ends only when the bank holds all the currency in the economy, and the only money held by the public is in the form of demand deposits. Notice also that the total amount of money created depends on the amount banks hold in reserve.

To see that you understand the process, say that banks suddenly get concerned about the safety of their loans, and they decide to keep **excess reserves**—*reserves held by banks in excess of what banks desire to hold*. What will happen to the money multiplier? If you answered that it will decrease, you've got it. Excess reserves decrease the money multiplier as much as desired reserves do. We mention this example because this is precisely what happened to the banking system in the early 1990s. Banks became concerned about the safety of their loans; they held large excess reserves, and the money multiplier decreased.

In summary, the process of money creation isn't difficult to understand as long as you remember that money is simply a bank's financial liability held by the public. Whenever banks create financial liabilities for themselves, they create financial assets for individuals, and those financial assets are money.

Calculating the Approximate Real-World Money Multiplier In the example we assumed that only banks hold currency. The simple money multiplier reflects that assumption. In reality banks are not the only holders of currency. Firms and individuals hold currency too, so in each round we must also make an adjustment in the multiplier for what people and firms hold. The math you need to calculate the money multiplier formally gets a bit complicated when firms and people hold currency. Since for our purposes a rough calculation is all we need, we will use an approximate money multiplier in which individuals' currency holdings are treated the same as reserves of banks. Thus, the **approximate real-world money multiplier** in the economy is:

$$\frac{1}{(r + c)}$$

where r = *the percentage of deposits banks desire to hold in reserve* and c is the *ratio of money people hold in currency to the money they hold as deposits*.[4] Let's consider an example. Say the banks keep 10 percent in reserve and the ratio of individuals' currency holdings to their deposits is 25 percent. This means the approximate real-world money multiplier will be

$$\frac{1}{(0.1 + 0.25)} = \frac{1}{0.35} = 2.9$$

Faith as the Backing of Our Money Supply

The creation of money and the money multiplier are easy to understand if you remember that money held in the form of a chequing account (the financial asset created) is offset by an equal amount of financial liabilities of the bank. The bank owes its depositors the amount in their chequing accounts. Its financial liabilities to depositors, in turn, are secured by the loans (the bank's financial assets) and by the financial liabilities of people to whom the loans were made. Promises to pay underlie any modern financial system.

The initial money in the story about the goldsmiths was gold, but it quickly became apparent that it was far more reasonable to use gold certificates as money. Therefore, gold certificates backed by gold soon replaced gold itself as the money supply. Then, as goldsmiths made more loans than they had gold, the gold certificates were no longer backed by gold. They were backed by promises to get gold if the person wanted gold in exchange for the gold certificate. Eventually the percentage of gold supposedly backing

When people hold currency the approximate money multiplier is $1/(r + c)$.

Q-6 If banks desire to hold 20 percent of their deposits as reserves, and the ratio of money people hold as currency to deposits is 20 percent, what is the approximate money multiplier?

Q-7 If people suddenly decide to hold more currency, what happens to the size of the approximate money multiplier?

---

[4]The precise money multiplier when individuals hold currency is $(1 + c)/(r + c)$.

APPLYING THE TOOLS

The Real-World Money Multiplier and Recent Reforms in Banking

Life keeps getting tougher. In the old days (as recently as the 1980s), economics students only had to learn the simple money multiplier. Recent reforms in the Canadian banking system have made that impossible. In the late 1980s and early 1990s, the Bank of Canada eliminated required reserves. Required reserves were set as a complicated fraction of a chartered banks' deposits, with the fraction set higher than the bank would otherwise want to hold. Required reserves were supposed to provide a degree of liquidity to the banking system because they forced the banks to hold more cash than they would like. Non-bank financial institutions such as credit unions and caisses populaires didn't face the same requirement. They weren't forced to tie up large sums of cash as reserves that weren't paying interest. Remember that financial institutions profit by lending out their excess reserves, so reserve requirements actually constrained the way that banks could behave. In fact, the chartered banks had been crying foul for some time, arguing they faced an unfair "reserve tax."

The government decided they were right. Members of the Canadian Payments Association (chartered banks and other financial intermediaries) simply need to maintain an average clearing balance of zero (on a daily basis) with the Bank of Canada over the specified period. *Clearing* refers to the process in which claims drawn against different chartered banks and other financial intermediaries are satisfied by transferring funds between their accounts at the Bank of Canada.

If you insert a value for the reserve ratio of zero into the simple money supply multiplier, you get a multiplier approaching infinity (any number over a very small number tends to be a very large number). The real-world money multiplier is much lower than that because banks always want to hold a certain proportion of their deposits as reserves against the clearing process and the demand for currency from the public.

the money became so small that it was clear to everyone that the promises, not the gold, underlay the money supply.

Today, all that backs the modern money supply are bank loan customers' promises to pay and the guarantee of the government to see that the bank's liabilities to individuals will be met.

All that backs the modern money supply are bank loan customers' promises to pay and government guarantees of banks' liabilities to individuals.

REGULATION OF BANKS AND THE FINANCIAL SECTOR

You just saw how easy it is to create money. The banking system and money make the economy operate more efficiently, but they also present potential problems. For example, say that for some reason suddenly there's an increase in money (that is, in promises to pay) without any corresponding increase in real goods and services. As the money supply increases without an increase in real goods and services to buy with that money, more money is chasing the same number of goods. The result will be a fall in the value of money (inflation), meaning real trade will be more complicated. Alternatively, if there's an increase in real goods and services but not a corresponding increase in money, there will be a shortage of money, which will hamper the economy. Either the price level will fall (deflation) or there will be a recession.

Financial Panics

Societies have continually experienced these problems, and the financial history of the world is filled with stories of financial upheavals and monetary problems. For example, there are numerous instances of private financial firms that have promised the world, but whose promises have been nothing but hot air. One instance occurred in the 1800s when banks were allowed to issue their own notes (their own promises to pay). These notes served as part of the money supply. Sharp financial operators soon got into the process and issued notes even though they had no deposits, hoping that no one would cash the notes in. Many such banks defaulted on their promises, leaving holders of the notes with only worthless pieces of paper. Merchants quickly caught on, and soon they began checking in a "book of notes" that told whether the notes the buyer was offering were probably good or not.

Anatomy of a Financial Panic

Financial systems are based on trust that expectations will be fulfilled. Banks borrow short and lend long, which means that if people lose faith in banks, the banks cannot keep their promises.

Banking and financial systems are based on promises and trust. People exchange their currency for other financial assets (such as demand deposits) and believe that these demand deposits are as good as currency. In normal times, demand deposits really are as good as currency. When times get bad, people become concerned about the financial firms' ability to keep those promises and they call on the firms to redeem the chequing account promises. But banks have only their reserves (a small percentage of their total deposits) to give depositors. Most of the depositors' assets are loaned out and cannot be collectively gotten back quickly, even though the banks have promised depositors that their deposits will be given back "on demand." Put another way, banks' borrowing is short-term while its lending is long-term; banks borrow short and lend long.

Q.8 Why does borrowing short and lending long present a potential problem for banks?

When a lot of depositors lose faith in a bank and, all at one time, call on the bank to keep its promise to provide currency in exchange for their chequing account balances, the bank cannot do so. The result is that the bank fails when depositors lose faith, even though the bank might be financially sound for the long run. Fear underlies financial panics and can undermine financial institutions unless the banks can convert their earning assets into currency quickly.

Government Policy to Prevent Panic

To prevent such panics, various levels of government guarantee the obligations of many financial institutions. The Canada Deposit Insurance Corporation (CDIC) was created in 1967. It provides a guarantee of up to $60,000 on deposits at all chartered banks and federally incorporated trust and mortgage loan companies. The Quebec Deposit Insurance Board, also established in 1967, guarantees deposits in credit unions and caisses populaires and other institutions in Quebec (but not deposits in chartered banks operating in Quebec). A number of provinces also offer protection to depositers in local area financial institutions. In most cases the guarantees work as follows: The financial institutions pay a small premium for each dollar of deposit to the government-organized insurance company. That company puts the premium into a fund used to bail out banks experiencing a run on deposits. These guarantees have two effects:

Q.9 What are two effects that a government guarantee of financial institutions can have?

1. They prevent the unwarranted fear that causes financial crises. Depositors know that the government will see that they can get their currency back even if the bank fails. This knowledge stops them from responding to a rumour and trying to get their money out of a suspect financial institution before anyone else does.

2. They prevent warranted fears. Why should people worry about whether or not a financial institution is making reasonable loans on the basis of their deposits if the government guarantees the financial institutions' promises to pay regardless of what kind of loans the institutions make?

The Benefits and Problems of Guarantees

Government guarantees prevent unwarranted fears. The illusion on which banks depend (that people can get their money in the short run, even though it's only in the long run that they can *all* get it) can be met by temporary loans from the government. Guarantees can prevent unwarranted fears from becoming financial panics. The guarantee makes the illusion a reality. If people can indeed get their money in the long run, seeing to it that this illusion is reality isn't expensive to the government. As long as the bank has sufficient long-term assets to cover its deposits, the government will be repaid its temporary loan.

Unfortunately, covering the unwarranted fear can also mean preventing the warranted fear from putting an effective restraint or discipline on banks' lending policies. If deposit liabilities are guaranteed, why should depositors worry whether banks have adequate earning assets to cover their deposits in the long run? Thus, when the short-run illusion is also a long-run illusion, and depositors can't get their money even in the long run because of excess loan defaults (that is, their fears were warranted), guaranteeing deposits can be expensive indeed for the taxpayers who must bear the cost of the guaranteed payouts to bank depositors.

Costly Failures of the 1980s and 1990s As we said, various levels of government have guaranteed the deposits of a variety of financial institutions. Since its inception, the CDIC has been called onto provide assistance to depositors in more than 20 failed financial institutions. Two events were particularly costly, one in 1985, and the other in 1992.

In the late 1970s and early 1980s, a number of new financial institutions opened in Alberta and British Columbia, partially due to the resource boom that resulted from high commodity prices (particularly for oil). The western provinces offered attractive opportunities for investment, but when oil prices fell and the economy went into recession in 1982, several banks found themselves in financial difficulty. Bad loans and poor management practices led to the collapse of two small banks—the Northland Batik and the Canadian Commercial Bank. These banks went under even though the Bank of Canada intervened to provide short-term assistance through a coordinated effort that included many of the other chartered banks. Unfortunately the Bank of Canada's actions were misinterpreted as evidence that the Canadian financial system was weak, and public confidence in financial institutions fell like a rock. By 1985 this had led to the failure of a number of small financial institutions, as depositors fled to what they perceived to be safer havens. The CDIC eventually paid out the full value of deposits up to and even exceeding the stipulated $60,000 maximum. They settled claims on deposits above the $60,000 limit since the ill-conceived government bailout led some depositors to believe that their funds were safe—they believed the government was going to take care of the problem.

These events led to the Estey Commission whose 1986 report formed the basis of reforms to financial regulations. In 1987 a new position—the Superintendent of Financial Institutions—was created to ensure that financial institutions were undertaking safe and sound practices.

In 1992 there were other costly failures. The CDIC settled the claims of over a million depositors, totalling over $14.1 billion. Most of this went to cover the collapse of Central Guaranty Trust Company, which was Canada's fourth-largest trust company at the time. Over $10.6 billion went to almost 900,000 of its depositors. These failures put the CDIC in a difficult financial position, because the rates they had been charging for

The fact that deposits are guaranteed doesn't serve to inspire banks to make certain deposits are covered by loans in the long run.

Q-10 Should governments guarantee deposits?

This 18th-century etching by Robert Goez, "The Speculator," captures a popular view of financial activities. It shows a man reduced to rags by bad speculation.

insurance just weren't high enough to cover their expenses: Losses almost doubled in just one year.

CONCLUSION

We'll stop our consideration of money and the financial sector there. As you can see, money is central to the operation of the macroeconomy. If money functions smoothly, it keeps the outflow from the expenditure stream (saving) and the flow back into the expenditure stream at a level that reflects people's desires. Money can be treated simply as a mirror of people's real desires.

When money doesn't function smoothly, it can influence the flows, sometimes creating too large a flow back into the expenditures stream, causing inflationary pressures, and other times creating too small a flow back in, causing a recession.

Chapter Summary

- The financial sector is the market where financial assets are created and exchanged. It channels flows out of the circular flow and back into the circular flow.

- Every financial asset has a corresponding financial liability.

- Money is a highly liquid financial asset.

- Money serves as a unit of account, a medium of exchange, and a store of wealth.

- There are various measures of money: M_1, M_2, M_2+, and M_2++. M_1 consists of currency in circulation and chequing accounts at chartered banks. M_2 is M_1 plus personal savings deposits, nonpersonal notice deposits at chartered banks. Measures of money like M_2+ and M_2++ add nonchartered bank, or near bank, deposits

and other assets to get a wider and more accurate measure of money in Canada.

- Since money is what people believe money to be, creating money out of thin air is easy. How banks create money out of thin air is easily understood if you remember that money is simply a financial liability of a bank. Banks create money by loaning out deposits.

- The simple money multiplier is $1/r$. It tells you the amount of money ultimately created per dollar deposited in the banking system.

- The approximate real-world multiplier is $1/(r + c)$.

- Financial panics are based on fear. They can be prevented by government guaranteeing deposits but only at a cost.

Key Terms

approximate real-world money multiplier *(320)*

asset management *(315)*

bank *(308)*

Bank of Canada *(308)*

bond *(307)*

desired reserve ratio *(317)*

excess reserves *(320)*

financial assets *(307)*

interest rate *(307)*

liability management *(315)*

M_1 *(311)*

M_2 *(312)*

money *(308)*

reserves *(317)*

simple money multiplier *(318)*

Questions for Thought and Review

1. If financial institutions don't produce any tangible real assets, why are they considered a vital part of the economy?

2. Money is to the economy as oil is to an engine. Explain.

3. List the three functions of money.

4. Why doesn't the government pay for all its goods simply by printing money?

5. What are two components of M_2 that are not components of M_1?

6. Write the equations for the simple and the approximate real-world multipliers. Which multiplier is most likely to be larger?

7. If paper money is backed by nothing but promises and is in real terms worthless, why do people accept it?

8. If the government were to force banks to hold a reserve requirement of 100 percent, what would likely happen to the interest rate banks pay on deposits? Why?

9. Name one benefit and one cost of government's guarantee of bank deposits.

10. What was the cause of the banking crisis in the 1980s? What role did government guarantees play in that crisis?

11. Is the current banking system susceptible to panic? If so, how might a panic occur?

Problems and Exercises

1. Calculate the money multipliers below:
   a. Assuming individuals hold no currency, calculate the simple money multiplier for each of the following: 5%, 10%, 20%, 25%, 50%, 75%, 100%.
   b. Assuming individuals hold 20 percent of their money in the form of currency, recalculate the approximate real-world money multipliers in *a*.

2. While Bill is walking to school one morning, a helicopter flying overhead drops a $100 bill. Not knowing how to return it, Bill keeps the money and deposits it in his bank. (No one in this economy holds currency.) If the bank keeps 5 percent of its money in reserves:
   a. How much money can the bank now lend out?
   b. After this initial transaction, by how much is the money in the economy changed?
   c. What's the money multiplier?
   d. How much money will eventually be created by the banking system from Bill's $100?

3. Categorize the following as components of M_1, M_2, both, or neither.
   a. Provincial and municipal government bonds.
   b. Chequing accounts.
   c. Money market mutual funds.
   d. Currency.

   e. Stocks.
   f. Corporate bonds.
   g. Trust company chequing accounts.

4. For each of the following, state whether it is considered money in Canada. Explain why or why not.
   a. A cheque you write against deposits you have at the National Bank.
   b. Brazilian reals.
   c. The available credit you have on your MasterCard.
   d. Reserves held by banks at the Bank of Canada.
   e. Bank notes in your wallet.
   f. Gold bullion.
   g. Grocery store coupons.

5. State the immediate effect of each of the following actions on M_1 and M_2:
   a. Barry writes his plumber a cheque for $200. The plumber takes the cheque to the bank, keeps $50 in cash, and deposits the remainder in his savings account.
   b. Maureen deposits the $1,000 from her CD in a money market mutual fund.
   c. Sylvia withdraws $50 in cash from her savings account.
   d. Mark cashes a $100 cheque issued on his Nova Scotia bank at a Toronto bank.

Web Questions

1. Beenz was advertised as the Web's currency. But was it money? Go to www.beenz.com and check it out.
   a. What were beenz? How did you earn them and how did you spend them?
   b. Did beenz fulfil the three functions of money? Explain your answer.
   c. Was beenz money?

2. Go to the Bartercard Web site (www.bartercard.com) and answer the following questions:
   a. What are the benefits of barter? Do they depend on whether you are buying or selling goods and services?
   b. Suppose you run a restaurant that is very busy at noon, but experiences a decline in traffic in the evenings. How might barter help your business?

   c. How does barter actually work? Can anyone join a barter exchange? Does one exist in Canada?

3. Go to the Bank of Canada's Web site (www.bankof-canada.ca) and find the section dealing with Weekly Financial Statistics. Answer the following questions:
   a. What were measures of M_1, M_2, M_2+, and M_2++ last month?
   b. How is M_2++ different from M_2+? What does it include that M_2+ does not include?
   c. What has happened to currency in circulation over the last year?

Answers to Margin Questions

1. We would respond by saying that the financial sector is central to the macroeconomy. It facilitates the trades that occur in the real sector. *(306)*

2. For money to have value, it must be in limited supply. People will use paper money as a medium of exchange, unit of account, and store of value only as long as it is limited in supply, which means that the Bank of Canada cannot print up lots of money and maintain its use as money. *(310)*

3. Money provides liquidity and ease of payment. People hold money rather than bonds to get this liquidity and hold down transactions costs. *(311)*

4. M_2 would be the larger number, since it includes all of the components of M_1 plus additional components. *(312)*

5. Banks operate on the law of large numbers—which says that, on average, many fluctuations will affect each other, and hence their effect will be much smaller than the sum of all fluctuations—so that they will have some money flowing in and some money flowing out at all times. This allows them to make loans on the "float," the

average amount that they are holding. If there is one big depositor at a bank, the law of large numbers does not necessarily hold, and the bank must hold larger reserves in case that big depositor withdraws that money. *(316)*

6. The approximate money multiplier is $1/(r + c)$, which is equal to $1/0.4 = 2.5$. *(320)*

7. The approximate real-world money multiplier would decrease since individuals holding cash makes the denominator of the money multiplier larger. *(320)*

8. When banks borrow short and lend long, they are susceptible to a financial panic. Unless they have a place where they can borrow, they may not have the liquidity to pay off depositors immediately. *(322)*

9. Government guarantees of financial institutions can prevent unwarranted fears that cause financial crises, but they can also prevent warranted fears and thereby undermine financial institutions. *(322)*

10. It depends; government guarantees have both costs (they eliminate warranted fears) and benefits (they eliminate unwarranted fears). *(323)*

APPENDIX A

A Closer Look at Financial Institutions and Financial Markets

FINANCIAL ASSETS AND FINANCIAL LIABILITIES

To understand the financial sector and its relation to the real sector, you must understand how financial assets and liabilities work and how they affect the real economy.

An *asset* is something that provides its owner with expected future benefits. There are two types of assets: real assets and financial assets. Real assets are assets whose services provide direct benefits to their owners, either now or in the future. A house is a real asset—you can live in it. A machine is a real asset—you can produce goods with it.

Financial assets are *assets, such as stocks or bonds, whose benefit to the owner depends on the issuer of the asset meeting certain obligations.* **Financial liabilities** are *liabilities incurred by the issuer of a financial asset to stand behind the issued asset.* It's important to remember that *every financial asset has a corresponding financial liability*; it's that financial

liability that gives the financial asset its value. In the case of bonds, for example, a company's agreement to pay interest and repay the principal gives bonds their value. If the company goes bankrupt and reneges on its liability to pay interest and repay the principal, the asset becomes worthless. The corresponding liability gives the financial asset its value.

For example, a **stock** is *a financial asset that conveys ownership rights in a corporation.* It is a liability of the firm; it gives the holder ownership rights that are spelled out in the financial asset. An equity liability, such as a stock, usually conveys a general right to dividends, but only if the company's board of directors decides to pay them.

A debt liability conveys no ownership right. It's a type of loan. An example of a debt liability is a bond that a firm issues. A **bond** is *a promise to pay a certain amount of money plus interest in the future.* A bond is a liability of the firm but an asset of the individual who holds the bond. A debt liability, such as a bond, usually conveys legal rights to interest payments and repayment of principal.

Real assets are created by real economic activity. For example, a house or a machine must be built. Financial assets are created whenever somebody takes on a financial liability or establishes an ownership claim. For example, say we promise to pay you $1 billion in the future. You now have a financial asset and we have a financial liability. Understanding that financial assets can be created by a simple agreement of two or more people is fundamentally important to understanding how the financial sector works.

Financial Institutions

A **financial institution** is *a business whose primary activity is buying, selling, or holding financial assets*. For example, some financial institutions (depository institutions and investment intermediaries) sell promises to pay in the future. These promises can be their own promises or someone else's promises. When you open a savings account at a bank, the bank is selling you its own promise that you can withdraw your money, plus interest, at some unspecified time in the future. Such a bank is a **depository institution**—*a financial institution whose primary financial liability is deposits in chequing or savings accounts*. When you buy a newly issued government bond or security from a securities firm, it's also selling you a promise to pay in the future. But in this case, it's a third party's promise. So a securities firm is a financial broker that sells third parties' promises to pay. It's a type of marketing firm for financial IOUs.

As financial institutions sell financial assets, they channel savings from savers (individuals who give other people money now in return for promises to pay it back with interest later) to borrowers (investors or consumers who get the money now in return for their promise to pay it and the interest later).

As economists use the term, *to save* is to buy a financial asset. *To invest* (in economic terminology) is to buy real, not financial, assets that you hope will yield a return in the future.[1] How do you get funds to invest if you don't already have them? You borrow them. That means you create a financial asset that you sell to someone else who saves.

Some financial institutions serve several purposes and their various functions may have various names. For example, a depository institution, such as a chartered bank, may also serve as a **contractual intermediary**—*a financial institution that holds and stores individuals' financial assets*. Contractual intermediaries intermediate (serve as a go-between) between savers and investors. For example, a pension fund is a financial institution that takes in individuals' savings, relends those savings, and ultimately pays back those savings plus interest after the individuals retire. It uses individuals' savings to buy financial assets from people and firms who want to borrow. Similarly, a chartered bank is a financial institution that relends an individual's chequing account deposits. A chequing deposit is a financial asset of an individual and a financial liability of the bank.

Types of Financial Institutions

Table A13-1 lists three types of financial institutions and shows the percentage of total Canadian financial assets each holds, along with the sources and uses of funds for each. These percentages give you an idea of the institution's importance, but institutions' importance can come in other ways. For example, although investment dealers hold only 0.6 percent of the total financial assets held by financial institutions, they're important because they facilitate buying and selling such assets. Let's consider each grouping separately.

Depository Institutions

Depository institutions, the first category listed, are financial institutions whose primary financial liabilities are deposits in chequing accounts. They hold about 38 percent of all the financial assets held by financial institutions in Canada. This category includes chartered banks, trust and mortgage loan companies, caisses populaires, and credit unions. As already noted, banks in Canada are referred to as chartered banks because they must obtain a charter from the federal government to operate as a bank. Trust companies engage in some depository functions, but they are primarily involved in administering trusteed pension plans (pension plans where a trustee is responsible for managing and investing the funds).

You might wonder why there are so many different types of depository institutions. Why not just have banks? The reason is related to the evolution of the Canadian financial system. At one time, trust companies flourished because there were legal restrictions that precluded chartered banks from acting as trustees. Similarly, mortgage loan companies initially sprang from restrictions on the ability of a chartered bank to offer mortgages on residential property. Credit unions and caisses populaires popped up around the country because small investors had limited access to financial institutions—you have to have a lot of

---

[1]This terminology isn't the terminology most laypeople use. When a person buys a stock, in economic terms that person is *saving*, though most laypeople call that *investing*.

TABLE A13-1   Holdings of Selected Financial Institutions, 2000

Financial Institutions	Percentage of Total Financial Assets Held by Financial Institutions	Primary Assets (Uses of Funds)	Primary Liabilities (Sources of Funds)
Depository Institutions			
Chartered banks	33.0	Bank loans, mortgages, and consumer credit	Currency and bank deposits
Credit unions and Caisses populaires	4.5	Mortgages, consumer credit	Deposits
Trust companies	0.4	Mortgages, consumer credit	Deposits
Contractual Intermediaries			
Trusteed pension funds	16.7	Bonds, short-term paper	Life insurance, pensions
Life insurance business	6.2	Mortgages, bonds, and shares	Life insurance, shares
Segregated funds of life insurance companies	2.8	Bonds, short-term paper	Life insurance
Sales finance and consumer loan companies	2.7	Loans, consumer credit	Short-term paper, bonds
Property and casualty insurance companies	2.3	Bonds, short-term paper`	Insurance, pensions, shares
Investment Intermediaries			
Mutual funds	13.5	Short-term paper, shares, and foreign investment	Shares
Investment dealers	0.6	Short-term paper	Loans
Other	17.3		Short-term paper

Source: Statistics Canada, National Balance Sheet Accounts, CANSIM II, Table 378-0004.

money in your account before a bank is very interested in you. Locally owned and operated intermediaries such as credit unions and caisses populaires developed as community-based financial institutions.

As you can see in Table A13-1, chartered banks hold the greatest proportion of financial assets among the depository institutions. The primary financial liability of each is deposits. For example, the amount in your chequing account or savings account is a financial asset for you and a financial liability for the bank holding you deposit.

A13.1

see page 335

Banks make money by lending your deposits (primarily in the form of business and commercial loans), charging the borrower a higher interest rate than they pay the depositor. Those loans from banks to borrowers are financial assets of the bank and financial liabilities of the borrower.

Over the years there have been significant changes to federal and provincial laws governing financial institutions. When the first Canadian banks came on the scene in the 19th century, some provinces wouldn't allow a bank to have more than one branch. That's in stark contrast to the current system of multibranch banking. Other arcane regulations include the restriction that cheques had to be written in blue fountain pen ink. Now you can use passion pink pencils, if that's your fancy.

These restrictions were usually aimed at constraining the behaviour of chartered banks, who were able to use their size to exert control over to whom funds were channelled. Regulations affect the activities that financial institutions undertake, and they allow us to make sharp, clear distinctions among financial institutions.

Changes in the laws have eliminated many of these restrictions, blurring the distinction between the various types of financial intermediaries. In Canada, the main banking legislation is revised, on average, about every 10 years. The Bank Act essentially sets the rules that chartered banks have to follow. The most recent changes to the act were aimed at establishing safeguards to reduce the potential for bank failures and at eliminating the legal differences between chartered banks and other financial institutions. For example, trust companies can offer commercial loans—something they were not permitted until mid-1992. Also, chartered banks can own trust and insurance companies, and they are allowed to offer life insurance. Some economists argue that banks should be excluded from offering life insurance. Why? Let's say you

F inancial assets are neat. You can call them into existence simply by getting someone to accept your IOU. *Remember, every financial asset has a corresponding financial liability equal to it.* So when you say a country has $1 trillion of financial assets, you're also saying that the country has $1 trillion of financial liabilities. An optimist would say a country is rich. A pessimist would say it's poor. An economist would say that financial assets and financial liabilities are simply opposite sides of the ledger and don't indicate whether a country is rich or poor.

To find out whether a country is rich or poor, you must look at its *real assets.* If financial assets increase the economy's efficiency and thereby increase the amount of real assets, they make society better off. This is most economists' view of financial assets. If, however, they decrease the efficiency of the economy (as some economists have suggested some financial assets do because they focus productive effort on financial gamesmanship), financial assets make society worse off.

The same correspondence between a financial asset and its liability exists when a financial asset's value changes. Say stock prices fall significantly. Is society poorer? The answer is: It depends on the reason for the

KNOWING THE TOOLS

Do Financial Assets Make Society Richer?

change. Let's say there is no known reason. Then, while the people who own the stock are poorer, the people who might want to buy stock in the future are richer since the price of assets has fallen. So in a pure accounting sense, society is neither richer nor poorer when the prices of stocks rise or fall for no reason.

But there are ways in which changes in the value of financial assets might signify that society is richer or poorer. For example, the changes in the values of financial assets might *reflect* (rather than cause) real changes. If suddenly a company finds a cure for cancer, its stock prices will rise and society will be richer. But the rise in the price of the stock doesn't cause society to be richer. It reflects the discovery that made society richer. Society would be richer because of the discovery even if the stock's price didn't rise.

There's significant debate about how well the stock market reflects real changes in the economy. Classical economists believe it closely reflects real changes; Keynesian economists believe it doesn't. But both sides agree that the changes in the real economy, not the changes in the price of financial assets, underlie what makes an economy richer or poorer.

---

have a medical condition that will raise the likelihood of your death at an early age. If your bank has that information as part of the medical history it requires for your life insurance policy, there's a chance you'll never be able to secure a mortgage, even if conventional medical wisdom changes and your life expectancy returns to normal.

Some differences remain that reflect their history. Chartered bank's primary assets are loans, and their loans include business loans, mortgages, and consumer loans. Trust and mortgage loan companies' primary assets are the same kind as those of commercial banks, but their loans are primarily mortgage loans.

Contractual Intermediaries

The most important contractual intermediaries are insurance companies and pension funds. These institutions promise, for a fee, to pay an individual a certain amount of money in the future, either when some event happens (a fire or death) or, in the case of pension funds and some kinds of life insurance, when the individual reaches a certain age or dies. Insurance policies and pensions are a form

of individual savings. Contractual intermediaries manage those savings. As the average age of the Canadian population increases, the share of assets held by these contractual intermediaries will increase.

Investment Intermediaries

Investment intermediaries provide a mechanism through which small savers pool funds to invest in a variety of financial assets rather than in just one or two. An example of how pooling works can be seen by considering a mutual fund company, which is one type of investment intermediary.

A mutual fund enables a small saver to diversify (spread out) his or her savings (for a fee, of course). Savers buy shares in the mutual fund which, in turn, holds stocks or bonds of many different companies. When a fund holds many different companies' shares or bonds, it spreads the risk so a saver won't lose everything if one company goes broke. This is called **diversification**—*spreading the risks by holding many different types of financial assets.*

A finance company is another type of investment intermediary. Finance companies make loans to individuals

The market for financial instruments is sometimes rather hectic, as suggested by this famous painting, "The Bulls and Bears on Wall Street."

and businesses, as do banks, but instead of holding deposits, as banks do, finance companies borrow the money they lend. They borrow from individuals by selling them bonds and commercial paper. Bonds are promissory notes specifying that a certain amount of money plus interest will be paid back in the future. **Commercial paper** is *a short-term promissory note that a certain amount of money plus interest will be paid back on demand.*

Finance companies charge borrowers higher interest than banks do, in part because their cost of funds (the interest rate they pay to depositors) is higher than banks' cost of funds. (The interest rate banks pay on savings and chequing accounts is the cost of their funds.) As was the case with depository institutions, a finance company's profit reflects the difference between the interest rate it charges on its loans and the interest rate it pays for the funds it borrows.

Why do people go to finance companies if finance companies charge higher interest than banks? Because of convenience and because finance companies' loan qualifications are easier to meet than banks'.

The final investment intermediary is the investment dealer. These dealers assist companies in selling financial assets such as stocks and bonds. They provide advice, expertise, and the sales force to sell the stocks or bonds. They handle such things as *mergers* and *takeovers* of companies. A merger is the joining of two or more companies to form one new company. A takeover occurs when one company buys out another company.

Many investment dealers are closely associated with brokerage houses. They assist individuals in selling previously issued financial assets. Brokerage houses create a sec-

ondary market in financial assets, as we'll see shortly. A **secondary financial market** is *a market in which previously issued financial assets can be bought and sold.*

FINANCIAL MARKETS

A **financial market** is *a market where financial assets and financial liabilities are bought and sold.* The stock market, the bond market, and bank activities are all examples of financial markets.

Financial institutions buy and sell financial assets in financial markets. Sometimes these markets are actual places, like the Toronto Stock Exchange, but generally a market simply exists in the form of a broker's Rolodex files, computer networks, telephone lines, and lists of people who sometimes want to buy and sell. When individuals want to sell, they call their broker and their broker calls potential buyers; when individuals want to buy, the broker calls potential sellers.

Primary and Secondary Financial Markets

There are various types of financial markets. A **primary financial market** is *a market in which newly issued financial assets are sold.* These markets transfer savings to borrowers who want to invest (buy real assets). Sellers in this market include *venture capital firms* (which sell part ownerships in new companies) and *investment banks* (which sell new stock and new bonds for existing companies). Whereas investment banks only assist firms in selling their stock, venture capital firms often are partnerships that invest their own money in return for part ownership of a new firm.

Many new businesses will turn to venture capital firms for financing because only established firms can sell stock through an investment bank. Risks are enormous for venture capital firms since most new businesses fail. But potential gains are huge. A company that's already established will most likely use an investment bank to get additional funds. Investment banks know people and institutions who buy stocks; with a new stock offering they use those contacts. They telephone those leads to try to *place* (sell) the new issue.

Generally new offerings are too large for one investment bank to sell. So the bank contracts with other investment banks and brokerage houses to sell portions of the new stock or bond issue.

There are many different types of buyers for newly issued financial assets. They include rich individuals and financial institutions, such as life insurance companies, pension funds, and mutual funds.

The floor of the New York Stock Exchange often is chaotic.

A *secondary financial market* transfers existing financial assets from one saver to another. (Remember, in economics, when an individual buys a financial asset such as a stock or bond, he or she is a saver. In economics, investment occurs only when savings are used to buy items such as machines or a factory.) A transfer on a secondary market does not represent any new saving; it is saving for one person and dissaving for another. One cancels out the other. The Toronto Stock Exchange is probably the best-known secondary financial market. It transfers stocks from one stockholder to another.

The secondary market does, however, have an important role to play in new saving. The existence of a secondary market lets the individual buyer of a financial asset know that she can resell it, transferring the asset back into cash at whatever price the secondary market sets. **Liquidity** is this *ability to turn an asset into cash quickly.* Secondary markets provide liquidity for financial assets holders and thereby encourage them to hold financial assets. If no secondary market existed, most people would hesitate to buy a stock or a 30-year bond. What if they needed their money in, say, 10 years? Or 10 weeks?

The secondary markets one hears the most about in Canada are the Toronto Stock Exchange and the Canadian Venture Exchange, and in the United States are the New York Stock Exchange and the National Association of Security Dealers Automated Quotations (Nasdaq). These stock exchange markets are undergoing significant change as the Internet eliminates the need for a place-specific stock market and replaces it with a virtual stock market that simply exists in the computer. More and more people are buying and selling stocks on the Internet because they can do so quickly and at low costs. (A thousand shares can be bought or sold for less than $10.) Large stockholders can now easily bypass the stock market and trade directly with others, eliminating the intermediaries. As that happens the stock markets are changing too. Trading hours are expanding; soon 24-hour trading will be the norm.

Money Markets and Capital Markets

Financial markets can also be divided into two other categories: **money markets** (*in which financial assets having a maturity of less than one year are bought and sold*) and **capital markets** (*in which financial assets having a maturity of more than one year are bought and sold*). Maturity refers to the date the issuer must pay back the money that was borrowed plus any remaining interest, as agreed when the asset was issued.) For example, say the federal government issues an IOU (sometimes called a *Treasury bill*) that comes due in three months. This will be sold in the money market because its maturity is less than a year. Or say the government or a corporation issues an IOU that comes due in 20 years. This IOU, which is called a *bond*, will be sold in a capital market.

TYPES OF FINANCIAL ASSETS

Now that you've been introduced to financial institutions and markets, we can consider some specific financial assets. Financial assets are generally divided into money market assets and capital market assets.

Money Market Assets

Money market assets are financial assets that mature in less than one year. They usually pay lower interest rates than do longer-term capital assets because they offer the buyer more liquidity. A general rule of thumb is: The more liquid the asset, the lower the return. As in the over-the-counter market, money market and capital market transactions are made over the phone lines using computers. Newly issued money market assets are sold through an investment or securities dealer. Table A13-2 gives you a sense of some of the most important money market assets. Let's briefly discuss each one.

Canada Treasury Bills

These are Canadian government IOUs that mature in less than a year. Since it's unlikely the Canadian government will go broke, IOUs of the Canadian government are very secure, so Canada treasury bills pay a relatively low rate of interest.

TABLE A13-2 Principal Money Market Instruments

Instruments	Maturity
Canada treasury bills	90–365 days
Short-term Canada bonds	Less than three years
Provincial and municipal bonds	90–365 days
Bank of Canada advances	Several days
Bankers acceptances	10–365 days
Day-to-day loans	Callable any time
Commercial paper	30–365 days

Where do the IOUs come from? Think back to the discussion of fiscal policy in which the government spent more than it took in in revenues. That deficit must be financed by borrowing. Selling Canada treasury bills is one way the Canadian government borrows money.

Short-Term Canada Bonds

Canadian government bonds with maturities of less than than three years are almost as liquid as treasury bills. These bonds usually carry fixed interest rates, but have fallen in relative importance since the early 1970s.

Provincial and Municipal Bonds

Canadian provincial and municipal governments also issue bonds to finance large expenditures on things such as hydro-electric plants, waste treatment, and other areas of spending that cannot be financed out of current revenues. They fund these large projects by borrowing from domestic and international markets, usually by issuing bonds denominated in Canadian dollars. Sometimes these bonds are issued in foreign currencies to entice foreigners to invest in Canada. The only problem with this is that if the Canadian dollar loses a lot of value against the foreign currency, in 20 or 30 years when it is time to repay the principal, a foreign currency loan may turn out to be more expensive than anyone had ever imagined. This happened in Nova Scotia when funds to build a large bridge were borrowed in Swiss francs. The total cost of the loan was much more than expected, leading to ever-increasing tolls on the bridge.

Commercial Paper

Why borrow from a bank if you can borrow directly from the public? Why not cut out the intermediary? Large corporations often do precisely that. The borrowings are called commercial paper. Commercial paper is a short-term IOU of a large corporation. It pays higher rates of interest than Canada treasury bills, but a lower interest rate than banks would charge the corporation. The same reasoning holds for a person who buys commercial paper. Commercial paper generally pays a higher interest rate than a term deposit, which is why people are willing to lend directly to the firm. Since the bank is an intermediary between the lender of funds and the borrower, the firm's action in this case is called **disintermediation**—the process of lending directly and not going through a financial intermediary.

Differences among Money Market Assets

Money market assets differ slightly from each other. For example, treasury bills are safer than commercial paper (usually there's more chance of a firm defaulting than a government) and pay slightly lower interest. For the most part, however, they are interchangeable, and the interest rates paid on them tend to increase or decrease together.

Capital Market Assets

Capital market assets have a maturity of more than one year. Table A13-3 shows several important capital market instruments and their maturities. Let's briefly discuss stocks and bonds.

Stocks

A stock is a partial ownership right to a company. A stock owner can vote on company policy and can attend stockholder meetings. Stocks have no maturity date, nor do they necessarily pay dividends (periodic payments to stockholders). People buy stocks because it gives them ownership rights to a percentage of the profits of the company. Firms issue stock to raise the cash necessary to invest in production. Stockholders can sell their stocks on secondary markets.

Bonds

A bond is an IOU, of either the government or a firm, that matures in more than one year. Unlike a stock, a bond must be repaid at maturity. Some bonds, called zero-coupon bonds, do not pay interest at periodic intervals. Most bonds, however, do pay a certain amount of interest at specified intervals. Like stocks, bonds can be bought and sold on the secondary market.

TABLE A13-3 **Principal Capital Market Instruments**

Instruments	Maturity
Government of Canada bonds	From 3 years and up
Provincial and municipal	From 3 years and up
Corporate bonds	From 3 years and up
Debentures	From 3 to 20 years
Stocks	Variable

LEADING YOU THROUGH TWO FINANCIAL TRANSACTIONS

We've covered a lot of material quickly, so the institutions discussed may be a bit of a blur in your mind. To get a better idea of how these financial markets work, let's follow two transactions you'll likely make in your lifetime and see how they work their way through the financial system.

Insuring Your Car

You want to drive. The law requires you to have insurance, so you go to two or three insurance companies, get quotes of their rates, and choose the one offering the lowest rate. Say it costs you $800 for the year. You write a cheque for $800 and hand the cheque to the insurance agent, who keeps a commission (let's say $80) and then sends her cheque for $720 to the insurance company. The insurance company has $720 more sitting in the bank than it had before you paid your insurance premium.

The insurance company earns income in two ways: (1) in the difference between the money it receives in payments and the claims it pays out, and (2) in the interest it makes on its financial assets. What does the company use to buy these financial assets? It has payments from its customers (your $720, for example) available because payments come in long before claims are paid out.

Because earnings on financial assets are an important source of an insurance company's income, your $720 doesn't stay in the insurance company's bank for long. The insurance company has a financial assets division that chooses financial assets it believes have the highest returns for the risk involved. Bond salespeople telephone the financial assets division offering to sell bonds. Similarly, developers who want to build shopping malls or ski resorts go to the financial assets division, offering an opportunity to participate (really asking to borrow money).

The financial assets division might decide to lend your $720 (along with $10 million more) to a mall developer who builds in suburban locations. The division transfers the $720 to the mall developer and receives a four-year, 12 percent promissory note (a promise to pay the $720 back in four years along with $86.40 per year in interest payments). The promissory note is a financial asset of the insurance company and a financial liability of the developer. When the developer spends the money, the $720 leaves the financial sector and re-enters the spending stream in the real economy. At that point it becomes investment in the economic sense.

Buying a House

Most people, when they buy a house, don't go out and pay the thousands of dollars it costs in cash. Instead they go to a bank or similar financial institution and borrow a large portion of the sales price, taking out a mortgage on the house. A **mortgage** is simply *a special name for a secured loan on real estate*. By mortgaging a house, you are creating a financial liability for yourself and a financial asset for someone else. This financial asset is secured by the house. If you default on the loan, the mortgage holder can foreclose on the mortgage and take title to the house.

The funds available in banks come primarily from depositors who keep their savings in the bank in the form of savings accounts or chequing accounts. Balances in these accounts are often small, but with lots of depositors they add up and provide banks with money to lend out. If you're planning to buy a house, you'll most likely go to a bank.

The bank's loan officer will have you fill in a lengthy form, and the bank will send an appraiser out to the house to assess its value. The appraiser asks questions about the house: Does it meet the electrical code? What kind of pipes does it have? What kind of windows does it have? All this information about you and the house is transferred onto a master form that the loan officer uses to decide whether to make the loan. (Contrary to what many laypeople believe, in normal times a loan officer wants to make the loan. Remember, a bank's profits are the difference between what it pays in interest to its depositors and what it receives in interest from loans and investments; it needs to make loans to make profits. So the loan officer often looks at hazy answers on the form and puts an interpretation on them that's favourable to making the loan.)

In a month or so, depending on how busy the bank is, you hear back that the loan is approved for, say, $80,000 at 9 percent interest. A bank credits your account with $80,000, which allows you to write a cheque to the seller of the house at a meeting called the *closing*.

Summary

We could go through other transactions, but these two should give you a sense of how real-world financial transactions work their way through financial institutions. Financial institutions make money by the fees and commissions they charge for buying and selling loans, and on the difference between the interest they pay to get the money and the interest they receive when they lend the money out.

Key Terms

bond   *(326)*

capital markets   *(331)*

commercial paper   *(330)*

contractual intermediary   *(327)*

depository institution   *(327)*

disintermediation   *(332)*

diversification   *(329)*

financial assets   *(326)*

financial institution   *(327)*

financial liabilities   *(326)*

financial market   *(330)*

liquidity   *(331)*

money markets   *(331)*

mortgage   *(333)*

primary financial market   *(330)*

secondary financial market   *(330)*

stock   *(326)*

Questions for Thought and Review

1. If the government prints new $100 bills and gives them to all introductory students who are using this text, who incurs a financial liability and who gains a financial asset?

2. Is the currency in your pocketbook or wallet a real or a financial asset? Why?

3. Anselm, your study partner, has just said that, in economic terminology, when he buys a bond he is investing. Is he correct? Why?

4. Nancy, your study partner, has just made the following statement: "A loan is a loan and therefore cannot be an asset." Is she correct? Why or why not?

5. What is the difference between an investment dealer and a chartered bank?

6. The difference between primary and secondary financial markets is that the primary markets are more important. True or false? Why or why not?

7. A company's stock is selling for three times earnings. How is the market valuing the prospects of that company?

8. Which market, the primary or secondary, contributes more to the production of tangible real assets? Explain why.

9. Why do money market assets generally yield lower interest payments than capital assets?

10. For the following financial instruments, state for whom it is a liability and for whom it is an asset. Also state, if appropriate, whether the transaction occurred on the capital or money markets.

    a. Lamar purchases a $100 term deposit at his credit union.
    b. The Bank of Nova Scotia grants a mortgage to Sandra.
    c. Sean purchases a $100 jacket using his credit card with the Royal Bank.
    d. City of Toronto issues $1 billion in municipal bonds, most of which were purchased by Toronto residents, to build a community centre.
    e. Investment broker sells 100 shares of existing stock.
    f. Investment broker sells 1,000 shares of new-issue stock.

11. State whether you agree or disagree with the following statements:
    a. If stock market prices go up, the economy is richer.
    b. A real asset worth $1 million is more valuable to an individual than a financial asset worth $1 million.
    c. Financial assets have no value to society since each has a corresponding liability.
    d. Canada has much more land than does Japan. Therefore, the value of all Canadian land should significantly exceed the value of land in Japan.
    e. Canadian GDP exceeds Italy's GDP; therefore, the stock market valuation of Canadian-based companies should exceed that of Italian-based companies.

Web Question

1. In 2001 Parliament passed legislation affecting the Canadian financial system. Visit the Department of Finance's home page (www.fin.gc.ca) and find the section on Canada's Financial Sector.
   a. How many domestic banks and how many foreign banks operate in Canada today? What is a foreign bank subsidiary?
   b. What will the new definition of "widely held ownership" imply for the Canadian financial system?
   c. Will it be easier for banks to merge under the new rules? Why?

APPENDIX B

Creation of Money Using T-Accounts

In this appendix we use T-accounts to demonstrate the example of the creation of money given in the text of the chapter.

The basis of financial accounting is the T-account presentation of balance sheets. The balance sheet is made up of assets on one side and liabilities and net worth on the other. By definition the two sides are equal; they balance (just as the T-account must).

To cement the money creation process in your mind, let's discuss how banks create money using transactions that affect the balance sheet. To keep the analysis simple, we limit the example to the case where only banks create money.

Table B13-1 shows the initial balance sheet of an imaginary Textland Bank, which we assume is the only bank in the country. As you can see, Textland has $500,000 in assets: $30,000 in cash, $300,000 in loans, and $170,000 in property. On the liabilities side, it has $150,000 in chequing deposits and $350,000 in net worth. The two sides of the balance sheet are equal.

The first thing to notice about this balance sheet is that if all holders of chequing accounts (demand deposits) wanted their currency, the bank couldn't give it to them. The currency it holds is only a portion—20 percent—of the total deposits:

$$\frac{\$30,000}{\$150,000} = 0.20$$

Banks rely on statistical averages and assume that not all people will want their money at the same time. Let's assume that Textland Bank has decided 20 percent is an appropriate reserve ratio.

Now let's say that Jean Finder finds $10,000 in currency. He deposits that $10,000 into Textland Bank. After he does so, what will happen to the money supply? The first step is seen in Transaction 1, which shows the effect of Jean Finder's deposit on the bank's account. The bank gains $10,000 in currency, but its liabilities also increase by $10,000, so, as you can see, the two sides of the balance sheet are still equal. At this point no additional money has been created; $10,000 currency has simply been changed to a $10,000 chequing deposit.

TABLE B13-1   **Textland Bank Balance Sheet**

Assets	Beginning Balance	Liabilities and Net Worth	
Currency	$ 30,000	Chequing deposits	$150,000
Loans	300,000	Net worth	350,000
Property	170,000		
Total assets	$500,000	Total liabilities and net worth	$500,000

Now let's assume the bank uses a reserve ratio of 20 percent, meaning it lends out 80 percent of the currency it receives in new deposits. Say it lends out 80% × $10,000 = $8,000 to Fred Baker, keeping 20 percent × $10,000 = $2,000 in reserve. The change in the bank's balance sheet is seen in Transaction 2. This step creates $8,000 in money. Why? Because Jean Finder still has $10,000 in his chequing account, while Fred Baker has $8,000 currency, so, combining Jean's chequing account balance with Fred's currency, the public has $8,000 in money. As you can see, loans have increased by $8,000 and currency in Textland Bank has decreased by $8,000.

Fred Baker didn't borrow the money to hold onto it. He spends it buying a new oven from Mary Builder, who,

in turn, deposits the $8,000 into Textland Bank (the only bank according to our assumptions). Textland's balance sheet now looks like Transaction 3.

Mary Builder has a demand deposit of $8,000 and Jean Finder has a demand deposit of $10,000. But Textland bank has excess reserves of $6,400, since it wants to keep only $1,600 of Mary's $8,000 deposit as reserves:

$$80\% \times \$8,000 = \$6,400$$

So the bank is looking to make a loan.

At this point the process continues in the fashion described in the chapter text. A good exercise to see that you understand T-accounts is to use T-accounts to demonstrate the next two rounds of the process.

TABLE B13-1 (continued)

Transaction 1					
Assets			**Liabilities and Net Worth**		
Currency (beginning balance)	$30,000		Chequing deposits (beginning balance)	$150,000	
Currency from Jean	10,000		Jean's deposit	10,000	
Total currency		$ 40,000	Total demand deposits		$160,000
Loans		300,000	Net worth		350,000
Property		170,000			
Total assets		$510,000	Total liabilities and net worth		$510,000

TABLE B13-1 (continued)

Transaction 2					
Assets			**Liabilities and Net Worth**		
Currency (after Trans. 1)	$ 40,000		Chequing deposits (after Trans. 1)		$160,000
Currency loaned to Fred	− 8,000		Net worth		350,000
Total currency		$ 32,000			
Loans (beginning balance)	300,000				
Loans to Fred	8,000				
Total loans		308,000			
Property		170,000	Total liabilities and net worth		$510,000
Total assets		$510,000			

TABLE B13-1   (continued)

	Transaction 3		
Assets		**Liabilities and Net Worth**	
Currency (after Trans. 2)	$32,000	Chequing deposits	$160,000
Currency from Mary	8,000	Mary's deposit	8,000
Total currency	$ 40,000	Total demand deposits	$168,000
Loans	308,000	Net worth	350,000
Property	170,000		
Total assets	$518,000	Total liabilities and net worth	$518,000

Questions for Thought and Review

1. Assume that there's only one bank in the country, that the desired reserve requirement is 10 percent, and that the ratio of individuals' currency holdings to their bank deposits is 20 percent. The bank begins with $20,000 in currency, $225,000 in loans, $105,000 in physical assets, $200,000 in demand deposits, and $150,000 in net worth.
   a. An immigrant comes into the country and deposits $10,000 in the bank. Show this deposit's effect on the bank's balance sheet.
   b. The bank keeps enough of this money to satisfy its reserve requirement, and loans out the rest to Ms. Entrepreneur. Show the effect on the bank's balance sheet.
   c. Ms. Entrepreneur uses the money to pay Mr. Carpenter, who deposits 80 percent of what he gets in the bank. Show the effect on the bank's balance sheet.
   d. Show the bank's balance sheet after the money multiplier is all through multiplying (based on the appendix).

2. Assume there is one bank in the country whose desired reserve requirement is 20 percent. It has $10,000 in currency; $100,000 in loans; $50,000 in physical assets; $50,000 in demand deposits; and $110,000 in net worth. Mr. Aged withdraws $1,000 from the bank and dies on the way home without spending a penny. He is buried with the currency still in his pocket.
   a. Show this withdrawal's effect on the bank's balance sheet.
   b. What happened to the bank's reserve ratio and what must the bank do to meet its desired reserve requirements?
   c. What is the money multiplier? (Assume no currency holdings.)
   d. What will happen to total money supply because of this event after the money multiplier is through multiplying?

3. Assume desired reserve requirements are 15 percent. Textland Bank's balance sheet looks like this:

Assets		Liabilities	
Currency	$ 30,000	Deposits	$150,000
Loans	320,000	Net Worth	550,000
Property	350,000		
Total	$700,000	Total	$700,000

   a. How much is the bank holding in excess reserves?
   b. If the bank eliminates excess reserves by making new loans, how much new money would be created (assuming no currency holdings)? Show using T-accounts.

Monetary Policy and the Debate about Macro Policy

14

After reading this chapter, you should be able to:

- Summarize the structure and duties of the Bank of Canada.

- List two tools of monetary policy and explain how they work.

- Define the overnight financing rate and discuss how the Bank of Canada uses it.

- Explain how monetary policy works in the *AS/AD* model.

- List five problems often encountered in conducting monetary policy.

> *There have been three great inventions*
> *since the beginning of time:*
> *fire, the wheel and central banking.*
>
> Will Rogers

Monetary policy is a policy that influences the economy through changes in the money supply and available credit.

Monetary policy is *a policy of influencing the economy through changes in the financial system's reserves that influence the money supply and credit availability in the economy.* Monetary policy is one of the two main traditional macroeconomic tools (the other is fiscal policy, discussed in an earlier chapter) by which government attempts to control the aggregate economy. Unlike fiscal policy, which is controlled by the government directly, monetary policy is controlled by the central bank in Canada, the Bank of Canada (the Bank). We'll discuss the Bank in more detail later in this chapter when we discuss the specific tools through which monetary policy is conducted. For now let us give you a sense of monetary policy and how it fits into our macro model.

Our familiar macro policy model is shown in Figure 14-1. What is the effect of monetary policy in the *AS/AD* model? Expansionary monetary policy shifts the *AD* curve to

Figure 14-1 (a and b)   THE EFFECT OF MONETARY POLICY IN THE AS/AD MODEL

Expansionary monetary policy shifts the *AD* curve to the right; contractionary monetary policy shifts the *AD* curve to the left. In (a) we see the effect of expansionary monetary policy when the price level is fixed. The *SAS* curve is horizontal and the effect of expansionary monetary policy is entirely on increasing real output to Y_1. If there are inflationary pressures, the *SAS* curve will shift up somewhat and the effect of expansionary monetary policy will be split between increases in real output and increases in the price level. If the economy is in the Classical range, as in (b), the *SAS* curve shifts up enough so that real output remains unchanged. The effect of expansionary monetary policy when prices are perfectly flexible is to increase the price level.

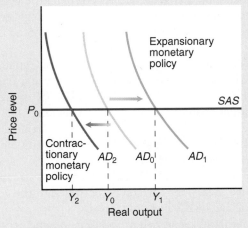

(a) **Monetary policy when prices are fixed**

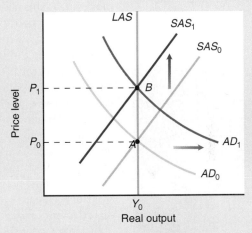

(b) **Expansionary monetary policy in the Classical range**

the right; contractionary monetary policy shifts it to the left. Changes in nominal income will be split between changes in real income and changes in the price level. That split will be determined by the effect of the policy on the price level—how inflationary pressures will be affected.

Let's consider the effect of expansionary monetary policy. If the economy is in the Keynesian range (price level doesn't change) and there are no inflationary pressures, as in Figure 14-1(a), the primary effect of expansionary monetary policy will be to increase real income to Y_1. If the economy is in the intermediate range (the price level is somewhat flexible), the *SAS* curve will shift up somewhat, and real income will increase to less than Y_1 because some of the effect of the expansionary monetary policy is to increase nominal income and the price level rather than real income.

If the economy is in the Classical range (the price level is completely flexible), monetary policy affects only nominal income and the price level, as in Figure 14-1(b). The economy begins at potential output Y_0 and expansionary monetary policy shifts the *AD* curve to AD_1. Because prices are perfectly flexible, inflationary pressures shift the *SAS* curve from SAS_0 to SAS_1. Real output does not rise at all and the price level rises from P_0 to P_1.

The general rule is: Expansionary monetary policy increases nominal income. Its effect on real income depends on how the price level responds:

%ΔReal income = %ΔNominal income − %ΔPrice level

Thus, if nominal income rises by 5 percent and the price level rises by 2 percent, real income will rise by 3 percent.

DUTIES AND STRUCTURE OF THE BANK OF CANADA

It is the bank's ability to create money that gives the central bank the power to control monetary policy.

Monetary policy is conducted by a **central bank**—*a type of bankers' bank*. If banks need to borrow money, they go to the central bank, just as when you need to borrow money, you go to a neighbourhood bank. As we explained in the last chapter, if there's a financial panic and a run on banks, the central bank is there to make loans to the banks until the panic goes away. Since its IOUs are cash, simply by issuing an IOU it can create money. It is this ability to create money that gives the central bank the power to control monetary policy. A central bank also serves as a financial adviser to government. As is often the case with financial advisers, the government sometimes doesn't like the advice and doesn't follow it.

Besides being a banker's bank and a financial adviser, the Bank of Canada also conducts monetary policy for the government. *Monetary policy* is a policy of influencing the economy through changes in the money supply and the availability of credit in the economy. You'll recall from an earlier chapter that credit simply represents savings made available to be borrowed, so when we say that monetary policy aims to affect the availability of credit, we mean that the central bank attempts to make available an appropriate level of savings to the economy. Monetary policy is one of two main macroeconomic tools (the other is fiscal policy) by which government attempts to control the aggregate economy. Unlike fiscal policy, which is controlled by the government directly, monetary policy is controlled by the Bank of Canada.

In many countries, such as Germany, Great Britain, and France, the central bank is a part of the government, just as Canada's Department of Finance is a part of the Canadian government. In Canada the central bank is not part of the government in the same way as in some European countries. The Bank of Canada is a Crown corporation, not under the direct day-to-day control of the federal government.

The Bank of Canada in Ottawa.

Structure of the Bank

The head of the Bank of Canada is the Governor of the Bank. The Governor is appointed by the federal Cabinet for a seven-year term. So far the Bank of Canada has had seven governors:

1934–54	Graham Towers
1955–61	James Coyne
1961–73	Louis Rasminsky
1973–87	Gerald Bouey
1987–94	John Crow
1994–2001	Gordon Thiessen
2001–	David Dodge

The governor cannot be removed from office and, since midway through Rasminsky's term, must agree to follow the government's direction or resign if he cannot support its policy. This is the result of the "Coyne Affair." Governor Coyne refused to expand the money supply at a time when the federal government was undertaking expansionary fiscal policies. Coyne was convinced that expansionary monetary policy would make the recession of the late 1950s worse. He eventually resigned (just before the government declared the Governor's seat to be vacant—they couldn't fire him so they decided to eliminate the position), and in the mid-1960s Rasminsky agreed that the government had final say in matters of monetary policy.

This is not to say there's been harmony in the setting of monetary policy since 1961. The most recent conflicts arose between 1987 and 1994 when John Crow embarked on

Q.1 Who appoints the Governor of the Bank of Canada?

14.1

see page 357

a policy that was aimed at stabilizing the price level. As we'll see shortly, in the long run all that monetary policy can do is provide an anchor for the nation's unit of account. That is, all it can do is affect the price level. In the long run, it can't really affect employment or the level of output. Crow was convinced that monetary policy should take this long-run view even though monetary policy might have some short-run effects capable of perhaps reducing unemployment during a recession. The debate over price stability as the only objective for monetary policy was high-pitched and, as we'll see in the next chapter, monetary policy contributed to the recession of the early 1990s. While John Crow achieved price stability—interpreted to mean a low and stable rate of inflation—it didn't help him win reappointment to a second term as Governor, and in 1994 Gordon Thiessen took over the position.

Price stability is interpreted to mean a low and stable rate of inflation.

John Crow's quest for price stability and his unwillingness to respond to double-digit unemployment by "priming the monetary pumps" of the economy led to calls for a change in the structure of the Bank of Canada. Monetary policy is set by the Governor with the advice of his senior advisers. The bank has a Board of Directors made up of 12 nonspecialists in monetary economics from a variety of backgrounds, but it has little say in the direction and conduct of monetary policy. Proponents of change argue that too much power is concentrated in the hands of unelected officials, and that those charged with operating the nation's monetary policy should be ultimately responsible to the people. They also suggest that the Board of Directors should be composed of persons specializing in monetary policy and that the Directors receive a salary that would encourage their active participation in the design of monetary policy. There have also been calls for regional representation in the structure of the Bank of Canada, particularly during the recession of the early 1990s. As we'll see in a later chapter, Governor Crow raised Canadian interest rates in an effort to restrain inflationary pressures that were located primarily in central Canada. This had the desired effect of reducing aggregate demand in Ontario and Quebec, but it crippled many industries in regional areas that were already operating at the margin. Critics of the Bank of Canada want to see more public input into the design and implementation of monetary policy.

Opponents of change at the Bank of Canada point to the relationship between the Governor and the Minister of Finance. The Governor must take direction from the federal Finance Minister, or resign. The fact that Governor Crow was not forced to resign, opponents argue, shows the government's tacit agreement with Crow's policies. Furthermore, the critics suggest that if the Governor has to worry about electoral politics, he won't follow monetary policies that might reduce his chances of re-election or reappointment. If he has to worry about being re-elected for another term, he may not undertake policies that are in the best interests of the nation. Having an independent central bank that is ultimately subservient to the Minister of Finance (if push comes to shove), it is argued, is the best of both worlds.

All of this does not mean that the Governor is impotent. As the government's banker, the Governor of the Bank of Canada can make running a budget deficit difficult for the government. He can exercise control over the amounts the government is allowed to borrow from the central bank, and the rates at which they can borrow. If push came to shove, and the Governor resigned, there would be serious implications for financial stability, particularly with respect to international investment. This would ultimately come back to haunt the government. Maintaining reputation and credibility are essential elements of any institutional arrangement, so if the Governor resigns, there's a price to pay in rebuilding the central bank's image in international markets.

Let's briefly touch on how international considerations affect the design and implementation of monetary policy in Canada. We'll see that exchange rates play a critical role in the process.

In Canada, the central bank is the Bank of Canada, and much of this chapter is about its structure. But the Bank is only one of many central banks. Let's briefly introduce you to some of the others.

APPLYING THE TOOLS

Central Banks in Other Countries

The United States
The central bank in the U.S. is called the Federal Reserve Bank. It's made up of 12 regional reserve banks and is run by the Board of Governors. It uses reserve requirements and open market operations to control the ability of banks to create money. The Chairman of the Board of Governors is appointed by the President for a four-year term. Affectionately known as the Fed, its actions have repercussions around the world, which we'll discuss in a later chapter.

Bundesbank
In Germany, the central bank is called the *Bundesbank*. It has a reputation as a fierce inflation fighter, in large part because of the historical legacy of the German hyperinflation of the late 1920s and early 1930s. To fight inflation in the mid-1990s, it maintained high interest rates relative to the rest of the world, causing international monetary disruption, which will be discussed in a later chapter. In the late 1990s it gave up much of its policymaking power to the European Central Bank.

European Central Bank
In the late 1990s a number of European Union countries formed a monetary union, creating a common currency called the euro, and a new central bank called the European Central Bank (ECB). It has 12 governors, one from each individual country's central bank. These governors hold a majority of the 18 seats on the ECB General Council, which decides monetary policy for the member countries.

The primary objective of the ECB is not much different from the Bank's; the ECB is focused solely on maintaining price stability, as was the German Bundesbank. Its tools and its directives are similar to the Bundesbank's, and some economists have considered it as an expansion of the Bundesbank for the entire EU.

Most economists held a wait-and-see attitude about the bank. They point out that the ECB is a new bank and it will take time for its operating procedures to become established. We can expect significant political infighting as the various countries attempt to influence the decisions of the ECB to favour them.

The Bank of England
The Bank of England is sometimes called the Old Lady of Threadneedle Street (because it's located on that street, and the British like such quaint characterizations). It does not use a required reserve mechanism. Instead, individual banks determine their own needed reserves, so any reserves they have would, in a sense, be excess reserves.

How does the Old Lady control the money supply? With the equivalent of open market operations and with what might be called "tea control." Since there are only a few large banks in England, the Old Lady simply passes on the word at tea as to which direction she thinks the money supply should be going. Alas for sentimentalists, "tea control" is fading in England, as are many of the quaint English ways.

The Bank of Japan
The Bank of Japan uses reserve requirements and open market operations to control the money supply. Reserve requirements are similar to those in the United States, but because banks are allowed a longer time to do their averaging, excess reserves are much lower in Japan than in the U.S. and Canada. Until the early 1990s the Bank of Japan held the Japanese interest rate far below the world rate, which caused an international outflow of savings and a corresponding trade surplus. In 1990 the Japanese interest rate increased substantially, in part due to the actions of the Bank of Japan, but by the mid-1990s and into the early 2000s the Japanese interest rate was once again very low.

Clearly, there's more to be said about each of these central banks, but this brief introduction should give you a sense of both the similarities and the diversities among the central banks of the world.

International Considerations   We said that the dismissal or resignation of the Governor of the Bank of Canada could have disastrous effects on international investment. To understand why, we first need to talk a little bit about exchange rates. An **exchange rate** is simply *the value of one nation's currency expressed in terms of another nation's currency.* It tells us how much of one currency it takes to buy a unit of another currency. For example, the exchange rate between the U.S. dollar and the Canadian dollar tells us

An exchange rate expresses the value of one currency in terms of the value of another.

TABLE 14-1   **Exchange Rates**

Currency	in C$	in US$	Daily % chg	Currency	in C$	in US$	Daily % chg
Antigua,Gr.EC$	0.6010	0.3745	nil	Kuwait (Dinar)	5.2118	3.2478	nil
Argentina (Peso)	0.74464	0.46404	-0.70	Lebanon (Pound)	0.001060	0.000661	-0.02
Austria (Euro)	1.3896	0.8660	0.19	Luxemb. Euro	1.38960	0.86596	0.19
Bahamas (Dollar)	1.6047	1.0000	nil	Malaysia (Ringgit)	0.4223	0.2632	-0.01
Bahrain (Dinar)	4.2565	2.6525	nil	Malta (Lira)	3.4817	2.1697	0.07
Barbados (Dollar)	0.8064	0.5025	nil	Netherlands (Euro)	1.3896	0.5460	0.19
Belgium (Euro)	1.3896	0.8660	0.19	Neth. Ant. Guilder	0.9015	0.5618	nil
Bermuda (Dollar	1.6047	1.0000	nil	New Zealand $	0.6767	0.4217	0.52
Brazil (Real)	0.6802	0.4239	0.25	Norway (Krone)	0.1801	0.1122	0.07
Bulgaria (Lev)	0.713835	0.4448	0.29	Pakistan (Rupee)	0.02677	0.01668	-0.08
Chile (Peso)	0.002388	0.001488	0.31	Panama (Balboa)	1.6047	1.0000	nil
Colombia (Peso)	0.000697	0.000434	0.22	Philippines (Peso)	0.03137	0.01955	0.23
Costa Rica Colon	0.004624	0.002881	-0.04	Poland (Zloty)	0.3798	0.2367	-0.73
Cuba (Peso)	0.0764	0.0476	nil	Portugal (Euro)	1.3896	0.8660	0.19
Cyprus (Pound)	2.4145	1.5047	0.32	Peru (New Sol)	0.46265	0.28831	0.07
Czech (Koruna)	0.0440	0.0274	0.56	Romania (Leu)	0.000049	0.000031	-0.23
Denmark (Krone)	0.1870	0.1165	0.19	Russia (Ruble)	0.051836	0.032303	nil
Dominican Rep Peso	0.0973	0.0606	nil	Saudi Arabia Riyal	0.4279	0.2667	nil
Egypt (Pound)	0.3473	0.2165	-0.22	Slovakia (Koruna)	0.0334	0.0208	0.49
Finland (Euro)	1.3896	0.8660	0.19	Slovenia (Tolar)	0.0062	0.0039	0.23
Greece (Euro)	1.3896	0.8660	0.19	S. Africa (Rand)	0.1415	0.0882	0.45
Guyana (Dollar)	0.00889	0.00554	nil	S. Korea (Won)	0.001221	0.000761	0.27
Hong Kong (Dollar)	0.2058	0.1282	nil	Spain (Euro)	1.3896	0.8660	0.19
Hungary (Forint)	0.00567	0.00354	0.09	Sri Lanka (Rupee)	0.01717	0.01070	nil
India (Rupee)	0.03298	0.02055	nil	Sweden (Krona)	0.1533	0.0956	0.14
Indonesia Rupiah	0.000158	0.000099	0.39	Taiwan (Dollar)	0.04584	0.0286	nil
Ireland (Euro)	1.3896	0.8660	0.19	Thailand (Baht)	0.03674	0.0229	0.23
Israel (N Shekel)	0.3444	0.2146	-1.16	Trinidad & Tob. $	0.2626	0.1637	nil
Italy (Euro)	1.3896	0.8660	0.19	Turkey (Lira)	0.0000012	0.0000007	1.08
Jamaica (Dollar)	0.03385	0.02110	-0.11	Jordan (inar)	2.2665	1.4124	3.94
Jordan (Dinar)	2.2665	1.4124	nil	Spec Draw Right SDR	1.9924	1.2416	0.06

Source: *The National Post*, March 1, 2002.

the value of a Canadian dollar in terms of U.S. dollars, and the value of a U.S. dollar in terms of Canadian dollars. Since there are two currencies involved, it's possible to measure exchange rates two different ways. That explains why, for example, you might turn on your TV and see that the Canadian dollar is trading for US$0.65 while today's newspaper says the exchange rate is $1.54. Why are the numbers different? The answer is simple: One is measuring how many Canadian dollars it takes to buy a U.S. dollar (1.54), while the other tells us how many U.S. dollars a Canadian dollar will buy (0.65). If you look carefully at these numbers you'll see that one is simply the reciprocal (inverse) of the other: The reciprocal of 0.65 is 1.54.

We'll define the exchange rate to be *the domestic currency price of foreign exchange*— that is, it tells us how many Canadian dollars it takes to buy a unit of the foreign currency. So, if we're looking at the Canadian dollar–U.S. dollar exchange rate, it tells us how many Canadian dollars it takes to buy one U.S. dollar (in our example, CAN$1.54 buys US$1). If we look at the Canadian dollar–Japanese yen exchange rate, it tells us how many dollars it takes to buy one yen. Similarly for the Canadian dollar–Swiss franc exchange rate. Table 14-1 presents information on exchange rates.

For a time, the development of the Canadian banking system closely followed what was happening in the United States. The Bank of Montreal was Canada's first bank, established in 1817 by a group of Montreal merchants. In the next 50 years more than 20 banks opened their doors, and by Confederation there were almost 30 chartered banks. Each bank had the power to issue its own paper notes, which circulated as currency. When you wanted to buy something you could either use one of these bank notes, or you could write a cheque against your deposits in a chartered bank. Before the introduction of bank notes, "money" took several forms, ranging from playing cards (altered by the colonial authorities to act as currency) to gold and silver.

In the United States banks expanded along regional lines, and there were few truly national banks. This is in stark contrast to the development of the Canadian banking system, which was characterized by centrally managed banks that spanned provincial borders. These differences between the U.S. and Canadian banking systems remain today: There are thousands of banks in the United States, each with relatively few branches, whereas Canada has relatively few banks, each with many branches.

Canadian banks provided the "lubrication" necessary for economic development. They gathered savings and lent them out to entrepreneurs and governments. Banks also provided the vehicle for foreign currency transactions, which were of vital importance to the development of the Canadian economy.

The Great Depression changed public confidence in financial institutions, and in 1933 the MacMillan Commission was charged with investigating whether Canada needed a central bank. Canadian politicians looked south of the border in their quest for a solution, since the United States had created their central bank, the Federal Reserve Bank, in 1913. While many Canadians wondered whether Canada really needed a similar institution, critics of the Canadian financial system blamed the chartered banks for contributing to the Depression. Not surprisingly, the financial community lobbied against the introduction of a central body that would regulate their activities. In the end, the MacMillan Commission recommended the establishment of a central bank for Canada, and in 1934 the Bank of Canada was officially created by the Bank of Canada Act.

The Bank of Canada was initially a private corporation that was later nationalized in 1938. It was given power to replace the existing currency with Bank of Canada bank notes, force chartered banks to hold a certain proportion of their deposits as cash or on deposit at the Bank of Canada, make advances to the chartered banks when appropriate, and act as the federal government's banker.

Why do exchange rates matter? For a country such as Canada, international trade is important. The trade sector of the economy directly employs more than 2 million people, or about 15 percent of Canada's workforce. Exchange rates matter because they allow people with different currencies to buy goods and services from each other. When Canadians want to buy foreign goods and services, they need to trade Canadian dollars for foreign currency, which is then used to buy the foreign goods and services. When foreigners want to buy Canadian goods and services, they need to trade their currency for Canadian dollars. They then use those dollars to buy what they want from Canada.

The importance of all of this has to do with our previous definition of monetary policy. Recall that we said monetary policy influences the economy through changes in the money supply and the availability of credit. From what we've just discussed, it's clear that monetary policy—*changes in the money supply*—will affect international trade, since the relative price of one nation's currency (the exchange rate) depends critically on how much of it is in circulation. For example, consider a world that includes only two nations, Canada and Great Britain. If the Canadian money supply rises while the British money supply remains fixed, the Canadian dollar will lose value against the British pound—there are relatively more Canadian dollars around, so each is worth less than before.

If the dollar loses value, what will this do to international trade? What will it do to employment in industries that produce goods for export to other countries? The answer

The relationship between the Prime Minister and the Bank of Canada is often more friendly than it appears to be in the press. The Prime Minister and the Bank of Canada sometimes play good cop/bad cop: The central bank undertakes a politically tough decision. The Prime Minister screams and yells to the press about how awful the Bank of Canada is (off the record), while privately encouraging it. The Bank of Canada takes the political heat since it doesn't have to face an election, while the Prime Minister seems like a nice guy (or gal).

It's Parliamentary folklore that each Prime Minister who takes up residence receives three letters from the outgoing Prime Minister. The letters are to be opened only in a dire economic emergency. Letter Number 1 says, "Blame it on the Opposition." Letter Number 2, to be opened only if Letter Number 1 doesn't work, says, "Blame it on the Bank of Canada." If Letter Number 2 doesn't work either, Letter Number 3 is to be opened. It says "Prepare Three Letters!"

depends on many factors, including what happens to prices, interest rates, and incomes, both at home and abroad. If the Governor of the Bank of Canada is forced to resign, this might create increased levels of uncertainty in international markets, and the dollar could lose a lot of value (or gain value, if the market consensus was that the Governor had to go!). This has implications for where international investors choose to place their funds; it could lead to changes in the pattern of international trade, thereby affecting the equilibrium level of income and employment in the Canadian economy.

All of this means that monetary policy cannot be set without consideration of international issues. We'll discuss this in much greater detail in Chapters 16 to 18.

Duties of the Bank

The Bank of Canada is responsible for:

1. Conducting monetary policy (influencing the supply of money and credit in the economy).
2. Providing central banking services, including the implementation of monetary policy and services to government, banks, and other central banks.
3. Issuing bank notes and ensuring their authenticity.
4. Administering public debt.

The Importance of Monetary Policy

Not only is monetary policy the most important function of the Bank, but it is probably the most used policy in macroeconomics. Although the Governor of the Bank of Canada must follow a directive from the Minister of Finance, in practice the Bank of Canada conducts and controls monetary policy, whereas fiscal policy is conducted directly by the government. Both policies are directed toward the same end: influencing the level of aggregate economic activity, hopefully in a beneficial manner. (In many other countries institutional arrangements are different and the central bank is part of government, so both monetary and fiscal policies are directly conducted by the government, albeit by different branches.)

Actual decisions about monetary policy are made by the Governor in consultation with senior staff. The Board of Directors meets with the Governor on a regular basis, and minutes of their discussion are included in the *Bank of Canada Review*, published quarterly (with monthly supplements). The financial press and business community dissect every word uttered by the Governor, looking for information that will set the course of the economy over the near term.

Q-2 What is the difference between monetary and fiscal policy?

The Conduct of Monetary Policy

You've already seen that monetary policy shifts the *AD* curve. Let's now consider how it does so. We need to look more specifically at the institutional structure of the banking system and the role of the Bank in that institutional structure.

Think back to our discussion of the banking system. Banks take in deposits, make loans, and buy other financial assets, keeping a certain percentage of reserves for those transactions. Those reserves are IOUs of the Bank—either vault cash or deposits at the Bank. *Vault cash, deposits of the Bank, plus currency in circulation make up the* **monetary base.** The monetary base held at banks serves as reserves of the banking system. By controlling the monetary base, the Bank can influence the amount of money in the economy and the activities of banks.

The actual tools of monetary policy will affect the amount of reserves in the system. In turn, the amount of reserves in the system will affect the interest rate. Other things equal, as reserves decline, the interest rate will rise; and as reserves increase, the interest rate will decline. So monetary policy will also be associated with interest rates.

Let's now turn to the main tools of monetary policy and see precisely how they influence the amount of reserves in the system.

TOOLS OF MONETARY POLICY

The basic tools of monetary policy evolve over time and depend on the structure of the financial system. In Canada, early in the new millennium, the central bank's policy tools include:

1. Changing the target range for the overnight financing rate
2. Cash management operations

Let's discuss each in turn.

The Overnight Financing Rate

Even though the percentage of Canadians using debit cards is the highest in the world, we still use cheques when we buy things. You buy a car, you write a cheque. Where does that cheque go, and how does your bank get the funds to the car dealer's bank (if they don't have an account at your bank)? Well, all chartered banks and many other intermediaries are members of the Canadian Payments Association. Among other things, this association runs an electronic funds transfer system called the *Large Value Transfer System* (LVTS), where payments clear and settle daily. So, the car dealer's bank puts your cheque into the system and the funds magically appear in their account (and disappear from yours).

Every day the members of the LVTS settle millions of dollars' worth of claims. Some days, participants might find that other members of the system owe them more funds than they owe, and so will find themselves with positive balances as a result of the clearing and settlements process. Other members may find that they owe more than they are owed. This requires them to come up with the cash to meet their obligations. One way this can be accomplished is by liquidating some of their interest-earning assets, such as treasury bills. They could sell a treasury bill—forgoing the interest income it provides—to solve their problem. Alternatively, they could call in some loans and top up their cash holdings to satisfy their LVTS positions. Of course, they could also approach the central bank and ask for a loan, since the Bank of Canada is a banker's bank, but the Bank is going to charge a relatively high rate of interest on the advance. The central bank does this to discourage intermediaries from looking for an advance in favour of having them find a private market solution.

Margin notes:

Reserves include vault cash or deposits at the central bank.

The tools of monetary policy are:
1. Changing the overnight financing target rate
2. Cash management operations.

The LVTS is the system through which large transactions clear and settle.

None of the options we've discussed so far is particularly satisfying to a chartered bank, since they all involve the bank losing an interest-earning asset. Chartered banks, after all, earn much of their income from the interest payments they receive on loans and securities in their portfolios, so we shouldn't be surprised that they would prefer to find another way to satisfy their cash requirements. Is there an alternative?

Yes! Members of the Canadian Payments Association who have surplus balances resulting from the clearing and settlements process in the LVTS can loan these surplus funds on a very-short-term basis to those members who are in a deficit position. These loans occur in the overnight market, and *the interest rate associated with these very-short-term loans is known as the* **overnight financing rate**.

The rate of interest on overnight loans is the overnight financing rate.

Changes in the overnight financing rate are important because all other interest rates are related to it through the **term structure of interest rates**—*the structure of yields on financial instruments with similar characteristics (such as risk), but different terms to maturity*. When the overnight financing rate changes, we usually see changes in many other interest rates. These changes reflect how investors view the prospect for long-term securities relative to short-term securities.

We know there is more than just one interest rate in the economy—there are hundreds of interest rates, each related to a particular financial claim. A Government of Canada 10-year bond carries with it a certain interest rate, and this differs from interest rates on 30-day commercial paper and a short-term treasury bill. The term structure of interest rates describes a relationship between short-term and long-term interest rates. For example, it links short-term Government of Canada bond rates to long-term Government of Canada bond rates (remember the similar risk assumption), or short-term corporate bond rates to long-term corporate bond rates (which are more risky than Government of Canada bonds because there's little chance the government will default). **Arbitrage**—*the buying and selling of similar goods and services across different markets*—provides the link between interest rates on dissimilar assets (such as Government of Canada bonds and corporate bonds). Figure 14-2(a) illustrates the link between short-term and long-term bonds while Figure 14-2(b) shows the relationship between the three-month treasury bill rate and the three-month commercial paper rate.

Arbitrage is the buying and selling of similar products across different markets.

The Bank of Canada has a target for the overnight financing rate, specified in terms of a 50-basis point range (a basis point is 1/100 of a percent). The **bank rate**—*the rate at which members of the Canadian Payments Association can borrow from the Bank of Canada*—is at the upper end of this target range. This is the interest rate at which an advance can be drawn from the central bank. An institution that needs funds to satisfy its obligations to the LVTS could borrow from the central bank at that rate.

The bank rate is the interest rate charged on advances from the central bank.

The bottom of the target range for the overnight financing rate is also an important component of monetary policy. It's the rate of interest the Bank of Canada will pay to LVTS participants who want to leave their surplus funds with the Bank of Canada. Can you see why it is important?

Suppose there are two banks in the economy, the Bank of Kingston and the Bank of Victoria. Further, assume that the Bank of Kingston has $10 million at the end of the LVTS process, while the Bank of Victoria needs $10 million to satisfy the demands it faces for clearing and settlements purposes. The Bank of Victoria could liquidate some of its interest-earning assets, or it could borrow from the central bank at the top of the target range for the overnight financing rate (the bank rate) through an advance. The Bank of Kingston could leave its surplus funds at the central bank and earn the bottom of the target range.

Both banks could do better by agreeing to borrow and lend from each other. The Bank of Victoria would like to pay a lower interest rate than the bank rate (the top of the overnight financing range), while the Bank of Kingston would like to earn more

Q-3 Why would a chartered bank use the overnight market rather than cash in a treasury bill?

Figure 14-2 (a and b)   RELATIONSHIPS AMONG INTEREST RATES

In **(a)** you can see the term structure sometimes inverts, with short-term rates above long-term bond rates. In **(b)** you can see that the short-term interest rates on treasury bills and corporate paper follow each other.

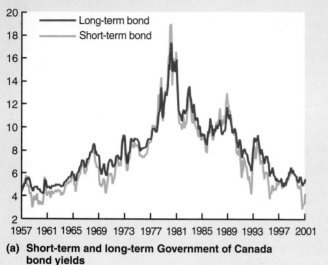

(a) Short-term and long-term Government of Canada bond yields

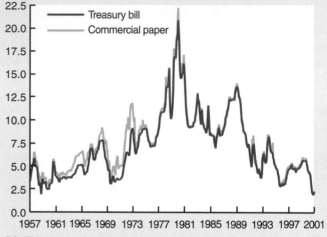

(b) Three-month treasury bill and corporate paper rates

Source: Statistics Canada, CANSIM II, Table 176-0043.

than the lower range of the overnight financing target. The two chartered banks have an incentive to interact, with the overnight financing rate being the rate at which the Bank of Kingston will lend the Bank of Victoria $10 million.

The main tool of monetary policy in Canada is the target range for the overnight financing rate. Through raising or lowering the target range, the Bank of Canada relies on the term structure of interest rates to filter changes into interest rates across the maturity spectrum. If investment and consumption decisions are financed over the long term (who buys a house and expects to pay off the mortgage in two years?), the central bank might be able to reduce long-term rates and stimulate aggregate demand by reducing the target range for the overnight financing rate. Similarly, if the Bank of Canada wants to restrain aggregate demand, it raises the target range for the overnight financing rate; this should filter through to all other maturities and eventually affect the level of aggregate demand in the economy.

Cash Management Operations

The second major tool of monetary policy in Canada involves cash management. **Cash management operations** *are the main techniques for implementing monetary policy in Canada.* Through intervening in the clearing and settlements processes, the central bank is able to maintain the overnight financing rate within its target band. Cash management techniques include a variety of **open market operations**—*buying and selling of government bonds and bills*—as well as the transfer of government deposits between chartered banks (and others) and the Bank of Canada. All of these activities involve the same basic principle: give the chartered banks more or less cash and allow their entrepreneurial spirit to determine the effects on deposits. This directly affects the money supply, as banks lend their excess reserves or call in loans when they find themselves short of cash. Let's look at some examples.

Open market operations involve the central bank in buying or selling federal securities.

Sometimes you'll hear or read about the changes in interest rates as changes in basis points. A basis point is simply ⅟₁₀₀ of 1 percent, so 25 basis points is just ¼ of 1 percent. In many bond markets the minimum change in interest rates is 1 basis point. That might not look like much to you, but multiply any 1-basis-point change in interest rates by a large amount of money (say $1 billion at 7.00 percent versus 7.01 percent), and you've got a tidy sum. Would you rather receive 7.00 percent or 7.01 percent interest on principal of $1 billion?

KNOWING THE TOOLS

Fancy Lingo

Open Market Operations Open market operations involve the purchase or sale of federal government securities such as treasury bills and Government of Canada bonds. When the Bank of Canada buys bonds, it deposits the funds in federal government accounts at chartered banks. You'll recall from the previous chapter that chartered banks can create money by lending their excess reserves. When the Bank of Canada pays the government for its bonds, chartered bank cash reserves rise. Chartered banks don't like to hold excess reserves, so they loan the excess, thereby expanding the deposit base of the economy. The money supply rises. Thus, an open market purchase is an example of **expansionary monetary policy** (usually defined as *one that tends to raise income and reduce interest rates*), since it raises the money supply (as long as the chartered banks strive to minimize their excess reserves).

An open market sale has the opposite effect. Here, the Bank of Canada sells bonds, and in return receives a cheque drawn against a chartered bank. The chartered bank loses demand deposits (since the Bank of Canada "cashes" the cheque and takes the money away from the chartered bank) and the money supply falls. This is an example of **contractionary monetary policy**—*lowering income and raising interest rates*.

What happens to bond prices and interest rates during this process? Figure 14-3(a) illustrates the effects of an open market purchase. The Bank of Canada buys bonds, thereby raising the demand for bonds. Bond prices rise, and since we know that bond prices and interest rates are inversely related (when one goes up, the other goes down), interest rates fall. That's what we'd expect of an expansionary monetary policy.

Figure 14-3(b) shows us what happens to bond prices in an open market sale (from that you can figure out the change in interest rates). As the Bank of Canada sells bonds, the supply of bonds shifts right, leading to lower bond prices. What happens to interest rates? If you said they go up, you're on track.

> *To expand the money supply, the Bank of Canada buys bonds.*
> *To contract the money supply, the Bank of Canada sells bonds.*

Government Deposits A transfer of government deposits from the chartered banks (and other financial institutions) to the Bank of Canada reduces liquidity in the banking system and tends to place upward pressure on interest rates. A transfer in the opposite direction from the Bank of Canada to the chartered banks (and others) has the opposite effect. Through these techniques the Bank of Canada is able to exert control over the liquidity of the banking system and, ultimately, the money supply.

As the government's banker, the central bank needs to predict government deposit flows so it can achieve the changes in liquidity that it desires. In the last few years the Bank of Canada has changed the manner in which it implements monetary policy on a daily basis. It relies more heavily on private incentives to encourage financial institutions to act in their own best interests. For example, it holds a daily auction of "excess" government deposit balances to help chartered banks meet their own internal liquidity targets. This helps financial institutions manage risk without direct intervention—the banks' quest for profits motivates their decisions.

Expansionary monetary policy is monetary policy aimed at increasing the money supply and raising the level of aggregate demand.

Q.4 Is an open market purchase a contractionary or an expansionary policy?

Contractionary monetary policy is monetary policy aimed at reducing the money supply and thereby restraining aggregate demand.

Q.5 How does a transfer of government deposits to the central bank affect interest rates?

 14.2

see page 357

Figure 14-3 (a and b) OPEN MARKET OPERATIONS

In (a) you can see that an open market purchase raises existing bond prices. That increase in bond price is the equivalent to a decrease in the interest rate. In (b) you can see that an open market sale reduces existing bond prices. That reduction means that the interest rate rises.

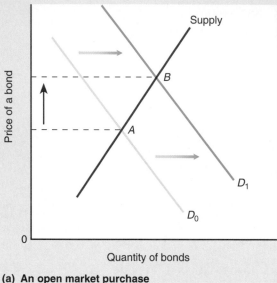

(a) An open market purchase

(b) An open market sale

MONETARY POLICY IN THE AS/AD MODEL

Q-6 If the economy is operating at potential output, does expansionary monetary policy raise real output?

In the *AS/AD* model, monetary policy works primarily through its effect on interest rates. As the government changes the money supply, the interest rate changes. Increasing the money supply increases the amount of money banks have to lend. To attract borrowers, banks offer lower interest rates. Lower interest rates lead businesses to borrow more, expanding investment expenditures, which increases aggregate demand. Decreasing the money supply reduces the amount of money banks have available for loans and increases the interest rate. Higher interest rates lead businesses to borrow less, and to decrease investment expenditures, which decreases aggregate demand.

Through the multiplier effects, aggregate demand and equilibrium income decrease by a multiple of the decrease in investment. Figure 14-4(a) shows the effect of a fall in investment on equilibrium income. A decrease in investment shifts the *AD* curve to the left by a multiple of the decline in investment. Thus, *contractionary monetary policy* tends to *decrease* the money supply, *increase* the interest rate, *decrease* investment, and *decrease* income and output.

$$M\downarrow \rightarrow i\uparrow \rightarrow I\downarrow \rightarrow Y\downarrow$$

Q-7 Demonstrate the effect of expansionary monetary policy in the *AS/AD* model when there are no inflationary pressures.

Expansionary monetary policy works in the opposite manner, as Figure 14-4(b) shows. *Expansionary* monetary policy tends to *increase* the money supply, *decrease* the interest rate, *increase* investment, and *increase* income and output:

$$M\uparrow \rightarrow i\downarrow \rightarrow I\uparrow \rightarrow Y\uparrow$$

Let's go through the reasoning again, only this time focusing on trying to provide an intuitive feel for what is happening. Say the Bank of Canada uses open market operations. As the Bank either injects or pulls out liquidity, it influences the amount of money banks have to lend and the interest rate at which they can lend it. When banks have more reserves than they planned, they want to lend. (That's how they make their profit.) To get people to borrow more from them, banks will decrease the interest rate they charge on loans. So expansionary monetary policy tends to decrease the interest rate banks charge their customers; contractionary policy tends to increase the interest rate banks charge customers. Expansionary monetary policy increases the amount of money banks have to lend, which tends to increase investment and leads to an increase in income. Contractionary monetary policy decreases the amount of money banks have to lend, which tends to decrease investment and leads to a decrease in income.

Monetary Policy in the Circular Flow

Figure 14-5's familiar circular flow diagram shows how monetary policy works in the AS/AD model. It works inside the financial sector to help equate the flow of saving with investment. When the economy is operating at too low a level of income and when saving exceeds investment, in the absence of monetary policy, income will fall. Expansionary monetary policy tries to channel more saving into investment so the fall in income is stopped. It does so by increasing the available credit, lowering the interest rate, and increasing investment and hence income.

Contractionary monetary policy is called for when saving is smaller than investment and the economy is operating at too high a level of income, causing inflationary pressures. In this case, monetary policy tries to restrict the demand for investment and consumer loans.

Figure 14-4 (a and b) **CONTRACTIONARY AND EXPANSIONARY MONETARY POLICY WHEN PRICES ARE FIXED**

Assume that the short-run aggregate supply curve is flat, so the price level is fixed. With a decrease in the money supply, the interest rate will rise, decreasing investment. The fall in investment shifts the aggregate demand curve from AD_0 to AD_1. Income decreases from Y_0 to Y_1, as shown in (a), which decreases savings sufficiently so that savings equal investment. In (b), expansionary monetary policy is shown working the opposite way. It shifts the AD curve to the right, from AD_0 to AD_1. Income increases from Y_0 to Y_1.

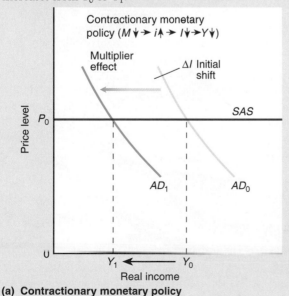

(a) Contractionary monetary policy

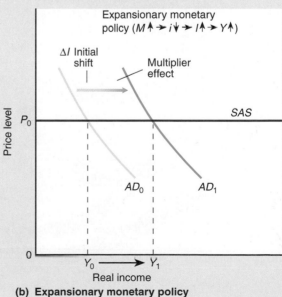

(b) Expansionary monetary policy

The Emphasis on the Interest Rate

Because in the *AS/AD* model monetary policy works through the effect of interest rates on investment, our analysis focuses on the interest rate in judging monetary policy. A rising interest rate indicates a tightening of monetary policy. A falling interest rate indicates a loosening of monetary policy.

A natural conclusion is that the Bank should target interest rates in setting monetary policy. For example, if the interest rate is currently 6 percent and the Bank wants to loosen monetary policy, it should buy bonds until the interest rate falls to 5.5 percent. If it wants to tighten monetary policy, it should sell bonds to make the interest rate go up to, say, 6.5 percent.

Real and Nominal Interest Rates

There is a problem in using interest rates to measure whether monetary policy is contractionary or expansionary. That problem is the real/nominal interest rate problem. **Nominal interest rates** are *the rates you actually see and pay*. When a bank pays 7 percent interest, that 7 percent is a nominal interest rate. What affects the economy is the real interest rate. **Real interest rates** are *nominal interest rates adjusted for expected inflation*.

For example, say you get 7 percent interest from the bank, but the price level goes up 7 percent. At the end of the year you have $107 instead of $100, but you're no better off than before because the price level has risen—on average, things cost 7 percent

---

Figure 14-5   MONETARY POLICY IN THE CIRCULAR FLOW

If monetary and fiscal policy are needed, it is because the financial sector is, in some ways, clogged and is not correctly translating saving into investment. Monetary policy works to unclog the financial sector. Fiscal policy provides an alternative route for saving around the financial sector. A government deficit absorbs excess saving and translates it back into the spending stream. A surplus supplements the shortage of saving and reduces the flow back into the spending stream.

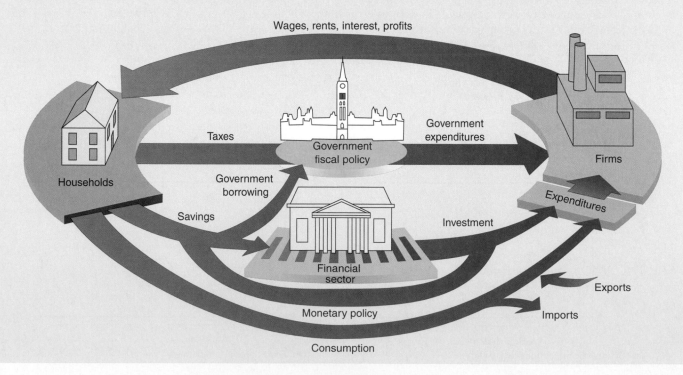

more. What you would have paid $100 for last year now costs $107. (That's the definition of *inflation*.) Had the price level remained constant, and had you received 0 percent interest, you'd be in the equivalent position to receiving 7 percent interest on your $100 when the price level rises by 7 percent. That 0 percent is the *real interest rate*. It is the interest rate you would expect to receive if the price level remains constant.

The real interest rate cannot be observed because it depends on expected inflation. To calculate the real interest rate, you must subtract what you believe to be the expected rate of inflation from the nominal interest rate. For example, if the nominal interest rate is 7 percent and expected inflation is 4 percent, the real interest rate is 3 percent. The relationship between real and nominal interest rates is important both for your study of economics and for your own personal finances:

Nominal interest rate = Real interest rate + Expected inflation rate

Q.8 If the nominal interest rate is 10 percent and expected inflation is 3 percent, what is the real interest rate?

Real and Nominal Interest Rates and Monetary Policy

What does this distinction between nominal and real interest rates mean for monetary policy? It adds yet another uncertainty to the effect of monetary policy. In the *AS/AD* model we assumed that expansionary monetary policy lowers the interest rate and contractionary monetary policy increases the interest rate. However, if the expansionary monetary policy leads to expectations of increased inflation, expansionary monetary policy can increase nominal interest rates (the ones you see) and leave real interest rates (the ones that affect borrowing decisions) unchanged. Why? Because of expectations of increasing inflation. Lenders will want to be compensated for the inflation (which will decrease the value of the money they receive back) and will push the nominal interest rate up to get the desired real rate of interest.

The distinction between nominal and real interest rates and the possible effect of monetary policy on expectations of inflation has led most economists to conclude that a monetary regime, not a monetary policy, is the best approach to policy. A **monetary regime** is *a predetermined statement of the policy that will be followed in various situations*. A monetary policy, in contrast, is a response to events; it is chosen without a predetermined framework.

Monetary regimes are now favoured because rules can help generate the expectations that even though in certain instances the Bank is increasing the money supply, that increase is not a signal that monetary expansion and inflation are imminent. The monetary regime that the Bank currently uses involves feedback rules that centre on the overnight financing rate. If inflation is above its target, the Bank raises the target range (by reducing liquidity, thereby decreasing the money supply) in an attempt to slow inflation down. If inflation is below its target, and if the economy is going into a recession, the Bank lowers the target range (by increasing liquidity, thereby increasing the money supply).

Q.9 How does the distinction between nominal and real interest rates add uncertainty to the effect of monetary policy on the economy?

PROBLEMS IN THE CONDUCT OF MONETARY POLICY

In an earlier chapter, after discussing fiscal policy's structure and mechanics, we presented the problems with using fiscal policy. Now that you've been through the structure and mechanics of monetary policy, let's consider the problems with using it, too.

Knowing What Policy to Use

To use monetary policy effectively, you must know the potential level of income. Otherwise you won't know whether to use expansionary or contractionary monetary policy.

Five problems of monetary policy:

1. Knowing what policy to use.
2. Understanding what policy you're using.
3. Lags in monetary policy.
4. Political pressure.
5. Conflicting international goals.

Let's consider an example: Late in 2001, the economy seemed to be in the doldrums, with most economists convinced that North America was in a relatively minor recession. Certainly the manufacturing sector had faced more than two quarterly declines in real output, so at a minimum it met the formal definition of being in a recession. The consensus was that across the economy, output was below potential. Then the terrorist attacks occurred in the United States. Financial markets closed for an unprecedented period. Concern over the stability of the insurance and transportation industries was widespread. To bolster confidence, the Federal Reserve Bank in the United States cut its key interest rate, with the Bank of Canada following suit. Liquidity was pumped into the system, without regard for the inflationary consequences that might follow. This was done to assure investors, financial institutions, and the general public that the financial system would continue to allocate society's savings to the best investments possible. As society came to grips with what had happened, central banks across the world acted to provide the liquidity required to maintain orderly markets. As time passed, central banks stood ready to tighten their belts at the first signs of inflationary pressure, but their primary concern was to foster a sense of economic security.

Understanding the Policy You're Using

To use monetary policy effectively, you must know whether the monetary policy you're using is expansionary or contractionary. You might think that's rather easy, but it isn't. In our consideration of monetary policy tools, you saw that the Bank doesn't directly control the money supply. It indirectly controls it, generally through open market operations by changing the *monetary base* (the vault cash and reserves banks have at the Bank). Then the money multiplier determines the amounts of M_1, M_2, and other monetary measures in the economy.

> The Bank only indirectly controls the monetary base.

That money multiplier is influenced by the amount of cash that people hold as well as the lending process at the bank. Neither of those is the stable number that we used in calculating the money multipliers. They change from day to day and week to week, so even if you control the monetary base, you can never be sure exactly what will happen to M_1 and M_2 in the short run. Moreover, the effects on M_1 and M_2 can differ; one measure is telling you that you're expanding the money supply and the other measure is telling you you're contracting it.

And then, of course, there are changes in the interest rate. If interest rates rise, is it because of expected inflation (which is adding an inflation premium to the nominal interest rate) or is it the real interest rate that is going up? There is frequent debate over which it is. Combined, these measurement problems make the Bank often wonder not only about what policy it should follow, but what policy it is following.

Lags in Monetary Policy

Monetary policy, like fiscal policy, takes time to work its way through the economic system. The Bank can change the money supply or interest rates; people don't have to borrow, however. An increased money supply may simply lead to excess reserves and have little or no influence on income. This is most likely when interest rates are very low. This is what happened in Japan in the late 1990s. The Bank of Japan (the Japanese central bank) lowered the interest rate (the one similar to the overnight financing rate in Canada) to 0.01 percent with little effect on investment spending. The belief that increases in the money supply would be ineffective in the 1930s led early Keynesians to focus on fiscal policy rather than monetary policy as a way of expanding the economy. They likened expansionary monetary policy to pushing on a string. The same problem exists with using contractionary monetary policy. Banks have been very good at figuring out ways to circumvent cuts in the money supply, making the intended results of contractionary monetary policy difficult to achieve.

It's also possible that there are asymmetries in the effect of a change in interest rates on investment. When interest rates are high, a small reduction may have a substantial impact on investment. The same rate cut experienced when rates are already low may have little or no impact on the level of investment in the economy. So, changing liquidity to alter interest rates, which should ultimately affect investment and aggregate demand, is an inexact science. Economists spend much of their time trying to figure out how the puzzle fits together. That's hard to do when the puzzle keeps changing shape.

Political Pressure

While the Bank is partially insulated from political pressure by its structure, it's not totally insulated. Politicians place enormous pressure on the Bank to use expansionary monetary policy (especially during an election year) and blame the Bank for any recession. When interest rates rise, the Bank takes the pressure.

Conflicting International Goals

Monetary policy is not conducted in a vacuum. It is conducted in an international arena and must be coordinated with other governments' monetary policy. Similarly, as we've already mentioned, monetary policy affects the exchange rate and trade balance. Often the desired monetary policy for its international effects is the opposite of the desired monetary policy for its domestic effects.

Q-10 What are five problems in the conduct of monetary policy?

CONCLUSION

We could continue with a discussion of the problems of using monetary policy, but the above should give you a good sense that conducting monetary policy is not a piece of cake. It takes not only a sense of the theory; it also takes a feel for the economy. In short, the conduct of monetary policy is not a science. It does not allow the Bank to steer the economy as it might steer a car. It does work well enough to allow the Bank to *influence* the economy—much as an expert rodeo rider rides a bronco bull.

 14.3

see page 357

The Bank can influence, not steer, the economy.

Chapter Summary

- Monetary policy is the policy of influencing the economy through changes in the banking system's reserves that affect the money supply and credit availability in the economy.

- The Bank of Canada is a central bank; it conducts monetary policy for Canada.

- The two tools of monetary policy are:
  1. Changing the target range for the overnight financing rate.
  2. Cash management operations.

- A change in liquidity changes the money supply by the change in reserves times the money multiplier.

- Open market operations are an important tool:
  To expand the money supply, the Bank buys bonds.
  To contract the money supply, the Bank sells bonds.

- The Bank of Canada's Governor and his advisers make the actual decisions about monetary policy.

- When the Bank buys bonds, the price of bonds rises and interest rates fall. When the Bank sells bonds, the price of bonds falls and interest rates rise.

- In the *AS/AD* model, contractionary monetary policy works as follows:
  $M\downarrow \rightarrow i\uparrow \rightarrow I\downarrow \rightarrow Y\downarrow$

- Expansionary monetary policy works as follows:
  $M\uparrow \rightarrow i\downarrow \rightarrow I\uparrow \rightarrow Y\uparrow$

- Because in the *AS/AD* model, monetary policy affects the economy through the effect of a change in the interest rate on investment, the interest rate is an indication of the direction of monetary policy. A higher interest rate indicates contractionary monetary policy; a lower interest rate indicates expansionary monetary policy.

- Nominal interest rates are the interest rates we see and pay. Real interest rates are nominal interest rates adjusted for expected inflation: Nominal interest rate = Real interest rate + Expected inflation.

- Because monetary policy can affect inflation expectations as well as nominal interest rates, the effect of monetary policy on interest rates can be uncertain. This uncertainty has led the Bank to follow monetary regimes.
- Problems of monetary policy include knowing what policy to use, knowing what policy you are using, lags, political pressure, and conflicting international goals.

Key Terms

arbitrage *(347)*

bank rate *(347)*

cash management operations *(348)*

central bank *(340)*

contractionary monetary policy *(349)*

exchange rate *(342)*

expansionary monetary policy *(349)*

monetary base *(346)*

monetary policy *(338)*

monetary regime *(353)*

nominal interest rates *(352)*

open market operations *(348)*

overnight financing rate *(347)*

real interest rates *(352)*

term structure of interest rates *(347)*

Questions for Thought and Review

1. Is the Bank a private or a public agency?
2. Name the two tools the Bank has to affect the money supply and explain how the Bank would use each tool to increase the money supply.
3. What happens to interest rates and the price of bonds when the Bank buys bonds?
4. Define the *overnight financing rate* and explain why it is the interest rate that the Bank most directly controls.
5. You can lead a horse to water, but you can't make it drink. How might this adage be relevant to expansionary (as opposed to contractionary) monetary policy?

6. Investment increases by 20 for each interest rate drop of 1 percent. The expenditures multiplier is 3. If the money multiplier is 4, and each change of 5 in the money supply changes the interest rate by 1 percent, what open market policy would you recommend to increase income by 240?
7. If the nominal interest rate is 6 percent and inflation is 5 percent, what's the real interest rate?
8. "The effects of open market operations are somewhat like a stone cast in a pond." After the splash, discuss the first three ripples.
9. Why would a bank hold treasury bills when it could simply hold cash?

Problems and Exercises

1. Demonstrate the effect of expansionary monetary policy in the *AS/AD* model when the economy is in the:
   a. Keynesian range.
   b. Classical range.
   c. Intermediate range.
2. The Bank wants to increase the money supply (which is currently 4,000) by 200. The money multiplier is 3. For each 1 percentage point the overnight financing rate falls, banks borrow an additional 20. Explain how the Bank can achieve its goals using the following tools:
   a. Change the overnight financing rate.
   b. Use open market operations.

3. Suppose the Bank decides it needs to pursue an expansionary policy. Assume people hold no cash, the desired reserve ratio is 20 percent, and there are no excess reserves.
   a. Show how the Bank would increase the money supply by $2 million if they could change the desired reserve ratio.
   b. Show how the Bank would increase the money supply by $2 million through open market operations.
4. Suppose the Bank decides that it needs to pursue a contractionary policy. It wants to decrease the money supply by $2 million. Assume people hold 20 percent of their money in the form of cash balances, the desired reserve ratio is 20 percent, and there are no excess reserves.

a. Show how the Bank would decrease the money supply by $2 million if they could change the desired reserve ratio.

b. Show how the Bank would decrease the money supply by $2 million through open market operations.

c. Go to your local bank and find out how much excess reserves it holds. Recalculate *a* and *b* assuming all banks held that percentage in excess reserves.

5. Some individuals have suggested that all banks must have a 100 percent reserve ratio.

a. What would the money multiplier be if this change were made?

b. What effect would such a change have on the money supply?

c. How could that effect be offset?

d. Would banks likely favour or oppose this proposal? Why?

6. The central bank pays interest on reserves held at the bank.

a. What effect does this have on excess reserves?

b. Would banks generally favour or oppose this policy? Why?

c. Would central banks generally favour or oppose this policy? Why?

d. What effect would this policy probably have on interest rates paid by banks?

Web Questions

1. Go to the Bank of Canada's Web site (www.bankof-canada.ca) and answer the following questions:

a. When was the last Monetary Policy Report?

b. How many times during this calendar year (before this month) has the Bank of Canada changed the target range for the overnight financing rate?

c. How many Deputy Governors are there at the Bank of Canada?

d. How many people sit on the Board of Directors of the Bank, and from which provinces are they drawn?

2. The Bank of Canada's Web site (www.bankofcanada.ca) contains information on how the LVTS operates and its role in the day-to-day operation of monetary policy (check out the link to *Publications and Research*).

a. At what point during the day are Receiver General balances auctioned?

b. What is a special purchase and resale agreement?

c. How does the LVTS allow the Bank of Canada some control over the overnight financing rate? If the market were pushing the overnight financing rate above the upper end of the target band, how would the central bank respond?

d. If the overnight financing rate falls below the lower end of the target band, does the Bank have to increase or decrease liquidity to bring the rate back up?

3. Check out the Backgrounder on the Transmission of Monetary Policy at the Bank of Canada's Web site (www.bankofcanada.ca).

a. How long does it take for monetary policy actions to affect the economy?

b. What is the process by which changes in interest rates affect the level of inflation in the economy?

c. How does the Bank adjust monetary conditions to achieve its objectives?

d. Is monetary policy predictable?

Answers to Margin Questions

1. The federal Cabinet appoints the Governor of the Bank of Canada.   *(340)*

2. Monetary policy is conducted by the Bank and involves changing the money supply or interest rates. Fiscal policy is conducted by the government, and involves running a surplus or deficit.   *(345)*

3. A treasury bill provides interest income to a bank so it would try to borrow in the overnight market rather than lose that interest income.   *(347)*

4. An open market purchase raises liquidity and is therefore an expansionary policy.   *(349)*

5. A transfer of government deposits to the central bank reduces liquidity and places upward pressure on interest rates.   *(349)*

6. No. Nominal output rises because the price level rises, but real output remains at potential.   *(350)*

7. Expansionary monetary policy makes more money available to banks for loan. Banks lower their interest rates to attract more borrowers. With lower interest rates businesses will borrow more money and increase investment expenditures. The multiplier shifts the *AD* curve to the right by a multiple of the increase in investment expenditures. Since the economy is in the Keynesian

range, real output increases to Y_1 and the price level remains constant.   *(350)*

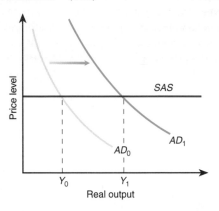

8. The real interest rate is 7 percent, the nominal interest rate (10) less expected inflation (3).   *(353)*

9. Because expansionary monetary policy can lead to expectations of higher inflation, expansionary monetary policy can lead to higher nominal interest rates. Because real interest rates cannot be observed directly, interest rates are not always a good guide for the direction of monetary policy.   *(353)*

10. Five problems of monetary policy are:
    1. Knowing what policy to use.
    2. Understanding what policy you're using.
    3. The lags in monetary policy.
    4. Political pressure.
    5. Conflicting international goals.   *(355)*

APPENDIX A

The Effect of Monetary Policy Using T-Accounts

The Bank uses the overnight financing rate and open market operations to change the money supply. Each of these tools works initially by affecting the amount of reserves in the banking system. Here we will show you exactly how the Bank changes the money supply using T-accounts. To simplify things, say there's only one bank, Textland Bank, with branches all over the country. Textland is fully loaned out at a 10 percent desired reserve requirement. For simplicity, assume people hold no cash. Textland's beginning balance sheet is presented below in Table A14-1.

Now say the Bank sells $10,000 worth of treasury bills to individuals. The person who buys them pays with a cheque to the Bank for $10,000. The Bank, in turn, presents that cheque to the bank, getting $10,000 in cash from the bank. This step is shown in Table A14-2.

As you can see, bank reserves are now $290,000, which is too low to meet the desired level on demand deposits of

$2,990,000. With a 10 percent desired reserve requirement, $2,990,000 in deposits would require $0.1 \times \$2,990,000 = \$299,000$, so the bank is $9,000 short of reserves. It must figure out a way to meet its desired reserve requirement. Let's say that it calls in $9,000 of its loans. After doing so it has assets of $299,000 in cash and $2,990,000 in demand deposits, so it looks as if the bank has met its desired reserve requirement.

If the bank could meet its desired reserve requirement that way, its balance sheet would be as shown in Table A14-3. Loans would decrease by $9,000 and cash would increase by the $9,000 necessary to meet the reserve requirement.

Unfortunately for the bank, meeting its desired reserve requirement isn't that easy. That $9,000 in cash had to come from somewhere. Most likely, the person who paid off the loans in cash did it partly by running down her chequing account, borrowing all the cash she could from

TABLE A14-1   Textland Bank Balance Sheet

Assets	Beginning Balance	Liabilities and Net Worth	
Cash (reserves)	$ 300,000	Demand deposits	$3,000,000
Loans	2,000,000	Net worth	1,000,000
Treasury bills	400,000		
Property	1,300,000		
Total assets	$4,000,000	Total liabilities and net worth	$4,000,000

others, and using whatever other options she had. Since by assumption in this example, people don't hold cash, the banking system was initially fully loaned out, and Textland Bank was the only bank, the only cash in the economy was in Textland Bank's vaults! So that $9,000 in cash had to come from its vaults. Calling in the loans cannot directly solve its reserve problem. It still has reserves of only $290,000.

But calling in its loans did *indirectly* help solve the problem. Calling in loans decreased investment which, because it decreased aggregate demand, decreased the income in the economy. (If you're not sure why this is the case, think back to the macro policy model.) That decrease in income decreases the amount of demand deposits people want to hold. As demand deposits decrease, the bank's need for reserves decreases.

Contraction of the money supply in this example works in the opposite way to an expansion of the money supply. Banks keep trying to meet their desired reserve requirement by getting cash, only to find that for the banking system as a whole the total cash is limited. Thus, the banking system as a whole must continue to call in loans until that decline in loans causes income to fall sufficiently to cause demand deposits to fall to a level that can be supported by the smaller reserves. In this example, with a money multiplier of 10, when demand deposits have fallen by $100,000 to $2.9 million, total reserves available to the system ($290,000) will be sufficient to meet the desired reserve requirement.

Questions for Thought and Review

1. Demonstrate, using T-accounts, the effect of the Bank selling $1 million of treasury bills when the desired reserve requirement is 10 percent and people hold no cash.

2. Demonstrate, using T-accounts, the effect of the Bank buying $2 million of treasury bills when the desired reserve requirement is 10 percent and people hold no cash.

TABLE A14-2

Transaction 1			
Assets		**Liabilities and Net Worth**	
Cash (reserves)	$ 300,000	Demand deposits.	$3,000,000
Payment to central bank (person's		Deposits for cash (person's cheque) . .	(10,000)
treasury purchase)	(10,000)	Total deposits.	$2,990,000
Total cash	$ 290,000	Net worth.	1,000,000
Loans	2,000,000		
Treasury bills.	400,000		
Property	1,300,000		
Total assets.	$3,990,000	Total liabilities and net worth	$3,990,000

TABLE A14-3

Transaction 2			
Assets		**Liabilities and Net Worth**	
Cash (reserves)	$ 290,000	Demand deposits	$2,990,000
Loans (repaid).	9,000	Net worth.	1,000,000
Total cash	$ 299,000		
Loans	2,000,000		
Loans called in	(9,000)		
Total loans.	1,991,000		
Treasury bills.	400,000		
Property	1,300,000		
Total assets.	$3,000,000	Total liabilities and net worth	$3,990,000

Inflation and Its Relationship to Unemployment and Growth

15

After reading this chapter, you should be able to:

- State some of the distributional effects of inflation.

- Explain how inflation expectations are formed.

- Outline the quantity theory of money and its theory of inflation.

- Outline the institutional theory of inflation.

- Differentiate between long-run and short-run Phillips curves.

- Explain the different views on the relationship between inflation and growth.

The first few months or years of inflation, like the first few drinks, seem just fine. Everyone has more money to spend and prices aren't rising quite as fast as the money that's available. The hangover comes when prices start to catch up.

Milton Friedman

Politicians tend to get re-elected when the economy is doing well. Thus, it should not surprise you that political pressures exert a strong bias toward expansionary policy. What prevents politicians from implementing the expansionary policies is inflation, or at least the fear of generating an accelerating inflation. It is for that reason that inflation and its relationship to unemployment and growth come to centre stage in any discussion of macro policy. Hence this chapter. It extends our earlier consideration of inflation and considers the trade-offs between inflation, unemployment, and growth.

SOME BASICS ABOUT INFLATION

We introduced you to inflation in an earlier chapter. There, you saw the definition of *inflation* (a continuous rise in the price level) and how inflation is measured (with price indexes). We also explained that expectations of inflation can become built into individuals' behaviour and economic institutions and cause a small inflation to accelerate, and that inflation creates feelings of injustice and destroys the informational value of prices and the market. (If any of those concepts seem a bit vague to you, a review might be a good idea.) We now build on that information to give you more insight into inflation.

The Distributional Effects of Inflation

Who wins and who loses in an inflation? The answer to that is simple: The winners are people who can raise their wages or prices and still keep their jobs or sell their goods. The losers are people who can't raise their wages or prices. Consider a worker who has entered a contract to receive 4 percent annual wage increases for three years. If the worker expected inflation to be 2 percent at the time of the agreement, she was expecting her real wage to rise 2 percent each year. If instead inflation is 6 percent, her real wage will *fall* 2 percent. The worker loses, but the firm gains because it can charge 4 percent more for its products than it anticipated. The worker's wage was fixed by contract, but the firm could raise its prices. On average, winners and losers balance out; inflation does not make the population richer or poorer. Most people, however, worry about their own position, not what happens to the average person.

Lenders and borrowers, because they often enter into fixed nominal contracts, are also affected by inflation. If lenders make loans at 5 percent interest and expect inflation to be 2 percent, they plan to earn a 3 percent real rate of return on their loan. If, however, inflation turns out to be 4 percent, lenders will only earn a 1 percent real rate of return, and borrowers, who were expecting to pay a real interest rate of 3 percent, end up paying only 1 percent. Lenders will lose; borrowers will gain. In other words, unexpected inflation redistributes income from lenders to borrowers.

The composition of the group winning or losing from inflation changes over time. For example, before indexation, people on pensions lost out during inflation since pensions were, on the whole, fixed in nominal terms. Inflation lowered recipients' real income. In the 1970s many pensions were changed to adjust automatically for changes in the cost of living, so pensioners are no longer losers. Their real income is independent of inflation. (Actually, because of the adjustment method, some say that pension recipients actually now gain from inflation since the adjustment may more than compensate them for the rise in the price level.)

What we can say about the distributional consequences of inflation is that people who don't expect inflation and who are tied to fixed nominal contracts will likely lose during an inflationary period. However, if these people are rational, they probably won't let it happen again; they'll be prepared for a subsequent inflation. That is, they will change their expectations of inflation.

Expectations of Inflation

Expectations of inflation play a key role in the inflationary process. When expectations of inflation are high, people tend to raise their wages and prices, causing inflation. Expectations can become self-fulfilling. For this reason, economists have looked carefully at how individuals form expectations. Almost all economists believe that the expectations that people have of inflation are in some sense rational, by which we mean they

Q.1 True or false? Inflation makes an economy poorer. Explain your answer.

15.1

see page 380

Unexpected inflation redistributes income from lenders to borrowers.

Expectations of inflation can have profound effects on economic activity. If inflation hurts consumers' purchasing power, economic activity could be dampened.

are based on the best information available, given the cost of that information. But economists differ on what is meant by rational and thus on how those expectations are formulated. Some economists take a strong stand and argue that rational people will expect the same inflation that is predicted by the economists' model. Thus, **rational expectations** are *the expectations that the economists' model predicts*. If inflation was, say, 2 percent last year and is 4 percent this year but the economists' model predicts 0 percent inflation for the coming year, individuals will rationally expect 0 percent inflation.

Other economists argue that there are many different economists' models and they are imperfect, so rational expectations cannot be defined in terms of economists' models. These economists instead focus on the process by which people develop their expectations. One way people form expectations is to look at conditions that already exist, or have recently existed. Such expectations are called **adaptive expectations**—*expectations based in some way on the past*. Thus, if inflation was 2 percent last year and 4 percent this year, the prediction for inflation will be somewhere around 3 percent. Adaptive expectations aren't the only type that people use. Sometimes they use **extrapolative expectations**—*expectations that a trend will continue*. For example, say that inflation was 2 percent last year and 4 percent this year; extrapolative expectations would predict 6 percent inflation next year. There are many other types of expectations, and individuals use various combinations of them, shifting suddenly from one type to another.

Since expectations play a key role in policy, shifts in the process of forming expectations can change the way the economy operates. It was precisely such a shift in the formation of expectations that played a key role in the recent expansion without inflation. Sometime in the early 1990s in Canada, individuals stopped expecting high inflation and began expecting low inflation, and those expectations became self-fulfilling.

Q.2 Name three different types of expectations.

15.2

see page 380

Productivity, Inflation, and Wages

Two key measures that policymakers use to determine whether inflation may be coming are changes in productivity and changes in wages. Together these measures determine whether or not the aggregate supply curve will be shifting up. The rule of thumb is that wages can increase by the amount that productivity increases without generating any inflationary pressure:

Inflation = Nominal wage increase − Productivity growth

For example, if productivity is increasing at 2 percent, wages can go up by 2 percent without generating any inflationary pressure.

THEORIES OF INFLATION

Economists hold two slightly different theories of inflation: the quantity theory and institutional theory. The quantity theory emphasizes the connection between money and inflation; the institutional theory emphasizes market structure and price-setting institutions and inflation. There is significant overlap between the two theories, but because they come to different policy conclusions, it is helpful to consider them separately.

The Quantity Theory of Money and Inflation

The quantity theory of money can be summed up in one sentence: *Inflation is always and everywhere a monetary phenomenon*. If the money supply rises, the price level will rise. If the money supply doesn't rise, the price level won't rise. Forget all the other stuff—it just obscures the connection between money and inflation.

KNOWING THE TOOLS

Demand-Pull and Cost-Push Inflation

Quantity theory and institutional theories of inflation are sometimes differentiated as demand-pull inflation and cost-push inflation. When the majority of industries are at close to capacity and they experience increases in demand, we say there's demand-pull pressure. The inflation that results is called *demand-pull inflation*—inflation that occurs when the economy is at or above potential output. Demand-pull inflation is generally characterized by shortages of goods and shortages of workers. Because there's excess demand, firms know that if they raise their prices, they'll still be able to sell their goods, and workers know if they raise their wages, they will still be employed.

When significant proportions of markets (or one very important market, such as the labour market or the oil market) experience price rises not related to demand pressure, we say that there is cost-push pressure. The resulting inflation is *cost-push inflation*—inflation that occurs when the economy is below potential output. In cost-push

inflation, because there is no excess demand (there may actually be excess supply), firms that raise their prices are not sure demand will be sufficient to sell off their goods and workers are not sure that after raising their wage they will all be employed. But the ones who actually do the pushing are fairly sure they won't be the ones who can't sell off their goods or the ones fired. A classic cost-push example occurred in the 1970s when OPEC raised its price on oil, triggering cost-push inflation.

Notice that in the text we do not use these distinctions. The reason is that although demand-pull and cost-push pressures can be catalysts for starting inflation, they are not causes of continued inflation. The reality is that in an ongoing inflation cost-push or demand-pull forces become intertwined. As Alfred Marshall (the 19th-century English economist who originated supply and demand analysis) said, it is impossible to separate the roles of supply and demand in influencing price, just as it is impossible to say which blade of the scissors is cutting a sheet of paper.

The Equation of Exchange The quantity theory of money centres on the **equation of exchange,** *an equation stating that the quantity of money times velocity of money equals the price level times the quantity of real goods sold.* This equation is:

$$MV = PQ$$

where:

M = Quantity of money

V = Velocity of money

P = Price level

Q = Quantity of real goods sold

Q is the real output of the economy (real GDP) and P is the price level, so PQ is the economy's nominal output (nominal GDP). V, the **velocity of money,** is *the number of times per year, on average, a dollar goes around to generate a dollar's worth of income.* Put another way, velocity is the amount of income per year generated by a dollar of money. Since MV = PQ, MV also equals nominal output. Thus, if there's $100 in the economy and velocity is 20, nominal GDP is $2,000. We can calculate V by dividing nominal GDP by the money supply. Let's take Canada as an example. In Canada in 2001, nominal GDP was approximately $1,100 billion and M was approximately $120 billion (using M_1), so velocity was about GDP/M = 9.2, meaning each dollar in the economy circulated enough to support approximately $9.20 in total income.

Velocity Is Constant The equation of exchange is a tautology, meaning it is true by definition. What changes it from a tautology to a theory are two assumptions. The first assumption is that velocity remains constant. Money is spent only so fast; how fast is determined by the economy's institutional structure, such as how close individuals live to stores, how people are paid (weekly, biweekly, or monthly), and what sources of credit

In the quantity theory model, inflation is caused by growth in the money supply. It focuses on the equation of exchange:

$$MV = PQ$$

Money can affect real output (Q) in the short run, but in the long run it affects only the price level (P).

Q.3 What's the difference between the equation of exchange and the quantity theory of money?

Something that is determined outside the model is called exogenous.

Three assumptions of quantity theory:
1. Velocity is constant.
2. Real output is independent of money supply.
3. Causation goes from money to prices.

The quantity theory view that printing money causes inflation is seen in the 18th-century satirical drawing by James Gilray showing William Pitt spewing paper money out of his mouth while gold coins are locked up in his stomach.

are available. (Can you go to the store and buy something on credit, that is, without handing over cash?) This institutional structure changes slowly, quantity theorists argue, so velocity won't fluctuate very much. Next year, velocity will be approximately the same as this year.

If velocity remains constant, the quantity theory can be used to predict how much nominal GDP will grow if we know how much the money supply grows. For example, if the money supply goes up 6 percent, the quantity theory of money predicts that nominal GDP will go up by 6 percent.

Real Output Is Independent of the Money Supply The second assumption is that Q is independent of the money supply. That is, Q is exogenous, meaning real output is determined by forces outside those forces in the quantity theory. If Q grows, it is because of incentives that affect the real economy. Thus, policy analysis based on the quantity theory focuses on the real economy—the supply side of the economy, not the demand side.

This assumption makes analyzing the economy a lot easier than if the financial and real sectors are interrelated and if real economic activity is influenced by financial changes. It separates two puzzles: how the real economy works, and how the price level and financial sector work. Instead of having two different jigsaw puzzles all mixed up, each puzzle can be worked separately. The quantity theory doesn't say there aren't interconnections between the real and financial sectors, but it does say that most of these interconnections involve short-run considerations. The quantity theory is primarily concerned with the long run.

With both V (velocity) and Q (quantity or output) unaffected by changes in M (money supply), the only thing that can change is P (price level). In its simplest terms, the **quantity theory of money** says that *the price level varies in response to changes in the quantity of money*. If the money supply goes up 20 percent, prices go up 20 percent. If the money supply goes down 5 percent, the price level goes down 5 percent.

Examples of Money's Role in Inflation Let's consider an example of the relationship between money growth and inflation from the 1980s when significant inflation—over 10 percent—had become built into the economy.

In late 1979 and the early 1980s, the Bank of Canada decreased the money supply growth significantly. This led to a leap in unemployment from 7.5 to nearly 12 percent, but initially no decrease in inflation. By 1984, however, inflation had fallen to about 4 percent, and it remained low throughout the 1980s and 1990s.

Now let's consider a couple more recent examples. In the early 1990s, the German central bank felt Germany's inflation rate was too high. It cut the money supply growth considerably. Initially, the impact was on output, and the tight money pushed the German economy into a recession. Germany remained in that recession through early 1996, and inflation fell in the late 1990s. A second recent example is Russia in the early 1990s. The Russian government was short of revenue and was forced to print money to finance its debt. As a result, inflation blew up into hyperinflation, and the Russian economy continued in a serious slump.

Despite these and many other examples, the simple view connecting inflation with money supply growth lost favour in the late 1970s and 1990s as formerly stable relationships between certain measurements of money and prices broke down in Canada. Consider Figure 15-1, which shows the relationship between prices and the money supply for Canada.

Figure 15-1   **PRICE LEVEL AND MONEY IN CANADA, 1953–2001**

From the 1950s until the late 1970s prices and the money supply were closely linked. Beginning in the late 1970s and again in the late 1990s the relationship broke down. Whether the breakdown in the relationship is temporary or permanent is debatable. Most economists agree that enormous changes in financial institutions and the increased global interdependence of financial markets contributed to the breakdown.

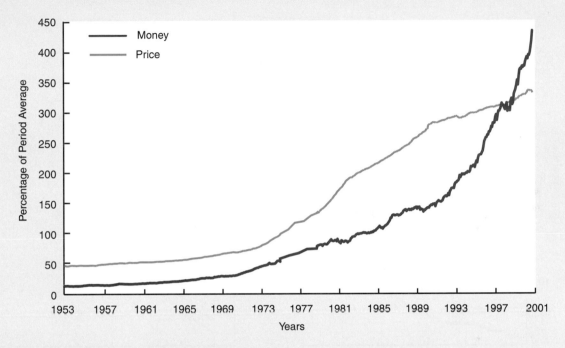

Source: Statistics Canada, CANSIM II, Tables 176-0025 and 326-0001; authors' calculations.

Notice that in the 1970s and 1990s the close relationship ended. Some economists argue that this breakdown was temporary; others argue that it was permanent. Both sides agree the breakdown was caused by (1) the enormous changes in financial institutions that were occurring because of technological changes and changing regulations, and (2) the increased global interdependence of financial markets, which increased the flow of money among countries. Where the two sides differ is in whether these changes will permanently alter the close relationship between money growth and inflation. In the 1990s it seemed that, for low inflation, the random elements (called noise) in the relationship between money and prices overwhelmed the connection between the two.

For large inflation of the type experienced by many developing and transitional economies, the connection is still evident, and the quantity theory remains the central theory of inflation in such countries. Some empirical evidence consistent with the quantity theory's relevance for developing countries can be seen in Figure 15-2, which shows the relationship between the increase in money and the increase in prices in two countries, Brazil and Chile. Notice that both money and prices have increased closely together.

The Inflation Tax The reason why central banks in countries such as Brazil and Chile sometimes increase the money supply so much is complicated. The goal that most often tops their list is to keep the economy running. They are also generally far less independent of political pressures than central banks in developed countries. Finally, developing countries

Figure 15-2   PRICE LEVEL AND MONEY RELATIVE TO REAL INCOME IN BRAZIL, 1912–1987, AND CHILE, 1940–1997

The empirical evidence that supports the quantity theory of money is most convincing in countries that experience significant inflation. Brazil and Chile are examples where high money growth has accompanied high rates of inflation.

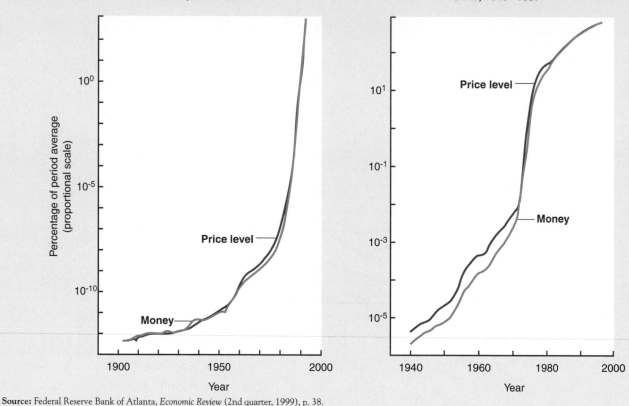

Source: Federal Reserve Bank of Atlanta, *Economic Review* (2nd quarter, 1999), p. 38.

lack broad-based government bond markets. So if the government runs a budget deficit and is financing it domestically, the central bank often must buy the bonds to finance that deficit. If it does not, the government will default. In this case we can say that the increase in the money supply is caused by the government deficit.

Financing the deficit by expansionary monetary policy is not costless. It causes inflation. The inflation that results from the increases in the money supply works as a type of tax on individuals and is often called an **inflation tax** (*an implicit tax on the holders of cash and the holders of any obligations specified in nominal terms*). Inflation is considered a tax because it reduces the value of cash and other nominal obligations.

Let's consider an inflation tax in relation to the transitional economies of the former Soviet Union. With the end of central planning, the currency circulating far exceeded the amount necessary to purchase the real goods the economy could produce at market prices. Why? Most individuals had stored their financial wealth in the currency of their country. This currency represented the enormous past obligations of the former socialist governments—obligations that far exceeded the governments', or the economies', ability to meet them.

As they moved to a market economy without an acceptable tax base, these governments had no way to meet their current obligations, let alone their past obligations. The

BEYOND THE TOOLS

The Keeper of the Classical Faith: Milton Friedman

The quantity theory is generally associated with Classical economics, and the most famous advocate of the quantity theory was Milton Friedman. By most accounts, Milton Friedman was a headstrong student. He didn't simply accept the truths his teachers laid out. If he didn't agree, he argued strongly for his own belief. He was very bright, and his ideas were generally logical and convincing. He needed to be both persistent and intelligent to maintain and promote his views in spite of strong opposition.

Throughout the Keynesian years of the 1950s and 1960s, Friedman stood up and argued for the quantity theory, keeping it alive. During this period Classical economics was called *monetarism,* and because Friedman was such a strong advocate of the quantity theory, he was considered the leader of the monetarists.

Friedman argued that fiscal policy simply didn't work. It led to expansions in the size of government. He also opposed an activist monetary policy. The effects of monetary policy, he said, were too variable for it to be useful in guiding the economy. He called for a steady growth in the money supply, and argued consistently for a laissez-faire policy by government.

Friedman has made his mark in both microeconomics and macroeconomics. In the 1970s, his ideas caught hold and helped spawn a renewal of the quantity theory. He was awarded the Nobel Prize in economics in 1976.

central banks generally chose to keep the governments operating (which isn't surprising, since they were often branches of the government). To do that, they increased the money supply enormously, causing hyperinflation. The hyperinflation soon took on a life of its own. The expectation of accelerating inflation created even more inflationary pressure as individuals tried to spend any money they had quickly, before the prices went up. This increased the velocity of money, the nominal demand for goods, and inflationary pressures. Eventually the hyperinflation wiped out (taxed away) the excess currency and allowed most of the transitional countries to rein in their inflation, getting it down to double digits (less than 100 percent per year). This was possible because, with the excess currency wiped out, the inflation tax only had to make up for the government budget deficit; it no longer had to be used to eliminate past obligations.

Central banks know that issuing large quantities of money will cause inflation. What they don't know, and what the policy discussions are about, is whether it's worse to have the inflation or the unpleasant alternatives of recession—or perhaps even a breakdown of the entire economy. Thus, the debate is not about whether the inflation is caused by the issuance of too much money but whether countries' budget deficits are absolutely necessary or not. Should the central bank bail out the government?

Q.4 Why do some central banks issue large quantities of money if they know that doing so will cause inflation?

Policy Implications of the Quantity Theory In terms of policy, the quantity theory says that monetary policy is powerful but unpredictable in the short run. Because of this unpredictability monetary policy cannot, and should not, be used to control the level of output in the economy. Thus, paradoxically, supporters of the quantity theory oppose an activist monetary policy. Instead they generally favour a monetary policy set by rules, not by discretionary monetary policy.

As discussed in the previous chapter, many central banks are now using monetary regimes, or feedback rules. A feedback rule might specify that the money supply will be contracted by 1 percent (or the interest rate will be raised by 1.5 percentage points) when inflation rises by 3 percent, and the money supply will be expanded by 1 percent when real output increases but remains below potential output. (This is only an example; the feedback rules can become much more complicated.) A monetary rule takes monetary policy out of the hands of politicians. Quantity theorists feel that politicians

Quantity theorists favour a feedback rule because they believe that the short-run effects of monetary policy are unpredictable and the long-run effects of monetary policy are on the price level, not on real output.

will not be able to hold the money supply down because of the expansionary tendencies in politics, and thus a rule is better than discretion.

The quantity theory has convinced many economists to exert pressure to create independent central banks so that politicians are separated from the control of the money supply. That way the government will not follow its political instincts and run expansionary monetary policy. Let's consider an example: New Zealand, which has legally mandated a monetary rule, based on inflation. Beginning in 1989, the Reserve Bank of New Zealand was required to keep consumer price inflation between 0 and 2 percent a year, a target agreed on by the government and the central bank. After averaging 10 percent a year in the 1980s, New Zealand's inflation rate fell in the early 1990s and averaged below 2 percent per year thereafter. An important reason New Zealand instituted monetary rules was to establish credibility in its central bank's resolve to lower the inflation rate.

In Canada the story was very similar. In 1991 the Bank of Canada and the federal government announced targets for the inflation rate based on the CPI. At the time, the rate of inflation in Canada was nearly 6 percent, and expectations of inflation were beginning to build into wage agreements. To combat these pressures, the authorities announced a series of inflation objectives that progressively lowered the target range for the rate of inflation in Canada. Using interest rates to dampen aggregate demand, the Bank of Canada was able to make the transition to a low-inflation environment. By 1994 the actual inflation rate had fallen to 2 percent, well within the central bank's target band. Given the success of the policy, in the mid-1990s the inflation targets were extended to 1998, then again to 2001 in the late 1990s, and once more to 2006 in May 2001. Canadian monetary policy is aimed at maintaining a low and stable rate of inflation of between 1 and 3 percent, and it seems to be working. Inflation has, for the most part, remained low and stable over the last decade.

The U.S. Federal Reserve Bank does not have such a strict rule, but the Fed works hard to show that it is serious about fighting inflation, regardless of the consequences to unemployment or output. Many economists felt that by the mid-1990s the Fed had established its credibility, and that credibility allowed the economy to expand without generating inflation. Inflation expectations fell, lowering interest rates, which contributed to the investment boom of the late 1990s.

A final example of the importance of the quantity theory concerns the European Central Bank. The constitution states that the European Central Bank's sole goal is to fight inflation. This will significantly reduce political considerations in the central bank's policies. We will have to wait to see the effectiveness of this approach to establishing central bank independence and low inflation.

The Institutional Theory of Inflation

Q.5 Use the equation of exchange to demonstrate the difference between quantity theory and institutional theory of inflation.

The alternative to the quantity theory is the institutional theory of inflation. Supporters of the institutional theory of inflation accept much of the quantity theory—money and inflation do move together. Where they differ is in what they see as the cause and the effect. According to the quantity theory of money, changes in the money supply cause changes in the price level. The direction of causation goes from left to right:

$$MV \rightarrow PQ$$

Institutional theorists see it the other way around. Increases in prices force government to increase the money supply or cause unemployment. The direction of causation goes from right to left:

$$MV \leftarrow PQ$$

According to the institutional theory of inflation, the source of inflation is in the price-setting process of firms. When setting prices, firms and individuals find it easier to raise prices rather than lower them and do not take into account the effect of their pricing decisions on the price level. To see the argument, let's consider firms' pricing decisions.

Focus on the Price-Setting Decisions of Firms Since all income is ultimately paid to individual owners of the factors of production, the revenue that firms receive is divided among profits, wages, and rent. Firms are simply intermediaries between individuals as owners of the factors of production and individuals as consumers. Given the institutional structure of our economy, it's often easier for firms to increase wages, profits, and rents to keep the peace with their employees and other owners of the factors of production than it is to try to hold those costs down. Firms then pay for that increase by raising the prices they charge consumers. That works as long as, in response to the rising price level, the government increases the money supply so that there is sufficient demand to buy the goods at the higher prices.

Let's consider an example of a lip balm company. It is happy with its competitive position in the market, and it expects 0 percent inflation. Productivity (output of lip balm per unit of input) is increasing by 2 percent, the same as the increase in productivity in the economy as a whole, so the firm can hold its nominal price of lip balm constant even if it increases wages by 2 percent. Since the price level isn't expected to change, the firm can maintain its share of the market by holding the price of its lip balm constant. The firm offers workers a 2 percent pay increase.

The firm meets with its workers to discuss the 2 percent offer. At the meeting it becomes clear to the firm that its workers will push for a 4 percent pay increase. What should the firm do? It is here where labour markets and the product market come in. Let's first consider the product market.

If the product market is highly competitive, what the firm can charge for its lip balm is set by the market; if other firms do not experience a 4 percent wage increase, and have a similar 2 percent productivity increase, giving in to the wage increase will ensure that the firm will incur losses and eventually go out of business. So, in a highly competitive market in which supply and demand forces alone determine prices, there's strong pressure to increase wages only 2 percent and hold the price constant. However, real-world firms generally are not in such a highly price-competitive market. They have some power to raise their price. Raising the price will make selling their goods more difficult, but not impossible. Thus, if the product market is only somewhat competitive, the lip balm firm may consider paying the 4 percent and raising the price of its product.

Price-Setting Strategies Depend on the Labour Market Whether the firm chooses this price-raising strategy depends on the state of the labour market. If the labour market is tight (unemployment is low) the firm knows that it will lose employees if it does not give the wage increase. Productivity may fall. Moreover, the firm can figure that if its workers are asking for such an increase, so too are workers of competing firms. Firms often meet workers' demands under the expectation that other firms will do so too. Meeting these demands helps maintain morale and prevents turnover of key workers. Thus, the state of the labour market plays a central role in firms' decisions on whether to give in to the wage demand or not, which is the reason economists look at unemployment to measure inflationary pressures.

Changes in the Money Supply Follow Price-Setting by Firms The institutional theory sees the nominal wage- and price-setting process as generating inflation. As one group pushes up its nominal wage or price, another group responds by doing the same.

The institutional theory of inflation focuses on the institutional and structural aspects of an economy, as well as the money supply, as important causes of inflation.

Institutional theorists see the nominal wage- and price-setting process as generating inflation.

More groups follow until, finally, the first group finds that its relative wage or price hasn't increased. Then the entire process starts again. Once the nominal wage and price levels have risen, government has two options: It can either ratify the increase by increasing the money supply, thereby accepting the inflation, or it can refuse to ratify it. If it refuses to ratify it, firms will not be able to sell all they want at the higher price and will cut production and lay off workers (firms generally don't lower nominal wages). Unemployment will rise.

Supporters of the institutional theory of inflation argue that in most sectors of the economy, competition works slowly. Social pressures, as well as the invisible hand, influence wages and prices. The result is that even when there is substantial unemployment and considerable excess supply of goods, existing workers can still put an upward push on nominal wages, and existing firms can put an upward push on nominal prices. Consider Finland in late 1999. Its economy was booming with unemployment at 10 percent, and growth in output was 3.5 percent per year. This was in stark contrast to the 18 percent rate of unemployment in 1993, which many economists attributed to the loss of exports to the former Soviet Union. Restructuring and the growth of the high-tech industry contributed to Finland's recovery, yet inflation remained low. That's because the key focus of policymakers was on workers' demands.

Consider also the following excerpt from *The Wall Street Journal* of July 26, 1999, which demonstrates the reasoning that follows from an institutional theory of inflation:

> Although unions have largely shown restraint in their wage demand in past years, there are signs that they will reach for a bigger slice of the pie during the next round of wage negotiations in December, when the hundreds of businesses from various industries, their unions and the federal government jointly negotiate wage scales.
>
> If the unions are successful, the larger paychecks, some economists argue, could cause the already skyrocketing real-estate market to spin out of control, triggering an inflationary spiral.

Q-6 How would a quantity theorist likely respond to an insider/outsider model of inflation?

The Insider/Outsider Model and Inflation To get a better picture of how existing workers can push up wages despite substantial unemployment, let's consider the **insider/outsider model,** *an institutionalist story of inflation where insiders bid up wages and outsiders are unemployed.* Insiders are current business owners and workers who have good jobs with excellent long-run prospects. Outsiders are everyone else. Insiders receive above-equilibrium wages, profits, and rents. If the world were competitive, their wages, profits, and rents would be pushed down to the equilibrium level. To prevent this from happening, according to the insider/outsider model, insiders develop sociological and institutional barriers that prevent outsiders from competing away those above-equilibrium wages, profits, and rents. Such barriers include unions, laws restricting the firing of workers, and brand recognition. Because of those barriers, outsiders (often minorities) must take low-paying dead-end jobs or attempt to undertake marginal businesses that pay little return for many hours worked. Even when outsiders do find better jobs or business opportunities, they are first to be fired and their businesses are the first to suffer in a recession. Thus, outsiders have much higher unemployment rates than insiders. For example, in the United States blacks tend to be outsiders; black unemployment rates have consistently been twice as high as white unemployment rates for the same age groups.

In short, our economy is only partially competitive. The invisible hand is often thwarted by social and political forces. Such partially competitive economies are often characterized by insiders' monopolies. Insiders get the jobs and are paid monopoly wage levels. Outsiders are not employed at those higher wages. Imperfect competition allows workers (and firms) to raise nominal wages (and prices) even as unemployment (and ex-

The debate on what to do about inflation has an analogy to dieting. Fasting will cause you to lose about one-half of a kilogram a day. Want to lose 14 kilograms? A dietitian who follows the quantity theory would say, "Fast. Fourteen kilograms equals 105,000 calories. When you've managed to complete a period in which you've eaten 105,000 fewer calories than are necessary to maintain your present weight, you'll have lost 14 kilo-

grams." An institutionalist dietitian would offer a variety of diets or would explore your psyche to discover why you want to overeat, and would perhaps suggest a liquid protein plan. Following the institutionalist diet, you would also take in 105,000 fewer calories than if you'd continued to overeat. But, institutionalists argue, you can't stick with a diet unless you've discovered what makes you want to overeat.

cess supply of goods) exists. Then, as other insiders do likewise, the price level rises. This increase in the price level lowers workers' real wages. In response, workers further raise their nominal wages to protect their real wages. The result is an ongoing chase in which the insiders protect their real wages, while outsiders (the unemployed) suffer. (If the ideas of nominal and real are unclear to you, a review of earlier chapters may be in order.)

Policy Implications of Institutional Theory As we saw above, the quantity theory says that monetary policy should follow a prescribed feedback rule. To stop inflation, reduce the rate of growth of the money supply. Control the money supply and you will control inflation. According to the institutional theory, governments can institute policies other than reducing the money supply that either prevent inflation or stop it in its tracks. Supporters of the institutional theory agree that contractionary monetary policy will ultimately control inflation, but they argue that it will do so in an inefficient and unfair manner. They argue that tight monetary policy usually causes unemployment among those least able to handle it.

Supporters of the institutional theory ask, "Why should the unemployed and the outsiders bear the cost of fighting inflation?" Putting a brick wall in front of a speeding car will stop the car, but that doesn't mean that's how you *should* stop a car. Instead, institutional theorists suggest that contractionary monetary policies be used *in combination with* additional policies that directly slow down inflation at its source. Such an additional policy is often called an **incomes policy,** *a policy that places direct pressure on individuals to hold down their nominal wages and prices.* Formal incomes policies have been out of favour for a number of years, but informal incomes policies exist in many European countries and in many smaller countries throughout the world. In these countries the government plays an important role in the wage negotiations.

In Finland, for example, the government meets with the major unions and companies and attempts to convince workers to hold down wage demands and firms to hold down price increases, promising both sides certain policies if they moderate their positions. Supporters of the institutional theory argue that such an incomes policy can hold down inflation and thereby reduce the unemployment necessary to fight inflation.

Institutionalists believe that, under current conditions, the costs of unemployment are borne more heavily by minorities and other outsiders.

Q-7 What measures would a quantity theorist suggest government use to reduce inflation? What measures would an institutionalist suggest government use?

15.3

see page 381

INFLATION AND UNEMPLOYMENT: THE PHILLIPS CURVE

Policy discussions are usually based on a trade-off between inflation and unemployment. You saw that trade-off in the discussion of policy with the *AS/AD* model. Recall that the effect of expansionary aggregate demand depends on how close to potential output the economy is. The further beyond potential output the economy is, the more inflation expansionary aggregate demand policy would cause. Thus, the economy has a temporary trade-off between unemployment and inflation.

That trade-off can be represented graphically, as shown in Figure 15-3(a). The **short-run Phillips curve** is *a downward-sloping curve showing the relationship between inflation and unemployment when expectations of inflation are constant.* In a Phillips curve diagram, unemployment is measured on the horizontal axis; inflation is on the vertical axis. The Phillips curve shows us the possible short-run combinations of those two phenomena. It tells us that when unemployment is low, say 4 percent, inflation tends to be high, say 4 percent (point A in Figure 15-3(a)). It also tells us that if we want to lower inflation, say to 1 percent, we must be willing to accept high unemployment, say 7 percent (point B in Figure 15-3(a)).

History of the Phillips Curve

The Phillips curve began as an empirical relationship and was discovered by, you guessed it, an economist named Phillips. In the 1950s and 1960s, when unemployment was high, inflation was low; when unemployment was low, inflation was high. Exhibit 15-3(b) shows this empirical relationship for Canada for the years 1952–1975, when the short-run Phillips curve became part of how economists looked at the economy.

Because the short-run Phillips curve seemed to represent a relatively stable trade-off, in the 1960s the short-run Phillips curve began to play a central role in discussions of macroeconomic policy. Conservatives (often advised by supporters of the quantity theory) generally favoured contractionary monetary and fiscal policy, which maintained high unemployment and low inflation (a point like B in Figure 15-3(a)). Liberals (often advised by supporters of the institutional theory) generally favoured expansionary monetary and fiscal policies, which brought about low unemployment but high inflation (a point like A in Figure 15-3(a)).

The Breakdown of the Short-Run Phillips Curve

In the late 1970s, the empirical short-run Phillips curve relationship seemed to break down. The data no longer seemed to show a trade-off between unemployment and inflation. Instead, when unemployment was high, inflation was also high. This phenomenon is termed **stagflation**—*the combination of high and accelerating inflation and high unemployment.* Figure 15-3(c) shows the empirical relationship between inflation and unemployment from 1976 to 1988.

Notice that the relatively stable relationship up until 1975 breaks down in the late 1970s. In the late 1970s, there doesn't seem to be any trade-off between inflation and unemployment at all. Something clearly changed. In the 1980s, inflation fell substantially and, beginning in 1989, a Phillips-curve-type relationship began to reappear, as can be seen in Figure 15-3(d).

The Long-Run and Short-Run Phillips Curves

This continually changing relationship between inflation and unemployment has economists somewhat perplexed. We know that a number of forces are at work, but the strength of these forces varies from one time period to another.

The Importance of Inflation Expectations One of the key forces at work is expectations of inflation. Actual inflation depends both on supply and demand forces and on how much inflation people expect. If people expect a lot of inflation, they will ask for

Figure 15-3 (a, b, c, and d)   **THE PHILLIPS CURVE TRADE-OFF**

Analyzing the empirical relationship between unemployment and inflation from 1952 to 1975—shown in (**b**)—led economists to believe there was the relatively stable Phillips curve which, for policy choices, could be represented by the smooth Phillips curve in (**a**). In the late 1970s the empirical Phillips curve relationship between inflation and unemployment broke down, leading many economists to question the existence of any Phillips curve relationship that allowed policymakers to choose between inflation and unemployment. In (**c**) you can see how in the late 1970s, no stable Phillips curve existed, while in (**d**) you can see how in the 1980s and 1990s, the evidence is mixed. From 1990 onwards a Phillips curve relationship appeared to exist in Canada.

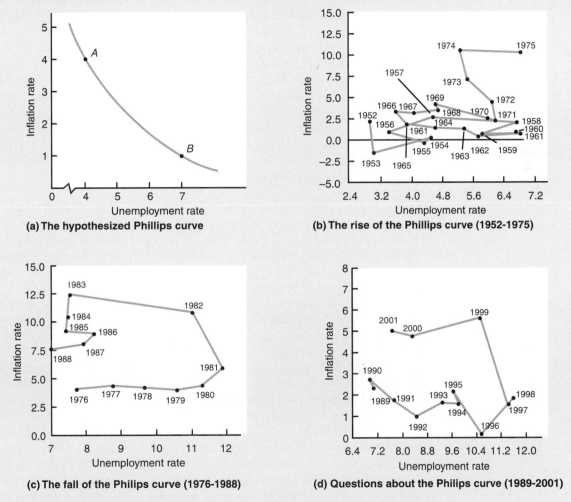

(a) The hypothesized Phillips curve

(b) The rise of the Phillips curve (1952-1975)

(c) The fall of the Philips curve (1976-1988)

(d) Questions about the Philips curve (1989-2001)

Source: Statistics Canada, CANSIM II, Tables 326-0001 and 279-0001; Canadian Historical Statistics series D491.

higher nominal wage and price increases. Expectations have been incorporated into the analysis by distinguishing between a short-run Phillips curve and a long-run Phillips curve.

At all points on the short-run Phillips curve, *expectations of inflation (the rise in the price level that the average person expects) are fixed.* Thus, on the short-run Phillips curve expectations of inflation can differ from actual inflation. At all points on the long-run Phillips curve *expectations of inflation are equal to actual inflation.* The **long-run Phillips curve** is thought to be *a vertical curve at the unemployment rate consistent with potential*

Q-8 Draw the long-run Phillips curve. Why does it have its shape?

output. It shows the trade-off (or complete lack thereof) when expectations of inflation equal actual inflation. Economists used expectations of inflation to explain why the short-run Phillips curve relationship broke down in the late 1970s.

Let's consider how expectations of inflation can explain high inflation and high unemployment in reference to both our AS/AD model and the Phillips curve model. Say the economy starts out with a rate of unemployment consistent with potential output. So there is no inflation, and the economy is at its potential output. (Wages can still be going up by the rate of productivity growth, say it's 3 percent, but the price level is not rising.) Further assume that individuals are expecting zero inflation; that is, if they get a 3 percent wage increase, they expect their real income to rise by 3 percent. This starting point is represented by point A in Figure 15-4 (a and b).

In Figure 15-4(a) you can see that aggregate supply and aggregate demand intersect at potential income at point A. Since the economy is in both short-run and long-run equilibrium, there are no forces moving the economy away from point A in the AS/AD model. Point A in Figure 15-4(b) is also on both the long-run and short-run Phillips curve. This means that point A is a sustainable combination of inflation and unemployment—the situation can continue indefinitely. The only sustainable combination of inflation and unemployment rates on the short-run Phillips curve is at points where it intersects the long-run Phillips curve, because that is the only unemployment rate consistent with the economy's potential income.

Moving Off the Long-Run Phillips Curve Now let's say that the government decides to increase aggregate demand, shifting the AD curve from AD_0 to AD_1. This pushes output above its potential, as in Figure 15-4(a). That will increase the demand for labour, and that competition for labour will push wages up by more than the increase in productivity as firms compete for the small pool of unemployed workers. Say wages rise by 7 percent. Initially that increase is enough to satisfy workers who are still assumed to expect zero inflation. But notice that, unless potential output increases, there is a problem—their expectation will not be met. Since productivity is still rising by only 3 percent while wages are rising by 7 percent, the higher wage costs force firms to raise their prices by 4 percent, shifting the SAS curve up from SAS_0 to SAS_1. The economy moves to point B. This same point B is shown in the Phillips curve diagram where the economy is still on the short-run Phillips curve. Unemployment falls from 5.5 to 4.5 percent and inflation rises from 0 to 4 percent. But point B is not on the long-run Phillips curve and actual inflation exceeds expected inflation.

Moving Back onto the Long-Run Phillips Curve Point B is not a sustainable position. Since it is beyond potential income, the SAS curve will continue to shift up. Eventually workers realize that their real wages aren't increasing by 7 percent; they are rising by only 3 percent. As workers come to expect the 4 percent inflation (they increase their inflationary expectations), they ask for higher wages to compensate for that inflation. The short-run Phillips curve will shift up from PC_0 to PC_1 since each short-run Phillips curve represents the trade-off for a given level of inflationary expectation. As wages increase, the SAS curve shifts up to SAS_2. As the price level rises, the dollars that people hold are worth less, causing the quantity of aggregate demand to decline and the economy to move to point C. Output returns to its potential, unemployment returns to its target rate and the economy returns to a long-run equilibrium at point C on the long-run Phillips curve. Unemployment is once again at its target rate, but inflation, and expectations of inflation, are now 4 percent.

A general relationship is the following: Any time unemployment is lower than the target level of unemployment consistent with potential output, inflation and expecta-

Figure 15-4 (a and b)   **INFLATION EXPECTATIONS AND THE PHILLIPS CURVE**

Both (a) and (b) show how an increase in aggregate demand can increase output initially. Eventually, however, the economy will return to potential output, but with a higher rate of inflation. The economy begins at point A. Initially, the aggregate demand curve moves from AD_0 to AD_1, pushing output above its potential in (a). As firms compete for labour, wages increase. To cover increasing costs, firms raise their prices. The combination of lower unemployment and higher inflation is shown by point B in (b). As workers realize that inflation is not 0 percent, but rather 4 percent, they will ask for further wage increases. This shifts the SAS curve to SAS_2 and the short-run Phillips curve to PC_1 and the economy to point C. The economy is once again in equilibrium. Unemployment has returned to 5.5 percent, but inflation is now 4 percent.

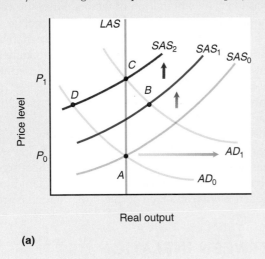

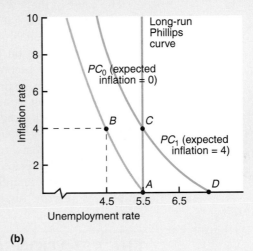

(a)

(b)

tions of inflation will be increasing. That means that the short-run Phillips curve will be shifting up. The short-run Phillips curve will continue to shift up until output is no longer above potential. Thus, any level of inflation is consistent with the target level of unemployment if the cause of that inflation is expectations of inflation. Economists used these expectations of inflation to explain the experience in the 1970s. The economy had been pushed beyond its potential, which had caused inflation to accelerate. (This explanation was supplemented with discussions of supply-side inflationary pressures caused by the large rise in oil prices that occurred at that time.)

Stagflation and the Phillips Curve

The problem with point C is that although the economy is back at potential output, inflationary expectations are built into people's price-setting behaviour. That expectational inflation can be eliminated if either aggregate demand falls or if the target rate of unemployment decreases, causing potential output to increase. That is how economists explained the stagflation in the late 1970s and early 1980s. Government attempted to push down the inflation through contractionary aggregate demand policy. The lower aggregate demand (shifting aggregate demand from AD_1 to AD_0) pushed the economy to a position such as point D. At point D, unemployment exceeds the target rate. The higher unemployment puts downward pressure on wages and prices, shifting the short-run Phillips curve down.

As you can see, the long-run Phillips curve tells us whether there will be upward pressure on the price level (when the economy is to the left of the long-run Phillips curve, and unemployment is below the target rate) or downward pressure on inflation (when the economy is to the right of it and unemployment is above the target rate).

A rise in crude oil prices for a country that is dependent on oil can cause difficulties for the economy, by imposing inflationary pressures, causing a retrenchment in economic activity and, consequently, a rise in unemployment—stagflation

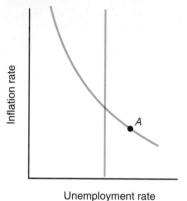

Q.9 If the economy is at point *A* on the Phillips curve below, what prediction would you make for unemployment and inflation?

The New Economy: The Late 1990s and Early 2000s

The above story is the one that most economists have in the back of their minds when they advise on policy. But that story did not fit the last half of the 1990s and beginning of the 2000s very well. Output expanded significantly above what economists had predicted potential output to be, and unemployment rates were lower than most economists thought consistent with potential output. Despite this, wages did not rise significantly. Instead, productivity grew at a faster than expected rate, and inflation remained low. Everything was going better than economists had previously thought possible.

The cause of these good times was likely a combination of factors. First, the economy was experiencing a temporary positive productivity shock because Internet growth and investment were shifting potential output out. Second, competition increased because of globalization and the price comparisons made possible by e-commerce. Third, workers had become less concerned with real wages and more concerned with protecting their jobs, so firms did not raise wages even with extremely tight labour markets. What was most amazing to economists was that in 1999 oil prices increased substantially but inflation did not rise, as it did in the 1970s.

Some economists argued that this combination of factors was permanent, and that the Canadian economy was entering a new era, in which we could have both lower inflation and lower unemployment than was previously thought possible. Others argued that the forces were temporary and that the economy would come out of its "Goldilocks period." As we write this, in early 2002, it is unclear which of these two views is correct.

THE RELATIONSHIP BETWEEN INFLATION AND GROWTH

We can understand the debate mentioned above by thinking back to the price/output path of the *AS/AD* model, shown in Figure 15-5(a). As the economy expands, input prices begin to rise (the Intermediate range) and when it exceeds potential output prices rise very quickly (the Classical range). At that point the *SAS* curve shifts up and both inflation and expectations of inflation rise. The problem is that no one knows precisely where potential output is. The government wants to choose as high an output level as possible yet keep inflation low and prevent it from accelerating. At what point it can do that is the subject of much debate. Supporters of the institutional theory of inflation tend to argue that it is best to err on the high side, and use a high estimate of potential output in Figure 15-5(a). Economists who focus on the quantity theory tend to argue that it is best to err on the low side, and use a low estimate of potential output.

Quantity Theory and the Inflation/Growth Trade-Off

We suspect many of you will agree that erring on the high side makes the most sense. If that were the entire trade-off, such a reaction is probably right. But the quantity theory points out a problem with that reasoning, which might be called the "little bit pregnant problem." At the beginning of a pregnancy, it's true you are only a little bit pregnant, but that "little bit" has initiated a set of cellular changes that will fundamentally alter your life. Supporters of the quantity theory say it is the same with a small rise in the price level: You can't have a "little bit" of inflation. That little bit is setting in motion a series of events that will make the inflation grow and grow, unless the government gives up its attempt to achieve a high rate of output. Their solution to prevent inflation is abstinence—just say no to any rise in the price level.

Those who support the quantity theory argue that erring on the low side pays off— it stops any chance of inflation. It establishes credibility of the Bank of Canada's resolve

Figure 15-5 (a and b)   THE TRADE-OFF BETWEEN INFLATION AND GROWTH

Quantity theorists are much more likely to err on the side of preventing inflation, arguing that an ongoing inflation will begin at low levels of output. They justify erring on the side of preventing inflation by arguing that there is a high cost of allowing inflation. For them, inflation undermines the economy's long-run growth and hence its future potential income. They emphasize the trade-off shown in (b). Institutionalists are more likely to argue that the inflation threshold is at higher estimate of potential output.

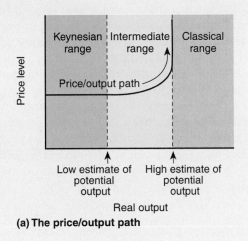

(a) The price/output path

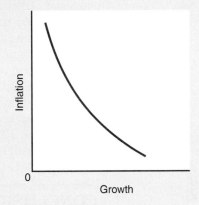

(b) Growth/inflation trade-off

not to increase the money supply. If some inflation is allowed and the Bank of Canada loses credibility, that inflation undermines the long-run growth prospects of the economy, and hence causes future levels of potential income to be lower than they otherwise would be. Put another way, inflation undermines long-run growth; abstinence creates the environment for long-run growth. Thus, for quantity theorists, while there is no long-run trade-off between inflation and unemployment, there is a long-run trade-off between inflation and growth: High inflation leads to lower growth.

Low inflation leads to higher growth for a variety of reasons. Low inflation reduces price uncertainty, making it easier for businesses to invest in future production. Businesses can more easily enter into long-term contracts when inflation is low, which lowers the cost of doing business. Low inflation also makes using money much easier. When inflation is high, people spend more time trying to avoid the costs of inflation, which diverts their energies away from productive activities that would lead to growth.

The hypothesized relationship between inflation and growth is shown in Figure 15-5(b). For quantity theorists, even if there is a short-run relationship between inflation and unemployment, it is precarious for government to try to take advantage of it, because doing so can undermine the long-run growth potential of the economy. For quantity theorists, government policy creating an environment of price-level stability is the policy most likely to lead to high rates of growth. They suggest that the reason for the success of the economy in the late 1990s and early 2000s was that people believed that the Bank of Canada would fight inflation should it appear.

Q-10 Why do quantity theorists believe that government should err on the side of lower output and a lower chance of inflation?

Institutional Theory and the Inflation/Growth Trade-Off

Other economists, mainly supporters of the institutional theory of inflation, are less sure about this negative relationship between inflation and growth. They agree that price-level rises have the potential of generating inflation, and that high accelerating inflation undermines growth, but they do not agree that all price level increases start an inflationary process. The lower unemployment rate accompanying the inflation is so nice, and if the government is really careful—we mean really, really careful—it can avoid reaching the point where the little bit of rise in price level starts the monster of inflation growing within the economy. And besides, if inflation gets started, the government has some medicine to give the economy that will get rid of the inflation relatively easily.

The real-world difference between the two views can be seen in the debate about monetary policy in the early 2000s, when the unemployment rate fell to just over 6.5 percent. Until then, potential income had been estimated at an unemployment rate that was much higher. So it seemed as if the economy were operating significantly beyond its potential output. But inflation remained low, at about 2 to 3 percent. Economists who focus on the quantity theory argued that inflation was just around the corner, and that unless the government instituted contractionary aggregate demand policy, the seeds of inflation would be sown. Other economists argued that institutional changes in the labour market had reduced the inflation threat and that more expansionary policy was called for. The Bank of Canada followed a path between the two, and the economy kept on its path of low inflation, low unemployment, and moderate growth.

CONCLUSION

The quantity and institutional theories of inflation, growth, and unemployment reflect two consistent but different worldviews. The institutional theorists see a world in which sociological and institutional factors interact with market forces, keeping the economy in a perpetual disequilibrium when considered in an economic framework. The quantity theorists see a world in which market forces predominate and institutional and sociological factors are insignificant. The overall economy is in continual equilibrium. These two theories carry over to economists' analyses of the central policy issue facing most governments as they decide on their monetary and fiscal policies: the trade-off between inflation and unemployment and growth. These different worldviews are an important reason why there are disagreements about policy, and the debate will likely continue for a long time.

Chapter Summary

- The winners in inflation are people who can raise their wages or prices and still keep their jobs or sell their goods. The losers are people who can't raise their wages or prices. On average, winners and losers balance out.

- Three types of inflationary expectations are rational (expectations based on economic models), adaptive (expectations based on the past), and extrapolative (expectations that a trend will continue).

- A basic rule of thumb to predict inflation is: Inflation equals nominal wage increases minus productivity growth.

- The equation of exchange is $MV = PQ$; it becomes the quantity theory when velocity is constant, real output is independent of the money supply, and causation goes from money to prices. The quantity theory says that the price level varies in direct response to changes in the quantity of money.

- The inflation tax is an implicit tax on the holders of cash and the holders of any obligations specified in nominal terms.

- Quantity theorists tend to favour a policy that relies on rules rather than on discretionary policy.

- The institutional theory of inflation sees the source of inflation in the wage-and-price setting institutions; it sees the direction of causation going from price increases to money increases.

- Institutional theorists tend to favour supplemental policies such as incomes policies to supplement tight monetary policies when fighting inflation.

- The long-run Phillips curve allows expectations of inflation to change; it is generally seen as vertical.

● The short-run Phillips curve holds expectations constant. It is generally seen as downward sloping and shifts up when expectations of inflation rise and shifts down when expectations of inflation fall.

● Quantity theorists see a long-run trade-off between inflation and growth; the higher inflation, the lower the growth rate. Institutional theorists are less sure about this trade-off.

Key Terms

adaptive expectations   *(362)*

equation of exchange   *(363)*

extrapolative expectations   *(362)*

incomes policy   *(371)*

inflation tax   *(366)*

insider/outsider model   *(370)*

long-run Phillips curve   *(373)*

quantity theory of money   *(364)*

rational expectations   *(362)*

short-run Phillips curve   *(372)*

stagflation   *(372)*

velocity of money   *(363)*

Questions for Thought and Review

1. Why do lenders lose out in inflation? Under what conditions would they not lose out?

2. If you base your expectations of inflation on what has happened in the past, what kind of expectations are you demonstrating?

3. If productivity growth is 3 percent and wage increases are 5 percent, what would you predict inflation would be?

4. What is the equation of exchange?

5. What three assumptions turn the equation of exchange into the quantity theory of money?

6. What one sentence best summarizes the quantity theory of money?

7. What does the quantity theory predict to happen to inflation if the money supply rises 10 percent?

8. Why did the relationship between the money supply and the price level break down in the 1970s and 1990s?

9. For what countries is the connection between the growth in the money supply and inflation still evident? What accounts for this?

10. If governments are aware that increases in the money supply cause inflation, why do some countries increase the money supply by significant amounts anyway?

11. Define the inflation tax. Who pays it?

12. Who is more likely to support monetary rules—a quantity theorist or an institutionalist? Explain your answer.

13. What is the direction of causation between money and prices according to the institutional theory of inflation?

14. Why do institutional theories of inflation focus on the state of the labour market?

15. What is the insider/outsider theory of inflation? Would quantity or institutional theorists likely believe this theory?

16. How do the policy implications of the quantity theory and the institutional theory of inflation differ?

17. Draw both a short-run and a long-run Phillips curve. What does each say about the relationship between inflation and unemployment?

18. If people's expectations of inflation didn't change, would the economy move from a short-run to a long-run Phillips curve?

19. The Phillips curve is just a figment of economists' imagination. True or false?

20. What is the reasoning behind the view that there is a trade-off between inflation and growth?

Problems and Exercises

1. Assume the money supply is $500, the velocity of money is 8, and the price level is $2. Using the quantity theory of money:
   a. Determine the level of real output.
   b. Determine the level of nominal output.
   c. Assuming velocity remains constant, what will happen if the money supply rises 20 percent?
   d. If the government established price controls and also raised the money supply 20 percent, what would happen?

   e. How would you judge whether the assumption of fixed velocity is reasonable?

2. Congratulations. You've just been appointed finance minister of Inflationland. Inflation has been ongoing for the past five years at 5 percent. The target rate of unemployment, 5 percent, is also the actual rate.
   a. Demonstrate the economy's likely position on both short-run and long-run Phillips curves.
   b. The prime minister tells you she wants to be re-elected. Devise a monetary policy strategy for her that

might help her accomplish her goal.

   c. Demonstrate that strategy graphically, including the likely long-run consequences.

3. In the early 1990s, Argentina stopped increasing the money supply and fixed the exchange rate of the Argentine austral at 10,000 to the U.S. dollar. It then renamed the Argentine currency the "peso" and cut off four zeros so that one peso equalled one dollar. Inflation slowed substantially. After this was done, the following observations were made. Explain why these observations did not surprise economists.

   a. The golf courses were far less crowded.

   b. The price of goods in dollar-equivalent pesos in Buenos Aires, the capital of the country, was significantly above that in New York City.

   c. Consumer prices—primarily services—rose relative to other goods.

   d. Luxury auto dealers were shutting down.

4. Grade inflation is widespread. Students' grades are increasing but what they are learning is decreasing. Some economists argue that grade inflation should be dealt with in the same way that price inflation should be dealt with—by creating a fixed standard and requiring all grades to be specified relative to that standard. One way to accomplish this is to index the grades professors give: specify on the grade report both the student's grade and the class average, and deflate (or inflate) the grade to some common standard.

   a. Discuss the advantages and disadvantages of such a proposal.

   b. What relationship does it have to economists' proposals for fixed exchange rates?

5. In the mid-1990s, Japan's annual money supply growth rate fell to 1–2 percent from an average annual rate of

10–11 percent in the late 1980s. What effect did this decline have on:

   a. Japanese real output?

   b. Japanese unemployment?

   c. Japanese inflation?

6. People's perception of inflation often differs from actual inflation.

   a. List five goods that you buy relatively frequently.

   b. Looking in old newspapers (found in the library on microfiche), locate sales prices for these goods since 1950, finding one price every five years or so. Determine the average annual price rise for each good from 1950 to today.

   c. Compare that price with the rise in the CPI.

7. Suppose an economy is operating at a low and stable rate of inflation and suddenly experiences an autonomous increase in investment that raises aggregate demand. Using short-run and long-run Phillips curves, demonstrate the immediate and long-run impacts on inflation and unemployment:

   a. When the central bank does not raise the money supply in response to the increase in investment.

   b. When the central bank increases the money supply when investment rises.

   How is the long-run equilibrium in your answer to *a* different from the long-run equilibrium in your answer to *b*? Explain why they are different.

8. Late in 2001 gasoline prices fell to less than $0.60 per litre in Ontario. Assuming that there are more gasoline users who would benefit from low prices than gasoline producers who would be hurt by low prices, how might this affect unemployment and inflation? Why? Use short-run and long-run Phillips curves in your analysis.

Web Questions

1. Most academic institutions subscribe to the CANSIM II database. Ask your instructor how to do this, or try to load the following Web page: www.datacenter2.chass. utoronto.ca/cansim2/. Click on "retrieve multiple series" and download the M_1 series V37124 (convert this to quarterly data) and nominal GDP series V498086. Save this as a spreadsheet data file.

   a. Use a spreadsheet to calculate the velocity of money for each year from 1961 to the most recent year available.

   b. How much income did $1 support in 1980? In 1990? In 2000?

   c. What happened to the velocity of money over this time period?

   d. What implications does the variability of the velocity of money have for the quantity theory of money?

2. Visit the CANSIM II database Web site (www. datacenter2. chass.utoronto.ca/cansim2/) and download data on the U.S. and Canadian consumer price indexes (CANSIM II numbers V11123 and V735319, respectively).

   a. Calculate the inflation rate as this month this year minus this month last year, divided by this month last year, and multiply by 100.

   b. Has inflation been higher in Canada or the U.S. over the last year?

   c. Look at a plot of inflation rates from January 1990 to December 2001. Estimate what the inflation rates will be during 2002 based on your plot.

d. Were your guesses close to the actual inflation rates during 2002? What kind of expectations did you create? Rational? Adaptive? Extrapolative?

3. Visit the "monetary policy" section of the Bank of Canada's Web site (www.bankofcanada.ca) and read some of the backgrounders on monetary policy. Answer the following questions:

Answers to Margin Questions

1. False. Inflation does not make an economy poorer. It redistributes income from those who do not raise their prices to those who do raise their prices. *(361)*

2. Three types of expectations are rational expectations, adaptive expectations, and extrapolative expectations. *(362)*

3. The equation of exchange, $MV = PQ$, is a tautology. What changes it to the quantity theory are assumptions about the variables, specifically that velocity remains constant, that real output is determined separately, and that the causation flows from money to prices. With these assumptions added, the equation of exchange implies that changes in the money supply are reflected in changes in the price level—which is what the quantity theory of money says. *(364)*

4. Central banks sometimes issue large quantities of money for a number of reasons. One reason is that in their estimation the benefit of doing so (avoiding a breakdown of the government and perhaps the entire economy) exceeds the cost (starting an inflation). Another reason is that some central banks lack the independence to maintain low inflation as a goal. *(367)*

5. According to the quantity theory, the direction of causation goes from money to prices ($MV \rightarrow PQ$)—increases in the money supply lead to increases in the price level. According to institutional theory, the direction of causation goes from prices to money ($MV \leftarrow PQ$)—increases in the price level are ratified by government, which increases the money supply. *(368)*

6. A quantity theorist would likely say that the insider/outsider model of inflation tends to obscure the central cause of inflation—increases in the money supply. *(370)*

7. A quantity theorist would recommend that the growth in the money supply be reduced. An institutionalist would recommend that the government hold prices down directly with an incomes policy as well as reduce the growth in the money supply. *(371)*

8. As you can see in the graph, the long-run Phillips curve is perfectly vertical. Its shape is dependent on the assumption that people's expectations of inflation com-

a. What is the relationship between interest rates and inflation?
b. Would you characterize the materials as reflecting an institutionalist or quantity theory viewpoint? Explain your answer.
c. What kind of feedback rule does the material suggest the Bank of Canada follows?

pletely adjust to inflation in the long run, and that adjustment is not institutionally constrained. *(374)*

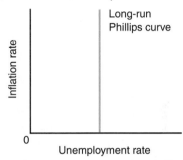

9. If the economy is at point A on the Phillips curve below, inflation is below expected inflation and unemployment is higher than the target rate of unemployment. If this were the only information we had about the economy, we would expect both unemployment and inflation to fall. *(376)*

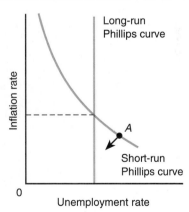

10. Quantity theorists believe that government should err on the side of low output and a lower chance of inflation because any amount of inflation sets into motion a series of changes in the economy that will likely lead to higher inflation. *(377)*

Open Economy Macro: Exchange Rate and Trade Policy

16

After reading this chapter, you should be able to:

- Describe the balance of payments and the trade balance, and relate them to the supply and demand for currencies.

- List three important fundamental determinants of exchange rates.

- Explain how a country fixes an exchange rate.

- Define purchasing power parity and explain its relevance to the debate about whether to have a fixed or flexible exchange rate.

- Differentiate fixed, flexible, and partially flexible exchange rates, and discuss the advantages and disadvantages of each.

- Describe the pros and cons of monetary union with the United States.

- List five important international trade restrictions.

- Explain why economists generally support free trade.

- List three international trade agreements affecting Canada.

A foreign exchange dealer's office during a busy spell is the nearest thing to Bedlam I have struck.

Harold Wincott

It's impossible to talk about macroeconomic policy in Canada without talking about international issues. So in this and the next chapter, we discuss international macroeconomic goals and policies. This discussion should not be totally new to you since earlier chapters introduced you to many international concepts and touched on international issues. But now it's time to put those discussions together and consider the issues more carefully. This chapter will provide you with the international base necessary for understanding the macroeconomic policy you'll be reading about in the newspapers.

The chapter starts with an in-depth consideration of the balance of payments, showing how it relates to the trade balance and exchange rates. That discussion is then tied to a consideration of the supply of and demand for currencies. Next we discuss exchange rate policy in some depth and present the arguments for and against various exchange rate regimes, including some form of monetary union with the United States. Finally, we consider trade policies, to which countries often resort when they have trade deficit problems.

THE BALANCE OF PAYMENTS

The best door into an in-depth discussion of exchange rates and open economy macro is a discussion of **balance of payments** (*a country's record of all transactions between its residents and the residents of all foreign nations.*)[1] These include a country's buying and selling of goods and services (imports and exports) and interest and profit payments from previous investments, together with all the capital inflows and outflows. Table 16-1 presents the 2001 balance of payments accounts for Canada. These accounts record all payments made by foreigners to Canadian citizens and all payments made by Canadian citizens to foreigners in those years.

Goods that Canada exports must be paid for in dollars; they involve a flow of payments into Canada, so in the balance of payments accounts they have a plus sign. Similarly, Canadian imports must be paid for in foreign currency; they involve a flow of dollars out of Canada, and thus they have a minus sign. Notice that the bottom line of the balance of payments is $0. By definition, the bottom line (which includes all supplies and demands for currencies, including those of the government) must add up to zero.

As you can see in Table 16-1, the balance of payments account is broken down into the current account, and the capital and financial account. The **current account** (lines 1–14) is *the part of the balance of payments account in which all short-term flows of payments are listed*. It includes exports and imports, which are what we normally mean when we talk about the trade balance. The **capital and financial account** (lines 15–23) is *the part of the balance of payments account in which all long-term flows of payments are listed*. If a Canadian citizen buys a German stock, or if a Japanese company buys a Canadian company, the transaction shows up on the capital account.

The government can influence the exchange rate (the rate at which one currency trades for another) by buying and selling **official reserves**—*government holdings of foreign currencies*—or by buying and selling other international reserves, such as gold. Such buying and selling is recorded in the **financial account** (line 19)—*the part of the balance of payments account that, among other components, records the amount of its own currency or foreign currencies that a nation buys or sells*.

To get a better idea of what's included in the accounts, let's consider each of them more carefully.

The balance of payments is a country's record of all transactions between its residents and the residents of all foreign countries.

The current account is the part of the balance of payments account that lists all short-term flows of payments.

The capital and financial account is the part of the balance of payments account that lists all long-term flows of payments.

---

[1]Balance of payments records are not very good. Because of measurement difficulties, many transactions go unrecorded and many numbers must be estimated, leaving a potential for large errors.

TABLE 16-1   The Balance of Payments Account, 2001 ($ millions)

1. **Current Account**			
2. Merchandise			
3. Exports	+412,510		
4. Imports	-351,003		
5. Balance of Trade		+61,507	
6. Services			
7. Exports	+55,095		
8. Imports	-61,926		
9. Balance of Services		-6,831	
10. Balance of Goods and Services		+54,676	
11. Net Investment Income	-27,446		
12. Net Transfers	+1,870		
13. Investment Transactions Balance		-25,576	
14. **Balance on Current Account**			+29,100
15. **Capital Account**			
16. Inflows	+6,482		
17. Outflows	-804		
18. **Balance on Capital Account**		+5,678	
19. **Financial Account**			
20. Assets	-107,388		
21. Liabilities	+80,889		
22. Net Financial Account		-26,499	
23. **Total Capital and Financial Account Balances**			-20,821
24. Statistical Discrepancy			-8,279
25. **Total**			0

Source: Statistics Canada, CANSIM II, Tables 376-0001 and 376-0002.

The Current Account

At the top of Table 16-1, the current account is composed of the merchandise (or goods) account (lines 2–5), the services account (lines 6–9), the net investment income account (line 11), and the net transfers account (line 12).

Starting with the merchandise account, notice that in 2001 Canada imported $351 billion worth of goods and exported $412.5 billion worth of goods. *The difference between the value of goods exported and the value of goods imported* is called the **balance of merchandise trade.** Looking at line 5, you can see that Canada had a balance of merchandise trade surplus of $61.5 billion in 2001.

The merchandise trade balance is often discussed in the press as a summary of how Canada is doing in the international markets. It's not a good summary. Trade in services is just as important as trade in merchandise, so economists pay more attention to the combined balance of goods and services.

Thus, the **balance of goods and services**—*the difference between the value of goods and services exported and imported*—(line 10) becomes a key statistic for economists. Notice that in 2001 most of the Canadian trade surplus resulted from an imbalance in the merchandise account. The service account worked in the opposite direction. It was slightly negative in 2001. Such services include tourist expenditures and insurance payments by

The balance of goods and services is the difference between the value of goods and services a nation exports and the value of goods and services it imports.

foreigners to Canadian firms. For instance, when you travel in Japan, you spend yen, which you must buy with dollars; this is an outflow of payments, which is a negative contribution to the services account.

There is no reason that the goods and services sent into a country must equal the goods and services sent out in a particular year, even if the current account is in equilibrium, because the current account also includes payments from past investments and net transfers. When you invest, you expect to make a return on that investment. The payments to foreign owners of Canadian capital assets are a negative contribution to the Canadian balance of payments. The payment to Canadian owners of foreign capital assets is a positive contribution to the Canadian balance of payments. These payments on investment income are a type of holdover from past trade and services imbalances. So even though they relate to investments, they show up on the current account.

The final component on the current account is net transfers, which include foreign aid, gifts, and other payments to individuals not exchanged for goods or services. If you send a $1,000 bond to your aunt in Taiwan, it shows up with a minus sign here.

Adding up the pluses and minuses on the current account, we arrive at line 14, the current account balance. Notice that in 2001 Canada ran a $29.1 billion surplus on the current account. That means that, in the current account, the demand for dollars greatly exceeded the supply of dollars. If the current account represented the total supply of and demand for dollars, the value of the dollar would have risen. But it doesn't represent the total. There are also the capital and financial account, and statistical discrepancies.

Q.1 If you, a Canadian citizen, are travelling abroad, where will your expenditures show up in the balance of payments accounts?

The Capital and Financial Account

The capital and financial account consists of the capital account and the financial account. The capital account measures transactions such as international inheritances, federal debt forgiveness, and the transfer of intangible assets (such as the value of patents and leases). The financial account measures transactions in financial assets and liabilities, and includes Canadian portfolio investment abroad and foreign investment in Canadian stocks and bonds. From Table 16-1 you can see that in 2001 Canada had a relatively small capital inflow of about $5.7 billion. You can also see that this was swamped by a large deficit on the financial account of $26.5 billion. This was the result of Canadians investing in foreign stocks and bonds (which appears as a negative entry of $107.4 billion on line 20) and foreign investment in Canadian securities of about $80.9 billion (which appears as an increase in liabilities on line 21).

To buy these Canadian stocks and bonds foreigners needed dollars, but Canadians needed foreign currencies to increase their holdings of foreign securities. The current account surplus can be interpreted as a net demand for dollars (since we are exporting more than we are importing; hence foreigners need more dollars than Canadians need foreign currencies—that is, there is an excess demand for dollars). You can think of the capital and financial account balance as capturing "the other side of the market," with Canadians supplying dollars so they can buy foreign currencies that are then used to buy foreign securities.

In thinking about what determines a currency's value, it's important to remember both the demand for dollars to buy goods and services and the demand for dollars to buy assets.

Common sense dictates that demand should equal supply, but if you look closely you'll see that the current account balance is not fully offset by the capital and financial account balance. Why? Many international transactions, especially in financial assets, go unrecorded and must be estimated. With these discrepancies taken into consideration through the adjustment on line 24, the statistical discrepancy, the accounts balance. This gives us balance of payments equilibrium.

There is, of course, a difference between the long-run effects of the demand for dollars to buy currently produced goods and services and the demand for dollars to buy assets. Assets earn profits or interest, so when foreigners buy Canadian assets, they earn income from those assets just for owning them. The net investment income from foreigners' previous asset purchases shows up on line 11 of the current account. It's the difference between the income Canadian citizens receive from their foreign assets and the income foreigners receive from their Canadian assets. If assets earned equal returns, we would expect that when foreigners own more Canadian capital assets than Canadian citizens own foreign capital assets, net investment income should be negative. And when Canadian citizens own more foreign capital assets than foreigners own Canadian capital assets, net investment income should be positive. Why is this? Because net investment income is simply the difference between the returns on Canadian citizens' assets held abroad and foreign citizens' assets held in Canada.

Balance of Payments Equilibrium

The current account and the capital and financial account measure the supply and demand for dollars. The concepts *balance of payments* and *surplus* or *deficit* refer to the balance of payments when we exclude a country's official reserve transactions and the amount designated as the statistical discrepancy. Remember that central banks sometimes intervene to dampen volatility in currency markets and to assure an adequate level of liquidity in their financial systems. In Canada, these transactions are included in the financial account. For example, in 2001 the Bank of Canada increased its reserve assets (foreign currencies it uses to buy dollars) by about $3.4 billion. This amount is included in the financial account under the net asset flow, line 20 of Table 16-1. Since Canada increased its holdings of foreign reserves, it sold dollars for those foreign currencies, so the net asset flow is negative to denote a net outflow of Canadian assets.

Central banks know exactly the amount of their reserve transactions, so the statistical discrepancy is calculated as the residual required to set the balance of payments to zero. Table 16-1 demonstrates that this discrepancy was about $8.3 billion in 2001, and it highlights some of the difficulties in working with balance of payments data. These data problems are much more severe in developing countries that don't enjoy the resources available to the various statistical agencies in Canada. Remember this the next time you hear pundits pontificate over the appropriate setting of monetary and fiscal policies in less-developed nations; they may be basing their advice on figures that bear little resemblance to reality.

Why is this important? Well, a balance of payments surplus will put upward pressure on the value of a country's currency. Other things being equal, this appreciation will reduce the demand for that country's goods and services and assets, returning the balance of payments to equilibrium. If a country wants to prevent that from happening, it can sell its own currency. This will increase its supply and tend to reduce the pressure on the currency to appreciate. Similarly, a balance of payments deficit will put downward pressure on the value of a country's currency. This would tend to increase foreign demand for domestic goods and services and assets, leading again to balance of payments equilibrium. The central bank could prevent this by purchasing its own currency and taking those funds out of circulation. The money supply would fall and the pressure on the currency to depreciate would be reduced.

Now let's return to the point made at the beginning of the chapter. By definition, the current account and the capital and financial account must sum to zero. Why? Because they are an accounting identity. The identity becomes something more than an identity if the currencies are freely exchangeable. In that case, anybody can take his or her currency and trade it for another whenever desired. The quantity of currency supplied, including the government's, must equal the quantity demanded, including the government's. This means that any deficit in the balance of payments (which you'll re-

Q.2 How can net investment income be positive if a country is a net debtor nation?

As part of its official reserves, the Bank of Canada has millions of dollars of gold, Canadian dollars, and various other international currencies.

A balance of payments deficit will put downward pressure on the value of a country's currency.

member is measured by excluding the statistical discrepancy and the government's official reserve transactions) must be offset by an equal surplus in official reserve transactions (this also assumes that we have perfect records, so the statistical discrepancy is zero). In reality, there are data leakages in reporting, and the statistical discrepancy is a catch-all designed to force the balance of payments to be zero.

EXCHANGE RATES

Supply and demand are two central forces of economics, so it shouldn't be surprising that our initial discussion of the determination of exchange rates uses supply and demand curves. As already stated, an **exchange rate** is *the rate at which one currency can be traded for another currency.*

Q-3 Show graphically the effect of an increase in demand for euros on the value of the euro.

At first glance, the analysis of foreign exchange rates seems simple: You have an upward-sloping supply curve and a downward-sloping demand curve. But what goes on the axes? Obviously price and quantity, but what price? And what quantity? Because you are talking about the prices of currencies relative to each other you have to specify which currencies you are using.

In Figure 16-1, we present the supply of and demand for euros in terms of dollars. Notice that the quantity of euros goes on the horizontal axis and the dollar price of euros goes on the vertical axis. When you are comparing two currencies the supply of one currency equals the demand for the other currency. To demand one currency you must supply another. In this figure we are assuming that there are only two currencies. This means that the supply of euros is equivalent to the demand for dollars. The Europeans who want to buy Canadian goods or assets supply euros to buy dollars. Let's consider an example. Say a French person wants to buy an IBM computer made in Canada. She has euros, but IBM wants dollars. So, in order to buy the computer, she or IBM must somehow exchange euros for dollars. She is *supplying* euros in order to *demand* dollars.

To demand one currency you must supply another.

The supply curve of euros is upward sloping because the more dollars European citizens get for their euros, the cheaper Canadian goods and assets are for them and the greater the quantity of euros they want to supply for those goods. Say, for example, that the dollar price of one euro rises from $1.30 to $1.40. That means that the price of a dollar to a European person has fallen from 0.769 euros to 0.714 euros. For a European person, a good that cost $100 now falls in price from 769 euros to 714 euros. Canadian goods

Figure 16-1   THE SUPPLY OF AND DEMAND FOR EUROS

As long as you keep quantities and prices *of what* straight, the standard, or fundamental, analysis of the determination of exchange rates is easy. Exchange rates are determined by the supply of and demand for currency. Just remember that if you're talking about the supply of and demand for euros, the price will be measured in dollars and the quantity will be in euros, as in this figure.

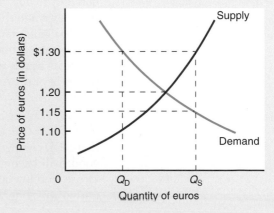

are cheaper, so the Europeans buy more Canadian goods and more dollars, which means they supply more euros.

The demand for euros comes from Canadians who want to buy European goods or assets. The demand curve is downward sloping because the lower the dollar price of euros, the more euros Canadian citizens want to buy, for the same reasons we just described.

Equilibrium is where the quantity supplied equals the quantity demanded. In our example, equilibrium occurs at a dollar price of $1.20 for one euro. If the price of euros is above or below $1.20, quantity supplied won't equal the quantity demanded and there will be pressure for the exchange rate to move to equilibrium. Say, for example, that the price is $1.30 The quantity of euros supplied will be greater than the quantity demanded. People who want to sell euros won't be able to sell them. To find buyers, they will offer to sell their euros for less. As they do, the price of euros falls.

Exchange Rates and the Balance of Payments

The supply/demand framework directly relates to the balance of payments. When quantity supplied equals quantity demanded, the balance of payments is in equilibrium. If the currency is overvalued, there will be a deficit in the balance of payments; if the currency is undervalued, there will be a surplus in the balance of payments. Thus, in Figure 16-1, when the price of euros is $1.30, the quantity of euros supplied exceeds the quantity demanded, so the euro area is running a balance of payments deficit. When the price of euros is $1.15, the quantity of euros demanded exceeds the quantity supplied, so the euro area is running a balance of payments surplus.

Fundamental Forces Determining Exchange Rates

Exchange rate analysis is usually broken down into fundamental analysis and short-run analysis. In this section we discuss fundamental analysis—a consideration of the fundamental forces that determine the supply of and demand for currencies, and hence cause them to shift. These fundamental forces include a country's income, a country's prices, and the interest rate in a country. That means that changes in a country's income, changes in a country's prices, and changes in interest rates can cause the supply of and demand for a currency to shift. Let's consider how they do so.

Changes in a Country's Income The demand for imports depends on the income in a country. When a country's income falls, demand for imports falls. Hence demand for foreign currency to buy those imports falls, which means that the supply of the country's currency to buy the foreign currency falls. That's why, in our presentation of the *AS/AD* model, we said that imports depend on income.

How important is this relationship? Very important. For example, in the mid-1990s the German economy went into recession and, as it did, its demand for imports fell and hence its supply of marks fell. This decrease in the supply of marks tended to push up the price of the mark relative to foreign currencies.

Changes in a Country's Prices Canada's demand for imports and foreign countries' demand for Canadian exports depend on prices of Canadian goods compared to prices of foreign competing goods. If Canada has more inflation than other countries, foreign goods will become cheaper, Canadian demand for foreign currencies will tend to increase, and foreign demand for dollars will tend to decrease. This rise in Canadian inflation will shift the dollar supply outward and the dollar demand inward.

Changes in Interest Rates People like to invest their savings in assets that will yield the highest return. Other things equal, a rise in Canadian interest rates relative to those abroad will increase demand for Canadian assets. As a result, demand for dollars will increase, while simultaneously the supply of dollars will decrease as fewer Canadians sell their dollars to buy foreign assets. A fall in the Canadian interest rate or a rise in foreign interest rates will have the opposite effect.

One of the ways economists like to think about interest rates and exchange rates is through asking what determines where an investor will place her savings. Suppose your sister has one Canadian dollar; she can invest this dollar in Canada and earn an interest rate of i percent, or she can trade that dollar for a euro at the exchange rate E and invest it in a euro-denominated security paying an interest rate of i^* percent. Where should she invest her funds?

If we disregard differences in the way interest income is taxed in the euro area and in Canada, and if we assume that the securities have similar characteristics such as risk and liquidity, we know that arbitrage—the simultaneous buying and selling of assets across different markets—should force the return to both securities to be the same. Otherwise investors could make excessive profits by placing their funds in one of the securities; this would place pressure on securities prices and interest rates to change and ultimately there wouldn't be any gains to investing in one country or another.

What return would that \$1 generate in Canada if invested for one year? That's simple: $\$1 \times (1 + i)$. What return would that \$1 generate in the euro area? That's simple, too! Remember that the exchange rate is the domestic currency price of foreign currency, so E is measured in Canadian dollars per euro. This means that $(1/E)$ measures the number of euros one Canadian dollar will buy. So, \$1 would buy $1 \times (1/E)$ euros. Investing this amount for a year at an interest rate of i^* percent yields:

$$\$1 \times \left(\frac{1}{E}\right) \times (1 + i^*)$$

That's how many euros the security would be worth at the end of the year.

To be indifferent between the two investment strategies, both of these returns would have to be the same. However, we cannot directly compare these figures because the euro-area security is valued in euros, so we need to express this in Canadian dollars to be able to compare it to the option of leaving the funds in Canada (alternatively, we could express the Canadian dollar values in terms of euros). A problem arises because we don't know what the exchange rate will be in a year when the euro-denominated security matures! This makes it difficult to compare the two investment options, but luckily economists have figured out a few ways to solve this problem.

The first involves using financial derivatives such as futures contracts and options to set the rate at which euros can be traded for Canadian dollars when the security matures. Using this approach leads to a **covered interest parity** relationship, where the term "covered" means *the investor has entered into a derivative market to lock in the exchange rate at which the foreign currency can be traded for the domestic currency.*

The second approach assumes that people form expectations of the exchange rate a year from now, and that based on those expectations the expected return from investing at home should be equal to the expected return from investing abroad. If we denote E^e_{t+1} as the expected exchange rate at time $(t + 1)$, the **uncovered interest parity** condition states that *the expected return from investing at home and abroad should be identical.* Remember that E is Canadian dollars per euro, so we need to multiply the euro figures by the expected exchange rate to convert units to Canadian dollars. We can express this as:

$$\$1(1 + i) = \$1 \times \left(\frac{1}{E}\right) \times (1 + i^*) \times E^e_{t+1}$$

Three shift factors relevant to the fundamental analysis of the supply and demand for currencies are:

1. Changes in a country's income.
2. Changes in a country's prices.
3. Changes in interest rates.

With a bit of algebraic manipulation[2] we can express this as approximately equal to:

$$i = i^* + \frac{E^e_{t+1} - E}{E}$$

where the second term is the expected depreciation (if positive) or appreciation (if negative) of the Canadian dollar. If the Canadian dollar is expected to lose value, Canadian securities will have to offer a higher rate of return than euro-area securities. The interest rate differential between the two countries is a function of the expected change in the value of the dollar.

If we solve for the exchange rate (we'll leave this for you to do on your own) you'll see that exchange rates depend on interest rates at home and abroad, as well as on expectations over future exchange rates. That's one reason why central bankers are so careful with what they say in public—they don't want to inadvertently affect exchange rate expectations by saying something they didn't mean to say, or by not saying something they meant to say. Remember this the next time you hear a central banker speak!

As you can see, interest rates play an important role in affecting the value of the dollar.

Some Examples To make sure that you have the analysis down pat, let's consider some examples. First, the Canadian economy goes into recession with interest rates remaining constant. What will likely happen to exchange rates? Second, the Mexican economy has runaway inflation—what will likely happen to exchange rates? And third, the interest rate on yen-denominated assets increases—what will likely happen to the exchange rate? If you answered: The value of the dollar will rise, the value of the peso will fall, and the value of the yen will rise, you're following the argument. If those weren't your answers, a review is in order.

16.1

see page 411

Q-6 Why don't most governments leave determination of the exchange rate to the market?

Why Exchange Rate Determination Is More Complicated Than Supply/Demand Analysis Makes It Seem

In day-to-day trading, fundamentals can be overwhelmed by expectations of how a currency will change in value. The supply and demand curves for currencies can shift around rapidly in response to rumours, expectations, and expectations of expectations. As they shift, they bring about large fluctuations in exchange rates that make trading difficult and have significant real effects on economic activity.

Let us outline just one potential problem. Say you expect the price of the currency to fall one-half of 1 percent tomorrow. What should you do? The correct answer is: Sell that currency quickly. Why? One-half of 1 percent may not sound like much, but, annualized, it is equivalent to a rate of interest per year of 617 percent. Based on that expectation, if you're into making money (and you're really sure about the fall) you will sell all of that currency that you hold, and borrow all you can so you can sell some more. You can make big money if you guess small changes in exchange rates correctly. (Of course if you're wrong you can lose big money.) This means that if the market generally believes the exchange rates will move, those expectations will tend to be self-fulfilling. Self-fulfilling expectations undermine the argument in favour of letting markets determine exchange rates: When expectations rule, the exchange rate may not reflect actual demands and supplies of goods. Instead, the exchange rate can reflect expectations and rumours. The resulting fluctuations serve no real purpose, and cause problems for international trade and the country's economy.

---

[2]To write this we need to assume that the ratio of the expected future exchange rate to the current exchange rate is approximately 1. Make sure you can see this!

A government can simply pass a law outlawing international currency trading and prohibiting the buying and selling of foreign currencies except at a rate determined by the government. Many developing countries set their exchange rates in this manner. When governments do so, they make international trade difficult because their currencies can't be freely exchanged with other currencies—that is, their currencies are nonconvertible.

Nonconvertible currencies' exchange rates don't fluctuate in response to shifts in supply and demand. Often the only legal way to deal in such currency is to buy it from the government and sell it to the government. It is illegal to trade nonconvertible currencies privately or even to carry large amounts of nonconvertible currency out of the country. Such prohibitions against currency flowing freely into and out of a country are called *capital controls*. If one country's currency can't be exchanged for another's at anything reflecting a market price, it's very difficult for countries to buy each other's goods.

If nonconvertible currencies make trade so difficult, why do countries use them? The answer is: To avoid making the economic adjustments that international considerations would otherwise force on them. Say that a country is running a large balance of payments deficit and the value of its currency is falling. This fall is pushing up the

KNOWING THE TOOLS

Exchange Rates Set by Law: Nonconvertible Currency and Capital Controls

price of imports, causing inflation, and making the country's assets cheaper for foreigners. Foreigners can come in and buy up the country's assets at low prices.

The country can avoid this political problem simply by passing a law that fixes the exchange rate at a certain level. This action indirectly limits imports, since most foreign firms won't sell their goods at the official exchange rate. They don't want the country's currency at the official exchange rate. It also limits exports since the price of a country's exports is held high. The government can and often does give favoured firms special dispensation to import and export. Thus, having a nonconvertible currency enables the government to control what can and can't be imported and exported. Generally when there's a nonconvertible currency, there is a large incentive for people to trade currencies illegally in a black market.

An example of the pressures leading to capital controls occurred in Asia during its 1998 currency crisis. At that time, investors were selling large volumes of Asian financial assets—capital was flowing out of a number of Asian countries. That lowered the value of the Asian countries' currencies precipitously. In response there was a significant push for strong capital controls that would limit outflows of currency.

16.2

see page 412

International Trade Problems from Shifting Values of Currencies

Suppose that a firm decides to build a plant in Canada because costs in Canada are low. But suppose also that the value of the dollar then rises significantly; the firm's costs rise significantly too, making it uncompetitive.

In a real-world example, from July to September 1997, the value of the Thai baht fell nearly 40 percent. Goodyear (Thailand), which had been one of the five most profitable companies on the Stock Exchange of Thailand, suddenly faced a 20 percent rise in the costs of raw materials because it paid for those raw materials in dollars. It also faced a decline in tire prices because the demand for tires had fallen 20 to 40 percent when the Thai economy contracted. Within just two months, a highly profitable venture had become unprofitable. Other firms were closing shop because they were unable to pay the interest on loans that were denominated in dollars.

In summary, large fluctuations make real trade difficult and cause serious real consequences. It is these consequences that have led to calls for government to fix or stabilize their exchange rates.

Figure 16-2 A DEMONSTRATION OF DIRECT EXCHANGE POLICY

If the government chooses to hold the exchange rate at $1.30, when the equilibrium is $1.20, there is an excess supply given by $Q_2 - Q_1$. The government purchases this excess (using official reserves) and closes the difference, thus maintaining equilibrium.

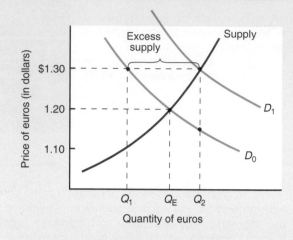

How a Fixed Exchange Rate System Works

> A fixed exchange rate policy is policy in which the government commits to holding the exchange rate at a specified rate.

One way the government can set the exchange rate is by law, making its currency nonconvertible. Major Western economies have agreed not to use this approach, so in what we discuss here we assume that this is not an option. (See the Knowing the Tools box on the previous page for a discussion of how nonconvertible currencies work.) Another way is for the government to adopt a fixed exchange rate policy.

Fixing the Exchange Rate The government can fix its exchange rate by *exchange rate intervention*—buying or selling a currency to affect its price. Let's consider an example of exchange rate intervention.

> A country can maintain a fixed exchange rate only as long as it has the reserves to maintain this constant rate. Once it runs out of reserves, it will be unable to intervene, and must then either borrow or devalue its currency.

Direct Exchange Rate Intervention Suppose that, given the interaction of private supply and demand forces, the equilibrium value of the euro is $1.20 a euro, but the European Central Bank wants to maintain a value of $1.30 a euro. This is shown in Figure 16-2. At $1.30 a euro, quantity supplied exceeds quantity demanded. The European Central Bank must buy the surplus, $Q_2 - Q_1$, using official reserves (foreign currency holdings). It thus shifts the total demand for euros to D_1, making the equilibrium market exchange rate (including the European Central Bank's demand for euros) equal to $1.30. This process is called **currency support**—the *buying of a currency by a government to maintain its value at above its long-run equilibrium value.* It is a direct exchange rate policy. If a government has sufficient official reserves, or if it can convince other governments to lend it reserves, it can fix the exchange rate at the rate it wants, no matter what the private level of supply and demand is. In reality governments have no such power to support currencies in the long run, since their reserves are limited. For example, in 1997 the Thai government ran out of foreign reserves and was forced to let its currency decline in value.

> A country fixes the exchange rate by standing ready to buy and sell its currency anytime the exchange rate is not at the fixed exchange rate.

A more viable long-run exchange rate policy is **currency stabilization**—the *buying and selling of a currency by the government to offset temporary fluctuations in supply and demand for currencies.* In currency stabilization, the government is not trying to change the long-run equilibrium; it is simply trying to keep the exchange rate at that long-run equilibrium. The government sometimes buys and sometimes sells currency, so it is far less likely to run out of reserves.

Successful currency stabilization requires the government to choose the correct long-run equilibrium exchange rate. A policy of stabilization can become a policy of support if the government chooses too high a long-run equilibrium. Unfortunately, government has no way of knowing for sure what the long-run equilibrium exchange rate is, so how much stabilizing it can do depends on its access to reserves. If it has sufficient reserves, the government buys up sufficient quantities of its currency to make up the difference.

Once the government has dried up the sources of borrowing foreign currencies, if it wants to hold its currency's value above the private equilibrium value it must move to indirect methods affecting its economy in order to affect private supplies and demands for its currency. (These indirect measures are discussed in the next chapter.) In short, if a country wants to maintain a fixed exchange rate, it must adjust its economy to the fixed exchange rate.

The same argument about running out of reserves cannot be made for a country that wants to maintain a below-market value for its currency. Since a government can create all the domestic currency it wants, it's easier for the European Central Bank to push the value of its currency down by selling euros than it is for the government to hold it up by buying euros. By the same token, it's easier for another country (say, Japan) to push the value of the euro up (by pushing the value of the yen down). Thus, if the two countries can decide which way they want their exchange rates to move, they have a large incentive to cooperate. Of course, cooperation requires an agreement on the goals, and often countries' goals conflict. One role of the various international economic organizations discussed in Chapter 3 is to provide a forum for reaching agreement on exchange rate goals and a vehicle through which cooperation can take place.

Notice that, in principle, any trader could establish a fixed exchange rate by guaranteeing to buy or sell a currency at a given rate. Any "fix," however, is only as good as the guarantee, and to fix an exchange rate would require many more resources than an individual trader has; only governments have sufficient resources to fix an exchange rate, and often even governments run out of resources.

In reality, given the small level of official reserves compared to the enormous level of private trading, significant amounts of stabilization are impossible. Instead governments use *strategic currency stabilization*—buying and selling at strategic moments to affect expectations of traders, and hence to affect their supply and demand. Such issues are discussed in depth in international finance courses.

Stabilizing Fluctuations versus Deviating from Long-Run Equilibrium The key to whether exchange rate intervention is a viable option or not involves the long-run equilibrium exchange rate. Direct exchange rate policy can succeed if the problem is one of stabilization. If, however, the problem is long run, or if the government estimates the wrong equilibrium, eventually the government will run out of official reserves. Here's the rub: While in theory it is important to make the distinction, in practice it is difficult to do so. The government can only guess at the long-run equilibrium rate, since no definitive empirical measure of this rate exists. The long-run equilibrium must be estimated. If that estimation is wrong, a sustainable stabilization policy becomes an unsustainable deviation from long-run equilibrium policy. Thus, a central issue in exchange rate intervention policy is estimating the long-run equilibrium exchange rate.

Estimating Long-Run Equilibrium Exchange Rates: Purchasing Power Parity Purchasing power parity is one way economists have of estimating the long-run equilibrium rate. **Purchasing power parity (PPP)** is *a method of calculating exchange rates that attempts to value currencies at rates such that each currency will buy an equal basket of goods.* It is based on the idea that the exchange of currencies reflects the exchange of real

Q.7 In general, would it be easier for Canada to lower the value of the dollar or raise it? Why?

Strategic currency stabilization is the process of buying and selling at strategic moments to affect the expectations of traders, and hence affect their supply and demand.

Q.8 Ms. Economist always tries to travel to a country where the purchasing power parity value is lower than the market value. Why?

The accompanying figure contains information on the number of Canadian dollars it takes to buy one Canadian dollar, as well as the C-6 exchange rate, or index—a weighted average of the value of the Canadian dollar against the U.S. dollar, the euro, the yen, the U.K. pound, the Swedish krona, and the Swiss franc (the weights are calculated using the trade flows between Canada and the countries and is based on a value of 1.00 in 1992). An increase in the number of Canadian dollars it takes to buy one U.S. dollar represents a depreciation of the Canadian dollar. Similarly, a decline in the C-6 index shows a reduction in the value of the Canadian dollar.

While there are some periods when the value of the Canadian dollar against our major trading partners deviates from its value against the U.S. dollar, it's the exchange rate with the United States that matters most for Canadian trade flows.

The increase in the value of the Canadian dollar throughout the late 1980s reflected changing interest rates both in Canada and abroad. The quest for price stability in Canada began during this period, with real interest rates in Canada rising above those in the rest of the world. As monetary conditions eased in the early 1990s so too did Canadian interest rates, with the resulting depreciation against the U.S. dollar and many other major currencies. In

2002 the Canadian dollar hit historic lows, with the uncertainty resulting from terrorist events creating destabilizing speculation in currency markets. Expectations play a critical role in setting prices in international markets and sometimes there's nothing a central bank can do but hang tough and ride out the storm.

As you can see, after the fact we economists are pretty good at coming up with explanations for why exchange rates move the way they do. Alas, before the fact we aren't so good, because often speculative activities make the timing of movements unpredictable.

Canada–U.S. Exchange Rate and C-6 Index

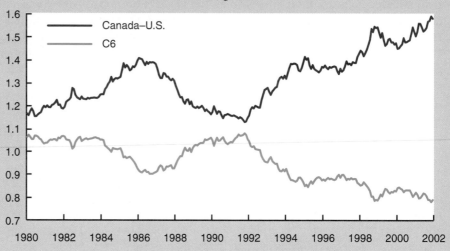

Source: Statistics Canada, CANSIM II, Table 176-0064.

goods. If you are able to exchange a basket of goods from country X for an equivalent basket of goods from country Z, you should also be able to exchange the amount of currency from country X that is needed to purchase country X's basket of goods for the amount of currency from country Z that is needed to purchase country Z's basket of goods. For example, say that the yen is valued at 100 yen to $1. Say also that you can buy the same basket of goods for 1,000 yen that you can buy for $7. In that case the purchasing power parity exchange rate would be 143 yen to $1 (1,000/7 = 143), compared to an actual exchange rate of 100 yen to $1. An economist would say that at 100 to the dollar the yen is overvalued—with 100 yen you could not purchase a basket of goods equivalent to the basket of goods you could purchase with $1.

Table 16-2 shows various calculations for purchasing power parity for a variety of countries. The second column shows the 2000 actual exchange rates. The third column

TABLE 16-2   **Actual and Purchasing Power Parity Exchange Rates for 2000**

Country	Actual Exchange Rate (Currency per Dollar)	PPP Exchange Rate (Currency per Dollar)	Under (−)/ Over (+) valuation
Switzerland	1.08	1.58	- 32
Japan	76.21	128.11	-40.5
Germany	1.38	1.62	-14.7
U.K.	0.44	0.54	-18.8
U.S.	0.66	0.84	-20.8
Portugal	142.27	109.50	+30
Korea	843.17	521.83	+61.6
Mexico	6.40	5.12	+25

Source: OECD Main Economic Indicators, 2001, Bank of Canada, and authors' calculations.

shows purchasing power parity exchange rates. The fourth column shows the difference between the two, or the 2000 distortion in the exchange rates (if you believe the PPP exchange rates are the correct ones).

Criticisms of the Purchasing Power Parity Method For many economists, estimating exchange rates using PPP has serious problems. If the currency is overvalued and will eventually fall, why don't traders use that information and sell that currency now, making it fall now? After all, they are after a profit. So if there is open trading in a currency, any expected change in the exchange rate will affect exchange rates now. If traders don't sell now when there are expectations that a currency's overvaluation will eventually make its value fall, they must believe there is some reason that its value won't, in fact, fall.

Critics argue that the difficulty with PPP exchange rates is the complex nature of trade and consumption. They point out that the PPP will change as the basket of goods changes. This means that there is no one PPP measure. They also point out that, since all PPP measures leave out asset demand for a currency, the measures are missing an important element of the demand. Critics ask: Is there any reason to assume that in the long run the asset demand for a currency is less important than the goods demand for a currency? Because the asset demand for a currency is important, critics of PPP argue that there is little reason to assume that the short-run actual exchange rate will ever adjust to the PPP exchange rates. And if that rate doesn't adjust, then PPP does not provide a good estimate of the equilibrium rate. These critics further contend that the existing exchange rate is the best estimate of the long-run equilibrium exchange rate.

Purchasing power parity is a method of calculating exchange rates such that various currencies will each buy an equal basket of goods and services. Those exchange rates may or may not be appropriate long-run exchange rates.

ADVANTAGES AND DISADVANTAGES OF ALTERNATIVE EXCHANGE RATE SYSTEMS

The problems of stabilizing exchange rates have led to an ongoing debate about whether a fixed exchange rate, a flexible exchange rate, or a combination of the two is best. This debate nicely captures the macro issues relevant to exchange rate stabilization, so in this section we consider that debate. First, a brief overview of the three alternative regimes:

Fixed exchange rates: If the government chooses a particular exchange rate and offers to buy and sell currencies at that price, it is imposing a fixed exchange rate. For example,

Three exchange rate regimes are:

1. Fixed exchange rate: The government chooses an exchange rate and offers to buy and sell currencies at that rate.
2. Flexible exchange rate: Determination of exchange rates is left totally up to the market.
3. Partially flexible exchange rate: The government sometimes affects the exchange rate and sometimes leaves it to the market.

suppose the Canadian government says it will buy euros at $1.20 per euro and sell dollars at 0.833 euros per dollar. In that case, we say that Canada has a fixed exchange rate of 0.833 euros to the dollar.

Flexible exchange rates: When governments do not enter into foreign exchange markets at all, but leave the determination of exchange rates totally up to currency traders, the country is said to have a flexible exchange rate. The price of its currency is allowed to rise and fall as market forces dictate.

Partially flexible exchange rates: When governments sometimes buy or sell currencies to influence the exchange rate, while at other times letting private market forces operate, the country is said to have a partially flexible exchange rate. A partially flexible exchange rate is sometimes called a dirty float because it isn't purely market-determined or government-determined.

Fixed Exchange Rates

The advantages of a fixed exchange rate system are:

1. Fixed exchange rates provide international monetary stability.
2. Fixed exchange rates force governments to make adjustments to meet their international problems.

The disadvantages of a fixed exchange rate system are:

1. Fixed exchange rates can become unfixed. When they're expected to become unfixed, they create enormous monetary instability.
2. Fixed exchange rates force governments to make adjustments to meet their international problems. (Yes, this is a disadvantage as well as an advantage.)

Let's consider each in turn.

Fixed Exchange Rates and Monetary Stability To maintain fixed exchange rates, the government must choose an exchange rate and have sufficient official reserves to support that rate. If the value it chooses is too high, its exports lag and the country continually loses official reserves. If the value it chooses is too low, it is paying more for its imports than it needs to and is building up official reserves, which means that some other country is losing official reserves. A country that is continually gaining or losing official reserves must eventually change its fixed exchange rate.

The difficulty is that as soon as the country gets close to its official reserves limit, foreign exchange traders begin to expect a drop in the value of the currency, and they try to get out of that currency because anyone holding that currency when it falls will lose money. For example, in December 1997, when traders found out that South Korea had only $10 billion in reserves instead of the official government announcement of $30 billion, they sold the Korean won and its value dropped. False rumours of an expected depreciation can become true by causing a "run on a currency," as all traders sell that currency. Thus, at times fixed exchange rates can become highly unstable because expectation of a change in the exchange rate can force the change to occur. As opposed to small movements in currency values, under a fixed rate regime these movements occur in large, sudden jumps.

Fixed Exchange Rates and Policy Independence Maintaining a fixed exchange rate places limitations on a central bank's actions. In a country with fixed exchange rates, the central bank must ensure that the international quantities of its currency supplied and demanded are equal at the existing exchange rate.

Say, for example, that the United States and the Bahamas have fixed exchange rates: $1 B = $1 U.S. The Bahamian central bank decides to run an expansionary monetary policy, lowering the interest rate and stimulating the Bahamian economy. The lower interest rates will cause financial capital to flow out of the country, and the higher income will increase imports. Demand for Bahamian dollars will fall. To prop up its dollar and to maintain the fixed exchange rate, the Bahamian government will have to buy its own currency. They can do so only as long as they have sufficient official reserves of other countries' currencies.

Because most countries' official reserves are limited, a country with fixed exchange rates is limited in its ability to conduct expansionary monetary and fiscal policies. It loses its freedom to stimulate the economy in response to a recession. That's why, when a serious recession hits, many countries are forced to abandon fixed exchange rates. They run out of official reserves, and choose expansionary monetary policy to achieve their domestic goals over contractionary monetary policy to achieve their international goals.

Fixed exchange rates provide international monetary stability and force governments to make adjustments to meet their international problems. (This is also a disadvantage.) If they become unfixed, they create monetary instability.

Flexible Exchange Rates

The advantages and disadvantages of a flexible exchange rate (exchange rates totally determined by private market forces) are the reverse of those of fixed exchange rates. The advantages are:

1. Flexible exchange rates provide for orderly incremental adjustment of exchange rates rather than large, sudden jumps.
2. Flexible exchange rates allow government to be flexible in conducting domestic monetary and fiscal policies.

The disadvantages are:

1. Flexible exchange rates allow speculation to cause large jumps in exchange rates, which do not reflect market fundamentals.
2. Flexible exchange rates allow government to be flexible in conducting domestic monetary and fiscal policies. (This is a disadvantage as well as an advantage.)

Let's consider each in turn.

Flexible Exchange Rates and Monetary Stability Advocates of flexible exchange rates argue as follows: Why not treat currency markets like any other market and let private market forces determine a currency's value? There is no fixed price for TVs; why should there be a fixed price for currencies? The opponents' answer is based on the central role that international financial considerations play in an economy and the strange shapes and large shifts that occur in the short-run supply and demand curves for currencies.

When expectations shift supply and demand curves around all the time, there's no guarantee that the exchange rate will be determined by long-run fundamental forces. The economy will go through real gyrations because of speculators' expectations about other speculators. Thus, the argument against flexible exchange rates is that they allow far too much fluctuation in exchange rates, making trade difficult.

Flexible exchange rate regimes provide for orderly incremental adjustment of exchange rates rather than large sudden jumps, and allow governments to be flexible in conducting domestic monetary and fiscal policies. (This is also a disadvantage.) They are, however, susceptible to private speculation.

Flexible Exchange Rates and Policy Independence The policy independence arguments for and against flexible exchange rates are the reverse of those given for fixed exchange rates. Individuals who believe that national governments should not have flexibility in setting monetary policy argue that flexible exchange rates don't impose the discipline on policy that fixed exchange rates do. Say, for example, that a country's goods are uncompetitive. Under a fixed exchange rate system, the country would have to contract its money supply and deal with the underlying uncompetitiveness of its goods. Under a flexible exchange rate system, the country can maintain an expansionary monetary policy, allowing inflation simply by permitting the value of its currency to fall.

Advocates of policy flexibility argue that it makes no sense for a country to go through a recession when it doesn't have to; flexible exchange rates allow countries more flexibility in dealing with their problems. True, policy flexibility may lead to inflation, but inflation is better than a recession.

Partially Flexible Exchange Rates

Faced with the dilemma of choosing between these two unpleasant policies, most countries have opted for a policy in between: partially flexible exchange rates. With such a policy they try to get the advantages of both fixed and flexible exchange rates. Sometimes these are referred to as "managed" exchange rates or a "dirty" float.

When policymakers believe there is a fundamental misalignment in a country's exchange rate, they will allow private forces to determine it—they allow the exchange rate to be flexible. When they believe that the currency's value is falling because of speculation, or that too large an adjustment in the currency is taking place, and that that adjustment won't achieve their balance of payments goals, they step in and fix the exchange rate, either supporting or pushing down their currency's value. Countries that follow a currency stabilization policy have partially flexible exchange rates.

If policymakers are correct, this system of partial flexibility works smoothly and has the advantages of both fixed and flexible exchange rates. If policymakers are incorrect, however, a partially flexible system has the disadvantages of both fixed and flexible systems.

> Partially flexible exchange rate regimes combine the advantages and disadvantages of fixed and flexible exchange rates.

Which View Is Right?

> **Q-9** Does government intervention stabilize exchange rates?

Which view is correct is much in debate. Most foreign-exchange traders we know tell us that the possibility of government intervention increases the amount of private speculation in the system. In the private investors' view, their own assessments of what exchange rates should be are better than those of policymakers. If private investors knew the government would not enter in, private speculators would focus on fundamentals and would stabilize short-run exchange rates. When private speculators know government might enter into the market, they don't focus on fundamentals; instead they continually try to outguess government policymakers. When that happens, private speculation doesn't stabilize; it destabilizes exchange rates as private traders try to guess what the government thinks.

Many of our economics colleagues who work for central banks aren't convinced by private investors' arguments. They maintain that some government intervention helps stabilize currency markets. We don't know which group is right—private foreign exchange traders or economists at the central banks. But to decide, it is necessary to go beyond the arguments and consider how the various exchange rate regimes have worked in practice. Appendix A gives you an introduction to the history of exchange rate regimes.

MONETARY UNION IN NORTH AMERICA

Now that we have a firm understanding of the benefits of fixed and flexible exchange rate systems it's time to turn to the question of whether Canada and the United States should adopt a common currency. The impetus for this proposal was the adoption of the

APPLYING THE TOOLS

The Euro

Over the last 50 years Europe has been integrating its economies, first with a common market, then with a loose federation called the European Union, which opened borders among member countries. The next step was the adoption of a common currency, the euro. This step was completed in 2002, at which time the euro is the only legal tender in a set of countries of the European Union.

As the euro has been adopted, it will be almost impossible for the countries to eliminate the fixed exchange rates. An analogy might be the two types of marriage in Louisiana—the normal marriage and the committed marriage. Normal marriages can be ended by divorce, but committed marriages are much more difficult to end. A single currency is like a committed marriage. Once it is established, there is no going back.

The European Union moved to a single currency to increase trade among countries and to create a financial asset and currency unit that can challenge the U.S. dollar on world markets. Thus, the euro has major positive aspects. It also has negatives; once they adopt the euro, these countries will no longer be able to run an independent monetary policy, which may mean that significant inflation or unemployment will exist in particular countries whose governments have no policy to deal with it. The verdict is still out on whether the advantages of the euro outweigh the disadvantages.

euro by 12 members of the European Union. No more Deutschmarks; no more French francs—on February 28, 2002, only euro-denominated notes and coins began to circulate in Europe. Should the North American economy follow suit and create a common currency for use in Canada, the United States, and perhaps even Mexico? What would the advantages be? Are there any disadvantages? What does economic theory have to say about these issues, and what is the political reality? What are some of the other suggestions for integrating monetary systems, and how would they work?

The European Union adopted the euro in January 1999.

Possible Options

Setting aside the political dimensions to the issue for now, we first need to identify the range of possible options associated with some form of monetary union in North America. While anyone with some imagination and a bit of training in economics can come up with suggestions for accomplishing monetary union, we'll focus on the three most popular proposals:

1. Moving back to fixed exchange rates.
2. Creating a new North American currency (the amero).
3. Adopting the U.S. dollar.

Fixed Exchange Rates Some economists advocate moving back to a fixed exchange rate system. We've already outlined the benefits of this action, and also have considered its downside, so you should be fairly comfortable with the economics of this proposal. We know that more than 80 percent of our exports are destined for the United States and that approximately 75 percent of our imports come from the United States. Fixing the value of the Canadian dollar to the U.S. dollar makes sense from a practical standpoint. However, there are some issues we haven't yet discussed that directly relate to the potential benefits and costs of re-establishing a fixed Canada–U.S. exchange rate.

On the benefit side, some economists point to the exchange rate system when trying to explain why Canadian productivity growth has lagged so far behind American productivity growth. They believe that Canadian firms have had less of an incentive to keep their costs down and innovate as a result of a fairly steady depreciation of the Canadian dollar over the last decade. Competitive pressures and globalization have led to relatively low prices for many products. If a firm cannot respond to lower prices by reducing its costs, it won't be in business much longer. The "lazy firm" hypothesis states that Canadian firms have been able to retain their markets without investing in productivity enhancements because the value of the Canadian dollar has fallen, making Canadian goods relatively inexpensive for foreigners. These Canadian firms have been able to stay in business as a result of the flexible exchange rate—it has sheltered firms from the forces of competition, with many continuing to produce only because the value of the dollar has fallen.

The solution, some economists advocate, is to move back to a fixed exchange rate system. This would reduce the buffer the exchange rate offers inefficient firms, and society's resources would be allocated to their best possible uses as these firms shut down and leave uncompetitive industries. It would force Canadian firms to be as innovative as their American counterparts, leading to a substantial increase in productivity. So, a return to fixed exchange rates, at least with respect to our trade with the United States, would be a "good thing."

The evidence as to whether the exchange rate has actually sheltered Canadian firms is somewhat mixed, and the argument does contain a number of flaws. It assumes that the managers of many Canadian firms are lazy and that they operate inefficiently, but Canadian shareholders wouldn't stand for this kind of behaviour, would they? It also presumes that comparative advantages persist indefinitely. However, we know that as technology changes and society's endowment of resources changes, opportunity costs change. This leads to shifts in comparative advantage and the distribution of the gains from trade across nations (if you need a refresher, review Chapter 2). The structure of trade *is supposed to change* as opportunity costs evolve.

Fixing the Canadian dollar to the U.S. dollar might help our trade with the United States, but we also trade with other nations. Any advantages a flexible exchange rate would provide us vis-à-vis making our goods more attractive to someone in Europe than goods priced in U.S. dollars would be lost if we moved to a fixed exchange rate system. Finally, there are the practical considerations: At what rate do we fix the value of the Canadian dollar? At the current nominal exchange rate? At the rate we calculate using PPP?

16.3

see page 412

Many economists believe a return to fixed exchange rates is not in the cards, although at least one prominent Canadian economist (Robert Mundell, who won the Nobel Prize in Economics in 1999) thinks we're already at an exchange rate of US$2 for CAN$3.

A New Currency If fixed exchange rates aren't the solution, then why not follow the European model and adopt a common currency—let's call it the amero. All goods and services in Canada and the United States (and even in Mexico) would be denominated in ameros. A North American central bank would be created from the existing central banks to design and implement monetary policy. Seems like a good idea.

Now answer the following questions: At what rate would countries enter the system; that is, at how many U.S. dollars to the amero, and at how many Canadian dollars to the amero? We could solve this "entry" problem, as they had to in Europe when countries decided the rates at which euros, drachma, and other currencies could be traded for euros. Which central bank gets to determine monetary policy as well as implement the strategy? Again, Europe solved this problem by creating a European Central Bank, with control rotating among different members over time. However, one might not expect the Federal Reserve to be as willing as, say, the Bank of Greece, to relinquish control over its monetary policy. Nor would a national government be particularly thrilled with losing its ability to respond to macroeconomic challenges through the use of fiscal policies that require monetization of government debt.

The benefits of having a common currency are greatest when the two (or more) nations respond in a similar fashion to disturbances such as shifts in commodity prices. Research at the Bank of Canada has indicated that the best candidates for adopting a common currency in North America are Alberta and Texas, since as oil producers they respond in generally the same way to shocks in oil prices. The other provinces and states respond to changes in energy prices in much different ways, so it isn't clear that forcing all provinces and states to use a single currency provides many benefits.

Let's think about this last point. Suppose energy prices rise. Provinces that are energy producers benefit from increased economic activity as firms pump more natural gas and oil from the ground, while provinces that are heavy energy consumers and rely on interprovincial energy flows face higher costs. These costs hurt the energy-importing provinces, while the energy-exporting provinces flourish. Alberta and Texas, as energy exporters, would gain from having a common currency. This currency would gain value as other provinces and states demand more energy (and hence more of the Alberta–Texas currency) and allow these energy producers to buy more goods and services from the other provinces and states.

A common currency also has benefits when an economy is relatively open so that much of what it produces is sold in other countries. Suppose the Canadian dollar depreciates. This raises the price of imports and import-competing goods (as people buy at home rather than import). The domestic price of exports also rises, since foreigners want more domestic goods (they are cheaper). The price of tradable goods—goods that are traded with the rest of the world—rises. If most goods produced are traded goods, domestic inflation rises—and we know that central banks abhor inflation. Having a common currency would eliminate exchange rate–induced changes in the price level.

Note that these benefits are much smaller if the economy is relatively closed (a small proportion of production is in traded goods). A domestic depreciation has little impact on the economy: The price of traded goods still rises, but since they don't make up a large fraction of domestic production, the inflation rate may not rise by very much.

Now ask yourselves some additional questions: Why would the United States be interested in a monetary union with Canada? What would they gain? Would they be willing to share equally the responsibility for designing and implementing monetary policy? What role do you think Canada would play in assessing the need for monetary intervention? Whose regulatory structure for the financial system would be adopted for the new system, Canada's or that of the U.S.? What would happen to the Canadian government's ability to fund fiscal policy? Would Canadian social programs and tax systems continue into the future or would they need to change to accommodate the new environment? Would there be pictures of presidents or prime ministers on the new currency? When you consider these questions reasonably and realistically, you may conclude that a common North American currency is out of the question today. Perhaps it will be viable in the future.

Adopting the U.S. Dollar Why not just adopt the U.S. dollar, get rid of the Canadian dollar, and be done with it? This suggestion takes the first two proposals we've considered—fixing the exchange rate and adopting a common currency—to the extreme. It would eliminate the buffering role that a flexible exchange rate offers Canada (which we've argued is both an advantage and a disadvantage), it would eliminate speculative activities and the resources they draw on as people try to guess what exchange rates are going to be, and Canada wouldn't need a central bank. We could go on and on (and on).

Do you think Canadians would be comfortable losing control over monetary policy? What about Canada's national identity? Can you think of other reasons Canada might not want to adopt the U.S. dollar (assuming we could)?

David Dodge, the Governor of the Bank of Canada, perhaps said it best:

> Research by the Bank of Canada and by many outside analysts confirms that Canada benefits significantly from having a separate currency and a floating exchange rate. It is true that Canada and the United States share many characteristics. But when it comes to economic structure, there are many important differences. Not only is our economy far more open than that of the United States, but Canada is also more dependent on raw materials. Moreover, while we are net exporters of primary commodities, the Americans are net importers. Sharp swings in world commodity prices have a much greater impact on economic activity in Canada and, more importantly, they affect us differently than our neighbours. It is very clear that the structure of our economy is sufficiently distinct from that of the United States that a flexible exchange rate can play a key role in facilitating the domestic economic adjustment to such shocks.
>
> From a strictly economic perspective, it is always possible that, at some future time, the structures of our two economies could converge to a point that the benefits of a common currency could outweigh the macroeconomic costs of abandoning our flexible exchange rate. But it is also possible that those structures could diverge further (if more trade led to greater specialization). We simply do not know. I would emphasize, however, that the crucial factor here is not the extent of the integration between Canada and the United States, but rather how close or how far apart our economic structures are, or will be.[3]

ADJUSTING THE ECONOMY TO THE EXCHANGE RATE VIA TRADE POLICY

Three types of trade restrictions are: (1) tariffs, (2) quotas, and (3) trade embargoes.

Government trade policy involves creating trade restrictions on imports in order to meet the balance of payments constraint without using traditional macro policy or exchange rate policy. Economists generally oppose such trade restrictions because (1) they prevent competition, (2) they lower world welfare, and (3) they lead other countries to retaliate. Despite economists' opposition, the world has many trade restrictions, and there is continual political pressure to institute more.

Varieties of Trade Restrictions

The most common trade restrictions are tariffs and quotas. Others are voluntary restraint agreements, embargoes, regulatory trade restrictions, and nationalistic appeals. Each of these restrictions will tend to reduce the private supply of a currency.

Some important international trade restrictions include tariffs, quotas, voluntary restraint agreements, and regulatory trade restrictions.

Tariffs **Tariffs,** also called customs duties, are *taxes governments place on internationally traded goods—generally imports*. Tariffs are the most used and most familiar type of trade restriction. Tariffs operate in the same way a tax does: They make imported goods relatively more expensive than they otherwise would have been, and thereby encourage the

---

[3]"Canada's Monetary Policy Approach: It Works for Canadians," remarks by David Dodge to the Edmonton Chamber of Commerce, June 26, 2001.

consumption of domestically produced goods. How tariffs affect prices and quantity was presented in Chapter 5; Figure 16-3 provides you with a brief review.

As you can see, a tariff paid by the supplier shifts the foreign supply curve back from S_0 to S_1. This raises price from P_0 to P_1 and reduces the quantity of imports from Q_0 to Q_1.

The dismal failure of tariffs in the early 20th century was the main reason the **General Agreement on Tariffs and Trade (GATT),** *a regular international conference to reduce trade barriers*, was established immediately following the Second World War. Since then, rounds of negotiations have resulted in a decline in worldwide tariffs and the establishment of GATT's successor, the **World Trade Organization (WTO)—***an organization committed to getting countries to agree not to impose new tariffs or other trade restrictions*. The WTO does allow retaliatory tariffs by countries it finds to have suffered from unfair trade practices. The WTO, and the free trade it stands for, is not supported by everyone. Some people oppose free trade because of the effect they believe it has on domestic jobs, the environment, and social justice. In late 1999, this opposition surfaced with demonstrations against the WTO when it met in Seattle, and who can forget what happened in Quebec City in 2001?

A tariff makes imported goods more expensive compared to domestically produced goods.

Quotas Quotas are *quantity limits placed on imports*. Their effect in limiting trade is similar to a tariff's effect. One big difference is in who gets the revenue. With a tariff, the government gets the revenue as tariff payments; with a quota, revenues accrue as additional profits to producers of the protected good. For example, if Canada places quotas on foreign textiles, producers of textiles will receive the proceeds of the resulting higher price. If Canada places a tariff on textile imports, the prices will also rise, but the Canadian government will receive the revenue.

A second big difference is that under a quota, any increase in domestic demand will be met by the less-efficient domestic producers (who would otherwise lose in the competition) since a quota places strict numerical limitations on what can be imported. Under a tariff, part of any increase in domestic demand will be met by more-efficient foreign producers since a tariff places a tax on imports but does not restrict their quantity. Needless to say, foreign producers prefer quotas to tariffs. A good exercise to make sure you understand the reason why foreign producers prefer quotas is to graphically show the relationship between a tariff and quota. (If you're not sure of the relationship you might review Chapter 5's discussion of tariffs and quotas.)

Figure 16-3   THE IMPACT OF TARIFFS ON IMPORTED GOODS

You can see how tariffs affect the price and quantity of imports. A tariff raises the price of foreign goods because the foreign supplier cuts down his supply (shown by the shift in the supply curve from S_0 to S_1). The price to domestic consumers rises to P_1. As the price rises, demand shifts toward domestic goods.

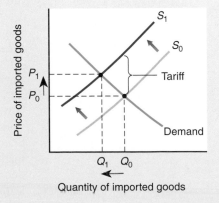

Voluntary Restraint Agreements Imposing new tariffs and quotas is specifically ruled out by the WTO, but foreign countries know that following WTO rules is voluntary and that if a domestic industry brought sufficient political pressure on its government, the WTO rules would be forgotten. To avoid the imposition of new tariffs on their goods, countries often enter into **voluntary restraint agreements**—*agreements in which countries voluntarily restrict their exports*. That's why Japan has agreed informally to limit the number of cars it exports to North America.

The effect of voluntary restraint agreements is similar to the effect of quotas: They directly limit the quantity of imports, increasing the price of the good and helping domestic producers. For example, when Canada and the United States encouraged Japan to impose voluntary restrictions on exports of its cars to North America, Toyota benefited from the restrictions because it could price its limited supply of cars higher than it could if it sent in a large number of cars, so profit per car would be high. Since they faced less competition, North American car companies also benefited. They could increase their prices because Toyota had done so. Consumers lost because they paid higher prices both for domestic and imported cars.

Embargoes An **embargo** is *a restriction on the import or export of a good*. Embargoes are usually established for international political reasons rather than for primarily economic reasons.

An example is the embargo of trade with Iraq. The government hoped that the embargo would so severely affect Iraq's economy that Saddam Hussein would lose political power. It did make life difficult for Iraqis, but it has not brought about the downfall of the Hussein government.

Regulatory Trade Restrictions Tariffs, quotas, and embargoes are the primary direct methods to restrict international trade. There are also indirect methods that restrict trade in not-so-obvious ways; these are called **regulatory trade restrictions**—*government-imposed procedural rules that limit imports*. One type of regulatory trade restriction has to do with protecting the health and safety of a country's residents. For example, a country might restrict import of all vegetables grown where certain pesticides are used, knowing full well that all other countries use those pesticides. The effect of such a regulation would be to halt the import of vegetables.

A second type of regulatory restriction involves making import and customs procedures so intricate and time-consuming that importers simply give up. For example, France requires all imported VCRs to be individually inspected in Toulouse. Since Toulouse is a provincial city, far from any port and outside the normal route for imports after they enter France, this inspection process can take months.

Some regulatory restrictions are imposed for legitimate reasons; others are designed simply to make importing more difficult and hence protect domestic producers from international competition. It's often hard to tell the difference. A good example of this difficulty occurred in 1988 and continued in the late 1990s when the EU disallowed all imports of meat from animals that had been fed growth-inducing hormones.

Nationalistic Appeals Finally, nationalistic appeals can help to restrict international trade. "Buy Canadian" campaigns and Japanese xenophobia are examples. Many Canadians, given two products of equal appeal except that one is made in Canada and one is made in a foreign country, would buy the Canadian product. To get around this tendency, foreign and Canadian companies often go to great lengths to get a MADE IN CANADA classification on goods they sell in Canada. For example, components for many autos are made in Japan but shipped to Canada and assembled in Ontario so that the finished car can be called a Canadian product.

Economists' Dislike of Trade Restriction Policies

When successful, these trade restriction policies decrease the demand for imports and decrease the private supply of domestic currency, thereby reducing its value relative to foreign currencies. The effect of trade restrictions on imports and a country's exchange rate is easy for politicians to explain, which is one reason why trade restrictions are so politically popular.

Despite the political popularity of trade restrictions, most economists support **free trade**—*a policy of allowing unrestricted trade among countries*. The reason is that, in their considered judgment, the harm done by trade restrictions outweighs the benefits.

Economists' first argument for free trade is that, viewed from a global perspective, free trade increases total output. From a national perspective, economists agree that particular instances of trade restriction may actually help one nation, even as most other nations are hurt. But they argue that the country imposing trade restrictions can benefit only if the other country doesn't retaliate with trade restrictions of its own. Retaliation is the rule, not the exception, however, and when there is retaliation, trade restrictions cause both countries to lose.

A second reason most economists support free trade is that trade restrictions reduce international competition. International competition is desirable because it forces domestic companies to stay on their toes. If trade restrictions on imports are imposed, domestic companies don't work as hard, and they become less efficient. For example, in the 1950s and 1960s Canada imposed restrictions on imported steel. Canadian steel industries responded to this protection by raising their prices and channelling profits from their steel production into other activities. By the 1970s the Canadian steel industry was a mess, internationally uncompetitive, and using outdated equipment to produce overpriced steel. Instead of making the steel industry stronger, restrictions made it a flabby, uncompetitive industry.

Economists' final argument against trade restrictions is: Yes, some restrictions might benefit a country, but almost no country can limit its restrictions to the beneficial ones. Trade restrictions are addictive—the more you have, the more you want. Thus, a majority of economists take the position that the best response to such addictive policies is "just say no."

> Economists generally support free trade because trade restrictions lower aggregate output, reduce international competition, and often result in harmful trade wars that hurt everyone.

Q.10 Why do many economists advocate free trade?

Strategic Trade Policies

While most economists favour free trade, at times trade restrictions can be used to promote free trade. For example, in the mid-1990s China was allowing significant illegal copying of Canadian software without paying royalties on the work. The United States exerted pressure to stop such copying but felt that China was not responding effectively. To force compliance, the United States made a list of Chinese goods that it threatened with 100 percent tariffs unless China complied.

The United States did not want to implement these restrictions, but felt that it would have more strategic bargaining power if it threatened to do so. Hence the name **strategic trade policies**—*threatening to implement tariffs to bring about a reduction in tariffs or some other concession from the other country*.

The potential problem with strategic trade policies is that they can backfire. One rule of strategic bargaining is that the other side must believe that you'll go through with your threat. Thus, strategic trade policy can lead a country that actually supports free trade to impose trade restrictions, just to show how strongly it believes in free trade.

> Strategic trade policies are threats to implement tariffs to bring about a reduction in tariffs or some other concession from the other country.

Even though most economists support free trade, they admit that in bargaining it may be necessary to adopt a strategic position. A country may threaten to impose trade restrictions if the other country does so. When such strategic trade policies are successful, they end up eliminating or reducing trade restrictions. When they are unsuccessful, they can lead to a trade war. Thus, in response to the United States' threat, China made a threat of its own—to put prohibitive tariffs on American goods. Just before the deadline the two countries had set, they agreed to avoid a trade war. China agreed to increase copyright enforcement and the United States agreed that China's proposed increased enforcement met American objections.

When should trade restrictions be used for strategic purposes—and, just as important, when should they not be used for strategic purposes? Economic theory does not tell us. That question is part of the practice of the art of economics. (It should be pointed out that economic game theorists are adding insights into the issue and that the area of strategic trade policies is a hot one for research.)

INTERNATIONAL TRADE AGREEMENTS AFFECTING CANADA

Now that we have a pretty good understanding of several different types of trade restrictions and why economists generally favour a free trade environment, it's time to look at several trade agreements that have transformed the Canadian economy.

The Canada–U.S. Free Trade Agreement

The **Canada–U.S. Free Trade Agreement** (FTA) was signed by the United States and Canada in 1987 and came into effect in 1989. It *set into motion a process in which most tariff and nontariff barriers would be eliminated over a 10-year period.* Today, nearly all trade between the United States and Canada is tariff-free. Canada entered into the agreement because throughout the 1980s protectionist sentiments in the U.S. were on the rise. Since most of Canada's exports are to the United States, Canadian firms lobbied the government to enter into the agreement so they would have secure access to U.S. markets. Otherwise Canadian goods could have been subject to the protectionist measures that were being considered by many American politicians at that time. It also allowed Canadian firms to benefit from the economies of scale associated with large U.S. markets. With a relatively small market it just wasn't profitable for many Canadian firms to expand their product lines given the associated increase in costs. With a potentially much larger market, Canadian firms could take advantage of gains in productive efficiency through the use of much larger production facilities. A frequently cited example is the production of beer. Production on a large scale allows firms to reduce their unit costs and benefit from expanding their product lines.

At about the time the FTA came into force the Canadian economy experienced a protracted recession, which didn't help the FTA's proponents. The elimination of protective tariffs displaced a large number of workers as uncompetitive firms left some industries, and it took several years for unemployment to return to pre-recession levels. Did everyone win as a result of the FTA? Let's look at how a reduction in tariffs might affect firms in an economy.

Tariff Reduction: The Winners and Losers Let's examine how a reduction in tariffs might affect two firms in a Canadian industry—say textiles. Figure 16-4 provides a view of the market, where a tariff raises prices above the world price, P_w to P_t. The elimina-

Figure 16-4   **THE BENEFITS OF TARIFF REDUCTION**

The elimination of a tariff will reduce prices to P_w and imports will rise from $Q_4 - Q_3$ to $Q_2 - Q_1$. Society will recapture areas A and B. An inefficient firm whose costs exceed P_w will be forced out of business.

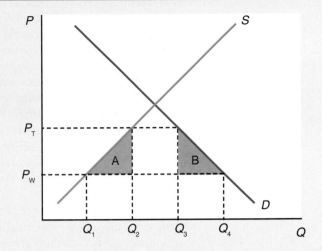

tion of the tariff would allow domestic prices to fall to the world price. Canadian textile imports would rise, and consumers would be better off.

The Free Trade Agreement reduces tariffs of both countries, causing problems for producing firms. We can see this if we think about two textile firms operating with different costs of production—perhaps due to the use of different technologies. Suppose the world price of cloth is $1.50 per metre, and the tariff raises the domestic price to $2.00 per metre. Say firm A, Walcloth, operates with costs of $1.50 per metre while firm B, Zellcloth, operates with costs of $1.75 per metre. The tariff ensures that both firms earn positive profits: $0.50 per metre for Walcloth; $0.25 per metre for Zellcloth. When the tariff is eliminated and cloth prices fall to the world price of $1.50 per metre, Walcloth will just break even, whereas Zellcloth will make losses ($0.25 per metre) and eventually leave the industry (they can't cover their costs per metre). So, when the tariff is removed and the domestic price falls to the world price, the marginal (high cost) firm will shut down. Domestic cloth production will fall.

Under any trade agreement there will be winners and losers. Policymakers spend a great deal of effort in attempting to identify the benefits and the costs of alternative trade arrangements. Unfortunately, economists' empirical estimates of the gains to free trade vary considerably, and sometimes there's little agreement on how the economy will respond to changes in trade policy. For example, estimates of the grains to Canada under the FTA varied by as much as 50 percent (from 2.5 percent to 5 percent of output). And, with respect to NAFTA, estimates of the gains to Mexico vary between 1.6 percent and 5.0 percent of Mexican output; for Canada the gains were calculated to be somewhere between 0.7 percent to 6.75 percent of Canadian output; and for the United States, gains were expected to be between 0.5 percent and 2.55 percent of U.S. output. When there's this much uncertainty in the numbers, it is difficult to design a set of economic policies that will mitigate the deleterious effects of structural change. (The FTA debate played a significant role in the 1988 federal election, and when the Tories were given a second mandate, opponents of the deal—mainly Liberals and New Democrats —admitted defeat.)

Faulty Reasoning Many economists pointed to a fundamental flaw in the economic reasoning of the opponents of the deal—the critics appeared to deny the principle of comparative advantage. From earlier in this chapter, we know that if Canada has a comparative advantage in the export of raw materials, we should seize that opportunity. Yet opponents of the deal went so far as to talk about scrapping it. For instance, some Canadians saw it as a U.S. attempt to get its hands on Canada's fresh water—that is, they predicted Canada's fresh water would be one of the natural resources that Canada would end up exporting. The critics appeared to argue that we should sacrifice economic efficiency for *short-term* employment. We say *short-term* employment because any industry that requires protective barriers for its existence won't survive the process of globalization. Competitive pressures will eventually lead to the production of the same products, at lower cost, somewhere else. World demand for our uncompetitive goods would be attracted to foreign soil, and Canada would be left with an inefficient industry with no market for the product. Firms would shut down, contributing further to the unemployment problem.

Many opponents of the deal argued that competition would put pressure on Canadian social programs—specifically, our health care system—to change. Universal medical coverage in Canada is the norm—not so in the United States. While there's an ongoing debate over the reform of the U.S. health care system, it's hard to say what will happen there. While it's true that the Canadian health care system faces a number of fiscal challenges, for now there's no serious talk about eliminating universality. User fees for certain medical procedures and services, yes. But every Canadian will still have access to basic health care.

The North American Free Trade Agreement

In 1993 Canada and the United States, and eventually Mexico, signed the **North American Free Trade Agreement (NAFTA)**. It *extended the FTA to Mexico and enhanced the FTA to eliminate other impediments to international trade*. The importance of trade in services had risen substantially since the FTA was signed and, among other things, NAFTA attempted to lubricate trade flows in services. It also aimed to provide a framework in which competition policies could be brought into the trade policy arena. In each country there were industries that enjoyed preferential treatment—or at least that were perceived by other nations as having received preferential treatment—and NAFTA expanded the dispute settlement provisions of the FTA.

You will have heard about one contentious trade issue in the news—the softwood lumber dispute. American producers alleged that Canada unfairly subsidized Canadian softwood lumber producers, and in 2001 the United States placed a punitive duty on exports of softwood lumber from Canada. Under American law, American softwood lumber producers would receive the revenues from these duties, so Canada placed an export tax on softwood sales to the United States to keep the funds in Canada. The conflict decimated the softwood lumber industry in British Columbia and Atlantic Canada. Late in 2001 both the federal government and Canadian softwood lumber producers revisited Canadian policies with a view to assuaging American producers in the hope that they would withdraw their complaints of unfair practices.

There were just as many critics of NAFTA as there were of the FTA. Indeed, many commentators believed that the FTA and NAFTA were the first steps down the slippery slope of "Americanizing" Canada. This concern has been renewed recently with plans for a Free Trade Areas of the Americas Trade Agreement.

Free Trade Areas of the Americas

If free trade is so great, why not extend agreements to every nation in the Americas to reduce trade impediments? That's the essence of the **Free Trade Areas of the Americas**

(FTAA) agreement. You might recall the riots and protests in Seattle and Quebec City—those took place when negotiators from 34 nations met to hammer out the details of the FTAA, which is scheduled to come into effect no later than 2005.

On the surface the FTAA appears to be a no-brainer. Encouraging trade, fostering economic development, securing basic human rights, protecting the environment, building democratic institutions—all of these seem to be a "good thing," as Martha Stewart might say. However, there are a number of criticisms of how the agreement will affect small developing countries. Free trade isn't necessarily the same thing as **fair trade,** by which we mean *a country is equitably compensated for its products,* so that farmers, for example, earn a decent wage and enjoy a safe working environment.

There are nine negotiating groups dealing with issues involving dispute settlement, agriculture, competition policy, government purchasing, market access, services, investment, intellectual property rights, as well as anti-dumping and countervailing duties. Many critics of the FTAA have expressed concern that relatively rich nations will dictate terms and take advantage of small developing nations. For example, they point to relatively weak environmental standards in some countries as being attractive to industries that create substantial amounts of pollution. If these firms face high costs of meeting environmental regulations in developed nations, it may be optimal for them to relocate to areas lacking effective regulatory controls. In the long run, this would be to the detriment of the developing nation. Hence, critics contend that a trade agreement that does not take into account these issues will broaden the gap between the have and have-not countries in the Americas.

16.4

see page 412

Of course, in economics, there's usually an "on the other hand" argument to consider. The Government of Canada signed trade agreements with Costa Rica, Israel, and Chile, arguing that relatively large, developed countries can enter into responsible arrangements with much smaller and less industrialized nations. Agreements with Singapore and four Central American nations (El Salvador, Guatemala, Honduras, and Nicaragua) were being negotiated late in 2001. The federal government uses these negotiations to demonstrate its sensitivity to issues of fair trade. Whether the FTAA comes into effect as planned, given renewed concerns over national security, is the subject of ongoing debate as we write this chapter early in 2002.

CONCLUSION

As we hope has been apparent from reading the chapter, the issues in open-economy macro are extraordinarily interesting, but they are even more complicated, and even more politically charged, than the issues in domestic macro. Whatever the correct answers to the questions are, we can expect that the problems will become more and more important for Canada. With international transportation and communication becoming easier and faster, and with other countries' economies growing, the Canadian economy will become even more interdependent with the other economies of the world, making the macroeconomics focus more and more on issues within an open-economy framework.

Chapter Summary

- The balance of payments is made up of the current account and the capital and financial account.

- Exchange rates in a perfectly flexible exchange rate system are determined by the supply of and demand for a currency.

- An increase in a country's income increases the demand for foreign currency and leads to a decline in the value of the country's own currency. An increase in a country's price level reduces the demand for one's own currency and increases the demand for foreign currency and leads to a decline in the value of one's own currency. A decrease in a country's interest rates reduces the demand for that country's currency and increases the demand for foreign currency, leading to a decline in the value of one's own currency.

- A country can maintain a fixed exchange rate by either directly buying and selling its own currency or adjusting its monetary and fiscal policy to achieve its exchange rate goal.

- It is easier technically for a country to reduce the value of its currency than it is to support its currency.

- It is extraordinarily difficult to correctly estimate the long-run equilibrium exchange rate; one method of doing so is the purchasing power parity approach.

- Fixed exchange rates provide international monetary stability but can create enormous monetary instability if they become unfixed. Fixed exchange rates force governments to make adjustments to meet their international problems.

- Flexible exchange rates allow exchange rates to make incremental changes, but are also subject to large jumps in value as a result of speculation. Flexible exchange rates give governments flexibility in conducting domestic monetary and fiscal policy.

- Some important international trade restrictions include tariffs, quotas, voluntary restraint agreements, and regulatory trade restrictions.

- Economists generally support free trade because trade restrictions lower total world output, reduce international competition, and often result in harmful trade wars that hurt everyone.

Key Terms

balance of goods and services   (384)

balance of merchandise trade   (384)

balance of payments   (383)

Canada–U.S. Free Trade Agreement   (406)

capital and financial account   (383)

covered interest parity   (389)

currency stabilization   (392)

currency support   (392)

current account   (383)

embargo   (404)

exchange rate   (387)

fair trade   (409)

financial account   (383)

fixed exchange rate   (395)

flexible exchange rate   (396)

free trade   (405)

Free Trade Areas of the Americas (FTAA) agreement   (408)

General Agreement on Tariffs and Trade (GATT)   (403)

North American Free Trade Agreement (NAFTA)   (408)

official reserves   (383)

partially flexible exchange rates   (396)

purchasing power parity (PPP)   (393)

quota   (403)

regulatory trade restrictions   (404)

strategic trade policies   (405)

tariff   (402)

uncovered interest parity   (389)

voluntary restraint agreements   (404)

World Trade Organization (WTO)   (403)

Questions for Thought and Review

1. If a country is running a balance of trade deficit, will its current account be in deficit? Why?

2. When someone sends 100 British pounds to a friend in Canada, will this transaction show up on the capital or current account? Why?

3. Support the following statement: "It is best to offset a capital account surplus with a current account deficit."

4. Support the following statement: "It is best to offset a capital account deficit with a current account surplus."

5. What are the advantages and disadvantages of a non-convertible currency?

6. In Figure 16-2, a foreign government chooses to maintain an equilibrium market exchange rate of $1.30 per unit of its own currency. Discuss the implications of the government trying to maintain a higher fixed rate—say at $1.40.

7. If you were the finance minister of Never-Never Land, how would you estimate the long-run exchange rate of your currency, the neverback? Defend your choice as well as discuss its possible failings.

8. Which is preferable: a fixed or a flexible exchange rate? Why?

9. Dr. Loonie believes price stability is the main goal of central bank policy. Is the doctor more likely to prefer fixed or flexible exchange rates? Why?

10. If currency traders expect the government to devalue a currency, what will they likely do? Why?

11. Distinguish between the three types of regulatory trade restrictions and discuss their pros and cons.

12. What is the difference between a tariff and a quota?

13. Demonstrate graphically how the effects of a tariff differ from the effects of a quota.

14. How might a country benefit from having an inefficient customs agency?

15. If you were an economic adviser to a country that was following your advice about trade restrictions and that country fell into a recession, would you change your advice? Why or why not?

Problems and Exercises

1. Draw the fundamental analysis of the supply and demand for the British pound in terms of dollars. Show what will happen to the exchange rate with those curves in response to each of the following events:
    a. The U.K. price level rises.
    b. The Canadian price level rises.
    c. The U.K. economy experiences a boom.
    d. The U.K. interest rates rise.

2. The government of Never-Never Land, after much deliberation, finally decides to switch to a fixed exchange rate policy. It does this because the value of its currency, the neverback, is so high that the trade deficit is enormous. The finance minister fixes the rate at $10 a neverback, which is lower than the equilibrium rate of $20 a neverback.
    a. Discuss the trade or traditional macro policy options that could accomplish this lower exchange rate.
    b. Using the laws of supply and demand, show graphically how possible equilibria are reached.

3. Will the following be suppliers or demanders of Canadian dollars in foreign exchange markets?
    a. A Canadian tourist in Latin America.
    b. A German foreign exchange trader who believes that the value of the dollar will fall.
    c. A Canadian foreign exchange trader who believes that the value of the dollar will fall.
    d. A Costa Rican tourist in Canada.
    e. A Russian capitalist who wants to protect his wealth from expropriation.

    f. A British investor in Canada.

4. You've been hired as an economic adviser to Yamaichi Foreign Exchange Traders. What buy or sell recommendations for Canadian dollars would you make in response to the following news?
    a. Faster economic growth in the EU.
    b. Expectations of higher interest rates in Canada.
    c. Canadian interest rate rises, but less than expected.
    d. Expected loosening of Canadian monetary policy.
    e. Higher inflationary predictions for Canada.

5. State whether the following will show up on the current account or the capital account:
    a. IBM's exports of computers to Japan.
    b. IBM's hiring of a British merchant bank as a consultant.
    c. A foreign national living in Canada repatriates money.
    d. Ford Motor Company's profit in Hungary.
    e. Ford Motor Company uses that Hungarian profit to build a new plant in Hungary.

6. One of the basic laws of economics is the law of one price. It says that given certain assumptions one would expect that if free trade is allowed, the prices of goods in multiple countries should converge. This law underlies purchasing power parity.
    a. Can you list what three of those assumptions likely are?
    b. Should the law of one price hold for labour also? Why or why not?
    c. Should it hold for capital more so or less so than for labour? Why or why not?

Web Questions

1. The Big Mac index is an index of purchasing power parity created by a magazine called *The Economist*. *The Economist* publishes the exchange rate value of various currencies that would make the Big Mac cost the same as in other countries. Go to www.economist.com/editorial/freeforall/focus/big_mac_index.html and look up the purchasing power parity of the dollar for five currencies and compare them with the actual exchange rates.

    a. Which currencies were undervalued? Which were overvalued?
    b. What are the shortcomings of the Big Mac index?
    c. If you were to design your own index, what types of goods would you use in your basket of goods? Explain your answer.
    d. How could you check the validity of the Big Mac index?

2. Visit the CATO Institute Web site and read the article at this link (www.cato.org/pubs/pas/pa-403es.html).
   a. Do capital controls encourage reform of financial markets?
   b. During the Asian crisis of 1998, which nation implemented capital controls?
   c. What impact did the controls have on foreign investment in that nation?

3. Visit the Nobel Web site for Robert Mundell's award (www.nobel.se/economics/laureates/1999/mundell-video.html):
   a. Which currencies does Mundell believe will persist indefinitely?
   b. Does Mundell believe we need an international currency?
   c. Which currencies make up "the three islands of monetary stability"?

4. The Department of Foreign Affairs and International Trade Web site (http://www.dfait-maeci.gc.ca/menu-e.asp) contains a section on international trade agreements. The Fair Trade Federation Web site (http://www.fairtradefederation.com) also contains information on international trade.
   a. Provide some facts on fair trade. Choose one issue and see if it is discussed on the federal government's Web site on the FTAA.
   b. Does Canada support inclusion of labour, human rights, and poverty reduction issues in the FTAA negotiations? Explain.
   c. Do you believe the FTAA will raise the standard of living in developing countries? Support your answer using information from both of the Web sites.

Answers to Margin Questions

1. The expenditures of a Canadian citizen travelling abroad will show up as a debit on the services account. As tourism or travelling, it is a service. *(385)*

2. Net investment income is the return a country gets on its foreign investment minus the return foreigners get on their investment within a country. A country is a net debtor nation if the value of foreign investment within a country exceeds the value of its investment abroad. A country can be a net debtor nation and still have its net investment income positive if its foreign investment is undervalued at market values (valuation is generally done at book value), or if its foreign investment earns a higher rate of return than foreigners' investment within that country. *(386)*

3. As in the following diagram, an increase in the demand for euros pushes up the value of the euro in terms of dollars. *(387)*

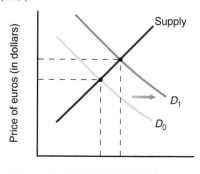

4. An increase in the demand for dollars is the equivalent of an increase in the supply of euros, so an increase in

the demand for dollars pushes down the price of euros in terms of dollars, as in the following diagram. *(388)*

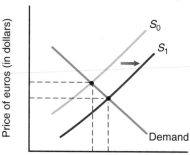

5. A recession reduces income, and since imports are directly related to income, imports fall. The demand for the foreign currency falls since people aren't buying as many imports. This leads to a reduction in the value of the foreign currency or, alternatively, an increase in the value of the domestic currency. *(388)*

6. In the short run, normal market forces have a limited, and possibly even perverse, effect on exchange rates, which is why most governments don't leave determination of exchange rates to the market. *(390)*

7. In general, it would be easier for Canada to push the value of the dollar down because doing so involves Canada buying up foreign currencies, which it can pay for simply by printing more dollars. To push the dollar up requires foreign reserves. *(393)*

8. When a foreign country's purchasing power parity value is less than the market value, the price of goods in that

country tends to be relatively cheaper than at home. This tends to make travelling there less expensive. (393)

9. There is much debate about whether government intervention stabilizes exchange rates—private traders tend to believe it does not; government economists tend to believe that it does. (398)

10. Economists generally support free trade because trade restrictions lower aggregate output, reduce international competition, and often result in harmful trade wars that hurt everyone. (405)

APPENDIX A

History of Exchange Rate Systems

A good way to give you an idea of how the various exchange rate systems work is to present a brief history of international exchange rate systems.

THE GOLD STANDARD: A FIXED EXCHANGE RATE SYSTEM

Governments played a major role in determining exchange rates until the 1930s. Beginning with the Paris Conference of 1867 and lasting until 1933 (except for the period around the First World War), most of the world economies had a system of relatively fixed exchange rates under what was called a **gold standard**—*a system of fixed exchange rates in which the value of currencies was fixed relative to the value of gold and gold was used as the primary reserve asset.*

Under a gold standard, the amount of money a country issued had to be directly tied to gold, either because gold coin served as the currency in a country or because countries were required by law to have a certain percentage of gold backing their currencies. Gold served as currency or backed all currencies. Each country participating in a gold standard agreed to fix the price of its currency relative to gold. That meant a country would agree to pay a specified amount of gold on demand to anyone who wanted to exchange that country's currency for gold. To do so, each country had to maintain a stockpile of gold. When a country fixed the price of its currency relative to gold, it fixed its currency's price in relation to other currencies as a result of the process of arbitrage.

Under the gold standard, a country made up the difference between the quantity supplied and the quantity demanded of its currency by buying or selling gold to hold the price of its currency fixed in terms of gold. How much a country would need to buy and sell depended on its balance of payments deficit or surplus. If the country ran a surplus in the balance of payments, it was required to sell its currency—that is, buy gold—to stop the value of its currency from rising. If a country ran a deficit, it was required to buy its currency—that is, sell gold—to stop the value of its currency from falling.

The gold standard enabled governments to prevent short-run instability of the exchange rate. If there was a speculative run on its currency, the government would buy its currency with gold, thereby preventing the value of its currency from falling.

But for the gold standard to work, there had to be a method of long-run adjustment; otherwise countries would have run out of gold and would no longer have been able to fulfil their obligations under the gold standard. The **gold specie flow mechanism** was *the long-run adjustment mechanism that maintained the gold standard.* Here's how it worked: Since gold served as official reserves to a country's currency, a balance of payments deficit (and hence a downward pressure on the exchange rate) would result in a flow of gold out of the country and hence a decrease in the country's money supply. That decrease in the money supply would contract the economy, decreasing imports, lowering the country's price level, and increasing the interest rate, all of which would work toward eliminating the balance of payments deficit.

Similarly a country with a balance of payments surplus would experience an inflow of gold. That flow would increase the country's money supply, increasing income (and hence imports), increasing the price level (making imports cheaper and exports more expensive), and lowering the interest rate (increasing capital outflows). These would work toward eliminating the balance of payments surplus.

Thus, the gold standard determined a country's monetary policy and forced it to adjust any international balance of payments disequilibrium. Adjustments to a balance of payments deficit were often politically unpopular; they led to recessions, which, because the money supply was directly tied to gold, the government couldn't try to offset with expansionary monetary policy.

The gold specie flow mechanism was called into play in the United States in late 1931 when the Federal Reserve, in response to a shrinking gold supply, decreased the amount of money in the economy, deepening the depression that had begun in 1929. The government's domestic goals and responsibilities conflicted with its international goals and responsibilities.

That conflict led to partial abandonment of the gold standard in 1933. At that time the United States made it illegal for individual citizens to own gold. Except for gold used for ornamental and certain medical and industrial purposes, all privately owned gold had to be sold to the government. Dollar bills were no longer backed by gold in the sense that citizens could exchange dollars for a prespecified amount of gold. Instead dollar bills were backed by silver, which meant that any citizen could change dollars for a prespecified amount of silver. In the late 1960s that changed also. Since that time, for U.S. residents, dollars have been backed only by trust in the soundness of the U.S. economy.

Gold continued to serve, at least partially, as international backing for U.S. currency. That is, other countries could still exchange dollars for gold. However in 1971, in response to another conflict between international and domestic goals, the United States totally cut off the relationship between dollars and gold. After that a dollar could be redeemed only for another dollar, whether it was a U.S. citizen or a foreign government who wanted to redeem the dollar.

THE BRETTON WOODS SYSTEM: A FIXED EXCHANGE RATE SYSTEM

As the Second World War was coming to an end, the United States and its allies met to establish a new international economic order. After much wrangling they agreed upon a system called the **Bretton Woods system,** *an agreement about fixed exchange rates that governed international financial relationships from the period after the end of the Second World War until 1971.* It was named after the resort in New Hampshire where the meeting that set up the system was held.

The Bretton Woods system established the International Monetary Fund (IMF) to oversee the international economic order. The IMF was empowered to arrange short-term loans between countries. The Bretton Woods system also established the World Bank, which was empowered to make longer-term loans to developing countries. Today the World Bank and IMF continue their central roles in international financial affairs.

The Bretton Woods system was based on mutual agreements about what countries would do when experiencing balance of payments surpluses or deficits. It was essentially a fixed exchange rate system. For example, under the Bretton Woods system, the value of the U.S. dollar for the British pound was set at slightly over US$4 to the pound.

The Bretton Woods system was not based on a gold standard. When countries experienced a balance of payments surplus or deficit, they did not necessarily buy or sell gold to stabilize the price of their currency. Instead they bought and sold other currencies. To ensure that participating countries would have sufficient reserves, they established a stabilization fund from which a country could obtain a short-term loan. It was hoped that this stabilization fund would be sufficient to handle all short-run adjustments that did not reflect fundamental imbalances.

In those cases where a misalignment of exchange rate was determined to be fundamental, the countries involved agreed that they would adjust their exchange rates. The IMF was empowered to oversee an orderly adjustment. It could authorize a country to make a one-time adjustment of up to 10 percent without obtaining formal approval from the IMF's board of directors. After a country had used its one-time adjustment, formal approval was necessary for any change greater than 1 percent.

The Bretton Woods system reflected the underlying political and economic realities of the post–Second World War period in which it was set up. European economies were devastated; the North American economy was strong. To rebuild, Europe was going to have to import North American equipment and borrow large amounts from Canada and the United States. There was serious concern over how high the value of the U.S. dollar would rise and how low the value of European currencies would fall in a free market exchange. The establishment of fixed exchange rates set limits on currencies' relative movements; the exchange rates that were chosen helped provide for the rebuilding of Europe.

In addition, the Bretton Woods system provided mechanisms for long-term loans from the United States to Europe that could help sustain those fixed exchange rates. The loans also eliminated the possibility of competitive depreciation of currencies, in which each country tries to stimulate its exports by lowering the relative value of its currency.

One difficulty with the Bretton Woods system was a shortage of official reserves and international liquidity. To offset that shortage, the IMF was empowered to create *a type of international money* called **Special Drawing Rights (SDRs).** But SDRs never became established as an international currency and the U.S. dollar kept serving as official reserves for individuals and countries. To get the dollars to foreigners, the United States had to run a deficit in its current account. Since countries could exchange the dollar for gold at a fixed price, the use of dollars as a reserve currency meant that, under the Bretton Woods system, the world was on a gold standard once removed.

The number of dollars held by foreigners grew enormously in the 1960s. By the early 1970s, those dollars far exceeded in value the amount of gold the United States had. Most countries accepted this situation; even though they could legally demand gold for their dollars, they did not. But Charles de Gaulle, the nationalistic president of France, wasn't pleased with the U.S. domination of international affairs at that time. He believed France deserved a much more prominent position. He demanded gold for the dollars held by the French central bank, knowing that the United States didn't have enough gold to meet his demand. As a result of his and other countries' demands, on August 15, 1971, the United States ended its policy of exchanging gold for dollars at US$35 per ounce. With that change, the Bretton Woods system was dead.

THE PRESENT SYSTEM: A PARTIALLY FLEXIBLE EXCHANGE RATE SYSTEM

International monetary affairs were much in the news in the early 1970s as countries groped for a new exchange rate system. The makeshift system finally agreed on involved partially flexible exchange rates. Most Western countries' exchange rates are allowed to fluctuate, although at various times governments buy or sell their own currencies to affect the exchange rate.

Under the present partially flexible exchange rates system, countries must continually decide when a balance of payments surplus or deficit is a temporary phenomenon and when it is a signal of a fundamental imbalance. If they believe the situation is temporary, they enter into the foreign exchange market to hold their exchange rate at what they believe is an appropriate level. If, however, they believe that the balance of payments imbalance is a fundamental one, they let the exchange rate rise or fall.

While most Western countries' exchange rates are partially flexible, certain countries have agreed to fixed exchange rates of their currencies in relation to rates of a group of certain other currencies. For example, a group of European Union countries adopted irreversible fixed exchange rates among their currencies, by electing to have one currency—the euro—beginning in 2002. Other currencies are fixed relative to the dollar.

Deciding what is, and what is not, a fundamental imbalance is complicated, and such decisions are considered at numerous international conferences held under the auspices of the IMF or governments. A number of organizations such as the Group of Eight, introduced in Chapter 3, focus much of their discussion on this issue. Often the various countries meet and agree, formally or informally, on acceptable ranges of exchange rates. Thus, while the present system is one of partially flexible exchange rates, the range of flexibility is limited.

Key Terms

Bretton Woods system *(414)*	gold specie flow mechanism *(413)*	gold standard *(413)*	Special Drawing Rights (SDRs) *(415)*

International Dimensions of Monetary and Fiscal Policies

17

After reading this chapter, you should be able to:

- Discuss why there is significant debate about what Canadian international goals should be.

- Explain how a country influences its exchange rate by using monetary or fiscal policy.

- Describe the paths through which monetary policy affects exchange rates and the trade balance.

- Explain the paths through which fiscal policy affects exchange rates and the trade balance.

- Summarize the reasons why governments try to coordinate their monetary and fiscal policies.

- State the potential problem of internationalizing a country's debt.

*The actual rate of exchange is largely governed
by the expected behavior of the country's
monetary authority.*

Dennis Robertson

In the last chapter we learned about the balance of payments and exchange rates. We saw how a country can influence exchange rates directly—by intervening in foreign exchange markets—or indirectly, through trade policy. We also saw how a trade surplus or deficit could exist if the other international accounts offset that surplus. In this chapter we put that knowledge to work, exploring the policy issues surrounding international goals in reference to the standard macro tools of monetary and fiscal policy.

THE AMBIGUOUS INTERNATIONAL GOALS OF MACROECONOMIC POLICY

Macroeconomics' international goals are less straightforward than its domestic goals. There is general agreement about the domestic goals of macroeconomic policy: We want low inflation, low unemployment, and high growth. There's far less agreement on what a country's international goals should be.

Most economists agree that the international goal of Canadian macroeconomic policy is to maintain the Canadian position in the world economy. But there's enormous debate about what achieving that goal means. Do we want a high or a low value for the dollar? Do we want a balance of trade surplus? Or would it be better to have a balance of trade deficit? Or should we not even pay attention to the balance of trade? Let's consider the exchange rate goal first.

The Exchange Rate Goal

There is a debate over whether a country should have a high or a low value for its currency. A high value for the dollar makes foreign currencies cheaper, lowering the price of imports. Lowering import prices places competitive pressure on Canadian firms and helps to hold down inflation. All of this benefits Canadian residents' living standard. But a high value for the dollar encourages imports and discourages exports. In doing so, it can cause a balance of trade deficit that can exert a contractionary effect on the economy by decreasing aggregate demand for Canadian output. So a high value for the dollar also has a cost to Canadian residents.

A low value for the dollar has the opposite effect. It makes imports more expensive and exports cheaper, and it can contribute to inflationary pressure. But, by encouraging exports and discouraging imports, it can cause a balance of trade surplus and exert an expansionary effect on the economy.

Many economists argue that a country should have no exchange rate policy because exchange rates are market-determined prices that are best left to the market. These economists question whether the government should even worry about the effect of monetary policy and fiscal policy on exchange rates. According to them, government should simply accept whatever exchange rate exists and not consider it in its conduct of monetary and fiscal policies.

Q.1 What effect does a low value for its currency have on a country's exports and imports?

Exchange rates have conflicting effects and, depending on the state of the economy, there are arguments for both high and low exchange rates.

The Trade Balance Goal

A deficit in the trade balance (the difference between imports and exports) means that, as a country, we're consuming more than we're producing. Imports exceed exports, so we're consuming more than we could if we didn't run a deficit. A surplus in the trade balance means that exports exceed imports—we're producing more than we're consuming. Since consuming more than we otherwise could is kind of nice, it might seem that a trade deficit is preferred to a trade surplus.

But wait. A trade deficit isn't without costs, and a trade surplus isn't without benefits. We pay for a trade deficit by selling off Canadian assets to foreigners—by selling Canadian companies, factories, land, and buildings to foreigners, or selling them financial assets such as Canadian dollars, stocks, and bonds. All the future interest and profits on these assets will go to foreigners, not Canadian citizens. That means eventually, sometime in the future, we will have to produce more than we consume so we can pay them *their* profit and interest on *their* assets. Thus, while in the short run a trade deficit allows more current consumption, in the long run it presents potential problems.

The trade balance is the difference between a country's exports and imports.

In the late 1990s and early 2000s the Canadian economy seemed to defy belief. Growth continued at higher than expected rates, unemployment fell below 7 percent, inflation was low, and the government budget went into surplus. Much of this was attributed to U.S. growth spilling over into Canada. During this period trade in goods and services between Canada and the United States amounted to $622.7 billion. That's an average of $1.7 billion a day! Trade with the United States accounted for about 80 percent of our exports, while the U.S. produced about 75 percent of our imports. That's one reason why Canadian forecasters spend a lot of time trying to predict where the American economy is going to go—we won't know where Canada will be headed without having a good idea of what's going on south of the border.

As long as a country can borrow, or sell assets, a country can have a trade deficit. But if a country runs a trade deficit year after year, eventually the long run will arrive and the country will run out of assets to sell and run out of other countries from whom to borrow. When that happens, the trade deficit problem must be faced.

The debate about whether a trade deficit should be of concern to policymakers involves whether these long-run effects should be anticipated and faced before they happen.

Opinions differ greatly. Some say not to worry—just accept what's happening. These "not-to-worry" economists argue that a trade deficit will end when Canadian citizens don't want to borrow from foreigners anymore and foreigners don't want to buy any more of our assets. They argue that the inflow of financial capital (money coming into Canada to buy our assets) from foreigners is financing new investment that will make the Canadian economy strong enough in the long run to reverse a trade deficit without serious disruption to the Canadian economy. So why deal with a trade deficit now, when it will take care of itself in the future?

Others argue that, yes, a trade deficit will eventually take care of itself, but the accompanying economic distress will be great. By dealing with the problem now, Canada can avoid a highly unpleasant solution in the future.

Both views are reasonable, which is why there's no consensus on what a country's trade balance goal should be.

International versus Domestic Goals

In the real world, when there's debate about a goal, that goal generally gets far less weight than goals about which there's general agreement. Since there's general agreement about our country's domestic goals (low inflation, low unemployment, and high growth), domestic goals generally dominate the Canadian political agenda.

Even if there weren't uncertainty about a country's international goals, domestic goals would likely dominate the political agenda. The reason is that inflation, unemployment, and growth affect a country's citizens directly. Trade deficits and exchange rates affect them indirectly—and in politics, indirect effects take a back seat.

Often a country responds to an international goal only when the international community forces it to do so. For example, in the 1980s when Brazil couldn't borrow any more money from other countries, it reluctantly made resolving its trade deficit a key goal. Similarly, when other countries threatened to limit Japanese imports, Japan took steps to increase the value of the yen and decrease its trade surplus. When a country is forced to face certain economic facts, international goals can become its primary goals.

Running a trade deficit is good in the short run but presents problems in the long run; thus, there is debate about whether we should worry about a trade deficit or not.

Q.2 Why do some people argue that we should not worry about a trade deficit?

Domestic goals generally dominate international goals because (1) international goals are ambiguous, and (2) international goals affect a country's population indirectly and, in politics, indirect effects take a back seat.

17.1

see page 430

As countries become more economically integrated, these pressures from other countries become more important.

MONETARY POLICY AND FISCAL POLICY WITH FIXED EXCHANGE RATES

How fast a country must respond to international pressure depends on the exchange rate regime it follows. If an economy sets fixed exchange rates, its monetary and fiscal policies are much more restricted than they are with flexible exchange rates. The reason is that the amount of currency stabilization that can be achieved with direct intervention is generally quite small, since a country's foreign reserves are limited. When this is the case, to keep its currency fixed at the desirable level it must adjust the economy to the exchange rate. Specifically, it must undertake policies that will change either the private supply of its currency or the private demand for its currency. It can do so by traditional macro policy—monetary and fiscal policy—influencing the economy, or by trade policy to affect the level of exports and imports.

To see the issues involved, consider the case of the European Union that we examined in the previous chapter. That case is shown in Figure 17-1. Europe's problem here is that it wants the value of the euro to be $1.30, not $1.20 as it currently is. The European Central Bank has three options for raising the value of the euro: decrease the private supply of euros (shifting the supply curve in from S_0 to S_1), increase the private demand for euros (shifting the demand curve out from D_0 to D_1), or use some combination of the two. Let's see how it could accomplish its goal with monetary or fiscal policy.

Q.3 If a country wants to fix the value of its currency higher than the market value, what monetary or fiscal policy must it use?

Increase the Private Demand for Euros via Contractionary Monetary Policy

To increase the demand for euros, the European Central Bank must create policies that increase the private foreign demand for European assets, or for European goods and services. In the short run the European Central Bank can increase the interest rate by running contractionary monetary policy. A higher interest rate increases the foreign demand for the area's interest-bearing assets. The problem with this approach is that to maintain an exchange rate at a certain level, the area must give up any attempt to target its inter-

---

Figure 17-1   TARGETING AN EXCHANGE RATE WITH MONETARY AND FISCAL POLICY

To increase the value of the euro from $1.20 per euro to $1.30 cents per euro, the European Central Bank will have to either shift the supply curve for euros from S_0 to S_1 or shift the demand curve for euros from D_0 to D_1. To increase the private demand for euros, the European Central Bank could increase interest rates by running contractionary monetary policy. To decrease the private supply of euros the European Central Bank could induce a recession by running either contractionary monetary or contractionary fiscal policy.

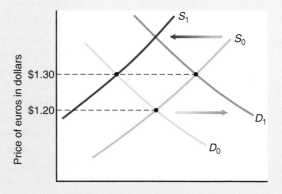

Quantity of euros

est rate to achieve domestic goals. To put it another way: An area can achieve an inter-est rate target or an exchange rate target, but generally it cannot achieve both at the same time.

Decrease the Private Supply of Euros via Contractionary Monetary and Fiscal Policy

To decrease the private supply of euros that comes from imports, the European Central Bank can run contractionary monetary and fiscal policy, slowing down the domestic economy and inducing a recession. This recession decreases the demand for imports and thereby decreases the private supply of euros. Governments are usually loath to use con-tractionary policy because politically induced recessions are not popular.

MONETARY AND FISCAL POLICY WITH FLEXIBLE OR PARTIALLY FLEXIBLE EXCHANGE RATE REGIMES

It is because of the constraints that fixed exchange rates place on domestic monetary and fiscal policy that many countries choose flexible, or at least partially flexible exchange rate regimes. In this section we shall take an in-depth look at the effect of monetary and fiscal policy on the exchange rate and the trade balance. Those effects often can significantly influence the choice of policies. We begin by considering the effect of monetary policy.

Monetary Policy's Effect on Exchange Rates

Monetary policy affects exchange rates in three ways: (1) through its effect on the in-terest rate, (2) through its effect on income, and (3) through its effect on price levels and inflation.

Q.4 What effect does the low-ering of a country's interest rates have on exchange rates?

The Effect on Exchange Rates via Interest Rates Expansionary monetary policy pushes down the Canadian interest rate, which decreases the financial capital inflow into Canada, decreasing the demand for dollars, pushing down the value of the dollar, and decreasing the value of the dollar via the interest rate path. Contractionary mone-tary policy does the opposite. It raises the Canadian interest rate, which tends to bring in financial capital flows from abroad, increasing the demand for dollars and increasing the value of the dollar. This interest rate effect is the dominant short-run effect, and it often overwhelms the other effects.

To see why these effects take place, consider a person in Japan in the late 1980s, when the Japanese interest rate was about 2 or 3 percent. He or she reasoned, "Why should I earn only 2 or 3 percent return in Japan? I'll save (buy some financial assets) in Canada where I'll earn 8 percent." If the Canadian interest rate goes up due to contrac-tion in the money supply, other things equal, the advantage of holding one's financial assets in Canada will become even greater and more people will want to save here. Peo-ple in Japan hold yen, not dollars, so in order to save in Canada they must buy dollars. Thus, a rise in Canadian interest rates increases the demand for dollars and, in terms of yen, pushes up the value of the dollar.

It's important to recognize that it is relative interest rates that govern the flow of fi-nancial capital. In the mid-1990s Taiwan kept its money supply tight, raising its inter-est rates to keep the value of the new Taiwan dollar high. In 1997 Taiwan cut reserve ratios; interest rates fell and the value of the new Taiwan dollar fell.

The interest rate effect on ex-change rates is the dominant short-run effect.

The Effect on Exchange Rates via Income Monetary policy also affects income in a country. As money supply rises, income expands; when money supply falls, income contracts.[1] This effect on income provides another way in which the money supply affects the exchange rate. As we saw earlier, when income rises, imports rise while exports are unaffected. To buy foreign products, Canadian citizens need foreign currency, which they must buy with dollars. So when Canadian imports rise, the supply of dollars to the foreign exchange market increases as Canadian citizens sell dollars to buy foreign currencies to pay for those imports. This decreases the value of the dollar. This effect through income and imports provides a second path through which monetary policy affects the exchange rate: Expansionary monetary policy causes Canadian income to rise, imports to rise, and the value of the dollar to fall via the income path. Contractionary monetary policy causes Canadian income to fall, imports to fall, and the value of the dollar to rise via the income path.

The Effect on Exchange Rates via Price Levels A third way in which monetary policy can affect exchange rates is through its effect on prices in a country. Expansionary monetary policy pushes the Canadian price level up. As the Canadian price level rises relative to foreign prices, Canadian exports become more expensive, and goods Canada imports become cheaper, decreasing Canadian competitiveness. This increases the demand for foreign currencies and decreases the demand for dollars. Thus, via the price path, expansionary monetary policy pushes down the dollar's value for the same reason that an expansion in income pushes it down.

Contractionary monetary policy puts downward pressure on the Canadian price level and slows down any existing inflation. As the Canadian price level falls relative to foreign prices, Canadian exports become more competitive and the goods Canada imports more expensive. Thus, contractionary monetary policy pushes up the value of the dollar via the price path.

The Net Effect of Monetary Policy on Exchange Rates Notice that all these effects of monetary policy on exchange rates are in the same direction. Expansionary monetary policy decreases the value of a country's currency; contractionary monetary policy pushes the value of a country's currency up. Summarizing these effects, we have the following relationships for expansionary and contractionary monetary policy:

Q.5 What effect would contractionary monetary policy have on the value of a country's currency via the income and price routes?

Monetary policy affects exchange rates through the interest rate path, the income path, and the price level path, as shown in the accompanying diagram.

Expansionary monetary policy

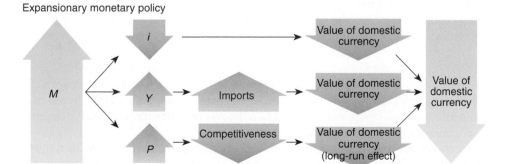

---

[1] When there's inflation, it's the rate of money supply growth relative to the rate of inflation that's important. If inflation is 10 percent and money supply growth is 10 percent, the rate of increase in the real money supply is zero. If money supply growth falls to, say, 5 percent while inflation stays at 10 percent, there will be a contractionary effect on the real economy.

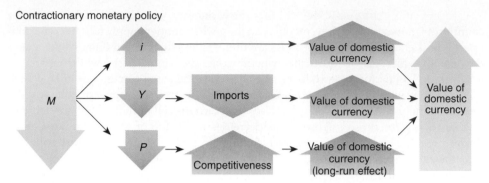

There are, of course, many provisos to the relationship between monetary policy and the exchange rate. For example, as the price of imports goes up, there is some inflationary pressure from that rise in price and hence some pressure for the price level to rise as well as fall. Monetary policy affects exchange rates in subtle ways, but if an economist had to give a quick answer to what effect monetary policy would have on exchange rates it would be:

Expansionary monetary policy decreases the relative value of a country's currency.

Contractionary monetary policy increases the relative value of a country's currency.

Monetary Policy's Effect on the Trade Balance

When a country's international trade balance is negative (in deficit), the country is importing more than it is exporting. When a country's international trade balance is positive, the country is exporting more than it is importing.

Monetary policy affects the trade balance in three ways: through income, through the price level, and through the exchange rate.

The Effect on the Trade Balance via Income Expansionary monetary policy increases income. When income rises, imports rise, while exports are unaffected. As imports rise, the trade balance shifts in the direction of deficit. So, via the income path, expansionary monetary policy shifts the trade balance toward a deficit.

Contractionary policy works in the opposite direction. It decreases income. When income falls, imports fall, while exports are unaffected, so the trade balance shifts in the direction of surplus. Thus, via the income path, expansionary monetary policy increases the trade deficit; contractionary monetary policy decreases the trade deficit.

The Effect on the Trade Balance via Price Levels A second way in which monetary policy affects the trade balance is through its effect on a country's price level. Expansionary monetary policy pushes a country's price level up. This decreases its competitiveness and increases a trade deficit. So, via the price path, expansionary monetary policy increases a trade deficit.

Contractionary monetary policy works in the opposite direction. It tends to push a country's price level down; this fall makes exports more competitive and imports less competitive. Both these effects tend to decrease a trade deficit. So, via the price path, contractionary monetary policy decreases a trade deficit.

Monetary policy's effect on the price level is a long-run, not a short-run, effect. It often takes a year for changes in the money supply to affect prices, and another year or two for changes in prices to affect imports and exports. Thus, the price path is a long-run effect. Price level changes don't significantly affect the trade balance in the short run.

The Effect on the Trade Balance via Exchange Rates A third path through which monetary policy influences the trade balance is the exchange rate. Expansionary Canadian monetary policy decreases the interest rate, which tends to push the value of the dollar down, increasing Canadian competitiveness. This decreases a trade deficit and hence works in a direction opposite to the effects of income changes and price level changes on the trade balance. Like the price level effect, the effect of the exchange rate on the trade balance is a long-run effect. This path doesn't have a significant effect in the short run.

Contractionary monetary policy works in the opposite direction. It raises the value of the dollar, increasing the relative price of Canadian exports and lowering the relative price of imports into Canada. Both effects tend to increase a trade deficit.

The Net Effect of Monetary Policy on the Trade Balance Since the effects are not all in the same direction, talking about the net effect of monetary policy on the trade balance is a bit more ambiguous than talking about its net effect on a country's exchange rate. However, only one of these paths—the income path—leads to a short-run effect. Thus, in the short run the net effect of monetary policy is relatively clear: Expansionary monetary policy tends to increase a trade deficit; contractionary monetary policy tends to decrease it. Since, in the long run, the price path effect and the exchange rate effect tend to offset each other, the short-run effects of monetary policy through the income path often carry over to the long-run effect.

Summarizing these three relationships, we have the following relationships for expansionary and contractionary monetary policy:

Q.6 What effect will contractionary monetary policy have on the trade balance through the price level and income paths?

Q.7 What will be the net effect of contractionary monetary policy on the trade balance?

Monetary policy affects the trade deficit through the income path, the price level path, and the exchange rate path, as shown in the accompanying diagram.

Expansionary monetary policy

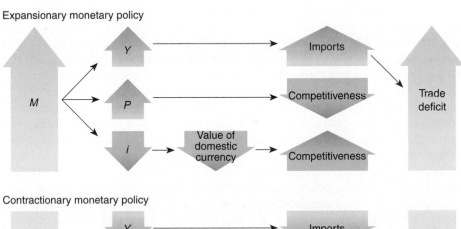

Contractionary monetary policy

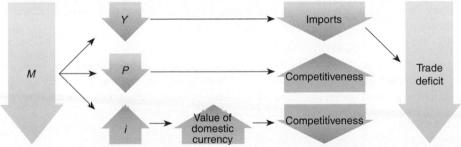

Expansionary monetary policy makes a trade deficit larger.

Contractionary monetary policy makes a trade deficit smaller.

While many complications can enter the trade balance picture, most economists would summarize monetary policy's short-run effect on the trade balance as follows:

Expansionary monetary policy makes a trade deficit larger.

Contractionary monetary policy makes a trade deficit smaller.

Fiscal Policy's Effect on Exchange Rates

Now we'll consider fiscal policy's effect on exchange rates. Fiscal policy, like monetary policy, affects exchange rates via three paths: income, price, and interest rates. Let's begin with its effect through income.

17.2

see page 430

The Effect on Exchange Rates via Income Expansionary fiscal policy expands income and therefore increases imports, increasing the trade deficit and lowering the value of the dollar. Contractionary fiscal policy contracts income, thereby decreasing imports and increasing the value of the dollar. These effects of expansionary and contractionary fiscal policies via the income path are similar to the effects of monetary policy, so if it's not intuitively clear to you why the effect is what it is, it may be worthwhile to review the slightly more complete discussion of monetary policy's effect presented previously.

The Effect on Exchange Rates via Price Levels Let's turn to the effect of fiscal policy on exchange rates through prices. Expansionary fiscal policy increases aggregate demand and increases prices of a country's exports; hence it decreases the competitiveness of a country's exports, which pushes down the the value of the dollar. Contractionary fiscal policy works in the opposite direction. These are the same effects that monetary policy had. And, as was the case with monetary policy, the price path is a long-run effect.

The Effect on Exchange Rates via Interest Rates Fiscal policy's effect on the exchange rate via the interest rate path is different from monetary policy's effect. Let's first consider the effect of expansionary fiscal policy. Whereas expansionary monetary policy lowers the interest rate, expansionary fiscal policy raises interest rates because the government sells bonds to finance that deficit. The higher Canadian interest rate causes foreign capital to flow into Canada, which pushes up the value of the dollar. Therefore expansionary fiscal policy's effect on exchange rates via the interest rate effect is to push up the value of the domestic currency.

Contractionary fiscal policy decreases interest rates since it reduces the bond financing of that deficit. Lower Canadian interest rates cause capital to flow out of Canada, which pushes down the the value of the dollar. Thus, the Canadian government budget surplus, which began in the late 1990s, put downward pressure on the interest rate and downward pressure on the value of the dollar.

Q.8 What is the net effect of expansionary fiscal policy on the exchange rate?

The Net Effect of Fiscal Policy on Exchange Rates Of these three effects, the interest rate effect and the income effect are both short-run effects. These two work in opposite directions, so the net effect of fiscal policy on the exchange rate is ambiguous. Let's summarize these three effects.

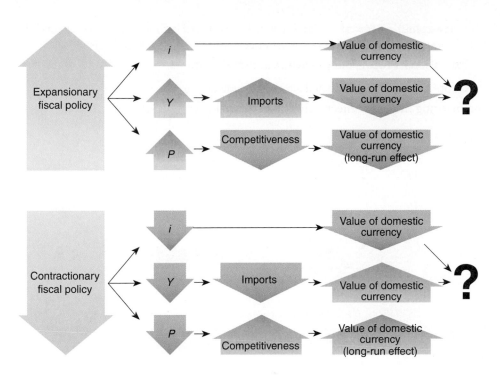

Fiscal policy affects exchange rates through the income path, the interest rate path, and the price level path, as shown in the accompanying diagram.

It's unclear what the effect of expansionary or contractionary fiscal policy will be on exchange rates.

Fiscal Policy's Effect on the Trade Deficit

Fiscal policy works on the trade deficit primarily through its effects on income and prices. (Since fiscal policy's effect on the exchange rate is unclear, there is no need to consider its effect on the trade balance through exchange rates.)

The Effect on the Trade Deficit via Income Let's begin by looking at the income path. As with expansionary monetary policy, expansionary fiscal policy increases income. This higher income increases imports, which increases the size of the trade deficit.

Contractionary fiscal policy decreases income and decreases imports. Hence it decreases the size of a trade deficit. These are the same effects as those of monetary policy.

The Effect on the Trade Deficit via Prices The effect via the price level route is also similar to the effects of monetary policy. Expansionary fiscal policy pushes up the price level, increasing the price of a country's exports and decreasing its competitiveness. Hence, it increases the trade deficit.

Contractionary fiscal policy pushes down the price level, decreasing the price of a country's exports, increasing its competitiveness, and decreasing the trade deficit. This effect via price is a long-run effect, as it is with monetary policy.

Expansionary fiscal policy
increases a trade deficit.

Contractionary fiscal policy
decreases a trade deficit.

Fiscal policy affects the trade
balance through the income path
and the price level path, as
shown in the accompanying
diagram.

The Net Effect of Fiscal Policy on the Trade Deficit Since these two effects work
in the same direction, fiscal policy's net effect on the trade balance is clear:

Expansionary fiscal policy increases a trade deficit.

Contractionary fiscal policy decreases a trade deficit.

Summarizing these two effects schematically, we have:

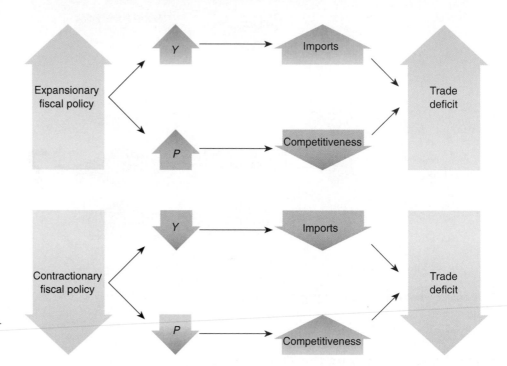

Q.9 What is the net effect of expansionary fiscal policy on the trade deficit?

INTERNATIONAL PHENOMENA AND DOMESTIC GOALS

So far, we've focused on the effect of monetary and fiscal policies on international goals.
But often the effect is the other way around: International phenomena change and have
significant influences on the domestic economy and on the ability to achieve domestic
goals.

For example, say that Japan ran contractionary monetary policy. That would increase the value of the yen and increase Japan's trade surplus, which means it would decrease the value of the dollar and increase a Canadian trade deficit, both of which
would affect Canadian domestic goals.

International Monetary and Fiscal Coordination

Governments try to coordinate
their monetary and fiscal policies
because their economies are
interdependent.

Unless forced to do so because of international pressures, most countries don't let international goals guide their macroeconomic policy. But for every effect that monetary and
fiscal policies have on a country's exchange rates and trade balance, there's an equal and
opposite effect on the combination of other countries' exchange rates and trade balances. When the value of one country's currency goes up, by definition the value of an-

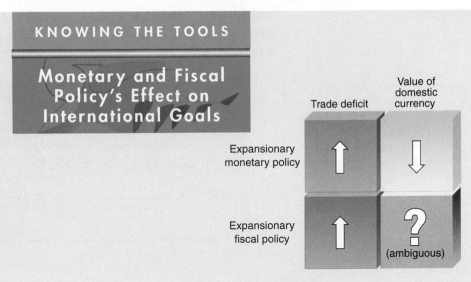

The effect of expansionary monetary and fiscal policy on international goals in the short run is summarized in the diagram below. In the short run, expansionary monetary policy tends to increase a trade deficit and decrease the value of the domestic currency. Expansionary fiscal policy tends to increase the trade deficit. Its effect on the exchange rate is ambiguous. The effects of contractionary policy work in the opposite direction.

KNOWING THE TOOLS

Monetary and Fiscal Policy's Effect on International Goals

other country's currency must go down. Similarly, when one country's balance of trade is in surplus, another's must be in deficit. This interconnection means that other countries' fiscal and monetary policies affect Canada, while Canadian fiscal and monetary policies affect other countries, so pressure to coordinate policies is considerable.

Coordination Is a Two-Way Street

Coordination, of course, works both ways. If other countries are to take the Canadian economy's needs into account, Canada must take other countries' needs into account in determining its goals. Say, for example, the Canadian economy is going into a recession. This domestic problem calls for expansionary monetary policy. But expansionary monetary policy will increase Canadian income and Canadian imports and lower the value of the dollar. Say that, internationally, Canada has agreed that it must work toward eliminating a trade deficit in the short run. Does it forsake its domestic goals? Or does it forsake its international commitment?

There's no one right answer to those questions. It depends on political judgments (how long until the next election?), judgments about what foreign countries can do if Canada doesn't meet its international commitments, and similar judgments by foreign countries about Canada.

Crowding Out and International Considerations

As a final topic in this chapter, let's reconsider the issue of crowding out that we considered in an earlier chapter, only this time we'll take into account international considerations. Say a government is running a budget deficit, and that the central bank has decided it won't increase the money supply to help finance the deficit. (This happened in Canada in the 1980s and 1990s.) What will be the result?

The basic idea of crowding out is that the budget deficit will cause the interest rate to go up. But wait. There's another way to avoid the crowding out that results from financing

Q.10 If domestic problems call for expansionary monetary policy and international problems call for contractionary monetary policy, what policy will a country likely adopt?

Each country will likely do what's best for the world economy as long as it's also best for itself.

While internationalizing a country's debt may help in the short run, in the long run it presents potential problems since foreign ownership of a country's debts means the country must pay interest to those foreign countries and that debt may come due.

TABLE 17-1 **Selecting Policies to Achieve Goals**

This table shows how alternative monetary and fiscal policies can be used to achieve the goal of a lower exchange rate and the goal of a lower trade deficit.

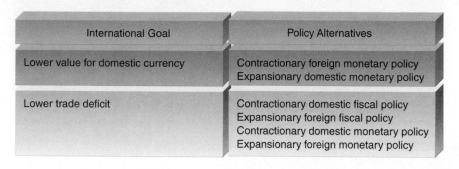

International Goal	Policy Alternatives
Lower value for domestic currency	Contractionary foreign monetary policy Expansionary domestic monetary policy
Lower trade deficit	Contractionary domestic fiscal policy Expansionary foreign fiscal policy Contractionary domestic monetary policy Expansionary foreign monetary policy

the deficit: Foreigners could buy the debt at the existing interest rate. This is called *internationalizing the debt*, and is what happened in the late 1980s.

In the 1980s, there were massive inflows to Canada of financial capital from abroad. These inflows held down the Canadian interest rate even as the federal government ran large budget deficits. Thus, those large deficits didn't push up interest rates because foreigners, not Canadian citizens, were buying Canadian debt.

17.3
see page 430

But, as we discussed, internationalization of the Canadian debt is not costless. While it helps in the short run, it presents problems in the long run. Foreign ownership of Canadian debt means that Canada must pay foreigners interest each year on that debt. To do so, Canada must export more than it imports, which means that Canada must consume less than it produces at some time in the future to pay for the trade deficits.

As you can see, the issues become complicated quickly.

Despite the complications, the above discussion gives you an understanding of many events that may have previously seemed incomprehensible. To show you the relevance of what we have said above about crowding out and international considerations, let's look at two situations.

The first concerned Germany and the EU in the early 1990s. For political reasons, Germany was running loose fiscal policy. Fearing inflation from this loose fiscal policy, the Bundesbank ran tight monetary policy, forcing both the German interest rate and the value of the German mark up. This disrupted the movement toward a European monetary system and a common European currency—the euro—as other European countries refused to go along. Here we see domestic goals superseding international goals.

The second concerns Japan in 1993 and early 1994. Japan was experiencing a recession, in part because its tight monetary policy had pushed up interest rates and hence pushed up the value of the yen. Other countries, especially the United States and European countries, put enormous pressure on Japan to run expansionary fiscal policy, which would keep the relative value of the yen high but simultaneously increase Japanese income, and hence Japanese demand for imports. In response, the Japanese ran expansionary fiscal policy and this helped to keep the value of the yen higher than it otherwise would have been. Soon thereafter, Japan simultaneously ran expansionary monetary policy, thereby offsetting the fiscal effect on the exchange rate.

There are many more examples, but these two should give you a good sense of the relevance of the issues.

Throughout this chapter we have organized the discussion around the effects of policies. Another way to organize the discussion would have been around goals, and to show how alternative policies will achieve those international goals.

Table 17-1 does this, and will serve as a useful review of the chapter. It shows alternative policies that will achieve specified goals.

You can see in the table why coordination of monetary and fiscal policies is much in the news, since a foreign country's policy can eliminate, or reduce the need for, domestic policies to be undertaken.

CONCLUSION

This brief chapter in no way exhausted the international topics. Countries use many policies to effect their international goals. But this chapter has, we hope, made you very aware of the international dimensions of our economic goals, and of how monetary and fiscal policies affect those goals. That awareness is absolutely necessary to discuss real-world macroeconomic policies.

Chapter Summary

- The international goals of a country are often in dispute.
- Domestic goals generally dominate international goals, but countries often respond to an international goal when forced to do so by other countries.
- To raise the value of one's currency a country can either increase private demand through contractionary monetary policy or decrease private supply through contractionary monetary and fiscal policy.
- Expansionary monetary policy tends to lower the value of a country's currency and increase its trade deficit.

- Contractionary fiscal policy has an ambiguous effect on a country's exchange rate but tends to decrease its trade deficit.
- For every effect that monetary and fiscal policies have on a country's exchange rate and trade balance, there is an equal and opposite effect on the combination of foreign countries' exchange rates and trade balances.
- International capital inflows can reduce crowding out.
- Internationalizing a country's debt means that at some time in the future the country must consume less than it produces.

Questions for Thought and Review

1. Look up the current dollar exchange rate relative to the yen. Would you suggest raising it or lowering it? Why?
2. Look up the current Canadian trade balance. Would you suggest raising it or lowering it? Why?
3. What effect on a Canadian trade deficit and exchange rate would result if Japan ran an expansionary monetary policy?
4. What would be the effect on a Canadian trade deficit and the value of the dollar if Japan ran a contractionary fiscal policy?
5. If expansionary monetary policy immediately increases inflationary expectations and the price level, how might the effect of monetary policy on the exchange rate be different than that presented in this chapter?
6. What effect will a combination of expansionary fiscal policy and contractionary monetary policy have on the exchange rate?
7. Is Canada justified in complaining of Japan's use of an export-led growth policy? Why?
8. How is the Bundesbank's running a tight monetary policy in the early 1990s an example of domestic goals superseding international goals?
9. In the 1990s, Japan's economic recession was much in the news. What would you suspect was happening to its trade balance during this time? What policies would you guess other countries (such as those in the Group of Eight) were pressuring Japan to implement?
10. How does internationalizing the debt reduce crowding out?
11. What are the costs of internationalizing the debt?

Problems and Exercises

1. Draw the schematics to show the effect of contractionary fiscal policy on exchange rates.

2. Draw the schematics to show the effect of expansionary monetary policy on the trade deficit.

3. You observe that over the past decade a country's competitiveness has been continually eroded and its trade deficit has risen.
   a. What monetary or fiscal policies might have led to such results? Why?
   b. You also observe that interest rates have steadily risen along with a rise in the value of the domestic currency. What policies would lead to this result?
   c. What policy might you suggest to improve the country's competitiveness? Explain how that policy might work.

4. Congratulations! You have been appointed an adviser to the IMF. A country that has run trade deficits for many years now has difficulty servicing its accumulated international debt and wants to borrow from the IMF to meet its obligations. The IMF requires that the country set a target trade surplus.
   a. What monetary and fiscal policies would you suggest the IMF require of that country?
   b. What would be the likely effect of that plan on the country's domestic inflation and growth?
   c. How do you think the country's government will respond to your proposals? Why?

5. Congratulations! You've been hired as an economic adviser to Textland, a country that has perfectly flexible exchange rates. State what monetary and fiscal policy you might suggest in each of the following situations, and explain why you would suggest those policies.
   a. You want to lower the interest rate, decrease inflationary pressures, and lower the trade deficit.
   b. You want to lower the interest rate, decrease inflationary pressures, and lower a trade surplus.
   c. You want to lower the interest rate, decrease unemployment, and lower the trade deficit.
   d. You want to raise the interest rate, decrease unemployment, and lower the trade deficit.

Web Questions

1. The Department of Foreign Affairs and International Trade Web site (www.dfait-maeci.gc.ca) provides data on Trade and Economic Analysis. Go to the Web site and answer the following questions:
   a. What are Canada's five largest trading partners?
   b. To what five countries does Canada export the most?
   c. What policies could Canada encourage those countries to implement to raise our exports?
   d. With what five countries does Canada have the largest trade surpluses?

2. The IMF is an international organization of 182 member countries, established to promote international monetary cooperation, exchange stability, and orderly exchange arrangements. In the late 1990s it came under increasing criticism. The Hoover Institution launched a public policy inquiry on the International Monetary Fund in 1999. Go to the official site of this inquiry (www.imfsite.org) to answer the following questions:
   a. What is conditionality?
   b. What are some typical IMF financing preconditions? If implemented, what would be the effect of these preconditions on the country's (a) exchange rate, (b) trade deficit, (c) domestic economy?
   c. Name five countries that have received IMF financing over the past five years.
   d. What is mission creep?

3. Many institutions provide access to the CANSIM II database to their students. Ask your instructor if you have access and visit the CANSIM II page (www.datacenter2.chass.utoronto.ca) and download Table 176-0021.
   a. What has happened to the ratio of nonresident to general public holdings of Government of Canada loans and securities over the past few years?
   b. Graph both series on the same plot. What does the figure tell you? When did nonresident holdings reach a peak?
   c. Download the Canadian–U.S. exchange rate. Did anything happen to the value of the Canadian dollar after nonresident debt holdings peaked? Why might this be interesting?

Answers to Margin Questions

1. A low value of a country's currency will tend to stimulate exports and curtail imports.   *(417)*

2. A trade deficit means a country is consuming more than it is producing. Consuming more than you produce is pleasant. It also means that capital is flowing into the country, which can be used for investment. So why worry? *(418)*

3. To increase the value of its currency, a country can increase the private demand for its currency by implementing contractionary monetary policy or it could decrease private supply of its currency by implementing contractionary monetary and fiscal policy.   *(419)*

4. A fall in a country's interest rate will push down the value of its currency.   *(420)*

5. Contractionary monetary policy pushes up the interest rate, decreases income and hence imports, and has a tendency to decrease inflation. Therefore, through these paths, contractionary monetary policy will tend to increase the value of the domestic currency.   *(421)*

6. Contractionary monetary policy will tend to decrease income and the price level, decreasing imports and increasing competitiveness. Since the income and price level paths work in the same direction, contractionary monetary policy is likely to decrease the trade deficit. The exchange rate path can, however, work in the opposite direction.   *(423)*

7. In the short run, the net effect of contractionary monetary policy on the trade balance is to decrease the trade deficit, or increase the trade surplus.   *(423)*

8. The net effect of expansionary fiscal policy on exchange rates is uncertain. Through the interest rate effect it raises the value of the domestic currency, but through the income and price level effects it pushes down the value of the domestic currency.   *(424)*

9. The net effect of expansionary fiscal policy on the trade deficit is to increase the trade deficit.   *(426)*

10. Generally, when domestic policies and international policies conflict, a country will choose to deal with its domestic problems. Thus, it will likely use expansionary monetary policy if domestic problems call for that. *(427)*

Tools, Rules, and Policy

18

After reading this chapter you should be able to:

- Summarize two micro models and explain their relevance to macro policy.

- Summarize four macro models and explain their relevance to macro policy.

- Distinguish Keynesian and Classical views of macro policy.

- Discuss the use of monetary and fiscal policy in practice.

- State why economists often talk about *policy regimes* rather than simply *policy*.

- Explain what is meant by the *new era economy*.

*The first task of the University teacher of any
liberal art is surely to persuade his students
that the most important things he will put
before them are questions and not answers.*

G. Shackle

We've come to the end of the book, and this final chapter will help you reflect on what you've learned. Here we'll tie together the tools, institutions, and policy discussions of the previous chapters, while relating them to recent macro policy discussions. The purpose is twofold: first, to give you a chance to place what you have learned in perspective and, second, to help you structure your studying for the final exam.

The main focus of the course has been on macro policy—how monetary, fiscal, and other macro policies work to achieve the goals of society. In the process of presenting these macro policy issues, we introduced a number of models because it is through models that economists understand the economy. Models capture certain key interrelationships in the economy in a highly simplified form. If you understand the models and the assumptions underlying them, you will have a good sense of both how economists approach macro policy questions and what their current thinking is.

Models capture certain key inter-relationships in the economy in a highly simplified form.

MODELS

The book started with a general discussion of economics, introducing you to the terminology and institutions that are central to economics. The discussion emphasized that economic reasoning is about costs and benefits and the inevitable trade-offs involved in making decisions. It discussed how the possibility of trade encourages individuals to develop their comparative advantage, and how specialization makes the entire society better off. Next, it placed the economy in a global setting and discussed the institutions that make up markets (consumers and producers) and the institution that is necessary for markets to function effectively (government). Finally, it introduced two primarily micro models—the production possibility model and the supply/demand model—which serve as building blocks for macro as well as micro.

As the issues in macro were developed, four other models were introduced: the aggregate supply and demand model, the multiplier model, the long-run growth model, and the quantity theory model. Together these six models serve as background information for discussing economic policy.

The reason macro has its own models is that the aggregate economy is so complicated that we cannot build up from micro supply and demand curves without encountering the fallacy of composition (that is, the false assumption that what is true for a part will also be true for the whole). Put simply: In economics, you cannot always understand the whole by studying the parts.

Macro models are needed because of the fallacy of composition.

The difference between micro and macro models is that micro models start by analyzing individual markets and build up to an analysis of the entire economy. Macro models start with an analysis of the aggregate economy and build down to an analysis of individual markets. (One hopes the two meet in the middle.) Macro avoids the fallacy of composition by focusing on empirical regularities, but does not always provide a clear analysis of what causes those empirical regularities.

Macro models build down; micro models build up.

Neither micro nor macro is the better way to analyze the economy. Models are simply tools to help us understand; the key is to use the right tool at the right time.

Micro Models

Let's now review the key models that we covered, starting with the two micro models.

The Production Possibility Model One of the early models that you learned was the production possibility curve—a model that shows the possible production of two goods given the technology and institutional structure of the economy. We demonstrate a standard production possibility curve in Figure 18-1. The bowed-out shape is caused by increasing opportunity cost (also known as decreasing marginal productivity) and comparative advantage. The production possibility curve is relevant to both macro and micro because it captures the *trade-off view* that is central to economists' policy perspective: To get more of something you must give up something else. In other words, everything has an opportunity cost.

Q.1 What would be the shape of the production possibility curve if there were constant opportunity costs?

Figure 18-1   **THE PRODUCTION POSSIBILITY CURVE MODEL**

The production possibility curve is a model that shows the possible production of two goods given the technology and institutional structure of the economy. It is bowed out because of increasing marginal opportunity cost. On this production possibility curve, an economy can increase the consumption of goods tomorrow only if it gives up consumption of goods today (moving from point A to point B).

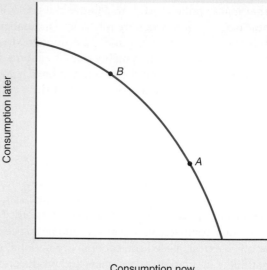

Consumption later

Consumption now

Suppose, for example, that society wants more growth; to achieve that growth, society must save and invest more (give up consumption now). You can see that in Figure 18-1. It has "consumption now" on the horizontal axis and "consumption later" on the vertical axis. By consuming less now (moving from point A to point B), we can consume more in the future.

Technological change shifts out the production possibility curve for a single time period. Long-run growth analysis concentrates on the causes of such outward shifts. In macro, since we focus on aggregate output rather than on combinations of goods, we often use potential output in lieu of the production possibility curve, but the concept is the same. When the economy is at its potential output it is operating on its production possibility curve.

When the economy is at its potential output it is operating on its production possibility curve.

The Supply/Demand Model   The supply/demand model is the primary micro model; it also serves as a fundamental building block of macro reasoning. The model consists of two curves—the supply curve and the demand curve—placed on a graph with price on the vertical axis and quantity of a single good on the horizontal axis, as in Figure 18-2. The supply curve slopes upward, and the demand curve slopes downward.

When talking about supply and demand it is important to distinguish a movement along the curve (caused by a change in price) from a shift of the curve caused by a shift factor. Supply/demand analysis is useful for answering questions about the effects a change in a shift factor will have on price and quantity. For example: What happens to price and quantity of apples if income increases? The answer is that price rises and quantity sold increases, as shown in Figure 18-2(a).

Another use of the supply/demand model is to show the effects of interferences with markets, in the form of price controls. Such interferences cause excess demand (in the case of price ceilings) and excess supply (in the case of price floors). We demonstrate the effect of a price ceiling in Figure 18-2(b).

One place where the supply/demand model plays a central role in macro is in discussions of foreign exchange rates. Exchange rates are determined by the supply and

Figure 18-2 (a, b, and c) | THE SUPPLY AND DEMAND MODEL

The supply/demand model is the primary micro model. It can be used when other things can reasonably be assumed to remain constant. In **(a)** you can see that an increase in income will increase the equilibrium price and quantity of apples. In **(b)** you can see that an effective price ceiling will cause a shortage of goods. In **(c)** an increase in Canadian interest rates will shift the demand for dollars to the right and the supply of dollars to the left. The value of the Canadian dollar, in this instance, will increase.

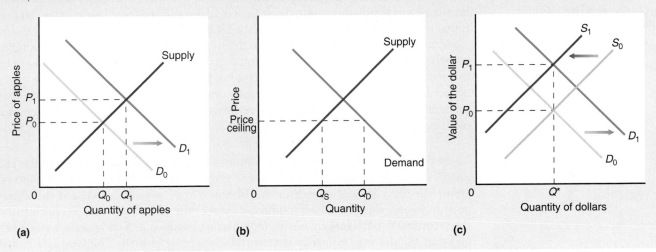

(a)   (b)   (c)

demand for currencies, as in Figure 18-2(c). The supply for Canadian currency comes from Canadian individuals demanding foreign goods (Canadian imports) or foreign assets (capital outflows from Canada). The demand for Canadian currency comes from foreign individuals demanding Canadian goods (Canadian exports) or foreign assets (capital inflows to Canada). As the demand and supply for dollars change, the exchange rate changes. Here is an example: If the Canadian interest rate rises, the demand for Canadian assets rises, shifting the demand for Canadian financial assets to the right, and hence shifting the demand for Canadian currency to the right and the supply of Canadian currency to the left (since fewer Canadians will want to invest abroad). The result is a rise in the value of Canadian currency relative to other currencies.

A number of different exchange rate regimes are possible. With flexible exchange rates, the exchange rate is determined by private supply and demand. With fixed exchange rates, the exchange rate is also determined by supply and demand, but in this case the government enters the foreign exchange markets and varies its supply and demand for its currency to ensure that the quantity supplied always equals the quantity demanded at the fixed exchange rate. Thus, fixed exchange rates are not price controls—that would be a nonconvertible exchange rate regime. Governments can fix their exchange rates as long as they have sufficient official reserves. The most common exchange rate regime is a partially flexible exchange rate system in which the government sometimes buys and sells its currency, and sometimes does not.

Q-2 If the European Union placed a tariff on Canadian imports, what would likely happen to the value of the Canadian dollar?

Fixed exchange rates are not price controls.

Macro Models

As we emphasized above, while supply/demand analysis is a building block of macro analysis, it must be applied carefully to policy issues because of the fallacy of composition. Supply/demand models apply directly only when other things can be expected to remain constant. In macro, supply and demand are enormously interdependent, so other things often cannot remain constant. It is for that reason that we have developed a separate macro analysis to complement micro analysis.

To apply macro models you must know the terminology and know about the institutions for which the terms have been designed. That means knowing what is meant by *growth, business cycles, unemployment,* and *inflation,* as well as having some knowledge of the stylized facts that have characterized experience in these areas. Key concepts to remember include real and nominal concepts (*real* is *nominal adjusted for inflation*) and national income accounting concepts such as GDP and its components.

Macro models are divided into two different types: long-run models focusing on growth, and short-run models focusing on coordination problems that can develop because of the fallacy of composition. The long-run models follow directly from microeconomics and are primarily micro in their orientation. The short-run models, while sometimes using micro building blocks, are oriented quite differently from the long-run models.

The Long-Run Growth Model The long-run growth model is a variation of the production possibility curve model adapted to macro. The foundation of long-run growth analysis is the Classical growth model, although recent work on what is called new growth theory offers a somewhat different view of the growth process. Both start from the premises that markets encourage individuals to make use of comparative advantage and that the division of labour is a central element of growth. The Classical growth model focuses on the sources of growth. Some specific sources of growth are investment, resources, appropriate institutions, technological development, and entrepreneurship.

The Classical growth model emphasizes diminishing marginal returns, saving, and investment. It predicts that an economy's growth rate is limited because, ultimately, as capital increases, it becomes less productive, and workers will not be able to keep up the pace of increased production. The Classical growth model also predicts income convergence for rich and poor countries and a slowing of the growth rate over time. Neither of these predictions has come true, and new growth theory has developed to explain why.

New growth theory focuses on increasing returns to scale and technology. It says there is no limit to the growth rate. New growth theory is closer to the empirical evidence than is the Classical growth model without adjustment, but that does not make it right and the Classical growth model wrong. Models are not right or wrong; they are simply tools that shed light on different aspects of a problem.

The Classical growth model focuses policy analysis on investment and saving; it leads us to look at policies such as investment tax credits or tax systems that do not tax savings. It also suggests that budget surpluses—government saving—temporarily increase growth and move the economy to a higher income than it otherwise would have. New growth theory focuses policy analysis on technology. It centres on policies that stimulate research and development, or create an environment conducive to entrepreneurship.

The Quantity Theory Model The other long-run model presented in the book is the quantity theory model of inflation. The quantity theory of money is based on the equation of exchange:

$$MV = PQ$$

By assuming that velocity (V) and real output (Q) are constant, we come to the conclusion that the price level (P) varies directly with the money supply (M). For example, if the money supply goes up 10 percent, prices will rise by 10 percent. The quantity theory

Real is nominal adjusted for inflation.

The Classical growth model emphasizes diminishing marginal returns, saving, and investment; new growth theory emphasizes increasing returns and technology.

Q.3 If the quantity theory holds true and prices go up by 15 percent, by how much would the money supply have had to rise?

assumes that the direction of causation is from money to prices; thus, it can be summed up as a model in which *inflation is always and everywhere a monetary phenomenon.*

Not everyone accepts the quantity theory model. Some economists hold an institutional theory of inflation, which says that inflation is caused by institutional factors, and increases in the money supply validate the inflation whose root causes are in the distributional fight for income shares. They see the direction of causation going the other way around. Whereas in the quantity theory the equation of exchange is read from left to right (money increases cause price increases: $MV \rightarrow PQ$), in the institutional explanation of inflation, it is read from right to left (price increases cause increases in money: $MV \leftarrow PQ$).

The AS/AD Model There are two central short-run macro models—the aggregate supply/aggregate demand (*AS/AD*) model and the multiplier model. Both tell the same story but emphasize slightly different aspects of it. The *AS/AD* model is a model of the aggregate economy. It has price level on the vertical axis and total output on the horizontal axis. Thus, it is a fundamentally different model from the micro supply/demand model that has the price of one good on the vertical axis and the quantity of that good on the other. The two models differ in what they hold constant, in what determines the shapes of the curves, and in how the curves shift when a shift factor changes.

The supply/demand model holds all other things, except the price of the good, constant. Specifically, it holds aggregate income constant. The *AS/AD* model does not hold aggregate income constant; that would be impossible, because GDP is on the horizontal axis and is equal to income. The *AS/AD* model is a model of how income changes. Thus, both the *SAS* and *AD* curves must be drawn in a way that allows aggregate income to change.

The shapes of the micro supply and demand curves are determined by opportunity cost and the possibility of substitution. The shape of the *SAS* curve is determined by the price-setting behaviour of firms, and the shape of the *AD* curve is determined by the interest rate effect, the wealth effect, the international effect, and the multiplier. The supply and demand curves shift by the *amount* of the shift factor; the *AD* curve shifts by a *multiple of the amount* of a shift factor. The *SAS* curve shifts as input prices change. How much and how fast input prices change both depend on how close the economy is to potential output and the related target rate of unemployment.

The *AS/AD* model can be used in a variety of ways. For example, it could be used to predict what will likely happen to the price level and real output if aggregate demand changes because of expansionary fiscal policy. For example, what would you expect to happen to an economy if it was close to its potential output and consumption increased significantly? The answer is shown in Figure 18-3(a). The increase in consumption would shift the *AD* curve to the right by a multiple of the initial increase in consumption, causing income to increase. However, because the economy is close to its potential income level, the expansion would push up input prices, shifting the *SAS* curve up and causing the price level to rise too.

How much the *SAS* curve rises depends on how close the economy is to its potential output. This works fine for predictions if we know where potential output is, but economists have not been especially good at measuring potential output in recent years. Thus, even though the economy has been at unemployment levels that were under those considered consistent with potential output and the target rate of unemployment, wages have not risen significantly more than the increases in productivity. There are different explanations why. Some economists believe that potential output was misestimated; others believe that prices have simply been slow to adjust, but they will adjust

The *AS/AD* model is fundamentally different from the micro supply/demand model.

How much the *SAS* curve will likely shift up or down depends on how close the economy is to potential output.

Q.4 If the central bank runs expansionary monetary policy and the economy is far from its potential income, what would happen to output and the price level?

Figure 18-3 (a and b)   THE AS/AD AND MULTIPLIER MODELS

If autonomous consumption rises in an economy, the aggregate demand curve shifts to the right by a multiple of the initial increase in consumption. If the economy began at a level of output close to potential, point A, in (a) and the increase in consumption pushes the economy to a point beyond potential, point B, then input prices will begin to rise and the SAS curve will shift up. As prices rise, the economy will move to point C. This same scenario is shown in (b), using the multiplier model. The increase in consumption expenditures shifts the AE curve up by the amount of the increase. Output rises by a multiple of the change in consumption expenditures to Y_1. As the price level rises, the AE curve shifts down and output falls to Y_2.

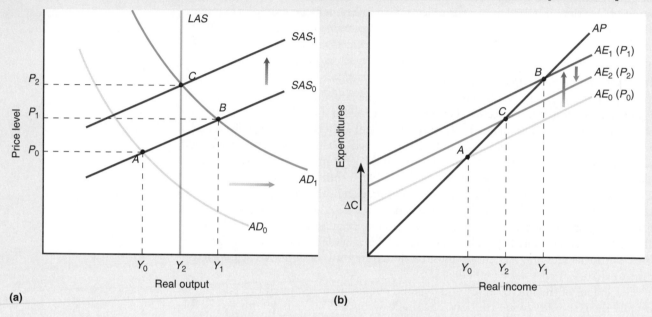

(a)   (b)

eventually; and still others believe that the economy has entered a new era in which the old views do not hold. (This issue will be discussed below.)

The Multiplier Model The multiplier model consists of two curves: the aggregate production (AP) curve and the aggregate expenditures (AE) curve. It is consistent with the AS/AD model in that it comes to the same conclusion about the effect of changes in aggregate demand, but it looks only at the short run and thus holds prices constant. It also shows the multiplier effects of expansionary demand policy better. In the situation above, the rise in autonomous consumption would shift the AE curve up, causing income to increase. However, because the economy is close to potential output, the price level would rise, causing the AE curve to shift back down some. We show this case in Figure 18-3(b). The net increase in output would be the same in both cases.

One difference is that the multiplier model gives specific numeric answers to questions. To determine a numeric answer, we use the multiplier equation:

$$\Delta Y = \left(\frac{1}{1 - mpc}\right) (\text{Change in autonomous shift factor})$$

Q.5 If government expenditures rose by 35 and the mpc was 0.8, what would happen to output?

For example, if autonomous exports increased by 20, and the marginal propensity to consume (mpc) was 0.5, income would increase by 40.

By dividing the effects of shift factors on income into two components—the initial shift factor and the repercussions—the multiplier model is designed to highlight the

Economists tend to teach using models. These models help structure their thinking about policy issues. Some of the important models in macro include:

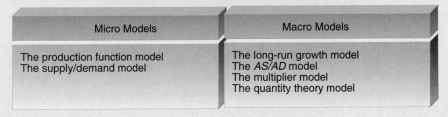

Micro Models	Macro Models
The production function model The supply/demand model	The long-run growth model The *AS/AD* model The multiplier model The quantity theory model

multiplier process, whereas in the *AS/AD* model we must remember that the *AD* curve will shift to the right by more than the initial shift factor. The multiplier model does not directly show what effect a rise in the price level will have on the economy. The *AS/AD* model is designed to include price-level effects; in doing so it combines the shift factor with the multiplier effects. The two models, however, come to the same conclusions.

USING MODELS TO UNDERSTAND AND DISCUSS POLICY

Now that we've reviewed the models, let's turn our attention to policy and how policy issues relate to the tools. The first point to emphasize is that the tools suggest policies, but they do not lead to policies. To apply the tools policymakers must use judgment about whether the circumstance fits the assumptions of the model sufficiently. Sometimes two models will suggest different policy advice and we must determine which model is more relevant. This is often the case when we are considering long-run models and short-run models. Suppose that you are trying to say what the effect of increasing the money supply will be. In the long-run quantity theory model, the effect will be an increase in the price level; in the short-run *AS/AD* model, the result could be an increase in real output if the economy is significantly below potential output.

Alternatively, consider the effect of a government deficit. In the short-run model, a deficit leads to an increase in output as aggregate demand shifts to the right. In the long-run growth model a deficit leads to less investment and less saving, less growth, and hence less output. Which of the models is right? Neither and both are; it depends on which of the assumptions of the two models better fit the real-world situation. The models simply focus on different relationships. In summary: Models are guides, not directives.

To apply the tools policymakers must use judgment about whether the circumstance fits the assumptions of the model.

Policies and Institutions

Policies are implemented through real-world institutions, and thus a study of real-world institutions becomes important to an understanding of macroeconomics. The institutions most relevant to macro are financial institutions, the parts of government that conduct fiscal policy, and international institutions that link together the economies of various countries. Let us briefly review each of these.

Financial Institutions The financial system plays a key role in macro policy. It determines the interest rate. It is through the financial system that monetary policy affects the economy. Monetary policy is undertaken by the Bank of Canada. The most important tool for conducting monetary policy is changing the target band for the overnight financing rate. Other tools the Bank can use involve directly affecting the liquidity of the financial system as well as open market operations. Buying bonds, decreasing the overnight financing rate, and injecting liquidity shift the AD curve to the right; selling bonds, increasing the overnight financing rate, and reducing liquidity shift the AD curve to the left.

> Changing the target band for the overnight financing rate is the Bank of Canada's most important policy tool.

The money supply changes by more than the amount of money that the Bank takes in or out of the economy. The relation between the change in the Bank's IOUs and the change in the money supply is determined by the money multiplier. The simple money multiplier, assuming no cash is held, is $1/r$, where r is the desired reserve requirement, and the approximate real-world money multiplier is $1/(r + c)$, where r is the desired reserve requirement and c is the cash to deposit ratio. For example, if the desired reserve requirement is 0.1 and the cash-to-deposit ratio is 0.4, the approximate real-world money multiplier will be $1/0.5 = 2$.

> **Q-6** If the central bank sells $100 worth of bonds and the reserve requirement is 0.1 and the cash-to-deposit ratio is 0.3, what would happen to the money supply?

Let's consider an example. Say the desired reserve requirement is 0.2 and the cash-to-deposit ratio, is 0.3. This makes the approximate real-world multiplier $1/0.5$, or 2, so if the Bank sells $100 worth of bonds, it decreases the money supply by $200. If the percentage of money that individuals hold as cash is zero, the multiplier would be the simple multiplier, $1/r$, or 5, in this case, and the money supply would be reduced by $500, not $200.

Currently, the Bank focuses its policy decision on the overnight financing rate, the rate that one bank charges another for loans of reserves. If inflation is above its target, the Bank raises the target band by selling bonds, thereby decreasing the money supply. If inflation is below its target, and if the economy is going into a recession, the Bank lowers the target band by buying bonds, thereby increasing the money supply.

Fiscal Institutions Fiscal policy involves changing taxes or expenditures to affect the level of income in the economy. Lowering taxes or increasing government expenditures shifts the AD curve to the right; increasing taxes or decreasing government expenditures shifts the AD curve to the left. These taxes and expenditures are controlled by the political structure and often are subject to enormous political fights, so the political structure of government becomes a central institution for any discussion of fiscal policy. The general consensus among policymakers is that the political structure is not able to implement fine tuning and fiscal policy should not be seen as an effective tool for stabilizing aggregate demand. (The government budget does, however, have automatic stabilizers built into it.)

> Politics limits the use of fiscal policy.

Fiscal policy can also affect aggregate supply. That was the idea behind Reaganomics—the economic policies of U.S. President Ronald Reagan. Reagan's advisers believed that targeted tax cuts would encourage firms to invest and expand their productive capacity. This would shift the long-run aggregate supply curve to the right as potential output increased with expansions in capacity. Some economists believe that Canadian fiscal policies should be targeted toward similar types of tax cuts to encourage Canadian firms to invest and expand their capacity. The difficulty is in tracking whether tax cuts are reinvested in Canada, and more importantly, whether they are reinvested in areas that will raise potential output. Some multinational firms may use those surplus funds outside of Canada, so there's no guarantee that a program of tax cuts will force the LAS curve to shift right.

This is one reason why the federal government implemented a system of tax credits for investment in certain industries. Only those firms investing in areas the government deems "worthy" receive the benefit. Of course, that opens up an entirely different can of worms—should the government try to pick industries that are, or will be, "winners"? Given shifts in comparative advantage and costs over time, it's not clear the government should get involved in that degree of micro-industry management. In fact, the Japanese government had a similar type of policy in effect throughout the latter half of the 20th century, and while it appeared to be successful, changes in comparative advantage and exchange rates demonstrated it wasn't a policy that could be relied on to provide sustained industrial growth. Late in 2001 the Japanese economy teetered on the brink of severe recession, partially as a result of its industrial policies of the 1980s and 1990s.

Much of the political debate about the budget centres on the existence of a deficit or a surplus. For economists, that surplus or deficit is less important than the general health of the economy.

The movement from a budget deficit to a budget surplus occurred for a number of reasons. One was the caps placed on government spending in the 1990s; a second was the boom that the economy experienced in the 1990s that increased tax revenue.

The elimination of the budget deficit has not solved all our fiscal problems. Canada still faces serious "real" problems. Once baby boomers start retiring in significant numbers, the real goods they are receiving will have to come from somewhere, which means that the percentage of goods produced and received by workers at that time will have to fall from what it otherwise would be.

International Institutions The Canadian economy is connected to the world through a system of international treaties and agreements. For example, Canada is a member of the International Monetary Fund (IMF) and the World Bank, as well as the Group of Eight. Through these organizations it attempts to coordinate its macro policy with other countries, and maintain orderly foreign exchange markets. Canada is also a member of the World Trade Organization (WTO), which is devoted to promoting free international trade.

The Canadian exchange rate system is a partially flexible system. That means that generally the exchange rate is determined by the private market, but once in a while the government intervenes, buying and selling foreign currencies to affect the value of the dollar. The government recognizes, however, that its reserves are too small to significantly affect the dollar on its own, and thus these interventions are primarily designed to work by affecting expectations.

Worldviews and Policy

In using models as guides you should be aware that long-run models and short-run models have certain biases built into them through their assumptions. Long-run models tend to guide you toward a laissez-faire policy. They emphasize the market's natural tendency to give people incentives to make use of their comparative advantage. As people do so, the economy will naturally tend to move to the frontier of the production possibility curve. Noneconomists often miss this important element of how markets work.

The logic behind the long-run position is sometimes described by using an analogy of a $20 bill on the ground. Rational people recognize that other individuals do not leave profit opportunities untouched. So if a rational person sees a $20 bill on the ground, with thousands of people seeing it but ignoring it, he or she can assume that it is a fake and is therefore not worth bending down to pick up. The same is true with government's attempt to make improvements in the economy; in the long-run view,

Long-run models tend to guide us toward a laissez-faire policy; short-run models tend to guide us toward an activist policy.

Q.7 Would a Keynesian or Classical be more likely to emphasize the view that there is no such thing as a free lunch?

opportunities for improvement through policy are often illusory. Following this analogy, the policy theme of micro and that of the long-run growth theory and the quantity theory in macro are the same: There ain't no such thing as a free lunch.

Short-run models have a bias in the opposite direction; they tend to direct us toward an activist policy. These models emphasize the aggregate market problems caused by coordination failures (which cause people not to do what is, collectively, in their best interest). When there are such coordination failures it is only natural that government action can improve the functioning of the economy. The situation pictured by short-run models is slightly different from that in the above analogy. The $20 bill is not on a city street where hundreds of people could see it, but instead on a lonely country road where few people walk. In such a situation there is far less reason to believe that it is a fake, so it is worthwhile to bend down and pick it up and buy yourself a lunch with it. The lunch is not free, but is paid for by the study of macroeconomics.

Most economists come out somewhere in between the two biases, which makes them relatively unbiased (at least from our perspective, and who could be more unbiased than us?). Mel Reder, a famous University of Chicago economist, summed up this in-between view by saying that although "there is no such thing as a free lunch, once in a while you can snitch a sandwich."

Keynesian and Classical Policy Views

In the past a Keynesian/Classical distinction has often been the centre of macro policy discussions. That distinction is less used today since more economists now consider themselves eclectic—neither Keynesian nor Classical.[1] Yet it is still important. In simple terms Keynesians are generally activist, and concerned about the short run. Liberals are more likely to be Keynesian than Conservatives. Classicals are generally laissez-faire and more concerned about the long run.

> Keynesians are generally more activist than Classicals.

The Classical View The Classical view of policy is centred on a profound distrust of government and the political process. Classical economists tend to believe that, even if theoretically the government might be able to help solve a recession, there's a serious question whether, given the political process, it will do so. Politics will often guide government to do something quite different from "furthering the general good." In the Classical view, real-world government intervention is more likely to do harm than good.

Classicals see democratic government as being significantly controlled by special interest groups. While, in theory, government might be an expression of the will of the people, in practice it's not. Thus, government is not a legitimate method of correcting problems in the economy. True, government sometimes does good, but this is the exception. Overall the costs of government action outweigh the benefits.

The Keynesian View Keynesians tend to have more faith that government not only is able to recognize what's wrong but also is willing to work to correct it. Thus, for a Keynesian, it's worthwhile to talk about a model that highlights an activist role for government.

---

[1]Whether your professor will focus on the distinction depends, we suspect, on when he or she was trained. The rough dividing line is economists who were trained before 1980, and those trained after 1990. (In the 10 years in between, it depends on where the economist was trained as well as on when.) Those trained before 1980 were brought up on a divergence of views among economists into Keynesian and Classical economists. Those trained after 1990 were brought up on a unified view. If you want to see if our dividing line holds true for your professor, you can generally find out when your professor was trained by looking in the back of the school catalogue or on your school's Web page. Then you can see how much he or she emphasized the Keynesian/Classical division in class. Better yet, ask your professor whether he or she thinks the distinction is important.

Figure 18-4 A COMPARISON OF CLASSICAL AND KEYNESIAN POLICIES

Problem	Keynesian Policy	Classical Policy
Inflation	• *Cause: Inflation is a combination institutional and monetary problem.* • Use contractionary monetary and fiscal policy. • Supplement above policy with policies to change wage- and price-setting institutions—possibly consider a temporary income policy. • Some small amount of inflation may be good for economy, and it is not worth trying to push inflation to zero if doing so involves significant unemployment.	• *Cause: Inflation is a monetary problem.* • Avoid inflation by relying on strict monetary rule—use contractionary monetary policy. • Be careful about expanding output too high and causing inflation. • Push inflation to zero by following strict monetary rule.
Slow Growth	• *Cause: Slow growth is a combination institutional and aggregate demand problem.* • Use expansionary monetary and fiscal policy. • Supplement above policy with policies to establish incentives for growth.	• *Cause: Growth rate reflects people's desires; probable cause of slow growth is too much regulation, too-high tax rates, and too few incentives for growth.* • Remove government impediments to growth; go back to laissez-faire policy.
Recessionary Unemployment	• *Cause: Recessionary unemployment is a combination institutional and aggregate demand problem.* • Use expansionary monetary and fiscal policy.	• *Cause: Recessionary unemployment was probably caused by earlier government policies that were too expansionary, causing inflation.* • If unemployment is very high, use expansionary monetary and fiscal policy. Generally, however, government policies should focus on the long run.

Keynesians tend to see government as an expression of the will of the people. Thus, they see it as a legitimate method of correcting problems in the economy. True, government is sometimes misled by special interest groups that direct it to do their own bidding rather than follow the general interest, but this is simply a cost of government. In the Keynesian view, the benefits of government generally outweigh the costs.

Contrasting the Keynesian and Classical Views Figure 18-4 contrasts the Keynesian and Classical views of policy in regard to the three central macroeconomic problems.

Monetary and Fiscal Policy

The primary short-run tools of macro policy are monetary policy and fiscal policy. Of
the two, monetary policy is the more important for short-run stabilization purposes. The
reason monetary policy has been emphasized is that the political and technical problems of using discretionary fiscal policy are major, and limit its use for small corrections
in the economy. As discussed above, politics, not the needs of the economy, generally
shape fiscal policy. Automatic stabilizers, such as unemployment insurance, have, however, built in an automatic fiscal response to fluctuations in the economy. Monetary policy has some of the same problems as fiscal policy but is more flexible, and less
influenced by politics. Both expansionary monetary and fiscal policy have long-run consequences, with monetary policy tending to lead to inflation, and expansionary fiscal
policy raising interest rates and decreasing investment in the long run.

The Trade-Off View of Macro Policy The primary goal of these macro policies is to
maintain the economy on this tightrope, with as high growth rates and as low unemployment rates as are consistent with low inflation. To stay on that tightrope, governments use monetary and fiscal policies as a balance bar. If the economy seems to be
falling into inflation, governments can use contractionary monetary and fiscal policies;
if it seems to be falling into recession, they can use expansionary monetary and fiscal
policies. If they face both problems simultaneously, they must choose between the two
strategies and hope for the best.

Thus, macro policy is often about trade-offs. In discussing the trade-offs economists
emphasize the limits of what can be achieved with macroeconomic policy. Economists
often tell governments that they're asking for too much. These governments are like a
patient who asks his doctor for a health program that will enable him to forget about a
training program, eat anything he wants, and run a four-minute mile. Some things just
can't be done, and it's important for governments to recognize the inevitable limitations
and trade-offs, at least with the monetary and fiscal policy tools currently available.
Good economists are continually pointing out those limits.

The trade-off view of economic policy is summarized in Figure 18-5.

Agreement about Macro Policy There is much agreement about macro policy, and
most economists would agree with the following statements:

1. Expansionary monetary and fiscal policies have short-run stimulative effects on
   income.
2. In the long run expansionary fiscal policy (running budget deficits) tends to
   slow the economy down because it means less saving.
3. Expansionary monetary and fiscal policies have potential long-run inflation
   effects.
4. Monetary policy is politically easier to implement than fiscal policy.
5. Expansionary monetary and fiscal policies tend to increase trade deficits.
6. Expansionary monetary policy places downward pressure on the value of a
   currency.

As you can see, the two key tools that macroeconomists have available to them are
monetary policy and fiscal policy, and each presents trade-offs between inflation on the
one side and unemployment and growth on the other.

Figure 18-5

MACROECONOMIC POLICY DILEMMAS

	Option	Advantages	Disadvantages
Monetary policy	Expansionary	1. Interest rates may fall. 2. Economy may grow. 3. Decreases unemployment.	1. Inflation may worsen. 2. Capital outflow. 3. Trade deficit may increase.
	Contractionary	1. Helps fight inflation. 2. Trade deficit may decrease. 3. Capital inflow.	1. Risks recession. 2. Increases unemployment. 3. Slows growth. 4. May help cause short-run political problems. 5. Interest rates may rise.
Fiscal policy	Expansionary	1. May increase output growth in the short run. 2. May help solve short-run political problems. 3. Decreases unemployment.	1. Budget deficit worsens. 2. Hurts country's ability to borrow in the future. 3. Trade deficit may increase. 4. Upward pressure on interest rate, discouraging growth.
	Contractionary	1. May help fight inflation. 2. May allow a better monetary/fiscal mix. 3. Trade deficit may decrease. 4. Interest rates may fall, stimulating investment and growth in the long run.	1. Risks recession. 2. Increases unemployment. 3. Slows output growth in the short run. 4. May help cause short-run political problems.

Policy Process and Credibility

One theme running throughout the entire discussion of modern macro policy is the importance of expectations, and economists have devoted a great deal of thought to expectations and their role in the economy. Changes in expectations can shift the *AD* curve; expectations of inflation can cause inflation. For this reason expectations are central to all policy discussions, and what people believe policy will be significantly influences the effectiveness of the policy.

Expectations complicate models and policymaking enormously; they change the focus from discussions about a mechanical policy—a response that can be captured by simple models—to much more complicated discussions in which any policy is seen as part of a broader policy regime.

Effective policy must be credible policy.

Rational Expectations People's expectations are generally rational, in the sense that they are forward looking. People aren't stupid, and will use available evidence to form their expectations about the future. Thus, it is reasonable to assume that rational expectations are based on the best current information available. That said, there is enormous debate about what rational expectations will be. The term *rational expectations* is interpreted by some economists to mean expectations consistent with economic models, but that definition is a technical one, and is not the one policymakers use. What's important for policymakers is the forward-looking aspect of rational expectations, and we use the term in this broader sense. Thus a reasonable way to think of **rational expectations** is as *forward-looking expectations that use available information*.

The influence of the rational expectations work is woven into much of the discussion of modern policy. It is why, for example, when we discussed monetary policy, we talked about the Bank posturing—*seeming* to be absolutely resolute about fighting inflation—in addition to *being* resolute. If the Bank convinces the public that its sole goal is to fight inflation, people will react differently than if they do not believe that. One central bank nicely summarized the distinction between making people believe the central bank's goal and the policy of actually pursuing that goal when it differentiated "bark policy" from "bite policy." If the Bank barks loudly and convincingly enough, it doesn't have to bite.

Uncertainty about the Effects of Policy The central role of expectations means that there is a great deal of uncertainty in the economy. Put simply: What people believe plays a central role in how they react to policy. Expectations can change the effect of a policy.

Most discussion of policy today assumes that people are forward looking, that they think strategically, and that they base their actions on expected policy actions. Thus, in some way their expectations are rational. But modern policy discussion is also built on the belief that the economy is complicated and that many possible expectations are rational. This includes adaptive and extrapolative expectations, and combinations of expectations strategies. The multiplicity of expectational strategies and the speed with which they can shift undermine our ability to develop deterministic models of the economy, and give the economy an unpredictability that precludes fine tuning. It was those assumptions that led us to talk about interpretative models rather than mechanistic models, and to constantly remind you that the models are not directly applicable but are simply for guidance of your thought process.

What the above assumptions mean in terms of policy is that depending on the beliefs that individuals hold, monetary and fiscal policy will work in different ways. People aren't stupid, and they aren't superintelligent; they are people. If the government uses an activist monetary and fiscal policy in a predictable way, people will eventually come to build that expectation into their behaviour. If the government bases its prediction of the effect of policy on past experience, that prediction will likely be wrong. But government never knows when expectations will change.

Let's consider an example. Say that everyone expects government to run expansionary fiscal policy if the economy is in a recession. In the absence of any expected policy response by government, people will lower their prices when they see a recession coming. Expecting government expansionary policy, however, they won't lower their prices. Thus, the expectation of policy can create its own problems. Such expectational problems can partially be avoided by establishing a set of rules that limits government's policy responses, but they cannot be totally avoided because people may or may not believe that the rules will be followed.

Q.8 Why does bark policy sometimes work better than bite policy?

18.1

see page 452

As people build expectations of policy into their actions, the effects of policy change.

Policy Regimes and Expectations A **policy regime** is a rule; it is *a predetermined statement of the policy that will be followed in various circumstances*. In contrast, a **policy** is a *one-time reaction to a problem*; it is chosen without a predetermined framework. As we stated above, these policy regimes can help generate the expectations that make the government's tools work.

An analogy to raising a child might make the point clear. Say that your child is crying in a restaurant. Do you hand out a piece of candy to stop the crying, or do you maintain your "no candy" rule? Looking only at the one situation, it might make sense to give the candy. But giving the child candy, even once, will undermine your credibility and consistency, and therefore has an additional cost. This emphasis on credibility is the primary effect modern theoretical work has had on macroeconomic policy. In conducting macro policy, we must consider the effect that expectations of that policy will have on the economy generally, and not only in a particular case.

Q.9 How does a policy regime differ from a policy?

Has the Economy Entered a New Era?

As you can see in Table 18-1, the mid- to late 1990s were wonderful years for the economy. These years, however, were trying ones for macroeconomics' trade-off view. During the 1990s economists have continually been suggesting that there were limits on economic growth and how low unemployment could go, and that to exceed them would cause inflation. Their predictions have not come true; inflation has not come, and the real economy, like the Energizer bunny, kept on going and going until 2001. These superb results—low inflation, low unemployment, and decent growth—were not predicted by economists. Thus, at the turn of the millennium there was much discussion about whether our economy has entered a *new era* in which the old laws don't apply.

The 1990s have been trying years for macroeconomics' trade-off view.

Economists' View of the New Era In dealing with this issue there are three views that economists hold. The first is that the low inflation was caused by the Bank following economists' policy recommendations and focusing on achieving low inflation, regardless of what the unemployment consequences were. By making its policy credible, the Bank has made it more effective. There is some truth to this view, but it must also be noted that almost no economist predicted that unemployment could go as low as it did

Q.10 What are three explanations economists give for why the predictions about inflation have not come true?

TABLE 18-1   The 1990s Economy

	Real GDP Growth	Inflation	Unemployment
1993	2.4%	1.9%	11.4%
1994	4.7	0.2	10.3
1995	2.8	2.1	9.4
1996	1.6	1.6	9.6
1997	4.3	1.6	9.1
1998	3.9	1.0	8.3
1999	5.1	1.7	7.6
2000	4.4	2.7	6.8
2001	0.5	2.6	7.2

Source: Statistics Canada, CANSIM II, Tables 279-0001, 326-0001, and 280-0002.

in the late 1990s without generating accelerating inflation.[2] The second view is that we are currently in the short run and that the long run will be coming, but has simply been slightly delayed. The third view is that the economy has entered a new era, in which the old trade-off view does not apply.

The majority of economists believe some combination of the first two explanations. They warn about the danger of the economy operating above its potential output, and talk about trade-offs. The current mood among the macroeconomists we talk to is a bit like the mood of parents whose child suddenly changes from being a normal kid to being a supergood kid. The parents ask themselves: "Has the kid really changed his fundamental nature, or is he simply preparing for a blowout such as we haven't seen in years?" (Believe us, with kids you never know which it is.) All we as parents can do is wait and see, and hope that our children have changed, but be prepared for the eventuality that they haven't. Modern macroeconomists have the same problem with the macroeconomy working perfectly as it did in the last part of the 20th century. All we, as economists, can do, is wait and see, and hope that the economy has changed, but be prepared for the eventuality that it hasn't.

18.2

see page 452

Most economists hope that the new economy has arrived, but they are concerned that policymakers will come to believe that the economy will always be good, and will forget the trade-offs. Thus, most economists argue that policy should not be based on the assumption that a new economy is here. They make an analogy to driving fast on a mountain road. Say that you know there is a 3 percent chance you will slide out of the curve at 100 kilometres per hour; that means the chances are 97 out of 100 that you will not slide out, but it doesn't mean that you should be going 100 kilometres per hour. True, the economy has had a string of good luck; productivity has increased more than expected, and tight labour markets have not led to labour-cost increases. But most economists argue that the balance is precarious, and that policy should be based on conservative estimates of the economy's potential. The trade-offs can appear suddenly. Tight labour markets can quickly lead to wage increases and thus, if those wage increases lead to expectations of larger increases, to accelerating inflation.

In voicing these concerns we feel the same way as we do when we give advice to our kids based on our considerable experience of what not to do. We know our words will most likely be forgotten or dismissed. Most students today have never experienced a recession or a serious bout of inflation. Most have never even experienced a significant bear market in the stock market. Since people's views are shaped by experiences, far more than by the framework they are presented within textbooks, students naturally think that recent experience will continue. The fear among economists is that the belief that the economy has a downside is disappearing from the collective memory.

Explanations for the New Era Economists might not be very good at predicting what will happen, but we are superb at explaining events after the fact. To explain the recent development, economists would focus on new growth theory. Its emphasis on technology provides a theoretical explanation of recent events—increases in technology in-

---

[2]Actually, not all economists emphasize trade-offs in the macroeconomy. Some economists argued throughout the 1990s that the economy could expand much faster, and operate at a much higher level without causing inflation, than other economists believed. One such economist was Bill Vickrey. Vickrey, who won a Nobel Prize for his work in micro (the Nobel committee did not mention his work in macro because it was considered so offbeat), was a strong advocate of the position that the economy could achieve a high growth rate and a low rate of unemployment without generating inflation. In doing so he was part of a group of economists, called post-Keynesian macroeconomists, whose predictions about the economy during the 1990s were much more on target than were the predictions of the majority of economists.

The late 1990s saw a boom in the stock market, with Internet stocks leading the way. Billions of dollars were being made every day in the stock market. This booming stock market was closely associated with the new-era economy predictions, and some people were predicting that the stock market prices were still undervalued, and would continue to rise through the new millennium.

BEYOND THE TOOLS

The Stock Market Boom and the Economy

span as "irrational exuberance." Others called it rational exuberance; since most investors felt that other investors believed that the economy would expand, they rationally didn't worry about inherent values of stock, since what mattered was that someone else would buy the stock from them at the high price.

Most economists disagreed; stock prices are grounded in the ability of the companies to make profits that warrant that price either now or in the future. Most felt that while the Internet revolution was a major revolution, the predicted earnings built into stock prices were highly unlikely. Thus, the stock market rise was a "bubble" driven by expectations in a process described by Alan Green-

The stock market boom increased consumption and investment spending throughout the 1990s, which kept the economy growing at a high rate. But that made some economists concerned about what would happen if the bubble burst, and everyone tried to sell their stock quickly. The result could be a sudden shift down in expectations, and with that a reduction in consumption and investment spending and a possible recession.

crease productivity, hold costs down, and thereby hold down inflation even as the economy grows.

Another argument for why the economy is a new economy involves international competition: even with tight labour markets domestically, wages are held in check by the threat of international competition. A further argument involves the policies Canada has followed—decreasing regulation, opening the economy further to trade, maintaining a balanced budget, and carefully limiting how expansionary monetary policy is. Supporters of the new-economy view argue that these policies have made our new economy immune to the trade-offs of the past.

Three recent explanations of why the economy has not experienced inflation include: (1) technology, (2) international competition, and (3) the policies Canada has followed.

A Potential Problem Area in the New Era One of the problems of the modern economy is its fragility. Prosperity is based on people having positive expectations about the future and acting on those expectations. When those expectations are brought into question, the economy can change quickly. That is precisely what happened in early 2001 when the U.S. economy, which had been the driving force of the Canadian economy, suddenly slowed. Initially, consumer spending remained strong, but then came a terrorist attack on the financial heart of the United States that destroyed the World Trade Center and several surrounding buildings, as well as part of the Pentagon, killing more than 3,000 people. The result for the North American economy was a sudden change in its prospects. Airlines lost passengers, and all industries dependent on travel—caterers, hotel and restaurant staff, and those working in tourist areas—lost customers. Mail contaminated by anthrax killed a small number of people in the U.S. and led thousands to demand prophylactic antibiotics.

The result was a sharp downward multiplier effect that slowed the U.S. economy even further. The Canadian economy wasn't far behind. Governments moved quickly to provide loan guarantees and assistance to airlines and to stimulate the economy with expansionary monetary and fiscal policy, but there was concern whether that policy response would be enough. Most economists felt that in the long run the economies were resilient and would be able to weather the storm, but many expected short-run problems. How international trade in goods and services will behave in the aftermath is not clear, although the additional scrutiny given to international shipments and travel is bound to impede the free flow of resources across borders.

Terrorist incidents and how governments respond are a major concern in the 21st century.

By late November 2001 it was official: The American economy was in recession (which economists say began in March of that year). You'll recall that a recession is formally defined as two successive quarterly declines in real output, although the agency that dates American business cycles doesn't always use this standard when defining recessions (for more on this see www.nber.org). This was bad news for Canada given that most of our exports are destined for American markets. When the U.S. economy slows, that country's demand for our products slackens, and employment in Canadian export industries falls. This, combined with trade disputes over softwood lumber, multiplied throughout the economy. Even though the Bank of Canada had cut the target band for the overnight financing rate by 3.5 percent during 2001, it wasn't enough to shelter the Canadian economy from this shock to aggregate demand.

The U.S. and its allies declared war on terrorism, which changed the fiscal regime into war footing in which less concern was given to deficits, as spending on war needs took priority. That stimulated the economy, but whether it will be sufficient to offset the decrease in consumption spending due to concerns about terrorism was unclear early in 2002. This is often the case; consumer spending can be so unpredictable that making any forecast about the economy is perilous.

CONCLUSION

We began this chapter with the quotation "The first task of the University teacher of any liberal art is surely to persuade his students that the most important things he will put before them are questions and not answers." The continuation of that quotation is the following: "He is going to put up for them a scaffolding, and leave them to build within it. He has to persuade them that they have not come to the University to learn as it were by heart things which are already hard-and-fast and cut-and-dried, but to watch and perhaps help in a process, the driving of a causeway which will be made gradually firmer by the traffic of many minds" (Shackle, 1953). Now that we've come to the end of the course, we hope that you agree that we have met that first task. Economic policy is not a cut-and-dried topic, but neither is it a totally subjective one. As Keynes once said, it is a method rather than a doctrine, an apparatus of the mind, a technique of thinking that helps the possessor to draw correct conclusions. The operative word there is *method*, not *doctrine*.

In economics you don't learn correct economic policy; what you learn is a method for thinking about economic policy that others have found useful. That method is to learn some models and then to judiciously apply them to a variety of situations. Past applications of these models have found that expectations and the policy process are often more important than the particular policy, which has led economists to talk about credibility and policy regimes when discussing policy. In such an uncertain world, tools, not rules, are what's needed for guiding policy, and it is our hope that it is tools, not rules, that you have learned in this book.

Chapter Summary

- Important micro models include the production possibility model and the supply/demand model.

- Four macro models include the long-run growth model, the quantity theory model, the AS/AD model, and the multiplier model.

- The Keynesian worldview of policy focuses on the short run and tends to have an activist bias; the Classical worldview of policy focuses on the long run and tends to have a laissez-faire bias.

- Economists take a trade-off view of macro policy. Their challenge is trying to find the appropriate mix of policy to see that unemployment is as low as possible, growth is as high as possible, and inflation is as low as possible.

● Policy is a process, not a one-time event, and policy regimes are often more important than any particular policy.

● The new era economy is characterized by high growth, low unemployment, and low inflation. There is much debate about the new era economy; most economists are cautious about basing policy on the assumption that a new era has arrived.

Key Terms

policy   *(447)*   policy regime   *(447)*   rational expectations   *(446)*

Questions for Thought and Review

1. Draw a production possibility curve for apples and oranges if there are (a) constant marginal opportunity costs and (b) increasing marginal opportunity costs.

2. If nominal GDP has risen by 8 percent, and inflation was 4 percent, how much did real GDP rise?

3. How does new growth theory differ from Classical growth theory?

4. A student from another school has just stated that since the government budget deficit has disappeared, our fiscal policy problems are solved. How would you respond to this statement?

5. The central bank of the economy has just increased the amount of reserves in the economy by $100. The desired reserve requirement is 20 percent and the cash-to-deposit ratio is 30 percent. By how much does the money supply change?

6. Assume that you are in a world with flexible exchange rates. Inflation is 6 percent in Canada, and the Cana-

dian nominal interest rate is 5 percent. World inflation is 3 percent and the nominal world interest rate is 4 percent. What do you expect to happen to the value of the Canadian dollar? Why?

7. The interest rate in Bulgaria is about 50 percent; John states that this is a high interest rate; Bob states that this is a low interest rate. Who is right, and why?

8. Which is considered the more effective tool: monetary or fiscal policy? Why?

9. Why is policymaking better seen as a process than as a one-time event?

10. How does a policy regime differ from a policy?

11. Has the Canadian economy entered a new era?

12. What are three explanations that have been given for why the Canadian economy did so well during the second half of the 1990s?

Problems and Exercises

1. Demonstrate, using supply and demand curves, what would happen to equilibrium price and quantity in the following cases.
   a. The market for cars when a major technological improvement occurs in the automobile industry.
   b. The market for avocados when a flood hits B.C., where many of them are grown.

2. Congratulations! You have just been appointed chairperson of the Economic Advisers for the Country of Funlandia. You are assigned a research assistant who provides you with the following information: (1) The marginal propensity to consume is 0.9. (2) Actual income is 4 percent below the government's targeted income of $10,000. The government wants to achieve its target income.
   a. Using the multiplier model, what change in government expenditures would you recommend to achieve this goal?

   b. What will happen to the budget deficit as a result of your policy proposal?

3. A decision has been made to increase income in the economy by $200 million. You are assigned to write the directive for what open market operation to undertake. Your research assistant tells you that the cash-to-deposit ratio is 0.2 and the desired reserve requirement is 0.1. You know that for each increase in the money supply of $50 million interest rates fall by a percentage point (e.g., from 6 percent to 5 percent) and that for each fall in the interest rate of one percentage point investment increases by $100 million. He also tells you that the marginal propensity to consume is 0.9. What open market operation will you suggest? Be specific.

4. Congratulations! You have just been appointed chairperson of the Economic Advisers for Textland. You are given the following information: The economy's potential real

income is 6,000. The economy's actual real income is 5,000, and the statisticians have determined that in response to changes in aggregate demand, the price level will remain constant up to 5,500, and then it starts slowly rising in response to increases in aggregate demand until potential income is reached. The marginal propensity to consume is 0.8.

a. The premier wants to increase real output to its potential. What advice do you give? Be as specific as possible.

b. The premier wants to know what his policy should have been if the price level were constant up until potential income is reached.

c. After discussing the policy a while with you, he tells you that he is a visual person and needs to see the argument put graphically on paper. You oblige with two diagrams, one using the multiplier model and the other using the AS/AD model. Also provide a short written explanation about what you are doing in the graphs. Assume the price level is fixed.

d. Now assume the price level is variable, so the SAS curve is upward-sloping. Revise your answer to c using this assumption.

5. Congratulations! You have been appointed adviser to the Bank of Canada.

a. The Governor decides that he must increase the money supply by 60. His staff tell you the desired reserve ratio is 0.1 and the cash-to-deposit ratio is 0.3. They ask you what directive they should give to the operations desk. You tell them, being as specific as possible, using the real-world money multiplier.

b. They ask you for two other ways they could have achieved the same end. You tell them.

c. Based on the quantity theory of money, tell them what you think the effect on the price level of your policy will be.

6. Explain what you expect to happen to the balance of trade and the value of the currency if a country undertakes the following policies:

a. Expansionary fiscal policy

b. Contractionary monetary policy

c. A combination of contractionary fiscal policy and expansionary monetary policy

7. Demonstrate, using supply and demand analysis, the likely effect on the value of the Canadian dollar of an increase in Canadian tariffs. Be sure to label your graphs carefully.

Web Questions

1. Go to the Bank of Canada Web site (www.bankof canada.ca) and the Department of Finance Web site (www.fin.gc.ca). Find their most recent forecasts for real economic growth. Is the forecast of the central bank identical to that of the Department of Finance? Explain why or why not.

2. In the Jokes for Economists Web site (www.etla.fi/pmk/ JokEc.html) find as many "bills lying on the pavement jokes" as you can. What is the meaning of each?

Answers to Margin Questions

1. It would be a straight, downward-sloping line.   (433)

2. The tariff would shift the demand for Canadian dollars to the left, causing the value of the dollar to fall.   (435)

3. The money supply would have had to rise by 15 percent.   (436)

4. We would predict that output would increase with very little, and possibly no, upward pressure on prices.   (437)

5. Output would rise by the multiplier $[1/(1 - mpc)]$ times the increase in government expenditures (35), or 175 (5×35).   (438)

6. The money supply would decline by 100 times the money multiplier. The money multiplier is $1/(r + c)$, or 2.5. So the money supply would decline by 250.   (440)

7. A Classical is more likely to emphasize the view that there is no such thing as a free lunch. Classical economists believe that expansionary monetary and fiscal pol-

icy may increase output in the short run, but it will only lead to inflation in the long run.   (441)

8. A bark policy sometimes works better than a bite policy because it is designed to convince people of the Bank's resolve to fight inflation and thus changes expectations of inflation. Changing the expectations of inflation is an important element to keeping inflation low.   (446)

9. A policy regime is a predetermined statement of a policy rule that will be followed in various circumstances. A policy is a one-time action taken by government; it may or may not follow a policy rule.   (447)

10. Three explanations by economists why predictions of inflation have not come true are (1) the low inflation was caused by the Bank's focus on achieving low inflation, (2) inflation will be coming eventually, and (3) the economy has entered a new era where the old trade-off view no longer applies.   (447)

GLOSSARY

A

Adaptive expectations. Expectations based in some way on the past.

Aggregate demand (AD) curve. Curve that shows how a change in the price level will change aggregate expenditures on all goods and services in an economy.

Aggregate demand management. Government's attempt to control the aggregate level of spending in the economy.

Aggregate expenditures (AE). Consumption (spending by consumers), investment (spending by business), spending by government, and net foreign spending on Canadian goods (the difference between Canadian exports and Canadian imports).

Aggregate expenditures (AE) curve. The graphical representation of the expenditures function.

Aggregate production (AP). The total amount of goods and services produced in every industry in an economy.

Annuity rule. The present value of any annuity is the annual income it yields divided by the interest rate.

Approximate real-world money multiplier. One divided by the sum of the percentage of deposits banks desire to hold in reserve (r) and the ratio of money people hold in currency (c) to the money they hold as deposits ($1 / (r + c)$).

Arbitrage. The buying and selling of similar goods and services across different markets.

Art of economics. The application of the knowledge learned in the achievement of the goals one has determined in normative economics.

Asset management. How a bank handles its loans and other assets.

Automatic stabilizer. Any government program or policy that will counteract the business cycle without any new government action.

Autonomous expenditures. Expenditures that are independent of income.

B

Balance of goods and services. The difference between the value of the goods and services a country imports and the value of the goods and services it exports.

Balance of merchandise trade. The difference between the value of goods exported and the value of goods imported.

Balance of payments. A country's record of all transactions between its residents and the residents of all foreign nations.

Bank. A financial institution whose primary function is holding money for, and lending money to, individuals and firms.

Bank of Canada. Canada's central bank, whose liabilities (bank notes) serve as cash in Canada.

Bank rate. The rate at which members of the Canadian Payments Association can borrow from the Bank of Canada.

Bar graph. Graph where the area under each point is filled in to look like a bar.

Bond. A promise to pay a certain amount plus interest in the future.

Bretton Woods system. An agreement about fixed exchange rates that governed international financial relationships from the period after the end of the Second World War until 1971.

Business. Private producing unit in our society.

Business cycle. The upward or downward movement of economic activity, or real output, that occurs around the growth trend.

C

Canada–U.S. Free Trade Agreement. An agreement between Canada and the United States to reduce trade impediments.

Capital and financial account. The part of the balance of payments account in which all long-term flows of payments are listed.

Capital markets. Markets in which financial assets having a maturity of more than one year are bought and sold.

Capitalism. An economic system based on private property and the market in which, in principle, individuals decide how, what, and for whom to produce.

Capitalists. Businesspeople who have acquired large amounts of money and use it to invest in business.

Cash management operation. Policies the Bank of Canada implements to change the liquidity of the financial system, such as open market operations.

Central bank. A type of bankers' bank.

Certificate of deposit (CD). A piece of paper certifying that you have a sum of money in a savings account in the bank for a specified period of time.

Classical growth model. A model of growth that focuses on the role of capital accumulation in the growth process.

Classicals. Macroeconomists who generally favour laissez-faire or non-activist policies.

Commercial paper. Short-term promissory note that a certain amount of money plus interest will be paid back on demand.

Comparative advantage. The ability to be better suited to the production of one good than to the production of another good.

Complements. Goods that are used in conjunction with other goods.

Constant returns to scale. Situation when long-run average total costs do not change with an increase in output. Also: Output will rise by the same proportionate increase as all inputs.

Consumer price index (CPI). Measure of prices of a fixed 'basket' of consumer goods, weighted according to each component's share of an average consumer's expenditure.

Consumer sovereignty. Principle that the consumer's wishes rule what's produced.

Consumer surplus. The value the consumer gets from buying a product less its price. Also: The difference between what consumers would have been willing to pay and what they actually pay.

Contractionary fiscal policy. Increase taxes or decrease government spending.

Contractionary monetary policy. Monetary policy that tends to raise interest rates and lower income.

Contractual intermediary. Financial institution that holds and stores individuals' financial assets.

Coordinate system. Two-dimensional space in which one point represents two numbers.

Corporation. Business that is treated as a person, legally owned by its stockholders. Its stockholders are not liable for the actions of the corporate "person."

Cost/benefit approach. Assigning costs and benefits, and making decisions on the basis of the relevant costs and benefits.

Countercyclical fiscal policy. Fiscal policy in which the government offsets any change in aggregate expenditures that would create a business cycle.

Covered interest parity. When an investor uses a derivative market to lock in the rate at which one currency can be traded for another; securites denominated in different currencies should offer the same rates of return, *ceteris paribus*.

Crowding out. The offsetting of a change in government expenditures by a change in private expenditures in the opposite direction.

Currency stabilization. Buying and selling of a currency by the government to offset temporary fluctuations in supply and demand for currencies.

Currency support. Buying of a currency by a government to maintain its value at above its long-run equilibrium value.

Current account. The part of the balance of payments account in which all short-term flows of payments are listed.

Cyclical unemployment. Unemployment resulting from fluctuations in economic activity.

D

Deadweight loss. The loss of consumer and producer surplus from a tax.

Debt. Accumulated deficits minus accumulated surpluses.

Debt service. The interest rate on debt times the total debt.

Decision tree. A visual description of sequential choices.

Decreasing returns to scale. Output rises by a smaller proportionate increase than all inputs.

Deficit. A shortfall of revenues under payments.

Demand. Schedule of quantities of a good that will be bought per unit of time at various prices, other things constant.

Demand curve. Graphic representation of the relationship between price and quantity demanded.

Demerit goods or activities. Goods or activities the government deems bad for people even though they choose to use the goods or engage in the activities.

Depository institution. A financial institution whose primary financial liability is deposits in chequing or savings accounts.

Depreciation. A decrease in the value of a currency or a decrease in an asset's value.

Depression. A large recession.

Desired reserve ratio. The ratio of reserves to total deposits.

Direct relationship. Relationship in which when one variable goes up, the other goes up too.

Disintermediation. The process of lending directly and not going through a financial intermediary.

Disposable personal income. Personal income minus personal income taxes and personal taxes.

Diversification. Spreading the risks by holding many different types of financial assets.

Division of labour. The splitting up of a task to allow for specialization of production.

Downsizing. A reduction in the workforce.

E

Economic decision rule. If the marginal benefits of doing something exceed the marginal costs, do it. If the marginal costs of doing something exceed the marginal benefits, don't do it.

Economic efficiency. Achieving a goal at the lowest possible cost.

Economic forces. The necessary reactions to scarcity.

Economic model. Framework that places the generalized insights of the theory in a more specific contextual setting.

Economic policy. An action (or inaction) taken by government, to influence economic events.

Economic principle. Commonly held economic insight stated as a law or general assumption.

Economic profit. Explicit and implicit revenue minus explicit and implicit cost.

Economically efficient. Method that produces a given level of output at the lowest possible cost.

Economics. The study of how human beings coordinate their wants and desires, given the decision-making mechanisms, social customs, and political realities of the society.

Economies of scale. Situation when long-run average total costs decrease as output increases. Also: Situation in which costs per unit of output fall as output increases.

Economies of scope. Situation when the costs of producing products are interdependent so that it's less costly for a firm to produce one good when it's already producing another.

Efficiency. Achieving a goal as cheaply as possible (using as few inputs as possible).

Efficiency wages. Wages paid above-the-going-market wage to keep workers happy and productive.

Efficient. Achieving a goal at the lowest cost in total resources without consideration as to who pays those costs.

Elastic. The percentage change in quantity is greater than the percent change in price (E > 1).

Embargo. A total restriction on the import or export of a good.

Employment rate. Number of people who are working as a percentage of the labour force.

Entrepreneur. An individual who sees an opportunity to sell an item at a price higher than the average cost of producing it.

Entrepreneurship. The ability to organize and get something done. Also: Labour services that involve high degrees of organizational skills, concern, oversight responsibility, and creativity.

Equation of exchange. Relates money, prices, real output, and velocity via the quantity theory.

Equilibrium. A concept in which opposing dynamic forces cancel each other out.

Equilibrium income. The level of income toward which the economy gravitiates in the short run because of the cumulative circles of declining or increasing production.

Equilibrium price. The price toward which the invisible hand drives the market.

Equilibrium quantity. The amount bought and sold at the equilibrium price.

European Union (EU). An economic and political union of European countries that is both an economic free trade area and a loose political organization.

Excess demand. Quantity demanded is greater than quantity supplied.

Excess reserves. Reserves held by banks in excess of what banks desire to hold.

Excess supply. Quantity supplied is greater than quantity demanded.

Exchange rate. The rate at which one nation's currency can be traded for another nation's currency.

Exchange rate policy. A policy of deliberately affecting a country's exchange rate in order to affect its trade balance.

Excise tax. A tax that is levied on a specific good.

Expansion. Upturn that lasts for at least two consecutive quarters of a year.

Expansionary fiscal policy. Decrease taxes or increase government spending.

Expansionary monetary policy. Monetary policy that tends to reduce interest rates and raise income.

Expected inflation. Inflation people expect to occur.

Expenditures function. A representation of the relationship between aggregate expenditures (which include both induced and autonomous expenditures) and income as a mathematical function.

Export-led growth policies. Policies designed to stimulate Canadian exports and increase aggregate expenditures on Canadian goods, and hence to have a multiplied effect on Canadian income.

Exports. The value of goods sold abroad.

External debt. Government debt owed to individuals in foreign countries.

Externality. An effect of a decision on a third party not taken into account by the decision maker.

Extrapolative expectations. Expectations that a trend will continue.

F

Fair trade. A policy of paying fair prices for goods produced in other nations.

Fallacy of composition. The false assumption that what is true for a part will also be true for the whole.

Feudalism. Economic system in which traditions rule.

Final output. Goods and services purchased for final use.

Financial account. The part of the balance of payments account that, among other components, records the amount of its own currency or foreign currencies that a nation buys or sells.

Financial assets. Assets such as stocks or bonds, whose benefit to the owner depends on the issuer of the asset meeting certain obligations.

Financial institution. A business whose primary activity is buying, selling, or holding financial assets.

Financial liabilities. Liabilities incurred by the issuer of a financial asset to stand behind the issued asset.

Financial market. Market where financial assets and financial liabilities are bought and sold.

Fine tuning. Fiscal policy designed to keep the economy always at its target or potential level of income.

Firm. An economic institution that transforms factors of production into consumer goods.

Fiscal policy. The deliberate change in either government spending or taxes to stimulate or slow down the economy.

Fixed exchange rate. The exchange rate is set and the government is committed to buying and selling its currency at a fixed rate.

Flexible exchange rate. The exchange rate is set by market forces (supply and demand for a country's currency).

Foreign exchange market. Market in which one currency can be exchanged for another.

Free rider. Person who participates in something for free because others have paid for it.

Free trade. A policy of allowing unrestricted trade among countries.

Free Trade Areas of the Americas agreement. An agreement by 34 nations in North, South, and Central America to reduce trade impediments, to come into effect by 2005.

Free trade association. Group of countries that have reduced or eliminated trade barriers among themselves, and, as a group, puts up common barriers against all other countries' goods.

Frictional unemployment. Unemployment caused by new entrants into the job market and people quitting a job just long enough to look for and find another one.

Fundamental analysis. A consideration of the fundamental forces that determine the supply of and demand for currencies.

G

GDP deflator. Index of the price level of aggregate output, or the average price of the components in total output (or GDP), relative to a base year.

General Agreement on Tariffs and Trade (GATT). Until recently, a regular international conference to reduce trade barriers. It has been replaced by the World Trade Organization (WTO).

General rule of political economy. When small groups are helped by a government action and large groups are hurt by that same action, the small group tends to lobby far more effectively than the large group. Thus, policies tend to reflect the small group's interest, not the interest of the large group.

Global corporations. Corporations with substantial operations on both the production and sales sides in more than one country.

Gold specie flow mechanism. The long-run adjustment mechanism that maintained the gold standard.

Gold standard. System of fixed exchange rates in which the value of currencies was fixed relative to the value of gold and gold was used as the primary reserve asset.

Government expenditures. Government payments for goods and services and investment in equipment and structures.

Government failures. Situations where the government intervenes and makes things worse.

Grandfather in. To pass a law affecting a specific group buy providing that those in the group before the law was passed are not subject to the law.

Graph. Picture of points in a coordinate system in which points denote relationships between numbers.

Gross domestic product (GDP). The total market value of all final goods and services produced in an economy in a one-year period.

Gross national product (GNP). Aggregate final output of citizens and businesses of an economy in a one-year period.

Gross private investment. Business spending on equipment, structures, and inventories and household spending on new owner-occupied housing.

Group of Eight. Group that meets to promote negotiations and coordinate economic relations among countries. The Eight are Japan, Russia, Germany, Britain, France, Canada, Italy, and the United States.

Group of Five. Group that meets to promote negotiations and coordinate economic relations among countries. The Five are Japan, Germany, Britain, France, and the United States.

Growth. An increase in the amount of goods and services an economy produces.

H

Households. Groups of individuals living together and making joint decisions.

Human capital. The skills that are embodied in workers through experience, education, and on-the-job training, or, more simply, people's knowledge.

Hyperinflation. Inflation that hits triple digits—100 percent or more per year.

I

Imports. The value of goods purchased abroad.

Income. Payments received plus or minus changes in value in one's assets in a specified time period.

Incomes policy. A policy that places direct pressure on individuals to hold down their nominal wages and prices.

Increasing returns to scale. Output rises by a greater proportionate increase than all inputs.

Induced expenditures. Expenditures that change as income changes.

Industrial Revolution. A time when technology and machines rapidly modernized industrial production and mass-produced goods replaced handmade goods.

Inefficiency. Getting less output from inputs which, if devoted to some other activity, would produce more output.

Inefficient. Achieving a goal in a more costly manner than necessary.

Inelastic. The percentage change in quantity is less than the percentage change in price ($E < 1$).

Infant industry argument. With initial protection, an industry will be able to become competitive.

Inflation. A continual rise in the price level.

Inflation tax. An implicit tax on the holders of cash and the holders of any obligations specified in nominal terms.

Inflationary gap. A difference between equilibrium income and potential income when equilibrium income exceeds potential income. Also: Aggregate expenditures above potential output that exist at the current price level.

Input. What you put into a production process to achieve an output.

Insider/outsider model. An Institutionalist story of inflation where insiders bid up wages and outsiders are unemployed.

Institutionalist economist. Economist who argues that any economic analysis must involve specific considerations of institutions.

Interest rate. The price paid for the use of a financial asset.

Interest rate effect. The effect that a lower price level has on investment expenditures through the effect that a change in the price level has on interest rates.

Intermediate products. Products used as input in the production of some other product.

Internal debt. Government debt owed to other governmental agencies or to its own citizens.

International effect. As the price level falls (assuming the exchange rate does not change) net exports will rise.

International Monetary Fund (IMF). A multinational, international financial institution concerned primarily with monetary issues.

Interpolation assumption. Assumption that the relationship between variables is the same between points as it is at the points.

Inverse relationship. A relationship between two variables in which when one goes up the other goes down.

Invisible hand. The price mechanism, the rise and fall of prices that guides our actions in a market.

Invisible hand theory. A market economy, through the price mechanism, will allocate resources efficiently.

J

Judgment by performance. To judge the competitiveness of markets by the behaviour (performance) of firms in that market.

Judgement by structure. To judge the competitiveness of markets by the structure of the industry.

K

Keynesians. Macroeconomists who generally favour activist government policies.

L

Labour force. Those people in an economy who are willing and able to work.

Labour force participation rate. Measurement of the labour force as a percentage of the total population at least 15 years old.

Labour market. Factor market in which individuals supply labour services for wages to other individuals and to firms that need (demand) labour services.

Labour productivity. The average output per worker.

Laissez-faire. Economic policy of leaving individuals' wants to be controlled by the market.

Law of demand. Quantity demanded rises as price falls, other things constant. Also can be stated as: Quantity demanded falls and price rises, other things constant.

Law of diminishing marginal productivity. As more and more of a variable input is added to an existing fixed input, eventually the additional output one gets from that additional input is going to fall.

Law of supply. Quantity supplied rises as price rises. Also can be stated as: Quantity supplied falls as price falls.

Learning by doing. As we do something, we learn what works and what doesn't, and over time we become more proficient at it. Also: To improve the methods of production through experience.

Liability management. How a bank attracts deposits and what it pays for them.

Limited liability. The liability of a stockholder (owner) in a corporation; it is limited to the amount the stockholder has invested in the company.

Line graph. Graph where the data are connected by a continuous line.

Linear curve. A curve that is drawn as a straight line.

Liquidity. Ability to turn an asset into cash quickly.

Long-run aggregate supply (LAS) curve. Curve that shows the amount of goods and services an economy can produce when both labour and capital are fully employed.

Long-run decision. Decision in which a firm chooses among all possible production techniques.

Long-run Phillips curve. A vertical curve at the unemployment rate consistent with potential output. (It shows the trade-off [or complete lack thereof] when expectations of inflation equal actual inflation.)

M

M1. Currency in circulation and chequing account balances at chartered banks.

M2. M1 plus other types of accounts at chartered banks.

Macroeconomic externality. Externality that affects the levels of unemployment, inflation, or growth in the economy as a whole.

Macroeconomics. The study of the economy as a whole, which includes inflation, unemployment, business cycles, and growth.

Marginal benefit. Additional benefit above what you've already derived.

Marginal cost. Additional cost to your overhead above the costs you have already incurred. Also, the increase (decrease) in total cost from increasing (decreasing) the level of output by one unit. Also, the change in total cost associated with a change in quantity.

Marginal propensity to consume (mpc). The ratio of a change in consumption, ΔC, to a change in income, ΔY.

Marginal propensity to save (mps). The percentage of income flow that is withdrawn from the income/expenditures flow of the economy in each round.

Market demand curve. The horizontal sum of all individual demand curves.

Market failures. Situations where the market does not lead to a desired result. Also, situations in which the invisible hand pushes in such a way that individual decisions do not lead to socially desirable outcomes.

Market force. Economic force that is given relatively free rein by society to work through the market.

Market incentive plan. A plan requiring market participants to certify that they have reduced total consumption—not necessarily their own individual consumption—by a specified amount.

Market structure. The physical characteristics of the market within which firms interact.

Market supply curve. Horizontal sum of individual supply curves. Also, the horizontal sum of all the firms' marginal cost curves, taking account of any changes in input prices that might occur.

Mercantilism. Economic system in which government determines the what, how, and for whom decision by doling out the rights to undertake certain economic activities.

Merger. The act of combining two firms.

Merit goods or activities. Goods and activities that government believes are good for you, even though you may not choose to consume the goods or engage in the activities.

Microeconomics. The study of individual choice, and how that choice is influenced by economic forces.

Minimum wage law. Law specifying the lowest wage a firm can legally pay an employee.

Monetary base. Vault cash, deposits at the Bank, plus currency in circulation.

Monetary policy. A policy of influencing the economy through changes in the financial system's reserves that influence the money supply and credit available in the economy.

Monetary regime. A predetermined statement of policy that will be followed in various situations.

Money. A highly liquid financial asset that's generally accepted in exchange for other goods, is used as a reference in valuing other goods, and can be stored as wealth.

Money markets. Markets in which financial assets having a maturity of less than one year are bought and sold.

Monopoly power. Ability of individuals or firms currently in business to prevent other individuals or firms from entering the same kind of business.

Mortgage. A special name for a secured loan on real estate.

Most-favoured nation. A country that will be charged as low a tariff on its exports as any other country.

Movement along a demand curve. The graphic representation of the effect of a change in price on the quantity demanded.

Movement along a supply curve. The graphic representation of the effect of a change in price on the quantity supplied.

Multiplier. A number that tells us how much income will change in response to a change in autonomous expenditures.

Multiplier effect. The amplification of initial changes in expenditures.

Multiplier equation. An equation that tells us that income equals the multiplier times autonomous expenditures.

N

National balance sheet. A balance sheet of an economy's stock of assets and liabilities.

National income (NI). The total income earned by citizens and businesses of a country.

National income accounting. A set of rules and definitions for measuring economic activity in the aggregate economy—that is, in the economy as a whole.

Net domestic product (NDP). The sum of consumption expenditures, government expenditures, net foreign expenditures, and investment less depreciation.

Net exports. Exports minus imports.

Net foreign factor income. Income from foreign domestic factor sources minus foreign factor income earned domestically.

Net private investment. Gross private domestic investment minus depreciation.

New growth theory. Theory that emphasizes the role of technology rather than capital in the growth process.

NIMBY. Not In My Back Yard. A mindset of approving a project but not wanting it to be nearby.

Nominal deficit. The deficit determined by looking at the difference between expenditures and receipts.

Nominal GDP. GDP calculated at existing prices.

Nominal interest rates. The rates you actually see and pay.

Nominal output. Output as measured at current prices.

Nonlinear curve. A curve that is drawn as a curved line.

Nontariff barriers. Indirect regulatory restrictions on exports and imports.

Normative economics. The study of what the goals of the economy should be.

North American Free Trade Agreement (NAFTA). A U.S.-Canada-Mexico free trade zone that saw reductions in tariffs.

O

Official reserves. Government holdings of foreign currencies.

Okun's rule of thumb (sometimes called Okun's Law). A 1-percentage point change in the unemployment rate will cause output to change in the opposite direction by 2 percent.

Open market operations. The Bank's buying and selling of government securities.

Opportunity cost. The benefit forgone by undertaking a particular activity.

Optimal policy. Policy in which the marginal cost of undertaking the policy equals the marginal benefit of that policy.

Output. A result of a productive activity.

Overnight financing rate. The interest rate on funds lent/borrowed on a overnight basis.

P

Partially flexible exchange rate. The government sometimes buys and sells currencies to influence the price directly, and at other times the government simply accepts the exchange rate determined by supply and demand forces.

Partnership. Business with two or more owners.

Passive deficit or surplus. The part of the deficit or surplus that exists because the economy is operating below or above its potential level of output.

Patent. A legal right to be the sole supplier of a good. (Note that a patent is good only for a limited time.)

Per capita growth. Producing more goods and services per person.

Per capita real output. Real output divided by the total population.

Perfectly competitive. Describes a market in which economic forces operate unimpeded.

Perfectly elastic. Quantity responds enormously to changes in price (E = infinity).

Perfectly inelastic. Quantity does not respond at all to changes in price (E = 0).

Permanent income hypothesis. Expenditures are determined by permanent or lifetime income.

Personal consumption expenditures. Payments by households for goods and services.

Personal income (PI). National income plus net transfer payments from government minus amounts attributed but not received.

Pie chart. A circle divided into "pie pieces," where the individual pie represents the total amount and the pie pieces reflect the percentage of the whole pie that the various components make up.

Policy. Action or inaction by government to achieve a desired outcome.

Policy regime. A predetermined statement of policy to be followed in various circumstances.

Positive economics. The study of what is, and how the economy works.

Positive externality. The effect of a decision not taken into account by the decision maker that is beneficial to others.

Potential income. The level of income that the economy technically is capable of producing without generating accelerating inflation.

Potential output. Output that would materialize at the target rate of unemployment and the target rate of capacity utilization.

Present value. A method of translating a flow of future income or saving into its current worth.

Price ceiling. A government-imposed limit on how high a price can be charged.

Price discriminate. To charge different prices to different individuals or groups of individuals.

Price elasticity of demand. The percentage change in quantity demanded divided by the percentage change in price.

Price elasticity of supply. The percentage change in quantity divided by the percentage change in price.

Price floor. A government-imposed limit on how low a price can be charged.

Price index. A number that summarizes what happens to a weighted composite of prices of a selection of goods (often called a market basket of goods) over time.

Primary financial market. Market in which newly issued financial assets are sold.

Principle of absolute advantage. A country that can produce a good at a lower cost than another country is said to have an absolute advantage in the production of that good. When two countries have absolute advantages in different goods, there are gains of trade to be had.

Principle of comparative advantage. As long as the relative opportunity costs of producing goods (what must be given up in one good in order to get another good) differ among countries, then there are potential gains from trade, even if one country has an absolute advantage in everything.

Principle of increasing marginal opportunity cost. To get more of something, one must give up ever-increasing quantities of something else.

Private good. A good that, when consumed by one individual, cannot be consumed by other individuals.

Private property rights. Control a private individual or a firm has over an asset or a right.

Producer surplus. Price the producer sells a product for less the cost of producing it.

Production. The transformation of the factors of production—land, labour, and capital—into goods.

Production function. The relationship between the inputs (factors of production) and outputs.

Production possibility curve. A curve measuring the maximum combination of outputs that can be obtained from a given number of inputs.

Production possibility table. A table listing the maximum combination of outputs that can be obtained from a given number of inputs.

Production table. A table showing the output resulting from various combinations of factors of production or inputs.

Productive efficiency. Achieving as much output as possible from a given amount of inputs or resources.

Productivity. Output per unit of input.

Profit. A return on entrepreneurial activity and risk taking. Alternatively, what's left over from total revenues after all the appropriate costs have been subtracted. Also: Total revenue minus total cost.

Profit-maximizing condition. $MR = MC = P$.

Progressive tax. Tax whose rates increase as a person's income increases.

Proletariat. The working class.

Proportional tax. Tax whose rates are constant at all income levels, no matter what a taxpayer's total annual income is.

Public assistance. Means-tested social programs targeted to the poor and providing financial, nutritional, medical, and housing assistance.

Public choice (conservative) model. A model that focuses on economic incentives as applied to politicians.

Public good. A good that if supplied to one person must be supplied to all and whose consumption by one individual does not prevent its consumption by another individual.

Purchasing power parity (PPP). A method of calculating exchange rates that attempts to value currencies at rates such that each currency will buy an equal basket of goods.

Q

Quantity demanded. A specific amount that will be demanded per unit of time at a specific price, other things constant.

Quantity supplied. A specific amount that will be supplied at a specific price.

Quantity theory of money. The price level varies in response to changes in the quantity of money.

Quantity-adjusting and price-adjusting markets. Markets in which firms respond to changes in demand by modifying both their output and their prices.

Quota. Limitation on how much of a good can be shipped into a country.

R

Rational. What individuals do is in their own best interest.

Rational expectations. Expectations that the economists' model predicts, which is that rational people base their decisions on the best information available, given the cost of that information.

Rational expectations model. All decisions are based on the expected equilibrium in the economy.

Raw materials price index. An index of producer prices for raw materials.

Real deficit. The nominal deficit adjusted for inflation.

Real GDP. Nominal GDP adjusted for inflation.

Real gross domestic product (real GDP). The market value of final goods and services produced in an economy, stated in the prices of a given period. Also: Nominal GDP adjusted for inflation.

Real interest rates. Nominal interest rates adjusted for expected inflation.

Real output. The total amount of goods and services produced, adjusted for price-level changes.

Real-business-cycle theory. A theory that views fluctuations in the economy as reflecting real phenomena—simultaneous shifts in supply and demand, not simply supply responses to demand shifts.

Recession. A decline in real output that persists for more than two consecutive quarters of a year.

Recessionary gap. The amount by which equilibrium output is below potential output.

Regressive tax. Tax whose rates decrease as income rises.

Regulatory trade restrictions. Government-imposed procedural rules that limit imports.

Rent control. A price ceiling on rents, set by government.

Rent-seeking activites. Activities designed to transfer surplus from one group to another.

Reserve requirement. The percentage a bank sets as its minimum amount of reserves.

Reserves. Currency and deposits a bank keeps on hand or at the central bank, enough to manage the normal cash inflows and outflows.

Retirement Income system. Social insurance programs that provide financial benefits to the elderly and disabled and to their eligible dependants and/or survivors.

Reverse engineering. The process of a firm buying other firms' products, disassembling them, figuring out what's special about them, and then copying them within the limits of the law.

Rosy scenario policy. Government policy of making optimistic predictions and never making gloomy predictions.

Rule of 72. The number of years it takes for a certain amount to double in value is equal to 72 divided by its annual rate of increase.

S

Say's law. Supply creates its own demand.

Scarcity. The goods available are too few to satisfy individuals' desires.

Secondary financial market. Market in which previously issued financial assets can be bought and sold.

Share distribution of income. The relative division of total income among income groups.

Shift in demand. The effect of anything other than price on demand.

Shift in supply. The graphic representation of the effect of a change in other than price on supply.

Short-run aggregate supply (SAS) curve. A curve that shows how firms adjust the quantity of real output they will supply when the price level changes, holding all input prices fixed.

Short-run decision. Decision in which the firm is constrained in regard to what production decisions it can make.

Short-run Phillips curve. A downward-sloping curve showing the relationship between inflation and unemployment when expectations of inflation are constant.

Simple money multiplier. The measure of the amount of money ultimately created per dollar deposited in the banking system, when people hold no currency.

Sin tax. A tax that discourages activities society believes are harmful (sinful).

Slope. The change in the value on the vertical axis divided by the change in the value on the horizontal axis.

Social capital. The habitual way of doing things that guides people in how they approach production.

Socialism. Economic system based on individuals' goodwill toward others, not on their own self-interest, and in which, in principle, society decides what, how, and for whom to produce.

Socioeconomic distribution of income. The allocation of income among relevant socioeconomic groupings.

Sole proprietorship. Business that has only one owner.

Soviet-style socialism. Economic system that uses administrative control or central planning to solve the coordination problems: what, how, and for whom.

Special Drawing Rights (SDRs). A type of international money.

Specialization. The concentration of individuals in certain aspects of production.

Stagflation. Combination of high and accelerating inflation and high unemployment.

State socialism. Economic system in which government sees to it that people work for the common good until they can be relied upon to do that on their own.

Stock. Certificates of ownership in a company.

Strategic decision making. Taking explicit account of a rival's expected response to a decision you are making.

Strategic pricing. Firms set their price based on the expected reactions of other firms.

Strategic trade policies. Threatening to implement tariffs to bring about a reduction in tariffs or some other concession from the other country.

Structural deficit (or surplus). The part of a budget deficit (or surplus) that would exist even if the economy were at its potential level of income.

Structural unemployment. Unemployment caused by economic restructuring making some skills obsolete.

Substitute. A good that can be used in place of another.

Sunk costs. Costs that have already been incurred and cannot be recovered.

Supply. A schedule of quantities a seller is willing to sell per unit of time at various prices, other things constant. Put another way, a schedule of quantities of goods that will be offered to the market at various prices, other things constant.

Supply curve. Graphical representation of the relationship between price and quantity supplied.

Surplus. An excess of revenues over payments.

T

Takeover. The purchase of one firm by a shell firm that then takes direct control of all the purchased firm's operations.

Target rate of unemployment. Lowest sustainable rate of unemployment that policymakers believe is achievable under existing conditions.

Tariff. Tax on imports.

Tax incentive program. A program of using a tax to create incentives for individuals to structure their activities in a way that is consistent with the desired ends.

Technological change. An increase in the range of production techniques that provide new ways of producing goods.

Technological development. The discovery of new or improved products or methods of production.

Technological lock-in. The use of a technology makes the adoption of subsequent technology difficult.

Technology. The way we make goods and supply services.

Term structure of interest rates. The structure of yields on similar assets by term to maturity.

Total cost. Explicit payments to the factors of production plus the opportunity cost of the factors provided by the owners of the firm.

Total revenue. The amount a firm receives for selling its product or service plus any increase in the value of the assets owned by the firm.

Total utility. The total satisfaction one gets from consuming a product.

Trade adjustment assistance programs. Programs designed to compensate losers for reductions in trade restrictions.

Trade deficit. An excess of imports over exports.

Trade surplus. An excess of exports over imports.

U

Uncovered interest parity. A relationship linking interest rates on securities denominated in different currencies in which investors' expectations of future exchange rates lead to identical expected returns to domestic and foreign investment, *ceteris paribus*.

Unemployment compensation. Short-term financial assistance, regardless of need, to eligible individuals who are temporarily out of work.

Unemployment rate. The percentage of people in the economy who are willing and able to work but who are not working.

Unexpected inflation. Inflation that surprises people.

Unit elastic. The percentage change in quantity is equal to the percentage change in price (E = 1).

Utility. The pleasure or satisfaction that one expects to get from consuming a good or service.

V

Value added. The increase in value that a firm contributes to a product or service.

Variable costs. Costs that change as output changes.

Velocity of money. The number of times per year, on average, a dollar goes around to generate a dollar's worth of income.

Voluntary restraint agreements. Agreements in which countries voluntarily restrict their exports.

W

Wealth. The value of the things individuals own less the value of what they owe.

Wealth effect. A fall in the price level will make the holders of money and of other financial assets richer, so they buy more.

Welfare capitalism. An economic system in which the market is allowed to operate but in which government plays dual roles in determining distribution and making the what, how, and for whom decisions.

Welfare loss triangle. A geometric representation of the welfare cost in terms of misallocated resources that are caused by a deviation from a supply/demand equilibrium.

World Bank. A multinational, international financial institution that works with developing countries to secure low-interest loans.

World Trade Organization (WTO). An organization whose functions are generally the same as GATT's were—to promote free and fair trade among countries. Also: Organization committed to getting countries to agree not to impose new tariffs or other trade restrictions except under certain limited conditions.

X

X-inefficiency. Firms operating far less efficiently than they could technically.

COLLOQUIAL GLOSSARY

A

Ads (noun). Short for "advertisements."

Ain't (verb). An ungrammatical form of "isn't," sometimes used to emphasize a point although the speaker knows that "isn't" is the correct form.

All the rage (descriptive phrase). Extremely popular, but the popularity is likely to be transitory.

Andy Warhol (proper name). American artist who flourished in the period 1960–1980. He was immensely popular and successful with art critics and the intelligentsia but, above all, he gained worldwide recognition in the same way and of the same quality as movie stars and sports athletes do. His renown has continued even after his death.

Armada (proper noun). Historic term for the Spanish navy. Now obsolete.

Automatic pilot (noun). To be on automatic pilot is to be acting without thinking.

B

Baby boom (noun). Any period when more than the statistically predicted number of babies is born. Originally referred to a specific group: those born in the years 1945-1964.

Baby boomers (descriptive phrase). People born in the years 1945 through 1964. An enormous and influential group of people whose large number is attributed to the "boom" in babies that occurred when military personnel, many of whom had been away from home for four or five years, were discharged from military service after the end of the Second World War.

Back to the drawing board (descriptive phrase). To start all over again after having your plan or project turn out to be useless.

Backfire (verb). To injure a person or entity who intended to inflict injury.

Bailed out (descriptive phrase). To be rescued. It has other colloquial meanings as well, but they do not appear in this book.

Balloon (verb). To expand enormously and suddenly.

Bear market (noun). Stock market dominated by people who are not buying (i.e., are hibernating). Opposite of a bull market, where people are charging ahead vigorously to buy.

Bedlam (noun). Chaotic and apparently disorganized activity. Today the word is not capitalized. A few hundred years ago in England the noun meant the Hospital of St. Mary's of Bethlehem, an insane asylum. The hospital was not in Bethlehem; it was in London. "Bedlam" was the way "Bethlehem" was pronounced by the English.

Beluga caviar (noun). Best, most expensive, caviar.

Benchmark (noun). A point of reference from which measurement of any sort may be made.

Better mousetrap (noun). Comes from the proverb, "Invent a better mousetrap and the world will beat a path to your door."

Bidding (or bid) (verb sometimes used as a noun). Has two different meanings. (1) Making an offer, or a series of offers, to compete with others who are making offers. Also the offer itself. (2) Ordering or asking a person to take a specified action.

Big bucks (noun). Really, really large sum of money.

Big Mac (proper noun). Brand name of a kind of hamburger sold at McDonald's restaurants.

Blow it (verb; past tense: blew it). To do a poor job, to miss an opportunity, to perform unsatisfactorily.

Blowout (noun). Serious release of pent-up emotions or of control over one's actions.

Boost (verb and noun). To give a sudden impetus, or boost, to something or someone.

Botched up (adjective). Operated badly; spoiled.

Bottleneck (noun). Situation in which no action can be taken because a large number of people or actions is confronted by a very small opening or opportunity.

Brainteaser (noun). Question or puzzle that intrigues the brain, thus "teasing" it to answer the question or solve the puzzle.

Bring home (verb). To emphasize or convince.

Broke (adjective). (1) To "go broke" or to "be broke" is to become insolvent, to lose all one's money

and assets. (2) Usually not as bad as to have gone broke—just to be (hopefully) temporarily out of money or short of funds.

Buffalo (adjective, as used in this book). "Buffalo chicken wings" are a variety of tempting food developed in, and hence associated with, the city of Buffalo. (Not all chicken wings are Buffalo chicken wings.)

Bus person (noun). Has no relation to transportation. It's a term for the person who clears the tables in a restaurant.

C

Call (verb). In sports refereeing, one meaning of "to call" is for the referee to announce his or her decision on a specific point.

Carriage maker (noun). Person or firm that makes carriages, a type of horse-drawn conveyance almost never seen any more except in films. Members of the British royal family ride in carriages on important ceremonial occasions, such as weddings.

Cellophane (noun). A transparent wrapping material. It differs from plastic wrap in that it is made of cellulose, not plastic.

Centre stage (noun). A dominant position.

CEO (noun). Abbreviation of "chief executive officer."

Charade (noun). A pretense, usually designed to convince someone that you are doing something that you are definitely not doing.

Chit (noun). Type of IOU (which see) or coupon with a designated value that can be turned in toward the purchase or acquisition of some item.

Chump change (noun). Insignificant amount of money earned by or paid to a person who is not alert enough to realize that more money could rather easily be earned.

Clear-cut (adjective). Precisely defined.

Clip coupons (verb). To cut coupons out of newspapers and magazines. The coupons give you a discount on the price of the item when you present the item and the coupon at the cashier's counter in a store. Sometimes you are directed to buy the item and then send the coupon and an identifying code from the item's package to the manufacturer, who will mail you the discount.

Clout (noun). Influence or power.

Coffer (noun). A box or trunk used to hold valuable items; hence, "coffers" has come to mean a vault or other safe storage place to hold money or other valuable items.

Coined (verb). "Invented" or "originated."

Coldhearted (adjective). Without any sympathy; aloof; inhuman.

Come up short (descriptive phrase). To be deficient.

Co-opted (adjective). Overwhelmed.

Cornrows (noun). Hair style in which hair is braided in shallow, narrow rows over the entire head.

Corvette (noun). A type of expensive sports car.

Couch (verb). To construct and present an argument.

Crack (noun). A strong form of cocaine.

Cry over spilt milk (verb). To indulge in useless complaint or regret. Note that there is a departure from standard English spelling in this phrase, which uses the spelling "spilt" instead of "spilled." Either is correct, but "spilt" is seldom used. (Another such variation is the rare "spelt" for usual "spelled.")

Cut and dried (descriptive phrase). Simple, obvious, and settled.

D

Deadbeat (noun). Lazy person who has no ambition, no money, and no prospects.

Deadweight (noun). Literally, the unrelieved weight of any inert mass (think of carrying a sack of bricks); hence, any oppressive burden.

Decent (adjective). One of its specialized meanings is "of high quality."

Doodle (noun and verb). Idle scribles, usually nonrepresentational and usually made while actively thinking about something else, such as during a phone conversation or sitting in a class.

Down pat (descriptive phrase). To have something down pat is to know it precisely, accurately, and without needing to think about it.

Drop in the bucket (noun). Insignificant quantity compared to the total amount available.

Dyed-in-the-wool (adjective). Irretrievably convinced of the value of a particular course of action or of the truth of an opinion. Literally, wool that is dyed after it is shorn from the sheep but before it is spun into thread.

E

'em (pronoun). Careless way of pronoucing "them". Written out, it reproduces the sound the speaker is making.

Energizer bunny (noun). Character in a television commercial for Energizer batteries. Just as the batteries are alleged to do, the Energizer bunny keeps going and going.

Esperanto (noun). An artificial language invented in the 1880s, intended to be "universal." It is based on words from the principal European languages, and the theory was that all speakers of these European languages would effortlessly understand Esperanto. It never had a big following and today is almost unknown.

Establishment (noun and adjective). As a noun, the prevailing theory or practice. As an adjective, something that is used by people whose views prevail over other people's views.

F

Fake (verb). To fake is to pretend or deceive; to try to make people believe that you know what you're doing or talking about when you don't know or aren't sure.

Fire (verb). To discharge an employee permanently. It's different from "laying off" an employee, an action taken when a temporary situation makes the employee superfluous but the employer expects to take the employee back when the temporary situation is over.

Fix (verb). To prepare, as in "fixing a meal." This is only one of the multiplicity of meanings of this verb.

Fleeting (adverb). This word's usage is elegant and correct, but rare. It means transitory or short-lived.

Flop (noun). A dismal failure.

Follow suit (verb). To do the same thing you see others do. Comes from card games where if a card of a certain suit is played, the other players must play a card of that suit, if they have one.

Follow the flag (verb). To be committed to doing business only with firms that produce in your own country or in your "colonies"—that is, territories that belong to your country.

Follow the leader (noun). Name of a children's game. Metaphorically, it means to do what others are doing, usually without giving it much thought.

Forest for the trees (descriptive phrase). To be so focused on details that you don't see the overall situation.

Free lunch (descriptive phrase). Something you get without paying for it in any way. Usually applied negatively: There is no "free lunch."

Funky (adjective). Eccentric in style or manner.

G

Gadget (noun). Generic term for any small, often novel, mechanical or electronic device or contrivance, usually designed for a specific purpose. For instance, the small wheel with serrated rim and an attached handle used to divide a pizza pie into slices is a gadget.

Gee (expletive). Emphatic expression signalling surprise or enthusiasm.

Get across (verb). To convince.

Get you down (desriptive phrase). Make you depressed about something or make you dismiss something altogether. (Do not confuse with "get it down," which means to understand fully.)

Glitch (noun). Trivial difficulty.

GM (noun). The General Motors automobile company.

Go-cart (noun). A small engine-powered vehicle that is used for racing and recreation.

Gold mine (noun). Metaphorically, any activity that results in making you a lot of money.

Goldilocks (fictional character). In a children's story, Goldilocks is a beautiful little girl with blonde curls who emerges unharmed from an encounter with three bears because she is so good and charming.

Good and ready (descriptive phrase). Really, really ready.

Good cop/bad cop (noun). Alternating mood shifts. It comes from the alleged practice of having two police officers interview a suspect—one officer is kind and coaxing while the other is mean and nasty. This is supposed to make the suspect feel that the nice cop is a safe person to confide in.

Good offices (descriptive phrase). An expression common in 18th century England, meaning "services."

Gooey (adjective). Sticky or slimy.

Goofed (verb). Past tense of the verb to goof, meaning to make a careless mistake.

Got it made (descriptive phrase). To succeed.

Grind (noun). Slang for necessary intense effort that may be painful but will likely benefit your understanding

Groucho Marx (proper name). A famous U.S. comedian (1885–1977).

Gung-ho (adjective). Full of energy and eager to take action.

Guns and butter (descriptive phrase). Metaphor describing the dilemma whether to devote resources to war or to peace.

H

Haggling (noun). Bargaining, usually in a petty and confrontational manner.

Handout (noun). Unearned offering (as distinct from a gift); charity.

Handy (adjective). Convenient.

Hard liquor (noun). Alcoholic beverages with a high content of pure alcohol. Beer and wine are not "hard liquor" but most other alcoholic drinks are.

Hard up (adjective). Seriously worried.

Hassle (noun). Unreasonable obstacle. As a verb, "to hassle" means to place unreasonable obstacles or arguments in the way of someone.

Hawking (adjective). Selling aggressively and widely.

Heat (noun). Anger, blame, outrage, and pressure to change.

Hefty (adjective). Large; substantial.

Hero sandwich (noun). A type of very large sandwich.

Highfalutin (adjective). American slang term, meaning pretentious, self-important, supercilious.

Hog bellies (noun). Commercial term for the part of a pig that becomes bacon and pork chops. (Also called "pork bellies.")

Holds its own (descriptive phrase). Refuses to give up, even in the face of adversity or oppostion.

Home free (descriptive phrase). Safe and successful.

Hot air (descriptive phrase). An empty promise. Also, bragging.

Hot dog (noun). A type of sausage.

Hot potatoes (noun). Slang term for anything that everyone wants to avoid confronting.

How come (expression). Why? That is, "How has it come about that . . . ?"

I

"In" (preposition sometimes used as an adjective). Placed within quotation marks to show it is used with a special meaning. Here it is used as an adjective, to indicate: "fashionable or popular, usually just for a short period." Compare, in this glossary, "all the rage."

Incidentals (noun). Blanket term covering the world of small items a person uses on a daily basis as the need happens to arise—that is, needed per incident occurring. Examples are aspirin, combs, and picture postcards.

IOU (noun). A nickname applied to a formal acknowledgment of a debt, such as a treasury bond. Also an informal but written acknowledgment of a debt. Pronounce the letters and you will hear "I owe you."

Iron Curtain (noun). Imaginary but daunting line between Western Europe and adjacent communist countries. After the political abandonment of Communism in these countries, the Curtain no longer exists.

It'll (contraction). "It will."

J

Jolt (noun). A sudden blow.

Junk food (noun). Food that tastes good but has little nutritional value and lots of calories. It is sometimes cheap, sometimes expensive, and it's quick and easy to buy and eat.

Just say no (admonition). Flatly refuse. This phrase became common in the 1980s after Nancy Reagan, the wife of the then-president of the United States, popularized it in a campaign against the use of addictive drugs.

K

Ketchup (noun). Spicy, thick tomato sauce used on, among other foods, hot dogs.

Kick in (verb). To activate; to start or begin. (Can also mean "to contribute to.")

Kickback (noun). A firm's giving part of the price it has received for its product or service back to the firm or individual who authorized the purchase of that product or service. In effect it is a type of bribe or blackmail demanded or expected by a purchaser's agent.

Klutz (noun). Awkward, incompetent person.

Knockoff (noun). A cheap imitation.

L

Laetrile (noun). Substance derived from peach pits, thought by some people to be a cure for cancer.

Late Victorian (adjective or noun). Embodying some concept typical of the late period of Queen Victoria. Also, a person from that period or who acts like someone from that period. (Queen Victoria was queen of England from 1837 to 1901.)

Lay off (verb). To discharge a worker temporarily.

Lead banker (noun). Primary or principal bank or banker in a joint undertaking.

Leads (noun). Persons or institutions that you think will be interested in whatever you have to sell. Also the information you have that makes you think someone or something is worth pursuing.

Left the nest (descriptive phrase). To have left one's parental home, usually because one has grown up and become self-sufficient.

Levi's (noun). Popular brand of jeans.

Like Greek to you (descriptive phrase). Incomprehensible (because in Canada, classical Greek is considered to be a language that almost no one learns).

Lion's share (noun). By far the best part of a bargain.

Lobby (verb and noun). To lobby is to attempt by organized effort to influence legislation. As a noun, a lobby is an organized group formed to influence legislation. A lobbyist is a member of a lobby.

Lord Tennyson (proper name). Alfred Tennyson, 19th century English poet who wrote a poem, *Ulysses*, about the nobility of effort ("To strive, to seek, to find and not to yield").

Lousy (adjective). Incompetent or distasteful.

M

Make it (verb). To succeed in doing something; for instance, "make it to the bank" means to get to the bank before it closes.

Mall (noun). Short for "shopping mall." A variety of stores grouped on one piece of land, with ample parking for all the mall's shoppers and often with many amenities such as covered walkways, playgrounds for children, fountains, etc.

MasterCard (proper noun). Brand name of a widely issued credit card.

MBA (noun). An academic degree: Master of Business Administration.

Messed up (adjective). Damaged or badly managed.

Mind your own business (admonition). Don't meddle in other people's affairs; don't ask intrusive questions.

Mind your Ps and Qs (expression). Pay close attention to distinctions. It comes from the similarity of the small printed letters "p" and "q" where the only visual distinction is the location of the downstroke. Also, the letters are right next to each other in our alphabet.

Mob (noun). Organized criminal activity. Also, the group to which organized criminals belong.

Moot (adjective). Irrelevant because the issue in question has already been decided.

Mousetrap (noun). Producing a better mousetrap is part of the saying, "Make a better mousetrap and the world will beat a path to your door." Metaphorically, producing a better mousetrap stands for doing anything better than it has previously been done.

N

NA (abbreviation). "Not available."

NASDAQ (also sometimes spelled "Nasdaq") (noun). Stock market operated by the National Association of Securities Dealers. The "AQ" stands for "Automated Quotations."

NATO (noun). North American Treaty Organization. Western alliance for joint economic and military cooperation. It includes the United States, Canada, and several European nations.

Nature of the beast (descriptive phrase). Character of whatever you are describing (need not have anything to do with a "beast").

Nicholas Apert (proper name). Nineteenth-century French experimenter who discovered how to preserve food by canning or bottling it.

Nirvana (noun). This word is adopted from Buddhism. Its religious meaning is complicated, but it is used colloquially to mean salvation, paradise, harmony, perfection.

No way (exclamation). Emphatic expression denoting refusal, denial, or extreme disapproval.

Not to worry (admonition; also, when hyphenated, used as an adjective). Don't worry; or, it's nothing to worry about.

Nudge (noun and verb). A little push (noun); to give a little push (verb).

O

Off the books (descriptive phrase). Not officially recorded (and hence it's an untaxed transaction).

Off-the-cuff (adjective). A quick, unthinking answer for which the speaker has no valid authority (comes from the alleged practice of writing an abbreviated answer on the cuff of your shirt, to be glanced at during an examination).

On her (his) own (descriptive phrase). By herself (himself); without any help.

On their toes (descriptive phrase). Alert; ready for any eventuality.

Op-ed (adjective). Describes an article that appears on the "op-ed" page of a newspaper, which is a page devoted to **OP**inion and **ED**itorials.

P

Ps and Qs. See under "Mind."

Park Avenue (noun). Expensive and fashionable street in New York City.

Pass the buck (descriptive phrase). Evade responsibility by forcing someone elso to make the relevant decision.

Peanuts (noun). Slang for a small amount, usually money but sometimes anything with a small value.

Pecking order. Hierarchy.

Peer pressure (descriptive phrase). Push to do what everyone else in your particular group is doing.

Penny-pincher (noun). Person who is unusually careful with money, sometimes to the point of being stingy.

Perks (noun). Short for "perquisites."

Philharmonic (adjective). A philharmonic orchestra is an orchestra that specializes in classical music. Sometimes used as a noun, as in "I heard the Philharmonic."

Phoenix from the ashes (descriptive phrase). Metaphor for coming to life after having been thought to be dead. In ancient Greek mythology, the phoenix was a bird said to (really) rise from the ashes after a fire. (Phoenix, Arizona, was so named because of the hot climate that prevails there.)

Pick up steam (verb). As steam pressure increases, the speed of a steam engine increases. When this happens, we say the engine has "picked up steam."

Pickle (noun). Dilemma.

Picky (adjective). Indulging in fine distinctions when making a decision.

Pie (noun). Metaphor for the total amount of a specific item that exists.

Piece of cake (descriptive phrase). Simple; easy to achieve without much effort or thought.

Pitt, (Sir) William (historical figure). Chief financial officer and prime minister of Britain in the 1780s. He is usually designated "the younger" to distinguish him from his father, who was also a high British government official.

Poorhouse (noun). Public institution where impoverished individuals were housed. These institutions were purposely dreary and unpleasant. They no longer officially exist, but they have a modern manifestation: shelters for the homeless.

Pop-Tart (noun). Brand name of a type of junk food. It's a sweet filling enclosed in pastry that you pop into the toaster and when the pastry is hot, it pops out of the toaster.

Populist (noun and adjective). As a noun, this means a member of a political party, that purports to represent the rank and file of the people. As an adjective, it means a political party, a group, or an individual that purports to represent rank and file opinion.

Pound (noun). Unit of British currency.

Practice makes perfect (expression). The grammar of this phrase is illogical but the meaning is clear.

Premium tires all round (descriptive phrase). Premium tires are tires of superior quality. When all the tires on your vehicle are premium tires, you have them "all round."

Presto! (exclamation). Immediately.

Proxy (noun). A stockholder can give a "proxy" to the firm. It is an authorization that permits the firm's officials to vote for the proposition that the stockholder directs them to vote for. By extension, proxy means a substitute.

Pub (noun). Short for "public house," a commercial establishment where alcoholic drinks are served, usually with refreshments and occasionally with light meals.

Q

Queen Elizabeth (proper noun). Here the author means Queen Elizabeth I (reigned in England from 1558 to 1603).

Quote (noun). Seller's statement of what he or she will charge for a good or service.

R

R&D (noun). Research and Development.

Rainy day (noun). Period when you (hopefully) temporarily have an income shortage.

Rainy day fund (descriptive phrase). Money set aside when you are doing well financially—i.e., in a financially sunny period—to use in case you have a period when you are doing less well financially—i.e., when you run into a financially rainy period.

Raise your eyebrows (verb). To express surprise, usually by a facial expression rather than vocally.

Red flag (noun). A red flag warns you to be very alert to a danger or perceived danger. (Ships in port that are loading fuel or ammunition raise a red flag to signal danger.)

Red-handed (adjective). Indisputably guilty. Comes from being found at a murder or injury scene with the blood of the victim on one's hands.

Red-lined (adjective). On a motor vehicle's tachometer, a red line that warns at what speed an engine's capacity is being strained.

Right on! (exclamation). Expression of vigorous, often revolutionary, approval and encouragement.

Ring up (verb). Before the introduction of computer-type machines that record each payment a retail customer makes—say at the supermarket or a restaurant—a "cash register" was used. When you pressed the keys representing the amount offered by the customer, a drawer sprang open and a bell rang.

Ritzy (adjective). Very expensive, fashionable, and ostentatious. Comes from the entrepreneur Caesar Ritz, a Swiss developer of expensive hotels, active in the first quarter of the 20th century.

Robin Hood (proper name). Semifictional English adventurer of the 12th or 13th century. He "stole from the rich and gave to the poor."

Rolodex file (noun). Manual—as opposed to electronic—device for organizing names, addresses, phone numbers, and e-numbers.

Rule of thumb (descriptive phrase). An estimate that is quick and easy to make and is reliable enough for rough calculations. Comes from using the space from the tip of your thumb to the thumb's first joint to represent an inch.

S

Sacred cow (noun). An institution or practice that social and/or political forces dictate is absolutely protected from change of any kind.

Saks (proper name). A mid-size department store that sells expensive, fashionable items. There are very few stores in the Saks chain, and Saks stores are considered exclusive.

Savvy (adjective). Slang term meaning very knowledgeable.

Adaptation of the French verb, "savoir," meaning "to know."

Scab (noun). Person who takes a job, or continues in a job, even though workers at that firm are on strike.

Scraps (noun). Little pieces of leftover food. Also little pieces of anything that is left over: for example, steel that is salvaged from a wrecked car.

Sears Catalogue (proper noun). Sears, Roebuck, and Co. is a large chain of stores that sells a wide variety of goods. Before shopping malls, highways, and the Internet, Sears used to have a huge mailing list to which it sent enormous catalogues. A person receiving such a catalogue would have information about, and access to, thousands of items, many of which the person might not have known existed before the catalogue provided the prospect.

Set up shop (verb). To go into business.

Shell out (verb). To pay money, often somewhat more than you want to pay for the item in question.

Shivering in their sandals (descriptive phrase). Adaptation of standard English idiom, "shivering in their shoes," which means being afraid.

Shorthand (noun). Any of several systems of abbreviated writing or writing that substitutes symbols for words and phrases. Shorthand was widely used in business until the introduction of mechanical and electronic devices for transmitting the human voice gradually made shorthand obsolete. Today it means to summarize very briefly or to substitute a short word or phrase for a long description.

Show up (verb). To put in an appearance, to arrive.

Shy away (verb). To decisively refrain from something. (Comes from

the world of horses, who are said to "shy at" things that startle them.)

Silk stockings (noun). Silk stockings for women denoted luxury and extravagance, almost like caviar or pearls. With the development of nylon in 1940, silk stockings for anyone, let alone the queens or factory girls mentioned in this book, joined the dinosaurs in oblivion.

Sixpence (noun). A British coin that is no longer in use. It represented six British pennies and its equivalent in the 2000s would be about a nickel.

Skin of one's teeth (descriptive phrase). To succeed, but just barely. A micromeasure less and one would not have succeeded.

Skyrocket (verb). To rise suddenly and rapidly. As a noun, it means the type of fireworks that shoot into the sky and explode suddenly in a shower of brilliant sparks.

Slow as molasses (descriptive phrase). Very slow. Molasses is a thick, sweet syrup made from sugar cane (known as "treacle" in the United Kingdom) that pours with agonizing slowness from its container.

Small potatoes (noun). An expression meaning insignificant or trivial.

Smoke screen (noun). Metaphorically, anything used intentionally to hide one's true intentions.

Smoking gun (noun). This term has come to stand for any indisputable evidence of guilt or misdeeds.

Snitch (verb). To engage in petty theft. (This verb has another meaning, which is to betray a person by divulging a secret about that person. If you do that, you are not only snitching, you are a snitch.)

Snowball (verb). To increase rapidly, like a ball of wet snow that grows and grows when it is rolled rapidly in more wet snow.

Soft drink (noun). Nonalcoholic beverage.

Sourpuss (noun). Dour; sulky; humourless. Derives from "sour," which is self-explanatory, and "puss," a slang word for "face."

Spending a penny (descriptive phrase). Spending any money at all. Do not confuse with usage in England, where the phrase means to go to the bathroom.

Squash (verb). To crush or ruin.

Squirrel away (verb). To hide or conceal in a handy but secret place (as a squirrel stores nuts).

Star Trek (proper name). Famous TV series about life in outer space.

Steady (noun). A person to whom you are romantically committed and with whom you spend a lot of time, especially in social activities.

Sticky (adjective). Resistant to change, as if glued on.

Strongarm (adjective). Repressive and violent.

Sucker (noun). A gullible person.

T

Tables were turned (descriptive phrase). The advantage of one side over the other reverses so that now the winner is the loser and the loser is the winner.

Tacky (adjective). In very poor taste.

Take the heat (verb). To accept all criticism of one's action or inaction, whether or not one is actually the person that should be blamed.

Take title (verb). Legal term meaning to acquire ownership.

Tea control (noun). A method of resolving differences by informal but powerful social mechanisms, such as inviting your opponents to tea and settling matters while passing teacups and plates of cake around.

Temp (noun). Worker whose job is temporary and who accepts the job with that understanding.

Time-and-a-half (noun). In labour law, 150 percent of the normal hourly wage.

Tombstone ad (noun). Newspaper advertisement announcing the completion of a stock or bond offering.

Ton (noun). A ton weighs 2,000 pounds and an English ton (often spelled "tonne") weighs 2,240 pounds. In this book the term is used most frequently to mean simply "a large quantity."

Tough (adjective). Very difficult.

Trendy (adjective). A phenomenon that is slightly ahead of traditional ways and indicates a trend. Something trendy may turn into something traditional, or it may fade away without ever becoming mainstream.

Truck (verb). To exchange one thing for another. This was Adam Smith's definition in 1776 and it is still one of the meanings of the verb.

Turf (noun). Territory, especially the figurative territory of a firm.

Turn of the century (expression). The few years at the end of an expiring century and the beginning of a new century. For example: 1998–2002.

Turn up one's nose (verb). To reject.

Twinkies (noun). Brand name of an inexpensive small cake.

U

Under-the-counter (adjective). Secret or concealed by an unscrupulous person. Also see "under the table" below.

Under the table (descriptive phrase). To accept money surreptitiously in order to avoid paying taxes on it or to conceal the income

for other reasons. Also, to proffer such money to avoid having it known that you are making a particular deal.

Union Jack (noun). Nickname for the British flag.

Up in arms (adjective). Furious and loudly protesting. Comes from the use of "arms" to stand for "firearms."

V

Vanity licence plate (descriptive phrase). One-of-a-kind motor vehicle licence plate issued to your individual specification. It might have your name, your profession, or any individual set of letters and numbers you choose that will fit on the plate.

Village watchman (descriptive phrase). Before modern communication technology, in small communities local news was gathered and reported by an official, the village watchman or town crier, who walked around collecting facts and gossip.

W

Wadget (noun). Term used by economists to stand for any manufactured good except goods designated as widgets, which see.

Wal-Mart (proper name). A very large store that sells thousands of inexpensive items. There are hundreds of Wal-Marts in the United States and Canada and the company is beginning to expand into foreign markets.

Wampum (noun). String of beads made of polished shells, formerly used by North American Indians as money.

Whatever (noun). Designates an unspecified generic item or action when the speaker wants to let you know that it doesn't matter whether you know the exact item or place.

Wheaties (proper noun). Name of a brand of dry breakfast cereal.

White knight (noun). A company that comes to the rescue of another company. The term comes from the game of chess—some chess sets have white pieces and black pieces—and from the children's book, *Alice Through the Looking Glass*, where the story is structured as a game of chess and a chess piece, the white knight, tries to rescue Alice.

Whiz (noun). An expert.

Whopper (proper noun). Brand name of a kind of hamburger sold at Burger King restaurants.

Widget (noun). The opposite of a wadget, which see.

Wild about (descriptive phrase). Extremely enthusiastic about undertaking a particular action or admiring a particular object or person.

Wind up (descriptive phrase). To discover that you have reached a particular conclusion or destination.

With-it (adjective). Current in one's knowledge.

Wodget (noun). A made-up term for a procuced good. Variation of "widget," which see.

Working off the books (descriptive phrase). Being paid wages or fees that are not reported to the tax or other authorities by either the payer or the payee.

Wound up (past tense of verb "wind up"). To have found oneself in a particular situation after having taken particular actions.

Writing on the wall (descriptive phrase). To see the writing on the wall is to realize that a situation is inevitably going to end badly. It comes from the Biblical story that Nebuchadnezzar, king of Babylon, saw a fatal predicition written on a wall.

Y

You bet! (exclamation). Expression meaning "It certainly is." or "Absolutely!"

PHOTO CREDITS

INDEX

A

activist policies, problems with, 272–277
AD curve. *See* aggregate demand (AD) curve
adaptive expectations, 362
aggregate demand (AD) curve
  defined, 215
  effect of shift factor, 219
  exchange rates, 217
  expectations, 217–218
  fiscal policies, 218–219
  foreign income, 217
  and income distribution, 218
  interest rate effect, 216
  international effect, 216
  monetary policies, 218–219
  multiplier effect, 216–217
  multiplier effects of shift factors, 219
  shifts, 217–219
  slope, 215–217
  wealth effect, 215–216
aggregate demand management
  defined, 262
  recessions, 261–262
aggregate economy
  beyond potential, 225–227
  equilibrium, 222–227
  inflationary gap, 225
  integration of frameworks, 223–227
  long-run equilibrium, 223
  policy examples, 227
  recessionary gap, 223–225
  short-run equilibrium, 222–223
aggregate expenditures (AE)
  autonomous expenditures, 237–239
  defined, 237
  expenditures function, 238–241
  induced expenditures, 237–239
  shifts, 247–249
aggregate expenditures (AE) curve, 240, 246, 249
aggregate income

curve, 237
  equilibrium level, 241–246
aggregate production (AP), 236–237
aggregate production curve, 237
aggregate supply/aggregate demand model. *See* AS/AD model
aggregate supply curve
  long-run. *See* long-run aggregate supply (LAS) curve
  short-run. *See* short-run aggregate supply (SAS) curve
Air Canada, 121
algebraic representations
  demand schedule shifts, 128–129
  equilibrium, 127
  equilibrium income, 242
  movements along supply and demand curves, 128
  multiplier model, expanded, 256–257
  price ceilings, 129
  price floors, 129
  quotas, 130
  subsidies, 129–130
  supply and demand, 127–129
  supply schedule shifts, 128–129
  taxes, 129–130
alternative measures of money, 311–314
annualized basis, 165
annuity rule, 79–80
approximate real-world money multiplier, 320
arbitrage, 347
Arkwright, Richard, 51
art of economics, 16
AS/AD model
  aggregate demand (AD) curve, 215–219
  aggregate economy, 222–227
  Canada in mid-1990s, 229
  curves, 214
  European Union in mid-1990s, 230
  fixed prices, 236
  formerly socialist countries in early 1990s, 230

historical model, 214
Japan in late 1990s, 229–230
long-run aggregate supply (LAS) curve, 221
macroeconomic policies, complicated nature of, 227–231
vs. microeconomic supply/demand model, 214
monetary policy, 339, 350–353
and multiplier model, 257–259
policy ranges, 228–229
potential output debates, 230–231
potential output estimation problems, 229
qualitative effects of aggregate demand shifts, 235
real-world examples of application, 229–230
recession, 263
review, 226–227
short-run aggregate supply (SAS) curve, 219–221
summary, 437–438
United States in mid-1990s, 230
asset management, 315
assets
  arbitrary nature in definition, 290–291
  capital market, 332
  financial. *See* financial assets
  money market, 331, 332
  real, 329
  relative to debt, 290–291
Astor, Nancy, 13
Austrian economists, 159–160
automatic stabilizer, 279
autonomous consumption policy, 270
autonomous expenditures, 237–239, 266

B

balance of goods and services, 384–385
balance of merchandise trade, 384
balance of payments
  balance of goods and services, 384–385
  balance of merchandise trade, 384
  capital and financial account, 383, 385–386

current account, 383, 384–385
defined, 383
equilibrium, 386–387
and exchange rate, 388
financial account, 383
official reserves, 383
balance of trade
Canada, 68, 70
defined, 68
merchandise trade balance, 69
services balance, 69
Bank Act, 328
Bank of Canada, 180, 310
see also monetary policy
Board of Directors, 341
cash management operations, 348–349
creation of, 344
credibility of resolve, 376–377
described, 308–309
duties, 345
government deposits, 349
governors, 340
increase of reserve assets, 386
international considerations, 342–345
open market operations, 348, 349
overnight financing rate, 346–348
political pressure, 355
structure, 340–345
vault cash, 346
Bank of England, 342
Bank of Japan, 342, 354
bank rate, 347
banks
asset management, 315
clearing, 321
contractual intermediary, 327, 329
defined, 308–309
demand deposits, 318
deposit insurance, 322–323
depository institution, 327–329
desired reserve ratio, 317
financial panics, 321–322
gold receipts, 316
goldsmiths, 316
government guarantees, 323–324
history, 316–317, 344
liability management, 315
and money creation, 314–321
money multiplier, 317–320
profitable nature, 317
reforms, 321
regulation, 321–324
reserves, 317
steps in money creation, 315–316
bar graph, 24
barter, 309
basis points, 349
Becker, Gary, 99
Bell, Alexander Graham, 204
benefits of growth, 137–138, 189
Bennett, R.B., 143
bias
discounting, 152
GDP, 168

new product, 152
quality improvement, 152
substitution, 152
Blinder, Alan, 224
Boettke, Peter, 160
bonds
defined, 307, 326, 330
described, 332
indexed, and inflation, 299
interest payments, 307
municipal, 332
provincial, 332
short-term Canada, 332
valuation, 78–81
zero-coupon bonds, 333
borrowing cycle, 202–203
Bouey, Gerald, 340
Bowles, Samuel, 161
Braudel, Fernand, 70
Bretton Woods system, 414–415
Bryce, R.B., 236
budget
deficit. *See* deficit
surplus. *See* surplus
surplus function, 300
Bundesbank, 342
business
in Canadian economy, 57–61
consumer sovereignty, 57
corporations, 58–59
defined, 57
digital economy, 60–61
e-commerce, 60–61
entrepreneurship, 57
and finance, 59–60
forms of, 58–59
partnerships, 58
profit, 57
sole proprietorships, 58
business cycle
boom, 139
contractions, 138
defined, 138
depression, 140
downturn, 139–140
economic debate, 138
expansions, 138, 140
leading indicators, 141
peak, 139
phases, 138–140
real-business-cycle economists, 230
reasons for occurrence, 140–141
recession, 140
recovery phase, 297

C

Canada Pension Plan, 123
Canada treasury bills, 332
Canada-U.S. Free Trade Agreement (FTA), 406–408
Canadian Airlines, 121
Canadian banking system, 344
Canadian Commercial Bank, 323

Canadian Deposit Insurance Corporation, 322–323
Canadian dollar, value of, 394
Canadian economy
business, 57–61
diagram, 56
global corporations, 66
in global setting, 65–71
government, 62–65
households, 61–62
invisible hand, 57
postindustrial economy, 58
trading partners, 68–69
Canadian Payments Association, 321, 347
Canadian Unemployment Assistance Act, 15
Canadian Venture Exchange, 331
capital
accumulation, and growth, 192–193
controls, 391
diminishing marginal productivity, 197–198
human, 193
physical, 192
social, 193
capital and financial account, 383, 385–386
capital consumption allowance, 171, 172
capital market assets, 332
capital markets, 331
capitalism
blending with socialism, 49
concept of, 52
defined, 28
evolution to, 50–51
laissez-faire policy, 51
price fluctuations, 29
private property rights, 28
use of term, 196
welfare, 48, 52–53
capitalists, 50–51
Carlyle, Thomas, 95
cash management operations, 348–349
central bank
see also Bank of Canada
defined, 340
in other countries, 342
central economic planning. *See* Soviet-style socialism
Central Guaranty Trust Company, 323
chartered banks, 313, 344
Chrétien, Jean, 235
Churchill, Winston, 13
circular flow
expenditures, 245
expenditures approach, 169
gross domestic product (GDP), 169
input, 169
model, 245–246
monetary policy, 351, 352
multiplier model, 245–246
output, 169
savings that escapes, 308
Clark, W. Clifford, 236
Clarke, J.M., 160
Clarke, Peter, 262
Classical economics

aggregate economy, 212
 Classical range, 228–229
 defined, 138
 development to Keynesian economics, 212
 inflation, 443
 and Keynesian economics, blended, 280
 laissez-faire policy prescription, 212
 policy views, 442, 443
 quantity theory of money and inflation, 367
 recessionary unemployment, 443
 slow growth, 443
 stock market, 329
 unemployment, 144, 147
classical growth model
 defined, 196
 diminishing marginal productivity of capital, 197–198
 diminishing marginal productivity of labour, 196–197
 empirical estimates of factor contribution to growth, 199
 factors of production, ambiguities in definition, 198–199
 failure of, 198–199
 summary, 436
 technology, 199
clearing, 321
closing, 333
commercial paper, 330, 332
Commons, John R., 160
comparative advantage
 defined, 34
 division of labour, 41–42
 explanation of, 39–40
competition, government role in, 120–121
composition, fallacy of, 118–119
compounding, 155n, 189
constant returns to scale, 195–196
consumer price index (CPI)
 composition of, 153
 defined, 153
consumer sovereignty, 57, 61
consumer surplus, 97–98
consumption
 autonomous consumption policy, 270
 expenditures approach, 169
 personal consumption expenditures, 169
contractionary fiscal policies
 crowding out, 274
 defined, 260
 euro supply, 420
 recession-fighting, 264
 and trade deficit, 269n
contractionary monetary policy, 349, 350, 351, 419–420
contractions, 138
contractual intermediary, 327, 329
coordinate system, 21
coordination failure, 224
coordination problems
 coercion and, 5
 in economics, 5, 27
 immensity of, 28
Cornwall, John, 160

corporations, 58–59, 205–206
cost-based pricing rules, 224
cost-push inflation, 363
costs
 factor, 171n
 of growth, 137–138
 inflation, 155–156
 marginal, 6
 menu, 224
 opportunity, 8–9
 see also opportunity cost
 sunk, 6
countercyclical fiscal policy, 266
covered interest parity, 389
Coyne, James, 340
"Coyne Affair," 340
credit, vs. money, 313–314
creditor nations, 69
Crow, John, 340, 341
crowding out
 contractionary fiscal policies, 274
 expansionary fiscal policies, 273
 fiscal policy, 272–274
 government expenditures, 298
 interest rate, 272–274
 international considerations, 427–428
 investment, 297
 surplus, 297–299
cultural forces, 9, 31
currency stabilization, 392
currency support, 392
current account, 383, 384–385
current account balance, 69
customs duties. See tariffs
cyclical deficit, 289
cyclical unemployment, 142

D

David, Paul, 201
Davidson, Paul, 160
debt
 arbitrary nature in definition, 291
 burden, 292–293, 294–295
 debt-to-GDP ratio, 303–304
 defined, 289
 external, 292
 federal, 297
 important points, 296
 individual vs. government, 291–292
 internal, 292
 management, 290–291
 municipal, 297
 provincial, 297
 relative to assets, 290–291
 service, 294
 as summary measure, 290
debt-to-GDP ratio, 303–304
debtor nations, 69
decision tree, 38
decreasing returns to scale, 196
deficit
 accounting and, 287
 arbitrary nature of definition, 286–287
 cyclical, 289

debt, defined, 289
debt burden, 292–293, 294–295
debt service, 294
 defined, 286
 external debt, 292
 federal, 297
 financing, 272–274, 286
 fiscal policy stance, measurement of, 299–300
 historical record, 292–296
 important points, 296
 and inflation, 287
 internal debt, 292
 municipal, 297
 nominal, 287–288
 passive, 289
 provincial, 297
 real, 287–288
 relative to GDP, 293
 relative to other countries, 293–294
 size of, 276
 structural, 289
 as summary measure, 287
 trade. See trade deficit
demand
 curve. See demand curve
 defined, 85
 excess, 95
 and expectations, 85
 individual, 88
 law of demand, 83
 "other things constant," 84
 and population, 86
 price adjustments, 95–96
 price changes, effect of, 86
 prices of other goods, 85
 quantity demanded, 85
 schedule shifts, 128–129
 shift factors, 85–86
 shifts in, 84–85, 105
 vs. supply, 89–90
 supply, relation to. See supply and demand
 table, 87
 tastes, 85
demand curve
 defined, 84
 from demand table, 87–88
 important considerations, 89
 individual, 88–89
 market, 88
 movements along, 84–85, 128
 sample, 84
demand deposits, 318
demand-pull inflation, 363
demerit goods or activities, 123
Denison, Edward, 199
deposit insurance, 322–323
depository institution, 327–329
depreciation, 169–170, 171
depression, 140
desired reserve ratio, 317
developing countries, and patents, 205
digital economy, 60–61
diminishing marginal productivity
 of capital, 197–198

of labour, 196–197
law of, 196
direct relationship, 21
directed investment policies, 267–268
discounting bias, 152
disintermediation, 332
distribution
and growth, 190–191
and markets, 190–191
and productive efficiency, 37
distributional effects of inflation, 361
diversification, 329
division of labour
comparative advantage, 41–42
defined, 190
and growth, 190
Dodge, David, 340, 402
Domar, Evsey, 262
domestic goals
international coordination of policies,
426–428
vs. international goals, 418–419
domestic trade, *vs.* international trade, 71–73
Dow Jones Industrial Average, 60
downward-sloping curves, 21

E

e-commerce, 60–61
econometric models, 235
economic decision rule, 6
economic fluctuations, decrease in, 280
economic forces, 8–11
economic geography, 67
economic insights
economic model, 11
economic principle, 11–12
economic theory, 13
invisible hand theory, 12
economic institutions, 14–15
economic model
defined, 11
graphs in, 21
interpolation assumption, 21
economic policies, 15
see also macroeconomic policies
economic principle, 11–12
economic reasoning
cost premise, 8
defined, 6
economic decision rule, 6
economic forces, 8–11
marginal benefits, 6–7
marginal costs, 6–7
market forces, 8–11
opportunity cost, 8–9
passion, 7–8
economic systems
capitalism, 28–29, 50–51
coordination, need for, 48
evolution, 47–49
feudalism, 47, 49–50
history of, 47–54
Industrial Revolution, 47
laissez-faire policy, 51

market-modified socialist economies, 48
mercantilism, 47, 50
and production possibility curve, 38–39
socialism, 29–30, 53
Soviet-style socialism, 53
state socialism, 53
welfare capitalism, 48, 52–53
economic terminology, 11
economic theory
inflation theories, 362–371
institutional theory of inflation, 368–371
Keynesian theory, 262
macroeconomics, 14
microeconomics, 13–14
quantity theory of money and inflation,
362–368
real-business-cycle theory, 231, 252
and stories, 13
economics
art of, 16
coordination problems, 5
defined, 5
history, 10
nonmainstream approaches, 159–161
normative, 16
and passion, 7–8
positive, 16
education policies, 204
efficiency
defined, 12, 36
and distribution, 37
productive, 35–36, 37
and technological change, 36
embargo, 404
employment
full, 144
full-employment level of income, 274
rate, 148
entrepreneurship
defined, 57
and growth, 195
equality of income and expenditure, 173, 174
equation of exchange, 363
equilibrium
in aggregate economy, 222–227
aggregate income, 241–246
algebraic representations, 127
balance of payments, 386–387
consumer surplus, 97–98
defined, 97
determination of, 127
income, 213, 242
long-run, 223
price, 97
producer surplus, 98
quantity, 97
short-run, 222–223
supply/demand, 97–99
equity capital, 59
Estey Commission, 323
euro, 387, 399, 419–420
European Central Bank, 342, 368, 419
European Union, 73, 206, 230
excess demand, 95

excess supply, 95
exchange rate
and *AD* curve, 217
and balance of payments, 388
Bretton Woods system, 414–415
capital controls, 391
complicated nature of determination, 390
country's income, changes in, 388
country's prices, changes in, 388
covered interest parity, 389
defined, 72, 342–343, 387
direct exchange rate intervention, 392–393
fiscal policy, effect of, 424–425
fixed, 395–397
fixed exchange rate system, 392–395
flexible, 396, 397–398
fundamental forces in determination, 388–390
goal of macroeconomic policy, 417
gold standard, 413–414
history of exchange rate systems, 413–415
importance of, 344
income, effect of, 421, 424
interest rate changes, 389, 420, 424
international trade problems, 391
intervention, 392
long-run equilibrium, 393–395
monetary policy, effect of, 420–422
monetary union in North America, 398–402
nonconvertible currency, 391
partially flexible, 396, 398, 420–426
policy, 269
price levels, effect of, 421, 424
set by law, 391
trade balance, effect on, 423
trade policy adjustments, 402–406
uncovered interest parity, 389
excise taxes, effect of, 116
expansionary fiscal policies
crowding out, 273
defined, 260
recession-fighting, 262–264
and trade deficit, 269n
war finance, 271
expansionary monetary policy, 349, 350, 351
expansions, 138, 140
expectations
and *AD* curve, 217–218
adaptive, 362
and demand, 85
directed investment policies, 267–268
extrapolative, 362
and financial panics, 322
forward-looking, and multiplier model, 252
inflation, 154–155, 361–362, 372–374, 375
policy regime, 447
rational expectations, 362
rational expectations model, 252
and supply, 92
expected inflation, 154–155
expenditures
aggregate, 237–241
autonomous, 237–239, 266
circular flow model, 245
equality of income and expenditure, 173, 174

induced, 237–239
more than current income, 252–253
shifts in, and supply and demand shifts, 252
expenditures approach
circular flow, 169
consumption, 169
government expenditures, 170
gross domestic product (GDP), 170–171
investment, 169–170
net domestic product, 170–171
net exports, 170
personal consumption expenditures, 169
expenditures function
aggregate expenditures (AE) curve, 240
defined, 238–239
graphs, 239–240
shifts, 240–241
export-led growth policies, 268–269
exports
defined, 68
net, 170
external debt, 292
externalities
defined, 121
government role in correction for, 121
macroeconomic, 122
negative, 121
positive, 121, 200
extrapolative expectations, 362

F

factor cost, 171n
factor incomes approach
capital consumption allowance, 172
factor payments, 171
farm income, 172
interest, 172
inventory valuation adjustment, 172
nonincorporated nonfarm income, 172
profit before taxes, 171
salaries, 171
supplementary labour income, 171
taxes less subsidies, 172
wages, 171
factor market, 56
factor payments, 171
factors of production, 198–199
fair trade, 409
fallacy of composition, 118–119
farm income, 172
Federal Employment and Social Insurance Act, 143
federal government
in Canada, 63–64
income and expenditures (2001), 64
federal interest payments relative to GDP, 295
Federal Reserve Bank, 342, 344, 354
Federal Unemployment Insurance Act, 143
feudalism, 47, 49–50
final output, 165
finance, and business, 59–60
finance companies, 329–330
financial account, 383
financial assets

bonds, 333
Canada treasury bills, 332
capital market assets, 332
commercial paper, 332
creation of, 315
defined, 307, 326
money, 308
money market assets, 331, 332
municipal bonds, 332
provincial bonds, 332
and rich society, 329
short-term Canada bonds, 332
stock, 326, 332
types of, 331–333
financial guarantees policy, 267–270
financial innovation, 315
financial institutions
contractual intermediary, 327, 329
defined, 327
depository institution, 327–329
depository institutions, 327
development of, and risk limitation, 205–206
finance companies, 329–330
holdings of selected financial institutions, 328
investment dealers, 330
investment intermediaries, 329–330
mutual funds, 329
and policy, 440
types of, 327
financial liabilities
bonds, 326–327
defined, 326
financial markets
capital markets, 331
described, 59–60
liquidity, 331
money markets, 331
primary, 330
secondary, 331
financial panics, 321–322
financial sector
as conduit for savings, 307
defined, 305
deposit insurance, 322–323
financial panics, 321–322
government guarantees, 323–324
importance in macroeconomics, 306–308
interest rate, role of, 307–308
necessity of, 306
regulation, 321–324
fine tuning, 266
fiscal policy
and AD curve, 218–219
alternatives, 266–270
automatic stabilizer, 279
built-in, 279
contractionary, 260, 264, 420
countercyclical, 266
crowding out, 272–274
deficit as measurement of stance, 299–300
deficit financing, and offsetting effects, 272–274
defined, 260
effect on other government goals, 276

effects, 440–441
exchange rate, effect on, 424–425
expansionary, 260, 262–264
fine tuning, 266
fixed exchange rate, 419–420
flexible price level, 277–278
government debt size, 276
government flexibility in changing taxes and spending, 275–276
inflation fighting, 265
into institutions, 279
international coordination, 426–428
international goals, effect on, 427
potential income level, 274–275
problems with, 272–277
questionable effectiveness, 264–266
recent, 271
in recession, 261–266
in Second World War, 270
summary of problems, 277
taxes as tool, 266
and trade deficit, 269n, 425–426
and trade surplus, 269n
and true situation, 274
fixed exchange rate
contractionary monetary policy, 419–420
defined, 395–396
fiscal policy, 419–420
"lazy firm" hypothesis, 400
monetary policy, 419–420
and monetary stability, 396
monetary union in North America, 399–400
and policy independence, 396–397
vs. price controls, 435
fixed exchange rate system
advantages, 396
Bretton Woods system, 414–415
currency stabilization, 392
currency support, 392
direct exchange rate intervention, 392–393
disadvantages, 396
fixing the exchange rate, 392
gold standard, 413–414
how it works, 392–395
long-run equilibrium exchange rates, 393–395
purchasing power parity (PPP), 393–395
strategic currency stabilization, 393
viability of option, 393
fixed output, and multiplier model, 251
flexible exchange rate, 396
advantages, 397
defined, 396
disadvantages, 397
monetary policy, 420–424
and monetary stability, 397
and policy independence, 397–398
foreign exchange markets, 72
foreign income, and AD curve, 217
free market in money, 160
free rider, 122
free trade
agreements. See international trade agreements
associations, 73

defined, 405
    international economic policy organizations, 74
    organizations, 73
Free Trade Areas of the Americas, 408–409
frictional unemployment, 143
Friedman, Milton, 16n, 367
full employment, 144
full-employment level of income, 274

G

gains from trade, 41
Galbraith, John Kenneth, 315
GDP deflator, 153, 177n
General Agreement on Tariffs and Trade (GATT), 73, 403
General Theory of Employment, Interest and Money (Keynes), 212, 262, 268
genuine progress indicator, 180–181
Gintis, Herbert, 161
global corporations, 66
global trade. *See* international trade
gold receipts, 316
gold specie flow mechanism, 413
gold standard, 413–414
goldsmiths, 316
goods
    demerit, 123
    market, 56
    merit, 123
    private, 122
    public, 122
government
    in Canadian economy, 62–65
    competition, promotion of, 120–121
    debt. *See* deficit
    deficit. *See* deficit
    deposits, 349
    economic stability and growth, 122
    externalities, correction for, 121
    failures, 123
    federal, 63–64
    guarantees, 323–324
    indexed bonds issue, 299
    institutions, 144
    local, 63
    macroeconomic externalities, 122
    and market failures, 123
    markets, undesired results, 122–123
    provincial, 63
    and public goods, 122
    as referee, 64–65
    roles of, 119–123
    stable institutional framework, 120
    "three letters," 345
    transfer payments, 63–64
    and unemployment, 143
government expenditures
    crowding out, 298
    defined, 170
    flexibility in changes, 275–276
government interventions
    excise taxes, 116
    minimum wage laws, 114–115

price ceilings, 111–113
price floors, 114–115
quotas, 117–118
rent control, 111–113
tariffs, 116
Grameen Bank, 203
graphs
    bar graph, 24
    coordinate system, 21
    defined, 20
    direct relationship, 21
    downward-sloping curves, 21
    in economic modelling, 21
    expenditures function, 239–240
    interpolation assumption, 21
    interpretation, 25
    inverse relationship, 21
    line graph, 24
    linear curve, 21
    maximum point, 23
    minimum point, 23
    nonlinear curve, 21
    number line, 20
    pie chart, 24
    real-world data presentation, 24
    slope, 21–23
    supply and demand, 96–97
    upward-sloping curves, 21
    ways to use graphs, 20–21
Great Depression, 48, 141, 143, 211, 344
grey market, 10n
gross domestic product (GDP)
    annualized basis, 165
    bias against women, 168
    calculation methods, 168–175
    calculation of, 164–167
    circular flow, 169
    comparisons among countries, 175–176
    debt-to-GDP ratio, 303–304
    deficit relative to GDP, 293
    defined, 163
    economic welfare over time, 176
    examples of calculations, 167
    expenditures approach, 168–171
    factor incomes approach, 171–172
    federal interest payments relative to GDP, 295
    final output measurement, 165
    as flow concept, 164–165
    GDP deflator, 153, 177n
    vs. gross national product (GNP), 164
    intermediate products, 165–166
    national income accounting identity, 168
    nominal GDP. *See* nominal GDP
    per capita GDP, 175
    purchasing power parity (PPP), 176
    real. *See* real GDP
    use of GDP figures, 175–177
gross national product (GNP)
    defined, 163
    vs. gross domestic product (GDP), 164
gross private investment, 169
Group of Eight, 74
Group of Five, 74
growth, 42

available resources, 193
    benefits of, 137–138, 189
    capital accumulation, 192–193
    classical growth model, 436
    compounding, 189
    cost of goods in hours of work, 191
    costs of, 137–138
    and distribution, 190–191
    empirical estimates of factor contribution to growth, 199
    and entrepreneurship, 195
    export-led growth policies, 268–269
    general observations, 188–192
    global experiences, 136–137
    growth-compatible institutions, 194
    history of, 135–136
    human capital, 193
    and inflation, 376–378
    and living standards, 188–190
    long-run growth model, 436
    and markets, 190–191
    per capita growth, 191–192
    see also per capita growth
    per capita growth rate, 136
    per capita real output, 136
    physical capital, 192
    potential output, 188
    production function, 195–196
    real GDP changes as measurement, 135
    Rule of 72, 189–190
    secular trend growth rate, 136
    slow, 443
    social capital, 193
    sources, 192–195
    and specialization, 190
    technological development, 194–195
    theories of. *See* growth theories
    through foreign investment, 203
growth theories
    classical growth model, 196–199
    new growth theory, 199–202

H

happiness index, 178
Hargreaves, James, 51
heterodox economics, 159–161
house purchase, 333
households
    in Canadian economy, 61–62
    consumer sovereignty, 61
    defined, 61
    labour supply, 62
    power of, 61
human capital, 193
hyperinflation, 155–156, 310

I

illegal activity, 180
implicit contracts, 224
import-led decline, 269
imports
    defined, 68
    tariffs, impact of, 403
incentives, 13

income
  equality of income and expenditure, 173, 174
  equilibrium, 213, 242
  exchange rate, effect on, 421, 424
  farm, 172
  foreign, 217
  full-employment level, 274
  interest, 172
  multiplier equation, 242–243
  national, 171
  net foreign factor, 163
  nonincorporated nonfarm, 172
  permanent income hypothesis, 253
  personal, 173–174
  personal disposable, 174
  potential, 213, 274–275
  supplementary labour, 171
  trade balance, effect on, 422
  trade deficit, effect on, 425
income distribution, and *AD* curve, 218
incomes policy, 371
increasing returns to scale, 196
indexed bonds, and inflation, 299
indicative planning, 160
induced expenditures, 237–239
Industrial Revolution, 47, 51, 142
inefficiency, 36
inertia, 31
inflation
  adaptive expectations, 362
  basics, 361–362
  in Canada since 1915, 151
  Classical view, 443
  consumer price index (CPI), 153
  cost-push, 363
  costs, 155–156
  and deficit value, 287
  defined, 149
  demand-pull, 363
  distributional effects, 361
  expectations, 361–362, 372–374, 375
  expected, 154–155
  extrapolative expectations, 362
  fighting, 371
  fiscal policies, 265
  GDP deflator, 153
  and growth, 376–378
  hyperinflation, 155–156, 310
  and indexed bonds, 299
  insider/outsider model, 370–371
  institutional theory, 368–371
  Keynesian view, 443
  measurement, 150–153
  money's role in, 364–365
  new economy, 376
  nominal output, 154
  Phillips curve, 371–376
  price index, 150–153
  and productivity, 362
  quantity theory of money and inflation,
    362–368
  rational expectations, 362
  raw materials price index, 152
  real output, 154

stagflation, 372, 375
  tax, 365–367
  theories, 362–371
  and unemployment, 371–376
  unexpected, 154–155
inflationary gap, 225, 278
initial public offerings, 59
input
  circular flow, 169
  defined, 31
  price of, 91
insider/outsider model, 370–371
institutional theory of inflation
  inflation/growth trade-off, 377–378
  insider/outsider model, 370–371
  labour market, 369
  money supply, 369–370
  policy implications, 371
  price-setting process of firms, 369
  vs. quantity theory, 368
  source of inflation, 369
institutionalist economists, 160
institutions, and policies, 439–441
insurance for car, 333
interdependencies in global economy, 269
interest
  factor incomes approach, 172
  income, 172
interest rate
  changes in basis points, 349
  covered interest parity, 389
  crowding out, 272–274
  and debt burden, 294–295
  defined, 307
  effect, 216
  and exchange rate, 389, 420, 424
  financial sector, role in, 307–308
  real, 352–353
  relationships among interest rates, 348
  term structure, 347
  uncovered interest parity, 389
intermediate products, 165–166
international coordination of policies, 426–428
international currency, 415
international economic policy organizations, 74
international effect, 216
international institutions, and policy, 441
International Monetary Fund (IMF), 74, 176,
    414, 415
international perspective
  and Bank of Canada governors, 342–345
  crowding out, 427–428
  growth, 136–137
international trade
  Canada's trading partners, 68–69
  and Canadian economy, 65–71
  creditor nations, 69
  current account balance, 69
  debtor nations, 69
  differences in importance of trade, 68
  vs. domestic trade, 71–73
  fluctuations, 66–68
  foreign exchange markets, 72
  global corporations, 66

interdependencies in global economy, 269
  and monetary policies, 344
  shifts in currency values, problems from, 391
  trade barriers, 71
  trading blocs, 71
international trade agreements
  Canada-U.S. Free Trade Agreement (FTA),
    406–408
  Free Trade Areas of the Americas, 408–409
  North American Free Trade Agreement
    (NAFTA), 408
Internet, overvaluation of stocks, 60–61
interpolation assumption, 21
inventory valuation adjustment, 172
inverse relationship, 21
investment
  autonomous, 245
  crowding out, 297
  dealers, 330
  directed investment policies, 267–268
  diversification, 329
  encouragement, through economic policy,
    202–203
  expenditures approach, 169–170
  flow, 192
  foreign, 203
  gross private investment, 169
  growth source, 192–193
  intermediaries, 329–330
  mutual funds, 315
  net private investment, 169
invisible hand, 9, 57, 370
invisible hand theory, 12

K

Kay, James, 51
Keynes, John Maynard, 212, 213, 236, 262, 268
Keynes, John Neville, 16*n*
Keynesian economics
  and Classical economics, blended, 280
  from Classical economics, 212
  defined, 138
  essence of, 213
  fiscal policy approach, 297
  inflation, 443
  national income accounting, 163
  paradox of thrift, 214
  policy views, 442–443
  recessionary unemployment, 443
  slow growth, 443
  stock market, 329
  unemployment, 144, 147
Keynesian theory, 262
Kuznets, Simon, 163

L

labour
  ambiguities in definition, 198–199
  diminishing marginal productivity, 196–197
labour force
  defined, 146
  participation rate, 147–148
labour market, and price-setting strategies, 369
labour supply, and households, 62

laissez-faire policy, 51, 120, 133n, 212
Large Value Transfer System (LVTS), 346
LAS curve. See long-run aggregate supply (LAS) curve
law of demand, 83
law of diminishing marginal productivity, 196
law of supply, 90
"lazy firm" hypothesis, 400
leading indicators, 141
learning by doing
    defined, 200
    new growth theory, 200–201
legal forces, 9
Lerner, Abba, 262
liability management, 315
libertarians, 159–160
limited liability, 59
line graph, 24
linear curve
    defined, 21
    slope, 21–22
Lipsey, Richard, 16n
liquidity, 331
living standards, and growth, 188–190
local government, 63
long-run aggregate supply (LAS) curve
    defined, 221
    vertical, 221
long-run equilibrium exchange rate, 393–395
long-run framework
    business cycles, 138–141
    growth issues, 135–138
    see also growth
    integration with short-run framework, 223–227
    vs. short-run framework, 135
    supply, 135
long-run growth model, 436
long-run Phillips curve, 372–375
Long-Term Capital Management, 268

M
M₁, 311–312
M₂, 312
M₂ "pluses," 312–313
MacKintosh, W.A., 236
MacMillan Commission, 344
macro models, 433, 435–439
macroeconomic externalities, 122
macroeconomic policies
    activist policies, problems with, 272–277
    art of economics, 16
    autonomous consumption policy, 270
    Classical economic view, 442, 443
    Classical range, 228–229
    complicated nature of, 227–231
    dilemmas, 445
    directed investment policies, 267–268
    education, 204
    encouragement of growth, 202–206
    exchange rate goal, 417
    exchange rate policy, 269
    export-led growth policies, 268–269
    financial guarantees policy, 267–270

and financial institutions, 440
and financial panics, 322
fiscal policies. See fiscal policy
incomes policy, 371
and institutions, 439–441
international goals, 417–419
international institutions, 441
international vs. domestic goals, 418–419
investment, encouragement of, 202–203
Keynesian economic view, 442–443
Keynesian range, 228
macroeconomic. See macroeconomic policies
monetary policies. See monetary policy
normative economics, 16
objective analysis, 16–17
options, 15–17
policy ranges, 228–229
policy regime, 447
political forces, 17
population growth control, 203
positive economics, 16
potential output estimation problems, 229
process and credibility, 445–446
research funding policies, 206
rosy scenario policy, 267
savings, encouragement of, 202–203
short-run tools, 444
social forces, 17
technological change, 204–206
trade balance goal, 417–418
trade-off view, 444
trade openness, 206
trade policy, 268–270, 402–406
uncertainty about policy effects, 446
worldviews, 441–442
macroeconomics
    defined, 14
    financial sector, importance of, 306–308
    historical development, 211–214
    paradox of thrift, 214
mad money, 285n
mainstream economists, 159
Malthus, Thomas, 10
marginal benefit, 6
marginal cost, 6
marginal opportunity cost, 33–35
marginal productivity
    diminishing marginal productivity of capital, 197–198
    diminishing marginal productivity of labour, 196–197
    law of diminishing marginal productivity, 196
marginal propensity to save (mps), 245
market basket comparison, 151
market demand curve, 88
market economic system. See capitalism
market failures, 123
market forces, 8–11
market supply curve, 93, 94
markets
    capital, 331
    and distribution, 190–191
    division of labour, 42
    financial, 59–60, 330–331

and financial sector, 306
foreign exchange, 72
and growth, 190–191
how they work, 28–29
money, 331
price-adjusting, 220
private property rights, 28
quantity-adjusting, 220
reliance on, 28–29
rise of markets, 32
role in economic decisions, 31
rules to clear markets, 224
specialization, 42, 190
structure of, 29
undesired results, 122–123
Marshall, Alfred, 10, 363
Marx, Karl, 10, 52, 53
math anxiety, 14
Mayhew, Anne, 160
measurement
    genuine progress indicator, 180–181
    inflation, 150–153
    national income accounting errors, 179
    necessity of, 180–181
    problems with consumer price index, 150–153
    summary measures of budget, 287
    total economic output, 163–164
    unemployment. See unemployment rate
the media, and present value, 80
medium of exchange, 309–310
menu costs, 224
mercantilism, 47, 50
merchandise trade balance, 69
merit goods or activities, 123
micro models, 433–435
microeconomics, 13–14
middle class tax breaks, 276
Mill, John Stuart, 10
minimum wage laws, 114–115
models
    AS/AD model, 437–438
    classical growth model, 436
    macro, 433, 435–439
    micro, 433–435
    multiplier model, 438–439
    production possibility model, 433–434
    quantity theory model, 436–437
    supply and demand, 434–436
monetarism, 367
monetary base, 346
monetary policy
    and AD curve, 218–219
    AS/AD model, 339, 350–353
    cash management operations, 348–349
    choice of policy, 353–354
    in circular flow, 351, 352
    conduct of, 346
    conduct problems, 353–355
    conflicting international goals, 355
    contractionary, 349, 350, 351, 419–420
    defined, 338, 340
    effect of, 358–359
    exchange rate, effect on, 420–422
    expansionary, 339, 349, 350, 351

fixed exchange rate, 419–420
flexible exchange rate, 420–424
government deposits, 349
importance, 345
interest rate, emphasis on, 352
international coordination, 426–428
international goals, effect on, 427
international trade and, 344
lags, 354–355
loss of control over, 402
open market operations, 348, 349
overnight financing rate, 346–348
political pressure, 355
real interest rate, 353
T-accounts, 358–359
tools, 346–349
trade balance, effect on, 422–424
understanding, 354
monetary regime, 353
monetary union in North America
adoption of U.S. dollar, 401
fixed exchange rate, 399–400
loss of control over monetary policy, 402
new currency, 400–401
possible options, 399–402
money
alternative measures, 311–314, 314
Bank of Canada, 308–309
creation of, 314–321
vs. credit, 313–314
defined, 308–309
functions of, 309–311
from gold receipts, 316–317
good, characteristics of, 312
inflation, role in, 364–365
M₁, 311–312
M₂, 312
M₂ "pluses," 312–313
medium of exchange, 309–310
and price level in Canada, 1953-2001, 365
and price level relative to real income, Brazil
and Chile, 366
quantity theory of money and inflation,
362–368
as store of wealth, 311
supply, and faith, 320–321
supply, and price-setting by firms, 369–370
T-accounts, 335–337
unit of account, 310–311
velocity of, 363
money market assets, 331, 332
money markets, 331
money multiplier
approximate real-world money multiplier, 320
calculation, 318
influences on, 354
money creation example, 318–320
real-world, calculation of, 320
and recent banking reforms, 321
simple, 318
monopoly, power of, 120
mortgage, 333
movement along a demand curve, 85, 128
movement along a supply curve, 91, 92–93, 128

multiplier, 242–243
multiplier effect
AD curve, 216–217
defined, 216
of shift factors, 219
multiplier equation, 242–243
multiplier model
in action, 246–249
aggregate expenditures (AE), 237–241
aggregate expenditures (AE) curve, 240
aggregate production (AP), 236–237
algebraic presentation of expanded model,
256–257
and AS/AD model, 257–259
assumptions, 235
autonomous expenditures, 237–239
Canada in 2000, 248–249
circular flow model, 245–246
depression in 1930s, 249
equilibrium level of aggregate income,
241–246
expenditures function, 238–241
fixed output, 251
flexible price level, 251
forward-looking expectations, 252
history of, 236
induced expenditures, 237–239
Japan in 1990s, 249
limitations, 249–253
multiplier, 242–243
multiplier equation, 242–243
multiplier process, 243–244
not complete economic model, 250
paradox of thrift, 249
and permanent income hypothesis, 253
price level changes, 250
quantitative effects of aggregate demand
shifts, 235
recession, 263
shifts in aggregate expenditures (AE),
247–249
shifts not as great as suggested, 250
steps of multiplier process, 247
summary, 438–439
supply and demand shifts, 252
multiplier process, 243–244, 247
Mundell, Robert, 400
municipal bonds, 332
mutual funds, 315, 329

N

National Association of Security Dealers
Automated Quotations (NASDAQ), 331
national balance sheet, 165
national income, 171
national income accounting
defined, 163
gross domestic product (GDP). See gross
domestic product (GDP)
identity, 168
income attribution, 173–174
limitations, 177–181
market activity measurement, 178–179
measurement errors, 179

measurement of total economic output,
163–164
misinterpretation of subcategories, 179–180
review of approaches, 175
welfare, nonmeasurement of, 178–179
nationalistic appeals, 404–405
net domestic product, 170–171
net exports, 170
net foreign factor income, 163
net private investment, 169
new economic era
economists' views, 447–448
explanations, 448–449
potential problem area, 449–450
new growth theory
defined, 199
learning by doing, 200–201
technological lock-in, 201–202
new product bias, 152
New York Stock Exchange, 331
NIMBY attitude, 28
nominal deficit, 287–288
nominal GDP
calculation, 185
defined, 176
vs. real GDP, 176–177
nominal output, 154
nonaccelerating inflation rate of unemployment
(NAIRU), 144
nonconvertible currency, 391
nonincorporated nonfarm income, 172
nonlinear curve
defined, 21
maximum point, 23
minimum point, 23
slope, 23
nonmainstream economic approaches
Austrian economists, 159–160
institutionalist economists, 160
post-Keynesian macroeconomists, 160
radical economists, 160–161
nontariff barriers, 71
normative economics, 16
North American Free Trade Agreement
(NAFTA), 73, 206, 408
Northland Bank, 323
number line, 20

O

objective analysis, 16–17
OECD, 176
official reserves, 383
Okun's rule of thumb, 149, 274
"Old Lady of Threadneedle Street," 342
oligopolistic markets, 224
Ontario Rental Housing Tribunal Web site, 113
open market operations, 348, 349
opportunity cost
and comparative advantage, 39
defined, 8
increase in, 35
marginal, 33–35
principle of increasing marginal opportunity
cost, 35

production possibility curve, 30, 33
    relevance, 8–9
"other things constant," 84, 118–119
output
    circular flow, 169
    constant returns to scale, 195–196
    decreasing returns to scale, 196
    defined, 31
    deflator, 153, 177n
    final, 165
    fixed, and multiplier model, 251
    increasing returns to scale, 196
    measurement of total economic output,
        163–164
    and money supply, 364
    nominal, 154
    Okun's rule of thumb, 149, 274
    per capita real output, 136
    potential, and unemployment, 148–149
    real, 154
over-the-counter trade, 59
overnight financing rate, 346–348

P

paradox of thrift, 214, 249
partially flexible exchange rate, 396, 398,
    420–426
partnerships, 58
passive deficit, 289
passive surplus, 289
patents, 200, 204–205
Peach, James, 160
per capita GDP, 175
per capita growth
    defined, 191–192
    education policies, 204
    encouragement through economic policies,
        202–206
    investment, encouragement of, 202–203
    population growth control, 203
    rate, 136
    research funding policies, 206
    savings, encouragement of, 202–203
    technological change, encouragement,
        204–206
    trade openness, 206
per capita real output, 136
permanent income hypothesis, 253
personal consumption expenditures, 169
personal disposable income, 174
personal income, 173–174
Phillips, Ronnie, 160
Phillips curve
    breakdown, 372
    described, 372
    history of, 372
    inflation expectations, 372–374, 375
    long-run, 372–375
    short-run, 372–375
    stagflation, 372, 375
    trade-off, 373
physical capital, 192
pie chart, 24
policies. See macroeconomic policies

policy regime, 447
political forces, 9, 11, 17
population
    and demand, 86
    growth control, 203
positive economics, 16
positive externalities, 200
post-Keynesian macroeconomists, 160
postindustrial economy, 58
potential income, 213, 274–275
potential output
    debates, 230–231
    defined, 148
    estimation problems, 229
    growth, 188
    and unemployment, 148–149
present value
    annuity rule, 79–80
    defined, 78
    formula, 78–79
    importance of, 80–81
    in media, 80
    rule of 72, 80
price
    adjustment, 95–96
    changes, effect of, 86
    equilibrium, 97
    fixed, 236
    in hyperinflation, 310
    inflexibility, 224
    of inputs, 91
    of other goods, and demand, 85
    supply and demand, effect of, 110
    tool, 83
    trade deficit, effect on, 425
price-adjusting markets, 220
price ceilings, 111–113, 129
price floors, 114–115, 129
price index
    consumer price index (CPI), 153
    creation of, 150–152
    defined, 150
    raw materials, 152
price level
    changes, 250
    exchange rate, effect on, 421, 424
    fiscal policy when price level flexible,
        277–278
    flexible, 251, 277–278
    inflationary gap, 278
    and money in Canada, 1953-2001, 365
    and money relative to real income, Brazil and
        Chile, 366
    recessionary gap, 277
    trade balance, effect on, 422–423
price mechanism, and invisible hand, 9
price-setting process of firms, 369
pricing coordination strategy, 224
primary financial markets, 330
principle of increasing marginal opportunity cost,
    35
Principles of Economics (Marshall), 10
private goods, 122
private property rights, 28

producer surplus, 98
production function
    constant returns to scale, 195–196
    defined, 195
    and growth, 195–196
production possibility curve
    and decision making, 38–39
    defined, 32
    difficult choices, 39
    and economic systems, 38–39
    efficiency, 35–37
    grades example, 32–33
    marginal opportunity cost, 33–35
    opportunity cost, relation to, 30, 33
    productive efficiency, 35–36
    shifts, examples of, 37–38
    trade, effect of, 41–42
production possibility model, 433–434
production possibility table, 31–32
productive efficiency, 35–36, 37
productivity
    defined, 188
    and inflation, 362
    marginal. See marginal productivity
    and wages, 362
profit
    defined, 57, 173
    before taxes, 171
progressive tax, 122
proletariat class, 52
property rights, 204–205
proportional taxes, 122–123
provincial bonds, 332
provincial government, 63
public goods
    defined, 122
    free rider, 122
purchasing power parity (PPP), 176, 393–395

Q

quality improvement bias, 152
quantity
    equilibrium, 97
    supply and demand, effect of, 110
quantity-adjusting markets, 220
quantity demanded
    change in, 86
    defined, 85
quantity supplied
    change in, 92
    defined, 91
quantity theory of money and inflation
    constant velocity, 363–364
    defined, 364
    equation of exchange, 363
    and inflation/growth trade-off, 376–377
    inflation tax, 365–367
    vs. institutional theory of inflation, 368
    money's role in inflation, 364–365
    policy implications, 367–370
    real output, independent of money supply, 364
    summary, 436–437
    velocity of money, 363
Quebec Deposit Insurance Board, 322

quotas
   algebraic representations, 130
   defined, 71, 117, 403
   effect of, 117
   vs. tariffs, 403
   tariffs, relationship with, 117–118
QWERTY keyboard, 201–202

R

radical economists, 160–161
Raleigh, Sir Walter, 70
Rasminsky, Louis, 340
rational expectations, 362
rational expectations model, 252
raw materials price index, 152
real-business-cycle economists, 230
real-business-cycle theory, 231, 252
real deficit, 287–288
real GDP
   defined, 176
   new method of calculation, 185, 186
   vs. nominal GDP, 176–177
   old method of calculation, 185–186
real gross domestic product (real GDP)
   changes in, as growth measurement, 135
   defined, 135
real interest rate, 352–353
real output, 154
real sector, 305
recession
   aggregate demand management, 261–262
   defined, 140
   fiscal policies, 261–266
recessionary gap, 223–225, 277
regressive tax, 122
regulatory trade restrictions, 404
rent control, 111–113
research funding policies, 206
reserves, 317
Retirement Income system, 287
Ricardo, David, 10
Rizzo, Mario, 160
Rosser, Barkley, 160
rosy scenario policy, 267
Rothbard, Murray, 160
Rule of 72, 189–190
rule of 72, 80
Russell 2000, 60

S

salaries, 171
SAS curve. *See* short-run aggregate supply (SAS)
   curve
savings
   encouragement of, 202–203
   financial sector as conduit, 307
   marginal propensity to save (*mps*), 245
   that escapes circular flow, 308
Say, Jean Baptiste, 188
Say's law, 188
scarcity
   defined, 5
   elements of, 5

Schumpeter, Joseph, 198
Second World War, fiscal policy in, 270
secondary financial markets, 331
secular trend growth rate, 136
services balance, 69
Sherman, Howard, 161
shift factors of demand, 85–86
shift factors of supply, 91–92
shifts in demand, 85, 105
shifts in supply, 91, 92–93, 105
short-run aggregate supply (SAS) curve
   defined, 219
   price-adjusting markets, 220
   quantity-adjusting markets, 220
   shifts, 221
   slope, 220–221
short-run framework
   inflation, 135, 149–156
   see also inflation
   integration with long-run framework, 223–227
   vs. long-run framework, 135
   unemployment, 135, 141–149
   see also unemployment
short-run Phillips curve, 372–375
short-term Canada bonds, 332
simple money multiplier, 318
slope
   aggregate demand (*AD*) curve, 215–217
   defined, 21
   linear curves, 21–22
   nonlinear curve, 23
   short-run aggregate supply (SAS) curve,
      220–221
Smith, Adam, 10, 51, 187, 190
social capital, 193
social forces, 9, 11, 17, 31
social philosophy, 10
socialism, 53
   blending with capitalism, 49
   defined, 29
   in practice, 30
   Soviet-style, 30, 53
   state, 53
   in theory, 29–30
sole proprietorships, 58
Soviet-style socialism, 30, 53
Special Drawing Rights (SDRs), 415
specialization
   defined, 42, 190
   and growth, 190
stagflation, 372, 375
Stalin, Joseph, 53
Standard and Poor's, 60
state socialism, 53
Statistics Canada, 57, 135, 138, 146
stock
   defined, 58–59, 326
   financial asset, 332
   valuation, 78–81
stock exchange, 59, 60
stock market, 60, 329
stock market boom, 449
stock market crash, future, 301
Stone, Richard, 163

strategic currency stabilization, 393
strategic pricing, 224
strategic trade policy, 405–406
structural deficit, 289
structural surplus, 289
structural unemployment, 142
subsidies
   algebraic representations, 129–130
   and supply, 92
   taxes less subsidies, 172
substitution bias, 152
sunk costs, 6
supplementary labour income, 171
supply
   curve. *See* supply curve
   defined, 91
   vs. demand, 89–90
   demand, relation to. *See* supply and demand
   excess, 95
   individual, 93
   law of supply, 90
   market, 93
   money, 320–321
   price adjustments, 95–96
   quantity supplied, 91
   Say's law, 188
   schedule shifts, 128–129
   shift factors, 91–92
   shifts in, 91, 92–93, 105
   table, 93–94
supply and demand
   algebraic representation of, 127–129
   vs. AS/AD model, 214
   for children, 99
   effect of shifts, 105–106
   equations, 127–129
   equilibrium, 97–99, 127–128
   for euros, 387
   fallacy of composition, 118–119
   graphs, 96–97, 109
   limitations of analysis, 118–119
   model, 434–436
   other-things-constant assumption, 118–119
   power of, 104–110
   price, effect on, 110
   quantity, effect on, 110
   real-world examples, 106–109
   shifts in, and expenditures shifts, 252
supply curve
   defined, 90
   important considerations, 94
   individual, 94–95
   market, 93, 94
   movements along, 91, 92–93, 128
   sample, 91
   from supply table, 94
supply-side economics. *See* long-run framework
surplus
   arbitrary nature of definition, 286–287
   cause of, 296–297
   crowding out, 297–299
   debt, defined, 289
   defined, 286
   function, 300

modern debate, 296–301
negative deficit, 288n
passive, 289
structural, 289
as summary measure, 287
trade. *See* trade surplus
surplus value of workers, 52

T

T-accounts
and creation of money, 335–337
monetary policy, 358–359
TANSTAAFL, 7, 138
target rate of unemployment, 143–144
tariffs
defined, 71, 402
effect of, 116
failure of, 403
imported goods, impact on, 403
vs. quotas, 403
quotas, relationship with, 117–118
reduction under FTA, 406–407
strategic trade policy, 405–406
tastes, 85
tax-based incomes policies, 160
taxes
algebraic representations, 129–130
excise, 116
failure to report, 180
as fiscal policy tool, 266
flexibility in changes, 275–276
less subsidies, 172
middle class tax breaks, 276
profit before, 171
progressive tax, 122
proportional, 122–123
regressive tax, 122
and supply, 92
technological age, 198
technological change
and efficiency, 36
and growth, 194–195
policies to encourage change, 204–206
and supply, 91–92
technological lock-in, 201–202
technology
classical growth model, 199
common knowledge effects, 200
defined, 194
new growth theory, 200
positive externalities, 200
term structure of interest rates, 347
theory. *See* economic theory
Thiessen, Gordon, 340, 341
Toronto Stock Exchange, 59, 60, 331
Towers, Graham, 340
trade
comparative advantage. *See* comparative
advantage
domestic, 71–73
fair, 409
free. *See* free trade
gains from trade, 41
international. *See* international trade

openness to, 206
and production possibility curves, 41–42
trade balance
exchange rate, effect of, 423
goal, 417–418
income, effect of, 422
monetary policy, effect of, 422–424
price levels, effect of, 422–423
trade barriers. *See* trade restrictions
trade deficit
defined, 68
fiscal policies and, 269n, 425–426
income, effect of, 425
prices, effect of, 425
trade policy, 268–270
strategic, 405–406
trade restrictions, 402–405
trade restrictions
economists' dislike of, 405
embargo, 404
nationalistic appeals, 404–405
nontariff barriers, 71
quotas, 71, 403
regulatory, 404
tariffs, 71, 402–403
voluntary restraint agreements, 404
trade surplus
defined, 68
fiscal policies, 269n
trading blocs, 71
tradition-based society, 31, 49–50
transfer payments, 63–64
TSX, 60

U

uncovered interest parity, 389
underground economy, 180
unemployment
categories, 145
Classical view, 443
cyclical, 142
frictional, 143
government's problem, 143
and inflation, 371–376
Keynesian view, 443
layperson's explanation, 212
measurement, 146–148
microeconomic categories, 149, 150
natural rate, 144
new economy, 376
nonaccelerating inflation rate of
unemployment (NAIRU), 144
Okun's rule of thumb, 149
Phillips curve, 371–376
and potential output, 148–149
recessionary, 443
responsibility of, 144–145
social problem of, 142–143
stagflation, 372, 375
structural, 142
target rate, 143–144
temporary assistance, 15
unemployment rate
accuracy, 147–148

calculation of, 146–147
Canadian *vs.* European, 144–145
defined, 141–142
employment rate, 148
labour force participation rate, 147–148
since 1946, 146
unexpected inflation, 154–155
unit of account, 310–311
United Nations (UN), 74
upward-sloping curves, 21
U.S. domination of Canadian trade, 418

V

valuation
bonds, 78–81
stocks, 78–81
value added, 166
vault cash, 346
Veblen, Thorstein, 160
velocity of money, 363
voluntary restraint agreements, 404
von Hayek, Friedrich, 159
von Mises, Ludwig, 159

W

wages
factor incomes approach, 171
and inflation, 362
and productivity, 362
war finance, 271
Watson, Thomas Sr., 204
Watt, James, 51
wealth
effect, 215–216
money as store of wealth, 311
Wealth of Nations (Smith), 10, 51, 187
welfare, nonmeasurement of in GDP, 178–179
welfare capitalism, 52–53
Western Union, 204
Whitney, Eli, 51
Wilshire index, 60
women
GDP bias against, 168
and property, 51n
target rate of unemployment, changes in,
143–144
World Bank, 74, 176, 414
World Court, 74
World Trade Organization (WTO), 73, 206, 403

Y

Yanus, Mohammed, 202–203

Z

zero-coupon bonds, 333